UNEQUAL RELATIONS
AN INTRODUCTION TO RACE, ETHNIC AND ABORIGINAL DYNAMICS IN CANADA
Second Edition

Augie Fleras and Jean Leonard Elliott

Prentice Hall Canada Inc.
Scarborough, Ontario

Canadian Cataloguing in Publication Data

Fleras, Augie, 1947–
  Unequal relations: an introduction to race,
ethnic, and aboriginal dynamics in Canada

2nd ed.
Authors in reverse order on 2nd ed.
Includes index.
ISBN 0-13-228743-9

1. Canada – Race relations. 2. Canada – Ethnic relations.
I. Elliott, Jean Leonard, 1941–95. II. Title.

FC104.E55 1996   305.8'00971   C95-931719-8
F1035.A1E55 1996

© 1992, 1996 Prentice-Hall Canada Inc., Scarborough, Ontario
A Viacom Company

Prentice-Hall, Inc., Englewood Cliffs, New Jersey
Prentice-Hall International (UK) Limited, London
Prentice-Hall of Australia, Pty. Limited, Sydney
Prentice-Hall Hispanoamericana, S.A., Mexico City
Prentice-Hall of India Private Limited, New Delhi
Prentice-Hall of Japan, Inc., Tokyo
Simon & Schuster Asia Private Limited, Singapore
Editora Prentice-Hall do Brasil, Ltda., Rio de Janeiro

ISBN 0-13-228743-9

Acquisitions Editor: Marjorie Munroe
Developmental Editor: Shoshana Goldberg
Production Editor: Avivah Wargon
Copy Editor: Lisa Penttila
Production Coordinator: Deborah Starks
Page layout: Hermia Chung

1 2 3 4 5   RRD   99 98 97 96 95

Printed and bound in USA

Every reasonable effort has been made to obtain permissions for all articles and data used in this edition. If errors or omissions have occurred, they will be corrected in future editions provided written notification has been received by the publisher.

To the memory of Sally M. Weaver

Contents

Preface to the Second Edition

Few domains in Canada are littered with as much conceptual debris as the field of race, aboriginal, and ethnic relations. Consider only these gaps in our understanding: Race continues to matter at a time when many think it shouldn't; racism, in turn, has proven much more tenacious than many would have hoped. Ethnicity is no longer about cuddly attachments for display in festivals and foodcourts, but a sometimes deadly business of "cleansing" or killing. On the political front, both the First Nations and the Québécois are probing the possibilities of a Canada so different that it may eventually exist on paper only. Immigrants and their associated cultural differences are proving no less contentious by their presence: Just watch temperatures soar whenever the concepts "multiculturalism" or "employment equity" are drawn into conversation. The fact that few Canadians can even agree on the meaning of the terms only complicates the turmoil.

The second edition of this book is designed to overcome these lacunae in our knowledge. Part analysis, part consciousness-raising, and part anti-racist, this introductory text comes at a time when the boundaries of our tolerance are being pushed to the limit by deep diversities and radical ethnicities. Several themes provide a unifying coherence to the text. Canada's race, aboriginal, and ethnic relations are portrayed as evolving patterns of group interaction within contexts both unequal and contested. The theme of group dynamics as unequal relations is particularly important. As sociologists we take an interest in how relationships of inequality between groups are created, supported, challenged, resisted, modified, and transformed by way of state policies and government practices. Special attention is aimed at the politics and practice of accommodating diversity as part of the society-building process. A viable Canadian society that can accommodate this diversity without repudiating the centre is perhaps the most formidable of the many challenges that confront Canada. That alone is sufficient rationale for a text on race, ethnic, and aboriginal relations.

The contents of the book are organized into three parts, as in the first edition. There is a certain logic and rationale to the sequence of topics: Concepts appear before application; theory before practice; the abstract before the concrete. Each section builds upon the other without necessarily invalidating the possibility of alternative arrangements for individual chapters. An overview and summary highlights appear at the end of each chapter, as do a list of key terms and questions for discussion and review. The first part (Chapters 1–6) provides a general conceptual framework for the study of race and ethnicity as unequal relations, with special emphasis on the constructs and perspectives employed by sociologists for sorting out intergroup relations. Topics for discussion include models of race and ethnic relations; race and racism; anti-racist strategies; ethnicity, ethnic identity, and ethnic nationalisms; inequality and minority stratification; and gendered diversity. The second part (Chapters 7–9) applies many of these concepts to the emergent realities of an evolving Canadian society. State policies and politics of government-minority interaction are examined with reference to the "three major forces," namely (a) the First Nations, (b) Charter groups (French- versus English-speaking colonizers), and (c) "multicultural" minorities. Each of these "diversities" is shown to occupy a distinct status in Canadian society: Not only does this influence their relationship with the state, it also defines the perimeters of their demands and proposed solutions. The third part (Chapters 10–12) looks at the complex and challenging world of multicultural relations in Canada. It begins by reviewing recent and proposed developments in the multicultural management of race and ethnic relations. It ends by analyzing the practices and perils of mainstreaming of diversity at institutional levels, with particular attention to policing, education, and the mass media. The book closes with a discussion of the paradoxes that confront society-building as Canada grapples with the uncertainties of diversity and change.

The second edition of this text resembles the first in both content and organization. Within this basic framework, the second edition has been updated and substantially revised. Much of the supporting evidence builds on the 1991 Census Canada data. Revisions are evident throughout — as might be expected in a domain where social patterns and conventional wisdom are rarely constant. The chapter on race, now Chapter 2, has been revised and retitled to "Race Matters" to reflect a renewed interest in the fallacy of race-based explanations. A reworking of the chapter on ethnicity, now Chapter 6, will better account for the emergence of radical ethnicity and ethnic nationalism as a global and national force. Extensive modifications are evident in the section on the "three major forces" because of revolutionary changes to the rules of engagement and entitlement. Chapter 9, now retitled "Multicultural Minorities," has shifted its focus from visible/nonvisible minorities to issues around immigrants and immigration. The concluding chapter, Chapter 12, "At the Crossroads: Reconstructing Canada," has been entirely rewritten in light of current developments.

Additional touches appear in the organization and presentation. The material on employment equity has moved over to Chapter 4, "Inequality and Stratification," while the concerns and aspirations of minorities are discussed in Chapter 5, "Gender and Race." Original case studies remain a central feature of the text, including new material on the genocide in Rwanda, experiences of women of colour in Canada, and racism on post-secondary campuses. Further illustration of key issues is provided through the addition of Research Clips, Applications, Voices, For the Record, and Question Boxes. Changes to terminology are no less apparent: the term First Nations, rather than Native Indians, is employed as often as aboriginal peoples;

visible minorities are usually referred to as people of colour; and racial and ethnic minorities are now labelled multicultural minorities in line with their policy status in Canada. We hope that these modifications, however modest, will improve the text by capitalizing on contemporary trends.

Any book of an introductory nature is written with the undergraduate and community college student in mind. Issues are selected for their timeliness and relevance. The language of the text is geared toward challenging the reader, without losing sight of basic rules for communication. Objectives for this book are varied as well, but generally geared toward personal growth through understanding, explanation, sensitization, criticism, empowerment, and action:

1) To acquaint the reader with an *understanding* of the subject matter encompassed by a sociology of race, aboriginal, and ethnic relations. The text seeks to clarify and to rethink perennial debates in this field, yet avoid sloppy reasoning, mindless clichés, oversimplification of issues, and common-sense assumptions at odds with reality.

2) To inform readers by *explaining* the pattern that undergirds race, ethnic, and aboriginal relations. The challenge rests in going beyond official explanations or pat description to recognize the value of multiple perspectives and flexible (sometimes contradictory) interpretations.

3) To *sensitize* readers to the problems and challenges associated with the pursuit of social equality and cultural retention. Those in positions of privilege must bolster their awareness levels by learning to empathize with minority experiences and perspectives.

4) To promote a *critical* perspective by confronting the myths and misconceptions about diversity issues. The debunking of illusions and half-truths is critical: Readers are encouraged to probe beneath the surface of often self-serving platitudes and mindless clichés in exchange for multi-textured answers and nuanced responses — not all of which toe the official line or conventional way of thinking.

5) To initiate a process of personal *empowerment*. Coping with diversity is no longer an option or luxury that any of us can blithely ignore. Race, ethnicity, and aboriginality are not abstract notions for analysis, but collectively have a powerful effect on Canada and Canadians (James 1995). Just as media literacy has grown in importance, so too is *diversity literacy* a prerequisite for personal careers and collective survival.

6) To encourage the reader to embark on a path toward personal *actions* of anti-racism and community. Personal awareness is great; involvement and action for meaningful change are better. The object is not wholesale global change, but improvement in one corner of the world (as the bumper sticker says, "think globally, act locally"). The struggle to eradicate racism and injustice even at local levels should never be underestimated, given the tenacity of the problem. Still, the rewards of an accommodating and equitable society are surely worth the efforts expended.

An embarrassment of riches confronted us when deciding on an appropriate title. After narrowing down our options, we decided to entitle our text *Unequal Relations: An Introduction to Race, Ethnic and Aboriginal Dynamics in Canada*. By this selection we tried to isolate the formative and distinctive properties of Canada's race, aboriginal, and ethnic patterns. Debates about diversity are ultimately discourses about inequality and power as unevenly matched groups jockey for position in a competitive game of "who gets what and why." Special attention is accorded to the means by which minorities are denied opportunities and power to accumulate resources they need for overcoming inequality. Gender relations and class relations are also relations of inequality, inasmuch as resources and power are differentially distributed. Our goal is to explore the common ground that fosters such inequities. We believe the context is as important as the process. To understand one, we must know the other.

There are several things the book is *not*. It is not a description of minority groups or Canadian ethnic lifestyles. Nor does it provide a platform for minority "voices" or "stories" by minority authors. Such a perspective is critical for intercultural understanding (see James and Shadd 1994), but our preference rests with the theme of group interaction within unequal contexts. The book begins with the assumption that race, ethnic, and aboriginal interactions are relations of inequality. It continues by emphasizing the manner by which group relationships are constructed, sustained, challenged, and modified by way of official policy and institutional practices. It concludes by focusing on the politics of race, ethnic, and aboriginal relations as they contribute to or detract from *Canadian* society-building. This nationalistic emphasis does not invalidate cross-national comparisons. It merely draws attention to the primacy of initially understanding what goes on in Canada before casting our net more widely.

Analysis in the text is decidely macro-sociological in orientation. Diversity issues are rarely framed around a micro-model of individual behaviour or psychological dispositions. Our intent is clearly toward the big picture, with its emphasis on the structure of society, its institutional arrangements, intergroup dynamics, distributions of power, and society-building processes (Frideres 1993). Social conditions and official policies that contribute to the construction, maintenance, and transformation of society are allocated special prominence. No less important are group dynamics: Attendant conflicts and confrontations associated with group life do not arise from individual ignorance or irrational fears, but from processes and paradoxes intrinsic to human social life (see Jaret 1995). A macro model not only provides a framework for conceptualizing issues in race, ethnicity, and aboriginality. It also sharpens our appreciation of group relations as essentially relationships of power and control.

It has been polite for Canadians to speak of our inequality by reference to assorted imagery. The expression "vertical mosaic" has been widely circulated to describe the unequal status of Canada's racial, aboriginal, and ethnic minorities. Equally popular has been the "two solitudes" metaphor. This image has accentuated the lack of understanding and communication between French- and English-speaking Canadians. Curiously there is no aphorism — however inadequate — to characterize the First Nations in Canada. Canada's past relations with aboriginal peoples have been so dismal that we lack even popular phrases to gloss over history. Our historical indifference to aboriginal concerns strikes a dissonant chord in the perception of ourselves as an open and generous people.

Metaphorical images are useful in alerting us to select features of Canada's diversity. Yet these representations are as likely to mislead as they are to inform. Our attention may be drawn toward certain aspects of social reality, but away from others. Social phenomena are squeezed into a somewhat static framework that is bereft of context and process. What we prefer instead is a dynamic perspective that conceptualizes race, aboriginal, and ethnic relations as patterned interaction within unequal and changing environments. We also need to take into consideration the broader political, economic, and social context in which intergroup life is embedded.

This focus on the emergent and negotiated will hopefully point toward a more egalitarian and multicultural ideal that we may strive for in Canada. To bridge this gap with an eye toward rebuilding Canadian society is a challenge that confronts each of us. We do not pretend to have all the answers. To think otherwise is not only arrogant and controlling; it mistakenly connotes the existence of an objective reality that readily unlocks its secrets to the privileged observer. We also want to avoid sermonizing and providing formulaic responses, without abdicating our responsibility to ask tough questions and take unpopular stands. In the end we hope to foster an appreciation of the ambiguities inherent in addressing issues about who we are and where we are going. The text has been written in this spirit.

The authors are grateful to those colleagues who acted as reviewers for this edition including Baha Abu-Laban, University of Alberta, Marilyn Bicher, Vanier College, and T. Callaghan, St. Clair College.

In Memoriam

Jean Leonard Elliott (1941-1995)

It is with deep sadness that I announce the death of my co-author and friend, Jean Leonard Elliott. Jean was the rarest of individuals, one who enjoyed life to the hilt, even when confronted with the spectre of death. In her role as a teacher and researcher, she was always the consummate professional who advanced the field of race, ethnic, and aboriginal relations at a time when many ignored these issues. Her varied writings across a spectrum of topics insisted on a feminist dimension, not because of "political correctness," but because of a passionate dislike for inequality and injustice of any kind. That Jean lived to see a Canada increasingly in the vanguard of societies for challenging racism, and sexism — in principle if not always in practice — is a credit to her tenacity and vision. Jean will be sorely missed by her colleagues and friends alike. It seems only fitting in light of our mutual interests to echo the words of the New Zealand Maori when bidding farewell, *"Haere ra e hoa"* — "Goodbye, good friend." May this second edition stand as a testimony to a keen academic, a champion of justice, and a courageous individual.

Introduction

The Good, the Bad, and the In-Between

Canada is a diverse and complex society composed of racially and ethnically different groups. Compared with other nation-states that routinely tolerate human rights abuses, Canada possesses an enviable reputation as a tolerant and compassionate country. The management of Canada's race, aboriginal, and ethnic relations is widely admired in global circles. People marvel at this capacity to forge unity from the shards of diversity, without foresaking prosperity or its reputation as a world-class society. Many are equally impressed by our collective threshold of toleration for seemingly endless debates over language, culture, and identity. Evidence of this high standing can be inferred from a list of global firsts: Canada was the first country to receive the UN-sponsored Nansen Medal in 1986 for its humanitarian response to the global refugee problem; Canada became the first country in 1982 to constitutionally enshrine aboriginal and treaty rights; and Canada remains the first and only country to officially endorse multiculturalism as a basis for the management of race and ethnic relations. This lofty reputation is further secured by Canada's consistently high placement in quality-of-life surveys — including its ranking as the world's best place to live when measured by a human development index related to wealth, education, and longevity (*Toronto Star*, 25 May 1994).

Some of these accolades are deserved; others, unfortunately, are not. From afar, Canada looks idyllic; up close, the picture changes. Dig deeper and one can unearth a country that has had little to boast about in the treatment of minorities. A partial list of shameful episodes would include: xenophobic attitudes and racist political responses to Chinese and East Indian immigrants from the mid-nineteenth century onwards (Baureiss 1985); the internment and dispossession of Japanese-Canadians during the Second World War (Berger 1981); the segregation of African-Canadians from mainstream institutions (Walker 1985; Henry 1994); and the pervasive anti-Semitism of the 1920s and 1930s, which culminated in the rejection of Jewish emigrés from Nazi Germany (Abella and Troper 1982). Much to our growing dismay, discrimination and racism are not relics from a bygone era. Anti-Semitism continues to plague the present, ranging in scope from Holocaust denial to defilement of Jewish properties, synogogues, and cemeteries. The current proliferation of white supremacist groups is no less disconcerting than in the past (Barrett 1987). People of colour continue to experience all manner of discrimination at personal and institutional levels (James 1995; Henry et al. 1995). The growing crisis in police-minority relations has also drawn attention to apparent injustices within the criminal justice system (Fleras and Desroches 1989). Mounting evidence of public backlash against the diversity agenda — from immigration to multiculturalism to employment equity — may signify a country in disarray.

Equally threatening to Canada's national fabric are the ongoing debates between the two "Charter groups" (French- and English-speaking colonziers). Relations between Quebec and Ottawa have hovered between the poles of the sullen indifference ("two solitudes") and open hostility ("two scorpions in a bottle"). This growing estrangement between the French and English is symbolized by seemingly inexhaustible language controversies. Much of the conflict can be interpreted as a power-struggle over jurisdiction and control within a federalist system. With the re-emergence of powerful separatist forces, English-speaking Canadians continue to fret over the very survival of Canada, from sea to shining sea. French-speaking Canadians, in turn, take exception to anglophone insensitivity over Quebec's demands for "distinct society" status within a reinvented federalism. Constitutional changes anticipated by the Meech Lake and Charlottetown Accords have done little to mollify debate over Quebec–Ottawa relations. If anything, the dashed expectations have aggravated public anxieties regarding the future of Canada — with or without Quebec.

Similarly, the actions and protests of Canada's aboriginal peoples have garnered political attention (Weaver 1981; Boldt 1993; Wotherspoon and Satzewich 1993). Decades of colonialist subjugation and neglectful stagnation have diminished Canada's lustre as a pacesetter in aboriginal affairs. No wonder that each annual report of Canada's Human Rights Commission since 1987 has pounced on aboriginal marginality as the country's most serious human rights violation. But the First Nations have challenged the status quo by engaging central authorities in a power-struggle over who controls what, and why (Fleras and Elliott 1992; Mercredi and Turpel 1993; Fleras 1996). The quest for self-determination through the implementation of inherent self-governing structures is central to this renewal and reform. Promotion of aboriginal and treaty rights has also proven pivotal in repositioning aboriginal-state relations (Little Bear et al. 1984). Yet compromises toward a workable agenda have proven to be elusive, despite lofty rhetoric to the contrary (Fleras 1996). Political responses are often rattled by the unconventional nature of aboriginal demands. Time and again government policies embody false assumptions and dubious tactics, many of which may inadvertently inflame political crisis and aboriginal cultural decline (Shkilynk 1985; Ponting 1986; Mercredi and Turpel 1993). To our discredit and profound embarrassment, aboriginal leaders have turned to world courts and international forums in last-ditch attempts to hasten the healing process. Even the prospect of violence to achieve aboriginal goals can no longer be rejected outright, with images of Oka still seared into our collective conscience.

This admittedly selective overview suggests a mixed verdict on Canadian race, aboriginal, and ethnic relations. Which is right or wrong? Different answers are possible because no one can agree on the criteria for assessment, with the result that right or wrong are assigned attributes on the basis of who is doing the evaluation, and why. That kind of equivocation suggests the possibility of a third position; that is, the notion of Canada as lying somewhere in between. Compared to a utopia, for example, Canada falls short of the mark. Yet Canada's record stands as a paragon of virtue compared with minority rights records elsewhere. Even the smallest incidents that would barely rate a mention in many global circles tend to be magnified in Canada because of our exacting standards. An appreciation for history also reveals an "in between" quality: Compared with our lofty expectations for the future, Canada leaves something to be desired. But in comparison with our past, we appear to have made substantial progress in the astute management of diversity — at least at the level of policy and promises. Canada today is substantially different from the one locked into the virtues of assimilation, white supremacy, open discrimination, and institutional segregation of a century ago. Proof of this shift reflects a growing commitment to accommodate diversity in ways that are workable and fair (Fleras 1994). Tangible indicators of a refurbished Canada are varied, but surely include the inception of official bilingualism and minority language rights, the implementation of multiculturalism from federal to municipal levels, and introduction of employment equity for accommodating diversity at institutional levels.

Collectively, of course, much needs to be done. We still have a long way to go in acknowledging minority needs and aspirations, let alone in implementing meaningful social reform. Relations between the Canadian state and minority groups tend to exist uneasily between grudging acceptance and qualified accommodation, with the spectre of public backlash in the background. This ambiguity is played out in the discord around government-minority restructuring. Many are confused by failure to grasp the rationale behind proposed changes in minority relations with the state. Others are frustrated by demands for entitlement and rules of engagement at odds with Canada's so-called national interests (Boldt 1993). Assumptions that once defined who got what are no longer applicable, but are superseded by provocative means for managing group relations. The margins are now competing with the centre for control over power, resources, and status — not by direct confrontation but by hugging the high moral ground of "victimhood" and "identity politics." With our conventional social moorings increasingly cast adrift, a comprehensive and up-to-date text is invaluable for sorting out what is going on, and why.

This book provides an introduction to the study of contemporary race, aboriginal, and ethnic relations in Canada. It takes as a point of departure the idea that race, aboriginality, and ethnicity are essentially relations of inequality between groups. That alone makes it imperative to appreciate how the social dimensions of this relationship are constructed, maintained, modified, or transformed at the level of state policy and government practices (Nelson and Fleras 1995). The presentation itself is organized around a macro-sociological approach, with its focus on intergroup dynamics within a highly charged yet uncertain context of diversity and change. Particular attention is also directed at those structural features ("class relations") and cultural values ("the dominant ideology") that impose a framework for intergroup relations. Efforts to classify and explain diversity begin with the division of Canada into three major forces (First Nations, Charter groups, and multicultural minorities). Each of these diversities not only occupies a distinct formal status in Canada because of history and politics; they also are locked in competition with central policy structures over access to power-sharing and group entitlements. Policy responses to these often contentious demands provide the catalyst for Canadian society-building. Finally, the book provides students with access to the burgeoning literature in this area by drawing on a wide range of sources (journals, newspapers, books, government reports), along with a variety of disciplines (sociology, anthropology, history, social psychology, and political science).

Content, Organization, and Scope

This textbook is partitioned into three major parts. The first provides a *conceptual* framework for the study of race, aboriginal, and ethnic relations. It covers the diverse concepts, definitions, theories, and perspectives that social scientists employ in dealing macro-sociologically with racial, aboriginal, and ethnic relations. Specific topics within this section are summarized below by way of major themes within each chapter. Part One covers the following topics:

Race and Ethnic Relations

What do we mean by the concept of "relations" when applied to race, aboriginality, and ethnicity? In what sense are such relationships (a) constructed, (b) patterned and predictable, (c) evolving, (d) assymetrical, and (e) unique to specific historical contexts? The management of such relations has historically revolved around the patterns of (a) genocide, (b) assimilation, (c) integration, (e) segregation, and (e) cultural pluralism. Diverse sociological perspectives for studying race, aboriginal, and ethnic relations are employed, including functionalism, conflict, and interactionism. A reliance on a macro-sociological perspective is defended as consistent with the notion of race, aboriginality, and ethnicity as intergroup relations, both constructed and unequal.

Race Matters

Why is it that race continues to "matter" even though many of us should know better? Races are socially constructed categories, created by those whose misunderstanding of human diversity and evolution plays into the hands of vested interests. The race concept is exposed as scientifically and intellectually bankrupt; yet we must account for its staying power and public appeal. The origins of the race concept is examined, followed by a discussion of race types and racial doctrines in the context of 19th century colonialism. Also included are the historical and conceptual links between race and racism, with its recent revival in debates over intelligence testing and race-based crime statistics.

Faces of Racism

Racism and worry over racism are a quintessentially Canadian trait. Yet the concept remains poorly understood by the public and vulnerable to shifts in meaning as contexts change. What do we mean by racism and how is it expressed? The concept of racism is examined along various dimensions including definition, properties, expression, impact, and implications. Different types of racism — from the overt and personal to the implicit and systemic — are compared and contrasted. Also discussed is the relationship of race to prejudice and discrimination at personal, institutional, and cultural levels. Likewise, strategies for the elimination of racism are explored. Anti-racist measures are shown to vary in magnitude and scope, ranging from those that focus on behavioral modification, to those that seek to modify institutional structures related to entry, participation, and reward systems.

Inequality and Stratification

Canada continues to be perceived as an open and egalitarian society. Both perceptions and ideals are marred by the realities of privilege distributed among racial, ethnic, and aboriginal minorities. The resultant stratification justifies a study of race, ethnicity, and aboriginality as relations of inequality involving cultures of dominance and subcultures of resistance. The relationship of inequality to race or class is scrutinized, especially since race and class (as well as gender) are important predictors of success or performance. We also want to know how and why racial and ethnic inequities continue to flourish despite moves to curb its worst excesses. The chapter concludes by examining the principles and practices associated with employment equity ("affirmative action") programs as one set of responses to inequality in a multicultural society.

Gender and Race

What is the relationship of diversity with gender when it applies to immigrant, aboriginal, and visible minority women? Attention is directed at the influence of gender in shaping the realities and opportunities for women of colour. Special attention is paid to the impact of race and ethnicity for women (and men) of colour as they struggle in a multicultural society where egalitarian pieties do not always match everyday practices. Also discussed are the hierarchies of subordination that profoundly influence minority lives and women's life chances. Finally, attention is directed at the strategies employed by women of colour to eliminate these mutually intersecting handicaps (race, ethnicity, gender, sexual preference, and social class).

The Ethnic Experience

Ethnicity has evolved into a complex and controversial social phenomena, with much second-guessing expended in determining its genesis, nature, properties, impact, and implications. This chapter explores the concept and challenges associated with the ethnic experience by reference to its expression at (a) group levels, (b) personal and collective identity, and (c) social movements up to and including secessionist ethnic nationalisms. Topics for discussion include the persistence of ethnicity; the scope of ethnic communities and groups; the upsurge in ethnicity; the nature and maintenance of ethnic boundaries; and the relationship of identity to ethnicity. Particular emphasis is focused on why ethnic groups and identities continue to persist and prosper, even when confronted by grinding pressures for assimilation and modernization. The implications of ethnicity are assessed against the backdrop of Canadian official multiculturalism and the process of society-building.

The second part of the text switches from conceptual issues in general, to their application for Canadian society. Response to the demands of demographic, political, and social changes has transformed Canada into an increasingly complex and contested site involving competition over power and scarce resources. Intergroup relations have become increasingly fraught with ambiguity and stress because of changes in the patterns of engagement (interaction) and rules for entitlements (who gets what, and why). The politics of this ongoing and negotiated interaction are reflected in government policy and institutional practices when applied to Canada's three major forces — namely, the Aboriginal First Nations, the Charter groups, and multicultural minorities (those with some non-British, non-French immigrants and non-aboriginal ancestry). Each of the major diversities is shown to occupy a relatively distinct status in Canadian society with respect to power, resources, claims and entitlements. All have taken the initiative recently to consolidate their agenda. Central authorities have responded to these often competing agendas by way of policy, constitutional, and legislative reform. The resultant interplay of vested interests and conflicting ideologies are central to capturing the essence of Canadian society-building as it evolves into as yet unexplored realms.

The First Nations

The fortunes of the First Nations in Canada have improved considerably. Irrelevancy has given way to that of primary-stakeholder status, with the result that the First Nations are poised on the brink of major breakthrough in redefining their relationship to Canada (Fleras and Krahn 1992; Mercredi and Turpel 1993). As the original occupants and a founding nation of Canada, aboriginal peoples define themselves as the "nations within" with an inherent right to self-determination across a spectrum of political, social, and cultural fronts (Fleras and Elliott 1992). Government unwillingness for political or economic reasons to concede this inherency adds to the bitterness behind state-aboriginal restructuring, but has scarcely diminished aboriginal resolve for a fundamental renewal in relational status. The chapter explores the rationale and logic that undergird these power struggles for greater control over jurisdiction (Fleras 1996). It also looks at the contemporary status of aboriginal peoples by way of policy developments and current socioeconomic standing. Discussions focus on whether aboriginal concerns are adequately addressed through existing legislation and the constitutional process; they also examine the extent to which an indigenous-based nationalism may provide solutions to the so-called Indian problem. The chapter concludes by attempting to reconcile the principles of aboriginality with the realities of Canadian federalism.

Charter Groups

Fewer dimensions in Canada consume more energy and mistrust than the politics of French-English relations. The conflict between Canada's two Charter nations is analyzed as part of an ongoing process to redefine Quebec's political status within a renewed Canadian federalism. Language debates serve as a major point of contention: They also may camouflage perhaps more fundamental issues pertaining to French and English struggles over power and jurisdictions. Special attention is devoted to how the politics of bilingualism continue to challenge Canadian unity. Proposals to constitutionally entrench a "distinct society" status for Quebec appear to have elevated the stakes in renegotiating who gets what in Canada. Finally, the concept of a sovereign Quebec as a contested domain is engulfed by the competing demands of Quebec's First Nations for recognition of inherent rights to self-determination.

Multicultural Minorities

The last force consists of racial and ethnic minorities, many of whom are immigrants or descendents of immigrants and refugees. Multicultural minorities are examined in terms of their evolving status as a "third wave" in Canadian society. Unlike the founding peoples of Canada, multicultural minorities do not have a distinct formal status in Canada. This omission thwarts their capacity to compete for attention or resources except as citizens under multiculturalism. Much can be gleaned by examining multicultural minority issues from the vantage point of immigration and immigrants, given the myths and misconceptions that litter the landscape. Topics for discussion include a review of immigration patterns; the logic behind government immigration policies both in the past and at present; Canada's national and international obligations; public perception of the merits and drawbacks of immigration; and the escalating backlash against the changing composition of Canadian immigration. The needs and concerns of immigrants of colour are also assessed and examined, as is the plight of refugees in Canada.

The third and final part addresses the concept of accommodating diversity by way of official multiculturalism as policy, principle, and practice. Our historical treatment of minorities is checkered at best, deplorable at worst, in spite of a carefully cultivated image of tolerance and acceptance. Neither the Canadian public nor its politicians have been especially receptive to minorities. Treatment has bordered on the openly hostile, with discriminatory segregation that rivalled that of South Africa or the southern USA. Assimilationist pressures were routinely endorsed: Once in Canada, immigrants were expected to discard their cultural past in exchange for anglo-conformity and institutional absorption. With multiculturalism, the status of diversity has gradually shifted from the margins to the centre, with a corresponding responsiveness on the part of mainstream institutions. The magnitude and scope of this mainstreaming has elicited debate over the entire diversity agenda.

The last section of the text deals with a variety of issues pertaining to multiculturalism as social policy and its implementation at institutional levels. We begin by exploring the concept of multiculturalism as policy and ideology. We conclude by analyzing the challenges associated with putting principles into practice. The extent to which multiculturalism contributes to or detracts from society-building is also examined.

Multiculturalism in Canada

Multiculturalism and its policy role in managing Canada's diversity is analyzed against the backdrop of government policy at federal, provincial, and municipal levels. Promotion of "official" multiculturalism is defined as a conflict management device for coping with the demands of increased diversity in the face of alternatives such as assimilation, integration, or segregation. Multiculturalism in Canada is interpreted at four levels of meaning: fact, ideology, policy, and practice. The origins and development of multiculturalism as policy and ideology are examined next, followed by its role as a resource in promoting political and minority interests. Legislative and constitutional changes have further elevated multiculturalism to the status of agenda-setting — for better or for worse (see Bissoondath 1994). Current debates and developments imply continued but uneven movement toward the ideal of "unity within diversity."

Putting Multiculturalism to Work

It is one thing to talk about multiculturalism as an ideology or policy. It is quite another to put these policy ideals into practice at institutional levels. The second last chapter of the text examines the challenges that await a mainstreaming of diversity within institutions such as the police, mass media, and education. The police have recognized a need to diversify the force; nevertheless, the combination of institutional inertia, subcultural resistance, and bureaucratic restrictions has hindered the implementation of culturally-sensitive and community-based policing. The mass media have historically mistreated minorities in terms of visual presentation and occupational representation. Recent efforts to treat minorities as more than social problems or as disposable stereotypes have captured some degree of success. Yet the logic of media continues to interfere with further adjustments. Finally, multiculturalism and education have evolved a partnership in pursuit of a more accommodative school environment. However useful these concessions, failure to address the structural barriers by way of anti-racist initiatives has impeded the process of inclusiveness. In short, each of these institutions has made progress in the multicultural management of diversity. Yet all continue to experience problems in mainstreaming diversity because of exclusionary structures, discriminatory practices, assimilationist values, and racist personnel.

Reconstructing Canada

Canada is at the crossroads in terms of its future growth. The forces of diversity and change are transforming the social landscape in profound and unprecedented ways. Nowhere is this crisis more evident than in the moves to accommodate such deep diversity. How does a society such as Canada, which constitutionally endorses the colour-blind equality of its individuals, incorporate the need to recognize and accommodate the identities and collective demands of particular racial, ethnic, or aboriginal groups without collapsing into disarray or open strife (Gutman 1996)? Debates over what constitutes citizenship strike at the sore of this dilemma. Efforts to restructure Canada along pluralist lines are gradually gaining momentum despite reactionary forces of an anti-politically-correct nature. Paradoxically, Canada's future as a diverse society looks bright, mainly because many of its perceived shortcomings may turn out to be strengths in the twenty-first century.

Objectives, Goals, and Rationale

The following objectives justify the need for a comprehensive look at Canadian race, aboriginal, and ethnic relations. First, we believe this book will foster a better appreciation of racial, aboriginal, and ethnic relations as a key catalyst in the unfolding of Canadian society. Our goal is to probe beneath surface events in search of recurrent patterns that logically account for intergroup relations. Relationships of power are analyzed and assessed in terms of how majority-minority relations are created, sustained, modified, dissolved — and resisted — within the shifting sands of an evolving and contested political field. Historical, anthropological, and social psychological perspectives are taken into consideration, but remain secondary to a sociological viewpoint. Diversity issues are not analyzed as psychological dispositions or cultural inventories. Concepts related to prejudice, discrimination, and harassment are conceptualized instead as social constructions and amenable to sociological analysis (Martin and Franklin 1973). A focus on group processes within wider contexts of structural inequality and social policy enhances a macro-sociological approach (Dashefsky 1975). Our interest lies in patterned and predictable relations *between* groups; it also extends to concerns over interaction *within* minority communities. This dual dimension enables us to reveal the tensions and conflict that exist internally, even within seemingly united or homogeneous groups, because of factional differences related to generations, gender, class, socioeconomic status, and levels of political involvement.

The second objective is related to the first. A textbook dealing with group-oriented issues is not intended to replace publications on ethnic cultures or ethnic processes (Herberg 1989; Driedger 1989). We readily concede a place in Canadian publishing for descriptions of the one-hundred-plus minority groups that reside in Canada. We also believe that minority voices have their own stories to tell of triumphs and failures in coping with Canada (James 1995; James and Shadd 1994). This book prefers a more analytic approach. The emphasis is on the dynamic and constructed components of group interaction, as well as on the inequality that is intrinsic to these relationships. Special prominence is accorded to a vision of society as a contested site involving competition among groups over scarce resources. To be sure, description is not dismissed altogether; after all, readers require sufficient detail to appreciate the direction and management of contemporary race, aboriginal, and ethnic relations. Nevertheless, the emphasis is on the centrality of power and inequality in shaping Canadian society.

A third objective addresses the possibility of empathy and tolerance toward diversity issues. All of us will come into contact with those who are ethnically and racially different at some point in our daily interaction. Each of us may also be a minority in some context or another. Fact and fiction mix uneasily in areas such as multiculturalism, immigration, racism, and bilingualism. Ambiguities can also interfere with public perception of minority concerns and aspirations. Racial and ethnic minorities are generally concerned with attainment of equality and justice. Many, however, find these goals are blocked as a result of social, political, ideological, and cultural barriers. Full participation in Canadian institutions is widely desired, but not necessarily at the cost of all continuity with the cultural past. If only for our collective survival, we must try to appreciate the social conditions that thwart minority aspirations. As well, we are morally bound to go beyond mere understanding. Empathy without local activism is a betrayal of the anti-racist principles upon which this book is organized. Unless we actively confront prejudice and discrimination in all its manifestations, many of us are destined to be part of the problem rather than part of the solution.

There are additional features that deserve comment. This book is not written with a view toward devising a theory of intergroup dynamics. The prospect of theory building is of marginal concern to most introductory students, even if our text is conceptually oriented. The testing of theoretical propositions is likewise beyond our interest or expertise. Our intent instead is largely analytical and substantive. We set out to analyze the relational status of Canada's three major forces in terms of who they are, what they want, why, and how they propose to achieve their goals. In addressing a need for clarity in a field of confusion, this book intends to decode many of the controversies and debates that distort the society-building process. Coverage is broad, but is refracted primarily through the prism of state policy (including constitutional and legislative initiatives) and government practices. References to specific groups such as the First Nations, Hutterites, Chinese, African-Canadians, and Québécois provide some grounds for illustrating key concepts.

Not everyone will agree with our treatment or assessment of many issues. But we believe an informed and critical response is possible when all sides of an issue are explored. This is not to suggest that tolerance and empathy are automatically bestowed on those who persevere through the text. Misconceptions and resistance are deeply entrenched within individuals and institutions. Common-sense notions often are resistent to efforts at debunking even under optimal conditions. Enlightened attitudes can only come about by undoing layers of socialization and unconscious reinforcement. Institutional and cultural practices need to be "deconstructed" if we are to expose hidden assumptions and structural barriers to genuine equality. An examination of the social forces that generate inequality and intolerance will foster an increased sensitivity to diversity. It will allow us to experience why racism is so difficult to detect, confront, and eradicate. We will acquire the conceptual tools to think through the basis of a genuinely multicultural and egalitarian society. We hope our book is a small contribution toward a society both accommodative and socially responsible, yet unmistakably Canadian in content and outlook.

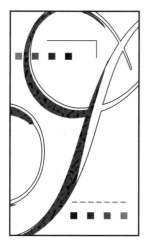

PART 1

CONCEPTUALIZING RACE, ABORIGINAL, AND ETHNIC RELATIONS

Any field of study is characterized by a distinctive subject matter. It is also distinguished from related fields by an appropriate set of assumptions, an inventory of key concepts, a range of perspectives, and a body of findings/conclusions. These criteria impart a unique basis for discussion and debate. They also provide a coherent and organizational framework for sorting out what is relevant for study.

The topic of race, aboriginal, and ethnic relations is no different. Sociologists have long gravitated toward a study of the diversity issues, often from a macro-sociological vantage point. A macro perspective concentrates on the "big picture," with a shared interest in group dynamics and social context as a unifying theme. But deep variations are found in the content and style of study. In place of consensus has appeared a seemingly inexhaustible inventory of constructs and concepts for studying diversity. This enlarged scope has broadened the depth and breadth of study; the profusion of material has also bewildered many novice readers.

Our aim in this section is to cut through the conceptual clutter by isolating recurrent themes in the field of race, ethnic, and aboriginal relations. A host of definitions and concepts are introduced for clarifying key issues in contemporary group dynamics. Concepts for discussion include, among others, race and racism; prejudice, discrimination, and harassment; anti-racism; ethnicity and the ethnic experience; diversity and gender; and inequality as ethnic stratification. Also discussed are the major sociological perspectives for sorting out patterns of intergroup behaviour. Functionalist, conflict, and interactionist perspectives embrace different visions of society, and how it works. Each, accordingly, has a distinct way of interpreting the status and role of diversity within society.

The goal of this exercise is twofold: First, we want to acquaint our readers with the conceptual tools for decoding the forces that generate group dynamics in Canada and abroad. We hope to convince how race, aboriginal, and ethnic relations are ultimately relationships of inequality. Failure to understand how this inequality is created, supported, or challenged can only diminish our knowledge of Canadian society-building. Second, we encourage a sensitivity to issues about majority-minority relations. Concepts such as racism and ethnicity are introduced not only as analytical exercises. We believe a knowledge of the basics are essential in coping with the diverse challenges of an increasingly post-modernist society. The application of this knowledge to everyday life is equally important. Canada will become an impoverished society unless we learn to "walk" that "talk" by putting principles into daily practice.

CHAPTER 1

UNEQUAL RELATIONS:
PATTERNS AND PERSPECTIVES

Q U E S T I O N   B O X

The Challenge of Studying Diversity in Canada

- Some Canadians remain adamantly opposed to accommodating turban-wearing Sikhs within the RCMP or the Canadian Legion. *What is it about about such ostensibly minor adjustments that seems to bring out the worst in a society where multiculturalism prevails? Why can't we just all get along?*

- People of colour compared with the general population appear to be underpresented in Canadian television programming. Those who make it remain locked into stereotypical roles as villains or victims. *Why are institutions, including the mass media, reluctant to accommodate diversity in a manner that is proportionate or progressive?*

- The Innu of Labrador protest against "southern justice" as too punitive in orientation and adversarial in style, preferrring instead a more traditional focus on reconciliation and healing. *Should the Innu (or any aboriginal people) be subject to the same laws and judicial systems as all Canadians? How and why are mainstream institutions often inappropriate for addressing aboriginal concerns?*

- The Québécois have threaten to leave Canada if English-speaking Canadians reject their demands for "distinct society" status. *Why is it so difficult to keep Quebec within the confederation? What do the Québécois want, and is there anything that English-speaking Canada can do to accommodate these demands, short of condoning secession?*

- White supremacist groups continue to proliferate at grassroots levels by tapping into a groundswell of discontent created by harsh economic times. *What combination of personal and institutional reforms are required to eliminate racism in all its forms, from the overt and the ugly to the subtle and the systemic?*

- The First Nations demand an end to colonialist dependency in favour of greater jurisdictional control and self-determination over their lives and life chances. *Why is inherent self-government a key aboriginal plank? How will restoration of this right influence the restructuring of aboriginal-state relations? What are the anticipated effects should Canada decide to recognize inherent self-government rights of the First Nations?*

- Immigration into Canada stands at about 250,000 per year despite mounting public concerns. The government responds by threating to cut back on the family reunification category which currently accounts for about 45 percent of the total. *What is the right amount of immigration into Canada? Should family or independent class prevail? From where should immigrants arrive? Can we justify the criteria for each of these responses?*

- Certain minorities do well in Canada, both socially and economically. Others do not when measured by various socioeconomic indicators. Still others are perceived as a menace to Canadian society because of so-called criminal tendencies. *In what way has crime become "racialized" in Canada? How do we account for the "criminalization" of certain minorities? Are certain minorities likely to commit crime? Are race-based statistics a valid means of finding out?*

- Aboriginal males represent one of the most suicidal groups in the entire world, with rates at 56 per 100,000 compared with 14.6 for Canada's general population. *What is the cause of this worrying figure, and what can be done to reduce these rates of self-destruction?*

- A Revenue Canada office in downtown Toronto is occupied by aboriginal protesters who demand non-taxation for aboriginal peoples who live or work off the reserve. *Should aboriginal people have to pay taxes just like all Canadians? Or are they exempted from taxation because of constitutional guarantees to recognize existing aboriginal and treaty rights? Is civil disobedience an effective tactic to deal with the issue?*

- Surveys indicate that Canadians resolutely oppose employment equity initiatives as a means of moving over and making space for certain minorities. *What can we deduce from this negativity to employment equity? Are negative responses the function of survey questions, or do they reflect a genuine dislike of government-imposed social engineering?*

- There are growing fears that the forces of ethnicity have the potential to dismember Canadian society. *Why have forces of ethnicity replaced ideological conflicts as a primary source of intergroup confrontation? Does multiculturalism contribute to or detract from the ethnic experience in Canada?*

- In an attempt to become more inclusive, public institutions such as education have eliminated explicit Christian references and symbols from the annual Christmas celebrations. *Is this an example of accommodating diversity or does it represent a violation of majority rights that infringes on core Canadian values?*

- Canadians appear to have become increasingly concerned about the dizzying pace and scope of diversity. Many blame increased immigration while others chastise misguided government policies. *To what extent is diversity good or bad for Canada? Does diversity contribute to or detract from Canadian society-building?*

INTRODUCTION

All of the above are examples of group dynamics that have bolted to the forefront of Canadian society. Each of these incidents not only cuts to the core of how we see ourselves as Canadians; they also remind us of what needs to be done to enhance survival in a changing and diverse society. Each issue is specific to time and place, yet cumulatively they point to a specialized form of patterned interaction involving minority and majority groups. These interactional patterns neither originate in a social vacuum nor unfold outside of a wider political and economic context. They are constructed instead within a broader framework of political and historical forces. The fact that these relations are inseparable from patterns of power and inequality also contributes to the often confrontational nature of majority-minority interaction.

All interaction at individual or group levels is patterned. These patterns may be relatively equitable when social participants possess equivalent access to power, resources, and decision making. They become unequal, however, if power differentials pervade or intrude — as usually is the case with minority groups. In other words, race, aboriginal, and ethnic relations embody a network of patterned yet often unequal interactions involving diverse groups within a specific social and historical context (see also Rose 1957).

The notion of race, aboriginal, and ethnic relations as patterned process is critical for several reasons. First, social reality is created by the cumulative impact of complex group interaction. Second, reality is shaped by the social and political circumstances that support or negate patterns of intergroup behaviour. Third, in an era of instantaneous communication, the broader (national and international) context is an influential force on local dynamics. Fourth and last, we must select a perspective or perspectives that can account for the constructed and formative properties of intergroup relations. Responding to each of these imperatives will form the basis on which this chapter is structured. Key terms and concepts will also be introduced for sorting out the relational components of race, aboriginal, and ethnic dynamics in Canada.

INTERGROUP DYNAMICS: PATTERNS AND OUTCOMES

Our approach to race, aboriginal, and ethnic relations is decidely macro-sociological, that is, we focus on the actions of people as members of large groups or institutions — governments, ethnic groups, societies, and so on. We begin by assigning a higher priority to the study of intergroup relations than to the description of minority groups or ethnic cultures (see Martin and Franklin 1973). This emphasis on group dynamics draws attention to the wider context that anchors developments in collective behaviour (Dashefsky 1975). Approaches that deal with attitudes, beliefs, or intersubjective experiences are not dismissed outright. They simply are secondary to the social conditions that give rise to patterned dynamics and unequal relations.

Contact and Response

Race, aboriginal and ethnic relations do not materialize from nowhere. Patterns of interaction evolve instead when racially or ethnically different groups come into sustained contact. Several types of contact situations are possible, singly or in combination with others (Feagin 1984; See and Wilson 1988). First, a dominant group incorporates or annexes foreign territory by force or conquest. The British conquest of the French on the Plains of Abraham in 1763 serves as an example that even today continues to rankle and provoke. Second, colonization and frontier expansion results in the acquisition of land or resources through peaceful avenues. Territories may be acquired by purchase or treaties such as between Canada's aboriginal peoples and the federal government. Third, forced migration is another possibility. A subordinate group is forcibly brought into the country for essentially exploitative purposes. The importation of Africans into United States — and into Canada but on a more limited basis — as slave labour is a classic example. Finally, we have voluntary migration from overseas. Immigration entails the premeditated and regulated movement of immigrant populations into the host society. These scenarios are not mutually exclusive, of course, but may coexist or overlap without fear of contradiction.

Sustained contact invariably leads to a patterned set of responses and relations. The sorting out of these relations is "loaded" from the outset. Discrepancies in power transform the contact situation into a relationship of domination and/or exploitation (Schermerhorn 1956). The resulting interaction not only crystallizes into an asymmetrical social structure: It also gives rise to a limited number of patterned yet unequal outcomes. The range of outcomes can span the spectrum from genocide or subjugation on the one hand, to that of accommodation and assimilation on the other, with multi-layers of separation or pluralism in the middle. The exact response will vary with the nature of the contact situation — its purpose, timing, the relative strength of competing groups, and the magnitude and scope of the contact situation. In some cases, the responses exist as implicit government guidelines; in others, an explicit and formal government policy is articulated for the management of race, aboriginal, or ethnic relations. In other words, when two unequal groups interact, one (or more) of the following scenarios (as policy outcomes or interactional styles) will materialize: genocide, assimilation, integration, segregation, and cultural pluralism.

Genocide/Ethnocide

A militarily powerful group may embark on a course of action that obliterates a weaker group up to and including the point of extinction. **Genocide** (or ethnocide) lends itself to different definitions, but most include the notion of deliberate and systematic mass killings of a despised group who dwell in a territory occupied and controlled by the killers (McGarry and O'Leary 1994). This mass liquidation process is not an isolated event by poorly disciplined militia; it may well embody an orchestrated campaign of terror involving a network of institutions, operating procedures, and ideological assumptions that sanctions the dehumanization and destruction of the evil incarnate other. It does not necessarily reflect the result of natural differences but the manipulation of these differences by cynical elites who will stop at nothing to retain power or privilege (Ignatieff 1995).

The process of genocide can encompass varying strategies: from ones that explicitly seek to exterminate "troublesome minorities," to those that inadvertently erase the cultural basis of minority societies. This demolition may be attained directly at times through military means. Indirect means may entail the spread of disease or loss of livelihood or resocialization. The cumulative effect is the same: Customs, values, and identities that threaten dominant rule come under prolonged attack, in the process pushing remnants of the population to the brink of extinction from which recovery is difficult. Group survival is also jeopardized through the introduction of foreign practices such as education or organized religion.

INSIGHT

The Road to Hell...

The harm that people do does not necessarily stem from the malevolent actions of sinister characters. The evil that is inflicted on others may arise from the logical consequences of often well-meaning actions based on faulty logic or ethnocentric assumptions. Coping with "the banality of evil" is not an isolated event, but encompasses a variety of regressive situations, ranging in scope from the genocidal machine of Nazi Germany, to more contemporary expressions in systemic racism.

A similar line of thinking can apply to the impact of missionization on indigenous peoples. Missionaries of the nineteenth century may have landed with a genuine interest in the well-being and conversion of aboriginal people. They also carted around a set of cultural blinkers with a self-righteous sense of Euroamerican superiority. This perceptual bias proved destructive: Securing the conditions for domination and control implicated the missionaries as accomplices in the conquest and colonization of indigenous peoples. Failure to separate the gospel from the sociocultural baggage of Western society culminated in the cultural genocide of many aboriginal tribes, the effects of which are still being experienced at present.

These assumptions and conclusions are consistent with the theme of missionization as a systemic evil. Pre-modern missionaries did not set out deliberately to destroy aboriginal communities. As a rule, they were not evil or unprincipled scoundrels, but well-intentioned individuals, many of whom underwent extreme privations in pursuit of their evangelical goal. Nor can they be blamed for their ethnocentrism: Like all individuals, they were people of the times who could not possibly have an awareness or understanding beyond what was culturally permissable, much less appreciate the long-term consequences of their actions. They embraced a specific culture that furnished a habitual frame of reference, not only for understanding the context, but also for proposing solutions to problems in line with Euroamerican interests. Euroamerican superiority in culture and religion ("civilization") was taken for granted; by contrast, aboriginal peoples were sometimes portrayed as savages, other times as childlike and innocent, but always as culturally inferior. Blinded by this cultural myopia, in other words, missionaries were no different from others who promulgated the Western illusion of world superiority as inevitable and the unquestionned standard to aspire to.

However well-intentioned but misguided, many argue, cultural naivete is unacceptable as an excuse to exonerate missionaries from the devastation and death that was inflicted. In the final analysis, they must take responsibility for the demoralizing consequences of their actions as partners in genocide — whether deliberate or unintentional. The act of missionization consistently lent legitimacy and theological justification to European colonization, even when missionaries protested to the contrary. The act of pacifying tribal communities simplified the political subjugation of tribal communities while fostering the conditions for economic exploitation. Prosyletization by missionaries did not simply mean conversion to Christ through the scriptures. It also involved the intentional or unwitting removal of aboriginal structures and their replacement with Euroamerican equivalents.

The social-psychological effects were equally devastating to say the least: Conversion and forced alienation from tradition inexorably led to the internalization of inferiority as well as the devaluation of aboriginal spirituality, in effect leading to self-loathing and hatred that lingers into the present. The horrific statistics that chronically plague aboriginal communities and reflect their dysfunctions and dependencies are part of the continuing legacy of missionization. To be sure, less attention is devoted to the positive dimensions of missionization as a buffer for coping with the demands of inevitable change. Nevertheless, the road to earthly hell is frequently paved with a history of good intentions often masquerading under self-serving doctrines such as "God's work," "divine will," and "white man's burden."

How accurate and believable is this attack on missionization? Is it logical to accuse missionaries of cultural genocide; or is the notion of missionaries as partners in genocide a case of polemics or hyperbole? Historically, the concept of genocide has referred to the systemic and deliberate mass killings of a group in the territory in which the killers reside. Critics, however, juxtapose the adjective "cultural" with genocide, then proceed to define cultural genocide as destruction of a people — both systematic and systemic — through elimination of those cultural values that provide meaning, identity, security, commitment, community, and continuity. Cultural genocide is consistent with the concept of systemic racism: Both scenarios emphasize context and consequences rather than motive and formality as the source of wrongdoing. As a result, even good intentions can lead to the logic of annihilation. But if everything is defined as genocide, as many are inclined to believe, then nothing is genocide. Such inclusiveness may have the effect, however unintended, of trivializing the suffering of those — from Stalinist purges to Serbian "ethnic cleansing" and Rwandan interethnic butchery — who have experienced ruthless extermination in the name of a godless humanism.

SOURCE: Tinker 1993

There are numerous examples of indigenous peoples who have (nearly) vanished. Australia's aboriginal populations were deliberated stalked and killed by European settlers in an effort to assert colonial control over what they saw as "pestiferous vermin." Likewise, aboriginal groups such as the Beotuck in Newfoundland became extinct as a result of contact with early European immigrants. The twentieth century record is no less disquieting: Ukrainians have suffered massive losses in famines engineered by Stalinist purges. Armenians were victimized by genocidal practices under the Turkish regime during the First World War. Millions of Jews and other despised minorities were liquidated under the Nazi banner. The blatant mistreatment of indigenous populations by settlers and miners in the Amazonian rainforest has proven destructive (Chagnon 1992). The Iraqi regime has also been accused of genocide and mass extinction (including the use of poison gas) in its efforts to squash the insurrectionist Kurdish populations in the north. The "ethnic cleansing" campaigns by Serbs against Moslem populations in Bosnia are likewise an incident of genocide, as are the murderous rampages in Rwanda where violence has been a recurrent feature in the struggle between the Hutu and Tutsi for control over government (Lemarchand 1993) (see Chapter 6, "The Ethnic Experience").

Assimilation

Assimilation can be defined as a one-way process of absorption — either deliberate or unconscious, formal or informal — whereby the dominant sector imposes its culture, authority, values, and institutions on the subordinate sector (Park 1950; Gordon 1964). The minority in turn loses its distinctiveness because of exposure to the forces of conformity. The concept itself was taken from biology, and reflected a scientific belief that social life could be better understood by drawing analogies with the natural processes of a living organism (Jaret 1995).

The process of assimilation occurs in those environments where the dominant group attempts to absorb (rather than physically obliterate) the subordinate group. Through assimilation, the dominant element seeks to (a) undermine the cultural basis of subordinate society, (b) transform minority members into patriotic and productive citizens, and (c) facilitate their entry and transition into the mainstream. The values, beliefs, and social patterns of the dominant group are defined as inevitable or desirable; conversely, subordinate sectors are dismissed as inferior or irrelevent. Collectively, members of this group are portrayed as "children" who need guidance, discipline, and control under the ever-vigilant eye of a judicious parent. Like children, they too are expected to abandon their "simple past" in exchange for outward compliance ("conformity") with so-called mature values and institutions.

As policy or practice, assimilation can be expressed or implemented in a variety of ways. Unobtrusive or informal means are employed at times to weaken prevailing cultural practices. One example is the promotion of the dominant ideology at the expense of alternate world views and values. Explicit or formal government regulations are also activated to hasten absorption. Assimilation may also happen involuntarily through repeated exposure to dominant values and institutions. The processes of assimilation are aptly illustrated in Canada throughout the text. For comparative purposes, we have chosen New Zealand as a case study for highlighting key points in the assimilationist drama.

CASE STUDY

He Iwi Kotahi Tatou — We Are All One People?

TRADITIONAL MAORI SOCIETY

The various Maori tribes collectively known as the *tangata whenua o Aotearoa* represent the indigenous inhabitants of Aotearoa having occupied New Zealand for up to a thousand years prior to European contact. The Maori tribes shared much in common with their Polynesian descendents, despite certain cultural differences created by historical and environmental circumstances. Like most Polynesians, the Maori lived in relatively self-sufficient communities (*hapu*) of related families (*whanau*). They subsisted by horticulture and foraging. The unit of political reality rarely extended beyond the tribal level (*iwi*) although, on occasion, a group of related tribes (*waka*) collaborated in a joint effort for military or economic reasons. As was common in pre-capitalist societies, Maori social organization was communal and organized around the dual principles of kinship and residence. Formal hierarchies of status and rank were important but not to the extent in Polynesians kingdoms such as Tonga or Hawai'i. A premium on personal honor, revenge, and generosity characterized interpersonal relationships. These virtues were often defined, expressed, and consolidated through inter-hapu warfare and competitive feasting (Parsonson 1981). Spiritual agents and the transcendental forces of *mana* (power) and *tapu* (prohibition) pervaded the Maori cosmos, reinforcing the prevailing distribution of power and authority (see Metge 1976; Davidson 1981 for overview).

EARLY EUROPEAN CONTACT AND SETTLEMENT (1840–65)

Maori tribes lived in relative isolation for many centuries. The explorations of James Cook and others paved the way for an influx of Europeans from whalers and traders to adventurers who arrived in hopes of striking it rich. These sojourners were dislodged eventually by the systematic colonizing efforts of missionaries and settlers. The ensuing patterns of interaction between Maoris and the *Pakeha* ("white Europeans and their descendents") was not altogether different from what evolved in other colonialist settings such as Canada (Armstrong 1987; also Fisher 1980). The cycle moved through the phases of initial cooperation, increased competition for land resources, escalation of conflict to the point of open skirmishes, and withdrawal of the vanquished aboriginal sectors from involvement in society.

The signing of the Treaty of Waitangi in 1840 established a blueprint for Maori-Pakeha relations that has continued into the present. A relatively enlightened social contract for its time between founding nations, the Treaty provided Maoris with British citizenship and rights to their resources in exchange for some kind of British sovereignty over New Zealand. Maori-Pakeha relationships were to be modelled under the slogan of *he iwi kotahi tatou* ("we are one people"). However lofty this rhetoric, it became quickly apparent that the one-people ideal was grounded on the priority of Anglo-

Saxon values and institutions. The Maori may have been highly regarded in the evolutionary scheme, but the Pakeha remained resolutely opposed to any social order at odds with Western racial and cultural superiority (Sinclair 1971). The spirit of accommodation which initially characterized Maori-Pakeha relations disappeared in the face of settler greed for land and control. The ensuing New Zealand Wars of the 1860s consolidated settler control over much of New Zealand at the expense of the Maori.

A CENTURY OF ASSIMILATION (1860-1960)

For much of the nineteenth and twentieth century, a commitment to assimilation furnished an ideological paradigm for defining government interaction with the aboriginal population. Then as now, the Maori were regarded for the most part as a "social problem." They either "had problems" or "created problems" because of cultural differences and competition over power and resources. Early British Maori policy revolved about the need to protect and assist the Maori, but with the eventual objective of assimilation into the mainstream always present. Assimilation as policy sought to establish government control over the Maori by phasing out as humanely as possible the cultural basis of their society. Virtually all legislation passed in Parliament concentrated on "the detribalization of the Maoris — to destroy if it were possible, the principle of communalism which ran through the whole of their institutions, upon which their social system was based, and which stood as a barrier in the way of all at-tempts to amalgamate the Maori race into our social and political system" (New Zealand Parliamentary Debates 1870:361).

Passage of the *Native Land Act* (1865) and the *Native School Act* (1867) hastened the demoralization of the Maori through the imposition of liberal-capitalist values (such as privatized land ownership and sales) at odds with a communal Maori culture. Nowhere was the irrelevance of Maoridom more evident than in the wholesale dismissal of Maori language as a tool of daily communication. Following New Zealand's assumption of responsible government during the 1860s, English emerged as the sole language of instruction at school. Maori was subsequently downgraded to the status of a rural folk language for use at home and around ceremonial occasions (Dewes 1968). Land continued to be alienated in the name of progress and civilization. The cultural basis of Maori society was dismissed as anachronism and subject to further suppression. Special measures such as the system of separate Maori seats in Parliament were later instituted when the assimilation of Maoris proved more difficult than anticipated.

Few disputed the inevitability and desirability of assimilation as government policy. Underlying assumptions were regarded as too obvious to require defence or analysis. Only questions related to means, pace, or scope of absorption — whether rapid or gradual, piecemeal or wholescale — were left open for debate. As a result of this assimilative pressure, the Maori population consequently declined to a point where its demise was widely accepted as unfortunate but inevitable in the face of relentless evolutionary progress.

ASSIMILATIONIST WINE IN INTEGRATION BOTTLES (1961–78)

National and international events led to the replacement of assimilation by the late 1950s with the principles of integration. Unlike assimilation which sought to absorb Maoris with complete loss of culture, an integration model espoused the retention of Maoritanga (Maori culture) within an overall Pakeha framework (Hunn and Booth 1962). Government commitment to integration was formally launched in 1961 with the publication of the Hunn Report. Integration sought to break down the social isolation of the Maori, while removing those discriminatory barriers that precluded equal treatment and basic human rights. It envisioned the achievement of equal rights and opportunities for the Maori, but not at the expense of depriving them of the right to cultural pursuits of their choice. Ideally, it sought to combine Maori and Pakeha elements into one ongoing New Zealand culture without destroying the cultural distinctiveness of either.

The rhetoric of integration did not match reality. There was much in the assumptions and objectives of integration that upheld assimilation as the preferred policy ideal. Maori leaders, in particular, were skeptical of any appreciable difference in content. As far as they were concerned, a policy of integration merely served to disguise the assimilative intent of government policy in the same way that appeals to assmilation had concealed earlier motives for divesting the Maori of their land. As aptly put in a Maori proverb, "'Let's integrate!' the shark said to the kahawai,

then swallowed the small fish for breakfast." Nor did a commitment to integration acknowledge a tenacious Maori pride in their cultural heritage, combined with a general dislike of Pakeha values despite high levels of admiration (Report, "A Maori View of the Hunn Report," 1961). To Maori leaders, the conclusion was inescapable: both assimilation and integration shared a common political objective, that is, the creation of a uniform society with a conformist set of political and social values. Maori cultural space was devalued except in the most trivial sense of the term. Growing Maori activism during the 1970s illustrated the extent to which the government had miscalculated the tenacity of assimilation and its growing irrelevance for managing diversity.

ASSIMILATION — PROBLEM OR SOLUTION?

Evidence suggests the Maoris have paid a high price as victims of assimilation. Despite recent improvements, Maoris as a group persist at the bottom of the socioeconomic ladder (Spoonley et al. 1991). They continue to be underrepresented in terms of educational and employment achievement. By contrast, many are overrepresented in areas related to crime, incarceration, morbidity and mortality. Compounding this physical impoverishment is the continued decline of Maori language, culture, and identity. Numerous urban Maori youth have lost any ability to speak or think in Maori terms, much less to identify with their cultural background. Although recent efforts at revival such as the recognition of Maori as an offi-

cial language alongside English are encouraging (Fleras 1987), it remains to

be seen if the costs of assimilation can
be reversed.

An unflagging commitment to assimilation evolved as the tacit framework for justifying government actions in settler colonies. An enlightened social policy for its times, assimilation gradually lost its lustre as an organizing principle, but has continued to play a prominent role in managing diversity even into the present.

The concept of assimilation has undergone a rethinking in recent years (see Jaret 1995). Assimilationist policies are rarely are intended to transform the subordinate sector in its entirety. The complete absorption of minority members as mainstream equals is neither attainable nor always desirable. Few majorities possess either the resources or the political will to enforce total conformity and wholescale conversion. What is subsumed under assimilation instead are the virtues of **dominant-conformity** (or **anglo-conformity** in areas under British control). Subordinate group members need only express outward compliance with dominant values and practices. Select elements of their cultural lifestyle are tolerated as long as they (a) are restricted to the private or personal realm, (b) involve only the "cultural" (aesthetic) realm, (c) conform to majority commercial, political, or ideological interests, and (d) do not violate basic moral principles or the law.

The refurbishing of assimilation is evident in other ways. Once most discussions of race and ethnic relations were couched in an assimilationist framework, with different groups plotted on a continuum from contact to absorption (Park 1950). Assimilation is now viewed as a process of social change involving several different but interrelated dimensions (Gordon 1964). Behavioural assimilation consists of minority acceptance of majority values; structural assimilation refers to minority incorporation into mainstream organizations and general civic life. The two patterns may not coincide. Nor does growing acceptance or incorporation automatically reduce attachments to ethnic cultures or engagement with ethnic community members. This issue will be explored more carefully in the chapter on ethnicity. Suffice at this point to remember that assimilation is a complex and multidimensional process that unscrolls at a varying pace, involves different intensities of absorption, and entails varying magnitudes of conformity (Gordon 1964; Fleras 1984).

Segregation and Separation

The patterns associated with segregation go beyond a physical separation of unequal groups. The dominant groups defines itself as superior because of technological, military, social, or moral properties. The others are dismissed as inferior or irrelevant to the nation-building process. Interaction between the segregated sectors is kept to minimum except in situations of obvious benefit to the controlling sector.

In other words, segregation is not only about a geographical relationship; it is also about a social relationship involving patterns of power and domination (Jaret 1995). Various reasons may account for this enforced isolation, for example, ethnocentrism and supremacist ideologies, group preference, socioeconomic differences, fear and hatred of others, resource competition, and discrimination.

One type of segregationist system is known as **plural society** (Furnival 1937; Smith 1965). Plural societies (not to be confused with cultural pluralism) are segmented into relatively autonomous dominant and subordinate groups. Each sector possesses a distinct and parallel set of institutions except at political or economic levels where a limited degree of interaction must occur. Contact between the two realms is kept to an absolute minimum. Both the dominant and subordinate group live apart as sharply divided and culturally distinct groups. Interaction is conducted primarily in the marketplace ("selective incorporation") where the dominant group exercises monopolistic control over the economy and distribution of wealth. Compliance and citizenship are not secured by value consensus or social norms, but by coercion (van den Berghe 1970). In the absence of any morally legitimate basis to govern, the dominant group must rely on (the threat of) physical force to compel obedience and order. In short, this system of segmentation and limited incorporation is bound by a combination of racist ideologies, political and economic self-interest, military might, and the long arm of the law.

Examples of segregationist policies are commonplace. Such a system existed in southern United States before and after the Civil War. Blacks and whites were separated by law and custom into different communities prior to the desegregation movements of the 1950s and 1960s. Segregation was enforced in restaurants, in public transport, and in major social institutions such as hospitals, churches, and schools. The labour force was racially stratified. Inter-racial marriages were prohibited in many states. The colour bar lead to inferior levels of developments among blacks; this in turn became a self-fulfilling prophecy and increased discrimination against a segregated population. It should be noted that segregationist laws existed in Canada despite our lofty reputation as the antithesis of the States (Walker 1995).

The Civil Rights movements of the 1960s dismantled many of the egregious dimensions of segregation. African-Americans received formal equality before the law, while discriminatory barriers were eased with the introduction of affirmative action programs during the 1960s. Despite de-segregation, many African-Americans continue to be plagued by the aftermath of segregation such as confinement to economic ghettos. The fact the vast majority of whites continue to live in exclusively white areas (less than 1 percent black), while most African-Americans reside in predominantly black residential areas, attests to the fact that segregation is alive and well in the USA (see Jaret 1995).

Few cases of segregation are as highly profiled as that of apartheid in South Africa. The implementation of a comprehensive set of segregationist laws and practices virtually segregated blacks from whites into separate groups at social, economic, and political levels. The next case study reveals the magnitude and scope of segregation, its impact on South African society, and recent moves to dismantle the system of apartheid.

CASE STUDY

Apartheid in South Africa

Of the many paradoxes inherent within South African race relations, none is as notorious as the political, economic, and social gap between the 4.5 million whites and the 27 million blacks. This gap can be attributed in large part to the effects of a system of institutionalized separation known as apartheid. Apartheid, only recently ended, imposed the organizing framework around which black and white relationships were defined and ranked. Historically, apartheid was formally instituted as law in 1948 by the Afrikaaner-based Nationalist Party. Its creation merely codified what had existed informally at political, social, economic and political levels — the escalating separation of South Africa into blacks and whites. Emphasis was focused on managing the presence of a large black population without undermining white power and privilege.

Two paradoxes sought refuge in the rationale for apartheid. On the one hand, whites wanted to maintain the integrity and unity of their cultural lifestyles, without relinquishing political control and economic domination to the black majority. On the other, they were surrounded by blacks who could not be expelled for a variety of demographic and economic reasons. While whites wanted to incorporate blacks as menial labourers into a resource-based economy, they did

not want to include them as equals at the social and political realm. This ambivalent desire to economically incorporate the blacks within a framework of political and cultural separation stimulated the appearance of **apartheid**.

Apartheid refers to the process of separate development between blacks and whites. It envisioned a complex and cooperative social system in which white South Africa would be surrounded by a relatively independent set of satellite black nations or homelands (bantustans). The bantustan model was inspired allegedly by the system of reserves established in Canada and the United States. Each black belonged to one of these states, such as Transkei; this, in effect, denied individual access to the benefits and privileges of South African citizenship. These homelands provided white South Africa with the labour it required without having to move over and share power.

To implement the principles of apartheid, a series of laws were passed to separate the races at the political, economic, social, and cultural level. The *Population Registration Act* was passed in 1950 to regulate the influx of migrant labourers. Provisions of the Act imposed compulsory registration according to race and ethnic group. The *Group Areas Act* then outlined where blacks could or could not live, although inevitably some breakdown occurred. This was especially evident with the proliferation of black suburbs in Sharpeville and Soweto. These black townships were not intended as permanent residences: the Bantustans existed for that. But in light of the need for an accessible labour force, the authorities ignored these violations. Finally, a series of discriminatory practices were instituted to deny black access to normal amenities. These included white-only beaches, the prohibition on mixed marriage or even mixed sexual relationships, and "pass laws" on where people could go or live. Many of these were either modified or eliminated in response to national and international pressure.

A new era has dawned in South Africa. With the release of black leader Nelson Mandela from prison, conferral of universal enfranchisement, and multiparty elections, apartheid has been dismantled and replaced by a democratic rule and a non-segregationist system of race relations. Intertribal tranquility appears to have been established in the wake of violence that claimed up to 12,000 blacks. An interim national unity government under Nelson Mandela and dominated by the ANC (African National Congress) is making slow progress in jobs, schools, health, and housing (Cook 1995). Nevertheless, the legacy of apartheid continues to flourish in the social and economic sector. Black workers earn about one-eighth of the monthly income of whites; black infants are six times more likely to die than whites; and illiteracy rates are 1 percent among whites, 46 percent among blacks, (*Newsweek*, May 9, 1994). Nor is there any mechanism in place to transfer economic power from four million white to 27 million blacks in a country of 4.5 million taxpayers, of high deficits and labour costs, with a poor track record in attracting foreign investment (Cook 1995). In other words, the painful reality is sinking in: It will taken more than ballot-box democracy to smash the chains of dependency and impoverishment after three centuries of colonialist domination (Watson 1995). Even the relatively smooth shift from apartheid to majority rule may experience a bumpy ride if reality clashes with expectations.

Segregation can be imposed as noted above. It can also be generated from "below" by groups who prefer **voluntary separation** from society. For example, the Hutterites of Western Canada and other communal religious sects have voluntarily divorced themselves from the outside world through expressions of religion, language, communal lifestyle, dress, and social interaction. Only contacts at the marketplace level are maintained. This separation is reinforced by the friction which develops from time to time between conflicting sovereignties (for more on Hutterites, see Chapter 6, "The Ethnic Experience.")

Elsewhere a separatist relationship can arise from secessionist movements. The emergence of a new global order has opened opportunity for separation from sovereignties once artificially frozen in time because of colonialism or strategic interests (McGarry and O'Leary 1994; Nelson and Fleras 1995). The integration of societies in global economies has paradoxically (or perhaps logically) bolstered demands for local self-determination. Emboldened by these post-modernist ideologies, racial, ethnic, or aboriginal minorities are currently seeking new arrangements within existing state systems. Prime examples consist of threats by Quebec and the First Nations to separate from Canada if demands for "distinct society" status are rebuffed.

Integration

A fourth outcome reflects a commitment to the principles of **integration**. The shift towards integration in Canada and elsewhere represented a mid-twentieth century reaction against colonialism and assimilation as official government policy. Few have dismissed the notion of any distinction between assimilation or integration in impact or intent. Many are not sure of how to assess integration: Some associate integration with the positive goals of equality and participation; others conjure up images of unwanted conformity (UNRISD 1994). Nevertheless, the processes and discourses associated with these techniques for managing diversity are sufficiently distinct to warrant a closer look.

Generally speaking, the concept of integration stands in opposition to segregation. Segregation is defined by forced separation among people who live apart from each other, social and geographically. Integration by contrast refers to a process whereby individuals intermingle with each other at all institutional levels (Jaret 1995). A distinction between de-segregation and integration is also useful. De-segregation entails a dismantling of physical or social barriers and formal equality before the law; integration involves the unification of disparate parts into a cooperative and functioning whole. One is about formal equality (equality before the law), the other concerns substantive equality.

Two variations underly the integration theme. Integration represents a two-way process by which the dominant and subordinate sectors are brought together in a single comprehensive lifestyle, without either losing its sense of distinctiveness. Each is expected to contribute to the construction of the new reality, yet retain a distinguishable presence within the new configuration. Related to this is the variant in which dominant and the subordant groups are encouraged to fuse (merge) together like paints in a bucket. The result of this "blending" process is a new cultural entity comprising both elements is constructed from this admixture. This fusion ("synthesis") of the "modern" with the "traditional" into a relatively homogeneous entity is metaphorically equivalent to the concept of the **melting pot**, an image which is often invoked to describe the ideal underlying American race and ethnic relations.

INSIGHT

Melting Pots and Mosaics

The path to social harmony can follow different avenues of knowledge and understanding. Both Canada and the United States are thought to rely on divergent paths to achieve the goal of harmonious race and ethnic relations. Canadians are reknown for their multicultural commitment to national unity through promotion of diversity; Americans are equally famous for efforts to integrate differences, albeit through the denial of differences. The language of metaphors is frequently employed to accentuate this distinctiveness. Canada's cultural **mosaic** is perceived as superior a discourse about diversity to the **melting pot** in the United States. Compared with their neighbours to the south, Canadians consider themselves to be more tolerant of minorities, more welcoming of immigrants, more accommodative in terms of participation and opportunity, and more respectful toward cultural differences. Canadians also believe that minorities here receive better treatment because of policies and practices that encourage retention of traditional cultures; by contrast, immigrants to the United States are expected to abandon all ethnic community ties by melting into the mainstream.

Not everyone agrees with this conventional wisdom. Prominent social scientists in Canada, such as Howard Palmer and John Porter, have long disputed the reality of these vaunted differences, in effect arguing that Americans are more diversity-oriented than implied by the melting pot metaphor. Conversely, Canadians are less enamored of diversity than repeated mantras about the cultural mosaic would imply. Recently this thesis was put to the test by two prominent sociologists from University of Toronto, Jeffrey Reitz and Raymond Breton. In their book, *The Illusion of Difference: Realities of Ethnicity in Canada and the United States*, published in 1994 by the C.D. Howe Institute of Toronto, Reitz and Breton confirm what a few had suspected: The differences between Canada and the United States are largely illusory when matched against the *realities* of the situation. Even the widely touted opposition between the mosaic and the melting pot is overstated, as far as they are concerned, since the two countries are similar in their treatment of ethnic minorities. Canadians are no more inclined than Americans to value or encourage cultural diversity: Polls even suggest Americans endorse higher levels of cultural retention — at least in intent if not in subjective measures such as ethnic identification or objective criteria such as intermarriage. Other convergences are noted by Reitz and Breton. Rates of assimilation in Canada are comparable to those in the United States: So too are degrees of occupational mobility, levels of racial discrimination, and patterns of minority economic incorporation — with neither country showing much improvement despite government expenditure. To be sure, there are differences in the tone of ethnic and race relations; for example, Canadians tend to be more low key in their debates over diversity, in part because of their historical commitment to tolerance. But many of the widely touted disparities tend to reflect degree rather than kind. Nor have government-mandated initiatives had much of an impact on minority experiences.

Reitz and Breton perform a timely service in debunking certain myths and misconceptions about North American race and ethnic relations. Essentially four major points are subjected to revision:

- Neither the mosaic nor the melting pot are an accurate depiction of historical reality; repeated references can only camouflage the gap between the real and the ideal.
- Canada's cherished cultural mosaic does not stand up to scrutiny; nor does it correspond with the practices and patterns of intergroup relations.

- Canada and the United States are more alike than different when managing race and ethnic relations. Minor differences do not justify the wide disparities implied by the melting pot or cultural mosaic as polarized metaphors. That being the case, the cultural mosaic is not altogether dissimilar from the melting pot in terms of outcomes and consequences.

- Canada's commitment to multiculturalism has not substantially altered public perception of diversity; nor has it enhanced minority cultural retention or life chances. The fact that public support for cultural retention has remained relatively constant since the early 1970s, the study concludes, further diminishes the relevance and/or usefulness of multiculturalism as public policy.

These conclusions are by no means unique or unprecedented. Perhaps Reitz and Breton's contribution resides in quantifying this thesis through use of several national surveys. They base much of their findings on a 1989 Decima survey involving 1000 respondents from Canada and another 1000 from the United States. Problems arise because of obvious pitfalls in any cross-national comparisons given the dynamics that animate each country (see also Weaver 1984). Problems of validity and reliability are no less formidable when dealing with race-related issues. The study itself may be highly selective and subjective, with numerous judgement calls and use of terms which are difficult to define operationally for a variety of reasons.

Still, initial reaction to the findings was favourable. In a lead editorial in The Globe and Mail (June 13, 1994 "The Myth of Canadian Diversity") the editor agreed with Reitz and Breton in repudiating the essential diversity of Canada. Canadians are more homogeneous than many think despite regional, linguistic, and ethnic/racial differences. Focusing on these differences, the editorial moralized, not only detracts from what we share, including a commitment to Canada's social system, tolerance for minorities, and respect for government and law. It also threatens Canada's survival, imperils our governability, distorts the political process, and mangles our self-image as a progressive society.

How valid are these findings? The importance of this study does not lie in what it says, but in what it *doesn't* say. Efforts to equate contemporary multiculturalism with the goal of cultural mosaic as the authors have done may not be accurate. Such a linkage conveniently overlooks the decade-long shift in multiculturalism from a focus on celebrating differences to managing diversity through removal of discriminatory barriers. Nor is there any evidence to promulgate the view that immigrants and refugees rely on multiculturalism to establish distinct ethnic enclaves. With few exceptions, new Canadians are anxious to participate in the mainstream, without necessarily abandoning all identification with their cultural past as the cost of entry (James and Shadd 1994).

In short, a mosaic metaphor does not exist to augment minority cultural retention as living realities. The multicultural mosaic is aimed at de-politicizing diversity as a potent political force. It is concerned with constructing a coherent and equitable society in which diversity can flourish without undermining either the integrity of the whole or uniqueness of the constituent units. Ethnocultures are permissable under multiculturalism; nevertheless, their expression is restricted to the level of individual identification or confined to private or personal domains — provided this does not interfere with the rights of others or violate the laws of the land.

Repeated mantras about the mosaic may confuse or distract. Yet the tolerance and acceptance implied by the mosaic metaphor are potentially liberating. The "slippage" inherent in the mosaic can create flexibilities and toeholds that in turn provide a catalyst for positive change. A social environment is established in which a diversity agenda can be introduced without fear of wholesale public backlash or outcries of cultural apartheid. Moreover, unlike the American melting pot that at best can only *tolerate* differences, the multicultural mosaic has the potential to *bolster* a political and public climate receptive to diversity as a *legitimate* and *integral* component of Canadian society-building. Those who insist on ignoring these nuances are unlikely to appreciate how metaphors — no less than symbols — have the power to move mountains.

In theory, a commitment to integration differs from that of assimilation. Assimilation endorses a one-way process of absorption and conformity with the mainstream. Integration upholds a two-way system of synthesis which ultimately yields a unique cultural fusion. In practice, however, the outcomes of either may be indistinguishable. In both cases, the subordinant group is absorbed into the basic framework as defined by the dominant sector. For example, although immigrants into United States are expected to melt into the American pot, this cauldron remains irrefutably white, male, English-speaking, and middle class in orientation. Any restructuring of American society is recast along the lines and priorities of the dominant sector. The prevailing institutional framework (and the corresponding distribution of power and resources) remains essentially intact. The subordinate sector merely adds a "dash of colour" to an otherwise pre-existing stew.

Cultural Pluralism

Government policies that once diminished the value of diversity are now giving way to alternate arrangements for engaging diversity in a meaningful way. Acceptance of diversity within a national framework is called **cultural pluralism**. Several distinctions are in order: **Cultural plurality** refers to the presence of individuals who are socially and culturally diverse because of international migration or appropriation of indigenous land (Helly 1993). Cultural *pluralism* by contrast is a prescriptive (rather than descriptive) statement that endorses diversity as a key component of an egalitarian society. Ingredients of a cultural pluralism consist of a commitment to secular tolerance, cosmopolitan worldliness, civic nationalism, and rational scientism (Ryan 1995). Neither social inequality nor unequal rights are consistent with a pluralistic society. The state has little choice but to intervene to address minority needs by reaffirming individual rights, rectifying past injustices, reducing social inequities through removal of discriminatory barriers, providing positive actions through affirmative (employment equity) action programs, and protection of traditional language and culture (Helly 1993).

Canada is widely perceived as a cultural pluralistic society. It pays lip service to the legitimacy of ethnic diversity as legitimate and integral. But racial and ethnic minorities are *not* incorporated equally into Canadian society. Their inability to gain access to political, economic, or social rewards can be attributed to racism, class conflict, and cultural differences (Breton et al. 1990; Henry 1994). One set of responses to these inequities is known as **multiculturalism**. (see also Part 3, "Accommodating Diversity"). Multiculturalism as philosophy or policy does not actively promote pluralism per se: Rather it seeks to establish a society that accommodates diversity without destroying the interconnectedness of the parts. Certain patterns and outcomes follow upon pluralist assumptions: Foremost is the right for diversity to take its place as a legitimate and integral component of a national framework. This in and of itself constitutes a departure from the past when dominant-subordinate relations revolved around the nexus of anglo-conformity.

To be sure, numerous perils inhere in a pluralistic philosphy. Many have criticized official multiculturalism as nothing less than a sophisticated variation of assimilation. Others have downgraded multiculturalism as a conflict management device to appease, defuse, and coopt minority groups. Still others pounce on multiculturalism as under-theorized romanticism out of touch with reality. It is seen as a recipe for disaster that inflames ethnic hostilities, incites social cleavages, and undermines the unity and identity at the core of society (Bibby 1990; Bissoondath 1994). These criticism deserve our attention. They also remind us that catchy slogans or metaphors are a poor substitute for a true reflection of the reality of social relations. Nevertheless, as we shall see in the penultimate chapter, a commitment to multiculturalism has payed dividends in redefining the discourse over government-ethnic minority relations (Fleras and Elliott 1992).

To sum up: Diverse responses and patterned outcomes are established when competitively different groups come into sustained contact. The sorting out of this contact situation results in a network of patterned relations, many of which become formalized into explicit government policy that deny differences (assimilation), reject minorities (segregation), demonize outgroups (genocide), tolerate variation (integration) and accommodate diversity (cultural pluralism). To be sure, political strategies for regulating minorities are often mixed and aimed at different target groups rather than discreet or exhaustive (McGarry and O'Leary 1994). As well, some degree of co-existence and duplication are inevitable since social reality cannot possibly be carved into mutual discreet and exclusive categories. Nor is there any definitive proof of which pattern is superior. The policies of genocide, assimilation, integration, or segregation may seek to eliminate ethnic and racial differences. But with the exception of genocide, there is no obvious moral hierarchy that asserts the superiority of one line of response, assuming of course there is widespread consent within the minority group for one option instead of another (McGarry and O'Leary 1994). Table 1.1 highlights some of the key features by way of comparison and contrast.

How do we account for the appearance of one rather than another policy outcome? A complex set of historical and social factors are responsible for variations in patterned interaction. The nature of the contact situation itself can dictate the process of interaction. Outcomes will vary depending on whether the contact is directed at resource exploitation or settler colonization. Responses can reflect ideologies prevalent at the time of contact. For example, early European attitudes respected the Maori of New Zealand. Maoris were eulogized as an evolutionarily sophisticated group, not only because they displayed considerable military prowess, but also because they embraced the arts of civilization (agriculture, Christianity, and literacy). By contrast, the Aborigines in Australia were contemptously vilified as

TABLE 1.1   Patterns of Interaction

	Definition	Objectives	Means	Outcomes
Genocide/ Ethnocide	deliberate mass killing	eliminate or destroy	direct (violent) or indirect (peaceful)	ethnic or racial purity
Assimilation	absorption, Anglo-conformity,	compliance	undermine + transform + incorporate	a white man's world
Segregation	forced separation	colour bar + discriminatory codes	threat of force	separate but unequal
Integration	incorporate + fuse	formal equality	civil rights + education	melting pot
Cultural Pluralism	accept differences	incorporate diversity	removal of discriminatory (both social and cultural) barriers	mosaic

worthless and beyond the pale of civilization. They were perceived as a physically unattractive species with minimal potential for advance. Their crude technology and seemingly random migratory patterns, coupled with an inability to grasp the fundamentals of civilization and Christianity, only confirmed the worst suspicions.

Both examples demonstrate how the social and cultural context can shape majority-minority interaction when mediated by government policy. The highly competitive nature of group interaction in unequal settings becomes clearly apparent. Certain sectors seek to consolidate power and access to resources. Others attempt to redefine an unjust system through peaceful or violent means. Our immediate objective is to examine how different sociological perspectives can address these and related issues with respect to race, aboriginality, and ethnicity.

SOCIOLOGICAL PERSPECTIVES AND MODELS OF DIVERSITY

Sociology as a discipline is often defined as the scientific study of human society (Macionis et al. 1994). Three key components of society are taken as axiomatic: the social dimensions of interpersonal and group behaviour; the social forces underlying consensus or dissensus and stability or change; and the social dynamics in the construction, maintenance, and transformation of social reality. Several conceptual frameworks are available that furnish a unique perspective on society and how it works. These perspectives can also be employed to explore the relationship of diversity to society.

Sociological perspectives of **functionalism**, **social conflict**, and **symbolic interactionism** provide complementary ways of looking at minority-majority relations. (In addition, we briefly attend to alternative approaches such as biological determinism, race prejudice, structuralism, and race relations cycle). Each perspective highlights certain features of society with respect to intergroup dynamics while excluding others. Obvious differences stem from the questions asked, the foundational premises, rules of proof, and supporting data. Each perspective contains a distinctive subject matter in conjunction with a corresponding set of assumptions and key terms. Nevertheless they all have one thing in common: When it comes to explaining group behaviour, each concentrates on the "bigger picture" as a basic point of reference and explanation. Taken together, these multiple perspectives emphasize the relevance of social forces in shaping the character and outcome of race, aboriginal, and ethnic relations. They also assist in explaining why race, ethnicity, and aboriginality constitute formidable forces in their own right, with the capacity to define, regulate, or destroy.

Functionalist Models

As suggested above, each sociological perspective contains foundational premises about the nature of society and human interaction (Burrell and Morgan 1979). For functionalists, society is viewed as a complex whole comprised of interrelated parts that singly and in unison contribute to maintenance and survival. Functionalist perspectives argue that these interrelated parts must work smoothly for the system to operate efficiently. Under optimal conditions, all elements of a society are intermeshed to enhance order and stability. But stresses associated with rapid social change may unravel these relationships to a point of temporary disarray. Countervailing measures are activated to restore a sense of equilibrium and order within society. These self-righting mechanisms provide relief by isolating and removing potentially disruptive situations. In other words, dysfunctions such as conflict and contradiction are viewed as potentially disruptive to an otherwise harmonious society (Parillo 1990). Corrective measures are thus required to reestablish the consensus and deep-seated values at the core of a stable social system.

A functionalist perspective on race, aboriginal, and ethnic relations approaches diversity as a potential threat to a stable, cooperative, and consensual social order. An example might be useful for illustrative purposes. The arrival of immigrants to Canada has proven beneficial to the economic and cultural well-being of society. Immigrants often provide a valuable source of labour to fulfill the needs of an expanding economy. They enliven Canadian society through the richness of their cultural heritages. Yet their entry into Canada can create problems ("dysfunctions") in terms of costs or disruptions. Many are pushed to the socioeconomic margins of society. They frequently are targeted as victims of prejudice and discrimination — both blatant or polite. Their cultural heritage may be inconsistent with the prevailing value system in Canada, further contributing to problems of incorporation and adjustment. In brief, while their contribution to Canadian prosperity is rarely disputed, certain immigrant groups may be viewed as a potential source of conflict ("dysfunction") to an otherwise stable and integrated society.

To rebuff potential conflicts, societies in general (and Canada in particular) have established devices for damage control and conflict management. A variety of institutional arrangements are in place to facilitate the entry of new Canadians. Assimilationist agencies (such as education) are in the forefront to ensure consenus and shared values. Initiatives are implemented to eliminate discrimination or segregration for the good of society. After all, failure to maximize human capital is not only a waste of human potential, but may lower productivity and sow seeds of disarray (Jaret 1995). Other mechanisms such as employment equity or multiculturalism are introduced in hopes of fostering an inclusive environment for accommodating diversity. Only by taking an active and interventionist role in controlling potential conflict, it is argued, can the government establish the climate for improved consensus, cooperation, and sense of community.

Functionalist perspectives are useful in drawing attention to government responses to diversity. It also pays dividends by raising questions about the society-building potential of diversity within society. For example: Is diversity worthwhile? How much diversity can be incorporated without undermining the integrity and character of society? What is the absorptive capacity of society? Will racial, aboriginal, or ethnic diversity persist in the face of pressures for modernization and assimilation? How can we achieve cooperation and consensus in a system of competitive free enterprise? In answering these questions, functionalist perspectives focus on the mechanisms employed by society to cope with potential disruptions and "troublesome" constituents. It remains to be seen whether functionalist thought is capable of addressing issues pertaining to conflict and change at intergroup levels.

Conflict Models

A conflict perspective on society is useful for addressing the dynamics of social life. In contrast with functionalist approaches (with an emphasis on system equilibrium, normative consensus, and institutional integration), a conflict perspective portrays society a complex system of unequal yet competing groups in perpetual competitive over scarce and valued resources, including power, wealth, prestige, and sovereignty (Collins 1975; Kinloch 1977; Boulding 1962; also Coser 1956; 1967). The groups themselves are organized around varying criteria. In some cases groups are identified by virtue of religious, social class, territorial, and language markers. In others, they are classified and organized along the racial and ethnic lines.

For conflict theorists, the normal state of society is conflict and change rather than consensus or stability. Because resources are unequally distributed, society is held together by force or the threat of coercion. Conflict sociologists are not especially anxious to study open confrontation as much as what happens to secure patterns of domination and inequality during periods of relative calm. Nor is conflict perspective intended to portray society in a perpetual state of conflict and confrontation. What is potentially more interesting is how order is maintained without resorting to heavy-handed tactics. At times, the dominant group is powerful enough to defuse the potential for overt conflict. At other times, group hostilities are open, but may subside during periods of relative stability or consensus. A temporary truce may materialize when opposing groups find it mutually advantageous to lay aside their differences in pursuit of common or specific interests. This in turn suggests that conflict and cooperation can be seen best as aspects of a single process involving accommodation and conflict, stability and change, and cooperation and confrontation (Gelfand and Lee 1973).

Two variants prevail: According to "moderate" conflict theorists (Simmel 1950; Coser 1954; Dahrendorf 1959), conflict is a normal and natural component in all societies. Relations between race and ethnic groups are sorted out along poles of domination and subordination (Gelfand and Lee 1973). Groups that are politically or economically dominant will take steps to advance and legitimize their own interests — by coercive means if necessary. They will seek control over key institutions through coalition building or divide and conquer strategies to influence the values and attitudes necessary for status quo (Jaret 1995). By contrast, subordinate groups will take whatever measures are necessary to undermine an unfavourable status quo. Even the outbreak of hostilities in some cases can produce positive results related to social change or group cohesion (Coser 1956). Open conflicts can sharpen normative values, draw groups closer together, and accentuate boundaries between groups in society. Confrontation and conflict over "who gets what" are inevitable under these conditions.

A more radical version of conflict theory incorporates Marxist thinking. It argues that the fundamental contradiction in any complex society is the existence of two social classes: the working and the ruling class. The working class can only survive by selling its labour to the ruling class; the ruling class in turn owns the means of production and will do anything to facilitate the flow of profits from productive property. One tactic is to de-stabilize the workers by fomenting internal divisions based on lines of race or ethnicity. The working classes prefer to present a united front — at least in theory — by playing down the salience of race and ethnicity as secondary to class interests. In both cases, racial, aboriginal, and ethnic minorities are portrayed as pawns with little legitimacy beyond their usefulness to the class struggle.

For conflict theorists, then, society represents an "arena for struggles" (Collins 1975) where racial and cultural groups adopt strategies to dominate, control, and exploit. Situated squarely within the conflict perspective is a widely accepted model of intergroup relations known as **internal colonialism**. This major challenge to assimilation theory argues that the experiences of certain minorities differed from the experiences and eventual assimilation of European immigrants because of their colour (race) and relationship to the means of production (Pedraza 1994). A focus on power and inequality makes the notion of internal colonialism especially appealing for unpacking the politics of majority-minority relations (Hechter 1975). European expansion was directly responsible for the overseas colonization and control of indigenous minorities (Blauner 1972; Feagin 1984). The imposition of white-settler institutions and values may result in the decline of the indigenous group as a viable unit. Forces are brought into play that undermine the capacity of indigenous cultures to impart meaning and security to its adherents. Remnants of the population are relegated to the periphery where they are ignored or divested of their land, identity, or culture. A cultural division of labour is established: members of the subordinate sector are frequently employed as "hewers of wood and drawers of water." Racism is profiled as an ideology to justify the perpetuation of inequality and separatism. Indirect rule and control are facilitated by a system of bureaucracy and administration, such as the Department of Indian Affairs in Canada. The end result culminated in a highly colonialist relationship that is no less exploitative than blatant forms of plunder.

The internal colonialism perspective has contributed to our understanding of intergroup dynamics. Analytical limitations nevertheless remain in stretching the colonial analogy too far (Pedraza 1994; see also Blumer and Duster 1980). Dominant-subordinate relations are couched in deterministic or reductionist terms. Relations between dominant and subordinate groups are portrayed as conspiratorial or unidirectional. Less attention is devoted to the social processes underlying interaction either within or between the colonizers and the colonized. Particularly serious is the exclusion of subordinate groups from the ongoing interaction. Evidence suggests the subordinate sector are not necessarily passive in the face of threats to their lives and life chances (Burger 1987). Different strategies of resistance may be employed, ranging from outright confrontation to passive resistance. Nativistic movements from the Ghost Dance among the American Plains Indians to the "cargo cults" in the South Pacific are just a few of the examples. In some cases the subordinate group may seek a degree of involvement (assimilation) with the dominant sector at some risk to their collective identity. In others, colonized minorities may resort to negotiation and compromise in reclaiming what rightfully belongs to them. In those contexts where the dominant culture is undergoing change because of urbanism, post-industrialism, and social upheaval, the corresponding breakdown in the cultural division of labour may spark collective efforts at resource competition. Culturally specific identities are created and sustained as a basis for collective action, especially when there is a competitive advantage to group affiliation.

Interactionist Models

Both functionalist and conflict perspectives see society as a taken-for-granted point of departure. Society is portrayed as durable and real, existing above and beyond the individual, and exerting vast leverage over people's behaviour. By contrast, interactionist perspectives begin with the notion of society as an active and ongoing human accomplishment. Rather than something "out there" and determinative, society is constantly under construction through group interaction and exchange.

Central to interactionist models are the principles of symbolic interactionism (Blumer 1969). Symbolic interactionism portrays the social world we inhabit as constructed, negotiated, and meaningful. According to this outlook, we do not live in a predetermined world. Rather we create our reality by applying meanings (interpretations) in conjunction with others to a variety of situations. Once a situation has been defined, jointly linked lines of action are developed through negotiation, compromise, and adjustment. The totality of these joint linkages at a given point in time and place is called society.

Interactionist approaches are frequently employed at a micro-sociological level of intersubjective experiences. Race, ethnicity, and aboriginality are treated as resources by social actors in defining situations and acting out on the basis of these definitions. These approaches can also involve macro-sociological concerns involving group dynamics and collective responses at societal levels (Lyman 1984; Fleras 1990). Particular attention is devoted to how the social construction of race, aboriginal, and ethnic relations is typical of group interaction. Minority groups, as Louis Wirth recognized long ago, may seek one of four broad goals — pluralism, assimilation, separatism, or militarism. Conversely, the majority casts for ways to eliminate, isolate, absorb, tolerate, or incorporate.

A **collective definition** approach by Herbert Blumer and Troy Duster (1980) is especially effective in understanding the interactional components of dominant-subordinate relations. A collective definition approach emphasizes the process by which intra- and inter-group relations are defined and constructed as ongoing activities. It deals with the (a) dynamics of group classification and assessment, (b) enactment and accommodation of jointly linked interaction at group levels, and (c) emergent properties of group relations by virtue of adjustments within the defining process. Patterned interaction is thus generated and sustained by opposing elements who compete for definitional control of the situation in an effort to attract constituencies and promote interests. We believe a collective definition approach has much to recommend with its potential to capture the formative and dynamic properties of race, aboriginal, and ethnic relations (Fleras 1990).

The concept of **dualisms** strikes at the core of collective definition. Both the dominant and subordinate group may be internally divided into competing factions known as dualisms. To one side are the dualisms associated with inclusion and exclusion; to the other side are the dualisms of assimilation and separation. These dualisms apply to both the dominant and subordinate sector, creating four interactional possibilities:

> subordinate assimilation + dominant inclusion
>
> subordinate assimilation + dominant exclusion
>
> subordinate separation + dominant inclusion
>
> subordinate separation + dominant exclusion

Consider the possibilities: One faction within the subordinate sector is concerned with assimilation ("inclusion") into the dominant sector, especially when conditions are ripe for economic expansion. The other subordinate faction, however, may reject the legitimacy of the dominant sector, preferring instead to separate ("exclusion")

TABLE 1.2   Models of Collective Definition

	Dominant Inclusion (+)	Dominant Exclusion (–)
Minority Assimilation (+)	+ +	– +
Minority Separation (-)	+ –	– –

through the creation of parallel institutions. Separatist measures are invoked as a tactical strategy to pry concessions from the dominant sector. These dual responses — inclusion or exclusion — are neither mutually exclusive nor fixed perpetuity, but vary over time. Certain conditions may bring about closer identification with the dominant sector (inclusion). Other conditions may activate exclusionary tactics to mobilize people for competition with the dominant group. Regardless of which prevails, these dualistic oppositions (inclusion-exclusion) serve to explain the diverse range of subordinate responses to majority rule.

Equally manifest are dualisms within the dominant sector. The dominant group too is confronted by the option of exclusion or inclusion in defusing challenges to its privilege. On the one hand, those dominant factions who wish to preserve the status quo are likely to engage in exclusionary actions. Elements within this sector may resort to tactics of closure by restricting access to resources and power. On the other hand, there are those who are not threatened by such demands. They are willing to be inclusionary toward subordinate claims and demands, especially if something can be gained by such conciliatory gestures. These dual tensions within the dominant sector give rise to an inner dynamic. When combined with corresponding dualisms within the subordinate group, they provide the transformative dimension to group relations.

The collective definition process is animated by the intersection of these two forces — assimilation/separation versus inclusion/exclusion as shown in Table 1.2. The pull and push of these two dualistic forces introduces an element of instability in intergroup dynamics, as any one of these dualisms may gain ascendency or decline in response to local, national or international developments. This portrayal of social reality as live and interactive makes collective definition a useful way of understanding group dynamics in unequal contexts, as the next case study reveals.

INSIGHT

Collectively Defining Aboriginal-State Relations

Recent trends in Canadian aboriginal-government relations can be examined by way of an interactionist perspective along the lines of collective definition (Fleras 1990). In employing this notion of group behaviour as socially constructed and collectively defined, aboriginal-government relations have undergone something of a reassessment by way of constitutional debate.

Constitutional efforts to redefine the relational status of aboriginal First Nations indicate quite clearly the prominence of competing images and definitions among opposing delegates, as well as shifting tactics and adjustments. The dualisms at play throughout this collective defin- ition process are also evident in these struggles to renew aboriginal-government relations along fundamentally different lines.

Redefining Aboriginal Constitutional Rights

Section 35 (1) of the Constitution Act of 1981 recognized and affirmed the "existing aboriginal and treaty rights" of Canada's First Nations. But inclusion of this clause did not specify the exact nature of these aboriginal rights. Nor did it elaborate on how they would be exercised, re- maining particularly silent over the design and scope of aboriginal self-governing rights. A se- ries of four First Ministers' conferences were convened between 1983 and 1987 to expand on the details of these constitutional rights. Subsequent debates focused on whether section 35 (1) represented an "empty box" clause (contingent rights) with no specific rights except those defined through prior negotiation. Alternately, did the clause entail a "full box" of rights (inherent rights) which only required clarification upon entrenchment within the constitution.

Aboriginal leaders endorsed an inherent (full box) right to self-government by virtue of what they called their priority status as sovereign occupants of land whose rights had never been extinguished by treaty or conquest. Aboriginal delegates proposed an initial constitu- tional entrenchment of self-government, followed by a negotiation of specifics at a later date. Federal and provincial authorities disagreed, and countered with what might be termed a con- tingent (empty-box) rights approach to aboriginal self-government. No proposal for self-gov- ernment would be constitutionally enshrined without first specifying costs, power-sharing, and jurisdictional issues. Many were prepared to negotiate the terms first, then constitutionally en- trench the principle (Opekokew 1987). Disagreement over the "principles-first" versus the "specific-agreement-first" approach to aboriginal self-government proved fatal in the end (Schwartz 1986).

Interactional Logjam

Few were surprised when talks collapsed, given the politics of power and conflict of irrecon- ciliable interests. Federal authorities seemed guardedly receptive toward inclusion of inherent aboriginal rights. Most provinces by contrast balked at the prospect of unrestricted right to self- government for fear of incurring excessive costs and administration. They expressed concern over relinquishing political control of the aboriginal agenda to the judicial sphere. Particularly wor- risome was the politics over power:

> The provinces are concerned with the possible transfer of powers to a third order of government....If there is a transfer of power to an aboriginal self-governing entity within a province, it can adversely affect other parts of the provincial powers (Opekokew 1987:45).

Several compromises were proposed, but federal and provincial leaders in the end rejected what they perceived as an unacceptable restructuring of Canadian society. Few doubted the in- tegrity of the participants. The costs of including aboriginal self-government within the con- stitution was too expensive. This left little recourse except to exclude aboriginal self-governing structures from constitutional debate.

The collective redefinition process failed for a variety of reasons. The lack of political will and imaginative leadership contributed to the breakdown. Failure also can be traced to a per- vasive colonialist mentality which has continued to compartmentalize First Nations as a social "problem" of concern for federal bureaucracy. In direct contrast with the fundamental redefinition proposed by aboriginal sectors, central authorities seem reluctant to treat aboriginal peoples as anything but a disadvantaged ethnic minority group (Shkilnyk 1985). Failure to elevate the collective definition process to a new level of discourse implied a lack of urgency in making ideological changes regarding the relational status of aboriginal peoples (George Erasmus, AFN, *The Toronto Star* 20 August 1987). Until such time as the collective dialogue process was reopened along fundamentally different lines, there appeared little chance of resolving the bottleneck in aboriginal-government relations.

Toward a Renewal

Collapse of talks resulted in government efforts to reincorporate Quebec's entry into Canada as a distinct society. The Meech Lake accord (see Chapter 8, "Charter Groups") proved pivotal in inadvertently drawing political attention to aboriginal issues when a First Nations member of Parliament from Manitoba, Elijah Harper, "de-feathered" the ratification process by voting against the accord while holding an eagle feather symbolizing his solidarity with the concerns of his people. The hostilities at Oka between reserve residents and police further sensitized central authorities to the unfinished business at the heart of aboriginal-state relations. Another collective definition process was set in motion with the Charlottetown Accord in 1992. The Accord not only acknowledged Quebec as a distinct society; it also guaranteed inherent aboriginal rights to self-government, with details to be worked out in consultation with key officials. The fact that aboriginal leaders sat with First Ministers confirmed that the First Nations had arrived as major players in Canadian society-building.

The Charlottetown Accord also crashed to defeat with the October 1992 referendum. The pattern of voting proved a suprise. The majority of aboriginal voters rejected the Accord despite its lofty promises and unprecedented level of power-sharing. A major reason for the rejection was aboriginal concern over the implementation and costs of this new inclusion. The tables had turned: The First Ministers of Canada (including the First Nations) were willing to accept what had been spurned five years earlier. The grassroots in turn had shown a decided preference to distance itself from the restructuring in favour of the status quo. The recent decision to implement a trial self-government arrangement in Manitoba suggests a compromise between the forces of separation versus those of inclusion.

The interactionist approach incorporates a process-oriented and non-deterministic view of inter-group dynamics. Intergroup relations are portrayed as continually emerging and undergoing change through the processes of formation, negotiation, accommodation, and definition. Interactional processes include power, conflict, bargaining, negotiation, adjustment, compromise and counter-claims as part of the ongoing and emergent adjustments. An interactional orientation rejects any kind of static or decontextualized analysis of race relations. Patterns of group associations persist instead in a state of constant flux, dynamic tension, mutual adjustment, and ongoing movement. They are also sustained, modified, and transformed by historical factors and institutional setting. Table 1.3 provides an overview of the interactionist perspective through comparison along different criteria with functionalist and conflict theories.

TABLE 1.3 Sociological Perspectives on Race, Ethnic, and Aboriginal Relations

	Functionalism	Conflict	Interactionism
Nature of Society	stable and integrated	competitive struggles between groups	reality as socially constructed
Status of Diversity	potential threat to consensus and survival	benefit to ruling classes	social actors/component of pluralistic environment
Official Reaction	neutralize negative aspects through government programs	activate to de-stabilize status quo	include or exclude depending on context
Intended Outcome	homogeneous, stable, and consensus-based society	preserve distribution of power and resources	a pluralistic/negotiated social order

Additional Perspectives

Functionalist, conflict, and interactionist perspectives provide a sound theoretical basis on which to study race, aboriginal, and ethnic relations. There are additional approaches that deserve mention. They include biological determinism, race prejudice, structuralism, and assimilation (Blumer and Duster 1980:212-218). Our coverage is brief since several receive additional mention in subsequent chapters. Others are losing favour as systems of explanation — replaced to a large extent by a focus on inequality and conflict perspectives as a preferred style of discourse (Jaret 1995).

Biological Determinism

One of the oldest theories, biological determinism attempts to explain race and ethnic relations in terms of the biological makeup of different groups. The theory is based primarily on the notion of innate and biologically fixed attributes among groups of people known as races. Races are viewed as distinct and discrete biological groupings. Biologically determined differences in intelligence, temperament, and other characteristics provide the raw material for subsequent interaction. These differences determine and explain the relative positions of racial groups in association with each other. That is, those groups with superior innate characteristics are destined to occupy the dominant positions in society. By contrast, racially inferior groups are relegated to the bottom. As we shall see in the next chapter, the theory of biological determinism does not hold up under scientific scrutiny. Points of weakness include difficulties in defining distinct and discrete groups, the dubious value of criteria employed in establishing hierarchies of superiority, and its poor explanatory value in accounting for human diversity over time and space.

Racial Prejudice

The racial prejudice perspective suggests race and ethnic relations stem from the action of racially assertive groups who define and enforce lines of acceptance and exclusion toward outgroups. The ways in which dominant and subordinate groups relate and interact with each other arise largely from attitudes of prejudice (both pre-judgements and misjudgements). These negative attitudes can originate from a variety of perceived sources including innate biological impulses, social conditions, and historical experiences. Conversely, eliminating prejudice can lead to improvements in race and ethnic relations. While the concept of prejudice is discussed more thoroughly in a later chapter, suffice to note that a race prejudice approach cannot adequately explain outgroup hostility in situations where discrimination is high, but prejudice is minimal ("systemic racism").

Structuralism

A third perspective on race and ethnicity is discussed in greater depth in Chapter 4, "Inequality and Stratification." Briefly, structuralism encompasses a diversity of viewpoints which includes both conflict and Marxist perspectives as well as functionalist thought. What is common to all these positions is the belief that race and ethnic relations must be analyzed within the framework of society or specific interests groups. For functionalists, it is the needs of society that dictate the treatment of minorities. For radical conflict theorists, majority-minority relations are inseparable from group competition over scarce resources. Also implicit is the subordination of race and ethnic relations under more basic structures such as class systems. Racial and ethnic activity thus constitute a byproduct of more fundamental social arrangements that account for the organization, differentiation, and exploitation of groups in society.

Assimilation/Race Relations Cycle

The prevailing discourse on American race relations has revolved around the principle of assimilation and its opposition to pluralism (Lyman 1994). America is viewed as a kind of universal and personal achievement-oriented society that liberates individuals from all hereditary claims related to race or ethnicity. Individual success is defined by what a person does, not by who she is or whom he belongs to. This vision focused on the process of social and cultural change that invariably absorbed minorities into the mainstream (Jaret 1995). Reflecting the experiences of immigrants in urban America, race and ethnic relations could be described within a cycle of development that implicated all minorities in a cyclical movement from entry to mainstream (Park 1950). This race relations cycle consisted of a linear and irrevocable progression from competition and conflict to accommodation and eventual assimilation. Topics for discussion might include how to facilitate the absorption of minorities; what barriers exist; why did some groups proceed faster than others. An assimilationist perspective today is poorly positioned to acknowledge the resurgence of ethnicity and ethnic conflicts in different parts of the world. Except perhaps in the United States, its legacy is largely historical in value.

CHAPTER HIGHLIGHTS

- This chapter provides an overview of race, aboriginal, and ethnic relations as socially constructed and patterned interaction involving diverse groups within contexts of inequality and change.

- Sociologists are interested in intergroup relations and may regard the competition and conflict associated with group dynamics as a necessary and normal component of interaction rather than pathalogical result of individual prejudices or irrational fears.

- A rephrasing of race, aboriginal, and ethnic relations as dominant-subordinate (majority-minority) interaction draws attention to the importance of power in shaping intergroup dynamics. Race and ethnic relations are treated as relationships of inequality between groups, and as sociologists we want to know how these inequities are constructed, supported, challenged, and transformed by way of state policies and government practices.

- Patterned interaction is likely to occur when racially and culturally different groups come into prolonged contact and compete over scarce resources. These relations between competitively different groups may crystallize around government policy and practices related to genocide, integration, assimilation, segregation, and pluralism.

- As systems for the management of diversity, genocide represents an orchestrated campaign to eliminate a devalued minority; assimilation consists of a framework for absorbing minorities into the mainstream without necessarily sharing power or cultural space; with its focus on fusion and melting, integration represents a more sophisticated form of assimilation as well as a reaction to segregation; segregation usually implies the rejection and forced separation of minorities from the mainstream; and cultural pluralism acknowledges the legitimacy of diversity and its accommodation within society.

- Various perspectives for the study of racial and ethnic relations are explored, with particular emphasis on functionalism, conflict, and interactionism. These perspectives provide distinct ways of looking at diversity, since each has different assumptions and asks different questions about the status, role, and impact of race, ethnic, and aboriginal relations. Inasmuch as group relations are constructed, patterned, and unequal, each of the models provides certain insights into sorting out diversity in Canada.

- With its focus on societal needs and the importance of consensus and shared values as a basis for stability and survival, functionalist models emphasize the devices for controlling (correcting or eliminating) diversity; conflict models envision society as a site of competition for scarce resources between groups; and interactionist models emphasize the socially constructed and contested nature of group interaction.

- Several other models of race and ethnic relations are briefly discussed, including biological determinism, race prejudice, structuralism, and race relations cycle.

KEY TERMS

Anglo-conformity
   (Dominant
   Conformity)
Apartheid
Assimilation
Collective Definition
Conflict Theory
Cultural Pluralism

Cultural Plurality
Dualisms
Functionalism
Genocide
Integration
Internal Colonialism
Melting Pot
Mosaic

Multiculturalism
Plural Society
Segregation
Symbolic Interactionism
Voluntary Separation

REVIEW QUESTIONS

1) What is meant by a sociology of race, aboriginal, and ethnic relations? Include the notion of patterned interaction in your answer.

2) Briefly compare and contrast the policies and principles of genocide, assimilation, integration, segregation, and cultural pluralism as strategies for managing race, aboriginal, and ethnic relations.

3) Why is it useful to rephrase race and ethnic relations as a relationship of inequality?

4) Compare and contrast the major sociological perspectives on society (functionalism, conflict, and interactionism) with respect to the perception on the status and role of racial, ethnic, and aboriginal minorities.

5) How does a collective definition perspective contribute toward an understanding of race, ethnic, and aboriginal relations?

6) Select any issue or incident involving racial, ethnic, or aboriginal groups. Analyze the issue or incident from one (or all three) perspectives on society.

GLOSSARY

Race can be defined as a socially constructed (rather than biologically valid) principle for classifying individuals into groups and differentiating them on the basis of largely arbitrary physical attributes. Ethnicity also encompasses a principle of organization and differentiation. In contrast with race, however, the criteria involves a common cultural heritage and a shared awareness of descent from common ancestry.

CHAPTER 2

RACE MATTERS

INSIGHT

White Privilege

"I don't think of myself as white," a friend described herself as a child, "I don't feel superior. I just felt normal."
                Quoted in Judith Levine "White Like Me" *MS* (March/April 1994:22-24)

Most Canadians are willing to admit that certain minorities are disadvantaged because of skin colour. Many are also willing to concede that social and economic disadvantages may not result from individual failure. Inequities flow instead from restricted opportunity structures rooted in racial discrimination. The disadvantages of race are widely acknowledged: As Henry and Tator (1993) remind us: "In a white dominated society, the colour of your skin is the single most important factor in determining life chances, as well as your dignity, identity, and self-esteem." But few Canadians are likely to acknowledge their privileged status because of skin colour (McIntosh 1988). Even fewer are prepared to concede how whiteness can directly contribute to the disprivilege of others.

Think for a moment about the privileges associated with whiteness, many of which are taken for granted and unearned by accident of birth. Being white means you can purchase a home in any part of town and expect cordial treatment rather than community grumblings about the neighborhood "going to pot." Being white saves you the embarrassment of going into a shopping mall with fears of being followed, frisked, monitored, or finger printed. Being white means you can comment on a variety of topics without someone impugning your objectivity or motives. You can speak your mind with little to lose if things go wrong. Being white enables you to display righteous anger in dealing with colleagues, yet not incur snide remarks about "aggression" or "emotional stability." Being white rescues you from taking responsibility or making excuses for the anti-social antics of your 'kind.' Being white gives you the peace of mind that your actions are not judged as a betrayal or a credit to your race. Finally, being white provides the satisfaction of cruising around late at night without attracting unnecessary police attention.

In other words, being white is a privilege that is wired into your skin. Whiteness is a kind of entitlement that opens doors and unlocks opportunities in the same way identity cards defined who got what under South Africa's apartheid system. The superiority implicit within whiteness is not openly articulated or deserved, but assumed and universalized as the norm; it is the culturally invisible environment that is never defined as white although non-whites are defined and judged by race (Stamm 1993). As Judith Levine (1994:22) puts it:

> Whiteness purports to be nothing and everything. It is the race that need not speak its name. Yet it defines itself as no less than whatever it chooses to exclude. To grow up white is to be the ground zero from which everything else differs...

In brief, whiteness is the frame of mind that needs no justification. Thus, racism is not about personal prejudices or open discrimination but of stubborn refusal to appreciate the privileges and advantages that adhere to people because of their whiteness, not necessarily because of their merit, ability, or viture. This tacitly accepted but unmarked (that is, unnoticed) category not only makes it difficult to see other viewpoints except as abnormal or deviant, but its unmarkedness also establishes the norm and the standard by which others are judged — and found wanting or in need of justification. Blackness, by contrast, represents the antithesis of whiteness — a stigma (or marked category) rather than a passport to privilege.

Not everyone equates whiteness with privilege. White supremacist groups have cleverly turned the tables by portraying whites as an endangered "race," under threat and challenge by minorities, in the same way men's movements have depicted males as victims of hardnosed feminism and misguided government policy (Farney 1994; Erlich 1994). The very existence of these grievances merely confirms the obvious: Systems of entrenched privilege exist and efforts to confront and challenge them are fraught with resistance and backlash. Herein, then, lies the genius of white privilege: Power and privilege are most secure when they are least intrusive (that is, unmarked) yet most pervasive (that is, act as the standard) sorting out who gets what.

INTRODUCTION: DOES RACE MATTER?

Race, aboriginal, and ethnic relations are inextricably linked with patterns of domination and control. The previous chapter argued that majority-minority relations cannot be considered apart from group dynamics. Nor do these relationships exist outside the general context in which group interaction takes its cue. Foremost to our analysis is the notion of group relations as patterned but unequal. But these patterns of inequality are not random; they tend to cluster around variations based on culture, language, or religious affiliation. No less important a factor is the concept of race.

Few will dispute the significance of race in shaping intergroup dynamics. The construction of race categories not only facilitated European colonialization, they also conferred a pseudo-scientific legitimacy on sometimes questionable schemes that classified humans into mutually exclusive categories on largely arbitrary grounds. Many have questioned the empirical validity of race as an explanatory principle. Critics argue that race is essentially a social construct rather than a biological reality, with next to no scientific value (Miles 1982; 1994). Nevertheless the concept of race continues to attract attention as a preferred means of (a) explaining group differences, (b) rationalizing unequal treatment, (c) condoning a lack of concerted action, (d) simplifying reality, and (e) vilifying scapegoats. Certain races are demonized as inferior because of a perceived propensity to violence, crime, or deviance. Others are typecast as victims in dire need of government intervention for righting historical wrongs. Still others see a gradual reversal: Race is increasingly portrayed as a subject of entitlement rather than an object of scorn for sorting out of who gets what, and why. That is, through such programs as racially based affirmative action, a distinction that once held people back is now employed as a criteria for promotion and group allocations.

Most Canadians appear ambivalent about the race concept. The concept carries a negative connotation that conflicts with the virtues of an achievement-oriented, upwardly-mobile society. Many dislike the underlying message of race: That is, the most important thing about a person is an accident of birth, something beyond control, and that alone should determine job, status, and privilege. Yet race as a source of disadvantage is difficult to dismiss. This ambiguity complicates public perception of race and renders the concept subject to different meanings and constant change (McCarthy and Critchlow 1993). As an explanatory system, it has evolved in meaning from that of (a) a fixed essence (biology = destiny); to (b) a byproduct of class struggles; to (c) an illusory ideological construct yet real in its consequences; and currently to (d) a variable in explaining differences and defining entitlements (McKague 1992; Apple 1993; Omi and Winant 1993). Admittedly, race is not a "thing" out there — a tangible object that can be isolated and measured as a fixed biological entity. It more accurately embraces a system of social relations and cultural constructions in line with human interests, needs, history, and strategies. Likewise, race is not especially well equipped to account for group inequities, in the same way that sex differences cannot explain gender inequalities. Perception of these differences as racial is the key. Nor should the study of race exclude whiteness as an unmarked category that stands outside history, convention, or valuation (McCarthy and Critchlow 1993). What is required instead is a proper appreciation of race as a social variable in explaining the discursive practices of everyday life (Essed 1991). The intersection of race with class and gender are examined in later chapters.

Regardless of its scientific or empirical validity, in other words, race continues to "count" in everyday discourse or public policy. Race matters not because groups of people are racially inferior or perceived as such by the dimwitted or politically inastute. Race "matters" because its presence provides privilege and power for some, privation for others. That makes race political, since ultimately it deals with who gets what in society. It also matters because people continue to rely on race as a basis for explanation and justification. Its salience is likely to expand even further with the intensification of radical ethnicities and ethnic nationalism. It is no small wonder that a wobbly and largely inaccurate Victorian construct appears in no danger of vanishing by the twenty-first century.

This chapter examines the race concept in terms of its (a) meaning and content, (b) genesis and rationale, (c) impact and implications, and (d) validity and value. We want to know what is meant by the concepts of race and race types/typologies; why these ideas originated in the first place; why they persist into the present; and how they justify entitlement and rules of engagement. Classifying the human population into race types once furnished a simple yet satisfying account of human diversity when conventional rules collapsed. Such a re-ordering was especially evident during the era of European exploration and expansion, the consolidation of capitalism, the colonization of new worlds, and the emergence of race consciousness following biological discoveries (Essed 1991). The fact that race explanations remain popular within certain circles for precisely the same reasons is cause for concern.

RACE STILL MATTERS: AMERICAN AND CANADIAN DIMENSIONS

The relevance of race to human affairs is hotly contested. Many would argue that race is worthless as a biological or explanatory concept, with no bearing whatsoever in the sorting out process. Others disagree: They believe the social world can be partitioned into a fixed and limited number of race types, each with a distinctive assemblage of cognitive and behavioural characteristics. Still others acknowledge the partial validity of both positions. Races do not exist in the conventional, concrete sense; nevertheless, perceptions of race are real. That is, people talk about race *as if* it had objective reality, regardless of its ontological status, with the capacity to determine or divide. Is this true of Canada and the United States?

America the Bad?

That race "matters" in the United States is taken as self-explanatory. Critics point to a country historically riddled with stains of slavery and segregation as well as lynchings and the Ku Klux Klan. Even today the race subtext is unmistakable in public discourses about crime, poverty, and urban decay. Statistical evidence confirms the notion that race matters when it comes to distinguishing "haves" from "have nots." The status for many African-Americans continues to deteriorate thirty years after the Civil Rights revolution. The real median household income for blacks has declined by five percent to $18,807 (US) in recent years. Nearly 32 percent of the black population compared with only 11 percent of whites reside in households below the federal poverty line of $13,400 for a family of four (Fraser 1994). By the end of 1993, 46 percent of black children lived in poverty, compared with only 16 percent of white children (*Kitchener-Waterloo Record* 15 September 1994). Race can also count in a different way as revealed in the Case Study, Race and Sport.

CASE STUDY

Race and Sport

Reference to race is frequently employed to explain group differences and similarities. Racial explanations possess a certain appeal: They are simple, conform with common sense, and pander to many of our stereotypes and prejudices. On the downside, explanations about race tend to ignore the social and historical dimensions of individual or group behaviour. The controversial link between race and sport is a case at hand. First the facts:

In 1993, African-Americans dominated three of the nations most popular spectator sports. Blacks comprised two thirds of the gridiron personnel in the National Football League; over three quarters of hoopsters in the National Basketball Association, and about one sixth of the major league ball players. These figures are striking, not only because they are vastly disproportionate to the number of African-Americans in United States (about 13 or 14 percent of the population), but also because the first black athletes did not breach the professional sports colour bar until 1947. How do we account for this relationship between race and success in certain sports, especially when including black domination in track and boxing (Peoples and Bailey 1994)?

A popular explanation is derived from black anatomical advantages. Black athletes perform well because of natural (biological) factors including bone structure, stamina, strength, coordination, and size. Anatomical differences include (a) leg and calf structures more suitable for jumping; (b) faster twitch muscles for sprinting; (c) more sweat glands (more body surface) for easing overheating; and (d) darker eye colours for excelling at reactive sports (Jaret 1995). Poor performance is related to biologically imposed limitations, for example, less buoyancy for swimming sports. While superficially appealing, the no-

tion that blacks rather than white are better endowed biologically cannot account for variations across sports. For example, blacks may excel in certain sports, but not others such as tennis or swimming. Nor can biological explanations explain the absence of blacks from professional team sports until after World War II — unless one reverts to some wildly implausible genetic shift in an impossibly short time span.

That leaves social factors to account for these discrepancies. It is not that biological factors are invalid; rather social factors are more compelling as systems of explanation. First, professional sports are one of the few opportunity structures open for African-Americans (Edwards 1971; 1984). Not only do blacks focus on sports to escape the poverty of the inner city, but they also gravitate to sports as an avenue to success beyond the business or professional fields. Success itself creates role models that provide additional incentive for youth. Second, American sports is a big business geared around winning at all costs. This post-war commitment put a premium on attracting the best athletes — regardless of colour or race. Black athletes were able to overcome discrimination by pursuing those sports whose performance levels could be evaluated objectively by way of statistics. Thus, highly quantifiable performances among black athletes (such as pass catching yardage or batting average) could dissolve preconceived reluctance. Third, entry occurred in team-oriented sports where black excellence could be diffused among white teammates and rationalized as integral to team success. Fourth, blacks did not excel in all sports. They tended toward those sports that were relatively cheap in terms of equipment, with readily accessible public facilities for practice.

Yet racism appears to linger on within professional sports. Blacks may do well in team numbers, but they are not randomly distributed across the playing field. Black players tend to cluster around certain positions in a phenomenon known as stacking. In the NFL, for example, blacks predominate in positions such as running back or wide receiver on offence, and cornerback and safety at defence (*USA Today*, 17 Dec 1991, C-6). Whites in turn prevail at quarterback and kicking on offence; they monopolize the positions of tackle, guard, and centre on defence. Despite a profusion of black college-level quarterbacks, few ever make it to the NFL in that position, with the first being James Harris of the Los Angeles Rams in 1975. Similarly, stacking occurs in baseball where pitchers and catchers are overwhelmingly white, with blacks predominantly in the outfield. That pattern is not entirely accidental: it reflects a view that whites should monopolize the thinking positions, while blacks should gravitate to those that can capitalize on their *natural* talents. Whites succeed as athletes through perseverance, brain power and strategic reasoning; black athletes are successful because of raw genetic prowess rooted in speed and power (see Brunt 1994). In other words, race matters regardless of its basis in reality, since perceptions of "who plays where" are based on such evaluations.

In contrast to this view, many believe that sport achievements among African Americans are primarily related to social rather than biological factors. Race matters when it comes to sports not because one race has more natural talent than another, but more likely because there is a dearth of opportunity structures for blacks outside of sport. However, we caution the reader from jumping to conclusions: Only a miniscule percentage of black athletes ever fulfill "hoop dreams" or achieve "gridiron success," much to the disappointment and frustration of the majority. Black managers and administrators are virtually unheard of in professional sports. Race matters even in ostensibly colour-blind systems.

For African-Americans, then, being black does matter. The primacy of race defines who you are, what you get, where you live, how you make a living, and when and how you die. Public debates about welfare mothers, inner city violence, urban decay, and hard drugs, are essentially code terms for "blackness." Race remains a significant factor even for middle class blacks. In a world of unremitting double standards, many continue to be rebuked for acting too white or too black. Conversely, race matters for whites since their whiteness is the norm that confers the privilege of being everything, yet nothing, if they choose.

Canada the Good?

Many believe that Canadians and Americans are poles apart when it comes to managing minority relations. Compared to the United States, the refrain "race doesn't matter here" is widely endorsed in Canada (James 1994:47). We exult in the myth that Canadians have a deep aversion to judging others by the colour of their skin. The focus on personality and merit as a basis for achievement is accepted as the Canadian way. A quick reality check suggests otherwise.

Historically, Canada's immigration policy rested on racial factors (Whitaker 1991). A constellation of mechanisms — from head taxes to continous passage requirements to climatic regulations — combined to protect Canada's perception of itself as a "white man's society" (Stasiulis 1992). The routine questions asked of native born racial minorities such as, "So, what island are you from?" attest to the continuing legacy of skin colour in defining who is a legitimate Canadian. Statements such as, "You're different...," "I'm not a racist but...," and "Some of my best friends..." connote a racial subtext that says more about prejudice and insensitivity than a desire for intercultural understanding (James and Shadd 1994). Minorities continue to bear the brunt of negative treatment, from local snubs to half-hearted service delivery. Historically as currently, people of colour were employed as cheap and disposable labour in often dangerous and always arduous tasks. Participation and decision making are influenced by prevailing stereotypes and racial prejudices, while social rewards are allocated on the basis of racial affiliation. Even the racialization of public discourse and the emergence of race-conscious state policies to ameliorate disadvantage has spawned a chorus of boos against racial groups for being too assertive, too exclusive, and just plain too uppity. The following case study reveals how race continues to intrude into Canadian society.

INSIGHT

Reality Bites: Tabulating Race and Crime

Racial and ethnic minorities have historically been accused of excessive criminal behaviour. From the nineteenth century Irish and Chinese to the Italians and Jews in the twentieth, certain groups were vilified as inherently depraved and in need of intense monitoring. Recent incidents in major Canadian urban centres have again singled out minorities for special attention, and resulted in renewed demands for keeping track of crime rates by racial origins. High profile crimes involving suspects of colour will invariably elicit additional calls to collect race-based crime statistics.

Those who support crime statistics by race argue that problem areas need to be identified to apply appropriate solutions. Crime statistics by colour classification would enable a profile of suspected criminals, the kind of crime they committed, what compelled them to do it, how to deal with these incidents, and the prevention of future occurences. Those against the collection of crime statistics based on skin colour, race, or origins, argue that such data are subject to abuse or manipulation. In an era of quantification, they warn, statistical data confer an air of authenticity and objectivity that may be unwarranted from the available evidence.

Consider only the dissemination of these data. Whether by intent or inadvertently, the circulation of this information may (a) reinforce stereotypes and legitimate a racist mindset; (b) promote ulterior motives and hidden agendas; (c) distract attention from the real source of the problem; and (d) strengthen policy monitoring powers. The collection of race-based statistics is equally problematic. Totals are skewed because only a small percentage of suspects who are arrested are eventually charged, and fewer still are convicted. Many crimes are never reported to the police, ranging from domestic crime to white collar crime, let alone make it to police occurence sheets. Making a racial identification for the report sheets is a mug's game in its own right: Who decides what category a suspect fits into — the victim, the suspect, the police officer? For example, the category of black can include recent immigrants from Jamaica or refugees from Somalia, or indigenous Canadian blacks, many of whom have been settled in Canada for generations. How will the data be collected? For what purpose? Are the police sufficiently trained and impartial to collect the data? How reliable are victims' perceptions for identification purposes, or have the victims been watching too much TV (Mitchell and Abbate 1994)?

In between are those who do not openly deny the relevance of such data but want safeguards to prevent abuse (Jansen 1994; Mitchell and Abbate 1994). In collecting *any* type of information it is important to know who is gathering the data, why these data being collected, how will these data be collected, who wants to know them and what is going to be done with them. This line of thinking can be applied to race related statistics on crime and race. Who wants to know, and why? Do the police want this information to justify bigger budgets or to secure more freedom of movement within minority communities? Do politicans hope to look tough on crime with collection of such data? What should be included in the count? Do we include white collar crime and other types of crime that are underreported? Can we be sure that fair procedures are in place for the arrest or conviction of people of colour? Until answers are forthcoming, we would be advised to move cautiously.

There is yet another reason for exercising caution in this area. No matter how accurate the survey or sound the interpretations, a causal relation between race and crime can never be proven. Crime cuts across all groups of people; only its detection may be influenced by race. The causes of crime are social and universal, not racial or restricted to a certain races. Recent studies suggest that immigrants do not commit more crimes (*Toronto Star* 23 July 1994). A federal study conducted with 20,000 inmates convicted of serious crimes found that foreign-born criminals were underrepresented in prison (5.5 per 10,000) in comparison with the population at large. The foreign-born may or may not commit more crimes in general, the study argued, but they commit fewer murders and rapes. Likewise, their rate of recidivism is lower than for Canadian-born criminals. Two exceptions are Caribbean- and Latin-American-born whose rate of crime stood at 18 per 10,000 and 14 per 10,000 (compared with 10.5 per 10,000 for the population at large). The relevance of social factors such as discrimination, biased criminal justice system, broken families, low employment, low incomes, and substandard housing should not be discounted as contributing factors.

As sociologists, we believe that priority should be assigned to the social dimensions of human behaviour. We prefer to focus on the environmental causes of social problems related to crime, including poverty, unemployment, hopelessness, police harassment, racism, dysfunctional families, disregard for the law, and absense of a work ethic (*The Toronto Star* 26 July 1994). Cultural values may lead to behaviour that is likely to attract police attention. The prevalence of stereotypes and prejudice may increase the likelihood of apprehension by race. In short, we have some real qualms about correlating race with crime. Race cannot account for crime but only public perceptions about "who's committing what." Statistics, in turn, can only measure levels of enforcement against targetted minorities. Race matters, to be sure — but not because some races carry an anti-social gene. Rather race matters because people act is if it did by assigning moral force to statistical computations.

These and related incidents remind us that race does matter when it "counts." Many Canadians appear to have an aversion to the race concept and everything that it stands for; yet they inadvertently employ it to explain or justify. Race looms even larger outside of Canada: Tribal violence in Rwanda and military repression in Bosnia are conducted and justified on the grounds of race and ethnicity. The globalization of race makes it more important than ever to scrutinize a term that has the potential to destroy society.

THE HUMAN RACE: SOCIAL OR BIOLOGICAL?

It is obvious that race has an existence beyond the biological or scientific. That alone generates problems because its casual use in the vernacular contradicts its marginal status in the sciences. Indiscriminate references to terms such as the "human race" or the "Irish race" compound the difficulty.

Human beings belong to a single biological species (*homo sapiens*) within a larger grouping or genus (*homo*). The term "species" is used in the genetic sense of an intrabreeding population whose members possess the capacity to naturally reproduce fertile offspring. Within the human species there are numerous populations that exhibit genetically diverse frequencies. These gene frequencies are manifest in readily observable characteristics including skin colour (*phenotypes*), in addition to less discernible attributes such as blood types (*genotypes*). Biologically speaking, then, the concept of race refers to this distribution of genes based on clusters of phenotypes or genotypes between populations. When applied to humans, it can be defined as a subpopulation of the species in which certain hereditary features appear more frequently in some population pools than others because of relative reproductive isolation (Jaret 1995).

On the surface, it might appear as if human diversity is too broad to qualify as a single species. But appearances in this case are deceiving. Judging by our capacity to propagate with each other, we all qualify as members of the human race (or more accurately, human species). Several reasons can account for the singularity of the human species:

1) **Speciation** (the process by which new species are generated) can only occur under conditions of relative isolation. With the possible exception of extremely remote areas such as Australia and interior New Guinea, human populations have remained in direct or indirect contact with each other. The creation of a generalized gene pool is a reflection of various social exchange process associated with migration, trade, or intermarriage between groups.

2) Speciation requires an extensive time period for genetically isolated populations to evolve. Although our ancestors arguably have been around for millions of years, this span of time may be insufficient even for the most isolated populations to speciate.

3) Speciation is likely to occur when organisms adapt to the environment by evolving the "appropriate" bio-physical characteristics. By way of contrast, humankind has relied on social and cultural characteristics as an adaptive response to evolutionary pressures. This reliance on culture and society as primary coping mechanisms has created a generalized rather than a specie-making gene pool.

We can conclude that human beings constitute a single intrabreeding species with phenotypic and genotypic variation at the subspecies (racial) level. Humans resemble other floral and faunal species in terms of population clusters with varying gene frequencies and distributions. Anatomical differences exist, of course, and span the spectrum from anatomical features such as skin color or ear wax (moist or crumbly), to genotypical attributes pertaining to blood chemistry (A, B, O, AB), metabolic rates, and physiological functions such as susceptibilities to disease (Jaret 1995). Most differences reflect adaptations to environmental niches in accordance with modern biological principles of mutation and natural selection. These differences presumably contributed to the survival of the human species.

No one should be surprised by scholarly interest in the study of human variation. Physical anthropologists and biologists have explored the limits of diversity in hopes of unravelling human secrets. What is unusual, however, has been an obsession by some to study human variation at the subspecies level (race). Plant and animal species also display an internal distribution of gene frequencies in response to evolutionary forces. Yet the concept of race is rarely applied to discussions about plant and animal populations. When was the last time you heard reference to tulip races or a race of dogs? By contrast, there has been no dearth of initiatives to (a) classify people into race categories, (b) attribute certain physical, social, psychological, and moral properties to these categories, and (c) evaluate and rank these categories in ascending/descending order. The following section addresses the paradox of why a biological concept of limited worth has altered the course of human history.

DEFINITION OF RACE

Definitions of race have proven to be elusive (Biddiss 1979). The term itself appeared in the English language as far back as the fifteenth century as a device to interpret and classify varied forms of human life, as well as to account for intergroup differences and similarities (Banton 1987). Such longevity notwithstanding, it is difficult to think of an English concept with greater ambiguity and emotional baggage than the concept of race (Martin and Franklin 1973). The term has also been applied indiscriminately to a jumble of sociopolitical units, including culture (Anglo-Saxons), religion (Jews), nationality (Irish, Chinese), language (French Canadians), polity (Irish), and geography (Mediterranean, European) (Stepan 1982). This lack of consensus is not surprising, given the politics and perils of extracting social significance from a concept of limited biological utility.

We can define race as the classification of people into categories on the basis of preconceived attributes. Under race, each group is defined as different by virtue of preconceived properties that are seen as fixed and permanent (van den Berghe 1967). This definition is unmistakably sociological in scope even if a biological dimension may be incorporated because of people's beliefs and perceptions of innate differences (Jaret 1995). We concur with Martin and Franklin (1973) in embracing a social rather than a biological emphasis:

> Sociologically, race tends to be whatever people define it to be; that is, one's racial group membership is largely a matter of how society classifies him, regardless of the biological validity of the classification.

Race represents a social rather than a biological (subspecie) category. Our interest resides in the concept of race as a social classification of people who are perceived as different from others by virtue of certain real or putative characteristics (van den Berghe 1970). This focus on the socially constructed and contested only partly explains the fascination and intensity generated by race. Its inclusion into systems of classification and evaluation provide insight into the emotional politics associated with race.

RACE TYPES AND RACIAL TYPOLOGIES

Early approaches to human variation drew inspiration from the race concept. This preoccupation reflected a nineteenth century quest for unitary schemes that explained the totality of human experience (Goldberg 1993). Just as Marx constructed an entire explanatory framework around the concept of class, so too did social theorists resort to race as an all-encompassing interpretive framework for understanding human differences and similarities (Biddiss 1979). The race concept classified human groups into a finite number of permanant **types**, each with a fixed and distinctive assemblage of physical and behavioural characteristics (Banton 1987). Individuals and groups were subsequently slotted into social rankings or **typologies** that reflected a predetermined hierarchy of superiority and inferiority (Feagin 1984).

A variety of classificatory schemes (or typologies) were hatched from the eighteenth century onwards. The Swedish naturalist, Carl von Linne (or Linneaus) posited 4 races in 1735; since then, the number of races has expanded to as many as thirty by Carleton Coon and even 150 by Quatrefages (Rensberger 1994; Jaret 1995). Typologists became preoccupied with measurement and quantification as proof of fundamental differences. Human skulls were endlessly measured for size while the contours of people's crania were were correlated with mental capacities ("phrenology") (Stepan 1982). The proliferation of racial typologies reflected a broad failure to agree on an appropriate typology. The most common and widely known system of classification endorsed a three-fold division of humanity into Caucasoid (white), Negroid (black), and Mongoloid (Asian or Oriental). Each of these categories was distinguished from the others by virtue of common physical features such as skin colour, hair colour and form (fuzzy, wavy, or straight), eye-lid shape, and so on (Garn 1946). Each had also evolved (or had had divinely be-stowed) its own unique and fixed bundles of characteristics. Only physical intermingling with other "stocks" could undermine the permanency of these types (Biddiss 1979).

Many social scientists are opposed to the race concept. They have rejected the validity of race as germane to the understanding of human diversity. Racial types and typologies have been discredited as pseudo science and dangerous politics, without any redeeming explanatory value or empirical merit. Aversion to the term "race" itself arose from global revulsion at the murder of six million Jews and gyp-sies in the name of Nazi racial purity (Stasiulis 1993). The common arguments against race thinking are numerous, but include the following:

1) Discrete and distinct categories of racially pure people do not exist. The inter-mingling effect of migration, social exchanges, and intermarriage has made it impossible to draw a line around human populations, with certain character-istics on one side, but not on the other (Martin and Franklin 1983). Explicit boundaries between so-called racial groups are non-existent (unlike political boundaries which are fixed at some point in time). Instead, populations with variable characteristics merge into one another, thus forming gradients (or clines). This makes any division between races a somewhat arbitrary exer-cise that reflects the whims of the investigator rather than anything intrinsic to reality itself. For example, picture ourselves moving from the north of Europe to the Mediterranean and across to Africa. Where do we draw the line beween white and and black populations? Any proposed demarcation is open to dispute as light-skinned northwestern Europeans merge into relatively darker Mediterranean populations and into progressively black-skinned pop-ulations in Africa. The picture is further complicated by the inclusion of mil-lions of Indo-Pakistanis who are defined as Caucasoids for racial purposes. Ultimately such a division is essentially a subjective decision on the part of the investigator. It becomes pointless, in other words, to devote countless studies to the notions of "racial superiority" or "pure races" when the nature of the units under study are inconsistent with reality (Banton 1987).

2) Related to this is the arbitrary manner of selecting traits for inclusion and eva-lution. The pigmentation of skin is the most widely used. Nevertheless, outside of convenience, one can justifiably ask, why skin colour? Why exclude eye colour or earwax type? Better yet, how about the weight of internal organs as criteria for categorization? Admittedly, skin colour is the most immediately

obvious feature. But it distorts the purpose of science to construct an elaborate system of classification based on skin pigmentation. It is equally fanciful to impute certain social attributes or psychological properties by virtue of this spurious correlation.

3) Even the integrity of racial typologies is open to question because of high rates of internal variation. Just as physical differences exist among persons whom we categorize as Caucasoid ("Nordic, Alpine, Mediterranian, and Indo-Pakistani"), so too is there equally signficant diversity within the Asian and Black categories. Differences *within* groups that are defined as races are often as great as differences between groups. Such internal diversity would appear to invalidate the credibility of any classificatory system that strives for universality and consistency. The options are lose-lose: Either an unwieldly large number of distinct categories are created to account for this diversity. Or a restricted number of classifications overlook the rich diversity within the human species. Yet no system of classification — large or small — can possibly include those that invariably fall outside any typology.

In addition to conceptual problems, there are practical and moral reasons for rejecting the validity of the race concept. Social scientists do not reject the reality of biogenetic differences between individuals or even groups (populations). Individual differences exist: What does *not* exist are defined populations with fixed inventories of common characteristics. Specific traits can be classified, but not particular groups of people, since all populations are bundles of different combinations of traits (Rensberger 1994). Nor do social scientists deny the validity of studying these differences in an objective and scholarly fashion. What they find objectionable are studies of race that isolate differences and rank diversity along an ascending/descending order. Equally reprehensible are doctrines that uphold the proposed superiority of one type over another without adequate biological justification. Many also object to the linking of select physical characteristics with certain behavioural, moral, or cognitive properties, thereby establishing an unwarranted relationship between culture and biology. The political fallout of such a linkage, it is argued, undermines the legitimacy of the race concept for public debate. The recent controversy over the right of Philippe Rushton of University of Western Ontario to promote racial supremacist theories will testify to a growing sense of outrage.

INSIGHT

Debunking the Rushton Myth

Biological theories of race and evolution have come and gone, and in all probability will continue to flourish into the foreseeable future. From the nineteenth century doctrines of Social Darwinism, to the pseudo-scientific racism of Herrnstein and Murray of the 1990s, efforts to link race with intelligence on an evolutionary hierarchy have proven tempting. A professor of psychology from University of Western Ontario, Philippe Rushton, has also entered the fray by unleashing a storm of controversy over issues pertaining to genetically-based determinants of human behaviour. The question of academic freedom has also moved to the forefront, as have debates over the roles and responsibilities of contemporary post-secondary education.

In his most notorious works, including the recent text *Race, Evolution, and Behavior: A Life History Perspective* (*NY Transaction* 1994), Rushton posits a theory of evolution to account for racial differences across a broad and hierarchical spectrum of physical, social, mental, and moral domains. Rushton argues that separate races, namely Oriental, Caucasoid, and Negroid, evolved a distinctive package of physical, social, and mental characteristics because of different reproductive strategies in diverse environments. Very simply, high reproductive strategies (many offspring, low nurturing) evolved in tropical climates; low reproductive strategies (few offspring, intense nurturing) in temperate climates. A racial pecking order can be observed, according to Professor Rushton, because of this evolutionary adaptation. Orientals are superior to Caucasoids on a range of sociobiological factors, who in turn are superior to Negroids on the grounds of measurements involving skull size, intelligence, strength of sex drive and genital size, industriousness, sociability, and rule following. Orientals as a group are proven more intelligent, more family-focused, more law abiding, but less sexually promiscuous than Negroids. Caucasoids happily occupy the terrain in between — neither too hot nor too cold. Table A summarizes this theory.

How valid is Rushton's thesis? Of course human differences exist at individual and group levels. But good reasons exist to reject a racial interpretation of human differences and achievement. Very simply, the concept of human race has long been discredited as scientifically valid or biologically meaningful. No empirical evidence supports the existence of discrete and well-defined categories of humans with unique assemblages of homogeneous and fixed properties. The credibility of Rushton's work has also plummeted because of funding links with a **eugenics**-based (improvement through genetic engineering) movement in United States. His conclusions are seen as an expression of classic racism: that is, behaviour is linked with genes;

TABLE A   Rushton's Evolutionary Typology

	Negroid	Caucasoid	Oriental
Evolutionary Branching from Hominid Line	200,000 years ago	110,000 years ago	40,000 years ago
Brain Size	1,330cc	1,408cc	1,448cc
IQ Score	85	100	107
Sexual Activity	intense	moderate	weak
Temperament	aggressive/excitable	moderate	calm/cautious
Marital Stability	brittle	moderate	strong
Social Organization: a) law abiding b) crime rates	a) low b) high	a) moderate b) moderate	a) high b) low

differences are ranked along a hierarchy; and an ideology of racial superiority is implied. Likewise, his data base has been denounced as outdated, simplistic, highly selective and calculated to achieve a singular dimension in the nature-nurture debate.

Many colleagues of Rushton have defended his right to speak on contentious issues — keeping in mind that freedom of speech is not an absolute right, but entails a degree of social responsibility. The University of Western Ontario also has defended his right to teach despite numerous protests. Others disagree; they are concerned that a preoccupation with race and racial differences is often a ruse for containment of minorities through the "politics of science" (Snyderman 1994:79) Still others are dismayed by the publicity and exposure Rushton has received, all of which has had the unfortunate affect of conferring both a public platform and a degree of legitimacy to his assertions. As to why this type of thinking finds a receptive audience, the answers are less clear. Perhaps simplistic and bio-reductionist explanations possess an appeal in times of social complexity and rapid change.

Concepts of race and racial types continue to attract interest despite unease within the scientific community. Not only do these concepts exercise a tenacious hold on our conscience; they also exert a powerful influence in shaping the lives and life chances of racial or indigenous minorities. This is a peculiar situation since neither race nor race types have any empirical validity. Both represent social constructs (ideologies) that reflect human interests rather than anything inherent or self-evident within reality itself (Miles 1982). The race concept also fails as a explanatory concept. An invention with no basis in reality cannot empirically account for human variations and societal inequality (Miles and Phizacklea 1984). Race relations are not biological relations; in the final analysis, they constitute relations of inequality between groups (Miles 1993).

But race continues to matter, even when fraught with political overtones and pernicious associations. This confirms that socially constructed perception *is* reality when it comes to impact. As grasped by the American sociologists, W.I. and D.I. Thomas in 1928: Social phenomena do not have to be real, to be real in their consequences. Merely defining a situation can make it "realistic." Argued in a parallel fashion, the race concept does not have to be real to exert an impact upon society. The renowned scholar, Michael Banton (1967:4), has claimed as much:

> Beliefs about the nature of race — whether true or false — still have considerable social significance, and, when a category is labelled in the popular mind by racial terminology rather than religious or class criteria, certain predictable consequences ensue. The social significance of the racial label ... forms part of the study of intergroup relations.

Evidence from around the world has revealed all too clearly the suffering and chaos generated by human fantasies and illusions. To what factors and forces can we attribute the origins, growth, and popularity of the race concept?

HISTORICAL ROOTS OF RACE

The race concept has enjoyed a long period of grace in the West. Its popularity runs counter to Enlightenment philosophies that extol the virtues of human progress and individual perfectibility. Even growing criticism over its conceptual and practical shortcomings has not dimmed its appeal. Several questions should immediately come to mind. Why did the race concept originate in the first place? How do we explain this compulsion to pigeon-hole human diversity into racial types that are fixed, permanent, and unequal? Why do pockets of openly racist thinking continue to linger on in the public domain? Why are they resistant to reform? Answers to these questions point to a constellation of social forces that have bolstered its legitimacy as an explanatory tool.

On the Origins of Race — European Exploration

A scientific approach toward the concepts of race and types originated in response to a variety of complex factors (Stepan 1982). These included the expansion of the slave trade after the fifteenth century, abolition movements at the end of the eighteenth century, the appearance of human and biological sciences (with their focus on comparative anatomy) around the turn of the nineteenth century, and the "estrangement" of Europeans from non-Europeans in the wake of international competition.

Particular interest in race relations was sharpened during the era of European exploration. European imaginations were intrigued by sustained contact with highly diverse populations whose appearance and culture stimulated an outpouring of amusement, fascination, and repulsion. Exposure to diversity encouraged a system of explanation that would impose a framework of coherence and order. The concept of race types (typologies) proved a "common-sense" approach to explaining and sorting out human diversity. This concept also helped to explain why non-Western populations lacked the political acumen and techno-military prowess of imperialistic minded Europeans. Taken to its logical conclusion, the race concept rationalized the control, domination, and exploitation of indigenous and immigrating populations. Its emergence is expressed by Martin and Franklin (1973:71) who wrote:

> [The] advent [of race] seemed to be due in large measure to the need for a rationalization of the exploitation of certain groups...This proposition was also advanced to justify the imperialism and colonialism that flourished....Racism became a convenient ideological defense for social practices which patently and flagrantly violated basic social and institutional principles.

To be sure, race as a social category existed prior to European exploration and expansion. Europeans had long relied on other criteria for demonizing those beyond the pale of Christianity. For instance, the Middle Ages world was divided into Christian and non-Christian sectors. Non-Christians were viewed as wild and untamed pagans ("the devils own handiwork") who had crawled out from beneath the flat world to test Christian patience. Heathens were dispatched to the lower rungs of the Creation ladder (a "chain of being") — a stable and static hierarchy which relegated lesser beings to one end, and superior races to the other. Primitives and savages were fortunate to have occupied the realms in between.

The magnitude and impact of the Christian/non-Christian dichotomy should not be underestimated. The intensity and cruelty of the violence espoused by the Crusades, the Inquistion, and the Protestant Reformation — all in the name of God — will verify that. Still, these earlier schemes were no match for the ruthless destruction unleashed by the race concept. After all, it was one thing to disparage non-westerners as worthless and unsalvageable for prosyletizing purposes. It was quite another to construct elaborate classificatory schemes that invoked pseudo scientific explanations to legitimize worldwide exploitation and domination. When sanctioned by human and biological sciences, these classifications made group differences appear more comprehensive, more entrenched, and more scientifically valid (Stocking Jr. 1968; Stepan 1982). When harnessed to military prowess and technological advances, the effects were much more deadly.

In other words, Europeans did not invent the concept of race and its ramifications. Ancient peoples possessed an intense aversion to those who were different — on the grounds of superstition or ignorance — rather than on comprehensive theories rooted in systematic observation and pseudo-scientific classification (Jaret 1995). Nor was Europe awash with racists who relished every opportunity to disparage and/or exploit distant peoples. To paraphrase Michael Biddiss (1979), many at this time were genuinely perplexed about the nature and significance of human diversity, but answers were limited. But Europeans were among the first to popularize the race concept as a scientifically-grounded formula for explaining away human diversity in an expansionist era. The concept of race emerged as a direct result of the European enlightenment, with its focus on the primacy and imposition of order through rational ("scientific") systems of thought (Goldberg 1993). For that reason Europeans must be held responsible for unleashing chaos and destruction of a magnitude previously unknown.

Putting Race to Work: Imperialism and Colonialism

It has been suggested that Europeans manipulated the concept of race as one way of domesticating global diversity. The proliferation of **racial doctrines** or dogmas stemmed from such a racial mindset. Racial doctrines originated to facilitate and condone the negative treatment of non-Western populations who were racially and culturally different from Europeans. Under the sway of these dogmas, many overseas populations found themselves susceptible to powerful external interests even after attaining nominal political independence.

The nineteenth century is often regarded as the age of **imperialism**. It represented a period of time when various European nations (including Russia and the

United States) assumed an inalienable right to conquer, colonize, and exploit overseas territories. A need for foreign markets, investment opportunities, cheap labour, and inexpensive resources reflected the requirements of an expanding capitalist system. It also embraced the stirrings of a religious fervor with its resigned commitment to prosyletize the world in the name of Christian duty ("the white man's burden"). In addition, imperialist expansion reflected an obsession among Europeans to accumulate foreign territories for nationalistic or military reasons. This fanaticism for colonial empires may have been perpetuated also for no other reason than to surpass the achievements of others in an ever-spiralling game of tit-for-tat which no side could realistically hope to win except at the expense of others.

A predatory approach toward global relations uncovered a set of existential dilemmas. First and foremost, how could so-called civilized and Christian nations rationalize and justify the blatant exploitation of others? Second, how could self-serving interests be sustained without contradicting the image of Europeans as a sophisticated and enlightened people with a moral duty to civilize and convert? Answers to these uncomfortable questions were provided by embracing an ideology that condoned the mistreatment of others as natural or normal — even necessary. This ideology not only explained and legitimated the sorting of populations along racial lines; it also set the tone for asserting absolute European supremacy on pseudo-scientific grounds.

Racial doctrines arose to "soften" the impact of imperialist encounters throughout Central and South America, the Caribbean, Africa, Australia, and New Zealand. By dismissing overseas peoples as inferior or subhuman, Europeans could exploit and oppress indigenous populations without remorse, guilt, or responsibility. Equal treatment was denied merely because of perceived deficiencies in the mental or moral makeup of primitives. Once racial differences were ingrained as fixed and immutable, moreover, Europeans were absolved of any compelling need for improving the plight of the less fortunate. With consciences salved, they were free to do whatever was expedient to expand or safeguard white privilege.

Neo-Colonialism and Race

Colonized minorities continued to be exploited even with the post-World War II collapse of colonialism. Whether through armed insurrection or relatively peaceful agreement, former colonies in Africa and Asia became liberated from overseas rule. In theory, the appearance of relatively independent political institutions provided a buffer to cushion against the worst abuses of colonialist exploitation. Notwithstanding a show of nominal independence, however, many of these nation-states continued to be economically dependent and underdeveloped. In many cases they remained firmly under economic control by outside interests.

Neo-colonialism represented colonialism by another name. Combining elements of old and new, neo-colonial exploitation was perpetuated primarily by European- and American-based multinational corporations. These highly monopolistic corporations were primarily interested in maximizing profits through cheap labour, markets, investments, and raw materials. But because of political contraints, they were restricted in their capacity to recklessly exploit indigenous workers. Restrictions were also implemented in the wake of expanding human rights awareness. Yet the overall effect was identical. Economic domination, dependency, and underdevelopment persisted in many areas. Racial doctrines, in turn, continued to justify systems of exploitation and control.

DOCTRINES OF RACIAL SUPREMACY

It did not take long for doctrines of racial superiority to appear once racial types were assigned a fixed moral value. Only a minimal cognitive shift was required to move from racial types, to their placement on rank orderings of superiority and inferiority (Biddiss 1979). These hierarchies were intrinsically racist in that they employed the authority of science to confirm the superiority of some groups over others on the basis of arbitrarily defined criteria (Stepan 1982). Their impact was devastating: Racial supremacist doctrines endorsed the dehumanization of minorities as objects for manipulations. In justifying inequality between races, the doctrines also embodied a set of practices and relationships that distorted group interaction during the colonizing process. The most notorious of these doctrines were Social Darwinism, Eugenics, and Scientific Racism.

Social Darwinism

Social Darwinism evolved into a widely acceptable doctrine of racial superiority during the final quarter of the last century. The doctrine itself borrowed a number of Darwin's biological propositions, then reworked them to further the aims of overseas exploitation. Foremost was the notion of a "struggle for survival" on a global scale and "survival of the fittest" by way of natural selection. Social Darwinism portrayed the social world as a a gladiatorial arena where populations were locked in mortal combat over scarce and valuable resources. Those who were better adapted to compete in this ongoing struggle prospered; those with less adaptive attributes lapsed into oblivion.

The nations of Europe and the United States defined themselves as evolutionarily advanced. Superior breeding had propelled Western Europe to the top of the unilinear evolutionary schemes that were in vogue at the time. The concept of unilinear evolution had proposed that populations evolved through predetermined and universal stages of savagery-barbarism-civilization. Those with the proper biological stock had progressed to the apex of the evolutionary ladder. Others, of course, were left behind in the competitive struggle for evolutionary survival. Racial groups were ranked along the evolutionary ladder on the basis of their likeness to standards of European civilization and Christianity. As mentioned earlier, the Maori of New Zealand were prominently ranked because of their military prowess and receptivity to Western customs. Australian Aborigines, by way of contrast, were banished to the bottom because of perceived immersion in a stone-age culture.

Social Darwinist philosophies played into the hands of western colonialism. They condoned the subjugation of colonized peoples on "natural" rather than conventional grounds. In the words of Nancy Stepan (1982:83):

> Evolutionism provided a new emotionally charged, yet ostensibly scientific language with which to express old prejudices. ... the "lower races" were now races that had "evolved" least far up the evolutionary ladder, had lost out in the "struggle for survival" and were "unfit" for the competition between tribes. Or they represented the evolutionary "childhood" of the white man.

These doctrines exonerated the colonialists of responsibility in the colonization of African blacks, East Asian populations, Aboriginal peoples, and Polynesian Islanders. Racial ideologies not only explained European superiority and justified outgroup exploitation, they also celebrated the virtues of capitalism and imperialism as integral to human progress and social enlightenment.

Eugenics

Racist doctrines assumed even more sinister proportions at the turn of the 20th century. A variety of social movements arose in United States, Britain, Russia, and Japan, with objectives often benign in intent, but deadly in consequence. Fortified by the discovery of hereditary laws, the eugenics movement collectively advocated the improvement of human stock by purging the species of unwanted specimens. Selective breeding procedures were proposed for their elimination: Eugenics operated on the assumption that the genetically unfit were a threat to society (Naureckas 1995). Defectives such as racial minorities, the congenitally deformed, and the retarded, would be sterilized as one way of curbing the further "bastardization" of the human species (Banton 1967). By contrast, racially superior stocks were encouraged to have larger families (Stepan 1982).

By the early 1930s, eugenics as a movement slipped into decline — with the exception of a final burst of compulsory sterilization and mass murder under the Nazi regime. Attacks on eugenics appeared in various circles. Prominent American anthropologists such as Franz Boas, Ruth Benedict, and Margaret Mead were instrumental in demolishing the validity of biological reductionist arguments. Eschewing racial explanations, they proposed instead the relevance of social and cultural forces as explanatory variables. Cultural explanations of human differences and similarities gained popularity once people understood the scope of Nazi atrocities under the white supremacist banner. Nevertheless, eugenicism has prevailed into the present as we shall shortly see, admittedly in diverse and somewhat more disguised forms and without the backing of an openly receptive social climate.

Scientific Racism in the United States

Doctrines of racial superiority were not applied exclusively to African, Asia, or South American countries. They also blossomed in North America where racial ideologies arose and evolved in response to the need for cheap and disposable labour, unrestricted access to land and mineral resources, and preservation of white privilege and power. Initially these dogmas were directed at indigenous peoples. Later they included successive waves of incoming immigrant groups. Powerful interests were thus able to exercise control and exploitation under these doctrines that dis-portrayed minorities as less than human.

Racial dogmas became especially marked in the United States. The existence of an indigenous native population, a more mobile black population, and the ongoing influx of European immigrants created a pressing need to scientifically sort out and impartially arrange this diversity. The search for an appropriate doctrine culminated with the discovery of so-called intelligence tests. The most popular of these was the **Intelligent Quotient (IQ) exam** which even today continues to fascinate or repel.

CASE STUDY

Testing for Race and Intelligence

American whites have long haboured racist sentiments towards African-Americans. This racism was manifest in a variety of ways during the pre-Civil war era: in the exclusion of blacks from the freedom and equality provisions within the American constitution, to the often brutal treatment of slaves on plantations. After emancipation, racism continued to flourish both in the North and the South. In the North this racism became increasingly focused in urban areas where blacks competed with white immigrants over jobs and housing. Blacks were resented for moving into neighbourhoods; they also were disliked even more for engaging in strike breaking activities at the expense of the European immigrants (van den Berghe 1967). Given such anti-black sentiments, American whites were ready to accept any scientific proof for putting blacks back into place.

The growing popularity of ideologies based on **scientific racism** provided racists with the proof they required. Scientific racism was built on the premise that racial capacities between populations could be measured and evaluated by statistical means. Eventually, the doctrine of scientific racism latched on to the comparative measurement of intelligence between blacks and whites by way of IQ exams. The IQ test itself was designed by Stanford Binet for the discovery of deficiencies in the cognitive skills of French pupils. It was never really intended to measure the amount of intelligence a person possessed. Stanford Binet himself believed intelligence could not be correlated with precise mathematical certainty. Nevertheless American interests applied the test indiscriminately during the latter stages of the First World War as a means of sorting raw recruits into two categories: officer rank or cannon fodder. Since blacks for a variety of reasons were more likely to perform poorly on these tests, the IQ exam quickly established itself as an instrument for proving racial inferiority.

Repeated testings revealed that blacks on the average scored about 15 percentage points less than whites on the IQ exam. This gap was taken as proof that blacks were intellectually inferior "stock" because of hereditary factors. With few exceptions, many believed this bio-genetic gap could never be bridged, even with environmental improvements or enrichment programs. That being the case the implications were obvious. Blacks were destined for menial occupations. They did not require a sophisticated education system since there was little hope for substantial improvement even with increased exposure or expenditure. In light of related theories such as Social Darwinism and eugenics, the biological deficit model of blacks was widely endorsed.

The IQ exam legitimized this popular conception of black inferiority. It invoked a set of statistics whose "halo effect" proved what many had secretly harbored. But in their hurry to promote white intellectual supremacy at the expense of blacks, the advocates of the IQ exam took some unwarranted liberties with the results. For example, while blacks scored consistently less than whites as a group, the range of variation between black and white scores was comparable. The highest and the lowest scores within each category was approximately the same. Also relevant but widely ignored were variations in group averages. While blacks on the average scored about 15% lower than whites, 15% of the blacks scored higher than the average score for whites, suggesting by inference that some blacks were intellectually superior to whites.

Recent testing continues to confirm a discrepancy between white and black scores. Then as now, several reasons can account for black failure to score as high as whites on these exams. First, many believe that the IQ exam is culture bound (Dewdney 1994). It has been produced by Eurocentric experts and geared toward white middle class children who are properly equipped to succeed because of in-school and out-of-class experience. Second, the IQ exam may not even measure intelligence. After all, what is intelligence? Does it consist of creativity, analytical skills, the ability to memorize and recall, the capacity to do well in school, or the ability to perform adequately in a non-educational environment? Put simply, IQ tests do not measure intelligence; rather they measure a person's ability to perform well in comparison with others in intensively competitive contexts. Third, blacks bring a series of environmentally imposed disadvantages with them to the testing experience that go beyond the stigma of slavery or trauma of oppression. Many continue to experience discrimination, racism, slurs, and violence, on a daily basis. Malnutritional deficiencies resulting from poverty or poor prenatal care also interfere with high performance levels. Put another way, the whole experience of blacks has been warped and strained by historical and social circumstances making it impossible to validate comparative results — even when family background and educational levels are held constant. Fourth, part of the environmentally imposed disadvantages that blacks bring with them to the IQ situation are deficiencies within the education system. Many blacks must cope with poor and unequipped schools, are taught by insensitive teachers, labelled as losers or failures (and streamed accordingly) and are forced to study curricula that are denigrating, alienating, and confusing. A self-fulfilling prophecy is set into motion: Not only do many begin to doubt their abilities, but often conform to the stereotypes, thereby confirming them (Cose 1994).

In short, the IQ exam should not be employed as a basis for comparing blacks and whites in the United States — even if such tests can enhance meritocracy by overcoming conventional means of distributing rewards based on inherited wealth, connections, and "old-boys" networks, and ascriptive qualities related to race (Wooldridge 1994). Differences in scores do not necessarily correlate with innate capacities. Sociologically speaking, differences in scores can be explained not as a result of genes, nature, or heredity, but primarily because of opportunity structures, social conditions, and cultural values. In addition grave concern is raised about the political implications of the IQ exam. Such negativity can only breed a negative public climate toward black achievements, and the responsibility of white America to do something about it.

The current social and political climate is less supportive of the old racial science with its emphasis on anatomy, morphology, typology, and hierarchy (Stepan 1982). Public and political perception of racial inferiority shifted with the Civil Rights movement: Increasingly, inequality was formulated around cultural differences and social conditions (Essed 1991). Nevertheless, support remains for doctrines associated with racism and intelligence (Browne 1994). During the 1960s, academics such as Arthur Jensen (1969), and Eysenck (1971) among others reincarnated the idea of intelligence as a function of heredity ("nature versus nurture"). The stubborn fifteen point gap in test scores confirmed to some whites that blacks as a group lacked the "raw" intelligence to take advantage of even compensatory intervention programs.

The most recent reincarnation of these debates stems from the publication of *The Bell Curve: Intelligence and Class Structure in American Life* (The Free Press 1994). The authors, Charles Murray and Richard J. Herrnstein, argue that intelligence (as measured by IQ) is inherited. Low levels of intelligence, in turn, are responsible for social problems such as poverty, lawlessness, and dysfunctional families. If this trend is allowed to continue, they warn, the eclipse of United States as a superpower is assured. This line of thinking puts Murray and Herrnstein in camp with others of similar conviction(see also Browne 1994). Key points in the argument are as follows:

- Intelligence is real and measureable;
- Intelligence can be quantified through IQ scores as measured by standardized testing;
- Intelligence is partly inherited; this makes it resistant to reform;
- Intelligence has a predictive value: that is, it correlates with positive (success) and negative (welfare or crime) achievement. Those with intelligence succeed; those without, fail. Those in between with I.Q. scores from 76-124) fall in the middle.
- Intelligence varies with ethnic and racial groups; some races or classes have high levels; others don't; whites, for example, are smarter than blacks and these differences are innate;
- The proliferation of intellectually-impoverished ethnic and racial groups (by migration or natural birth) will diminish a country's ability to produce, compete, or prosper;
- Innate differences in intelligence should serve as basis for social policy; why throw good money at bad when compensatory or affirmative-type programs are a losing proposition that no government can afford.

In other words, inequality and class (who is rich and who is poor) are not randomly distributed, but dependent on inherited measures of intelligence. Those at the top of their cognitive class are successful; those near the bottom are destined to be dysfunctional. Social problems will proliferate unless something is done to purge the country of the intellectually impoverished underclass.

Many social scientists would disagree with this assessment (Callahan 1995). Low IQ scores do not create social problems; rather social conditions such as class structure or racial discrimination are likely to create lower IQ scores. Even if intelligence were partly inherited and measureable, genetic and environmental factors are impossible to separate. Nevertheless, the assertion that biological pools rather than social conditions shape behaviour has altered how we think about social inequality. Two reasons may account for the tenacity of racial explanations. First, if intelligence is biologically innate and largely impervious to environmental modification, then white American cannot be held responsible for the plight of minority groups. Second, IQ exams are an effective device for explaining away differences in a simple, yet scholarly manner. They possess an aura of scientific validity that is substantiated by the "magic" of quantification and measurement. The results of these tests can be used to justify negative treatment of minorities, ranging from segregated facilities to inferior programs. They can also be employed to forestall progressive change.

The coupling of **intelligence and race** also represents a strategy (in consequence if not intent) for keeping minority groups "in their place." In a world where **race matters**, a genetic justification for the status quo and patterns of privilege remains a popular means for sorting out who gets what in society. The use of half truths in conjunction with reams of graphs and statistics can create mystification and can lead to negative social consequences (Callahan 1995). It can also create the impression that racism is a respectable intellectual position when grounded in "science," with a legitimate place in the national debate on race (Naureckas 1995). Even more frightening is the potential for such an undemocratic political agenda as the basis for public policy.

CHAPTER HIGHLIGHTS

- This chapter has examined the race concept, the origins of racial types and typologies, the role of racial doctrines as instruments of colonialist expansion, and its status in the comprehension and construction of human reality.

- Race continues to matter in terms of entitlement or engagement within contemporary society. Race remains a powerful social force that is instrumental in shaping intergroup dynamics since groups are likely to exploit, control, or dominate on the basis of what they "see" in others.

- Race matters when it comes to minority participation in sports. African-Americans excel in certain sports not because of physiological properties (although genetic differences may play a role) but because of social factors and opportunity structures.

- Race and crime do not necessarily correlate, notwithstanding public perception and political clamour to the contrary. Race cannot explain crime (crime transcends racial groupings); race-based crime statistics do not measure crime but rates of minority apprehension by law enforcement.

- The race concept is described in terms of its (a) definition and characteristics, (b) logic and underlying rationale, (c) origins and development during the age of imperialism, and (d) impact and implications on group dynamics.

- The race concept is primarily a social construct, without any biological basis or scientific validity, even if its consequences are real. In that sense, race is political because it is associated with debates over who gets what.

- Recourse to the race concept reflected a growing reliance on "scientific" techniques to (a) categorize people into racial groups on the basis of skin colour, (b) provide an explanation for internal diversity among humans, (c) explain the relative achievements of certain groups, and (d) predict the fate of the human species.

- Racism in United States was conveyed by the vehicle of scientific racism and its expression in intelligence (IQ) testing. The fact that such thinking remains today indicates that race matters as a system of explanation, exploitation, engagement, and entitlement.

- The controversy over IQ and race ultimately hinges on whether the tests measure innate intelligence or socially constructed measures of intelligence.

- The race concept originated and evolved in response to the needs of an expanding Western economy. As an ideology with powerful public appeal, it was employed to rationalize and condone exploitation of colonized groups.

- Doctrines of racial domination, including Social Darwinism, Scientific Racism, and Eugenics, were also invoked to establish the desirability and inevitability of white privilege.

- Racial differences exist but races do not — at least not in the sense of distinct and fixed categories of individuals, with a unique assemblage of characteristics that evolved over time.

- People are similar in essence but vary in certain surface differences, mostly in terms of single traits rather than as bundles of characteristics. That suggests that traits can be categorized, not groups of people with their different combination of traits.

- In theory, the concept of race is not the problem per se. The problem lies in arbitrarily dividing the world into fixed categories of people; linking physical differences with social and moral properties, arranging these assemblages of characteristics in ascending/descending order; and establishing ideologies of superiority to explain, justify, exploit, and control.

- Race has long been endorsed as a way of condoning inequality and domination while maintaining a veneer of morality and piety throughout. It has also been employed to explain human differences and similarities under a pseudo-scientific mantle.

• Race matters not because it is real, but because people respond to it as real. Race matters not because people are inherently different or unequal but because perceived differences serve as a basis for sorting out privilege and power. Race matters not because of biological differences but because an exclusive preoccupation with genes detracts from the social dimensions of the sorting process in society.

KEY TERMS

Colonialism/Imperialism	Race	Scientific Racism in
Eugenics	Race Matters	United States
Intelligence and Race	Race Types	Social Darwinism
IQ Exam	Racial Doctrines	Speciation
Neo-colonialism	Racial Typologies	

REVIEW QUESTIONS

1) How valid is the race concept from a scientific point of view?

2) Rather than a biological thing "out there," the concept of race is properly analyzed as a system of social relations and a set of cultural (ideological) productions that are historical and reflect a range of human interests, needs, and strategies. Explain what is meant by this statement.

3) Sociologists have an expression suggesting that, "phenomena do not have to be real, to be real in their consequences." Apply this sociological insight to a discussion of race and racial typologies in terms of their impact on targetted groups.

4) Indicate why racial doctrines emerged in the nineteenth century Europe, and why they continued to persist into the twentieth century.

5) Do you think there is any way to prove or disprove the existence of racially based differences in intelligence? Use the IQ exam controversy to assist you in your answer.

6) Write a brief essay (about 250 words) on the topic "race matters" in Canadian society.

7) Indicate whether there is any validity to the collection of crime statistics by race.

FACES OF RACISM

INTRODUCTION: RACISM EXISTS

From afar, Canada strikes many as a paragon of racial tranquility. Racism may lurk as the single most destructive force in many societies, including the United States (King III, 1994), but surely not in Canda where racism is a dirty word in many social circles. Open racists, including a host of white supremacists, are routinely charged and convicted for disseminating hate propaganda. Race riots are virtually unheard of, while blatant forms of racial discrimination have gone underground. The demographic revolution that has transformed stodgy provincial capitals such as Vancouver and Toronto into vibrant, racially heterogenous cosmopolitan centres without explicit racial confrontation is also a positive indicator.

Up close, the picture changes. Critics charge that racism is alive and well in Canada; only its worst effects are camouflaged by a teflon veneer of tolerance and politeness (Walker 1989; Philip 1992). Rather than an affliction among some isolated malcontents, racism in Canada is chronic and deeply embedded in the very core of our history and institutions, with little or no sign of diminishing. Racism provides the ideological life-support for capitalism at large (Bolaria and Li 1988; Satzewich 1991; McKague 1992; McKenna 1994). Hatemongers remain a social blight, while racist rules and institutional procedures have the effect (if not necessarily the intent) of excluding minorities (Henry et al. 1995). Certain institutions such as the police or mass media are condemned as regressive as their oft-criticized counterparts in the United States. Even Canada's efforts to accommodate diversity through government initiatives are denounced as thinly-veiled racism in defence of the status quo (Thobani 1995). That Canada has managed to escape wholesale race riots is less an tribute to enlightened policies, and more to exceptional good fortune and a powerful myth-making machine.

Which picture is more accurate? Is Canada as racist as critics say; or is Canada essentially an open and tolerant society, with only isolated and random incidents of racism? Can Canada be described as a society where individuals are rewarded on the basis of merit, where no group is singled out for special treatment, and where physical attributes are irrelevant in determining a person's status, or is reality completely different (Henry et al. 1995)? Perhaps the answer lies somewhere in between the poles of naive optimism and cynical pessimism. Canada contains an awkward and conflicting blend of hard-core racists and resolute anti-racists, with the vast majority of individuals parked somewhere in between these extremes. It makes no more sense to exaggerate the notion of Canada as irrevocably racist, with countless hate groups resorting to violence to achieve supremacist goals, than it is to underestimate the tenacity of racism in supporting white privilege and power. Racism exists, to be sure, yet its face is shifting in response to a changing and diverse society (McFarlane 1995).

This chapter will explore the many faces of racism in Canada from a variety of different vantage points. The chapter will analyze racism in terms of its nature and definition: A key distinction is between racism as *hate* versus racism as *power*. The magnitude and scope of racism will be assessed by dissecting its constituent elements, including prejudice (from ethnocentrism to stereotyping) and discrimination (including harassment). The different dimensions of racism are also compared: Those involving the personal, conscious, and deliberate are contrasted with the impersonal and systemic. Racism is also expressed at different levels, from the institutional and ideological to the individual and everyday. Understanding racism in its many guises provides a platform for exploring the concept of anti-racism. Anti-racist strategies are classified into personal or institutional, then examined with respect to differences in objectives, means, and outcomes.

Certain questions are inevitable in a field as highly charged as racism. These questions impart an organizational framework for sorting out issues of relevance to Canada. They also secure a basis for group discussion:

1) Are incidents of racism and racial conflict increasing across Canada? Or are Canadians more aware of racism and human rights, with a growing willingness to report violations to proper authorities?

2) Is racism a recent introduction to Canada? Or is racism deeply embedded in the cultural and structural make-up of Canada? Does contemporary racism represent a last-ditch effort by white privilege to resist minority initiatives for equality and justice?

3) To what extent is racism a case of individual ignorance or fear? Are we better off to analyze racism within the cultural context of Canada's institutional structures?

4) How valid is the charge that Canada is a racist society? When is racism an all purpose putdown for silencing opponents or closing debates? Can constant repetition diminish or trivialize the impact of racism on those who routinely suffer from its presence?

5) In what way is racism a "thing" out there? Or should racism be interpreted as a system of social relations, with a complex array of practices and discourses that are historically defined, embedded in patterns of power, and woven into the ideological fabric of society (Stamm 1993)?

6) How is it possible for persons to be colour-blind yet stand accused of racism? Conversely, why can colour-consciousness be regarded as progressive and non-racist?

7) Is racism something that is inherent in certain actions? Or is racism an attribute conferred on actions because of their context and consequences?

8) What, if anything, can be done about racism? To what extent have anti-racist initiatives succeeded in dealing with this social problem?

We could be smug about our race relations record if racism were a mere blip on Canada's social and historical landscape. This, sadly, is far from the truth. Minority populations have experienced varied degrees of intolerance and discrimination depending on when they came and from where they arrived. Many continue to feel it, albeit in more indirect ways. The manner in which we confront these issues says a lot about our approach to race, aboriginal, and ethnic relations. It also furnishes a framework for analyzing the many and changing faces of racism in Canada.

DEFINING RACISM

Expressions of **racism** have varied over time and place; accordingly, a widely accepted definition of racism has eluded our grasp. That is a surprising admission in light of its pervasiveness. As many definitions exist as specialists in this area. Certain actions are unmistakably racist; others are defined as such because of context or consequence. Such variance leads to a profusion of contradictory statements whose combined impact can generate more heat than light. Some define racism as a predisposition to "biologize" the intellectual, moral, and social characteristics of a person or group. Others prefer to define racism as an act of denial or exclusion against those perceived as inferior. Racism is defined by others still as any organized activity that unjustly diminishes others and justifies this discrimination by reference to race. Still others see racism as the exercise of power by some groups over others.

The scope of racism is bewilderingly elastic: It can span the spectrum from the openly defamatory to systemic patterns that confer institutional advantage to some, not to others. Certain types of racist behaviour are unplanned and unpremeditated, but expressed in isolated acts at irregular intervals because of individual impulse or insensitivity. Other racist actions are not spontaneous or sporadic; they are systemic and manifest instead through discriminatory patterns that are inextricably linked with society at large (University of Guelph 1994). Expressions of racism can be wilfull, intentional, or conscious; alternately, they can be involuntary, inadvertent, or unconscious. Racism can be expressed by individuals, or it can be deeply embedded within institutional frameworks. Some see racism as something individuals do or don't do, while others define it as structural arrangements that exclude and deny. Still others characterize racism as a property attributed to actions rather than an attribute inherent in reality. As a result, racism means whatever people want it mean. That can only play havoc with consensus.

Definitional difficulties also arise from an indiscriminate use of the term itself. Racism is as an omnibus concept with an remarkable capacity to bend, elude, twist, conceal, and shape, depending on context and consequences. Negative comments involving racially different persons are assumed to be racist; nevertheless, the remarks may more accurately reflect ignorance, bad manners, greed, fear, or laziness on the part of the speaker (Wieseltier 1989). Indiscriminate use of the term racism carries its own set of risks. Blaming racism for everything when race is irrelevant may be racist in its own right. Doing so may draw attention to racial rather than social causes of minority problems, in effect contributing to perceptions of minorities as victims or villains. Constant and repetitive use of the term runs the risk of turning it into a harmless cliché. The very act of calling everything racism eventually means that nothing is racist, thus trivializing its consequences for victims at large. Racism is also vulnerable to manipulation by various interests along the political spectrum. Used as a smokescreen, it can divert attention from the issues at hand; likewise, it may silence others or close debate because of the cringe factor associated with racism.

Racism as Hate

Part of the problem in securing a definition stems from reality itself. The word no longer has a meaning in the conventional sense of a word having a single, commonly understood definition (Editorial, *The Globe and Mail*, 12 May 1992). Definitions appear to sort themselves out into two streams. A narrow definition is derived from the root, "race", with its notion that biology is destiny. Definitions of **racism as hate** tend to partition the human world into fixed and discrete categories. Each of these racial categories contains a distinctive and inherited assemblage of social and biological characteristics that can be arranged in ascending/descending orders of importance. Unequal treatment of others is then justified on this basis. Racial doctrines not only define certain types as behaviour (such as intelligence) as bio-genetically programmed; a moral value of inferiority or superiority is also assigned to human differences. Certain races are judged as inherently unequal because of social or mental deficiencies, and subsequently denied rights and opportunities (Jaret 1995). As one prominent scholar in this field has noted in correlating racism with biological determinism:

> "[R]acism is an ideology which considers a group's unchangeable physical characteristics to be linked in a direct causal way to psychological or intellectual characteristics, and which on this basis distinguishes between superior and inferior racial groups" (van den Berghe 1967).

Racism, in short, can be defined as a relatively cohesive set of beliefs ("ideology") and practices that labels, classifies, evaluates, and ranks members of a group along a hierarchy by virtue of their inclusion in a predefined category. A preoccupation with biologically-focused inferiority is being replaced with assumptions about cultural inferiority. Minorities are denied or excluded because of technological or cultural deficiencies rather than because of their genetic makeup (Essed 1991).

Racism as Power

A more comprehensive definition focuses on the notion of **racism as power**. This broader definition approaches racism as virtually any type of exploitation or exclusion inherent in majority-minority relations. Racism refers to that package of beliefs and practices, both deliberate and inadvertent, that reinforces the superiority of one group over another. Like sexism, racism entails a set of beliefs about withholding equal treatment from "inferior" groups, along with a corresponding set of practices that provide "bite" to these beliefs (Alladin 1996). Intent and motive may be less important than the context of an action and its consequences on those without the power to deflect or defuse them. Racism also appears to be moving away from its ontological status as a "thing" out there, and toward a social construct involving relations of inequality.

At its most fundamental, then, racism is about power. That much is acknowledged by one of the better definitions available: *Racism refers to the power held by one group or individuals that results in dominance and control over another on the basis of appearance, intelligence, or moral worth* (University of Guelph 1994). This power is (a) expressed at the level of majority-minority interaction, (b) embedded within the institutional framework of society, (c) buttressed by a coherent system of ideas and ideals, and (d) perpetuated by vested interests. Minority group lives and life chances are limited by the superior power of those with the resources and the sanctions to ensure compliance. That raises an interesting and often controversial point of contention: Can minorities be racist?

QUESTION BOX

Is Racism a Two-way Street?

The correlation between racism and the power of dominant groups raises a vexing question. Can minority group members display racism against the majority sector? Is it a case of reverse racism when non-aboriginal writers are openly discouraged from filming or writing fiction about aboriginal themes? Is it racist for aboriginal peoples to accuse whites of genocide in undermining the political, social, and cultural grounds of aboriginal society? Is it racist for black militants to openly display hatred toward whites as an inferior race, deserving only of a one-way ticket back to Europe? Are black leaders who make defamatory remarks about Jews acting in a racist manner? How racist is it when a university stipulates that only a black person can sit as the inaugural chair of a Black Canadian Studies?

Consider the cry of reverse racism when the Writers Union of Canada sponsored a conference in Vancouver in the spring of 1994 that barred white Canadians from participation. Funded primarily through public monies, Writing Thru "Race" — A Conference for First Nations Writers and Writers of Colour sought a venue for minorities to explore the experiences of racism in a world where, national myths notwithstanding, race matters. The conference justified its decision to exclude whites from one session on the grounds of improving dialogue among the historically oppressed — in the same way women's consciousness raising movements frequently excluded men. Critics saw this as little more than reverse discrimination on the grounds of race. They resented the notion that people could be singled out on the basis of race or group affiliation rather than as unique individuals (*Alberta Report*, 25 April 1994). Others were irritated by the fact that it was supported by a government group in direct violation of the Canadian Charter of Rights (see McFarlane 1995).

Was this a case of racism? Much depends on how one defines racism, of course. A narrow reading of racism as race is destiny would imply, yes, it was. Majority members, for example, prefer to equate racism with racist ideologies or colour-conscious denial of equal opportunity or equality before the law (Jaret 1995). But there are certain difficulties in attributing racism to minority group members. A more comprehensive view of racism as power suggests, no, it wasn't. Accusations of racism must go beyond external appearances. Emphasis must be instead on the context of the actions and their social consequences. The essence of racism resides in the unequal distribution of power, combined with the denial of opportunity or privileges in a colour-conscious climate (Blauner 1991).

In short, racism is about power and its abuse. Statements made by a minority group — however distasteful or bigoted — should not be regarded as racist. They are merely slogans without the capacity for harm since minorities lack the power to put hateful slurs into practice. Racism is not oppression because of white prejudice but because of a system that promotes domination and subjugation; black prejudice by contast does not operate in a parallel context (hooks 1992). To be sure, minorities are not entirely powerless; after all, there is recourse to alternate sources of power broking such as boycotts, civil disobedience, and moral suasion. Still, minority hatred has neither the resources to topple the dominant sector nor the strength to harass, exclude, exploit, persecute, dominate, or undermine its collective self respect. Conditions of relative powerlessness reduce minority hostility to the level of rhetoric — a kind of protective buffer against the intrusive presence of the majority in defence of minority interests. In other words, reverse racism is a contradiction in terms, since those without access to power or resources cannot deny or exclude. Racism is not a two-way street; more accurately, it resembles an expressway with controlled access points for those privileged enough to occupy the driver seat.

In sum: We prefer a definition of racism that encompasses both perspectives. Racism is defined as *those ideas and ideals ("ideology") that assert the superiority of one race over another, together with the power to put these beliefs into practice in a way that denies or excludes on the basis of membership in a devalued category*. Racism is ultimately based on issues of power involving relations of dominance, control, and exploitation (Schermerhorn 1956). Those in positions of power are able to invoke a doctrine of hate to ensure a measure of *social control* over those deemed inferior in the competitive struggle for scarce resources. Even when correlated with social control, however, expressions of racism can be manifested in a variety of different ways. A look at the different components of racism provides further insights into the realities of Canadian society.

CONSTITUENTS OF RACISM

Racism does not exist as a monolithic reality. Nor is it a kind of thing out there that everyone can agree on. Racism ultimately touches on a variety of social processes, from the immediate and everyday to the remote and systemic. Each of the components that comprise racism contributes to its totality as an ideology and practice. The building blocks of racism consist of **prejudice** (including ethnocentrism and stereotypes) and **discrimination** (including harassment).

Prejudice

The concept of prejudice refers to negative, often unconscious, and preconceived notions about others. Prejudice arises because of our tendency to prejudge persons or situations as a way of imposing definition and order on the world around us. It consists of *pre+judgements* that are irrational and unfounded on the basis of existing or compelling evidence. Many regard prejudice as a psychological phenomenon with a corresponding set of rigid or authoritarian personality traits (Adorno 1950; Allport 1954). Others link these pre+judgements with a visceral and deepseated fear of those whose appearances, values, or practices threaten a cherished and comfortable status quo. Still others equate prejudice with (a) feelings of superiority, (b) a perception of subordinate groups as inferior, (c) belief in the propriety of white privilege and power, and (d) reluctance to share these prerogatives (Blumer 1958).

Without dismissing this experiential dimension, we prefer to analyze prejudice from a sociological approach. We see prejudice as a social construction, grounded in and derived from social processes, and amenable to analysis by sociological means. For example, the more powerful groups in a competitive environment will resort to prejudice for preserving privilege (Cox 1948; Blumer 1965). Individuals, of course, are the carriers of prejudicial attitudes. They are responsible for harboring prejudice; they must be held accountable for actions that stem from prejudice. But these prejudgements do not originate in a vacuum. Nor can they be separated from the restrictions and choices within the wider context. Prejudicial judgements are part and parcel of society, and failure to appreciate this social dimension is self-defeating.

National surveys confirm what many probably suspect (Henry and Tator 1985): Most Canadians are inclined to negatively prejudge others because of ignorance or visceral dislike. Prejudice is sufficiently widespread to foster fertile grounds for racial hatred and discrimination against identifiable groups under certain economic or social conditions (McKenna 1994). This prejudice is reflected in and reinforced by **stereotyping** — unwarranted generalizations about others; it also is expressed by **ethnocentrism** with its belief in the self-proclaimed superiority of one culture over others. It is quite possible that many references to racism are confused with stereotyping or ethnocentrism. Nevertheless, the net impact of such prejudicial attitudes may be racist and controlling, given their potential to perpetuate a racially-based social pecking order.

Ethnocentrism

Ethnocentrism can be defined as a belief in the superiority of one's own culture compared with others. It represents an uncompromising loyalty to and belief in one's own cultural values and practices as natural, normal, and necessary. Other values and practices are implicitly dismissed as inferior. There is nothing intrinsically wrong with thinking of your cultural lifestyle as self-evident and preferable. Difficulties arise when your standards are used as a frame of reference for negatively evaluating the behaviour of other groups. Not surprisingly, these groups will come across as backward, immoral, or irrational — a highly unenviable situation for that group when they have less power in society. In other words, favouritism towards one's group may promote cohesion and morale; it can also contribute to inter-group tension and hostility.

Stereotypes

Ethnocentrism often leads to a proliferation of stereotypes about outgroup members. Stereotypes are essentially generalizations about others, both unwarranted and unfounded on the basis of available evidence. Stereotyping reflects a universal tendency to reduce a complex phenomena to simple(istic) explanations that are generalized to a whole category without acknowledging individual differences (Rose 1957). Like ethnocentrism, stereotypes in themselves are harmless. Problems arise when these preconceived mental images give way to discriminatory practices. The dispossession of aboriginal peoples from their lands was facilitated by circulation of negative images of First Nations as savages, cannibals, or brutes (McKenna 1994). A pervasive anti-Orientalism in British Columbia fostered hatred against Asian populations, thereby simplifying the task of expelling 22,000 Japanese-Canadians from the West Coast in 1942.

All negative stereotypes are hurtful; nevertheless not all negative portrayals have an equivalent degree of impact (Stamm 1993). Context and consequence are crucial variables. Socially empowered groups need not be unduly concerned with negative stereotyping since they as a group have control over a wide range of representations of themselves. Even a constant barrage of negative images can be absorbed without harm or damage. Sterotypes might make white men uncomfortable, yet many possess the resources to resist or neutralize them. Power and privilege provide a protective layer. For minorities, however, stereotyping is a problem. Each negative image or unflattering representation reinforces their peripheral position within an unequal society. The media are a major source of stereotyping; so too are ethnic jokes. Ethnic jokes often portray minorities in a demeaning way, not out of intentional malice, but because such humour by definition is simplistic and prone to exaggeration. The consequences, while unintended, are damaging in unequal contexts: Minorities are portrayed in uni-dimension terms, for example, as comics, athletes, victims, or vixens. These images, in turn, can be employed to justify daily violence or structural oppression through the negative effects of a "chilly climate" (Ford 1994). In short, stereotypes are not an error in perception, at least no more so than prejudice. Think of them as yet another extension of *social control* (Stamm 1993).

Discrimination

Prejudice refers to attitudes and beliefs; by contrast, discrimination consists of the process by which these negative cognitions are put into practice. The term "discrimination," can be employed in different ways. Non-evaluative meanings indicate a capacity to distinguish (for example, a colour-blind person may not distinguish between blue and green). Evaluative meanings of discrimination can be used positively ("a discriminating palate") or negatively ("a differential treatment") depending on whether the distinction is appropriate or legitimate. Distinctions are discriminatory when constructed on unnecessary or irrelevant grounds for purposes of perpetuating disadvantage. In short, while some forms of discrmination are inevitable and acceptable — even essential to the functioning of society (MacQueen 1995), Section 15 of the Charter expressly prohibits discrimination on the basis of race, ethnicity, or origins. Discrimination as we use it here involves the differential treatment of minority groups not because of their ability or merit, but because of irrelevant characteristics such as skin colour and language preference. Individuals are lumped together as members of a devalued group rather than valued as individuals with skills and talents. Intrinsic to all types of discrimination are the realities of *power*: Those with power possess the capacity to put prejudice into practice in a way that denies, excludes, or controls. *Discrimination can be defined as any act, whether deliberate or not, that has the intent or the effect of adversely affecting others on grounds other than merit or acquired skills.*

Though discrimination is often twinned as the behavioral counterpart of prejudice, such a distinction or relationship is not as clearcut as appearances may suggest. Discrimination can exist without prejudice; conversely, prejudice may flourish without its expression in discrimination. Prejudice and discrimination are analytically distinct concepts that can vary independently under certain conditions (Rose 1957). That is, an individual can be prejudiced, yet may not act in a discriminatory manner for a variety of reasons (see LaPiere 1934).

QUESTION BOX

Prejudice versus Discrimination?

Do prejudicial attitudes lead to discriminatory behaviour? Social scientists have long pondered the nature of the link between prejudicial attitudes and discriminatory behaviour. One of the earliest studies in this area was conducted by Richard LaPiere and a Chinese couple who travelled throughout United States during the early 1930s. The pervasive anti-Oriental (Asian) prejudice at the time led LaPiere to assume that the travellers would be refused service in most hotels and restaurants they frequented. On the contrary, only one establishment out of over 200 refused service to LaPiere and his friends. Several months later LaPiere sent a letter to all the establishments they had visited. In the letter he asked if they would accept members of the Chinese race as guests in their establishment. An overwhelming number of establishments (92 percent) that earlier had accepted Chinese guests replied in the negative.

This study was held as proof that there was a poor correlation between attitudes (as manifest in verbal responses) and overt behaviour. But a certain amount of caution is necessary before jumping to conclusions from LaPiere's experiment. For example, no one could determine if the same individuals who provided services responded to the requests for reservations. Did the presence of a white person defuse a potentially discriminatory situation, whereas the letter only mentioned the needs of a Chinese couple? For these and related reasons, we must conclude that a correlation between prejudicial attitudes and discriminatory behaviour is tenuous at best. It is governed instead by a variety of situational cues and opportunity structures. We must also recognize that racism (as prejudice + discrimination) is a complex and situational concept.

In short, prejudice must be divorced from discrimination. Fear, threats, sanctions, company policy, or good sense may encourage individuals to compartmentalize their prejudice from everyday action. By way of contrast, discrimination can prevail in many domains where wilful malice is absent. What is critical in defining discrimination are the *context* in which the actions occur and the *consequences* of these actions in unequal situations. This is especially true in situations involving institutional or organizational settings (Mackie 1985). Here, negative treatment toward outgroups is deeply embedded within formal structures and rules — often beyond the consciousness or personalities of those who occupy organizational offices. Thus institutions can operate on racist principles even if the individuals themselves are free of prejudice. This notion of systemic bias will be explored shortly.

Harassment

Harassment is commonly appraised as a type of discrimination. Racial harassment consists of persistent and unwelcome actions of a racially oriented nature by those who ought reasonably to know that such attention is unwanted (UWO 1993). In the words of Monique Shebbeare (McGill 1994:6), harassment involves:

> [t]he abusive, unfair, or demeaning treatment of a person or group of persons that has the effect or purpose of unreasonably interfering with a person's or group's status or performance or creating a hostile or intimidating working or educational environment...

As is the case with discrimination, harassment constitutes an abuse of power that need not be explicitly directed at a specific target. The creation of a chilly climate or "poisoned environment" because of harassment can also have an adverse effect on work, study, involvement, or well-being (Waterloo 1994). Discrimination by harassment — ranging in scope from innuendo and name-calling to pin-ups and open threats — is now covered under laws and human rights codes.

To Sum Up: Racism = *Prejudice+Discrimination+Power*. We have seen how racism is made up of a complex interplay of ideas and actions, with its admixture of prejudice (stereotyping and ethnocentrism) and discrimination (harassment). It also encompasses an ideology with a patterned set of responses: These responses combine to explain, justify, rationalize, and legitimize the unequal treatment of minorities through political exclusion, economic exploitation, or social segregation. The key element in this equation is power. When combined with power, the interplay of prejudice and discrimination create fertile grounds for racism to thrive.

TYPES OF RACISM

Racism is not a uniform concept that reflects a singular experience or common reality. On the contrary, different modes of racism can be discerned which embody variations in intent, awareness, scope, channels of expression, depth of intensity, and consequences. These variations have led to the proliferation of diverse **types of racism**, including: (a) red-necked, (b) polite, (c) subliminal, (d) institutionalized, and (d) systemic. Comparing and contrasting these admittedly ideal types will reveal the complex and multi-dimensional nature of racism as principle and practice. The existence of different racisms should also point the way for diverse solutions if we are serious about purging racism from our midst.

Red-necked racism

Red-necked racism is the kind of racism that most of us think of when asked to comment on the topic. It refers to the kind of old-fashioned racism that prevailed (and continues to exist) in the American "deep South." It flourished during frontier expansion in Canada and United States, then escalated with the arrival of immigrants from outside northern Europe. Intrinsic to red-necked racism is the explicit, highly personalized character of its expression. Whether through physical or verbal abuse, red-necked racism consists of highly personal attacks on others who are perceived as culturally or biologically inferior. These personalized attacks often consist of derogatory slurs and minority name-calling.

Red-necked racism continues to penetrate the social corridors of Canadian society. Even a cursory glance over Canada's past will reveal that racism is a chronic component of Canada's post-Confederation history (Walter 1989; Henry et al. 1995). This may come as a shock to many readers. That the United States is synonymous with racism comes as no surprise to most (King 1994). A country with historical claims to slavery and convulsive urban riots is easy to single out as a bastion of racism. But Canada? Certain myths are deeply entrenched in our collective memories. We like to think of Canada as different when it comes to racial issues. Many Canadians believe these myths about our society, in part because of the existence of laws that expressly prohibit the display of hatred toward minority groups. They point to the absence of American-style race riots, the lack of racist symbols, the omission of prolonged slavery, and the entrenchment of multicultural philosophies within Canadian society. To be sure, slavery and a variety of racist organizations such as the Ku Klux Klan have flourished at certain times in Canadian history (Barrett 1987). However, their impact here is viewed as minimal when compared to their impact on our neighbours to the south.

How accurate are these perceptions? Are Canadians really superior to Americans when it comes to the treatment of racial minorities? Close scrutiny suggests no. Our treatment of racial, aboriginal, and ethnic minorities since Confederation has left everything to be desired. The Chinese, the Japanese, Indo-Pakistanis, First Nations, Jews, and blacks have been and continue to be the object of intense racism. Both the political and public sector have colluded to squelch minority threats against the prevailing order. This racism was especially virulent when directed at Asian populations — as described in the case study, "Controlling the 'Yellow Peril' in Canada."

CASE STUDY

Controlling the "Yellow Peril" in Canada

Early immigration of Chinese into Canada provides a disturbing example of blatant racism toward new Canadians (Baureiss 1985; Li 1988a). The Chinese first arrived in the mid nineteenth century as virtually indentured labour for the construction of the transcontinental railway. Upon completion of the rail-way, they secured other, highly unskilled employment, but were increasingly exposed to abusive treatment by the general public and politicians. The Chinese were frequently subjected to racial invectives by manual labourers who saw them as strike-breaking "scabs." Others perceived them as kind of "yellow peril" that would undermine the purity and integrity of this British outpost. Federal plans to import an additional 5,000 Chinese for the construction of the Grand Trunk Railway elicited this editorial response from the a September 1906 issue of *Saturday Night*:

> We don't want Chinamen in Canada. This is a white man's country and white men will keep it so. The slant-eyed Asiatic with his yellow skin, his unmanly humility, his cheap wants, would destroy the whole equilibrium of industry... We cannot assimilate them. They are an honest, industrious, but hopelessly inferior race (quoted from Fraser 1989:12).

As well, politicians often exploited the Chinese as a political football (scapegoats) to defuse electoral pressure. Chinese efforts to withdraw into their own communities for protection resulted in further dislike and suspicion. Under public pressure, successive government imposed a **head tax** on each incoming

immigrant, culminating with a fee of $500 in the early twentieth century — a sum that was equivalent to the price of new home in Vancouver. The federal government curtailed Chinese immigration in 1923 in response to public demands to stem the "yellow peril." This racist ban was not lifted until 1947 with repeal of the Chinese Immigration Act and passage of Canada's first Citizenship Act.

In recent years, the Chinese have moved from isolation within their communities to active involvement in staking a rightful claim to status as Canadian citizens (Fraser 1989). But prejudicial and racist attacks continue to linger. Chinese-Canadians have been accused of stirring up a host of social problems, from monopolizing spaces in medical schools to driving up real estate prices in Vancouver. These attacks are less direct than in the past; nevertheless the undercurrent of hostility is equally disconcerting.

Stark reminders of red-necked racism in Canada are readily available. Racial violence in recent years has been perpetuated by white supremacist groups ranging from the White Aryan Nation and Western Guard movements to neo-nazi skinheads in urban areas (Kinsella 1994; Barkun 1994). Racist groups such as the Ku Klux Klan have also relied on red-necked violence to cultivate an environment of fear and hatred against minorities throughout United States and Canada (Barrett 1987). The popularity and potential of white supremacist groups is difficult to gauge. Perhaps only 1,500 hard core supremacists operate in Canada, but these extremists have the potential to destabilize a society where prejudice is pervasive (McKenna 1994). Many supremacists may see themselves as white Christians, fusing race and religion in a single nationalist crusade against the forces of "evil" (Jaret 1995). Hate groups sustain their credibility and legitimacy by capitalizing on a poor economy and social instability. Disaffected youth are an obvious target because of their perception that the government is indifferent to the their plight in a changing and diverse world. Demographic imbalances resulting from immigration are likely to ignite supremacist ire, as is the perception that certain minorities have hijacked government business for self-serving purposes. White hate groups have infiltrated the social fabric of Canadian society in different ways, but primarily through telephone hotlines, computer internet, and disinformation campaigns by hatermongerers recruited by the movement (see Kinsella 1994). The courts in Canada have ruled these diatribes are "hate propaganda" and a violation of Canada's criminal code, but technicalities have often overturned such verdicts.

Why does red-necked racism survive? Red-necked racists are not intimidated by accusations of racism. Unlike many Canadians, they take considerable pride in — even boast about — such a label. Evidence, however, suggests that red-necked racism is less acceptable at present than was the case in the past. It has been displaced by more subtle forms of racism that may be somewhat less obtrusive yet equally destructive in impact. Polite racism is another case in point.

Polite Racism

> If racists as a category all wore horns, the battle against them would be a great deal easier. ...The type that chilled me the most, in fact, was not the hard-nosed bully who wanted to kick somebody's teeth in, but rather the highly educated man, wealthy and sophisticated, who sat sipping his cognac while elaborating on the nobility of the white race and the necessity of excising the "mud people" from our midst (Stanley R. Barrett, 1987).

Few people at present will tolerate the open expression of racial slurs. Blatant defamations were routinely hurled at minorities in the past; the risk of social or legal consequences serves as an inhibitor nowadays. The passage of constitutional guarantees such as the Charter of Rights and Freedoms and Human Rights Codes have eroded the legitimacy of red-necked racism from public discourse. But while blatant forms of racism have dissipated to some extent, less candid expressions of bigotry and stereotyping remain in force. Instead of disappearing in the face of social reprisals and legal sanctions as might have been expected, racist slurs ("those kinds of people...") are now couched in a way that allows us to talk around or disguise our criticism of others by using somewhat more muted (polite) tones.

Polite racism then can be seen as a contrived attempt to disguise a dislike of others through behaviour that outwardly is non-prejudicial in appearance. This politeness is especially evident when people of colour are ignored or turned down for jobs, promotions, or accommodation on a regular basis (Henry and Ginzberg 1985). For example, an employer may claim a job is filled rather than admit "no blacks need apply" when approached by an undesirable applicant. Polite racism may appear more sophisticated than its red-necked equivalent; nevertheless, the effect on victims is similar: It serves to sustain prevailing relationships of control, exclusion, or exploitation.

Canadian racism is often depicted as polite and subdued. Racism in Canada is rarely perpetuated by raving lunatics who engage in beatings, lynchings, or grafitti. Rather, racism among Canadians is unobtrusive, often implicit and embedded in words or actions. Derogatory references about minorities continue to be expressed, but they are usually restricted to remarks to friends in private locales. With higher education, individuals become more adept at compartmentalizing and concealing racist attitudes, lest they blurt out statements at odds with career plans or a sophisticated self-image (Fleras 1996). This subtlety makes it difficult to confront, let along eradicate, the expression of polite racism.

The next case study illustrates polite racism in practice by looking at the mistreatment of Indo-Pakistanis immediately prior to the First World War. It reveals the depth of hostility toward immigrants who did not match the demography of a white Dominion. It also demonstrates the convoluted logic behind Canada's racism toward people of colour. More importantly, it exhibits how outgroup hostility hid behind the polite mask of government laws and regulations.

CASE STUDY

The Komagata Maru Incident: Harboring Polite Racism

Canada's early immigration policies are a striking example of racial doctrines in action. Racist (white-only) immigration policies prevailed in Canada up to the end of the Second World War. These policies were directed at populations who were racially or culturally different from the ideal British immigrant.

Indo-Pakistanis in particular were viewed as a threat to the traditional social fabric of Canada. The first immigrants did not arrive until 1903, but the combination of cultural differences, competition for jobs, scapegoating, and unease over the unknown quickly culminated in racially motivated attacks (Buchignani and Indra 1985). By 1910, measures were enacted to curb further entry of East Indians. One law required

all immigrants to have $200 before clearance for landing in Canada; the other required all immigrants to arrive by direct passage ("continuous journey") from their country of origin. The fact that no direct shipping lines existed between India and Canada exposed the racist subtext of this law. The **Komagata Maru incident** is an example of this law in action.

On May 23, 1914, a ship carrying Indo-Pakistani immigrants arrived in Vancouver but passengers were not allowed to disembark. The passengers were refused permission for entry to Canada on the grounds they did not come directly to Canada. Canada had passed a law to that effect — precisely for the purpose of restricting the flow of

East Asians into this country. Since the steamer, Komagata Maru, had picked up passengers in various ports along the way, the mostly Sikh migrants did not meet the continuous journey requirements. For two months both the government and courts refused to grant landing rights. Eventually, on July 23rd, port authorities towed the ship out of the harbour. During the confinement, one passenger died and several contracted serious ailments from inadequate nutrition. Another 26 died in skirmishes when the steamer landed in India after being refused docking privileges in Singapore and Hong Kong.

In recent years, Sikh organizations have exerted pressure on the federal government to acknowledge the wrongdoing of the incident. The Ontario Council of Sikhs has also requested a $10 million compensation package for redress. Whether or not reparations will be forthcoming is difficult to predict, but the outlook is dim following a negative decision by the Minister of Multiculturalism. In short, the spirit or rejection, however polite, continues to fester into the present, as this editorial in the Kitchener-Waterloo Record (1994) poignantly reminds us: "We are the dead. Short days ago/We lived, felt dawn, saw sunset glow/Loved, and were loved; and now we lie In Flanders Fields."

On November 11, four Orthodox Sikhs who had served India in World War II donned their uniforms and medals to join their comrades at the Newton Branch of the Canadian Legion in Surrey B.C.

"Take up our quarrel with the foe!/ To you from failing hands we throw/ The torch; be yours to hold it high;"

The Sikhs were barred from entry into the Legion Hall after the ceremonies because they were wearing turbans as their religion dictates.

"If ye break faith with us who die/ We shall not sleep though poppies grow In Flanders Fields."

There is no denying that Asian populations were vulnerable to outright bigotry and racial intolerance in the past. Open discrimination against racial minorities has subsided in recent years. Since the shift toward human and individual rights awareness, in Canada it is now illegal to engage in overt acts of discrimination. More polite forms of racism continue to prevail, however. Few will openly admit to racist tendencies or beliefs; still, racism continues to hobble the lives and life chances of racial, ethnic, and aboriginal minorities.

Subliminal Racism

Subliminal racism bears a passing ressemblance to polite racism. Both types of racism are communicated at personal levels by indirect means. In neither case do people set out to openly put people down, but their actions or words somehow seem to have that effect. Differences stem from levels of intent: Only polite racism can be regarded as a conscious attempt to disparage minorities. By contrast, subliminal racism (alternatively, "democratic racism" [Henry et al. 1995]; "nonracist racism" [Elliott and Fleras 1991]; or "aversive racism" [Dovidio 1986]) constitutes an unconscious criticism of minorities. How can this be?

Evidence suggests that Canadians as a whole are receptive toward the principles of multiculturalism and racial equality (Fleras and Elliott 1992; Berry and Kalin 1993). Many Canadians express sympathy for the plight of those less fortunate than themselves; for example, immigrants are frequently portrayed as industrious contributors to Canadian well-being. Yet negative and prejudicial attitudes continue to distort our assessment and treatment of the foreign born. Antiracist activist demands are criticized as a threat to national identity (autonomy, norms, values) and social harmony (Dijk 1987:61). People of colour are chided for making too many complaints or demands, or for not taking advantage of the opportunities open to them. Affirmative or preferential action programs are disparaged as unfair to the majority.

How then do we explain this ambiguity toward minorities in Canada. Cynics would argue that Canadians are hypocrites whose deep-seated racism is camouflaged by platitudinous pieties. We disagree, but concede that critics may have a point in reminding us to "mind our gap." What we have instead is a style of outgroup hostility that goes undetected by conventional measures (Weigel and Howes 1985; McConohay 1986; Gaertner and Dovidio 1986; and Katz et al. 1986). Subliminal racism is not directly expressed but embodied in opposition to progressive minority policies and programs. The opposition is coded in terms that politely skirt the issue and that rationalize criticism of minorities on grounds of mainstream values, national interests, or appeals to a higher sense of fair play, equality, and justice. For example, refugee claimants are not condemned in blunt racist terminology; their landed entry into Canada is criticized on procedural grounds ("jumping the queue") or they are belittled for taking unfair advantage of Canada's generosity. Other examples such as the decision by the RCMP to accommodate the mandatory turban worn by religious Sikh males are denounced as unCanadian, an affront to majority values, illegitimate, excessively demanding, too costly, unacceptably rapid, or outside due process (See and Wilson 1988).

Clearly, then, a degree of racial ambiguity is apparent. Individuals may endorse progressive racial attitudes as a matter of principle, yet disapprove of policy implications (the "costs") or minority assertiveness to bring about the practice of racial equality (Essed 1991). Values that endorse racial equality are publicly reaffirmed; nevertheless, there is deep seated resentment at the prospect of moving over and making space for these newcomers. The subliminality of racism appears to reflect an inescapable dichotomy in our core values (see Myrdal 1944). On the one hand, we place a value on the public good, with its emphasis on collective rights, special treatment, equality of outcomes, and fair play. On the other, there remains a powerful commitment to competitive individualism, with its focus on personal freedom, self-reliance, meritocracy, and competition. Subliminal racism results from the interplay of these oppositional values. It enables individuals to maintain two apparently conflicting values — one rooted in the egalitarian virtues of justice and fairness; the other in beliefs that exclude or deny. These very values that define a democratic right to compete or receive are also used to denigrate or erect barriers (Henry et al. 1995). This conflict is not openly manifested except in terms of discomfort and uncertainty when values clash. Even many of those who profess egalitarian attitudes and a commitment to racial equality are unwilling — or incapable — of realizing the contradiction.

In effect, subliminal racism is located among that class of person who abhors openly discriminatory treatment of minorities. Yet these same individuals are incapable of escaping the cultural or cognitive influences that release dormant hostilities. The subliminality of this racism denounces the explicitness of old-fashioned racism while reinforcing racial inequality through muted criticism of racial minorities. Perpetrators may be oblivious to their attitudes and actions. Still, the net effect is the same, that is, minority groups are cast as troublemakers.

Institutionalized Racism

Much of the discussion to this point has dwelt on racism as an individual attribute. Other types of racism go beyond the interpersonal in terms of scope, style, and impact. Racism at the institutional level represents such a shift. Institutional racism involve rules and procedures that directly and deliberately prevent minorities from full and equal involvement within society. According to the sociologist, Peter S. Li (1988a, b), institutionalized racism appears when discriminatory practices are legally sanctioned by the state and formalized within its institutional framework. It consists of norms and corresponding activities that are embedded within the design (structure and function) of the organization to preclude minority entry or participation (Bolaria and Li 1988).

Institutional racism flourished in societies that endorsed racial segregation. The system of apartheid in South Africa was a classic example. While Canada may have had a reputation as a progressive society in the management of race and ethnic relations, it was not exempt from the tarnish of institutionally racist practices (Reitz and Breton 1994). Institutional racism was once a chronic and inescapable component of Canadian society (Sunahara 1981). Minorities were routinely barred from even partial participation in mainstream institutions. Predictably, they were subjected to verbal and physical harassment without much chance of recourse or retribution. This racism ranged from the slavery of blacks in Nova Scotia in the pre-Confederation era (Jones 1978), to the disenfranchisement of Japanese Canadians in British Columbia until 1949 (Sunahara 1981) and the differential admissions policy for Jewish students in Montreal at McGill University during the 1940s (Draper 1983). African-Canadians were routinely excluded from entry into theatres and restaurants until these odious distinctions were rescinded in the 1950s (Walker: 1989).

The abolition of institutional racism, however, did not automatically create a racism-free zone for minorities. Racism in many cases simply changed its face to comply with national myths and public laws. The next case study, "Anti-Semitism in Canada," exposes the changing face of racism over time in response to historical and social circumstances.

CASE STUDY

Anti-Semitism in Canada: From Institutional to Polite

As one might expect of a country peopled by numerous European immigrants, Canada has historically endorsed racist attitudes towards the Jews. This **anti-Semitism** has assumed many faces — ranging from violence and outright discrimination in the past, to more indirect expressions at present which are no less powerful in their impact. How does anti-Semitism express itself in a society that collectively takes pride in its tolerant and non-discriminatory ideals?

OPEN SEASON

Intolerance and bigotry toward Jews were openly tolerated in the prewar era (Abella 1989). This estrangement between Jews and non-Jews was displayed in numerous ways. One of Canada's only race riots exploded in Toronto in August, 1933 when the Swastika Club confronted some Jews at a baseball game in Christie Pits field, for example. In other areas Jews were routinely excluded from employment in banks, insurance companies, and department stores. Jewish professors, judges, doctors, engineers, and architects found it nearly impossible to get work. Universities imposed limits on the number of Jewish students who could enrol (Abella 1989; *Maclean's* 16 April 1990). Refusal by Canadian authorities in 1939

to accept 900 German-Jewish refugees who arrived by boat after rejection in Latin America and American ports of call reflected the depth of hostility. These refugees had no choice but to return to Nazi Germany where many were subsequently forced into concentration camps (Abella and Troper 1991).

SOFTENING THE STANCE

Jews in Canada have excelled in economic terms. Various factors have contributed, including (a) a religiously inspired emphasis on education, (b) a history as urbanites, (c) reliance on middle class values such as delayed gratification, and (d) experience with marginality as a basis for coping (Lipset and Raab 1995). Yet anti-Semitism persists. Modern anti-Semitism is more varied than in the past. In some cases, anti-Semitic feelings are invoked through racist slurs, vandalism, or acts of harassment. Incidents involving the defacing of Jewish synogogues with Nazi grafitti in Toronto and Vancouver have shown a marked increase in recent years as documented by the B'nai B'rith League. The destruction of property is thought to be the work of youthful skinheads some of whom are steeped in white supremacist ideologies. The fact that 290 cases of anti-Semitism were reported by B'nai B'rith in 1994 is worrying as is an increase of 11.7 percent from 1993 and the highest number of incidents since reporting begain in 1980.

In general, blatant expressions of anti-Semitism are no longer tolerated in Canada, although prejudicial attitudes appear deeply embedded in Canadian society. Where 50 percent of all Canadians once harbored anti-Semitic prejudice prior to the Second World War, the figure has dwindled to about 10 percent at present. Discrimination which denied Jews access to housing, employment, education, and club membership is illegal under the Charter of Rights and Freedoms and various Human Rights Codes. What we have instead are increasingly "polite" forms of racism as they are manifest in the circulation of dogmas and propaganda that victimize Jews. Holocaust-denial theories camouflage anti-Semitism by rejecting the historical fact of Nazi concentration camps in which millions of Jews were incarcerated and slaughtered. Two of the major proponents of this theory, Ernst Zundel, a Toronto publisher, and James Keegstra, an Alberta teacher, have been charged with acts against the Criminal Code for wilfully distributing

hate propaganda. Allegations continue to circulate about Zionist conspiracies to assert world-wide domination in the field of business and government.

TOWARD A NEW REALITY

We can see from the examples above that prejudice, discrimination, and racism can take on various guises, depending to some extent on the social, political, and cultural climate which shapes group dynamics (Brym et al. 1993). Generally speaking, the subtle and more sophisticated forms of anti-Semitism are more common, although explicit provocation and malicious destruction remain in effect. Affixing the modifier "polite" is not intended to trivialize the impact of racism on the Jewish population. On the contrary, these polite and more sophisticated expressions of racism are just as devastating as the old red-necked variety. After all, both the Holocaust-denial and Jewish-conspiracy theories deny to Jews their collective memory about suffering in the past (*Maclean's* 16 April 1990). They also libel Jews by repeating lies about their collective ambitions in society.

Evidence now suggests that minorities are unlikely to be directly victimized by blatant institutional racism. Openly racist platforms find little public acceptance or political support in Canada (Adam 1992). This injunction applies across the board, from institutions to interpersonal relations. Institutions can no longer openly discriminate against minorities, lest they attract negative publicity or incite consumer resistance. Nevertheless, institutional racism continues to exist. It can incorporate various discriminatory actions, from red-necked to polite or subliminal, all of which combine to preserve the prevailing distribution of power. The revelation that the

Denny's Restaurant chain (USA) went out of its way to discourage African-Americans from entry or service (Kohn 1994) provides an example of institutional racism in contemporary practice.

Systemic Racism

There is another type of institutional racism that comes across as impersonal and unconscious. Its unobtrusiveness makes it that much more difficult to detect, let alone to isolate and combat. **Systemic racism** is the name given to this subtle yet powerful form of discrimination within the institutional framework of society. It is entrenched within the structure (rules, organization), function (norms, goals), and process (procedures) of social institutions. The standards and expectations inherent within these organizations may be universal and ostensibly colour-blind. Yet they have the unintended but real effect of excluding those outside the mainstream.

With systemic racism, it is not the intent or motive that counts, but rather the *context* and the *consequences*. Policies, rules, priorities, and programs may not be inherently racist or deliberately discriminatory — that is, institutions do not go out of their way to exclude or deprive minorities. However, rules that are evenly applied may have a discriminatory effect in that they exclude certain groups, while conferring advantage to others. Minority experiences and needs are ignored under the guise of formal equality. For example, job experiences and employment credentials may be discounted because of company policy. In brief, we can define systemic racism as the adverse yet unintended consequences that result from applying seemingly neutral rules, but with dissimilar effects on different people.

Systemic racism rests on the belief that institutional rules and procedures can be racist in practice, even if the actors are themselves free of prejudicial discrimination. These barriers are unintentional, but hidden in institutional procedures and reward systems that penalize some individuals because of who they are, not what they can do. As such, systemic racism is rarely identified as such by those who benefit from such arrangements. Embedded within institutional rules and procedures, it remains (a) beyond our everyday consciousness, (b) undetected and disguised by universal standards and rhetoric to the contrary, (c) taken for granted, and (d) powerful. Minority opportunities are restricted and constrained by the rigid application of rules and procedures. The implicit character of systemic racism makes it difficult to isolate, let alone to confront and combat.

Even a few examples will demonstrate how this implicit bias can operate to support the prevailing distribution of societal power and resources. For years, a number of occupations such as the police, firefighters, or mass transit drivers retained minimum weight, height, and educational requirements for job applicants. In retrospect, we can interpret these criteria as systemically discriminatory because they favoured males over females, and white applicants over people of colour. Valid reasons may have existed to justify these restrictions; nevertheless, the imposition of these qualifications imposed a set of unfair entry restrictions, regardless of intent or rationale. No deliberate attempt is made to exclude anyone since standards are uniformly applied. But these criteria have the net effect (if not the deliberate intent) of excluding certain groups who lack these requirements for entry or promotion. Other examples of systemic racism may include an insistence on Canadian-only experience, the devaluation of minority experiences and credentials, unnecessarily high educational standards for entry into certain occupations, and other demanding qualifications that discourage membership into professional bodies.

Systemic racism can be illustrated in other ways. Minorities have long complained about the media's mistreatment of them. For the most part minorities are ignored or rendered irrelevant by mainstream presses (Report, *Equality Now*, 1984). When reported on, they are portrayed as a social problem (a state for which they are ultimately responsible) or as having problems in need of costly solutions. Some minority groups are depicted as volatile, prone to mindless violence, and having minimal regard for human life. While such violence does occur, the absence of balanced coverage results in a single and distorted image of that minority group. This one-sided coverage assists to perpetuate both negative images and global and domestic exploitation of racial and ethnic minorities.

In what way are media portrayals of minorities a case of systemic racism? In some ways, the misrepresentation stems from the media's preoccupation with readership, audience ratings, and advertising revenues. To satisfy audience and sponsorship needs, the mass media will usually focus on minorities only in situations of crisis, conflict, or catastrophe involving natural or human disaster. Otherwise, they are ignored as non-newsworthy. The end result is a portrayal of minorities as nothing more than threats to the social or global order. The mass media may not be aware of such discriminatory effects in this area, arguing they are only reporting the news. The net result, however, is an unflattering picture of minorities that distorts reality and people's perception under the guise of information or entertainment (Fleras 1993; Fleras 1995).

In short, rules and priorities that may seem neutral on the surface are not even-handed in terms of who gets what. This hidden agenda imposes certain handicaps on those who are inadequately prepared to cope with organizational demands and routines. The overall effect of excluding minorities is further aggravated when combined with additional disadvantages. The case of immigrant women in Canada provides a useful example of systemic racism in action.

INSIGHT

Systemic Racism and Sexism

Racial, aboriginal, and ethnic minorities are often exposed to discrimination in the public sector. Invariably, we tend to think of discrimination as behaviour whereby one individual intentionally bars another from access to valued goods and services. (For example, the case of a landlord who will not rent an apartment to a single mother who is also a women of colour.)

Attempts to combat such discrimination take the form of appeals to higher ideals such as justice and fair play or to human rights legislation.

At other times, women are exposed to systemic discrimination because of rules, programs, and priorities that are deeply embedded within the institutions of society. A useful example here is the treatment of immigrant women by Employment and Immigration Canada (EIC). It has been the policy of this federal department to offer language training only to those immigrants who are destined for the paid labour force and who are seeking jobs which require the use of an official language. Since more women than men come to Canada under the provisions of the "family class" category rather than as "independent workers," they have been denied access to language training, though many of these "family class" women do, in fact, work outside the home. Without fluency in either official language, they become targets for further discrimination in the workplace. Without language training, they tend to be confined to menial, non-unionized, low wage employment with no prospects for advancement. It is a further policy of EIC not to offer language training when the immigrant worker's job does not require knowledge of French or English. Jobs such as chamber maids or seamstresses fall under this category.

Employment and Immigration devised its language training policy in a rational manner with an eye toward providing training for the primary breadwinner, given the limited resources at its disposal. The by-product of this otherwise sound policy has been structural discrimination against women. No one in the federal government concerned with immigration policy ever consciously conspired to discriminate against women. But language training policies have had this effect. While some changes have been made in language training policies, limited funds prevent universal access to this program. When limited resources are available, what criteria — other than gender and ethnicity — should we apply in order to determine who shall receive what?

The above case has illustrated the "chilling effect" of systemic discrimination. Well meaning people may have drawn up the policies, and the policies may have been administered by caring and concerned employees. The architects and employees typically defend their actions as even-handed. They may be well-intentioned individuals adhering to guidelines which they feel are universal, justified and fiscally responsible. Nevertheless the logical consequences of these actions are systemically discriminatory because of misconceptions that underpin these initiatives. The systemic nature of this discrimination makes it even more difficult to expose and eliminate.

Table 3.1 briefly compares and contrast the different types of racism. Each type of racism is compared with others in terms of the "key slogan" (What), the degree of intent (Why), the style of expression (How), the magnitude and scope (Where), and level of expression (When).

Everyday Racism

It is obvious that racism operates at the level of *ideology* and *culture*. Certain ideas and ideals are widely circulated that explicitly or implicitly assert the superiority of some people at the expense of others. The internalization of these racist ideas and ideals is called **individual racism**. Individual expressions of racism can be explicit and open; conversely they can be implicit and conveyed through mixes signals.

TABLE 3.1   The Faces of Racism

	What: Core Slogan	*Why:* Degree of Intent	*How:* Style of Expression	*Where:* Magnitude and Scope	*When:* Locus of Expression
Red-Necked Racism	"X get out!"	conscious	personal and explicit	personal	interpersonal
Polite Racism	"Sorry, the job is taken."	moderate	discreet and subtle	personal	interpersonal
Subliminal Racism	"I'm not racist, but..."	ambivalent	oblique	cultural	value conflicts
Institutional Racism	"X need not apply."	deliberate	blatant	institutional	rewards and entitlements
Systemic Racism	"We treat everyone the same here."	unintentional	impersonal	societal	rules and proceedures

Racism is also manifest at the level of *institutions* or *structures*. Rules and priorities are socially constructed and organized in a way that confers privilege or power on some, not on others. These different domains of racism may be divided into the public and private (Oommen 1994). Racism can also be expressed at the *everyday* level. This level connects the micro-level (experiential or private) with the macro-level (structure, ideology, or public) to reveal the continuity between the two (Essed 1991; Oommen 1994).

The mechanisms of everyday racism are well established. Individuals interact with each other in a way that tolerates and reinforces racism, sometimes explicitly, other times in an implicit or oblique manner. As a process and social practice, racism is created and reconstructed through daily actions that are repetitive, systematic, familiar, and routine. Racist discourses is "prestructured" (Essed 1991) in a manner that constrains individual actors and everyday behaviour. This suggests the structures and ideologies that underpin racism are produced and reproduced through a complex and cumulative interplay of attitudes (prejudice) and practices (discrimination). This combination (a) is diverse in manifestation, but unified through constant repetition; (b) permeates daily life to the extent that it is viewed as normal or inevitable; and (c) exerts consequences that diminish minorities. It also implies the notion that the potential for racism exists in all of us, rather than reflecting a division of society into racists and nonracists.

Daily speech patterns embody the idea of racism as everyday and interactive. Words are a powerful way of conveying negative images and associations. Take the word "black," for example. While seemingly innocuous on the surface, the term comes across as derogatory in the context of everyday discourse. We frequently use the word black as synonymous with evil or mystery — black magic for example. Reference to "the black hole of Calcutta" is sufficient to arouse powerful images of despair and inhumanity. For this reason and others, some Canadians of African ancestry prefer to be called "African-Canadians" rather than "blacks." To be sure, the racism implicit in words and metaphors may not be intended or deliberate. Nor will the occasional use of such loaded terms explode into full-blown racism. Nevertheless, perils await those who trivialize the impact of language in perpetuating racism through its cumulative and quiet effect.

There is a kind of artificiality in distinguishing between the micro-racism at individual levels and the macro-racism at institutional levels (Essed 1991). The same line of reasoning applies to the conceptualization of racism in general. Racism from the personal to the institutional can be abstracted for purposes of analysis even if the distinctions overlap in reality. Similarly, individuals are not outside the institution and institutions are nonexistent without individuals. Reality is such that they are inescapably linked, though researchers separate them for analytic purposes. This intricate linkage creates certain challenges in confronting racism through anti-racist measures.

Anti-racism

"People, why can't we just get along?" (Rodney King, 1992). Well, why can't we?

That racism in one form or another exists in Canada is surely beyond debate at this point in our history. With the benefit of some prodding and sharp reminders, Canadians are increasingly facing up to our checkered past, with its curious mixture of tolerance and repression. What remain open for debate are questions about the magnitude and scope of this racism. For example, in what way is racism a key component in creating and supporting relationships of inequality? What are the causes and consequences of racism, both in the past and at present? The fact that these questions have not been answered to everyone's satisfaction attests to the varied and changing faces of racism.

Awareness of racism as a social problem is firmly secured in Canada. Anti-racism has emerged as a powerful and direct challenge that promises to go beyond conventional measures to correct racism. However, its potential for social and cultural change invariably raises concerns about the politics of anti-racism. That is, what — if anything — can be done to curb racism that does not undermine core Canadian values related to free enterprise, liberal values, freedom of speech, and tolerance for diversity? Negotiating a balance among these forces is easier said than done. The very act of defining something as a problem is no guarantee of finding a workable solution within the framework of a democratic society. Deciding on an appropriate level of response is shaped by how we define racism in terms of what it is, why it exists, how it is manifest, and what can be done about it.

THE ROOTS OF RACISM

Canada was founded on racist principles and continues to be so in organization and consequence if not intent, though there is evidence of collective denial and historical amnesia about this (Philip 1995; Henry et al. 1995). Racism is now widely condemned and detested, even by those who are indifferent toward diversity. Not confined to a certain segment of our society such as the working class or the uneducated, racism is endemic to Canada, with few signs of releasing its tenacious grip. No less worrying is why and how racism continues to fester despite public policies that guarantee equal rights and full participation. The threat of social condemnation only seems to have propelled racism to go underground. The fact that racism persists in the face of debilitating costs and destructive effects is cause for concern. Unless we properly define the magnitude and scope of racism, however, the likelihood of applying an appropriate solution is reduced.

The Costs of Racism

Racism does not come cheaply. It represents a blot upon Canadian society that has the capacity to squander our potential as an ordered and tolerant country. Racism costs all Canadians: To tolerate racism is to perpetuate inequality or to infringe on fundamental human rights; racism diminishes the number of people who can contribute to Canada; useless energy is expended that otherwise could be funnelled into more productive channels; institutions that cannot capitalize on a diverse workforce because of racism are destined to lose their competitive edge. Racism also adds an additional burden to minority lives (Ford 1994): Minorities live in perpetual fear of physical retaliation; they endure a restricted set of economic and social opportunities; and many are constantly burdened by psychological pressures. A few may even lash out from frustration in occasional acts of violence.

The danger of racism does not reside in creating racist attitudes where none existed before. Rather, the threat is three-fold: An environment is fostered where existing prejudices are articulated, legitimized, and defended as a basis for white privilege (McKenna 1994); mixed messages are delivered, many of which contradict the ideals of a socially progressive image; the costs of racism are absorbed unevenly across society, some capitalize on racism as a basis for preserving privilege or power; others suffer. The varied and intersecting sources of racism only complicate the anti-racist challenges.

Accounting for Racism

Many would be inclined to dismiss racism as a relic from the past, out of sync with the dynamics of a progressive contemporary society. Yet racism continues to flourish despite laws and social sanctions. How do we account for this anomaly? Is it because of people's inertia or disinterest, with the result that racism drifts along, irrespective of its dysfunctional effects on society? Some attribute the pervasiveness of racism to our biogenetic wiring — from an evolutionary past in which a fear of outsiders constituted a survival response in uncertain environments—that continues to operate in the present so that recoiling from what is different seems only natural. This visceral dislike of outgroups may explain the universality and emotional roots of racism.

Others like to think of racism as the byproduct of ignorance or fear of the unknown, not in the biogenetic sense, but in the sense of improper socialization. "Improve our stocks of knowledge," many will argue, "and racism will vanish accordingly." Others believe that racism persists because of its self-serving properties. Put bluntly, racism has a way of making the mainstream feel good about itself. Racism not only bolsters individual self-images, whether people are aware of it or not, it also has the effect of enhancing majority privilege by reducing uncertainty and imposing control. Simple but effective explanations are circulated to justify why people get what they deserve or deserve what they get. Still others look to social institutions as the primary culprit responsible for racism. These sources may be subtle and systemic but they are no less real and powerful as we shall see.

Racism as a Social Control

Each of these explanations of racism has its followers. But reference to racism as a function of biology or individual is secondary to most sociological analyses. Racism does not exist solely in the minds of demented individuals; nor is it an error of perception. The roots of racism go beyond the conduct of aberrant individuals even if individuals are the carriers and targets of this outgroup hatred. Racism persists because of its location within the capitalist structures of society (Satzewich 1991). The economic well-being, standard of living, and cultural history of Canada are constructed around hatred towards others, both in the formal and informal sense (McKenna 1994). Through its ideological underpinnings, racism has played and continues to play a formidable role in establishing and maintaining patterns of inequality and control. Those in positions of power will do anything to preserve privilege in the competition for scarce resources. Sowing the seeds of racism provides this advantage without drawing unnecessary attention to the contradictions and dysfunctions within the system.

More specifically, the root source of racism can be attributed to the imperatives of a profit-oriented society (Bolaria and Li 1988). Capitalism encourages racially-based class fractions as a part of the rational pursuit of profit. Racist ideologies are employed as rationalizations to foster acquisition of a cheap and disposable labour supply; to destabilize minority movements by undermining any potential show of unity or strength; and to justify intrusive devices for regulating the activities of troublesome minorities (Satzewich 1991; McKenna 1994). Invoking racist doctrines in defence of exploitation and social control reminds devalued minorities of the need to "stay in their place." Racism, therefore, cannot be understood apart from the social, cultural, economic, and political context in which it is embedded and nourished.

The prospect of eliminating racism in its entirety may not even be feasible in a capitalist society, despite loud protestations to the contrary. Racism as a form of destabilization is not inconsistent with class interests (McKenna 1994). To be sure, some measure of social tranquility is a prerequisite for capital accumulation through foreign investment and efficient production. Capital accumulation in the global economies of contemporary capitalism, Robert Miles (1982) notes, requires transnational labour mobility, the destruction of traditional societies for acquisition of cheap resources and ready markets, a regulation of labour supply especially in prestigious occupations, the allocation of labour to particular sites of production, and relatively high levels of unemployment (see also Satzewich 1991). Yet the interests of capitalism are also served by a degree of inner turmoil — from racial unrest to group instability — as long as this does not unduly interfere with wealth extraction or public order. Public resentment of immigration can be manipulated as a way to provide scapegoats for Canada's economic failures, thus diverting public scrutiny away from inherent defects in "doing business" (Brym et al. 1993; McKenna 1994). Some measures of minority marginalization and powerlessness are additional benefits for capitalist interests.

In short, racism is linked with patterns of social control in contexts pervaded by relations of unequal power. Racism in Canada is neither a transient phenomenon nor an anomolous and unpredictable feature. The orgins of racism have deep roots in Canadian society: That is, racism is intrinsic to Canada's historical and economic development; embedded within the institutional structures of society; endemic to core cultural values; and integral to Canadian society-building. That alone should remind us that racism is a majority (white) problem, rather than a minority problem. It should also alert us to the possibility that racism and racial hatred are not always perceived as dysfunctional (abnormal or deviant). Its "normalcy" within the context of a commodity-oriented society only complicates the process of solution.

Rephrasing the Question

This review of why racism exists provides a glimpse of its tenacious hold on society. Racism persists not only because of improper diagnosis of its causes. More to the point, racism continues to flourish because of its positive functions in support of white, ruling class interests. Cultural values and institutional structures have evolved on the strength of racially-based social cleavages. We are saturated by racist messages in society, with sources ranging from everyday language to stereotyping in the media, all of which have the effect, if not always the intent, of confirming unequal relations. That suggests that the struggle against racism faces formidable obstacles, a kind of resistance not altogether different from walking up a down escalator whose rate of speed is controlled by remote control.

In other words, we don't have the right answer because we've been asking the wrong question. Perhaps the question should be rephrased away from "why does racism exist" to "why should racism *not* exist in light of social pressures for preserving privilege and power." Rephrasing the question in this way alters our ap-

proach to solutions. Anti-racist initiatives that focus on racism as a self-evident social problem are doomed to fail. Misreading the problem creates inappropriate solutions, especially when disregarding the social conditions that give rise to negative
beliefs and behaviour. Anti-racist initiatives are a step in transforming the racist
dimensions of Canadian society.

ANTI-RACISM: PERSONAL AND INTERACTIVE

Anti-racism can be defined as the process that isolates and challenges racism
through direct action at personal and institutional levels. Two styles of anti-racist
strategy can be discerned: one is concerned with modifying individual behaviour
through education or sanctions; the other with removal of discriminatory structural
barriers through institutional reform. This distinction corresponds to some extent
with the concepts of *racism as hatred* versus *racism as power*. The differences are
briefly outlined in Table 3.2

The distinction between personal and institutional anti-racism is critical. Taken
at its most obvious level, racism is normally envisaged as a personal problem of
hatred. There is an element of truth to this assertion. Racism is ultimately rooted
in individual thoughts and expressed through hatred of others. Prejudice consists
of ignorance or a dislike of others because they are different or threatening.
Definitions of racism as a personal problem call forth strategies for containment
or control that focus on modifying defective attitudes related to prejudice and
stereotyping. Four strategies are normally included within the anti-racist package:
interaction, education, law, and language.

Improvement through Interaction

Learning through interaction represents one of the many anti-racist techniques
available for individual change. Interaction with others will remove barriers that stem
from ignorance or fear. Lack of knowledge is replaced with mutually reinforcing understanding. Yet contact in its own right is not necessarily beneficial. It is doubtful

TABLE 3.2   Styles of Anti-Racism

	Racism as Hatred	Racism as Power
Source	individual	institutional
Manifestation	attitude	behaviour
Scope	prejudice	discrimination
Solution	awareness	action
Outcome	cultural	structural

if the millions of tourists that pour into the Caribbean each winter have done much to ameliorate race relations given that such interactional patterns are restricted primarily to serving white interests. Under these potentially degrading circumstances, the degree of resentment and contempt escalates as the indigenous populations recreate colonialist patterns as hewers of wood and drawers of drinks.

Reduction of racism through interaction depends on the nature of the interactional setting. For any positive effect, interaction must be conducted between individuals who are relatively equal in status, who collaborate on a common endeavour in a spirit of trust and respect, whose interaction receives some degree of institutional and societal support, and who derive mutual benefit from cooperation (Jaret 1995). Interaction between unequals simply upholds the status quo by perpetuating stereotypes and confirms the worst prejudices in a negatively charged environment.

Education

It is widely assumed that formal instruction can reduce racism. Once aware of what they are doing and why, people are deemed sufficiently rational to make the appropriate adjustments. This notion of enlightenment through learning has put schools in the vanguard of institutions for dealing with diversity. Two styles prevail in accommodating diversity within schools: multicultural and/or anti-racist (Fleras and Elliott 1992). **Multicultural education** refers to a philosophy for "celebrating differences." It consists of activities or curricula that promote an awareness of diversity in terms of its intrinsic value to minorities and/or society at large (Ontario Ministry of Education and Training 1993). The aim of multicultural education is largely attitudinal — namely, to enhance sensitivity by improving awareness about cultural differences. Emphasis is directed at becoming more aware of ourselves as cultural carriers; of the customs that underpin non-Western cultures; and of the role of ethnocentrism and cultural relativism in supporting or denying diversity. Strategies for this kind of sensitivity awareness are varied, spanning the spectrum from museum approaches to immersion programs, with cross-cultural enrichment in between.

Multiculturally-based training sessions have proliferated at public and private levels. Training sessions may involve workshops for new and established employees, with content ranging from cultural awareness modules to cross-cultural communication sessions, to pointers about prejudice and ethnocentrism. Police forces in the larger metropolitan areas are increasingly involved in multicultural-relations training programs for cadets, patrol officers, and management (Fleras and Desroches 1989). Program sessions are generally geared toward the elimination of discrimination in policing, promotion of cultural diversity within the police force, development of sensitivity to culturally diverse constituencies, improvement of cross-cultural communication, and implementation of community-based policing principles. Yet diversity training programs can be counterproductive in the hands of poorly trained and inadequately motivated instructors. Blame-and-shame programs can backfire because they are openly confrontational and may humiliate, embarrass, and tend to foster resentment among participants. No one likes to be told what to do or to be manipulated because of guilt or shame (Jaret 1995). Even in the hands of skilled practitioners, there is no guarantee of positive change in attitude or behaviour. Still, education in the broadest sense remains a practical and attractive strategy to minimize the expression and impact of racism in Canadian society.

Law

Recourse to law is sometimes upheld an effective deterrent. Laws exist in Canada that prohibit the expression of racial discrimination against vulnerable minorities. The scope of these laws is broad: Some legal measures consist of protection for identifiable minorities through restrictions on majority behaviour. For example, the Supreme Court of Canada has ruled repeatedly that prohibition of racial pro-paganda is a justifiable and reasonable limitation on freedom of speech. Other measures are aimed at removing discriminatory barriers that deter minority participation within society. The objective is to make it illegal to discriminate by making people aware of the repercussions if they break the law.

Passage of these and related laws is not intended to alter people's attitudes — at least not in the short run. A democratic society such as ours entitles people to their own private thoughts, however repugnant or anti-social. But this right disappears when private thoughts become discriminatory behaviour: Legal sanctions apply at this point. To be sure, laws are limited in their effectiveness for modifying individual thought or behaviour. The legislative advances of the Civil Rights Act in 1964 in the United States neither resolved African-American inequities nor eliminated prejudice or discrimination. Nor can laws eliminate disadvantages by dispersing the concentration of wealth or distribution of power. Passage of laws may be designed to minimize majority inconvenience rather than assist minorities. But laws can modify peoples behaviour through the imposition of sanctions. On the assumption that most individuals are law-abiding because of the threat of punishment or social ostracism, passage of anti-racist laws will ensure compliance with the letter of legislation, at least outwardly if not by personal conviction. In time, however, people may bring their thoughts around to match behaviour in an effort to reduce the dissonance between thought and action.

Anti-Racist Language

The role of language in perpetuating racism is generally downplayed. Many think of language as a kind of postal or courier system, that is, a neutral system of conveyance between sender and receiver for the transmission of messages created independently through a process called thinking. In reality, language is inextricably linked with the social construction of reality. Language is intimately bound up with our experiences of the world and our efforts to convey that experience to others. Ideas and ideals are "trapped inside" language, with the result they influence how we think and act and relate to others. Nevertheless, it is inaccurate to say that language determines our reality; more precisely, it provides a cultural frame of reference for defining what is desirable and important.

The relationship between language and reality construction should be clearer. Language can be employed to control, conceal, evade issues, draw attention, or dictate agendas about what gets said. Words are not neutral; rather they have the capacity to hinder or harm when carelessly employed. Words also have a political dimension: They convey messages above and beyond what is intended. Inferences can (and are) drawn about who you are and where you stand in the competition for who gets what and why. Language may be used to degrade or ridicule minorities. Negative meanings can become part of the everyday speech as the following passage from Robert Moore (1992) demonstrates:

> Some may *blackly* (angrily) accuse me of trying to *blacken* (defame) the English language, to give it a *black* eye (mark of shame) by writing such *black* words (hostile) ... by accusing me of being *blackhearted* (malevolent), of having a *black* outlook (pessimistic; dismal) on life, of being a *blackguard* (scoundrel) which would certainly be a *black* mark (detrimental fact) against me.

The association of "blackness" with negativity illustrates how certain values are embedded in our everyday speech. The effect can be deadly. The effect is subtle and cumulative: One word is not going to make much difference; the combination of verbal insults over a span of time can result in the equivalent of "death by a thousand cuts."

INSIGHT

Challenging Racism

Intolerance or neutrality are indefensible positions when it comes to fighting racism. Doing nothing is not neutral but a kind of indifference that may be interpreted as support of the status quo. Do something! Whether you want them to or not, your actions or inaction will be interpreted as part of the problem or part of the solution. When each of us makes a contribution, perhaps we *can* get along. Listed below are sixteen things a person can do to combat their racism. Some of the recommendations are taken from Clyde Ford's book *We Can All Get Along*; others are taken personal experiences in the anti-racist field. All are designed to be within the grasp of the average student who has some degree of commitment.

1) **Watch your language.** Terms such as "coloured folk" or "those types" or "your people" are demeaning in their own right. They also reflect poorly on yourself. Terms such as Negro or black or African-Canadian are not interchangeable but can carry negative connotations. Loaded terms such as "race" should be avoided except in contexts where common agreement exists. "People of colour" is currently acceptable as a term of reference, with "world majorities" likely to replace "visible minorities" in the immediate future.

2) **Don't tell or listen to racist jokes.** Ethnic or racial jokes have the unfortunate effect of reinforcing stereotypes about identifiable groups. The cumulative effect of such putdowns is

a feeling of exclusion. That's called harassment. Let people know you are not interested in hearing demeaning racist jokes. If others tell you to "lighten up," remind them that racism is no laughing matter. If they reply that harassment was not intended, convince them that consequences, not just intentions, count in contexts that are manifestly unequal.

3) **Don't deny differences. Don't exaggerate them, either.** Few people will appreciate the phrase, "When I look at you I don't see your colour. You're just another person like I am," however well-intentioned it is. The underlying message is one of denial; it forces others to reject their identity, experiences, and realities, while it reinforces your status and standards as the norm. By the same token, don't exaggerate differences or inflate exclusion by blurting out, "Where did you come from?" as soon as you meet someone. Each one of us wants to be treated the same way yet have our uniqueness recognized and respected. Keep in mind that racial differences are just one of the many similarities and differences people have to each other. Talk about such differences in a way that keeps them in perspective.

4) **Enlighten yourself.** Prejudice is a state of mind. Change your mind by taking courses on the history of race relations in Canada. Properly taught, it could well be the best investment in yourself and your relations with others. Even a book on Canada's social history might be useful in appreciating the magnitude and scope of racism in this country.

5) **Be careful around young children.** Young children are extremely impressionable. Careless words and deeds may have a lasting impression on their approach to diversity. Even repeated references to the word "black" as "dangerous" may have a cumulative negative effect on their image of African-Canadians. With children, it is probably best to actively embrace diversity as natural and normal. Denying differences or assuming a colour-blind status can convey the wrong message. Read stories to children with positive minority role models. Prepare a meal with foods from around the world. Talk it up.

6) **Don't let it slide by.** However tempting, racist actions from slurs to jokes must be confronted. Otherwise the action is condoned and/or reinforced. Don't go beserk, however. Direct confrontation may have dramatic flair, but may not accomplish much except create resentment or defensiveness. Confront the perpetrator in private and convey your concerns accordingly. Remember, there is some truth to the adage that you can catch more flies with honey than with vinegar.

7) **Report it! If something happens to you, tell someone!** Most colleges and universities are firmly committed to a racist-free environment. Many have officials that investigate reports of offences while maintaining confidentiality. Become familiar with these channels of redress if informal means are inappropriate.

8) **Wear your politics.** The personal is political whether you like it or not. The act of wearing an anti-racist button (readily available from multicultural and anti-racist groups in the community) announces your commitment to an anti-racist society. Nothing intimidates racists as much as the perception of a community against racism. The same rationale can be applied to anti-racist bumper stickers or posters.

9) **Walk a mile in somebody else's shoes.** Many of us have never been forced to look at the world from another perspective. Technically speaking, it's probably impossible to share identical experiences with those who are different, since you run a very real risk of superimposing your experience on others'. That shouldn't stop you from trying to bridge differences through open-mindedness. Challenge your thinking by becoming involved in ethnic organizations, anti-racist networks, multicultural or First Nations festivals, and community

projects. The experience may be a bit daunting at first, even disruptive in some cases, but never underestimate the rewards of learning to see reality from another vantage point.

10) **Make your actions speak louder than your words.** It's one thing to be against racism in principle. It's quite another to put anti-racist principles into practice. In other words, it's not enough to be tolerant or outraged; this anger must be acted upon for justice to happen. Attend activities or demonstrations in support of racial and aboriginal issues. Active levels of involvement are important not only for moral support. They also convey a clear message of community commitment to anti-racism.

11) **Read!** Become informed about what is happening in Canada today, and why. The walls of racial ignorance can be surmounted by the acquisition of knowledge about immigration, multiculturalism, and racism. Reading can also help keep you abreast of shifting sands of meaning related to anti-racism.

12) **Travel.** Few things in this world can dismantle barriers as thoroughly as travel to other parts of the world. Get a backpack and go. Be prepared to live with indigenous populations for even a short period of time. Chances are you will learn more about yourself in this way than through reading all the quick-fix books on self-analysis and personal improvement. Remember: Self-understanding is the first step in the journey to anti-racism.

13) **Look within.** All improvements begin with self-awareness. De-construct the reasons behind why you see, think, experience, and relate to others as you do. Try to appreciate how whiteness confers privilege because of its status as the unmarked norm of acceptance in society. Make an effort to understand how your perceptions begin with a set of first principles that differ from those who are different. Take stock of yourself: do you see society as a treasure-trove for personal plunder, or a community to nurture for the benefit of all.

14) **Reach out.** It would be nice if each of us could cultivate deep and lasting friendships with people of different races and ethnic backgrounds. Failing that, take the time to initiate acquaintances with others who are different, even if this means simply extending an invitation to join in your plans at school or outside. Try to appreciate why some initially may rebuff your advances, or why others seem angry or frustrated about their minority status in society.

15) **Boycott! Put your money where your principles are.** Never underestimate the power of the dollar. Do not patronize establishments that are known to be racist in word or deed. Encourage others to do the same. None of this will have much effect unless the offending establishments are informed of your concerns. Many will listen only because your university or college status represents a potential source of income they can't afford to squander. You'll be surprised how quickly changes will materialize when the bottom line is on the line.

16) **Walk that talk.** Pontificating in private about racism is not going to do a lot of good. Challenge racists; combat apathy. Write a letter to the local paper about negative or positive developments within the community. Putting your thoughts into words may be personally therapeutic. It may also get a lot of people thinking and doing. Send a message to racists that they are under scrutiny.

WALKING UP A DOWN ESCALATOR

This list should be of some assistance in coping with racism at a personal level. The steps are reasonable; presumably they lie within the grasp of most people. Still, the reader must be cautioned against excessive optimism. The road to undoing the racist basis of Canadian society is strewn with hurdles. It is not a simple or straightforward route, but literally littered with cultural landmines and social pitfalls. The same line of reasoning applies to the struggle for personal anti-racism. The path of least resistance is to do nothing; after all, who wants to have a bad reputation or risk the loss of popularity — much less invite physical danger because of an unpopular stand. A resilient and flexible mindset is indispensable under these circumstances: Accept the inevitability of miscommunication or inadvertent miscues. Appreciate that there is no certainty about even learning from mistakes since the specifics of one situation may not apply to another. About the best we can hope for is the ability to bounce back from these miscues with graciousness and a firm commitment to try again.

We would also warn individuals about success in the anti-racist struggle. There remains uncertainty about what racism is, why it exists, how it is expressed, and what if anything should be done about it. No guarantees exist that racism is solvable as a social problem; Its roots in human evolution, its universality, its embeddedness in capitalism, and its visceral component make it largely resistant to rational reform. Compounding the problem is knowing that a small percentage (between 10 and 15 percent of Canada's population) are incorrigible racists (Henry and Tator 1985), perhaps even beyond redemption. Precipitating (that is, immediate or personal) causes can be addressed; root (remote or structural) may be much more difficult to access. Even more daunting is the prospect that racism is a "white problem." The fact that this hatred is enshrined in values, institutional rules, and everyday practices, makes the problem difficult to identify — let alone to eradicate or control.

In short, a sense of perspective is necessary when confronted by such formidable obstacles. Nobody is going to singlehandedly transform the world we live in, regardless of commitment or energy. Nor is anyone asking this of anyone. All we expect is for each person to do their little bit in their corner of the world. When each of us learns to think globally, but act locally, the critical mass alone should be sufficient to make a dent.

ANTI-RACISM: INSTITUTIONALIZED AND SYSTEMIC

There is room for cautious optimism when discussing the effectiveness of individually-tailored anti-racist programs. But are these initiatives of sufficient strength to expunge racism at its roots? Are the structures of society amenable to reform through personal transformation? Perhaps a word of clarification is needed about the sociological point of view. With the possible exception of sociobiologists (see van den Berghe 1985), most sociologists would argue that individuals are not biologically programmed to act in a racist manner. There are no genes that express themselves in racial discrimination. Nor is there reason to believe that people are born with a propensity to hate.

We do not dismiss outright biological or psychological perspectives. There may be good reasons for an evolutionary approach that acknowledges the fear of others as a survival value. Our preferences are directed at social explanations: People are conditioned to be racist by environments that foster ethnocentrism, outgroup antipathy, and racism. Racism is inextricably linked with the process of social control for preserving the status quo in complex societies. This assertion is consistent with a fundamental sociological premise: namely, social forces (culture + structure) not only transcend individual personalities, but can account for differences in people's attitudes and behaviour. Racism may be expressed in and through people (who may be regarded as precipitating causes), but individuals are merely the conduits of racial antipathy. It is the social context that counts.

Racism can only be resolved by attacking it at its source — namely, within the institutional structures that support a capitalist society. Personal solutions such as anti-racist training are comparable to applying a bandage to a cancerous growth — compassionate and humane to be sure, but ultimately self-defeating in light of the magnitude of the disease. The problem of racism cannot be eliminated except by confronting it within the wider confines of political domination and economic control. This comprehensive approach will entail a different set of assumptions and tactics than those focusing on personal initiatives.

Anti-racist measures may include fighting racist hate groups, direct action through protest or civil disobedience, boycotts, litigation, or legislation (Jaret 1995). The promotion of employment equity is one such measure. Employment equity programs are based on the premise that racially discriminatory barriers do not stem from ignorance, fear, or arrogance. These barriers are systemic and entrenched within existing structures: That embeddedness makes them amenable to reform only through institutional rather than personal change. Equity initiatives are directed at hidden rules and unconcious procedures that inadvertently distort the process of recruitment, entry, treatment, promotion, or reward allocation in favour of one group rather than another. These initiatives hope to identify and eliminate offending practices; they also intend to remedy the effects of past discrimination, to remove systemic barriers in pursuit of equal outcomes, and to ensure appropriate representation of identifiable groups at all workplace levels. The ultimate goal is the creation of a workplace environment where differences are embraced as a legitimate and integral component of "business as usual."

In short, anti-racism strategies consist of measures and mechanisms for dismantling the structural basis of institutional racism. The removal of discriminatory barriers is central: Selection and recruitment procedures as well as rules for promotion and reward are scrutinized for hidden bias in the interests of accessibility. Values and practices are monitored that historically have propelled the organization, but are irrelevant in a changing and diverse context. Anti-racist strategies must focus on dominant beliefs and values within the institution, the organizational system related to rules and practices, and the experiences and behaviours of organizational actors. These systemic biases are most apt to occur at the level of mission statement, culture and subculture, power and decision making, structures (including rules, roles, and relationships), and resources distribution of physical, financial, and human assets. Any institutional enterprise will foster racism intentionally or unintentionlly when it perpetuates mission statements that are exclusionary; refuses to share power or decision making; promulgates a monocultural set of values and beliefs as normal and necessary; maintains an inflexible or unresponsive set of structure and operations; and endorses unequal distributions of resources (Chesler and Crowfoot 1989). These multi-pronged anti-racist initiatives sound plausible in theory; their implementation may be another story.

TOWARD A COMPREHENSIVE SOLUTION: THINK GLOBALLY, ACT LOCALLY

It's relatively easy to dismiss racism as a personal problem. It is equally tempting to situate racism within a system of vast and impersonal forces that are largely beyond individual responsibility and outside the bounds of human agency. Neither of these positions is entirely correct. Individuals may not be the root cause of racism, but racism is represented within the person. Systems do not exist apart from individuals who interact to create, support, maintain, or transform societies. It is implicit in our daily encounters through the perpetuation of countless actions, gestures, and speech patterns. Each of us must be held accountable for our actions, no matter how powerful the social context and social forces. That much is critical: Unless we become aware of our contribution to the problem, it becomes difficult to be part of the solution. Put differently, when applied to the realm of racism and proposed solutions, the personal is indeed the political. The political in turn defines the personal. That is, changing the system invariably changes peoples attitudes; changing peoples attitudes may result in corresponding alterations in peoples behaviour and revisions to society.

Racism is a ubiquitous feature of our existence, although often beyond our awareness or consciousness. As individuals, we must reflect critically upon our degree of complicity in perpetuating racism. Racism is embedded in our capitalist society by way of social, economic, political institutions and practices. To combat the root cause of racism requires a sociological analysis and critique of how and why racism as ideology is widely perpetuated. Thus, strategies to combat racism must obviously take into account the interplay of social forces and intersubjective experiences of individuals. Only a comprehensive approach can deliver the goods with any hope of success.

CHAPTER HIGHLIGHTS

- Racism exists and has always existed in Canada: What is open to debate is its magnitude and scope. The many faces of racism, both past and present, provide a coherent theme for organizing the chapter.

- Racism is not a recent import into Canada. Even a cursory review of Canada's history reveals otherwise. Racism instead is a chronic and embedded feature of Canadian society.

- Defining racism can be a problem. Some of the difficulties flow from the fact that racism is not necessarily a "thing" out there, but rather an attribute conferred on a social relationship within a specific context and having certain consequences.

- Definitions of racism fall into a "narrow" and "comprehensive" category. Narrow definitions (racism as hatred) lean toward racism as a belief in a kind of biological determination and racial inferiority. More comprehensive definitions (racism as power) tend to focus on racism as the power of one group over that of another.

- Racism is defined as a relatively coherent set of *beliefs* about the innate inferiority of some racial groups, combined with the *power* to transform these ideas into *practices* that deny or exclude.

- With its focus on group dynamics within contexts of power and domination, racism is best envisaged as a socially constructed system of control between opposing groups in the competition for scarce resources.

- Racism represents a relatively coherent system of beliefs ("ideology") and practices that legitimates the expression of racial inequality in society. It also includes a behavioural component which may or may not entail some element of prejudice. Power underpins all forms of racism: Without it, racism is indistinguishable from a host of negative attitudes and practices.

- Prejudice consists of beliefs about a group, an emotional reaction to that group, and a motivation to act on the basis of these beliefs and attitudes. This consellation of thoughts, feelings, and motives is learnt, generalizable from one group to another, often indirect and coded, and does not necessarily lead to discriminatory behaviour (Pincus and Ehrlich 1994).

- Prejudice and discrimination continue to exist. But the once strongly held notion of biological inferiority and hateful stereotypes has given way to rejection on the grounds of cultural differences and unacceptable lifestyles (Pe Higrew 1994).

- Minorities are unlikely to be racist since they lack the power to put prejudice into practice in a way that denies, excludes, exploits, and controls. The notion of racism as folded into the institutional structures of dominant society also shifts blame away from minorities.

- There are many faces of racism, varying as they do along different criteria. Faces of racism discussed include red-necked, polite, subliminal, institutional, and systemic. The different types of racism can be compared and contrasted along diverse dimensions.

- Expressions of racism are embedded in the institutional structures of capitalist society; they also are grounded in the everyday experiences of people. This distinction between micro-racism and macro-racism is analytically useful; however, the interactive dimensions of racism between macro and micro levels provides it with its staying power.

- The different dimensions of racism make it difficult to precisely define the problem, where it is located, why it exists, and how it should be dealt with.

- Anti-racism is an emergent field both in study and practice that is concerned with the elimination of racism at personal and institutional levels. Anti-racism can be defined as the process by which those institutions, values, and practices that perpetuate racism at personal or systemic levels are identified, challenged, and modified through direct action.

• Anti-racist strategies vary with how racism is defined, the magnitude and scope of the racism that has been identified, and its impact. In general, anti-racism focuses on personal and institutional strategies for reform.

• Anti-racist strategies aimed at personal change are channelled into venues as varied as language, laws, interaction, and education.

• The roots of racism are challenged by anti-racist measures at institutional and structural levels. Formidable barriers confront those who want to change society by changing the system.

KEY TERMS

Anti-Racism	Head Tax	Stereotyping
Anti-Semitism	Komagata Maru Incident	Subliminal Racism
Discrimination	Multicultural vs Anti-	Systemic Racism
Ethnocentrism	Racist Education	Types of Racism
Everyday Racism	Prejudice	
Harassment	Racism	

REVIEW QUESTIONS

1) Compare and contrast the different types of racism that have been discussed in terms of style, level of expression, and degree of intent.

2) Demonstrate the linkages between racism and prejudice (including ethnocentrism and stereotypes) and discrimination (harassment).

3) Why does racism continue to exist? How does a sociological approach assist in providing the answer?

4) Define racism, and reveal key features that distinguish it from prejudice or discrimination.

5) Discuss whether or not you think Canada is a racist society. Use specific examples to support your answer.

6) Expand on the notion that racism exists in Canada.

7) Select several examples of recent incidents involving racial, ethnic, or aboriginal minorities, and indicate if the issue is one of racism. If yes, what kind of racism is involved?

8) How can we explain the existence of racism? Be sure to emphasize the social dimensions in your answer.

9) Compare and contrast the strategies of anti-racism at the personal level versus the institutional level.

CHAPTER 4

INEQUALITY AND STRATIFICATION

INTRODUCTION

Canada cherishes its image as an egalitarian and largely middle class society, with few extremes of poverty or wealth. This portrayal is arguably true in a relative sense, given the gross inequities and racial oppression elsewhere. By comparison, Canada indeed represents a remarkably open and pluralist society with a powerful commitment to equality before the law, regardless of a person's background or beliefs. Ideally, all parts of the national "mosaic" are envisaged as contributing equally to the whole. These diverse components are also viewed as deserving of a fair share of the entitlements of wealth or power.

Appearances, however, can be deceiving. Canada is more accurately a society of unequal shares with wealth concentrated in the hands of the few (the richest one percent holds 25 percent of Canada's wealth) (Goar 1995). Income and opportunity gaps involving dominant and subordinate sectors have created a situation the eminent Canadian scholar John Porter described in *The Vertical Mosaic* (1965). For Porter, Canada's tapestry of cultural differences was stratified vertically along ascending/descending lines of ethnicity and race. Inception of official multiculturalism and Employment Equity initiatives have not appreciably altered this arrangement. Racial, aboriginal, and ethnocultural groups continue to be sorted out unequally against a "mosaic" of raised (dominant) and lowered (subordinate) tiles (Tepper 1988). Pyramids of privilege exist that elevate white, male, middle-class, middle-aged, and the able-bodied to the top of scale, others to the bottom. Those of Northern European origin seem to have more options and opportunities when reflected in their place in the economy, different socioeconomic levels, and residential patterns (see Jaret 1995). In other words, all the deeply ingrained myths in the country cannot disguise the fact that Canada remains a stratified society where differences in skin colour or ethnic background continue to make a difference.

That Canada is stratified by race and ethnicity should come as little surprise (Curtis et al. 1993). Immigrants during Canada's historical past were usually imported as a source of cheap, expendable labour — either to assist in the process of nation-building (eg. the construction of the trans-Canada railway), or to provide manual skills in labour-starved industries such as the garment trade (Burnet and Palmer 1988). Entry of immigrants into the work force served to fragment the working class into competing sectors, thereby eliminating the potential for a cohesive and collective show of strength. Once in the country, many became convenient scapegoats for abuse or exploitation. Immigrants could be hired and fired with impunity, especially during periods of economic stagnation. Promotions, of course, were entirely out of the question. Political or civil rights were trampled upon without even so much as a murmur of public protest. The openly racist treatment of Asian immigrants during the twentieth century proved a lowpoint in a century of lowpoints.

The management of diversity has improved considerably thanks to the passage of human rights and multicultural legislation. Yet many Third World immigrants and refugees continue to be shunted into marginal employment sectors. Professional degrees and work experiences abroad are deemed irrelevant in Canada, with the result that highly skilled employees remain stuck in menial jobs. Work environments are such that minorities tend to be alienated rather than accommodated even when progressive policies are implemented (DIAND 1991). Domestics and "nannies" from Third World countries are subject to long hours and poor pay, with little recourse in case of disputes. Immigrant labourers from the Caribbean are brought over for seasonal jobs in agriculture that other Canadians disdain. The combined effect of this unequal treatment ensures the relegation of certain minorities to the bottom of Canada's socioeconomic heap.

This chapter draws on these themes by exploring the inequitable relationship of minority groups to society at large. It is based on the assertion that race, ethnic, and aboriginal relations are properly conceptualized as relationships of inequality. The mechanisms employed to create, sustain, and modify this inequality are essential to such an interpretation. The chapter argues that inequality in Canada is not randomly distributed but patterned around the poles of race, ethnicity, and aboriginality. Race and ethnicity not only reflect fundamental inequities in Canadian society; national origins and skin colour also have an effect in defining who gets what. Chapter content is organized around responses to such concerns: (a) what is the nature of minority inequality; (b) how is this inequality manifest; (c) why does it exist; and (d) what can be done about it. We begin by comparing the concept of inequality from functionalist and conflict perspectives. The scope of inequality is examined next in terms of stratification and social class as it applies to minorities. This is followed by a look at the debate between race and class as competing explanations of inequality. Evidence suggests that neither race nor class are reducible into each other, but intersect in mutually reinforcing ways in shaping personal and group success. The chapter concludes with a section on employment equity as a proposed solution to minority inequality. Opposed definitions of inequality are also discussed and assessed in light of a reconceptualized equality.

PERSPECTIVES ON INEQUALITY

Perspectives on social inequality vary among sociologists. Some regard inequality as a social problem for solution; others believe inequality is desirable. Each of these perspective differs in how inequality is defined with respect to minority groups. They also vary in what can be done to reduce this inequity to manageable proportions.

Functionalist Models

The economic division of labor is the starting point for functionalist models. For society to operate smoothly, functionalists argue, positions in the economic structure such as jobs and careers must be filled with suitable personnel. Since these jobs differ in skill and importance, people need to be rewarded appropriately for doing tasks of differing complexity. The occupational prestige hierarchy is the result of these differential rewards. We accept as "natural" that physicians are compensated more for their services than plumbers even though, arguably, both are crucial for our well-being (Davis, and Moore 1945). Leading sport figures are paid more than common laborers (in the United States the average major league baseball player earns about $1.2 million per year while a gas station attendant earns $13,400). This discrepancy arises not because one is more important to society. Salary and status gaps exist because certain skills are in short supply compared with the demand. Those skills that can generate more wealth are in even shorter supply, and paid accordingly.

The **status attainment model** is central to a functionalist view of inequality. Social status pertaining to wealth and power is acquired by individual effort through competition in an open market (Sewell and Hauser 1975). Status differences arise because individuals vary in their abilities and motivation. They are socialized differently to compete for and value certain goals. Class background is especially prominent in determining career success (Li 1988b). Cultural factors related to race and ethnicity may also affect the level of achievement: for example, those socialized into a "**culture of poverty**" (Lewis 1964) are thought of as deprived compared with the offspring of mainstream parents. Inasmuch as racial and ethnic groups may be disproportionately trapped in ghettos and on reserves, it is understandable that they are not able to achieve social mobility. They are locked into negative opportunity structures: They are conditioned by cultures that do not adequately prepare them for the demands of competitive corporate world. This is not to suggest racial or ethnic minorities are "inferior" in the absolute sense. Rather, their "**human cultural capital**" — namely, skills related to education, social class, experience, achievement orientation, and business culture — is defined as "deficient" in coping with the attainment of externally-defined success.

Functionalists acknowledge the existence of prejudice and discrimination. They argue the failure of minorities to penetrate the market may reflect this lack of human cultural capital. Efforts to boost human cultural capital would focus on improving minority education levels to those consistent with competitive labour force needs. Once opportunity is equalized, the modern forces behind a rational meritocracy will ultimately sort out people on the basis of ability. Cultural or racial considerations will be rendered superfluous when employers overcome bias and simply hire the best. A modern technological society — if it hopes to prosper in an intensely competitive and global market economy — has to be "colour blind" in capitalizing on the entire spectrum of brainpower and talent.

In sum, functionalists distinguish between inequality and racism. They recognize and decry the existence of racism and discrimination. Yet the pernicious effects of racial discrimination can be diminished by liberal appeals to fairness through objective testing for educational and job entry. Functionalists also accept the inevitability of innate differences, not necessarily in a racial way but in terms of what individuals bring to the marketplace. Wealth and poverty are equally functional for society — the rich because of what they do, and the poor as a grim warning to others of their fate should they fail to conform or play by the rules. In that sense, functionalists argue, inequality is necessary and desirable in society. But inequities by virtue of ascribed racial or ethnic differences are not. Society must take what steps are necessary to purge ascriptive indicators from determining who gets what. A fair and open competition demands nothing less.

Conflict Models

Conflict theorists share with functionalists the view that a capitalistic society is differentiated by competition. They differ in their assessment of the role played by inequality. For the functionalists, society exists as an on-going entity inasmuch as a consensus of values secures social cohesion. The inevitability of inequality — a basic tenet of functionalism — is an anathema to the Marxist variants of **conflict theory**. For Marx, inequality is an *not* natural to society, but normal and necessary only in societies geared toward the rational pursuit of profit. Private productive property and class relations that pit one class against another are largely responsible for these inequities.

Society, for conflict theorists, is composed of opposed groups who compete for scarce resources. One set of competing pairs has the ruling class on one side, the subordinate class on the other. Conflict theorists argue that ruling class interests are advanced by sowing the seeds of dissension within working class ranks. Racism is generated when people are denied human rights or excluded from full participation because of invidious distinctions based on assumed racial or ethnocultural characteristics (Kallen 1995). Fomenting racial prejudice and outgroup hostility helps to perpetuate the status quo, prevents the formation of worker solidarity, improves capital formation, destabilizes counter movements, and militates against the development of class consciousness. This infighting also has the effect of inhibiting the ability of workers to "unite and throw off their chains." Under conflict models, in other words, race-based inequalities are functional for some, dysfunctional for others.

Conflict models differ from functionalist models in other ways. Little credibility is attached to the functionalist credo (status attainment model) of individual competition as necessary and normal in an open job market. The labour force in a capitalist society operates in two markets, not one. The main market is monopolized by the mainstream sector. Minorities by contrast are systemically excluded from points of entry. The marginal workforce is composed largely of unskilled labourers, recent arrivals, people of colour, and minority women. This sector has been referred to by Marx as a "reserve army of labour." Many are hired as "cheap labour," then fired as the needs of the market contract. Such a dual labour market can lead to a cultural division of labour involving different minority groups. The existence of the reserve army also props up the survival of the capitalist class.

INEQUALITY IN CANADA

Canada is characterized by high levels of inequality among aboriginal, racial, and ethnic groups. Herein lies the genesis of what popularly is known as **ethnic strat-ification**. The term ethnic stratification can be employed in two ways. (See and Wilson 1988). First, it refers to hierarchical systems in which scarce resources are unequally and vertically distributed among diverse minority groups. Second, it consists of highly segmented systems in which minority groups occupy specialized occupational statuses (sometimes referred to as a cultural division of labour). Taken together, stratification can be thought of as a hierarchical structuring of society into "strata" or "layers" by which racial or ethnic minorities are unevenly ranked in descending/ascending order because of differences in wealth, status, or power. Any society predicated on unequal relations, regardless of the criteria employed including race or ethnicity, can be defined as a socially stratified society (Kallen 1995). These ranked differences are not randomly distributed across the population. Nor are they of a transitory nature, that is, reflecting the "costs" of initial adjustment. Rather these differences are patterned in the sense that they are accorded social significance, and their placement is predictable and enduring.

Inequality remains a fact of life in Canadian society (Hiller 1990; Curtis et al. 1993). This inequality is not distributed evenly or randomly; it concentrated among certain minority groups who tend to cluster around certain nodes on the socioeconomic continuum. John Porter's seminal study, *The Vertical Mosaic* (1965) provides a useful introduction to the concept of ethnic stratification. Based on an analysis of census data between 1931 and 1961, Porter set out to examine the nature of the relationship between ethnic origin, social class, and power in Canada. Power was conceptualized as decision-making in elite positions in the institutional structure stretching beyond the economic to include the mass media, schools, military, and government.

Porter convincingly argued that ethnic groups in Canada were arranged hierarchically with the British and to a lesser extent the French playing a gate-keeper role, regulating who would enter the corridors of power. Canada's Charter members occupied and controlled this privileged position by an accident of history. The other groups to emigrate to Canada occupied an "entrance status" inferior to the power and privilege of the charter groups. The vertical mosaic posed a paradox to immigrant groups. To achieve social mobility and shed their lowly entrance status, they would have to turn their back on their cultural background and assimilate into the mainstream. But loss of traditional culture could prove disruptive and create hardship. Maintenance of ethnic community ties, however, could block social mobility. The policy implications of this conflict between culture and equality are vexing. If an ethnic mosaic is a vertical one, will our multicultural policy hinder rather than aid immigrants and others in their mobility attempts?

Current tabulations bear out this out. The 1986 Census Canada income data (the 1991 data are not yet available as of this writing) indicate significant differences in the average income between racially and culturally different Canadians (of both single and multiple origins). Table 4.1 demonstrates these differences.

These findings are open to interpretation in light of social stratification theories. If one takes a functionalist point of view and adopts the status attainment model, it could be argued that income correlates with race and ethnicity. That is, some aspect of ethnicity rather than the nature of the labour market accounts for the findings. By contrast, knowledge of the dual labour market and conflict theory would predict the peripheral placement of African-Americans and Chinese because of class factors. Not all ethnic groups are affected equally. It is interesting to note that Greeks appear to be hindered by ethnicity but another Mediterranean group, the Italians, are not. The British and the French are minimally effected. While it would require more study to sort out the dynamics for each group, it is indisputable that the people of colour are the biggest losers in "open" competition among the groups studied. This empirical evidence of racial discrimination in the job market bolsters the view that our ethnic mosaic is, indeed, vertical.

TABLE 4.1   Average Income and Ethnic Origin by Gender, 1986

	Males	(single+multiple origins)	**Females**
Northern Europeans	$24,447		$13,025
Arabs	$24,172		$12,806
British	$24,160		$12,926
Western Europeans	$23,765		$12,546
Eastern Europeans	$23,480		$13,181
South Asians	$23,113		$12,256
South Europeans	$21,861		$11,995
French	$21,440		$11,930
West Asians	$21,421		$11,793
East and Southeast Asians	$20,567		$13,387
Caribbeans	$19,373		$12,783
Blacks	$18,362		$12,899
Pacific Islanders	$18,357		$11,844
Latin,Central, South Americans	$17,953		$10,423
Aboriginal	$15,760		$9,828

SOURCE: Statistics Canada, February, 1989.

Patterns of ethnic stratification prevail as well in the United States. Evidence is clear in confirming vast gaps in the income status of whites, blacks, and latinos. In 1960, the median income for white families stood at $5,835 and $3,230 for blacks, with a ratio of black to white income of .55 (US Bureau of the Census 1992.) By 1975, this figure had risen to $14,268 for white families and $8,779 for black families, a ratio of .61. The mean income for Hispanic families (the first year this figure was recorded) was $9,551 or .67 of the ratio to white families. In 1990, median income for white families had risen to $36,915 while the black family median income stood at $21,423, a ratio of .58. The ratio of Hispanic family median income to whites was .63 or $23,431. A similar gap is revealed by figures on percentage of American families with incomes below the poverty level. In 1959, 48.1 percent of all black families were below the poverty line, compared with 15.2 percent of whites. By 1990, the figure for black families had declined to 25.0 percent and 8.1 percent for white families. In 1975, the figure for Hispanic families was 19.8 percent, but by 1990 this too had increased to 29.3 percent. In other words, improvements are evident, but these tend to be glacial-like in pace and seemingly impervious to wholesale reform.

How do we account for racial and ethnic inequality in Canada? Only the foolhardy would discount the relevance of minority status for influencing a person's life chances. Ethnicity provides an advantage for some, but a disadvantage for others. A system of stratification exists that reflects the ability of some sectors to do well, while others perform poorly in economic terms. The case, "Ethnic Identity and Inequality in Toronto," is based on research whose findings yielded some interesting conclusions.

CASE STUDY

Ethnic Identity and Inequality in Toronto

Canadians have long debated whether ethnocultural persistence contributes to or detracts from class inequality and social stratification. John Porter (1965) posed this quintessential Canadian question: Does promotion of diversity along race or ethnic lines reinforce inequality and stratifications; does it improve the prospects for material advancement; or does it make no difference? The debate was put to the test by Raymond Breton and his associates (1990) in a study conducted among seven ethnic groups in Toronto—Jews, Ukrainians, Germans, Chinese, West Indians, Portuguese, and Italians. The authors focused on two dimensions of ethnicity: first, the notion of ethnic retention and societal incorporation among select ethnic groups in Toronto, second, the relationship between ethnic retention and the degree of incorporation (equality) in Canadian society. The results of the survey on ethnic identity and inequality are presented below.

1) The authors found certain ethnic minorities had achieved a high degree of incorporation as measured by economic rewards, job discrimination and socio-political acceptance into the culture and structure of Canadian society. Germans and Ukrainians exhibited a high degree of incorporation, while the Chinese and West Indians demonstrated the least. Italians and Portuguese fell in between. West Indians, Chinese, and Jews are most likely to experience job discrimination and social rejection; Germans and Ukrainians the least. It was noted that Jews had a high level of economic and political incorporation, but less so at a social level.

2) Ethnic minorities in Canada tend to be protective of aspects of their cultural background, including identities, select customs, and interpersonal relations. This commitment to ethnic retention is especially salient among the Jews, followed closely by Ukrainians. Despite high levels of incorporation, the individual and collective behaviour of both sectors has been shaped by their cultural background (as indicated by identity, cultural preferences, residential segregation, social ties and interaction, and political activity). The Germans displayed the lowest level of cultural retention, whereas the Portuguese and Italians were ranked intermediately. In the case of the Chinese and West Indian, both groups occupied the lower end of the ethnic salience scale.

3) The impact of ethnic concentrations in the labour market is variable. At times, labour market concentrations are discriminatory and serve to obstruct achievement, mobility, and incorporation. Such is the case among the Chinese, West Indian, and Portuguese whose concentration in low status occupations (for example, construction work among the Portuguese) is a barrier to the pursuit of equality. By way of contrast, the Jews who are highly concentrated in certain occupations display a high degree of occupational incorporation. The Germans and Ukrainians are equally incorporated occupationally, but, unlike the Jews, these two groups reflect low levels of labour market segregation. The Italians occupy an intermediate position. Finally, ethnic concentrations for women from the Italian, Portuguese, and Chinese sectors are correlated with low occupational status and incomes. In short, it is possible to have a high level of incorporation in society with or without ethnic occupational concentrations. It is also possible to exhibit high levels of occupational concentration with or without high incorporation levels.

4) With respect to social and political organization, the results are equally mixed. Two well-incorporated groups—the Jews and the Ukrainians—perceive themselves to be high in political cohesion with a capacity to act in a concerted fashion for collective interests. The Germans, however, are low on political or social cohesion although they, like the Jews and Ukrainians, are high on the scale of incorporation. Two of

the least incorporated groups, the Chinese and the West Indians, are also low on socio-political cohesion and organization. Lying in between the highest and lowest are the Italians and the Portuguese.

The authors make the following conclusions on the basis of their survey findings:

a) Some ethnic groups have little or no trouble becoming fully incorporated into Canada's social, political, and economic life (Ukrainians and Germans).

b) Other ethnic minorities such as Jews, visible races, and recent immigrants encounter obstacles to full incorporation despite their desire to blend into Canadian society. In the case of the Jews, they incorporate economically and politically but experience barriers to social acceptance.

c) Even with full incorporation into Canadian society, ethnic minority members are likely to retain some commitment to ethnicity. Jews, followed by Italians and Ukrainians, have the highest levels of ethnic retention, Germans the lowest. Hence, incorporation into wider society does not necessarily diminish ethnic salience as an organizing principle in the personal or social life of minority members. Still, there is some loss of language, community participation, and sense of obligation to the group. But other aspects, such as social ties and organization, are often retained. This suggests the dynamics of ethnic retention and societal incorpo-

ration are mutually distinct yet related social processes, and must be analyzed as such.

d) The retention of ethnicity can have either a positive or negative effect on the degree of societal incorporation. Ethnocultural persistence does not necessarily impede or retard incorporation into society as shown by Jews and Ukrainians. Nor does it necessarily facilitate incorporations, although, when properly mobilized, appeals to ethnicity may challenge the status quo and the prevailing distribution of power. This implies the relationship between ethnic persistence and social equality is contingent on a variety of factors.

e) General propositions about the evolution of ethnic minorities in Canada must be treated with caution. Causal schemes are of dubious value because different levels of incorporation are associated with different levels of retention, and vice versa. Nevertheless, certain regularities can be suggested. When it comes to levels of incorporation, a general distinction may be drawn between racial minorities (Chinese and West Indian) and ethnic minorities (Ukrainian and German).

f) A series of internal and external factors largely determine whether ethnicity is an asset or a liability for minority groups. Ethnicity (in terms of organization and mobilization) can facilitate access to resources (resource mobilization). It can also hinder minority aspirations through job discrimination. In other words, the effect of cultural retention on societal incorporation is highly variable. In some cases, ethnicity interferes with incorporation; yet, in others, the resources associated with ethnicity facilitate incorporation.

g) The dynamics of incorporation and retention do not unfold or develop uniformly across generations or sexes for all ethnic groups. Ethnicity as a social process involving incorporation and retention must be viewed in the context of history and contemporary social circumstances.

This study indicates how and why ethnicity persists in some shape or form over time and across generations. It demonstrates how various ethnic minorities are incorporated into Canada's social, political, and economic fabric. It also lays to rest the widespread belief

that, as one dimension of ethnic reality increases (incorporation), the other decreases (ethnicity). One is not necessarily the obverse of the other; namely, incorporation into society is not automatically linked with loss of ethnic attachments. Breton et al. (1990:9) state:

Incorporation does not necessarily mean that ethnicity is disappearing as a basis of social organization and individual identity. The existence of a vibrant ethnic community does not imply that incorporation is failing to occur. The variations of the two phenomena may be correlated; but they are not the same. Conversely, ethnic retention is not always a liability with regard to incorporation, but may be turned into an asset when dealing with problems of identity and socio-economic well-being.

Summary of *Ethnic Identity and Inequality. Varieties of Experience in a Canadian City*, by Raymond Breton, Wsevolod W. Isajiw, Warren E. Kalbach, and Jeffrey G. Reitz. Toronto: University of Toronto Press (1990).

INEQUALITY: RACE AND SOCIAL CLASS

We have already emphasized that race and ethnic relations are ultimately relationships of inequality. Class relations also constitute a type of unequal relation. Race and **social class** provide two of the grounds upon which inequality is constructed, organized, and perpetuated. What precisely is the nature of this relationship between *race* and *class* in explaining who gets what? Which of these key explanatory variables is logically prior in shaping intergroup dynamics and explaining social inequality? The debate touches on a number of related points regarding the true source of exploitation in society. Concern over which of these variables (race or class) logically precedes the other in structuring unequal relations reflects a growing interest in tracing the interlinkages among multiple dimensions of inequality (Kallen 1995; also Stasiulis 1990). Are people unequal because of who they are (race) or because of what they do (class)? Are group conflicts in Canada the result of racial or ethnic tensions? Or do conflicts reflect differences of productive property ownership (class)? For example, did nineteenth century Chinese immigrants experience discrimination because of a pervasive anti-Orientalism (race)? Or should the treatment of the Chinese be assessed because of their occupational status (class) as essentially disposable labour for Canadian nation-building purposes? Are both interpretations correct in part? Logically, three possibilities can exist:

Social Class

The first position argues that social class is logically prior to race as a source of inequality. Social class can be defined as a principle of organization that differentiates groups of individuals because of their unequal involvement in the economy. It consists of those who occupy a similar position in a stratified social order when measured by such criteria as income, education, occupational status, prestige, ownership of property, or socioeconomic power. With class at the core of capitalist society, race relations are simply an extension of a more comprehensive category of social dynamics (Li 1988b; Bolaria and Li 1988; Wotherspoon and Satzewich 1993).

The principles of capitalism are central to Canadian society. Capitalism can be defined as a system for the rational pursuit of profit and capital accumulation by way of privately owned means of production and the production of goods (commodities) for sale in an unlimited and competitive marketplace (Mandel 1979). Profits (or capital) are re-invested in factories and raw materials (rather than spent nonproductively), thereby sustaining the cycle of profit-making. The centrality of the profit motive culminates in the establishment of class relations, with the productive property owning class squaring off with the working class (or "proleteriat"). The affluent classes own the means of production such as factories and tools. They derive profit not only from the ownership of this private property, but also through the exploitation of the working class who must sell their labour power for survival. The difference between the cost of hiring workers and the selling price of the finished product ("surplus labour value") determines the profit.

Shared experiences, notwithstanding, the working class is neither homogeneous in composition nor uniform in outlook. It is internally divided since all workers by definition are exploited, but some more so than others because of gender or race. Class divisions or fractions exist that can be measured by levels of income or education. These divisions (or fractions) can then be ranked hierarchically on the basis of job segregation, wage discrimination, and promotional ceilings. For example, white male workers often are better paid than non-white workers. Males in general earn more than females of all ethnic groups. The lowest paid male groups earn more than the highest paid female group. In addition to income differentials, males generally have access to more secure types of employment with greater opportunities for promotion and career enhancement. Differences are also noticeable when dealing with mean income within specific groups: Ethnic minorities generally earn more than people of colour, while the men within each category outperform women within that category. Competition among the fractions serves to reinforce a system of stratification as well as a pattern of domination that is sustained through racist ideology (Cohen 1976).

The property owning and working classes are in a constant struggle for control over power and wealth. The ruling class enhances its profit-making capacity by fostering internal divisions along lines of race and ethnicity (Rex 1983). Racial factors serve primarily as a basis for de-stabilizing class relations (Li 1988b). This fragmentation and the corresponding ideology stigmatizes certain groups as undesirable and less marketable. It also provides a constant supply of cheap and unskilled labour. These class fractions can also be manipulated to foster what Marx termed "false consciousness." Instead of directing their hostility at the source of their exploitation and domination (ie. the capitalists), workers misplace their antagonism toward each other. This has the effect of fostering social cleavages within the working class. Nevertheless, class relations remain at the root of this conflict. Racial differences and confrontations are simply aspects of the wider struggle between classes. Minority concerns merely complicate the issue by distorting ("mystifying") the reality of domination and the true source of exploitation. Thus, conflicts between racial groups are ultimately conflicts within and between classes — whether people are aware of it or not.

Race

Can race and ethnic relations be reduced to the level of stratification and class conflict? Race theorists dispute the validity of this reductionist assertion. Race and ethnic relations are *not* reducible to class relations. Nor are they a derivative of economic forces. Race and ethnicity constitute forces in their own right, with a distinctive set of explanations (see, van den Berghe 1981). For example, Frances Henry (1994) has argued that the differential treatment of Caribbean Canadians can be attributed primarily (but not exclusively) to racism and racial discrimination, a refusal to appreciate visible minority needs, and failure to accommodate Caribbean cultural values within institutional structures. Class issues are subsumed under the more inclusive category of racial conflict.

Race has historically (and geographically) preceded class relations as an a classifying principle. Class divisions are merely superimposed on existing racial patterns without diminishing the significance of race as an antecedent force for organization, differentiation, and stratification. As well, attachments created by racial and ethnic ties are more durable than the "contrived" bonds generated by class affiliations. Ethnic connections are perceived as natural and "authentic" because of their conception from birth or descent. These relationships provide the basis for group affiliation, with its lure of emotional security, interest satisfaction, and accessible appeal for adherents (Brown 1989). Such is not necessarily the case with class. Members of a particular class may possess little in common except a similar relation to the means of production. Class ties are perceived as brittle, and subsequently prone to rupture in the face of concerted pressure.

How valid is this argument when applied to Canada? Public perception of group conflict in Canada is often couched in racial or ethnic terms. Reports of group confrontation are viewed as conflicts between racially or culturally different sectors, whether they be French-English strife, aboriginal-non-aboriginal tension, and police-visible minority hostility. Confrontation between groups is rarely framed within the discourse of class conflicts. Of course, one might argue that this merely represents the victory of the ruling class who owns the mass media in distracting us (through dominant ideologies) from the root cause of exploitation and domination ("false mystifications"). Difficulties obviously exist in attempting to prove or disprove this position.

In short, race and ethnicity are posited as relatively autonomous forces that exist independent of class factors. They were not created by economic forces alone. Discrimination and inequality in many cases predate the appearance and evolution of class-based capitalist systems. Neither reducible to class relations nor consistent with theories of economic determinism, in other words, race and ethnic relations embody group dynamics in their own right and must be analyzed accordingly.

Race and Class

A third possibility suggests that race and class represent separate yet interdependent forces for inequality in society. For example, it can be argued that race and class themselves are derived from fundamental forces of domination and control that appear in all human societies. Ranked differences among individuals or groups are reflected and reinforced through gradations in power and prestige even in tribal groups. Similarly, forces of domination and control in complex societies are exercised through differentials in authority, personal influence and ability, sex, age, and wealth. The concepts of race and class represent but two of several criteria for the exclusion and exploitation of certain sectors.

In acknowledging the primacy of domination and control as forces in society, race and class exist as alternate expressions of these generalized constraints. Race and class are analytically different expressions of oppression that require separate entries. These relations exist alongside of each other as distinct modes of domination or exploitation. One or the other may dominate at some point, depending on the social, political, or economic context (Wilson 1978). Yet these determinants of inequality are not necessarily mutually opposed dimensions (Jaret 1995). Both race and class interact with each other in a complex manner not only to define the position of minorities in society but also to create separate yet interrelated hierarchies. Class structures are likely to inflame racial conflicts.

The essentials of the race/class debate are sharply etched in South Africa where the system of apartheid prevailed until 1993. No one disputed that whites controlled and exploited the black population. To what extent did this unequal relation embrace a racial dimension? Or is it more accurate to speak about a class relation involving workers (most of whom happen to be blacks) and owners of production (who are largely white). Perhaps both race and class have equal explanatory status in South Africa.

INSIGHT

Race and Class in South Africa

The situation that existed in South Africa until recently furnishes a useful test case in highlighting the controversy over race and class as explanatory systems. This relationship between race and class in that country can be rephrased within the ideological framework of apartheid. Apartheid represented a prime example of racial and ethnic stratification — a caste system so entrenched in a racial division of labour that skin colour constituted the single overriding criterion of societal power and privilege (Marger 1994). Economically speaking, there were and are signficant differences in income and status along racial lines, though not all white South Africans belong to a prosperous propertied class. South African whites themselves are divided into a wealthy and working class by virtue of their relationship to the means of production. Cleavages exist between the rich and the poor as well as between blacks and whites. These anomalies create certain ambiguities in black-white relations that distort the possibility of reductionist arguments. In general, blacks tend to be unemployed at a higher rate, to earn considerably less than white workers do, and to be concentrated in certain occupations. Despite some improvements, domestics and rural workers continue to receive a fraction of the income of the average white worker.

Yet inconsistencies within the system were evident and continue to exist. In some cases, white workers themselves have been outflanked by blacks when assessed on income and occupational levels. Highly paid black workers in the car industry, for example, can earn up to twice as much as as poor white clerical workers. In other cases, not only have blacks assumed positions of power and authority, but they also have narrowed the gap in certain occupations. With the growing emergence of a skilled black work force, blacks now occupy approximately one-third of the country's total professional and managerial positions. In the mining industry where whites once earned eighteen times more than blacks, blacks have reduced the ratio considerably since the early 1970s. This reduction in income disparity can be attributed to a variety of reasons, including increased black involvement in trade unions. Equally important has been the pressure exerted by international corporations. In response to political and shareholder pressure, Canadian and American corporations in South Africa have introduced internal reforms for elevating the status, income, and life chances of black employees.

What we have then is a rather unusual situation in terms of capitalist class relations. There exists a duality or split between higher priced and lower priced labour (Bonacich 1972). Whites are pitted against whites, blacks against blacks, and lower earning white workers against higher earning black workers. This split in the labour market may ostensibly appear at odds with profit maximization. After all, reason dictates that all capitalist owners would prefer to impose a uniformly low wage to maximize the profit margins. While true in theory, advantages can exist with a fragmented labour market. This division between and among black and white workers can be used to depress wages, to provide a reserve labour force, to crush strike breakers, and to keep labour demands to within manageable proportions. A degree of fractionalization can ensure a degree of control and domination by undermining the development of a collective consciousness for mobilization. In opposing worker against worker rather than worker against owner, the labouring classes are divorced from the true source of oppression and exploitation.

How than do we assess the racial or class aspect of apartheid? On the one hand, apartheid represented a system that is racist in appearance, but economic in content. It constituted an ideology to mask the true nature of exploitation that persists between the largely white propertied class and predominantly black working class. The races are segmented into separate spheres, but incorporated differently at economic levels. On the other hand, apartheid can be viewed primarily as a racist ideology that advanced select economic interests. Afrikaaners take great pride in their history and culture, and some continue to resolutely defend an ideology that separates whites from blacks. The Afrikaan defence of apartheid was derived from scriptural readings to ensure the purity of the chosen people and their separation from the "pagans." They regard themselves as a "chosen people" with a legitimate right to existence in a promised land. Many believe that Afrikaaner toil and sacrifice transformed this country into the powerful and sophisticated nation it is at present. Thus, it is not surprising that racial antipathy has contributed to the inferior and exploited status of South African blacks. It also suggests that class relations are wholly a function of racial stratification (Marger 1994).

The case study, "Race and Class in South Africa" has focused attention on the racial and class dimensions of intergroup behaviour in unequal contexts. Both black and white South Africans are differentiated and exploited on the basis of racial as well as class origins. A similar line of reasoning can be applied to Canada. The exploitation of Chinese immigrants was based in part on skin colour (race); in other part on working class status (class). Chinese workers were allowed into the country as cheap reserve labour as long as they accepted their inferior racial position and did not compete with the host country for scarce resources. This suggests the merits of a comprehensive perspective. Race overlaps with class; at other times, it displaces class as a system of organization or differentiation. (Rex 1983). At still other times, neither race nor class determines the final outcome since additional factors (such as gender) may be involved in creating systems of inequality. It is our belief that a plurality of explanations best explains the diversity of forces at play within a societal context.

To sum up: The relationship between race and social class can be analyzed in three ways. In the first way, social class and the economy are logically prior to race as systems of exploitation. Race relations are an merely a sub-category of this more comprehensive system of domination and control. Class forces are integral in shaping intergroup dynamics within contexts of social inequality and stratification. Appeals to race and ethnicity merely obscure or complicate the true source of societal injustice. In the second way, race and discrimination are logically prior to class as systems of exploitation. Social class affiliation is simply superimposed on preexisting racial patterns and antagonisms. And in the third way, neither race nor class are logically prior, but are coexistent and interdependent forces of a more generalized domination. Each, accordingly, must be analyzed as separate yet mutually reinforcing principles in determining life chances and career opportunities. Each interpretation will influence proposed solutions. A racially-driven inequality will entail solutions around education and sensitivity training. Inequality as a class problem will focus on the exploitative nature of productive property ownership. An emphasis on both race and class will entail a more comprehensive package of tactics for solution.

RETHINKING INEQUALITY

The fact that racial and ethnic inequality exists in Canada is beyond dispute. What is open to conjecture is the nature and source of this inequality, in addition to what can be done about it. This section reveals how the concept of inequality is changing in response to emergent trends. Even the concept of equality is undergoing a shift in meaning that may be difficult to accept for most Canadians. The next section follows up by examining the concept of **employment equity** within the framework of an evolving Canadian society.

Ethnicity and Culture: The "Old" Vertical Mosaic

Under the **"old" vertical mosaic**, Canada is described as a bilingual yet pluralist federalist system, with a commitment to individual rights and formal equality as prerequisites for national unity and identity. Yet minorities historically have been excluded from full equality and equal participation. Ethnicity at one time was blamed as the source of minority inequality (see Agocs and Boyd 1993). Minorities steeped in ethnicity could hardly hope to make it in Canada. Majority prejudice against ethnic differences could also preclude acceptance. Solutions were proposed consistent with this reading of ethnicity as a major problem.

The process of ethnicity-blaming did not stop here. Many envisaged Canada as an open and competitive marketplace in which individuals sort themselves out on the basis of skills, credentials, or productivity. Individual success or failure reflected variation in human capital: Those individuals with training, skills (credentials), and resources (education) succeeded; those without, faltered. But ethnicity interfered with this sorting out process in a meritocracy. Ignorance and prejudice on the part of employers hindered a natural sorting out process. A process of mutual understanding and accommodation proved the solution. Once basically rational employers were shown the irrationality of hiring except by merit or credentials, ethnic discrimination would vanish. The role of the government in this orientation was essentially passive, and restricted largely to initiatives for eliminating negative attitudes and language barriers to participation. In short, the chief obstacles to success were individual prejudice and cultural ethnocentrism.

Equity and Structure: The "New" Vertical Mosaic

By the early 1980s, it was evident the ethnicity paradigm was not working according to plan. Racial and ethnic stratification remained as real and as entrenched for certain minorities as it did in the days of John Porter (1965; also Agocs and Boyd 1993). Compared with whites, people of colour occupied an unequal status in society above and beyond the "initial adjustment" phase. Therein lay the discriminatory component: discrimination was institutionalized in that it was supported by cultural values and social practices, reflected normal functioning of societal structures, and persisted as a pervasive feature of interpersonal contact (see Aguirre Jr. and Turner 1995). Minorities continued to experience difficulty in making their mark on Canada — with or without possession of impressive educational credentials. Nor did a personal commitment to assimilation seem to make much difference. Full participation was denied to some new Canadians because of ascribed characteristics reflecting race or nationality. Unless something was done about opening up these opportunity structures, the claim to equality was shallow and self-serving.

A new paradigm was articulated that redefined the problem and corresponding solutions. A commitment to equity replaced ethnicity as part of this transformation; similarly the focus shifted from culture to structure as the departure point for analysis. Where once it was thought that democratic guarantees and the tolerant rationality of Canadians were sufficient to destroy obstacles, the idea took hold that interventionist measures were required to overcome this inequality (see Puddington 1995). According to this perspective, the problem did not necessarily reside with cultural explanations or individual attitudes related to achievement values or human cultural capital. Social structures and systemic institutional barriers were the main culprits. Solutions could hardly arise from the open marketplace as had once been thought the case. The free market itself was a major contributor to the problem through the perpetuation of chilly workplace climates, racial harassment, dual labour markets, and systemic bias. These structures combined with relations of power to constrain minority life chances by circumscribing access, retention, reward allocation, and advancement. This paradigm is called the **"new" vertical mosaic.**

In short, inequality was embedded within the workings of a capitalist system (Bolaria and Li 1988; Jaret 1995). Barriers to advancement stemmed from structural constraints that were largely systemic or chronic, and reflected mainstream institutional biases. Solutions that focused on purging individual shortcomings ("blaming the victims") were doomed to fail. Such a reading could only apply cosmetic remedies to social problems of a substantial nature. Institutional reforms rather than behaviour modification were defined as the catalyst for genuine equality. This concept of institutional change through removal of systemic barriers is at the cutting edge for moves to manage diversity. Yet evidence is doubtful whether Canadians are convinced of these proposals. Nowhere is this more evident than in confusion over the "new" equality.

Redefining Equality

It is widely accepted that minorities are penalized socially or economically for their race or ethnicity. Most would also agree that minorities aspire to equality in

Canada's social and economic landscape. But the concept itself, equality, is problematic. The concept is subject to diverse interpretations, with meanings that depend on context and evolve over time. The net result can lead to confusion and misunderstanding, especially when dealing with issues over who gets what, and why ("entitlement"). Two schools of thoughts are predominant: **formal equality** versus **substantive equality**, each of which casts different light on how to improve minority status in Canada.

First, equality is used as equivalent to sameness. Everyone is treated the same regardless of their backgrounds or circumstances. Everyone is accorded the "same chances" in a system designed around equal opportunity and universal merit. This type of formal equality is based on the principle that everyone is equal before the law. Second, equality is used in the sense of numerical or proportional equivalence. Under systems of preferential hiring and promotion, each group is allocated positions on the basis of their numbers in society or the workforce. Under substantive equality, those with physical as well as social disadvantages require different treatment just to be able to compete with others on an equal basis. This "results-oriented" equality is concerned with fair shares and outcomes rather than the formalities of equality. Those properties align it with the principle of "different but equal." Consider for example the "special" treatment that extends to individuals with disabilities, including wheelchair ramps, closed caption TV, and designated parking spots. These concessions are not special as in preferred, but special as in necessary for achievement of a level playing field. A similar line of reasoning applies to people of colour who face equally daunting if less visible barriers. Treatment must be tailored accordingly to ensure an equality with substance rather than of promises.

Each of these perspectives on equality differs from the other in terms of objectives and scope. Equal opportunity focuses on the rights of individuals to be free from discrimination when competing for the good things in life. By contrast equal outcomes concentrates on the rights of individuals for a fair and equitable share of societal goods. A commitment to equal opportunity openly advocates as natural and inevitable the virtues of market-driven and inequality-generating competition. Opposed to this is the principle of a results-oriented outcomes, with its focus on justice and fairness through controlled distribution. Instead of treating everyone alike or the same, an equal outcomes perspective is concerned with treating certain groups differently as a basis for entitlement when the situation demands it. Distinctions that once were employed to deny or exclude are now used as a basis for sorting out who gets what. This perspective leans toward the priority of collective (or group) over individual rights as necessary if not altogether desirable. In short, *formal* equality is concerned with mathematic precision, equality of opportunities, and market forces. By contrast, *substantive* versions of equality focus on equivalence, outcomes, and intervention (Simpson 1992). Sometimes equality means treating people the same way despite their differences; sometimes it means treating people differently because of the difference.

Equality: Solution or Problem?

Many continue to support equal opportunity as a solution to minority problems. All discrimination based on race or ethnicity would vanish and be replaced with colour-blind criteria for assessment if everyone were treated equally. However, not everyone agrees with this line of reasoning. The application of equal standards to unequal situations merely freezes the prevailing distribution of inequality without any appreciable change in the status quo. After all, as minorities push forward to improve their socioeconomic status, those with the advantages of a head start are also moving upward. The numbers improve overall, to be sure, but the gap remains proportional and the pace of change glacial.

In the final analysis, equal opportunity principles do not really assist those sectors that historically have been excluded from full societal involvement. Nor can such a commitment overcome the debilitating effects of systemic discrimination and institutional racism. Certain groups require special assistance over and above that available to the general population. A results-oriented equality is high on the wish list for minority groups. This is not to reject equal opportunities as a basis for entitlement. To the contrary: A commitment to the principle of equal opportunity constitutes a necessary first step in overcoming entrenched racism and discrimination. But ultimately such a commitment is insufficient to achieve a fair and just equality. Only a dual advancement at outcomes and opportunity level can shake up the prevailing entrenchment of power and wealth. That principle, called **the new equality**, has been put into practice in Canada as we shall see next — with controversial results.

EMPLOYMENT EQUITY: PUTTING EQUITY INTO PRACTICE

Initiatives pertaining to a results-oriented equality derive legitimacy from the concept of **employment equity** (also known as affirmative action in the USA). Equity initiatives are aimed at proactively assisting minorities who have been excluded through no fault of their own from full and equal workplace participation. To its credit, the Canadian government has pioneered such measures through its *Employment Equity Act* of 1986, although the specifics of the law and its implementation leave much to be desired. With passage of Bill 79 in September, 1994, the Ontario government is equally committed to an employment equity programs.

Our experiences tell us that few social programs in Canada have generated as much dislike as employment equity. One Gallup poll found that 74 percent of Canadians (involving a telephone interviews with 1,000 Canadian adults, conducted December 3-14, 1993, with a margin of error of 3.1 percentage points, 19 times in 20) opposed job equity programs (*The Toronto Star* December 23, 1993). In all fairness to the debate, the question itself was loaded: The question asked whether the "Government should (a) actively hire more women and minority group members; or (b) hire new employees based on their qualifications." A negative response was virtually assured given the choice between either qualified candidates or minorities — as if the two categories were mutually exclusive.

This section will examine the concept of employment equity within the context of the new vertical mosaic. The discussion begins with a distinction between employment equity as a *principle* or *philosophy* (lower case employment equity) and its expression as official *government policy* and *program* (Upper Case Employment Equity). A distinction between principles and *practices* may also be useful in sorting out equity issues. Emphasis in this section is on the principles behind employment equity as an ideology for managing diversity at institutional levels. Attention will focus on (a) what is meant by employment equity; (b) why it exists in terms of its underlying rationale; (c) how it is officially expressed in law; (d) its impact and implications; (e) and public response to and official criticism of it. Our objective is to demonstrate how employment equity represents a plausible if imperfect solution to the problem of racial inequality.

WHAT IS IT? DEFINITION AND SCOPE

Employment equity has been defined in different ways. Definitions vary, reflecting variations in emphasis on what employment equity looks like and does, or should look like and should do. Problems have arisen from failure to distinguish principle from policy or practice. Employment equity as a philosophy is concerned with the principle of "institutional accommodation" through the removal of discriminatory barriers. It is based on the belief that all persons regardless of colour should be treated equally within the workforce. That is, they should be recruited, hired, promoted, trained, and rewarded like any other persons — assuming they are qualified on the basis of job-related skills and positions are available — without barriers that discriminate against them because of membership in certain devalued groups.

By contrast, Employment Equity as a policy constitutes a legislated program with a formal set of practices to achieve government goals. As principle, it points to a set of ideas and ideals; as policy, it embraces a political solution to a social problem. One is concerned with the principles of justice and fairness, the other with the principle that for justice to be done it must be *seen* to be done. Towards that end, Employment Equity consists of a comprehensive set of strategies designed to:

- ensure equitable representation of designated groups throughout all occupational and income levels at numbers consistent with their percentage in the regional workforce (Jain and Hackett 1989);
- identify and remove discriminatory and systemic barriers in employment policies and practices;
- remedy adverse effects of past discrimination through positive programs for the recruitment, selection, and training of minorities;

- to ensure reasonable progress in meeting numerical goals and timetables as proof of a more inclusive workplace (Jain 1988).

Why Employment Equity? Assumptions and Rationale

Employment Equity is ultimately concerned with institutions moving over and making space. Attainment of this goal is based on the notion of proportions, reasonable numerical goals and timetables, removal of discriminatory barriers, and proactive employment and promotion programs. Several assumptions underly this commitment; they also provide a rationale for its existence. These include:

1) *Lack of Equality of Opportunity?*
   Employment equity begins with the premise that equality of opportunity and the hiring of individuals on the basis of merit *eludes* the four targetted minorities (women, persons with disabilities, people of colour, and aboriginal people). These targets are thought of as disadvantaged victims of workplace discrimination because of race or gender (rather than class) (Levitt 1995). Conditions such as gender, race, or disability which are unrelated to merit and ability must be neutralized as a basis for equality of opportunity. Persons who are disadvantaged because of race need to be "empowered" by focusing on race-based solutions. Towards that goal, employment equity serves as a temporary means to advance disadvantaged groups through concrete results rather than abstractions about equal opportunities. The measures are expected to last until such time as a proportional workforce balance is achieved.

2) *Systemic Racism*
   Workplace discrimination was once viewed as a minority problem. It involved deliberate actions against hapless victims by misguided persons in positions of power. There is a growing move at present away from discrimination as a private trouble to a social problem at the level of impersonal organizational structures and procedures. It stands to reason that problems rooted in social structures will demand structural solutions. Discrimination may be defined systemically, that is, in the application of ostensibly neutral rules and conditions of employment that adversely affects certain minorities because of their culture or appearance. Systemic discrimination can vary in form and style. Often, it is inherent in universal employment policies and practices that uphold qualifications (such as those based on weight, height, gender, and experience). The rules when applied evenly have a dissimilar effect because they are unrelated to successful job performance, do not compensate for the disadvantages of a late start, and fail to incorporate minority needs or experiences. Positive and intrusive measures are required to redress what good will and best intentions cannot (Heath 1993). To achieve that long-range goal, moreover, may require temporary colour-conscious initiatives on the assumption that race problems only respond to racial solutions.

3) *Proportional Representation*

Employment Equity is built around the pursuit of proportional and equitable representation of minorities within institutions. If discriminatory employment barriers did not exist, proponents contend, all sectors of the workforce would be evenly distributed along all occupational and income levels in accordance with their numbers in the population (allowing of course for individual and cultural pressures which may restrict occupational choices) (Regional Municipality of Waterloo 1986). A reality check suggests otherwise. Certain minorities are locked out or unevenly segregated throughout occupational structures, even with the presence of anti-discrimination laws and human rights codes. Many have been denied employment and promotion for reasons unrelated to ability or credentials. This suggests the strong possibility of discriminatory employment barriers, both pervasive and entrenched, as well as difficult to isolate and remove. It also suggests that to get beyond racism, we must take race into account. Likewise, it confirms that left to their own, organizations will tend to reproduce themselves unless an outside force is applied to break the circularity (Kanter 1977; *Newsweek*, 27 March 1995).

4) *Demographic Changes*

Demographic trends indicate a shift away from white able-bodied males as the primary target population for the Canadian labour market. Predictions point to a growing reliance on women, persons with disabilities, people of colour, and aboriginal peoples. Coping with this shift in Canada's human resource pool is no longer an option or luxury. It constitutes instead a necessity in terms of our capacity to compete globally without loss of national interests. Yet these target groups suffer from long-term economic and employment disadvantage. Labour force adjustments have not occurred quickly enough; as a result, employment equity strategies are enacted to accelerate the representation and equitable treatment of target group members (Ontario Ministry of Citizenship 1989).

5) *Market versus Intervention*

Employment Equity takes a clear stand on the role of the government in softening the harshness of a market economy. The market is perceived as contrary to minority interests because of disadvantages related to late start and cultural handicaps. Applying unrestricted market forces as means for sorting out who gets what is inappropriate in contexts of pervasive and chronic inequality. By contrast, government intervention is seen as vital in hastening the entry of minorities into the workplace. Workplaces will continue to reproduce themselves until an outside force is applied to reverse the process. The normal rules of doing business are suspended until achievement of a numerical proportion of designated minorities.

6) *Charter of Rights*

The legitimacy of Employment Equity is derived from Canada's *Human Rights Act* and the *Charter of Rights and Freedom*. One of the fundamental principles of human-rights legislation is the belief that blanket definitions of equality are inappropriate. Individuals in different circumstances may require differential treatment for attainment of equality. Both declarations acknowledge the legality and fairness of special programs when designed to "overcome disadvantages" or to remedy the effects of past discrimination (Jain and Hackett 1989). The collective rights implied in such arrangements may override individual rights when employed to ameliorate minority disadvantage. Of particular significance, Section 41 (2) of the *Human Rights Act* confers authority on human rights tribunals to impose special programs in cases of systemic discrimination. This ruling was put to the test successfully in 1987 when the Supreme Court ordered CN to increase to 13 percent the proportion of women working in non-traditional occupations in the St. Lawrence region.

Implementation: Employment Equity Acts

The federal government proclaimed Employment Equity as law in August of 1986. Passage of this uniquely Canadian approach toward "affirmative action" was largely in response to the recommendations of the Royal Commission on Equality in Employment (1984). The act sought to

> ...achieve equality in the workplace so that no person shall be denied employment opportunities or benefits for reasons unrelated to ability...by giving effect to the principle that employment equity means nothing more than treating persons in the same way but also requires special measures and the accommodation of differences.

Terms of the Act applied to all federally regulated employers (with 100 or more employees), public sector companies, and crown corporations. These companies were obligated to publish annual reports on the composition of their workforce, with particular reference to the number of and type of work performed by women, visible minorities, differently able, and aboriginal peoples. Minorities were to be hired and promoted in numbers commensurate with their ratio in the general workforce. Also falling under Equity provisions are federal contractors of at least 100 employees. Each had to sign a certificate of commitment to comply with Equity provisions ("contract compliance") if they wished to bid on government goods or services contracts worth $200,000 or more. All organizations were expected to file an annual report outlining their progress in this area. However, no penalties for non-compliance appeared in the Act.

In addition to the federal level, Employment Equity has appeared in several provinces. Ontario's long awaited *Employment Equity Act* came into effect in late 1994. Bill 79 intends that women, people of colour, individuals with disabilities, and aboriginal peoples be hired, rewarded, and promoted like all other employees, provided they possess the qualifications for existing job openings. Employers are expected to draw up plans for diversifying the workforce. They also are required to set their own goals and time-tables within the limits laid down by the legislation (Gibb-

Clark 1994). Those private sector employers with more than 50 workers are required by law to conduct a survey to determine the number of individuals from each designated group in their workforce. Completion of the "self-identification" survey (within eighteen to thirty-six months depending on the size of the workforce) is followed by an employment systems review whose primary purpose is to identify discriminatory barriers, ie. the terms and conditions of employment that would have a negative effect on designated minorities. Employers are then expected to establish plans for the removal of discriminatory barriers, the implementation of positive measures, and the conferral of supportive assistance to accommodate designated groups (OCUFA 1994). Monitoring and ongoing evaluative measures are also stipulated as a basis for securing a more inclusive and representative workplace. The Conservative government elected in 1995 may overturn the *Equity Act*.

Setting the Record Straight

Confusion about Employment Equity continues to prevail. The three most common misconceptions are those that link it with **reverse discrimination,** with **merit,** and with **quotas.** Employment Equity is frequently accused of "reverse discrimination." If it was unfair to discriminate against minorities, critics say, it is just as wrong to to give preference to minorities and treat whites unfairly. Reference to context and consequences are important in sorting out this issue. Racial discrimination, by definition, is aimed at preserving privilege by denying or excluding minorities. Employment Equity measures, by contrast, are geared toward greater inclusiveness through removal of discriminatory barriers (see Fish 1993). Equity programs are not intended to discriminate against white able bodied males (although the unintended consequence of such actions would appear to disqualify whiteness and maleness from certain consideration). Nor are Employment Equity initiatives designed to confer preferential treatment for designated minorities. To the contrary, the objective is to expand the number of qualified candidates by eliminating bias that historically has rewarded certain sectors at the expense of disadvantaged groups. It is asking those with privilege to move over and make space to ensure everyone has a fair and equal chance to succeed on the basis of their merit as individuals rather than membership in a devalued group. That this is not happening without deep resentment and threats of a backlash reinforces the notion that neither power nor privilege are easily relinquished.

Employment Equity is not in business to hire or promote unqualified personnel. It does not set out to dilute competition by restricting the pool of qualified applicants. If anything, the removal of discriminatory barriers is intended to expand the number of qualified applicants in the competition for employment. Employment Equity also strives to make the competition more equal by opening it up to those formerly excluded from fair and just participation (Regional Municipality of Waterloo 1986). Merit remains the hiring principle for all employment decisions. Minorities under employment equity are now considered on the basis of merit or credentials, in contrast with the past when people were hired because they fit the right type. Under Employment Equity only the best candidates need to be hired; however, targetted minorities should get the nod only when candidates are of comparable quality in a minority-depleted occupation or institution. Moreover, even the concept of merit may need to undergo a rethinking in a world engulfed by rapid change, increased diversity, and painful uncertainty. Employment and promotions based on credentials are no longer guarantors of success. In fact, merit as a narrow set of abstract qualifications may well inhibit organizational effectiveness by obstructing other characteristics and criteria for employment, such as cross-cultural communication.

Finally, Employment Equity is not about quotas or deadlines. American-style quotas consisted of an externally imposed system of fixed percentages to be achieved within a certain time frame. Not surprisingly, unqualified personnel were hired to comply with the law or circumvent penalties (Heath 1993). By contrast, Employment Equity goals are much more flexible; they reflect "reasonable expectations" about hiring or promotion from qualified designated group members when and if available for employment. Employment equity is not about numerical representation. It is about who gets what in Canada. Nor is Employment Equity concerned with government-mandated quotas or reverse racism. It is about taking constructive steps to ensure that everyone has a stake in the system. In the final analysis, Employment Equity is aimed at creating a workplace culture, both inclusive and equitable, as well as progressive and productive.

Response and Reaction

Employment Equity has lept into the forefront of moves for the restructuring of Canada along pluralist, egalitarian lines. Its growing centrality in the workplace has not necessarily improved its acceptance or understanding. Reactions to employment equity are varied: Some support the principle as well as the practice; others reject one or both.

The *business community* has had little choice but to accept Employment Equity as the cost of doing business. Certain benefits are anticipated: employment equity may enhance productivity by enlarging the pool of qualified candidates for employment; it may allow businesses to expand into new markets, both nationally and internationally. Some business people tend to focus on the downside: they are concerned about the additional regulatory costs associated with employment equity; many are worried over the potential loss of global competitiveness because of a costly government intervention. Implementation costs may be a problem since some businesses have neither the sophistication nor resources to cope with a numbers-driven process. Finally, management fears losing control over decision making, thus sacrificing independence and versatility.

White males concur with many of the ambivalence voiced by the business sector. Some see Employment Equity as a well intentioned but ultimately misguided effort at managing diversity. Others accuse it of being a form of reverse discrimination since it fights racism by racist means (Walkom 1995). Still others condemn it as an infringement of equality rights, a violation of basic cultural values related to merit and colour-blind equality, as open to abuse, and unfair with respect to seniority principles (Schaffly 1995). Employment equity is wrong because it can create ghettoes, stigmatize beneficiaries, prompt a backlash, and squander productivity. There is too much danger of enforcing "...hiring quotas that give jobs to individuals that are not the best qualified, and proposals to make gender, race, and other considerations irrelevant to merit a crucial part of the hiring process (Groarke 1992:A-7). The very idea that white males be penalized in atonement for past misdeeds is no less disconcerting to many.

Politicians and *bureaucrats* appear resigned to Employment Equity. Many have jumped aboard the Equity bandwagon, in part because of its political value in terms of cooling out troublesome constituents. Employment Equity provides a useful indicator that the government is serious about managing diversity. Proof is in the statistical data related to minority hiring and promotions. That in turn creates a social climate that is conducive to international investment and export trade. For politicians, then, Employment Equity represents a political solution to a social problem. Not surprisingly, consensus in support of what many see as race preferential policies may exist only at the level of political elites (Puddington 1995).

Targetted minorities are equally mixed in their responses. Some find the whole exercise both odious and intrusive as well as demeaning and patronizing. It implies inferiority and incompetence because of undue dependence on government largesse. Others have an unshakable faith in merit as a basis for hiring, with an aversion to preferential promotion no less avid than among the mainstream (see Bissoondath 1994). Many also stand in fear a "pale-male" backlash of consequence to long-term interests (Grayson 1994). Others, however, condone Employment Equity as an overdue opportunity for a "fair shake at a good job" — a not inconsequential concession in a society where work is valued. Debate over Employment Equity has drawn public attention to institutional barriers, both hidden and beyond consciousness, yet real and discriminatory. Besides, as some proponents like to remind us, men have always enjoyed a de facto system of employment equity and preferential hiring (based on their maleness and whiteness). Now its time for women and minorities to be counted.

Who is right, and who is wrong? Nobody, really, if we accept a multi-perspective view of social realities. Each of these perspectives contains an element of truth, with a logic that is rational under the circumstance. Yet the combined impact of these diverse perspectives adds to the confusion and miscommunication. The end result is a volley of criticism that tends to generate more heat than shed light on the topic.

Criticism of Employment Equity: Is it Working?

Americans pioneered the concept of employment equity nearly thirty years ago. Supporters have defended affirmative action programs because they provide economic benefits, create a representative work force, furnish positive role models for minorities to aspire to, include minority perspectives, and compensate for past injustice (Fish 1993). While some progress has occurred, affirmative action initiatives have not mended the rift between whites and most blacks. Hopes of healing and reconciliation have given way to additional strains in the social fabric of American society. Critics are extremely vocal about their dislike of affirmative action. Affirmative action is criticized for contradicting core values and universally held ideals pertaining to the rights of individuals to be treated as individuals rather than as members of groups or to be judged for what they do instead of who they are (Puddington 1995). In criticizing affirmative actions as a form of tribalism, both premodern as well as morally retrograde, George Will (1993: 78) writes that America "... is a nation of grievance groups exploiting the coveted status of 'victims' (of American wickedness) to claim special rights and entitlement." Historical redress is seen as a form of "payback," with the potential to foster workplace resentment and public backlash (Schaffly 1995). In another hardhitting attack that examines consequences as well as goals and rationale, Thomas Sowell (1989) has critiqued affirmative action on the grounds of its social impact and implications. Affirmative action represents a politically attractive quick fix that rarely provides assistance for those in need. Sowell also notes that affirmative actions are counterproductive: they tend to become permanent or expand in scope over time, disportionately benefit certain members of a particular group, defuse activism through gestures of appeasement, and foster backlash from non preferred groups.

Ambivalence over affirmative action has spilled over into Canada. Some have described Employment Equity as medicine that is "too strong;" others see it as "too weak." One *Maclean's* columnist described Employment Equity as a kind of racism that makes the Third Reich seem benign by comparison (20 July 1993). Still others agree with the principle of employment equity but disagree with its practice: That is, there is support for employment equity initiatives that empower the disadvantaged by improving their qualifications and fostering equal opportunities through elimination of discriminatory barriers ("levelling up"). There is much less support for equity initiatives whose aim is on "handicapping" some through preferential treatment of others in the drive to achieve equal outcomes (levelling down") (Brown 1994). Many are disturbed by the race connotations. Employment Equity appears to focus on skin colour as the single most important feature in a person's existence (Walkom 1995). Yet its self-identification procedures are subject to abuse since no clearcut guidelines exist as to who may qualify as an equity target. Even something as seemingly simple as the concept of visible minorities is not well understood (Grayson 1994), nor is it widely accepted, given the negative connotation associated with the term. People of colour are refusing to identify themselves as "visible minorities" because of stigma or shame. Other groups such as Italians or Greeks are being identified as visible minorities even though they do not qualify for that status.

Critics have also taken Employment Equity to task for lack of (a) specific goals or timetables, (b) comprehensive monitoring mechanisms, and (c) effective sanctions for non-compliance (Jain 1987; Jain and Hackett 1989). Without mandatory targets and timetables, critics argue, employers have excelled at keeping track of numbers, but have been less successful at changing them. For example, according to the 1994 Annual Report of the Department of Human Resources Development, Canada department, aboriginal people working for federally regulated companies have made small employment gains since 1986 (1.04 percent of all employees in 1993 compared with 0.66 percent in 1987). The average salary compared with the average for all employers declined slightly (aboriginal men earned 85 percent of what all men earned in 1993, down from 90.3 percent in 1987; aboriginal women earned 88 percent in 1993 compared with 92 percent in 1987) (Platiel 1995). Paradoxically, Canada's federal sector is one of the most glaring violators — having already exempted itself from the provisions of the 1986 Act. Even though women comprised 46.1 percent of the federal public servants as of March 1993, they made up only 17.6 percent of the highest paid executive public servants. Only 2 of the 4,441 aboriginal peoples working for the federal government earned more than $100,000. Likewise, only 14 individuals with a disability and 11 people of colour among the 841 public servants earned six-figure salaries (*Kitchener-Waterloo Record*, 26 March 1994). Other statistics also seem to support this pattern of inequity. Unemployment rates for certain visible minority groups such as Latin Americans (19 percent), Southeast Asias (17 percent) West Asians and Arabs (16 percent), South Asians (16 percent), and blacks (15 percent) far exceeds that for other canadian adults (10 percent) — even though more people of colour (18 percent) hold university degrees compared with other Canadians (11%) (Mitchell 1995).

Nevertheless there is room for cautious optimism — at least in the private sector. Consider Canada's banking industry. Since 1987, the number of women in upper management has leapt from 2.6 percent to 11.6 percent in 1993 — an impressive figure but still below the number of women in upper management in the labour force at large (25 percent). Similarly, the number of visible minorities in middle management has grown from 5.7 percent in 1987 to 9.2 percent compared with the workforce average of 7.3 percent, according to the Canadian Bankers Association (*Toronto Star* 15 June 1994).

In short, the jury is still out on the effectiveness of Employment Equity as a tool for social engineering. Debate on the pros and cons will continue to confuse and alienate until greater research efforts are expended on identifying, isolating, and eliminating the processes underlying systemic discrimination (Jain and Hackett 1989). A sense of balance is required: Employment equity is neither the source of all evil nor the solution to all of Canada's problems. As Grant Brown puts it, "Those who defend Employment Equity to the hilt are vulnerable to criticism over flaws within the program or practice. Those who reject it altogether are equally guilty of procrastinating when basic justice demand otherwise." Still, the overall thrust of Equity initiatives appears to be in the right direction. Consider only the alternatives. We take some comfort in a statement attributed to Sir Winston Churchill who once claimed, albeit in an altogether different context: The virtues of employment equity may leave a lot to be desired but compared to the alternatives, they constitute a useful first step in blending what is necessary, what is fair, and what is workable.

CHAPTER HIGHLIGHTS

- The relationship between inequality and minority groups is a complex and evolving one. Generally speaking, Canada remains stratified by race and ethnicity despite moves to improve and accommodate. What is less well known is why this inequality exists, and what, if anything, should be done to bridge the gap.

- Functionalist and conflict perspectives differ in how they approach minority inequality. Functionalists tend to see inequality as necessary and normal in a complex society; conflict theorists prefer to think of inequality as inevitable only in capitalist type societies.

- The concepts of race and class represent two principles of organization in society, each of which can be employed to dominate, differentiate, and divide population groups — alone or together.

- Evidence suggests that minorities in Canada are not equal when it comes to income. People of colour and aboriginal people tend to gravitate toward the bottom; whites and European ethnics are at the top.

- Some explanations of inequality assign a priority to race as the source of domination. Others explain ethnic stratification primarily as a result of social class. Still others suggest that race and class originate simultaneously, in the process reflecting relatively independent systems of explanation and prediction.

- An analysis of apartheid as a system of race relations in South Africa indicates how both race and class as analytic concepts can account for patterns of inequality and stratification.

- The whole notion of racial and ethnic inequality is currently under reconsideration. This is especially evident in terms of *causes* and *cures*. The emphasis on ethnocultural differences or individual attitudes as the source of the problem (the ethnicity paradigm) is shifting toward structural factors as they relate to institutional rules, processes, and outcomes (the equity paradigm).

- This focus on structures of society as the problem has altered government solutions, with growing emphasis on institutional accommodation through removal of discriminatory barriers

- Employment equity can be interpreted as a solution to the structural problem of inequality. A distinction needs to be made between employment equity as a principle (which many accept) and its application as government program (which many reject).

- The new equality rejects the notion of equal in the sense of formal equality or mathematical precision. The application of equal ("identical") treatment to unequal situations simply "freezes" (however unintentionally) the status quo. It focuses instead on an equality that incorporates differences and focuses on equal outcomes (conditions) as a basis for entitlements.

KEY TERMS

Conflict Theory
Culture of Poverty
Employment Equity
Equity Paradigm
Ethnic Stratification
Ethnicity Paradigm

Formal Equality
Human Cultural Capital
Merit
New Vertical Mosaic
Old Vertical Mosaic
Quotas

Reverse Discrimination
Social Class
Status Attainment
    Model
Substantive Equality
The New Equality

REVIEW QUESTIONS

1) Describe patterns of stratification in Canada by race and ethnicity.

2) Race and class offer alternate means of explaining inequality. Would you describe the system of apartheid in South Africa as essentially a class (economic) phenomena with racial overtones, or a racial issue with economic overtones? Why?

3) Compare and contrast the approaches of conflict versus functionalist theory as means for explaining inequality and social stratification.

4) Point out how race and class offer different explanations about the source of group inequality. Which do you think is correct?

5) Our thinking on inequality has evolved in recent years. The equity paradigm (the new vertical mosaic) is replacing the ethnicity paradigm (the old vertical mosaic). Explain what has happened and why.

6) The concept of equality can mean different things. Discuss the different meanings of equality as they pertain to race and ethnicity.

7) Stanley Fish has posed an interesting question: Whites once set themselves apart from minorities and claimed privileges while denying them to others. Now on the basis of race and employment equity, people of colour are claiming special status and reserving for themselves privileges that they deny to others. Is one form of "discrimination" as bad as the other?

8) Employment Equity is an extremely controversial method for managing diversity. Explain what Employment Equity is trying to do (both as principle and as a program) and why. Do you agree with its objectives or means.

CHAPTER 5

GENDER AND RACE

TO BE SOLD, A BLACK WOMAN, named Peggy, aged about forty years; and a Black boy her son, named JUPITER, aged about fifteen years, both of them the property of the subscriber. The woman is a tolerable Cook and washer woman and perfectly understands making Soap and Candles. The Boy is tall and strong of his age, and has been employed in Country Business, but brought up principally as a House Servant — They are each of them Servants for life. The Price for the Wowan [sic] is one hundred and fifty Dollars — for the Boy two hundred Dollars, payable in three years with Interest from the day of Sale and to be properly secured by Bond &c. — But one fourth less will be taken in ready Money. PETER RUSSELL. York, Feb. 10th 1806

(adapted from Bristow et al. 1993).

INTRODUCTION

The previous chapter identified race and social class as important principles of social differentiation and organization. Both race and class provide the foundation upon which social inequities are constructed and maintained. Gender as a key explanatory variable is no less important in shaping intergroup relations. Women of colour, immigrant women, and aboriginal women tend to be penalized and put down for no other reason than to preserve mainstream power and privilege. Yet the literature on gender and race — at least compared with race and class — is not well established. Native-born and foreign-born women, as well as aboriginal women and women of colour, tend to be lumped together under a broad generic category, thus reinforcing and perpetuating their invisible status (Boyd 1993). This lack of analytic sophistication has created difficulties as acknowledged by Daiva Stasiulis (1990):

> ...the omission of gender in theories addressing the race-class question stems...from the real difficulties encountered in fashioning a coherent analysis that considers two or more different social dimensions — both separately and in their complex articulation.

Some of these difficulties of analysis will be examined in this chapter.

The incorporation of minority women imparts a gendered dimension to our understanding of group dynamics as unequal relations in Canada. We will focus primarily on the ways in which gender intersects with race, class, and ethnicity to shape the realities that confront immigrant, aboriginal, and visible minority women.

130

Particular attention is directed at the nature of the problem, how it is manifest, why it exists, and its impact on women and society at large. We will also deal with the concept of gender and diversity in terms of its implications for reform.

The chapter begins with various perspectives on gender, including an examination of its cultural underpinnings and the socially constructed nature of gendered relations. The economic base underlying gender inequality is discussed next, followed by a look at gender socialization with reference to sexism and ethnicity. Issues related to violence and ethnicity are addressed in light of recent incidents. In addition, we examine the relation between gender and inequality. We argue that both gender and class, in combination with race and ethnicity, constitute categories of control and containment. Emphasis is placed on the role of discrimination in shaping the lives and life chances of immigrant, aboriginal, and minority women. In the process, we hope to reveal why racism and sexism are are so prevalent and even taken for granted in many sectors of Canadian society. Finally, while minority women have served as objects of control and oppression, they also continue to be actively involved in creating their world as women and as minorities (Carty 1991). We review some of the mechanisms and strategies employed by women (both individually and collectively) to cope with varied pressures and contradictory demands. The concerns of women as minorities cannot be swept aside as redundant or irrelevant.

PERSPECTIVES ON GENDER

The terms *male* and *female* are biological distinctions which are referred to as **sex** in everyday language. The concepts *masculine* and *feminine*, however, take us beyond the realm of the physiological into the symbolic world of the cultural. Each culture has a unique set of definitions with regards to ideal masculine and feminine behaviour. These definitions or "blueprints" are known as as **gender**. The rules governing appropriate behaviour for each gender are called gender norms, while those idealized behaviours that characterize "true" masculinity or femininity are termed **gender roles** or **gender scripts**.

Gender Scripts

Given Canada's diverse and complex composition, there are numerous ways in which we may act out our gender roles. Scripts vary depending upon age, social class, religion, ethnicity, and region of the country, to name but a few of the more important variables affecting gender. Gender, like race and social class, involves status positions embedded within systems of stratification. Thus an examination of how gender "works" in a society is not a sharp departure from our previous look at race and class. These three concepts represent social constructions involving cultural definitions, especially since society assigns meaning to gender, race, and class. That is to say, sex has an objective reality that is denied to a social construction such as gender. Likewise differences in skin pigmentation exist apart from the concept of race, and wealth exists separately from class.

Through social interaction we witness the creation of the prestige hierarchies and power differentials associated with gender, race, and class. When a certain gender or particular race is deemed "superior" or "inferior," the dominant group possesses the power to impose its definition on the subordinate sector. The mere possession of this power, it could be argued, is itself evidence of "superiority." By this logic, Europeans historically have defined themselves as superior to indigenous peoples. Armed with this definition, they have justified their occupation of such areas as North America. Colonialism prospered under such definitions. Similarly, as capitalism developed, the work of women was arbitrarily assigned a lower value than the work of men. This differential evaluation made it acceptable not only to exempt women from wages for work done in the home, but also to roll back wages for work performed outside the home — even when tasks were similar to males". Just as racism is a belief in racial superiority, so too is sexism a belief in gender superiority. If we understand the origins, dynamics, and effects of racism, we are well on our way towards comprehending the manifestations of sexism in our society. A cursory review of the preceding chapters will demonstrate the interchangeability of "gender" for "race" in many of the key sentences, and "sexism" for "racism."

Biology and Culture

"Who am I?" Responses to this question often involve an identification with a gender role — man, woman, son, daughter, husband, or wife. They may also include a reference to nationality, religion, occupation, age, and special interests such as hobbies. Gender identification is usually a core dimension of our personality. Research shows that as early as eighteen months of age children think of themselves in terms of gender differences (Money and Ehrhardt 1972). All cultures differentiate by gender even though the meaning and values assigned to this construct are highly variable.

Theories based upon biological determinism have long distorted our thinking on gender and gender relations. Freudian thought, for example, rigidly characterized appropriate behaviour for each gender. Those who strayed out of line were thought to be maladjusted. For Freud, anatomy was indeed destiny. By the 1930s, anthropologists such as Margaret Mead (1963) began to challenge the main tenets of biological determinism. On the basis of her field experiences in New Guinea, patterns which we normally associate with gender roles in the West were linked instead with the "opposite sex" elsewhere. Certain cultural groups endorsed a spirit of aggression among women, but instilled an ideal of nurturance for men. Mead's field methods and findings have come under scrutiny in recent years (Freeman 1983), yet there is little doubt that her work sensitized people to the many possible ways of being male and female. As a result of this and other pioneering efforts, few scholars at present would deny the pivotal role of culture in shaping our gender identifications, roles, and norms.

While gender differentiation exists in all societies, we are unsure why male domination is so pervasive. It is inaccurate to speak of one sex or race being innately superior or inferior to another. Mental abilities follow a statistically normal distribution within each sex and so-called racial group. A similar range of abilities exists for each category. In addition, this range of abilities within each gender or racial group is greater than differences between men and women or between ethnic and racial groups. Duley (1986:78) after an exhaustive review of the literature concludes, "There is as yet no comprehensive, fully articulated, and agreed upon theory of the origin and perpetuation of gender inequalities, even among those who stress the importance of socio-economic systems or culture in shaping gender stratification." The case study "Gender and Diversity" explores this issue more deeply.

CASE STUDY

Gender and Diversity

SEXUAL DIVISION OF LABOUR: MAN THE HUNTER, WOMAN THE GATHERER?

Is anatomy destiny? There seems to be a global and generalized division of labour based on sex. Each society in theory assigns separate productive activities to men and women. The tasks performed by women and men, along with a corresponding division of labour, reflects a certain practical arrangement in how a society exploits its environment. Evidence suggests that men were the universal hunters; later in evolutionary development they monopolized the jobs of lumbering, smelting, and iron working (Peoples and Bailey 1994). These activities require those qualities that often are linked with men — namely speed, endurance, strength, and a lack of encumbrances associated with childbearing. Women were generally involved in work activities such as gathering that were compatible with the nursing and care of young infants. This division of labour was not always sharply defined.

Women were known to routinely hunt smaller game or on occasion cooperate with men in larger game drives (see Brettell and Sargent 1993). Nor does it mean that men were the breadwinners while women stayed near hearth and home. Women's contribution to community subsistence may easily have exceeded that of the males — a conclusion which in effect denys comfort to those who attribute male dominance to their disproportionate contributions to the domestic larder (Peoples and Bailey 1994). Nevertheless, there is a general pattern of hunting men and gathering women that cannot be casually brushed off.

GENDER INEQUALITY: WHO'S IN CHARGE HERE?

Anthropology reminds us that perfect equality probably never existed even in the simplest and most egalitarian foraging society. Inequities based on age or gender appear inevitable. But while gender inequality may be universal, the intensity and scope of male dominance and female subordination is relative to time, place, and circumstance. This assertion invariably leads to one of two questions: Are there any matriarchal societies that feature female dominance and male subordination? Most anthropologists would say *no*. To be sure, societies have existed in which individual women were extremely powerful and wielded economic clout, but none where women as a social category held power over men as a social category. Evidence also points to female power in societies where they contributed to the material well-being of society, controlled access to scarce resources, and were organized around female patterns of inheritance (Peoples and Bailey 1994). Second, are there societies in which men and women exist in a state of perfect equality? The simplest answer is that *we don't know*. As Peoples and Bailey observe, what exactly do we mean by perfect equality and how would we recognize total gender equality even if we stumbled across it? Does perfect equality mean everyone is the same or performs identical tasks, or does equality spring from a valuation of differences as legitimate and complementary?

What we *do* know is that most societies are portrayed as male-dominated. Yet male patterns of dominance and privilege are not what they might appear to be. Males are not uniformally or universally dominant although men do seem to possess formal authority and the right to impose sanctions. Recent ethnographic research suggests that women have power (both formal and informal) that they exercise on a daily or a public basis (Nelson 1974). Women also possess some degree of autonomy in the pursuit of personal goals. The scope of female inequality is openly contested since the concept of unequal status may be highly variable and reflect a variety of different factors, from property to reproductive control (Peoples and Bailey 1994). In other words, the key question is not whether or not men are dominant but under what conditions are women likely to experience patterns of inequality.

Different modes of adaptation to the environment may also account for status differences between women and men (Brettell and Sargent 1993). Generally speaking, gender relations in primitive societies were egalitarian — at least in principle if not always in practice. Egalitarian societies were not societies of formal equality, but societies that allowed all members equitable access to basic necessities. Where a distinction needs to be postulated is in separating gender relations between foraging societies (hunting, gathering, and fishing) and those organized around a agricultural-industrial nexus. Gender relations in a stateless, classless society of the hunter-gatherers shifted from an inequality based on social sanctions to one rooted in material grounds — with the domestication of plants and animals (Leacock 1978). Patriarchy emerged as the key ideology: core values revolved around male dominance and female subordination in spite of the unquestioned importance of women in productive and reproductive capacities. The emergence of industrial capitalism with its central state structures and class systems completed what the agricultural revolution had begun (Engels 1973). Formerly egalitarian and complementary relations declined with the emergence of productive private property and its ownership by men (Gailey 1987).

Karl Marx (1951) and Frederick Engels (1972) were among the first theorists to perceive the relationship between **capitalism and gender relations**. According to Marx and Engels, the importance of both women and the kin unit decreased following the growth of the modern state and rise of capitalism. The advent of capitalism concentrated wealth in the hands of a few. Private property and other valuables could be passed on from generation to generation within the family unit. Thus it was thought necessary for the woman to be monogamous in marriage so as to ensure the rightfulness of her heir. With industrialization, moreover, the home ceased to be the unit of production and became primarily a consumption unit. While entire families worked in factories, it was the men who tended to control the production of labour outside the home. The economic dependence of women on men developed in tandem with the social class system. The more women were restricted to labour in the private domain of the home, the lower their status vis-a-vis their male counterparts. Emergence of a patriarchal monogamous family also meant the relegation and restriction of women to roles around the domestic-maternal axis, the separation of private from public realms, and decline in the centrality of kinship groups. Those women who remained part of the working class saw their contribution squeezed into pink collar ghettoes, or deemed expendable in light of their role as a reserve labour force.

SEPARATE DOMAINS: "MAN THE AGGRESSOR/WOMAN THE NURTURER"

Does male privilege stem from the public domain that men occupy versus female monopoly of the private domain? In general, ethnographies have associated men with the privileged domain of politics, decision making and leadership, religious specialization, and economic trade. Women in turn were depicted as occupants of the private and highly maternal-domestic domains of gardening, gathering, childbearing, and hearth nurturing. That distinction, however, cannot account for male privilege or power, especially since women's activities arguably are more important to the survival of the community. Theories have arisen to explain this anomaly, including Sherry Ortner's (1974) widely discussed hypothesis that men = public = culture = superiority, while women = private = nature = inferiority. This line of thinking tends to portray men as the "movers and shakers" in a society, both competitive and aggressive, with the right stuff for the hurly burly of public life. Women by contrast are depicted as passive and peripheral pawns who are best suited for auxillary roles.

How widely applicable is the notion of a dual and separate world of women and men with respect to power or status? Evidence suggests that this dichotomization of the social world is overstated or oversimplified. Such a distinction may reflect an androcentric-Eurocentric interpretation of reality rather than anything inherent in tribal society itself (Leacock 1978). Not only is the concept of public versus private domain subject to scrutiny. A rethinking of first principles confirms that the lives of tribal women are much more complex, variable, and layered than originally envisaged. Rather than passive or peripheral pawns, they are seen as social actors actively involved in the construction, maintenance, and dissolution of reality — at times in tandem with men and other times in direct competition (Lamphere 1993).

ACCOUNTING FOR THE DIFFERENCES THROUGH ANTHROPOLOGICAL FILTERS

No consensus exists as to why this inequitable state of affairs exists or how it evolved. Explanations about male dominance and female subordination have varied in emphasis and scope, with many focused on biological differences due to simple brute strength, male bonding, and male aggressiveness on the one hand, and female maternity dependency and fertility rates, on the other. Many of the theories that endorse an "anatomy as destiny" determinism have been refuted or modified. Biological differences have no uniform or universal application for social roles and relations, but simply establish physical facts that are given meaning by a given culture (see Brettell and Sargent 1993). Besides, a condition that is constant among cultures cannot by itself explain conditions that vary among cultures (Peoples and Bailey 1994). Other theories exist to explain gender inequality, such as symbolic theories related to male public realms and patriarchy (Ortner 1974), and hypotheses related to psychological theories about latent fears and misplaced loyalties. That disagreement persists about the nature, scope, and intensity

of inequality only confirms the difficulty of consensus when dealing with cross-cultural interpretations.

Doubts, of course, linger about the accuracy of early ethnographies. An **androcentric bias** prevailed, at times bordering on openly sexist (Brettell and Sargent 1993). That is, most anthropological works are not sexist in openly asserting the superiority of one gender over another or the rigid allocation of roles and rewards on the basis of sex only. Many, however, are what is called androcentric (a less intentional form of sexism) in that they routinely look at reality from a male perspective. The legitimacy of female perspectives is ignored or rendered irrelevant because of this preoccupation with a "man's world" (Conkey 1993). Nor can we ignore the **Eurocentric bias** in most anthropological research. More often than not gender relations (when anthropologists were allowed to study them or showed any interest in the women's world) were filtered through the European lens related to gender hierarchy, preconceived notions of passive femininity, and primacy of the private/public spheres (Peoples and Bailey 1994). The power and resourcefulness of women were largely underreported by this contingent of largely male anthropologists (Harris 1993). The timing of anthrological research may also have distorted interpretations. Few anthropologist studied societies in their pristine state but in conditions already "contaminated" by European colonization or the indirect penetration of wealth or trade goods. Yet a colonized setting was virtually a precondition for ethnographers to study a given society. Structures and ideologies of colonial domination resulted in the decline of women's status, with generally egalitarian relations replaced by hierarchies and patterns that marginalized women because of a shift in the productive (both factory and cash crop industries), social (urbanization) and cultural (patriarchal) dimensions of society (Leacock 1978; Brettell and Sargent 1993). In other words, anthropologists may have exaggerated the degree of inequality in tribal societies, the separation of private from public domains, or patterns in sexual division of labour. The distribution of power and resources was such that women were not necessarily at

the mercy of men, any more than they were passive robots in the struggle for daily existence (Harris 1993). That line of thinking is consistent with the concept of feminist scholarship and the transformation of contemporary sociology. This assertion, however, asks uncomfortable questions about the data base that social scientists employ to explain human differences and similarities. It also reminds us of Carolyn Nelson's (1974) trenchant assertion that data are not *collected* per se, but *manufactured* and *grounded* in the foundational interaction of the research process.

It is clear that what it means to be male or female is culturally constructed. How we define masculinity or feminity differs across time and cultural space. Relationships between women and men are socially constructed and evolving according to environmental changes. It is also evident that societies usually have public and private domains with the private more or less off limits to the researcher. Inasmuch as the male's contribution may tend to be more visible (public) than that of women's, the latter's status and importance may not be as fully valued and understood. The much vaunted "male domination" may not be as empirically pervasive or as theoretically important as once assumed. At any rate, our interest is not necessarily in cross-cultural perspectives on diversity and gender. It is the variation in gender roles and status due to ethnicity in Canada that concerns us here.

DILEMMAS AND CHALLENGES:
WOMEN ARE A MINORITY, TOO

> Being a Canadian-born Chinese I tried to follow the ways of Canadians. Yet I found it difficult at times because of respect and obedience to my mother.
>
> *Mrs L. as quoted in Nipp in Burnet, 1986.*

Many fall into the trap of approaching minorities as if they represented a distinct and homogeneous category of people. Not only are they tarred with a similar brush; there is also a tendency to portray minorities as if they existed apart from the mainstream. Yet diversity, arguably, *is* the mainstream judging by the demographics in Canadian society. Moreover, many minority needs and concerns may converge with those of so-called mainstream Canadians: That is, racial and ethnic minorities are anxious to put down roots in Canadian society without necessarily foresaking all continuities with the past. They want an end to exploitation and discrimination with respect to employment, housing, education, and delivery of social services. Improved access to the good things in Canadian life is also desired, but without having to endure excessive government interference in the process. And all minorities demand the best for their children without abandoning everything that makes their families distinctive. In short, racial and ethnic minorities are not entirely different from people at large. A respect for basic human rights is foremost, and minorities hold Canada accountable for violation of these rights.

What minority groups want, however, is not what they always receive. Many minorities experience denial or exclusion because of their race or ethnicity, as well as their lower class status. Their lives are constrained by Eurocentrism and the centrality of Anglo-Canadian concerns to the exclusion of others (see Carty 1993). Formidable pressures exist to succeed in their adopted land, even if many are without the language skills or credentials to make an immediate adjustment. Many confront discrimination that stems from racism, class conflict, and ethnic putdown. Women of colour no less than their male counterparts encounter discrimination since their visibility compounds the difficulty of integration. With respect to class, both men and women of colour are usually ghettoized into menial, sometimes dangerous occupations, with low pay and lower chances for promotion. Even highly accredited persons may be forced to accept demeaning labour if they are without the requisite amount of Canadian experience or credentials .

It's obvious that Canada has much to offer minority women. Yet their liking of Canada is tempered by a longing for the language, culture, social patterns, familiarity, and routine from the past (Warren 1986; Philip1992). Nor should we underestimate the shock of cultural adjustment. Newcomers, for example, are handicapped in the job search because of culturally inbred norms of modesty, lack of assertiveness, and refusal to extol one's strengths at length (Tebege 1989). Effective communication is hindered also by customs that tolerate eye contact only between peers. In communicating with those in a higher status position, direct eye contact is avoided as a sign of respect. In our society the job applicant who does not maintain eye contact is dismissed as timid and perhaps untrustworthy. In short, new Canadians "may need to undergo substantial personality change and appreciate values and practices they previously regarded as taboos. They must also develop an attitude of aggressive competitiveness and develop a whole new understanding of work ethics" (Tebege 1986:6). With such pressures, it is not surprising that some individuals give up on the system, preferring instead a street life that may be nasty in outcome, but easier to understand and deal with in the short term.

Both men and women of colour suffer discrimination and drawbacks because of colour, country of origins, racial background, or ethnic traditions. But minority women are doubly disadvantaged as a result of their membership in additional devalued categories. Unlike men, minority women face sexist barriers that arise from their status as women in a predominantly patriarchical society. Their contributions to Canadian society are ignored or trivialized — even to the point of irrelevance. A year after her appointment of as President of the National Action Committee on the Status of Women (NACSW), Sunera Thobani, for example, continues to bear the brunt of accusations as a non-native born woman of colour in a position of authority. Critics have fixated on her ethnicity to the exclusion of other aspects, according to Beverly Bain, Executive Coordinator of NACSW, with the result that anything associated with Ms Thobani is twisted into a race issue (*Kitchener-Waterloo Record*, 27 July 1994).

Sexism and racism combine with social class to account for the social inequities so common in our society. The term "multiple jeopardy" refers to the fact that minorities who are low on more than one hierarchy are subject to additional discriminatory forces. Inclusion in several devalued categories inflates the handicaps. Women of colour in Canada may experience more discrimination on average than either minority group males or white females. Low status penalties are compounded by the forces of race, class, region, and gender. Women of colour, immigrant women, and aboriginal women are disadvantaged not only because of gender, but because of race, class, and ethnicity — not in the mechanical sense of three cumulative forces, but in a complex interplay of process and outcomes (Stasiulis 1990).

GENDER AND ETHNICITY

> Life here is much better for my family. In Canada there is more opportunity...But even with all these things I do not always feel happy in Canada. I feel I am far away from my home. I miss my own language and my own friends. I miss the simple lifestyle of Pula (near Zagreb in the former Yugoslavia), and I miss the freedom. Here, even with my own car, I don't feel as free as I felt in Pula. You see, I don't even speak the same language.
>
> Mary has been in Canada for 17 years. (Warren 1986).

Both **gender and ethnicity** are social constructions. As such they reflect cultural definitions that vary over time. Gender roles are changing with respect to rigid sex-typed occupational choice. Women are gradually gaining admission to the more lucrative non-traditional occupations. The increased representation of women throughout the work force has altered the role of males as "the primary breadwinner." In fact a growing number of men are taking a more active role in parenting and sharing domestic responsibilities. This is not to say that the "double day" (women working both in and outside of the home) has been eliminated or that men share equally in household chores. Likewise prejudice and discrimination as well as tradition continue to act as barriers to career selection.

Ethnicity has the same dynamic effect as gender. The values, attitudes, and beliefs of a particular ethnic group are not cast in stone, but tend to change and adapt with the times. Not only does the ethnicity change with distance from the country of origin, but the host society may be more or less tolerant with time. The exception to this statement are various communal religious sects such as Hutterites, Mennonites, and Doukhobors who pride themselves in their ability to preserve the traditions of the past unscathed by secular change. From this we can conclude a woman's life chances are potentially more favourable when gender and ethnicity are associated with power and prestige. Conversely, opportunities are diminished if gender and ethnicity are socially stigmatized and negatively labelled. Still, in order to determine how ethnicity and gender influence any particular group, we must examine the history, values, attitudes and beliefs of the group in question.

Minority women are subtly, yet profoundly undermined by ethnicity. Put bluntly, women in many ethnic communities are expected to know their place. Actions by women that do not conform with tradition or male values may be criticized as a betrayal to the cause or the community. For appearance's sake, many women of colour are expected to defer to the authority of tradition and community. Such passivity and submissiveness may foster the facade of unity and cohesion; it also inhibits the expression of skills necessary for women to excel in society at large. Assertiveness or freedom can lead to trouble when it interferes with deference to tradition-bound males. As a result, we shall see that women of colour remain the 'hushed-over' victims of violence: This violence results from cultural traditions that (a) endorse male abuse of women, (b) encourage body mutilation as a price of social acceptance, and (c) discourage public disclosure because of family honour.

Tradition may dictate a double duty for women: As well as outside employment, many are expected to maintain responsibility for raising children. That type of dual responsibility comes with its own set of problems: Many children want to become absorbed and accepted as quickly as possible into the mainstream. Their ethnicity is a constant reminder of how different they from the friends and routines they are trying to emulate. Parents, by contrast, may be anxious to impose more conservative, even rigid codes of behaviour, including strict sexual propriety, respect for authority, particular dress styles and appearances, and compliance with tradition. Youth are trapped in a complex balance between culture of the home and the culture of the peers. Some enjoy the challenge of picking and choosing the best of both worlds. Others find it a wearying struggle to reject parental values and authority, while endlessly explaining strange customs and practices to friends.

INSIGHT

Intergenerational Conflict: The Virginity Complex

Value conflict between generations which exists when adolescents are attempting to establish their independence from their parents is intensified if their parents are immigrants or members of an ethnic community which stands apart from the mainstream. The young people may feel cross-pressured. They may have one foot in the immigrant culture of their parents and one foot in the mainstream, but feel they have no solid ground to stand on that they can call their own.

Such marginality is most common in the second generation (Stonequist 1937). Some may resolve the conflict by accepting their parents' values and others may rebel against their parents in favour of the perceived values of their peers. Their children, the third generation, typically do not face as intense loyalty and identity problems as those encountered by the second generation or the first immigrant generation if they came as children.

While both genders may be caught up in inter-generational conflict, it may be particularly acute for young women. The divergence between parental and mainstream values is aptly illustrated by the value cluster referred to as the **virginity complex**. In North America, the expectation that girls will be virginal upon marriage is not as widespread or as strongly adhered to as it was a generation ago. Boys were never harshly judged by this standard which is why it is often referred to as a "double standard" — one set of rules for women and another for men. Not only were men not expected to be "pure" at the time of marriage, it was seen as advantageous for them to have sexual experience and knowledge so that they, in turn, could initiate their innocents wives.

Where were the men to acquire this experience? Women who were their social inferiors, "bad girls" (i.e., girls who did not follow the virginity norms), and professional prostitutes were acceptable targets. Men who made the "mistake" of falling in love with socially undesirable women were forbidden to marry or they would face ostracism from their families. Women, on the other hand, might find themselves exploited by men, perhaps promised a marriage that never occurred. Once a woman's reputation was "ruined," she was relegated to the "bad girl" category from which there was seldom escape. Consequently women were taught to repress their sexuality until the wedding ring was firmly placed on their finger. Meanwhile men, bragging about their own conquests, were expected to slip the ring on a finger of a "good girl"(Kleinman 1978).

Viewed through contemporary eyes, the virginity complex may appear to be a recipe for disaster. It supports a dishonest and exploitative sexuality which is hardly the basis for a sound marriage between equals. Versions of the virginity complex are still rigidly adhered to by Mediterranean area ethnic groups, for example. (Diamond 1989). The honour and respectability of the family, not merely the individual, hinges upon the young women in the family remaining chaste until marriage. Given this orientation, it is easy to see how a young woman in Canada with parents from "the old country" would be very confused. It would be awkward for her to negotiate with her parents such matters as clothing style, hair and make-up, late night hours, choice of friends and acceptable activities. Dating and courtship would be especially problematic if she wished to please both her parents and her boyfriend.

Perhaps anguish reaches its peak when parents seek to arrange a marriage. Parents may attempt to match their children with marriage partners from the "old country" much to the chagrin of the children who want to exercise the North American freedom of mate selection. The potential influence of the parents might extend to such matters as occupational choice and the newlyweds' place of residence. In this way, parental pressure could place an inordinate amount of strain on adolescents of both genders. Personal autonomy tends to be more highly valued in North America than in other cultural areas of the world where the welfare of the family or kin group takes precedence over the wishes or whims of the individual.

In short, ethnicity remains a powerful force for shaping the identities, status, importance, roles, and potential of women of colour, both within the community and in society at large. Women of colour have experiences that differ from their male counterparts. Their needs and aspirations are also different, even if many communities appear willing to sacrifice their women on the alter of expediency — for appearance sake. Minority women must walk a fine line between the past and present, without capitulating to either. Loyalties must be balanced between tradition, with its unique configuration of cultural and religious codes, and an acceptance of Canadian ways, with its own set of laws and customs (Raza 1994). That this balance can be difficult to achieve is illustrated in the box, "Pursuit of Happiness":

VOICES

Pursuit of Happiness

My best friend called me late on Saturday night to tell me she was leaving her husband. It was completely unexpected, but yes, she was definitely leaving him. Her mind was made up— 16 long years of marriage, 4 children— and she was leaving.

"Why? What happened?" I asked on reflex. Something must have happened; why else would she be so resolute. It had to be something devastating.

"Nothing really," she answered, "nothing I can put my finger on."

"Is he having an affair? Is he involved with someone else?" He didn't strike me as the cheating type, but why else would she be leaving?

"No, nothing like that." I was amazed at how calm she sounded.

"Did he beat you up?" I was not prepared yet to accept her dismissive attitude. Women don't end marriages for nothing. She just wasn't leveling.

"It's nothing in particular." She spoke haltingly, weighing every word. "All I know is that I've been very unhappy lately."

"Uhm, I'm listening," I nudged her, waiting for the litanies of abuse, of deprivation. But she said no more. "I just thought you should hear it from me," she added as we said our goodbyes.

I waited two days and called her back. I knew I had to tread very lightly. "Just tell me one thing and I'll leave you alone: Are *you* having an affair?" That wasn't the question I wanted to ask, but it popped out.

"No! Are you crazy? How can you even ask me that?" She laughed out loud. Then sensing my need to come to terms with her news, she said she'd call back after her husband was asleep.

As I waited, I pondered the inquisition our friends would put me through. My friend and I and both our husbands, like a majority of our friends, are Nigerians. While we've lived in the United States for most of our adulthood and for all intents and purposes live like Americans, we identify closely with our traditional Ibo culture. An Ibo woman is born (educated if she is lucky), marries, procreates (a definite must, male children preferably) and dies when her time comes, God rest her soul. Women of our generation, educated and all, are expected to live through our husbands and children as our mothers and grand-mothers did before us.

An Ibo woman has very little personal identity, even if she lives in the United States and has success in her career. Our culture takes very little pride in a woman's accomplishment. At an Ibo gathering a woman is more likely to be asked whose wife or mother she is before she is asked her name or what she does for a living. If the woman is accomplished but unmarried, people will say, "But where is she going with all that success?" Ibos cling to the adage that a woman is worth nothing unless she's married and has children.

I am as guilty as any other Ibo woman living in the United States in perpetuating this. Professionally, I am more successful than the majority of Ibo men I've met in this country, yet when we gather for a party, usually to celebrate a marriage or birth, I join the women in the kitchen to prepare food and serve the men. I remember to curtsy just so before the older men, looking away to avoid meeting their eyes. I glow with pride when other men tease my husband about his "good wife." I often lead the women in the Ibo wedding song: "It is as it should be; give her the keys to her kitchen." At birth ceremonies, I start the chant: "Without a child, what would a woman be?" It is a song my mother sang and one which every Ibo woman knows like her own name.

I know the rules and the consequences of breaking them. Our culture is unforgiving of a stubborn woman. She always gets the maximum punishment—ostracism. "She thinks she's smart; let's see if she can marry herself" is how mistreatment of a non-compliant woman is justified.

To the surprise of my American friends, I've never had difficulty separating my Ibo self from my professional and everyday American life. At work, I'm as assertive as any American-born female. I raise my voice as loud as necessary to be heard in meetings. At conferences where I present papers on "Women From the Third World," I make serious arguments about the need for international intervention in countries where women are deprived of all rights, where women are subjected to clitorectomies, where baby girls are killed to make room for boys. Yet as easily as I switch from speaking English to Ibo, I am content to slide into the role of the submissive and obedient wife. I never confuse my two selves.

Hundreds of thousands of women from the third world and other traditional societies share my experience. We straddle two cultures, cultures that are often in opposition. Mainstream America, the culture we embrace in our professional lives, dictates that we be assertive and independent—like men. Our traditional culture, dictated by religion and years of socialization, demands that we be docile and content in our roles as mothers and wives—careers or not.

But suddenly, my best friend, steeped in the Ibo culture as much as I am, tells me she's leaving her husband—not for any offenses he's committed but because she is unhappy. I think of the question my mother and her mother would ask: "What on earth does she want?" She has everything any woman (Ibo woman, that is) would want: a professional husband (from a good family back home) with a good income, who allows her to pursue her own career; not one, not two, but *three* sons and a daughter; a huge house in the suburbs. And she tells me she's unhappy.

"Whoever told her a woman needs to be happy?" her mother would ask. Everyone knows that the happy part of a marriage is brief. After the first child, she is well on her way to fulfillment. This may sour a little if her first and second babies are girls. Her husband will drop subtle hints that he'll marry someone who can produce a son. But a good Ibo woman devises ways to hold his interest until she produces a son. My friend has three sons, and she's not happy?

"What about the children?" I heard her muffled sobs and sensed her struggle to regain composure. "They'll stay with their father," she said. She has no right to the children. That is the Ibo tradition, American laws or not. A woman departs from her husband's home as she came into it—empty-handed. She must refund the bride price her husband paid—plus interest—and may even have to refund the cost of the master's degree she obtained during their marriage.

My friend knows all that. And now she was going to leave without the chil-

dren she had lived for, her guarantee of protection in her marriage. She had been lucky birthing three sons in a row, delighting her husband, winning praise in our community. Had she not consoled me when my first child was born female? "Don't worry, the next one will be a boy; you'll see." And when my second child was born male, had my friend not screamed louder than I with joy? Why would she now walk away from the secure future she had earned?

"How can you do this to yourself?" I lost all control. "Have you gone mad?"

"I need to try to find happiness. I really thought that you, of all people, would understand," she said coldly, hanging up before I could reply.

Later, I realized what was going on with my friend. She thinks herself American. She has bought into America's concept of womanhood — personal satisfaction no matter the cost. I wonder if she knows what she's getting into.

SOURCE: DympnaUgwu-Oju

GENDER AND CLASS

Minority males experience discrimination because of race and/or class. Both personal and systemic types of racism are pervasive, while class inequalities often compound their marginal status in society. Immigrant and minority women are also engulfed by discriminatory forces that reflect race and class. The average weekly wage of visible minority women is markedly less than non-visible minority women according to a 1986 study of females between the ages of 25 and 55 who lived in Census Metropolitan Areas of Toronto, Montreal, and Vancouver (Boyd 1995). Studies in United States also confirm that minority women not only receive less income than male counterparts, but also are excluded from most high paying occupations (Aguirre Jr. and Turner 1995). Women also face an additional type of gender-related discrimination that further jeopardizes their capacity for success in Canadian society. Gender dimensions of discrimination suggests problems confronted by women are different from those of men (King 1988). Instead, immigrant and minority women are victimized by a series of jeopardies, both distinctive yet powerful in controlling destinies.

A number of studies including the "Doubly Disadvantaged: The Women Who Immigrate to Canada" and the "Report of the Ontario Task Force on Immigration and Women" have documented many of the barriers confronting women in making an adjustment to Canadian society. These include isolation, racial prejudice, and employment related difficulties (Goudar 1989). Immigrant and minority women are often relegated to menial jobs for which they are overqualified. They are sometimes exploited by unscrupulous employers who capitalize on their unfamiliarity with Canadian laws to take advantage of them. Like many other working women, they are caught between the sometimes competing pressures of home and workplace. As well, immigrant and refugee women from Third World countries must cope with cultural shock when arriving in Canada. Much of their early socialization with its premium on passivity or submissiveness, puts many at a disadvantage when communicating with others or when competing in the job market.

Women of colour, especially black women, were historically segregated into jobs such as domestic servants or positions deemed either unsafe or unsuitable for white women — a situation further cemented when white women became employed in outside wage labour (Carty 1993). Their marginal status is further perpetuated by difficulties in obtaining training or access to second language learning. The exploitation of immigrant and ethnic minority women working as domestics under the Domestic Worker's Scheme in Canada underscores the intersection of race, class, and gender. In **1955**, the Canadian government instituted the **Domestic Scheme** (Henry 1968). Young, single female workers from the Caribbean would contract to come to Canada as live-in domestics. They were deemed to be landed immigrants and free to seek work in another field after a year's service as a domestic. The Domestic Scheme was not without problems but it was more humane than the policy that replaced it. Currently, domestics enter Canada with "temporary employment visas"; they are not landed immigrants and as such they are subject to deportation if they violate the terms of their visa. Many of them are virtually treated as slaves in the affluent homes where they reside (Silvera 1983). While Employment and Immigration has established minimum standards and guidelines for their living and working conditions, individual households tend to unilaterally set their own. Government regulations are rarely enforced. The temporary employment visas for domestic workers provide the conditions under which unscrupulous employers (often wealthy white women) exploit poor women (often black women). The situation illustrates exploitation within gender — rich women profiting from the "cheap labour" of poor women (Hurtado 1989).

Taken as a whole, immigrant women have had more trouble than immigrant men in gaining access to social services and programs for settlement and adaptation. Many are reluctant to accept outside assistance or to turn to formal authorities for fear of physical reprisals or social ostracism for the shame and dishonour inflicted on the family or community. Even the government may collaborate in the marginalization, however inadvertently this may be. It has been a usual policy of the federal department of Employment and Immigration to offer language training only to those immigrants who are destined for the paid labour force. More women (50%) than men (39%) come to Canada under the provisions of the "family class" category as opposed to "independent workers." These immigrant women typically have been denied access to language training (Ng 1988; Boyd 1993). Many of these "family class" women do in fact work outside the home. Lack of fluency in either official language makes them targets for further discrimination in the workplace. This lack of access to language training condemns many to menial, non-unionized, low wage employment with few prospects for advancement.

INSIGHT

Language Training Programs: A Case of Gender Discrimination

The category of immigrant and minority women is not homogeneous, but reflects considerable internal variation in terms of problems, needs, concerns, aspirations, and solutions. This is evident with respect to the status of immigrant women and their relationship with society as a whole. In addition, immigrant women face problems over and above those experienced by immigrant men. A recent case highlights the dilemmas which confront immigrant women.

Two immigrant women with the assistance of the Womens Legal Education and Action Committee (LEAF) have taken the Canadian Employment and Immigrant Commission to the Supreme Court for violation of their rights under the equality provisions of the Charter of Rights and Freedoms. According to the women and legal representatives from LEAF, the Commission's language training program which was subsidized for six months discriminates against women. It is a policy of Employment and Immigration not to offer language training when the immigrant worker's job does not require knowledge of French or English. While males are routinely accepted as "labour destined persons" who need English for employment, women are often turned down because English (in service as well as garment and textile industries) is perceived as superfluous to the job — although Settlement Language Programs provide basic coping language skills for persons not destined for the non-domestic job market. Arguing for the necessity of English as a second language for full societal participation, this exclusion has the effect of freezing immigrant women from the mainstream. Not knowing the language of the host country hinders the attainment of any employment outside of domestic, service, or productive industries; it also depresses both wages and levels of involvement in the labour market — especially when knowledge of the host language is critical for completion of the task (Boyd 1993). The role of language as social or human capital is further enhanced as a basis for obtaining information about services and benefits that are available.

In fairness to the Commission, they point out that nearly half the language trainees are women and that the amount spent on language training currently stands at $60 million — a considerable increase from the $38 million in 1983. Nevertheless, this is regarded as insufficient for meeting the special — and catch-up — needs of immigrant women.

A gender segregated labour force entrenches the problems of immigrant women. They share with all women economic discrimination in the market place. A recent study by two University of Guelph economic professors has underscored the wage rift (*Kitchener-Waterloo Record*, 20 June 1994). Professors Robert Swidinsky and Louis Christofides compared the wages of 28,000 Canadians using 1989 Statistics Canada data. They found that the average hourly wage for white males was $14.73; for visible minority men, $12.48; for white women, $11.33; and for women of colour, $10.97. The authors concluded that the wage-gap differences could be attributed in part to productivity factors (differences in experience, length of continuous employment, marital status, and education). Much of the discrepancy, they concluded, was due to discrimination by employers. Even highly educated women of colour were payed differently and relegated to domestic or service work, despite similar levels of education — if they received their degrees overseas.

To sum up. Women across Canada share a common set of problems related to poverty and powerlessness. These disadvantages arise from their status as aboriginal, visible, and ethnic minority women who must deal with the pressures of race and ethnicity in addition to those of class. As well as labour exploitation and racial slurs, they must cope with sexism which may exist within as well as outside their cultural group. Nor should we assume that immigrant and minority women constitute a single identifiable category with similar outlooks, needs, or aspirations. Noticeable differences can be found. Many aboriginal women occupy a distinct legal status which imposes a different set of constraints than those faced by non-aboriginal women. Visible minority women are equally handicapped by race and class although their problems may differ in degree and scope from majority group women. These disadvantages are not simply cumulative, but involve interdependent systems of control that multiply and compound the forces of domination and exploitation (King 1988). Triply disadvantaged, minority women face a series of seemingly insurmountable problems as part of their overall experience in dealing with the realities of a racist, classist, and sexist society.

GENDER AND VIOLENCE

Violence against women and children is a recurrent refrain in our society. While domestic abuse cuts across all racial and ethnic boundaries, women of colour compared to white women are confronted by additional burdens. Within certain ethnotraditions, the very concept of spousal violence may not be culturally coded as a social problem, let alone a criminal offence punishable by law. Pressure may be exerted on mothers and daughters to submit to violence as part of her duty; Resistance is one thing, but women are discouraged from going public for fear of dishonoring the family name or discrediting the community. Central authorities are rarely or reluctantly contacted in cases of violence. Such a person risks being stigmatized as a troublemaker; she may also be socially ostracized by friends or family for involving outside authorities, many of whom are perceived as hostile to minorities in cases of personal abuse (Raza 1994).

In short, minority women find themselves in an uncompromising position. Violence may be part of their lives, partly because of cultural traditions, and partly because of enraged husbands who are reluctant to share what little privilege or power they possess in the new country. Yet these same women have little in the way of recourse that will not bring them into disrepute. In this section, the discussion of violence will be focused around the death of Helen Betty Osborn.

INSIGHT

Justice Denied

Racism is something most minority women confront as part of their lives. When violence is combined with racism and sexism, it produces an especially lethal result. A tragic Canadian example which illustrates this point concerns the case of the young Cree woman, Helen Betty Osborne.

In 1971, a nineteen-year-old high school student, Helen Betty Osborne was kidnapped from the main street of Le Pas, Manitoba, and forced to enter a car with four young white men. When she refused their sexual demands, she was brutally stabbed to death. In the community at the time of the crime, it was an acknowledged practice for white men to harass and sexually assault native women. The practice was called "squaw-hopping." By applying this derogatory label to the behaviour, the men distanced themselves from the immoral and criminal activity. In effect, they were not with women but with "squaws." Although the townspeople in the community were aware of the identity of the four men, it was sixteen years before a trial took place. The jury consisted of ten men and two women; there were no natives on the jury. One man was convicted of second degree murder and sentenced to life imprisonment. A second man was acquitted, a third granted immunity, and a fourth never charged. The response of the chief of the Pas Indian Band, Oscar Lathlin, summed up the feelings of the native community, "I'm disgusted that three of the four got away..." (Priest 1989). The outcome of the trial and the circumstances preceding it were responsible in large measure for the 1989 Public Inquiry into the Administration of Justice and Aboriginal People. The inquiry was mandated to call witnesses in an attempt to determine whether the police, courts, and jails discriminate against aboriginal peoples. As with the Donald Marshall case in which another aboriginal person was wrongly accused of murder and imprisoned, the combination of race and class can lead to arrested justice. The injustices are perpetuated further when the element of gender is added.

In addition to overt acts of aggression, hatred and violence is reflected in racist terminology such as calling a woman a "squaw." This permits behaviour to take place which otherwise would not be condoned if it involved sisters, daughters, wives, or girl friends. A similar sort of psychological mind game is employed in time of war. We are able to kill the enemy once they have been demonized or dehumanized. Bombs do not kill humans but rather de-humanized types such as "gooks," "Japs," and "Krauts." Sexism along with race and class is thus a social process which reinforces exploitation of the weaker by the stronger.

MULTIPLE JEOPARDIES

At this point, it is difficult — if not unwise — to determine which of these handicaps is foremost in the lives of minority women— race, ethnicity, class, or gender. Does racism or sexism have a more powerful impact in shaping the lives of minority women? Are minority women more likely to be victims of discrimination because of gender or ethnicity? To what extent is working class status the culprit? While answers are not readily forthcoming, one can assume that each of these factors is important in its own right. Each not only remains a primary organizing principle in social relations, but also provides a basis for interaction with the world at large. We can also assert that the interplay of these dimensions not only mutually reinforce the effects of the others; a hierarchy of overlapping oppressions sometimes known as **multiple jeopardies** is also created. The following case study highlights this interplay of challenges that confront women of colour in Canada.

VOICES

Caribbean Women, Canadian Experience

There are many obstacles to achieving equality in the Canadian society for the Caribbean immigrant women. The two most prominent obstacles are the attitudes of some white Canadians, and some members of the Caribbean community both male and female. Unless the reasons behind these attitudes are understood, improvements and changes will be long in coming.

Most people dislike social change that immigrants create. These feelings occur because people in general fear that immigrants will not be able to cope successfully with the changes in culture and values of a new society. Some people also fear that immigrants may bring about changes to culture and norms of the society of their adopted country. Fear is common to humankind; different racial groups react similarly. Some whites as well as some blacks tend to oppose equality for black women — the whites because they fear that it threatens their privileged status, the blacks because of insecurities and conflict of interest. These fears and insecurities impact heavily on some Caribbean women.

Most Caribbean people love to travel. In my opinion it is because they have inherited the frontier and pioneering mentality from their ancestors who have travelled from various parts of the world to settle in the Carribean. It is said that, "their lives are portraits in movement." This quality manifests itself in their culture, which symbolizes movement by its enchanting music, dance, sports and rhythmic language. Thus, it is no surprise that migration is common among people from the Caribbean, who have been aptly described as "go-getters."

Between the early sixties and mid seventies there was an influx of immigrants from the Caribbean to Canada. They came in both genders and from all socio-economic strata. There were nurses, engineers, doctors, dentists, clerical workers, teachers, domestics, and short term migrant farm workers. Then in 1980, because of the fear of Jamaican Prime Minister Manley's version of socialism, there was a mass exodus of professional and business people from Jamaica to Canada. This scenerio best illustrates the "push" and "pull" factors in immigration — the "push" because of the political situation in Jamaica, the "pull" towards a stable lifestyle in Canada.

In no group were the "push" and "pull" factors more strongly felt than in that of Caribbean women. Caribbean women are an ambitious, industrious, and adventurous lot, who are always striving for a better lifestyle for themselves and their children. Their decisions to immigrate were often made with deep anguish; however, they were certain that they had no alternative if they wanted to improve their own and their children's lives. Consequently, many of them immigrated, some to join spouses already setled here, others coming independently, leaving spouses behind. But in most cases they left children behind with relatives — often grandparents.

Once in Canada these women found themselves in a strange, cold, and often hostile environment. The friendly white faces they saw in the Caribbean were now almost non-existent. They often encountered hostility, racial stereotyping, bias, discrimination, and prejudice in employment, education and housing. Sometimes there was even an overt anti-foreigner attitude which continues to come across today in a vicious backlash in Canada's national politics.

To many of these women Canada presents a contradiction in attitudes: on one hand they are welcome to low paying, low status jobs no one else wants, but on the other hand they are accused of taking away jobs from working class Canadian women. They are often bewildered by this attitude since many of them earn low wages, have poor working conditions, little work stability, and little or no chance for advancement. They perceive themselves as paying an exorbitant price to be members of Canadian society. Since many of them were teachers and clerical workers in their home countries, they feel cheated of the promise of a better lifestyle as they try to eke out a living working at jobs which are below the level of their social strata and educational qualifications.

Many of them have made the transition into the Canadian society successfully and are working as teachers, nurses, or office managers. Still, many others are relegated to jobs in service industries such as domestics, nannies, hospital aides, beauticians, and seamstresses in garment factories. These women realize their predicament as they try to adapt physically to the climate and housing, as well as psychologically adapt to a new social environment — different habits, social life, and social structure. They now find themselves in a society where gender, race, and class are deeply embedded in the structure and relationships among people. Their's is a double jeopardy — they are "black women."

Gender and race have made a significant impact on their lives. They are female as well as a racial minority. Like many other females, a large number of them are at the lower end of the income scale. In addition, many of them are single mothers and heads of their households. They are cut off from the support system they had in the Caribbean. Many of them have no friends, and they experience enormous stress and anxiety as they try to integrate in a new and different society on their own. They feel inadequate, homesick, depressed, hopeless, and helpless as they face the new reality. To combat these bad feelings most of them work relentlessly to amass money so that they can be reunited with the family they left behind. Others work to send remittance "back home" to support the children they left behind, until they are established and able to provide a home for them in Canada. Ironically some of their first jobs in Canada are looking after other women's children.

Those who are unattached work to buy houses here in Canada, or build their retirement homes back in the Caribbean. Notwithstanding the odds, they all stay and brave the cold, hostile physical and sometimes emotional environment — because they have no choice. The economic conditions are bet-

ter here in Canada than they are in the Caribbean. So, they amass physical goods to compensate for and to fulfill emotional needs.

There are many adjustment problems encountered by the Caribbean women and their children when they are reunited after the long separation. On arriving in Canada, the children must learn to adapt to the climate as well as a new and different culture. Sometimes the mothers are unable to assist them because they have not yet adjusted to the new culture either or because there is a cultural difference between mother and child. This difference could be at a generational or gender level, where mother and child are not sharing similar situational experiences, and so they have no common ground.

If the children are of school age, they attend school where most likely there are few peers with similar backgrounds with whom they can associate. They have to cope with a new education system which is biased against them, and peers who are prejudiced and sometimes hostile. They often find it difficult to understand their teachers and peers when they speak, and are frequently teased about their Caribbean accents. They desperately try to hide their differences by losing their accents and casting off any affiliation with the Caribbean as they come face to face with an identity crisis and culture shock. However, they cannot hide their physical characteristics.

As the chidren lose their Caribbean identities and assimilate, mothers and children become more and more estranged. Mothers try desperately and sometimes futilely to keep the culture alive in their children. The harder they try the more alienated their children become. This results in the mothers feeling disappointed, betrayed, and hated by their children. They perceive that their hard work and sacrifices were made in vain for children who have proven ungrateful. This creates conflict, tension, and stress in the household.

To compound their stress most Caribbean immigrant women worry about career opportunities for themselves as well as their chidren. Most working class Caribbean women are upset and humiliated by their own status. They see themselves as being exploited in the labour market, and do not want their children to become exploitable labour for the future. The professional women find many barriers and obstacles placed in their way toward upward mobility. There are hardly any black Headmistresses in the school system, black Members of Parliament, or nursing administrators, and only a handful of black women have advanced to lower and middle management in business. The working class women realize that at their socio-economic level they will not be able to finance postsecondary education for their children. They come to accept that the Canadian dream is "but a dream" for black women.

Caribbean immigrant children arriving in Canada are confronted with many shocking realities. While back in the Caribbean they thought that their mothers were wealthy and lived opulent and easy lives. In one mother's words: "They think money grows on trees here." Upon arrival, they quickly learn that blacks in general are denied acceptance and economic opportunities in their adopted country, and also that their mothers work long and hard just to make ends meet. Consequently, they

too feel cheated. They develop a sense of hopelessness which turns into rebellion against their mothers as well as the Canadian norms. Some of them become delinquents, join youth gangs, and engage in many anti-social activities. The failed dreams and hopes for their children are sources of great distress and anguish for Caribbean women.

Many Caribbean women are happily married and enjoy gratifying and fulfilling relationships with their Caribbean husbands. Nevertheless, a number of Caribbean women have little relationship with men. When they do, it is generally sexual in nature. Many of them are afraid to have relationships with Caribbean men whom they regard as unfaithful, fickle, and exploitative. Some of them feel this way from personal experiences: They have sponsored lovers and fiances, who have left them as soon as they established themselves in Canada.

It is extremely difficult for professional Caribbean women to find suitable unmarried partners of their peer among Caribbean men. Therefore, many of them are unmarried or have affairs with married men who are their professional peers. Frequently these women bear children for these men rather than establish relationships with other partners they deem "unsuitable," because they are not as educated, refined, and sophisticated as the women are.

Caribbean women who left spouses back home are eventually joined by them. These reunions are not always happy. They are sometimes the source of great disappointment and unhappiness because of the stress and strain that the adjustments place on the marriage. The Caribbean male has difficulty adjusting to the change in climate, lifestyle, and norms of the Canadian society. In the patriarchal Caribbean society male and female have the traditional sex roles. Thus, Caribbean men become confused when faced with the more egalitarian nature of sex roles in Canada. In one man's words: "Women in this country don't know their place, because they have too many rights."

Moreover, many of these men are torn between enforcing their traditional roles and losing their spouses, or conforming and losing face before their peers. To their male friends they have to appear to be in control of their households; if not, they run the risk of losing their respect and being teased that "their wives wear the pants in their families." Therefore, to save face, they live by the roles of the "old country." They refuse, or are reluctant to do household chores, to grocery shop, or participate in child rearing activities. As a result, enormous stress is placed on the women who have the double responsibilities of full time jobs in and outside the home.

Some Caribbean men feel out of control and inadequate in Canada, as they encounter racism, prejudice, stereotyping, and discrimination. Their self esteem becomes very low. More than anything else they want to feel in control and respected. To compensate for their lack of control outside the home they attempt to exercise control inside the home. Their families become their objects of control. This control extends not only to wives, but to children as well. Children growing up in Canada are not always as respectful as they are in the Caribbean, so they sometimes defy their fathers. This presents a source of great displeasure to the fathers who experience feelings of humiliation and disrespect. Hence, in a family scenario these men are constantly in situations where these feelings surface.

Some feel so threatened that they batter their wives and children in vain attempts to reassert their authority and masculinity and gain control of the family. These beatings are frequently not reported to the police. According to one source: "Caribbean women do not like to air their dirty laundry in public." This violent behaviour creates animosity, frustration, resentment and discontent in the family relationship. This behaviour is a double-edge sword: instead of gaining for these men the respect they so badly crave, it ends up costing them the love, trust, and respect of their families.

Caribbean men may become so disillusioned they leave their wives and children and go back home. Others experience impotence with their wives because of their inability to cope with their problems at home. Many leave the marriage to pursue extra marital relationships, sometimes with younger women in order to prove their virility. This most often compounds their problems, since they lack the financial resources to support two homes. As a result, they abdicate their responsibilities to their wives and children, and relegate them to a life of poverty. Others turn to women of different racial groups as a panacea for what ails them.

One major problem for the Caribbean immigrant woman is that Caribbean women are separated along the lines of length of residency in Canada, education, and socio-economic strata. They do not perceive themselves as sharing many common goals and interests. The established female immigrant sometimes looks unfavourably on the new arrivals and refers to them as "J J C" or "Jane Just Come," which is a term of disdain and derision. She has assimilated in the Canadian society, amassed some personal belongings. Therefore, she sees the new arrival as a constant reminder of her past, one of which she is no longer very proud and which she would like to forget. She makes no effort to get close to her, to point out pitfalls, explain or interpret the ways of life in the new country to help her to adapt. She keeps her distance, avoids all contacts, and behaves outwardly as if she was born in Canada and does not share a common cultural ancestry.

Friendships between the educated and uneducated are virtually non-existent. The educated woman finds the other ignorant, crude, and unsophisticated, someone with whom she has nothing in common apart from the colour of her skin. Although many professional Caribbean females immigrated to Canada, the majority of them came as domestics and went back to colleges and universities to acquire professional qualifications. Having worked so hard to get where they are, they are not sympathetic and responsive to the needs of women who did not bother to upgrade themselves or to "pull themselves up by the bootstrap." They see the working class women as lazy and unambitious, and therefore unworthy of their friend-

shp. The now professional women feel themselves to be "better" than the others are, because they have taken the time to improve themselves.

If some Caribbean men and women would only take the time to get together and relate they would discover common ground. They would realize that they are not each other's enemy, but that they have a common enemy: racism. If they could put aside their negative attitudes about gender and class and present a united front they could challenge the real enemy and work towards gaining equality for themselves and their children.

Finally, to address the present inequalities and difficulties of the Caribbean women, awareness of racial, gender, and class imbalance in the Canadian society is key. Only when Canadian society becomes aware of the inequalities can it work to make gender, race, and class irrelevant. Only when society questions its own notions of "better than" or "best" can people be fairly equated.

Hopefully, with knowledge and increased awareness of the plight of Caribbean women, attitudes and perceptions among white Canadians as well as members of the Caribbean community will change. Old barriers will start to go down, and new doors will open. Then, and only then will Caribbean women gain their equal and rightful place in the Canadian mosaic.

SOURCE: Marita Williams

COPING WITH GENDERED INEQUALITY

How do individuals react to the impact of gender and ethnicity on their lives? The response may be collective or individual. If collective, the individual aligns with others for the sake of a common cause. If the response is individualistic, a personal adjustment is sought. The role of the state in support of the individual is also a critical concern.

Collective Action

Individuals confronted with ethnic or gender discrimination may resort to collective action in an attempt to alleviate their predicament. Union activity is a classic example of collective action. For example, unions have taken up the struggle against sexual harassment in the workplace. At other times, legal recourse is sought through the various Human Rights Commissions in Canada. A woman's lobby group in Montreal, Action Travail des Femmes, using federal human rights legislation won its 1984 sex discrimination case against Canadian National Railways. A human rights tribunal found that the company had discriminated against women in its hiring practices. The company was ordered to increase to 13 percent the proportion of women working in non-traditional occupations in the St. Lawrence region (Pentney 1987). The CN case is significant because it occurred a year before the equal rights section of the Charter of Rights and Freedoms went into effect. It was the first time that hiring goals were specified in an affirmative action decision.

In the past decade the women's movement has sought to weld together divisions in its ranks caused by class, ethnicity, race, and sexual orientation. Considering the diversity of interests, ambitions, and backgrounds, we might expect the presence of conflicting interests and internal dissention. Yet the effectiveness of the movement depends upon their ability to put aside differences for the common cause of gender equity. Many women have not developed the collective consciousness necessary for sustained action. In addition to social factions within the movement, some women have not identified with the movement and do not espouse its cause. Other women such as the REAL Women organization are opposed to liberal feminism, especially lesbian feminists. Equally significant, some immigrant and minority women have rejected the women's movement as too white and too middle class. Issues of abortion on demand and universal child care services are not necessarily the concerns of immigrant women whose concerns focus on housing, employment, and discrimination. Many feminist groups have also been accused of fostering racism against "women of colour" by failing to confront ethnocentrism and bias within their ranks (Davis 1989; Thobani 1994). Lastly, both aboriginal and minority women run the risk of appearing "disloyal" to their male counterparts if they ally themselves with white feminist organizations (Joseph and Lewis 1986).

In short, women are not uniformly oppressed, as many believe, but possess contradictory interests that intersect along the lines of race, ethnicity, or class (Khayatt 1994). Even the expression "minority women" conceals fundamental differences in experience and life chances; it also fails to disentangle the different levels of oppression or resistance through class struggles. Rather than embracing those most marginalized in society or making a commitment to inclusiveness and diversity in general, women who have made the largest gains continue to exclude the voices and aspirations of those most silenced. It remains to be seen whether NACSW will respond to the charge of white domination by feminists of colour (*Ottawa Citizen*, 3 June 1993).

In response, immigrant and minority women have turned to alternate organizations whose goals and interests reflect their triple jeopardies. Nevertheless, co-operation continues to exist. The most noteworthy illustration of collaboration between the mainstream movement and aborignal women concerns the latter's struggle for equity with aboriginal men over such issues as who is and who isn't a status Indian. Native women were losing their status when they married non-natives, but this was not the case when native men married non-native women. First Nation women struggled to correct this inequity through support from such diverse groups as churches, women, and the United Nations (Weaver 1983).

Individual Coping Mechanisms

For the most part, the socialization of gender relations works quite smoothly. But when mistakes occur in gender scripting, a variety of individual coping mechanisms might be employed. Disguised identity, a phenomenon known as **passing** has been a ploy used by women and minority ethnic individuals. By disguising personal identity, one passes for a higher status gender or ethnic group. A change in name is commonly accepted among ethnic minority individuals to facilitate movement into a higher status ethnic group. The most drastic attempt to pass, or become more acceptable to a higher status group, involves alteration of one's physical appearance. For example, Jewish women have resorted to facial surgery in order to better conform to mainstream notions of beauty (Medjuck 1988). Similarly, before the Civil Rights Movement of the 1960s, black Americans would attempt to straighten their hair and lighten their skin. The slogan of the movement, "Black is beautiful," was an attempt to counter these negative self-attitudes.

What are the costs and benefits of passing? By successfully passing one hopes to reduce the penalties of minority status while securing the rewards associated with majority status. Such benefits are not always without costs. The psycho-social dynamics of passing tend to be associated with low self-esteem and self-hate. In other words, the motivation underlying passing tends to be dissatisfaction with oneself as well as with one's group. While the passer may solve one set of personal problems by passing, he or she must then cope with feelings of self-contempt and loathing. These guilt feelings stem from the fact that one knowingly has rejected a link with the past (Simpson and Yinger 1972).

Individual strategies for coping differ, depending on whether the source of the prejudice and discrimination stems from within either the ethnic group or the larger society. For example, if a Muslim woman is discontented because of the seclusion code which requires her to wear a veil and limits her behaviour in a variety of ways, she can renounce her religion and assimilate into the mainstream non-Muslim culture. Such a decision is never taken lightly. Shedding one's identity with the intent to develop another is a long-term process fraught with difficulty and second-guessing. In the intermediate stages the individual may experience confusion, self-doubt, and uncertainty.

For those unable to cope with discrimination, the result may be depression and addiction. It is no accident that prostitutes, drug addicts, and prisoners are disproportionately drawn from minority ethnic and racial backgrounds. The pressures of everyday life weigh more heavily on the economically impoverished who in Canada are overwhelmingly represented by women and children. When poverty is coupled with prejudice and discrimination, it is not surprising that personal break-downs and various self-destructive behaviours like addiction and prostitution occur.

State Reform

Ultimately, gender and race and ethnic relations are not an individual matter but ones which involves the state. How effectively has the Canadian state responded to the plight of individuals victimized by race and gender? The legal framework for gender and race and ethnic relations includes many components ranging from constitutional guarantees, federal and provincial statutes, policies and programs. In 1947, Saskatchewan was the first province to enact a comprehensive Bill of Rights. The first Human Rights Commission was created in Ontario in 1962. It was responsible for the enforcement of anti-discrimination legislation. Such Commissions were commonplace in all provinces and in the federal government by 1977. The grounds of prohibited discrimination expanded from the original ones of race and religion to cover such areas as sex and marital status (Flanagan 1985).

The **Charter of Rights and Freedoms** was heralded as an advance over human rights codes. Unlike parliamentary statutes (of which Human Rights codes are an example), Charter provisions are constitionally entrenched and cannot be easily repealed. Still, in 1983 the Social Credit government in British Columbia threatened to repeal the B.C. human rights codes and abolish the commission (Gonick 1987). Gender and race and ethnic relations are addressed in the Charter in the context of "fundamental freedoms" (s. 2), and especially Sections 15, 27, and 28. Section 15(1) provides for "equal protection...without discrimination...based on...sex," while s. 15(2) provides for what are often referred to as affirmative action programs; s. 27 provides that the Charter shall be interpreted in a manner "consistent with the preservation and enhancement of the multicultural heritage of Canadians." S. 28 states that Charter rights and freedoms are guaranteed equally to both sexes.

Employment Equity policies are permitted by the Charter in s. 15(2) and were enacted in the 1986 federal Employment Equity Act. They may have little effect on the vast majority of aboriginal, immigrant or poor women in general. Employment Equity programs do not articulate class based inequities with those based on gender, race, and ethnicity. Nor do they typically reach down to the lower rungs of the occupational structure where poor women are clustered (Sowell 1989). Since 1988, companies employing over 100 people under federal jurisdiction have been compelled to file yearly reports on the number of women, natives, disabled, and visible minority members they employ and information on their occupation and salary levels. Nothing in the legislation requires the companies to improve; there are no goals or timetables. The removal of barriers is voluntary. Without "teeth," one can not expect social change to occur in the wake of the Employment Equity Act.

In conclusion: the law embodies a set of ideals to which our society aspires. The legal underpinnings of gender and race and ethnic relations grow and expand in direct relation to initiatives from individuals and groups. The failure of our laws to accommodate aspirations may lead to frustration, despair and extra-legal action. To date those in our society struggling for gender equity, minority rights, and aboriginal self-determination have worked through legal channels. It is encumbent upon the larger society to continue to respond with a generous spirit to such initiatives.

CHAPTER HIGHLIGHTS

- This chapter on gender and ethnicity has built on the previous material which dealt with issues of race and class. Each chapter is concerned with the effects of race, ethnicity, class, and gender in shaping the lives and life chances of Canada's diverse populations.

- Gender and race interact regularly and cumulatively to create "gender stratification" — a kind of social hierarchy in which men as a group dominate women as a group not only in terms of power and resources ("patriarchy") but also by way of assessment and priority ("androcentrism").

- Immigrant and minority women confront many problems that also hinder men of colour. Women of colour also face additional obstacles as a consequence of gender-related discrimination.

- These additional hardships are termed "multiple jeopardies," and their analysis provides a glimpse into the pressures and demands encountered by women in coping with everyday reality.

- The concept "gendered relations" draws attention to the realities of minority women's lives and experiences as they are defined and controlled by the forces of race, ethnicity, and class.

- The notion of gendered relations is a social construction, ie., the status and role of women, and their relationship to male status and roles vary from time, and place, and circumstance.

- The section on gender and ethnicity clearly reveals the contradictory pressures that confront women of colour and immigrant women. Traditional values and relationships appear to collide with mainstream equivalents. This ambiguity creates additional barriers for minority women in their drive to full and equal participation in society.

- The fact that women of colour as a group are exploited in Canadian society is explored. On too many occasions, minority women are subject to discrimination in the workplace, denied access to skills and language training, vulnerable to pressures from employers and the ethnic community, and relegated to double duty as wives and mothers.

- Women of all colours continue to be victims of male violence. The magnitude and scope of this violence within minority communities is unknown, but evidence suggests that this has more to do with ethno-community politics rather than amiable gender relations. Not only are minority women victimized by husbands, but they are also denied recourse to proper authorities.

- There are several options open for women of colour in pursuing gender equity. Personal and collective strategies may be employed, some of which are more successful than others. Women of colour can also look to the Canadian state, especially the Charter of Rights, as a possible source of grievance resolution.

KEY TERMS

Androcentric Bias
Capitalism and Gender
  Relations
Charter of Rights and
  Freedoms
Domestic Scheme, 1955

Eurocentric Bias
Gender and Ethnicity
Gender Scripts
Gender versus Sex

Multiple jeopardy

"Passing"
The "Virginity Complex"

REVIEW QUESTIONS

1) Describe the nature of the relationship between sex (biology) and gender (culture).

2) Comment on the relationship between gender and ethnicity as it affects women of colour, immigrant women, and aboriginal women.

3) What problems do immigrant and minority women encounter in Canadian society? How have they tried to cope with these experiences?

4) How is the problem of gender and violence compounded in some minority contexts?

5) What is the role of the state in reducing gender prejudice and discrimination?

6) Describe some of the problems and challenges confronted by Caribbean-Canadian women in terms of coping with the demands of Canadian society.

THE ETHNIC EXPERIENCE

CASE STUDY

Ethnic Strife: Power Politics or Tribalism?

Rwanda is a small African country with a population of about 8 million, most of whom are subsistence farmers whose average personal income is about $350 per year (Canada's per capita income is about $22,000 per annum), making it one of the poorest countries in the world. It is also one of the most densely populated at 304 people per square kilometre. Two tribes predominate: the Hutu comprise about 85 percent of the population; the Tutsi most of the remainder. The fact that the numerically smaller Tutsi have historically dominated Rwanda's politics and economy creates a climate conducive to interethnic strife. To what extent are the conflicts in Rwanda (and elsewhere) the result of pent-up ethnic hatred, or is ethnicity a convenient label to justify power struggles between groups?

THE TURMOIL

Two decades of relative political tranquility came to end in 1990 when Rwanda was plunged into civil turmoil. The country was "invaded" by the Rwandan Patriotic Front, a force of about 10,000 guerillas/refugees predominantly from the outnumbered but politically powerful Tutsi. Prior to Rwandan independence from Belgium in 1962, the quality of Tutsi-Hutu relations had fluctuated over time and from place to place. A Hutu-driven rebellion ended Tutsi domination, with thousands fleeing to safety in neighboring countries. A military coup in 1973 resulted in further bloodshed, followed by yet another massive exodus of Tutsi. The Patriotic Front invaders reached the capital of Kigali before being repulsed by government forces, with considerable loss of life on both sides. A transitional government based on Tutsi-Hutu power sharing was proposed by the Hutu president. But the plans collapsed when a suspicious air accident killed both the Rwandan and Burundi presidents — an action that was seen by some as a deliberate effort to destabilize the country, that is, to sabotage any compromise process by a privileged clique of extremist Hutu who preferred the status quo.

A horrifying spasm of killing followed, instigated in large by Hutu military hard-

160

liners loyal to the president. Hundreds and thousands of unarmed Tutsi civilians and Hutu moderates were slaughtered on a scale perhaps unparalleled in recent human history. The Tutsi-led rebel forces eventually proved victorious and installed an interim government by mid 1994, but not before between 500,000 and 1,000,000 Rwandans had been butchered. These totals were subsequently swollen further still through vigilante violence in Rwandan refugee camps, coupled with reports of planned reprisals by Rwandan Patriotic Front. The UN has officially declared the killings in Rwanda an act of genocide — an orchestrated and methodical slaughter of undesirables rather than a random outburst by undisciplined soldiers.

WHY RWANDA?

There is no question that ethnic tensions and tribal hostilities are endemic to Rwanda. These conflicts did not materialize out of nowhere; they represent instead a legacy from the colonial past when European missionaries and ethnologists classified the Rwandan population into categories on the basis of physical appearance, social standards, and date of entry. This imposed classification not only violated the fundamental unity of Rwanda tribes and clans, it also re-aligned Rwandan group relations by bolstering Tutsi claims as the preferred and privileged ethnic group in control of the Hutu peasants. First the Germans, then the Belgians bestowed a most favoured status on the Tutsi, largely because of their attractive physical appearances. In return, the Tutsi chiefs were expected to do the "dirty" work in administering a colonialist system of di-

vide-and-indirect-rule. Superimposing the rule of one group over another inevitably set off a chain of events that culminated in open resentment and popular uprising. Tensions had existed in the past, to be sure, but such preferential treatment reinforced group differences and imparted a new dynamic to already existing frictions between the cattle owning "haves" (Tutsi) and the horticultural "have-nots" (Hutu). Conferral of Rwandan independence in 1959, followed by the departure of Belgian troops in 1962, unleashed an orgy of pent up ethnic hate and intertribal killing that festered unnoticed by an otherwise preoccupied world.

TRIBALISM OR POLITICS?

The carnage in Rwanda challenges some of our thoughts about the ethnic experience. Few of us will ever forget the horrific images of machete-wielding youths who dragged unarmed women and children from homes, then hacked them to death with a fury that went beyond human comprehension or sanity. Can we attribute this barbarism to yet another unfortunate outbreak of some inherent and primordial tribalism that occasionally flares to the surface? Does the rule of law and reason run counter to the human grain of violence and fanatacism, only to be acheived and maintained by an unremitting struggle to suppress basic human nature (Ignatieff 1994)?

Responses vary: Many have noted that much of the ethnic hatred is politically driven, with power and economics rather than ethnicity the root cause. Extremists in any conflict are known to use any method available to forestall progressive reforms. Even slaughtering members from one's own ethnic group is tolerable as a tactic for demonizing the "other." Rather than a spontaneous outburst of dormant ethnic hostilities, in other words, ethnicity is manipulated by ruthless or opportunistic elites who stop at nothing to achieve advantage, to secure political support, to conceal economic difficulties, and to distract from internal squabbles. Ethnicity is about power, not as a commodity possessed by one to the exclusion of the other, but as a process that resides in social relations.

In short, intergroup conflicts are inevitable in a pluralistic society. That, however, should not blind us to political undercurrents that animate groups dynamics. Ethnicity may inhere in conflicts that ostensibly are political or economic or religious; conversely, group relations rarely exist without an ethnic component. At any rate, it is not ethnicity per se that is the problem. Difficulties arise from its manipulation by those who will stop at nothing to procure their blood-soaked interests.

SOURCES: *The Globe and Mail* 8 April 1994; *New York Times* 17 April 1994; The Globe and Mail 26 May 1994; *The Globe and Mail* 14 April 1994

INTRODUCTION: GLOBAL IMPLOSION VERSUS ETHNIC EXPLOSION

The world we live in is engulfed by two distinct yet seemingly related forces. On the one hand are the unifying forces of globalization, with their potential to standardize and homogenize. Globalization consists of a process in which nation-states are inexorably drawn into a single world economy. This globalization of world economies is manifested in the creation of regional trading blocks such as the European Common Market or the North American Free Trade Agreement (NAFTA). The formidable presence of transnationals underscores this universalizing trend. Technological advancements have also contributed to this interdependence and integration. Mass communication and mass consumerism have diluted much of the distinctiveness that once flourished in many parts of the world. The cumulative impact of these centripetal forces intensifies the pressure for a single global village.

There is a second but equally compelling force that is pushing in an opposite direction, away from the general and the uniform, toward the specific and particular. The logic and calculation of globalization are juxtaposed by the forces of "hot blooded" **ethnicity**, with its tendency to embrace the irrational and emotional. Pressures for conformity and routinization have prompted like-minded people to rediscover their ethnic roots as a basis for continuity or competition. The two trends are not unrelated: The more similar people become because of global cultures and mass consumerism, the greater the urge to be special or claim differences (Behrens 1994; Fukuyama 1994). This force can be "regressive" in its capacity to unleash dormant hatreds and settle old scores. It can be "progressive" — even quaint — in terms of influencing how we think, who we marry, how we interact, what we do, and when we eat. It can also be "political" in the sense of open competition for scarce resources. Few will doubt the potential of ethnicity to mobilize individuals into the most formidable of action groups. More worrying still is its capacity to be manipulated as an excuse to settle old scores. The faith of even the most optimistic has been shaken with the demise of superpower restraints on intertribal blood-shed and the corresponding release of deeply rooted ethnic antagonism in once unknown colonial outposts (Schlesinger Jr. 1992).

Ethnicity has now catapulted to the forefront of contemporary society-building. Where once society was discussed in terms of a universal sense of common humanity, with differences attributed to uneven development or class conflict, there is growing awareness of ethnic pluralism as a bedrock of the human condition (Kromkowski 1995). Because of its capacity to empower or dismember, reaction to ethnicity as a social force is mixed to say the least. For some ethnicity is endorsed as a positive contributor to global survival, reflecting a fundamental fact that differences rather than similarities constitute the definitive feature of the human species. Others denounce ethnicity as an inexcusable reversion to "tribalism" and groupthink that panders to the basest instincts in women and men. Ethnicity is criticized for seeing people as members of a group rather than as individuals; for judging others by who they are rather than by what they do. Ethnically-based nationalisms are disparaged as a major contributor to international conflicts through challenges to the cohesion and integrity of sovereign states (Brown 1989). Still others are not sure how to respond. Many are resigned to ethnicity as a persistant presence in human affairs, with potential to harm or help, depending on the circumstances. That being the case, the preferred option is to determine how ethnicity can be put to good use, without capitulating to a worst case scenario. In other words, the challenge is to make the world safe *for* ethnicity, as well as make it safe *from* ethnicity (Schlesinger Jr. 1992).

Canada is no exception to this global trend. Recent years have witnessed an explosion of controversies and challenges that routinely are labelled as "ethnic" (Jaret 1995). What is this enigmatic force that threatens to dismantle the conventional in exchange for the unwanted or untried? Why and how has ethnicity come to assume such salience in shaping Canada's destiny and that of other societies? This chapter explores the "ethnic experience" as a formidable dynamic in reshaping Canada's political and cultural landscape. The chapter is concerned primarily with understanding (a) what ethnicity is, (b) why it exists, (c) how it is expressed, and (d) its impact and implications for society-building in general, and in Canada in particular.

Two themes provide conceptual bookends: Ethnicity as inequality/ethnicity and society-building. Ethnic relations are primarily unequal relations in that they deny basic human rights and exclude minorities from full participation in society (Aguirre Jr. and Turner 1995; Kallen 1995). Attention, accordingly, must focus on how ethnicity is employed to create, support, challenge, or modify these relationships of inequality. Ethnicity is also inseparable from questions of Canadian society-building. Ethnic issues are portrayed as a practical response to the demands of an increasingly diverse and changing society. Particular attention is devoted to the processes and outcomes associated with the (a) ethnic surge, (b) ethnic group and communities, (c) varied types of ethnic identities, including lived-in, symbolic, and radical; (d) ethnic nationalism as social movements; and (e) de-politicizing ethnicity. We conclude this chapter by discussing ethnicity in terms of its implications for the reconstruction of Canada along multicultural lines.

WHAT IS ETHNICITY?

The term "ethnicity" continues to infuriate and inflame. Widespread usage cannot disguise its relatively recent introduction into the popular vernacular. It hasn't taken long for ethnicity to displace the term race as the preferred category for sociological discourse. Ethnicity is employed as an adjective ("ethnic identity" or "ethnic cleansing"), or a noun (ethnicity or "professional ethnics") or even a verb ("ethnicize"). Such elasticity of usage weakens the case for a commonly accepted definition (see Proceedings 1992). The term itself seems immune to rational analysis: What else can we expect from a term that must contend with vagaries as disparate as Rwandan ethnocide on the one side, Québécois ethnic nationalism on the other, and the contrived ethnicity of Kitchener-Waterloo's annual Oktoberfest celebrations on still another.

There are additional problems. Ethnicity can be used as a putdown that entails some degree of derision, contempt, or condescension (Greenfield 1994). References to ethnicity may serve as a kind of verbal code that camouflages a majority disdain for something that "those other people have" (Jaret 1995:71; also Bissoondath 1994). The term ethnic may be wielded as a dodge to circumvent the more loaded term, race or racial. People have been known to pounce on the "R" word to smear or to silence; by contrast, the term ethnicity is less likely to ruffle feathers. Ethnicity can also be employed in the hyphenated sense to publicize one's political commitments. The increasingly politicized and oppositional nature of ethnicity cannot be dismissed lightly. As Myrna Kostash (1988:58) proclaims:

> "Anglo" and "ethnic" have become politicized designations in the same way that the designation "woman" has become politicized and represents a world view critical of and alternative to male-dominated identity...When I call my self an ethnic I am signalling that I situate myself obliquely in relation to Anglo-American culture ...

The term is also employed to label individuals of European descent ("white ethnics"); alternately, it may be applied to any social movement that has defined itself as a people or nation. Finally, a few rely on ethnicity to describe a people's sense of belonging to a particular group and specific territory. It evokes a pervasive mood of affinity in terms of a shared culture, language, social pattern, descent, kinship, and history among a "peoplehood." That is, ethnicity is a statement of affiliation or attachment, with like-minded people in pursuit of a social activity or goal.

We prefer a definition consistent with our sociological commitment to race and ethnicity as predominantly unequal group relations. Ethnicity, for our purposes, can be defined as a principle of organization whereby those who share a common sense of belonging are entitled to benefits on the basis of perceived commonality. Employed in this sense of belonging or "peoplehood," ethnicity is concerned with classifying persons who are related by birth or common symbols into goal-directed action groups. Generally speaking, ethnicity is seen as a form of ascriptive identity that provides a basis for social relations or political mobilization (Keating 1993). More specific referents incorporate a concept of group dynamics. Ethnicity as classification also consists of those distinctive attributes that typify and distinguish members of one group from another on the basis of beliefs, values, emotions, and practices (Glazer and Moynihan 1975). A distinction between **ethnicity** and **ethnic groups** is useful. More a social organization than an organizing principle, ethnic groups are defined as a kind of social collectivity comprised of people who see themselves as united by physical, social, cultural, and political attributes. The term **ethnic** connotes a very general label attached to groups who express this sense of belonging or distinctiveness (Jaret 1995).

Objective and Subjective Dimensions

At one time, ethnicity was discussed almost exclusively as a set of objective and specific cultural features. Canadian society, for example, was envisioned as a mosaic of relatively durable and distinct cultural entities. Ethnicity embraced an objective and immutable laundry list of cultural traits which could be employed to identify a person as belonging to "x" rather than "y." A set of appropriate symbols and artifacts was attached to a particular community of people (Brown 1989). Explicit and unbending boundaries were drawn around designated ethnic groups once the inventory of values, language, religion, and culture was identified. Focusing on the objective dimension of ethnicity culminated in a "cookie-cutter" approach toward the study of ethnicity.

This emphasis on objective ethnic content has waned in recent years. In its place has emerged an interest in the subjective experiences and "symbolic" boundaries that define and encircle. Subjectivists reject the notion of ethnicity as clearly demarcated cultural category with an easily defined set of morphological features. Emphasis is focused instead on ethnicity as a transactional process; that is, a socially constructed reality involving inter-ethnic relations in contexts of inequality (Barth 1969; Jenkins 1994; also Kallen 1995 for review). Ethnicity reflects a shared "we-feeling" within a collectivity ("groupness") whose symbolic components can vary from time to place. Marger and Obermiller (1987:4) expound to that effect:

> Stressing its subjective origins, ethnicity in this view is not a particular array of behaviors, attitudes, and values; but is rather a form of social organization, the boundaries of which are flexible in various social contexts. Cultural features are only symbolic and serve to mark out particular group boundaries...[S]o long as people

define themselves and are defined by others in ethnic terms, they constitute an ethnic group.

The argument for subjectivity is compelling. But just as a laundry list approach to ethnicity is inadequate, so too is a lopsided emphasis on subjective experience. Ethnicity is more than a feeling of apartness; select tangible markers are required to validate a sense of continuity and commitment. A limited number of objective features are subsequently incorporated in defining a distinction. These distinguishing markers become relevant only when deliberately chosen and promoted as such. A few of these symbolic markers are visible to the naked eye, such as clothing or lifestyle. Others are less apparent, including religious beliefs or attitudes on a wide variety of subjects from family obligations to sexual mores. Of those characteristics that serve as indices of ethnicity, few are as conspicuous as birthright, homeland, and language:

(a) *birthright*

Only persons with proven (or perceived) descent from a common source can claim membership to a particular ethnic group with a consequent entitlement to assistance and security. The notion that "blood is thicker than water" serves as a definitive trait.

(b) *homeland*

Many ethnic groups have a powerful attachment to a territory or homeland which they have left behind or which they are attempting to reclaim. This attachment is frequently couched in almost spiritual or reverential terms. Instead of viewing land as a commodity for purchase and profit, ethnic homelands are exalted as an embodiment of the past worth defending to death if necessary.

(c) *language*

Language represents a key component of group distinctiveness (Fishman 1989). It represents more than a routine way of communication for threatened minorities. As the French-speaking elements in Canada have shown, language retention is endorsed as a powerful symbol of identity, cohesion, distinctiveness, and boundary-maintenance. The issue of language and ethnic minority aspirations will be discussed later with French-English relations.

In short, ethnic groups select certain items as a basis for carving out a distinctive space in society. These criteria provide a rallying point around which to articulate and mobilize ethnic action. David Brown (1989) writes:

> Thus it is not that the possession of common cultural attributes generate community loyalty in themselves, but rather that these attributes provide outward manifestations and symbols with which to sustain the belief in common kinship.

The practice of ethnicity calls forth a combination of subjective and objective properties. Ethnicity refers to a category of persons who not only perceive themselves as different by virtue of certain attributes; they also are perceived by others as different. Certain elements are pivotal in defining the notion of in- and out-group perceptions, commonality of origins and characteristics, shared experiences, and historically-derived sense of belonging. These definable criteria establish the content and boundaries of an ethnic group, but nothing happens unless group members express a definite sense of who they are, where they came from, and what they want to become.

WHY ETHNICITY? THE ETHNIC SURGE

Virtually all societies are composed of racially and culturally diverse groups. The range of variation is almost limitless. Some societies are relatively homogeneous in terms of composition (Japan or Korea); others have a single dominant majority with numerous minorities in different stages of assimilation (United States or many European countries); still others consist of dominant and subordinate groups that are nearly equivalent in power (Fiji); and still others, including Canada, Australia, and New Zealand are white settler colonies with powerful indigenous or aboriginals sectors.

On the surface it might appear hopeless to extract pattern from such a remarkable range of social conditions. However, two patterns prevail: First, there is a prominence of dominant groups whose culture, language, values, and social patterns are upheld as normal and desirable. Such groups possess the power and resources to establish institutional arrangements and ideological systems consistent with their interests (Kallen 1995). Second is the equally impressive spread of subordinate groups. Occupying the margins of society in terms of power and resources, these groups are marginalized from the mainstream because of racial composition and cultural differences. Many are under constant pressure to conform with prevailing values, norms, and institutions. A situation is thus created where opposing groups enter into competition to define and protect, as well as promote collective interests. It is the tension between these competing forces that generates the dynamics of societal life and interethnic strife.

Dominant groups have dealt with racial and ethnocultural minorities in different ways. Most have sought to diminish ethnic differences through their assimilation into the mainstream. Few at one time doubted the inevitable dissolution of ethnic communities with the onset of modernization. Both socialism and liberalism have attacked particularist attachments as atavistic survivals at odds with rational, universal progress (Connor 1972). Common-sense assumptions rejected any place for ethnicity in this modern world. Such "primitive" attachments would erode in the face of social and cultural integration or recede under the relentless assault of an all pervasive modernist belief that people should be treated as individuals rather than as members of a group (Bell-Fialkoff 1994). Minority values and lifestyles were disparaged as immoral or unrealistic and irrelevant to the needs of contemporary society. Functionalists, for example, concurred with a belief in the eventual demise of ethnocultural minorities. Ascriptive differences such as race would diminish with exposure to contemporary forces of modernization such as urbanism, industrialization, mass education, and mass communication (Parsons 1951).

A Marxist perspective is equally contemptuous of any group organization with racial or ethnocultural overtones. Class relations constitute the fundamental dynamic in society. Everything else — race or ethnicity — is derivative (Bell-Fialkoff 1994). At the heart of this theory is the assumption that all working class members are (or should be) pitted against the property-owning class in the competitive struggle for survival. Once aware of the true source of exploitation in society, it is claimed, workers will reject racial or ethnic differences in favour of a realignment around common class interests. To act otherwise, namely in terms of race or culture, is to perpetuate false consciousness and postpone the inevitable reconstruction of a just and equal socialism. In short, both functionalist and conflict theorists alike treat race and cultural differences as glitches on the path to progress.

Predictions for the decline of racial and ethnic differences have proven premature to say the least. Rather than disappearing as anticipated, ethnic experiences have undergone nothing short of a spectacular surge. A new reality has evolved instead since the 1960s that permits minority mobilization as a basis for collectively challenging the status quo (Nagel and Olzak 1982; See and Wilson 1988). People have turned to ethnicity as a means of mobilizing in defence of their immediate interests, especially when state formations lose their power to regulate the social and economic conditions within their boundaries because of globalization and transnational corporations (Turner 1994). Ethnic forces have proven to be extremely resilient in the teeth of modernization. Perpetuated at times by individuals as genuine culture (enjoyed for its own right) or as an impetus for mobilizing people into goal-directed action, this surge of ethnic pride and group politics has had a profound effect in unsettling contemporary societies.

Ethnic forces are especially evident in Canada where political, demographic, and social changes have created an environment for diversity to flourish. Whether measured in terms of adherents or by the passions aroused, ethnic social movements are transforming how governments conduct their business and set agendas. No longer are ethnic attachments viewed as an anachronistic survival from the past — quaint and exotic, perhaps, but irrelevent to the demands and rigours of the twentieth century. To the contrary, this renewal of ethnic pride and identity has been endorsed as a positive and dynamic force, with the capacity to enhance personal growth or national interests. Its contribution to society-building is widely acknowledged even if the potential for society-bashing is ominous.

The rejuvenation of ethnicity in Canada and elsewhere has raised many questions. What do we mean by the term **ethnic surge**? Why has it occurred? How is it manifested? With what impact? What are the immediate or long-term implications? Answers to these questions require us to associate ethnicity with the growing assertiveness of once-downtrodden minorities. We must discover how the visceral appeal of ethnicity can supersede the cosmopolitan demands of a modern society. Why, indeed, do people prefer to affiliate along ethnic lines rather than political parties or trade unions? Put crudely, why would anyone want to be thought of as a Québécois or Aboriginal or Portuguese or Vietnamese when they have the opportunity to identify as non-hyphenated Canadians? This and subsequent sections will address the reasons why by examining the principles, processes, and outcomes of ethnicity as a social force in modern Canadian society. Three major explanations help to isolate the factors contributing to this explosion of ethnic pride and affiliation, They include the (1) **primordialist thesis** (2) **identity thesis** and (3) **resource mobilization theory**.

Primordialist Thesis: Blood is Thicker Than Water

The **primordialist thesis** argues that the boom in ethnicity is essentially an extension of primary sentiments that link past with present. Ethnicity is an ancient and deep-rooted impulse that reflects a tendency to seek out others of your "own kind" (Jaret 1995). This "survival" from an "primitive" past endorses a basic and fundamental need for belonging with others who are similar. It is only natural to exhibit such spontaneous feelings and emotional attachments with those of common birthright. People appear to have a genuine preference for confiding in and congregating with people of their own cultural background. Evolutionary adaptation and survival of the human species may have been contingent on this ethnic bonding. In short, individuals affiliate with one another not only because of personal gain; they also do so because of a "primitive" urge to advance related interests (Rex 1983). This intrinsic dimension may help to explain the magnitude of passions and emotions associated with ethnic fanaticism. It may also explain the popularity of fascist movements, with their rejection of modernist values and endorsement of ethnic primordial ties as a basis for collective harmony and group cooperation (Bell-Fialkoff 1994).

Within the primordialist camp are various biologically-slanted theories, the most popular of which is **sociobiology**. According to this perspective, ethnic interest is biogenetically "wired" into the human species as a mechanism for transmitting genes from one generation to the next. Pierre van den Berghe (1981), for example, traces the origins of ethnic sentiment and racial bonding to an extension of kinship group solidarity. Any kinship group with knowledge of its own common ancestry and descent tends to act in a manner that provides mutual aid and cooperation. Involvement with related others ensures the long term survival of the species — albeit at some expense to any specific individual. It follows from this that our actions serve to protect and promote our well-being through the welfare of our kin group. This assumption is called the principle of "inclusive fitness." Conversely, these actions may discourage interaction with outgroups.

On balance, the evidence is insufficient to confirm the validity of the sociobiology theory. While sociobiology may not be a readily "testable" thesis, it provides food for thought regarding our primordial nature and its relevance to race and ethnic relations. Sociologists themselves are split on the merits of sociobiology as an explanatory device, in part because of the ambiguous role assigned to social forces in shaping human behaviour. On the one hand there is something to recommend sociobiology. By casting ethnic feelings into our genetic and evolutionary past, sociobiology can explain the all-embracing and often emotional appeal to ethnicity, especially when compared to alternate explainations for affiliaton (Brown 1989). On the other, many are disturbed by the political implications of reductionist arguments that link biology and culture. Culture and environment, after all, intervene in any relationship between genes and behaviour. Our capacity for culture and learning releases people from the imprisonment of our genetic code. We may be genetically predisposed to reward and identify with our "own kind" in the interest of our own personal survival. Yet we are also free to choose otherwise, and many have done so in turning away from ethnic heritage.

Identity Thesis: Buffer Zones

The second set of explanations, the **identity thesis,** looks at ethnicity as a source of identity and meaning. Ethnicity and the search for identity is primarily an expression of a perhaps universal desire for social space and cultural location in a mass modern society (Ratner and Buenker 1991). This expressive perspective points to ethnicity as a buffer for insulating individuals from the pressures of a modern, changing, and complex society. A commitment to ethnicity allows an escape from feelings of irrelevance, powerlessness, alienation, and impersonality. Appeals to ethnicity foster a sense of relief, belonging, importance, and security — especially for those at the margins of society without alternate channels for coping with societal stress. Ethnicity constitutes a search for meaning and continuity, even relaxation and enjoyment, in a rapidly changing and complex urban-technological environment. Ethnic involvements, in other words, permit meaningful identity to be forged at a time when the influence of mass society has expanded. A quasi-kinship community is sustained that not only accounts for the tenacity of ethnic attachments in contexts of competition and change. It also helps to explain the intense and universal appeal of such affiliation (Brown 1989).

Resource Mobilization Thesis: Strength in Your "Own Kind"

A third source of explanation, the **resource mobilization thesis**, is firmly grounded in a sociology of group dynamics in unequal contexts. Ethnicity is defined as a catalyst for political mobilization and resource competition. As pointed out in earlier chapters, a cultural division of labour emerges in situations of uneven economic development (Hechter 1976). Dominant sectors monopolize the wealth and power at the expense of cultural/racially different subordinate groups, many of whom are locked into a position of inferiority because of their unskilled status. Racial and ethnic markers are devalued and employed to justify economic exploitation.

Resentment over this differential treatment may reach a boiling point. The cultural division of labour with its prevailing system of stratification may waver under pressure from the forces of mass education, mass communication, improved education, and ameliorative government policies. It is precisely at this point that ethnic activism and conflict is likely to escalate (Nagel and Olzak 1982; See and Wilson 1988). Action groups begin to mobilize around racial or cultural markers to improve their lot in the competitive struggle for scarce and valued items. Ethnic activism is further boosted by the mobilization activities of manipulative elites and leaders who may articulate personal concerns as group interests (Brown 1989).

The resource mobilization theory suggests that ethnic minorities will take united action not only to lay claim to rightful entitlement, but also to thwart state intrusion into their collective affairs (Adam 1989). Emphasis on collective rather than individual responses is a preferred course of action. Why do ethnic groups prefer to act on a collective basis rather than as individuals or neighbourhood associations to achieve their goals? Put simply, a collective basis is superior for coping with the demands of a complex and bureaucratized society. Only large scale social movements possess the human resources and critical mass to compete effectively at a national level or to influence central policy structures.

Equally important is the relevance of ethnic markers in securing the loyalty and commitment of members. What is the tactical advantage of relying on ethnicity in the competition for scarce resources? The mobilization of persons along racial or cultural lines represents one of several "trump cards" that ethnic leaders can use in forging a collective identity (Ross 1982). Recruitment by ethnic bonds is perceived as more natural and durable than the "artificial" linkages inherent in political or economic organizations. These bonds are cemented by emotional involvement with persons of one's own kind — a kind of "quasi-kinship" that needs no justification beyond its own existence (Brown 1989). These quasi-kinship ties infuse the movement with the commitment necessary to wage a protracted struggle in the competition for scarce resources. Ethnicity thus serves as a useful criteria for political mobilization since it combines an objective base (culture, language, religion, institutions) with a common symbolism and shared consciousness (Bell 1975).

This perspective should dispel any lingering notions about ethnicity as a romantic exercise in nostalgia. Ethnicity and ethnic movements constitute a practical response to an unacceptable situation or set of grievances. In many ways they resemble contemporary interest groups in function and process (Cohen 1969; Glazer and Moynihan 1970). Under the banner of ethnicity, members of an ethnic group seek to maximize social advantage in a rational and calculated manner (Olsen 1965; Hechter 1982). To the extent that such rational preferences are shared and shaped by structural constraints, the actions of ethnic groups are patterned and predictable and subject to sociological analysis.

In brief, then, the ethnic surge reflects the emergence of collective social movements that employ racial or cultural diacritics to galvanize minorities into more competitive action once the rules of the game begin to change. Ethnicity is manipulated as a strategic resource that allows more effective competition on a society-wide basis. Dispossessed minority members are organized into collective action groups through promotion of certain cultural symbols. Direction is provided by leaders who combine traditional myths with the virtues of group solidarity over individual action (See and Wilson 1988). This strategic resource model also emphasizes the situational and dynamic character of ethnic organization and the socially constructed aspects of ethnicity in terms of identities and actions (Nagel 1994). Yet engaging in this competition does not come at the expense of abdicating those cultural and spiritual values of relevance to ethnic minorities. Rather than a regressive or emotional response to modern challenges, in other words, ethnicity constitutes instead a rational choice for collective improvement in a world of uncertainty and scarcity.

EXPRESSIONS OF ETHNICITY

Ethnicity can be expressed in different ways. At one level, ethnicity is manifested in ethnic groups who live together in relatively self-sufficient communities. At another level, ethnicity manifests itself through expressions of identity from moderate to radical at personal or group levels. At a third level, ethnicity is expressed as a social movement, some of which culminate in ethnic nationalism.

Ethnicity as Community

Ethnicity refers to a principle of potential group formation. Ethnicity at times remains highly abstract and hardly extends beyond a symbolic role. It classifies persons with shared and felt identification into a category, but this "collective sentiment" rarely translates into an action group. At other times, ethnicity serves as a principle for uniting ethnically related persons into ongoing social units. Those with a common sense of history and peoplehood are united temporarily to further individual or collective claims. In still other circumstances, ethnicity provides a basis for relatively permanent communities and stable institutional settings of ethnically related individuals. Such group formation reflects both self- and other-identifications (Shibutani and Kwan 1965). In some cases, ethnic groups define themselves as unique and alike by virtue of common ancestry and select cultural symbols. In others such as the case of early Chinese immigrants to Canada, the host society imposes an ethnic label on migrants who then resort to cohesive bonds for adaptive purposes in an unfriendly environment.

The ethnic community can be conceptualized in different ways. It can be viewed as a collectivity with a distinctive set of values, traditions, and cultural patterns that have evolved and been transformed over time. Institutions are established that ensure some degree of completeness and control over the delivery of services (Breton 1964). Ethnic communities can also be seen as systems of social relations. These consist of interpersonal and kinship relations for emotional and material support; they also entail a framework for collective activities. Finally, the political dimension of ethnic communities deserves scrutiny. There is an interest in issues as varied as minority participation in mainstream political institutions, including voting behaviour and political involvement. Attention is also aimed at indigenous political structures and processes that relate to collective decision making, conflict resolution, and factional disputes.

Urban Canada is composed of numerous ethnic communities, including the widely reknown Chinatowns in Vancouver and Toronto. These communities provide a number of political, economic, and cultural functions for individuals who are related by descent or kinship (Reitz 1980). Those communities with a relatively high degree of "institutional completeness" (Breton 1964) furnish their members with mutual support, networks, services, and source of identity. Involvement in these institutions is seen as accelerating rates of integration into wider society without loss of cultural integrity. Ethnic communities may assist in the preservation of language and transmission of culture. They also establish a power base for advancing political consciousness and action. Recent immigrants in particular may find economic and cultural refuge in communities: That in turn may help bridge the gap between the society of origin and urban Canada. Similarly, ethnic communities provide a sense of security in a highly impersonal and mechanized society by buffering the old from the new, the individual from society, and the familiar from the strange (Isajiw 1978).

INSIGHT

New Communities for Old

Ethnic communities have a number of functions. Not only do they assist in preserving the past, but they can also serve as a link with the future. Chinatown communities in Toronto provide a useful glimpse into the dynamics of ethnicity in contemporary settings. Chinese-Canadians number about 350,000 in Greater Toronto's urban population of about 4 million. At one time, most Chinese-Canadians resided in the enclave located primarily but not exclusively in the Spadina-Dundas region of downtown Toronto (Gorrie 1991). There has been a recent exodus of Chinatown residents to suburbs such as Scarborough or Mississauga. Compared to the older generations who prefer the accessibility and intimacy of the downtown area, many new immigrants and younger Chinese-Canadians have opted for the spaciousness and amenities associated with suburban living. Life in the downtown ghetto is dismissed as quaint and as anachronistic as the archaic "ponytail" (Gorrie 1991:18). The suburbs provide a comparable range of benefits, but without the costs of congestion or fear of crime. All manner of services and transactions related to government services or private business are available in English or Chinese. Community centres provide a focal point for interaction and exchange. This suggests that, the lure of assimilation notwithstanding, Chinese-Canadians will remain a distinct population, with a unique constellation of lifestyles, patterns of interactions, and proposals for problem solution.

References to ethnic communities as ongoing entities should not obscure the prevalence of internal diversity. A common bond and cultural background are not a guarantee of community harmony or group consensus. Each community may embrace members who vary in outlooks and commitment. Political cleavages are readily apparent in some cases, with a potential for factional infighting because of differences in age, sex, income, education, and length of residence (Buchnignani and Indra 1985). Ethnic community members convene not only to promote corporate interests; they also congregrate to jockey for leadership and status. An image of corporate unity is maintained, but primarily for the benefit of the outside world. Beneath the constructed facade may lurk internal tensions that not only threaten community solidarity, but undermine consensus on important group issues.

In other words, the concept of ethnic community is not a constant and cannot be taken for granted. Nor is membership in an ethnic group a ticket to cooperation or solidarity. Ethnic ascription does not automatically consolidate bonds of consensus or commonality. What we see instead are internally diverse collectivities that capitalize on the ethnic dimension to promote respective interests (Stasiulis 1980). As well, this dynamic quality cannot be viewed apart from the historical and structural context. The ongoing and adjusted relationship with central authorities is especially important as we shall see shortly.

Preserving Ethnic Communities

Many ethnic communities find it difficult to survive in Canada's highly democratic, achievement-oriented, and relatively egalitarian system. Without external pressure or outside hostility, it is too easy to slip into the mainstream unless vigilance is constant (Abella 1995). **Ethnic boundaries** provide a protective canopy to preserve community differences and distinguish one group from another. They ensure ethnic group members do not lose the capacity to make a positive and distinctive identification. Such boundaries can be strengthened and sharpened, especially if competitive advantage can be gained through promotion of differences.

Ethnic boundaries can be defined as socially constructed barriers that provide some degree of separation between ethnic groups. Neither totally impenetrable nor excessively permeable, these boundaries can be likened to "membranes" that simultaneously inhibit or enhance the flow of individuals into or out of the group (Comeau and Driedger 1978). Ethnic boundaries are negotiated and adjusted through social interaction inside and outside ethnic communities (Barth 1969; Nagel 1994). These arise as part of a defensive response to limited political involvement, racist legislation, restricted economic opportunity, restrained cultural expression, and rejection by the majority group. The presence of stereotypes and prejudice can also lead to erection of boundaries for self-preserving reasons. They are maintained for as long as members of the group consider themselves to be distinct on the basis of self-defined characteristics. This protective role as the outer limits of defence against outside forces is conveniently illustrated by reference to exclusionary groups such as the Hutterites.

CASE STUDY

Keeping the Faith, Maintaining the Boundaries

The Hutterites can be described as a religiously inspired ethnic group whose distinctiveness springs from an agrarian lifestyle and communal ownership of property and possessions (Hostetler and Huntington 1980). Centuries of hostility and exposure to assimilationist pressures have not diminished Hutterite resolve to survive as an economically viable, biologically self-reproducing, and culturally distinct people (van den Berghe and Peter 1988). Much of their success can be attributed to the construction of social boundaries against the outside world. What boundary maintaining devices are employed to keep unwanted influences out? How does an ethnic group retain its membership while securing their loyalty and commitment?

ETHNIC DISTINCTIVENESS

Restricted largely to the west where about 200 colonies thrive, the Hutterites are one of three Anabaptist groups (the others being the Amish and the Mennonites) who reside in Canada. In common with the other sects, the Hutterites believe in the separation of state and church (in the process denying the legitimacy of secular authority) and the primacy of voluntary adult baptism as a basis for entry into the community. They survive as a pacifist people with orthodox Christian beliefs, frugal lifestyles, and austere appearances that have remained virtually intact since inception in the early sixteenth century. Social organization consists of predominately male-dominated colonies that are essentially self-sufficient, relatively egalitarian, rigidly ranked and classless. Reflecting a division of labour based on scriptural readings, only men have a say in the running of the colony's spiritual or material concerns. Activities and interaction are guided by a pervasive and preordained order, with God at the top followed by men, women, children, animals, and down the line. This order cannot be tampered with without incurring the wrath of God. This commitment to a foreordained order and religious injunction against violence may account for their steadfast refusal to limit family sizes or engage in war.

Unlike other Anabaptists, the Hutterites reside in communally-based communities of about ten to twelve families. Up to 200 persons live in these classless colonies in the belief that communal living provides them with the protection and support to fend off the blandishments of a secular world. Contrasting their simplicity elsewhere, the Hutterites display few qualms in utilizing modern productive technology to secure an economic base for all to share equally. Their willingness to take advantage of economic opportunities, but unwillingness to integrate into the wider community has created resentment, at times bordering on open hostility and resulting in persecution or death. Strangely enough, this hatred has had the effect of drawing

Hutterites closer together ("seige mentality") and strengthening their resolve to remain spiritually, culturally, and socially apart.

ETHNIC CLOSURE

Hutterites have relied on various strategies — both deliberate or unintended — to ensure an appropriate distance between themselves and the outside world. Arm-length distance, called ethnic closure is upheld by their appearance, styles of interaction, and patterns of communication. They defend their boundaries through structural endogamy ("marriage within the group") and high reproductive rates. Geographic and social isolation is also important. Access to the outside is restricted and carefully controlled by colony leaders (Kallen 1995). Large tracts of land are purchased at some distance from the general population; communities are then constructed in the centre of the tract to minimize contact. Considerable energy is expended on formal education and the indoctrination of their children as hardworking and godfearing followers of the colony (van den Berghe and Peter 1988). Equally important in maintaining ethnic closure and distinctiveness is the commitment to a central core of values involving a dualist ('spiritual versus materialist') world view. Hutterite religious world view furnishes an underlying rationale and charter myths for spurning the temptations of the outside world (Hostetler and Huntington 1980). An oral history rich with vignettes of persecution and martyrdom has also reinforced perceptions of the outside as evil, corrupt, godless, and untrustworthy. Strong leadership within the commune has kept the faithful in the fold (Boldt 1985). Small scale settings such as these allow religious leaders leeway in applying diffuse sanctions to ensure compliance with spiritual and social norms. The temptation for youths to stray from the path is defused through a moderate degree of pragmatic accommodation in making concessions to the outside world. This flexibility and moderate receptivity to change suggests Hutterite willingness to "bend rather than break" — provided these concessions do not interfere with the running of the colony or contravene scriptural doctrines (van den Berghe and Peters 1988; Kallen 1995).

In sum, the Hutterites have displayed remarkable success in sustaining a viable lifestyle in a large, unfriendly environment. Part of their success can be attributed to the construction of well-defined boundaries which are not entirely impenetrable to outside influences. Their lifestyle is based on self-sufficiency and independence, each colony exhibiting a degree of institutional completeness at political, social, economic, and educational levels, in addition to religiously legitimated mechanism for social control (Kallen 1995). A cradle-to-grave-and-beyond security not only diminishes any decision to leave, but also ensures loyalty and commitment. In erecting boundaries for protection against outside influences, the Hutterites hope to ensure that their young remain loyal and committed brethren to the cause.

This circling-the-wagon-train-mentality illustrates an additional characteristic of ethnic boundaries. The existence of external hostility (both real and imagined) is pivotal in keeping boundaries firm for minority survival. Perceived outside threats are useful in drawing a group of people closer together. Conflict between ethnic groups may be contrived to foster outgroup distance. A sense of solidarity and commitment to the ingroup is subsequently reinforced. This mutual interdependence demonstrates the interactional and dynamic aspects of race, aboriginal, and ethnic relations. That is, people define and sort themselves out by virtue of their opposition and differences with others.

Ethnic Identities

Many accept the existence of ethnicity as an organizing principle with the power to impart social cohesion and shared commitment. Ethnicity as principle establishes guidelines for acceptable behaviour. It also provides a sense of identity for individuals who wish to foster that affiliation. These identities can be broadly defined as positive and personal attachments to a group (or tradition) on the basis of commonly shared ancestry, experiences, and characteristics (Driedger 1989). They also furnish a basis for ethnic group formation in the competition for scarce societal resources. In certain cases, ethnic identities are imposed by outside sources; in others, they are voluntarily adopted on the basis of the way individuals or groups feel about themselves.

One of the identities open to many Canadians is derived from a racial or ethnic background. In a multicultural society such as ours, it comes as no surprise that many individuals regard their racial or cultural background as a component of identity. Ethnicity and ethnic identity can assume different levels of salience from person to person as well as from one region of Canada to the next (Edwards and Doucette 1987; also Mackie 1978; Mackie and Brinkinhoff 1984; Isajiw 1990). Some reject their ethnic background and want to be identified only as Canadians, except perhaps for special occasions; others maintain a dual identity without much difficulty; still others prefer to retain strong nationalistic feelings and can't wait to return home. The properties associated with ethnicity and ethnic identities are varied, but may (a) embrace both objective and subjective components, (b) be imposed or voluntarily selected, (c) acquire a variety of overlapping ascriptive loyalties, (d) be for genuine ("**expressive**") or practical ("**instrumental**") purposes, and (e) be situational and intermittent yet sufficiently durable to persist across a variety of domains (see Murphee 1988). Identities can be positive or negative: An emphasis on ethnicity may imperil mobility and opportunity, whereas an underemphasis may hinder self-esteem and identity (Fitzgerald 1977; 1989). Some researchers suggest a deep-rooted tendency for individuals to associate with members of their own group over others (Tajfel 1981; van den Berghe 1981). Others suggest ethnic identities arise, persist, and change in response to the vagaries of intergroup behaviour (See and Wilson 1988). This in turn implies the existence of different "styles" of ethnicity in modern settings.

Lived-in Ethnicity: Fulltime and Functional

Individuals with common cultural values or religious beliefs may acknowledge their belonging to a particular ethnic group. This affiliation with the norms, values, and institutions of this group constitutes a serious personal statement. Anabaptists sects such as the Hutterites, sociologically speaking, are real communities governed by rules, values, and sanctions. Here the principle of ethnicity is expressed in the organization of viable groups that continue to exert a pervasive influence in shaping members lives. These individuals admit that their identification with the cultural past makes a difference in how they think and behave. Involvement at this level presupposes a canopy of constraints, demands, and responsibilities for members of the group. Individuals are born into these primary groups and their membership is irrevocably assigned at birth (Watson 1987).

We refer to this type of identification and involvement as **lived-in ethnic identity** (Boldt 1985). There is good reason to believe this style of ethnicity is disappearing in Canada. Restricted largely to rural areas or in certain urban enclaves, the "old fashioned" style of ethnicity no longer appeals to those who are anxious to derive full benefit from a socially mobile and achievement-oriented society. Ethnic groups have lost much of their moral authority as a social force. They can no longer supply a common set of shared values, enforce mutual obligations or responsibilities, supply incentives or sanctions, or secure compliance from members. Ethnic groups are gradually being replaced by social categories (people who share one or two characteristics in common) and social aggregates (people who happen to be there) (see Jaret 1995). This lack of formality is creating the basis for a new kind of ethnic expression.

Situational (Symbolic) Ethnicity

Another kind of ethnic identity is common across Canada. This ethnicity is indeterminate and negotiated; it represents a strategic resource that allows individuals and groups to improve their life chances within a pluralistic environment (Lyman and Douglass 1973). The "new" ethnicity reflects a process of adaptation by immigrants in their adopted country. As incoming immigrants become established through work or social involvement, many become estranged from the behavioural aspects of their cultural heritage (in terms of language use, friendship circles, or residential patterns). Many are increasingly attracted to a lifestyle associated with consumerism, career enhancement, and materialism. Involvement in ethnic organizations declines (except on isolated occasions or in favourable circumstances) to the point of insignificance — if measured by the frequency or intensity of institutional participation.

This tendency toward behavioural assimilation is widely acknowledged. Yet many new Canadians may retain a strong emotional tie or cognitive commitment to their cultural past. In resisting the lure of total assimilation, they reveal an affective attachment to the community as a reference group. What is not accepted, however, are the sanctions, restrictions, or responsibilities of continuous interaction (Roberts and Clifton 1990). Individuals in other words do not so much belong to an ethnic group as they voluntarily affiliate with the symbols of that culture as preferences dictate and situations demand.

Social scientists (Gans 1979; Weinfeld 1985) refer to this as **symbolic** or **situational ethnic identity**. A person's degree of participation in ethnic clubs, knowledge of ethnic language, circle of friends, place of residence, and marital patterns, are largely irrelevant with situational ethnicity (Isajiw 1977). Involvement or frequency are not important; what is salient is an identification with that ethnicity and the symbols associated with its distinctiveness. Ethnic minority members do not necessarily share a common culture; more accurately, they possess a sense of identity or affiliation on the basis of perceived similarities and common cultural symbols (Edwards 1985; Edwards and Doucette 1987). Not everyone, of course, has this choice of identities: Because of the constraints of visibility, this option may be less applicable to people of colour. Nevertheless, ethnicity for most represents a resource that can be manipulated in the search for identity or struggle against inequality (Oommen 1994).

The situational nature of contemporary identity provides answers to vexing questions about Canadian ethnicity. Three questions prevail. First, can distinct ethnic identities survive in situations where the traditional past has disappeared or declined to meet the needs of modern society? Second, can individuals continue to identify themselves as "ethnics" long after abandoning all involvement in group activities? According to the logic of situational ethnicity, the answer to both question is "yes." The decline of a particular lifestyle will not necessarily diminish the intensity of the ethnic experience. After all, what is critical is the identification with select aspects of that cultural lifestyle — not the degree or intensity of involvement. This style of identity is relatively painless and voluntary as well as abstract and effortless. It is also well-suited to the needs of a socially mobile and competitive society.

Third, is a hyphenated-Canadian possible? Is it possible to identify and participate as a Canadian, yet retain an affiliation with a certain ethnic heritage such as Lithuanian (or black or aboriginal)? Again, the answer is in the affirmative. Dual identity entitles people to compartmentalize their secondary ("ethnic") identity from their primary ("citizen") identity. The demands of a particular context as well as the nature of the ethnic group will determine which identity is to be activated. Affiliation with select symbols should not be regarded as necessarily incompatible with involvement in mainstream values and lifestyles. Dual identities are not mutually exclusive; rather they may complement each other in fulfilling diverse personal needs and goals. Nor does identification with select symbolic elements necessarily interfere with the business of making a living — provided identification is restricted to the cognitive rather than the behavioural level. That allows everyone to regard themselves as an "ethnic" while maintaining full and active participation in the political, economic, and social institutions of Canadian society. Having the best of both worlds also helps to explain the popularity of ethnicity.

Radical Ethnicity: The New Tribalism

Both lived-in and situational ethnicities appear to be relatively innocuous. With few exceptions, these identities confirm the pluralist axiom of "live and let live" or "agreeing to disagree." **Radical ethnicity** by contrast is much more assertive about what it believes is right or wrong, is highly politicized in terms of what it wants, and aggressive in its approach to goal attainment. Affiliation with radical ethnicity transcends mere identification or celebration. In place of coexistence is a forceful assertion of peoplehood who want a share of power, access to resources, and a level of autonomy. Such a collectivity is willing to take whatever measures necessary, including the revival of dormant grievances, to achieve their goals of nationhood.

Radical ethnicities superficially resemble other types of ethnic identities. For example, radical ethnic identities compare with ethnicities that are lived-in and functional, given their mutual commitment to differences that really make a difference. The group takes precedence over the individual because of its capacity to enforce compliance through imposition of sanctions. Differences are also evident. Radical ethnicities are neither as durable as lived-in ethnicities nor as transitory as situational ethnicities. More importantly, an intense dislike of others, especially when religion or language differences are factored into the equation, provides a defining feature of radical ethnicity. Expressions of this deep-seated dislike of anyone outside your group can range from open hatred to violent actions, including references to a "final solution" or "ethnic cleansing" or "racial purification."

The notion of radical ethnicities may strike many of us as illogical or irrational, at least when interpreted from the perspective of the nation-state, with its commitment to civic nationalism and secular coexistence. Emotions run high with radical ethnicities and this affectivity often goes beyond rational analysis or behaviour modification. Not surprisingly, radical ethnicities rarely respond to rational solutions: Sanctions as varied as international censure or trade embargoes or military force do not carry as much moral authority as the ethnic imperative. Nor can such initiatives guarantee compliance; by definition, radical ethnicities refuse to play by conventional rules. That alone makes radical ethnicity a potent force in de-stabilizing a national or international order. Nowhere is this more evident than in the growth of social movements that are vehicles for the expression of radical ethnicity.

Social Movements: Ethnic Nationalism

"Hell Hath no Fury like a Nation Scorned" — Behrens (*Time*, 21 March 1994)

Ethnic nationalisms are a logical culmination of radical ethnicities: They also constitute the third manifestation of ethnicity.

There is little substance to the allegation that globalization will mold everyone into culturally homogeneous robots. Nor is there reason to believe in the eventual domination of liberal democracy, with its notion of a nation as a community of individuals, both secular and tolerant, with equal and inalienable rights, and united in patriotic attachment to a shared set of political practices and democratic values (Ignatieff 1994). What is increasingly evident, as Michael Ignatieff (1994) notes is an intensely parochial era in which the "key narrative of the new world order is the disintegration of nation states into ethnic civil war; the key architects of that order are warlords; and the key language of our age is *ethnic nationalism*" (emphasis mine). Old idiosyncracies and group differences have been resurrected by these national, non-immigrant groups who share a state with larger groups in spite of — or perhaps because of — global patterns, with a passion and a vengeance that verges on the terrifying in its capacity to stoke dormant hatreds (Behrens 1994; Kymlicka 1995).

This surge of ethnic nationalism has come about for various reasons. The principle of self-determination and nationality continues to provide a normative basis for the creation of a legitimate government and political claims against the state (Bell-Fialkoff 1994). Tribal conflicts, once suppressed by colonialist control and Cold War politics, have found a receptive market. The collapse of superpower colonialism gave rise to a host of social movements that emphasized ethnic loyalties rather than civic nationalism as a basis for society-building (Ignatieff 1994). This ethno-chauvinism has challenged the fundamental tenets of liberal society, including the commitment to cultural coexistence and a cosmopolitan internationalism.

Properties of Ethnic Nationalism

Ethnic nationalisms are not new social phenomena. Their origins can be traced to nineteenth century European Romanticism with its disavowal of Enlightenment ideals. Romanticists disagreed with Enlightenment ideals of universal human progress through reason and science. These "reactionaries" proposed instead the notion of a nation as a community of people who were racially uniform and culturally distinct (Jakobsh 1994). This nineteenth century ideal of a sovereign state as the politicized expression of a single people in a particular territory continues to be embraced, and is used to justify all manner of violence or oppression (Graff 1994). Membership is defined on the basis of birthright and descent from a common ancestry. Loyalty to the community or homeland ("nation") precedes loyalty to nation-states or social classes. The territorial rights, distinctive language, and shared ethnicity of this imagined political community must be defended at all costs from hostile outsiders. Recourse to violence may be permissable not only to preserve autonomy or authenticity, but also to consolidate the bonds of belonging.

Central to these nationalist movements is a guiding ideology with a set of national sentiments pertaining to a collective sense of peoplehood (Smith 1994). All present-day varieties of ethno-nationalism are grounded in this idealization of group exclusiveness and maintenance of internal cohesion and collective loyalty because of perceived external threats or unresolved grievances (Rothchild and Groth 1995). Claims to ethnic nationalism are based on the principle of self-determination: minorities strive to become majorities by revamping the existing political arrangement not only to establish jurisdictional control over a defined homeland, but also to achieve sovereign status denied to them as a subject people (Graff 1994). People want to be become "normal" as the Québécois remind us; they want to be a majority in their own homeland rather than a minority in somebody else's. Such an intense nationalism is based on the premise that the world can be divided into nations, rather than states, each with its own distinct character. Unlike a state that is comprised of numerous nations, a nation constitutes a moral community in which members feel themselves emotionally involved and responsible to each other, with a passionate attachment to a homeland as the site of preexisting ethnic entitlements (Mead 1993). This nation is the sole source of political power; group loyalty overrides others. The belief is that everyone belongs to the nation: Their full potential can only be realized under this community of like-minded individuals. Attainment of an ethnically pure community may entail removal or "cleansing" of those who do not fit the physical bill. Nations must be autonomous, it is believed, for full realization of national unity or achievement of global peace. This mosaic of different and separate nations represents a logical extension of ethnicity with its loose sense of identification and affiliation at one end, to a fully formed community with its shared commitments and group embeddedness on the other.

The path to ethnic self-determination can take different routes. Peaceful channels are pursued in some cases; in others, long suppressed grievances and a craving for settling scores is more important than scoring points with the UN. Nationalism may be most violent when there are small differences between groups, confirming once again that hatred between brothers (for example, Cain and Able) is more ferocious than between enemies (Ignatieff 1995). The violence factor may be heightened when religious differences are at play. At times, ethnic nationalism represents a revolt against the modern and the universal, with a preference for the traditional and particular. At other times, it is essentially looking forward to redefining status with a new global order at political and economic levels. Sometimes, expressions of hot blooded ethnicity are genuine; other times it represents a convenient front to camouflage or distract, to conceal or evade, or to deter or preserve. What is too often common among most of these movements is their unwillingness to recognize that others also have a comparable right to preserve and protect (Havel 1994).

In sum: No longer can we think of ethnicity as some primitive or transient whimsy in a cultural backwater outide the path of rational progress and liberal democracy. Ethnicity, especially when harnessed with a vibrant nationalism, is a powerful political force and potent social movement. Its potential for greatness or depravity is magnified even more in conjunction with religious grievances. It remains to be seen whether the new international order can cope with the multiplicity of ethno-jingoistic demands. To be sure, coexistence is not dependent on the need to understand or adapt to the others. What is critical, however, is the acceptance of others as legitimate and equal (Havel 1994). When differences are seen as absolute rather than relative, the chances for global survival are diminished.

IMPLICATIONS: DE-POLITICIZING ETHNICITY

A new international order is gradually taking shape. Even the very concept of a sovereign society is under scrutiny because of shifting global and ethnic trends. Once assumed to be the bedrock of international order as well as a natural focus of group solidarity, the nation-state can no longer automatically command the loyalty of its citizens. It is much less capable of preserving its boundaries against the forces of ethnicity "from below" or globalization "from above" (Smelser 1993). The very concept of a country (in terms of a sovereign nation-state) may drift into irrelevance because of capital mobility and ethnic jockeying (see Aguirre Jr. and Turner 1995). Nation-states may have little choice except to relinquish their legitimacy and control over citizens to ethnic formations. Negotiating the fine line between the forces of "implosion" versus "explosion" could result in a global order altogether different than the current arrangement. Instead of nation-states as we know now, boundary lines will be redrawn to reflect a loose confederation of ethnic communities within the framework of regional or global trading blocks.

Canada as the world's third oldest federal state is not unaffected by these pressures. The dual challenges of ethnicity and globalism have infiltrated every aspect of our social and personal existence. Rules that formerly defined right from wrong are openly challenged and increasingly irrelevant. Forces of change have shaken those institutions and values that once imposed security and meaning on social life, including the authority of the Church, the State, and elite politics. The abandonment of the conventional has exerted even greater pressure on people to snatch unity from the strands of diversity in one last ditch effort at society-building.

Multiculturalism represents Canada's response to the challenges and paradox of ethnicity. But endorsement of ethnocultural diversity poses a dilemma: How can national unity be secured in the face of forces whose potential to divide is legendary. Ethnicity may enrich a society or it may ignite a chain reaction of destruction and decline. The fact that no one can predict or control the outcome is no less perplexing. That raises the question of whether an ethnically diverse country such as Canada can remain cohesive when ethnic ties are becoming brittle, when the cultural centre appears to be eroding, and when group conflicts are escalating (see also Aguirre Jr. and Turner 1994).

Canada has chosen to pursue the path of unity through diversity. Its attachment to the "mosaic" as a egalitarian ideal departs from the "melting pot" blueprint of the USA with its commitment to unity within homogeneity (Reitz and Breton 1994; Kallen 1995). Yet protection and preservation of ethnocultural diversity comes with a qualifier: Canada's multiculturalism is planted firmly within the framework of symbolic ethnicity. Under official multiculturalism, all Canadian are encouraged to identify and participate as individuals in the cultural heritage of their choice. Multiculturalism in Canada is not concerned with the enhancement of ethnic communities, let alone the preservation of ethnic nationalities. Few societies could survive the strain of multiple competing groups with clearly demarcated sovereign boundaries, a separate power base, and parallel institutions. Ethnicity can only exist when stripped of its potency to divide or incite, then folded into the prevailing social and cultural system of society.

Herein lies the appeal of situated and symbolic identities within a multicultural society. Promotion of ethnic identity at situational or symbolic levels comes across as relatively harmless since the political and economic status quo is left intact. In that sense, multiculturalism does not exist to promote ethnicity. Multiculturalism is a means of creating a society in which ethnicity is accommodated as integral and legitimate but without undermining the interconnectedness of the core. Put baldly, multiculturalism is concerned with **de-politicizing ethnicity** as part of the society-building exercise. That is Canada's response to the challenge of making society safe for ethnicity, as well as safe from ethnicity.

CHAPTER HIGHLIGHTS

- The centrality of ethnicity in complex, urban societies ranks as one of the more remarkable features of the late twentieth century. Nevertheless, our understanding of ethnicity is subject to ongoing revision and new interpretations in light of uncovered evidence.

- Ethnicity is examined from three perspectives: as group relations in competition for scarce resources, as a key variable that constructs and maintains unequal relations, and as an exercise in society-building or society-bashing.

- The emergence of ethnicity represents a powerful theme in the reconstruction of contemporary societies like Canada. The world is being pushed and pulled by diametrically opposed forces. A multinational-driven globalism is pushing the world together ("homogenizing") in a rational and calculating way. The forces of ethnicity, in turn, are pushing it apart.

- Nation-states appear to be the main casualties in this world-wide tug of war between ethnicity and globalization. It remains to be seen if nation-states are indeed "too big" to handle "small" problems of ethnicity or "too small" to cope with big problems of a market-driven globalism.

- Ethnicity is a powerful force that is capable of arousing both deep and irrational feelings as well as a sense of identity and continuity in times of uncertainty and change. These emotional and cognitive dimensions can be manipulated as a political organizing tool.

- Ethnicity at personal levels involves a search for continuity, community, and commitment in a world of diversity, change, and uncertainty. At group level, ethnicity refers to a strategic device for improving advantage in a competitive context. At societal levels, ethnicity represents a way of organizing social relations in terms of who gets what.

- Ethnicity can be defined as a principle of organization for mobilizing individuals into action groups on the basis of self-definition and shared characteristics.

- Confusion can sometimes arise from failure to separate ethnicity as a "thing" (the objective components that comprise an ethnic group) versus ethnicity as a "process" (including subjective experiences and intergroup relations).

- From a sociological perspective, ethnicity arises primarily (but not exclusively) from intergroup conflict and competition. It represents a dynamic resource which can be called into action by emphasizing community, continuity, and identity during periods of stress or change. Individuals and groups rely on ethnicity to define an appropriate self-image, to articulate demands, or to express dissatisfaction.

- The surge in ethnicity can be explained. Inasmuch as ethnicity resembles a practical response to modern problems, the "instrumentalist" perspective provides an interpretation that complements the "primordial" and "identity" hypotheses.

- Ethnicity is manifested in several ways, including that of ethnic communities; ethnic identities; and social movements.

- Urban Canada continues to be the site of ethnic enclaves that provide a degree of community and continuity for more traditional members, as well as social and institutional support.

- One's ethnicity can provide an important component of identification for many Canadians. Ethnic identities can be expressed at the level of "lived-in," "symbolic," and "radical."

- Ethnicity is increasingly expressed in terms of social movements. Commonly called ethnic nationalism, the politicization of ethnicity has grave consequences for the survival of the modern nation-state.

- Civic nationalism differs from ethnic nationalism is several ways. At the core of civic nationalism is a belief that people should be identified and evaluated on the basis of what they do as individuals, not on who they are as members of a group.

- Ethnically diverse countries confront a challenge with respect to national identity and unity. Initiatives such as Canada's official multiculturalism are best seen as moves to de-politicize ethnicity as a means of national survival and society-building.

KEY TERMS

Cultural Division of Labour
De-politicizing Ethnicity
Ethnic Boundaries
Ethnic Closure
Ethnic Groups
Ethnic Nationalism

Ethnic Surge
Ethnicity
Expressive Thesis
Identity Thesis
Instrumental Thesis
Lived-in Ethnicity
Modernization Thesis

Primordial Thesis
Radical Ethnicity
Resource Mobilization Theory
Situational (or Symbolic) Ethnicity
Sociobiology

REVIEW QUESTIONS

1) Globalism and ethnicity represent two powerful trends at present. Explain the magnitude and scope of these forces in terms of their potential impact on a nation-state such as Canada.

2) Three major approaches — primordialist, identity, and instrumental ("resource mobilization") — have historically been utilized to explain the ethnic surge. Compare and contrast.

3) Using the Hutterites as a primary example, compare and contrast the concept of lived-in ethnic identity with that of situational ethnic identity.

4) How is ethnicity expressed? Focus on the notions of community, identity, and social movement.

5) What are the impact and implications for ethnicity in Canada's continuing efforts to make the country safe for ethnicity, as well as safe from ethnicity?

6) Explain the logic that prevails behind the notions of radical ethnicity and ethnic nationalism.

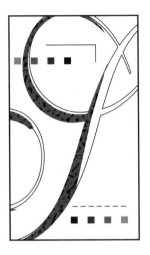

PART 2

THE MAJOR
FORCES IN CANADA

Canada encompasses a formidable array of racial, aboriginal, and ethnic minority groups. Such a profusion of riches poses a problem of who to incorporate in an introductory textbook. Should our sample of minorities include the descendents of the original First Nations who populated Canada thousands of years before the earliest European settlement? Logic would dictate, yes. How much attention should focus on the British or French component? Again, an adequate level of coverage would appear necessary to reflect their importance as Charter (founding) members of Canadian society. Who do we select among other racial and ethnic minority groups in Canada? The rationale for choosing one group over another cannot be taken lightly. Should coverage be geared toward numerically large groups such as those with Germanic or Ukrainian descent? Or should emphasis be directed at primary targets of Canadian racism such as Indo-Pakistani Canadians or African-Canadians (see Buckner 1993)? Can the inclusion of certain minorities be justified on the grounds of sympathy or visibility? Should the decision be based on practical concerns such as access to research material? How do we deal with ethnic groups from Europe ("white ethnics") whose appearance and lifestyle pose less of a threat to Canadian society-building? What about largely ethno-religious sects, namely, the Mennonites of southern Ontario or Hutterites in western Canada? The range of possibilities can be explored indefinitely. Nevertheless, the problem is self-evident at this point: In the face of bewildering array of diversity, who do we select for study and how do we justify our choices?

Specialists in this field have explored different ways to impose some semblance of coherence on an otherwise sprawling subject matter. They have tried to reduce this diversity to manageable proportions in hopes of achieving some degree of logic in the sorting and selection process. One solution suggests we classify Canadian diversity into a limited number of categories by virtue of shared similarities in historical problems, legal status, and contemporary aspirations (Elliott 1983). Our text follows this proposal. Canada is partitioned into three major sectors on the basis of their **relational status** in society. The three major "forces" in Canada include: (a) The First Nations (or Aboriginal Peoples); (b) Charter groups (descendents of the British and French); and (c) multicultural minorities (including immigrants, refugees, landed residents, European ethnics, and native-born people of colour). According to this classificatory scheme, most minorities in Canada can be analyzed on the basis of their representation in one category. Each category is associated with a set of distinctive yet shared properties including (a) legal status in society, (b) relationship with the Canadian state, (c) historical development within the federalist system, (d) problems, needs, concerns, and aspirations, and (e) proposed solutions. Collectively, each major force confronts unique problems: Each is also likely to espouse strategies commensurate with their interests and priorities. Table A compares and contrasts the three major forces on the basis of these criteria.

This table clearly demonstrates how Canada's three "diversities" differ in terms of formal status, fundamental problems, proposed solution, and anticipated outcome. The legal status of the First Nations as the original occupants of Canada defines the dynamics of aboriginal needs, concerns, and aspirations. Foremost on the aboriginal agenda is a commitment to decolonize their relational status through self-determination. Ottawa-Quebec relations are constructed around the constitutional status of founding nations. Failure of central authorities to concede the fundamental notion of this relationship, as manifested in Quebec's demands for distinct society status, provides a catalyst for English- and French-speaking conflicts. Finally, multicultural minorities confront a different set of pressures. Compared to First Nations or the Québécois, both foreign-born and native-born Canadians who are immigrants or descendents of immigrants possess less collective clout because of their non-indigenous status. All multicultural (immigrant) minorities are entitled to citizenship status; nevertheless, the distinct agendas of visible and nonvisible mi-

TABLE A   The Three Major Forces: Comparison and Contrast

	Legal Status	Basic Problem	Proposed Solutions	Anticipated Outcome
1. **Aboriginal Peoples**	First Nations	Colonialism = poverty and powerlessness	Self-determination	The Nations Within
2. **Québécois**	Charter (founding) Member	Blocked Nationalism and Federal Centralization	Separation or Flexible Federalism	Distinct Society
3a) **Multicultural Minorities (People of Colour)**	Immigrant or Descendent of Immigrants	Racial Discrimination	Institutional Accommodation	Substantive Equality
3b) **Multicultural Minorities (European Ethnics**	Immigrant or Descendent of Immigrants	Language and Culture Loss	Celebrate Diversity	Mosaic

norities clearly reveal differences in the worlds occupied by people of colour versus predominantly northern European ethnics.

We believe this system of classification provides a convenient organizing principle. Exceptions, of course, abound in this kind of typology. The very nature of "ideal types" is prone to exaggeration, as the sociologist Max Weber once noted, but such is the price of meaningful analysis or workable comparisons. After all, the goal of any typological exercise is not to replicate reality to its last detail, but to render it intelligible for analytical purposes. Foremost in terms of groups that are difficult to classify are religious ethnicities such as the Anabaptists (Hutterites). Unlike other immigrants to Canada, the Hutterites received special exemptions from central authorities as inducements for settlement (freedom from bearing arms and freedom to set up separate schooling). French-speaking Canadians outside of Quebec also fall between the cracks of our admittedly less than watertight scheme. Francophones who live outside the province of Quebec have no formal status. Yet their status as official language minorities entitles them to certain rights above and beyond normal citizenship.

Beyond its limitations, the classification of groups by virtue of **relational status** solves a major problem. It specifies convenient units of analysis for comparison and contrast. Recurrent themes and predictable patterns in group behaviour can be emphasized without lapsing into a welter of detail. Challenges that confront racial, aboriginal, and ethnic minorities will be highlighted in terms of (a) why they exist, (b) how they are manifested, and (c) what has been and can be done toward resolution. Specifics are sacrificed along the way; yet readers will benefit from exposure to the logic rather than the details behind evolving trends in Canada's diversity agenda. Exposure to the principles that are animating and re-shaping the contours of Canadian society is an additional benefit.

Part Two is organized around this level of analysis. The major diversities in Canadian society are analyzed in terms of (a) who they are, (b) what they want, (c) how they propose to achieve their goals, and (d) what barriers interfere with implementation. In Chapter Seven, we begin this section by examining recent developments in the field of aboriginal-government relations. Emphasis will focus on the dynamics of redefinition and restructuring as competing groups attempt to grapple with the "nations within" concept. Chapter Eight analyzes the politics of English-French (Charter group) relations as unequal power relations. A closer look at the language issue will demonstrate its ability not only to advance Québécois ethnicity, but also to address Quebec's perennial concerns against the backdrop of conceptually different Canadas. The last chapter in this part, Chapter Nine, looks at a variety of challenges and concerns that confront multicultural minorities as they cope with the demands of survival in Canada. Primary attention is centered on various issues pertaining to immigration, including a review of immigration policies and patterns as they apply to the past and resonate at present. Part Three on multiculturalism and society-building, will deal more specifically with the management of this diversity.

CHAPTER 7

FIRST NATIONS

If there is any single issue on which Canada cannot hold its head high in the international community, any single area in which we can be accused of falling down on our obligations, it is in the area of aboriginal relations.

(Canadian Human Rights Commission, 1989).

..by far the most serious human rights problem in Canada, and that failure to achieve a more global solution can only continue to tarnish Canada's reputation and accomplishments

(Canadian Human Rights Commission 1994:20).

INTRODUCTION

It is no accident that we begin Part Two with an analysis of First Nations people (also called **aboriginal peoples** or Native Indians as the context suggests). The term "aboriginal" itself refers to the first or original or indigenous occupants of this country. This status as first among equals provides First Nations with the credentials to press claims against the Canadian state for entitlement on the basis of inherent jurisdiction (Fleras 1996). The term "first" can also be used in a less flattering way. Aboriginal peoples are "first" in those social areas that count least (unemployment, undereducation, suicide, and morbidity rates), but last in realms that matter most. With the possible exception of French-English relations, they also are "first" in terms of total publicity — much of it reflecting a popular view of aboriginal peoples as "problem people" who "have problems" or "create problems" that cost or provoke. Some of this media exposure is sympathetic, but much reflects degrees of indifference or ignorance. Most coverage is inadequate to provide anything but a fleeting glimpse into changing realities. The circulation of this misinformation is unfortunate. A considerable amount of public sympathy and good will is squandered because most Canadians are abysmally unaware of what aboriginal peoples want, why they want it, and how they propose to get it (Ponting 1988).

Canadian treatment of the First Nations has been called a national tragedy and a disgrace with overtones of neglect, oppression, and expediency. Negative stereotypes prevail, in spite of nationally recognized accomplishments in fields as diverse as art, literature, and academics. Yet First Nation efforts at renewal and healing are often under-appreciated or under-reported. Inasmuch as such a reality gap hinders rather than helps, this chapter will examine the emergent status of aboriginal peoples as the "nations within." Equating aboriginal-state relations with internal colonialism enables us to explore how this relationship of inequality is defined, maintained, contested, and modified by way of state policy and government practices. The complex and difficult issues associated with this reconstruction process should never be underestimated. Aboriginal demands are organized around the principle of nationhood rather than social integration, and there is much to be gained by seeing indigenous efforts toward reconstitution of the elements of that nationality through restoration of aboriginal communities and cultural values as well as self-determination and territorial reappropriation (Alfred 1995; Salée 1995). That alone need not deter us from appreciating how these transformative dynamics may help or hinder Canadian society-building. It also points the way to aboriginal renewal and the start of a much delayed healing process.

The chapter begins with a brief overview of aboriginal peoples in terms of their legal and socioeconomic status. This is followed by an examination of policy changes that historically have shaped aboriginal-state relationships. Aboriginal policy is shown to have generated as many problems as it set out to solve, partly because of faulty premises and partly from concern with "national interests" (Boldt 1993). We attend to the politics of redesigning an appropriate working agenda for aboriginal-government relations by focusing on the actions and reactions of the **Department of Indian Affairs and Northern Development (DIAND)**. Aboriginal solutions to the so-called Indian problem are explored as part of an overall shift toward "aboriginality" as the source for a blueprint for reconstruction. Comparable initiatives by aboriginal peoples elsewhere in the world are also discussed as grounds for contextualizing Canada's experience with a broader perspective. Our intent is to equip students with the resources they need to decipher the underlying rationale behind aboriginal-state restructuring.

A word of warning to the reader. Neither of the authors is of aboriginal ancestry so we cannot speak from an aboriginal perspective. Our analysis cannot capture the experiences, aspirations, and constraints that routinely confront the original occupants of "Turtle Island" (North America) because of colonialist pressures. All we can do is reflect upon our research experience in Canada and elsewhere as a basis for assessing the contemporary situation. This limitation, of course, need not be fatal since an outsider's point of view can augment an insider's interpretation. Reliance throughout this chapter on the works of aboriginal scholars and colleagues will serve to lessen the potential for distortion.

Second, the limitations of space cannot be ignored. It is impossible to compress into a single chapter all there is know about aboriginal peoples, both past and present. The necessity to be selective leads us to concentrate on a single dimension of aboriginal life, namely, the evolving relationship of the First Nations with the Canadian state (or government) as embodied in official policy and administration. Admittedly, this decision to restrict ourselves to the politics of power may rob the reader of the richness associated with aboriginal existence. Nevertheless, we firmly believe that these political dimensions offer the most provocative challenges to society-building in Canada.

Third, our discussion of First Nations is confined to general terms. This increases the risk of ignoring the historical and social specifics of different tribes and bands. Aboriginal peoples themselves are legally divided into status, non-status, Metis, and Inuit — each with a specific set of problems and solutions. Variation can be found among aboriginal groups in the Atlantic provinces, Central Canada, the Western Plains, Yukon and the Northwest Territories, and the Pacific West. The diversity is conditioned by ecological adaptations to unique physical environments, along with corresponding differences in the symbolic and material cultures. Adjustment problems vary for aboriginal peoples in remote and rural reserves, in contrast with those who reside in towns and cities. Compounding geographical variation are individual differences based on age, gender, education levels, and socio-economic status. The political concerns of aboriginal "elites," with their focus on "inherency" and "self-governance," may be at odds with the more practical aspirations of community members. In short, there are numerous traps in discussing aboriginal peoples as if they were a relatively homogeneous entity with a common set of problems and a uniform set of solutions. Common sense will dictate they are as heterogeneous as non-native Canadians in political outlook and cultural aspirations. The reader must keep this in mind when sorting out the debates in a field of burgeoning complexity.

CONTEMPORARY STATUS

Aboriginal peoples comprise an extremely diverse constituency, with numerous tribes of varying size, access to resources, development levels, and social health. According to the 1991 Census, aboriginal peoples comprise about 3.7 percent of Canada's population, with 1,002,675 reporting aboriginal ancestry — up 41 percent since 1986 because of natural increases and different means of enumeration. Social and cultural differences among aboriginal tribes remain as real as they did prior to European contact (Frideres 1993). Aboriginal communities vary in terms of development and socioeconomic status; Differences also exist between rural and urban natives as well as between women and men. Even the term "aboriginal peoples" is misleading, since this constitutional status can be further subdivided into the categories of **status Indians**, **non-status Indians**, **Metis**, and **Inuit**.

Legal Dimensions

Aboriginal peoples with highest profile in Canada are **status Indians**. Membership to status Indians is defined by (a) admittance to a general registry in Ottawa, (b) affiliation with one of 605 bands, (c) entitlement to residence on band reserve lands, and and (d) jurisdiction under the Indian Act. The current population of status Indians stands at 553,316 — up from the 230,902 in 1967. These numbers are expected to increase to about 750,000 by 2005 primarily through reinstatement of individuals who had lost status through marriage or other means. Ontario has the largest population of status Indians with 121, 867 followed by British Columbia with 90,769 (Socioeconomic Status, DIAND, *The Globe and Mail* July 5, 1994). Status Indians reside on one of 2,597 reserves across Canada, ranging in size from a handful of people on one Pacific coast reserve to nearly 16,000 at the Six Nations Reserve near Brantford, Ontario. The majority of status Indians (59.2 percent in 1992) live on reserves created by one of 61 treaties signed with the Crown. These numbers can vary because of fluctuations in the pattern of rural-urban migration (Dosman 1972). The interests of status Indians are represented by 633 chiefs who comprise the Assembly of First Nations. These interests are supported by the federal government which targets over five billion dollars per year to this group because of treaty and fiduciary responsibilites. Only a small percentage (about four percent) of this amount is directed at aboriginal economic development, primarily in the form of loans for business (Buckley 1992), with the bulk monopolized by administrative costs and social spending.

The second category of aboriginal peoples are **non-status Indians.** The exact population is unknown, but estimates fluctuate from 75,000 to 750,000. Unlike status Indians, non-status Indians are exempt from provisions of the Indian Act or the Department of Indian Affairs. Some individuals, relinquished their official status in exchange for the right to vote, drink alcohol off the reserve, or (in the case of women) to marry a non-Indian. Others never entered into any formal treaty agreement with the federal government. Non-status Indians do not live on reserves (only status Indians are entitled to reserve life and receive band inheritance); they are scattered in small towns and large cities across Canada. This geographical and social isolation is not conducive to preserving language, culture, or identity. Despite this formal estrangement from their roots, many non-status Indians continue to identify themselves as aboriginal peoples because of shared affinities. Inclusion of non-status Indians as aboriginal peoples by the Canadian Constitution of 1982 has legitimated the identity and concerns of non-status Indians. Still, relationships between non-status and status Indians have been fraught with disagreement because of competition over limited federal resources. Currently, non-status Indians are represented by the Congress of Aboriginal Peoples.

The third class, the **Metis**, constitute a sprawling category comprising the offspring (and descendents) of mixed European-aboriginal unions. Numbering in the vicinity of between 100,000 and 400,000 persons, many dwell in relatively remote communities (in some cases, settlements, such as exist in Alberta) throughout the Prairie provinces. The 192,000 Metis across the Prairies are represented by the Metis National Council. The Metis (like non-status Indians) do not fall under the provisions of the Indian Act. Nevertheless, the Metis are officially regarded as aboriginal peoples with a corresponding right to claims upon the Canadian state. Proposed government land transfers involving Metis and non-status Indians may provide these groups full or partial control of much of Canada's northern land mass. The Alberta government has also recognized Metis self-governing rights along with the right to limited institutional autonomy.

The **Inuit** constitute the final category. With the population at about 40,000, the Inuit enjoy a special status and relationship with the federal government despite never having signed any treaty arrangements. Their interests at national levels are represented by the Inuit Tapirisat ("an association of various Inuit leaders") of Canada. The Inuit have recently concluded successful negotiations with Ottawa for control over their homeland — Nunavut — in the Eastern Arctic. The first case study highlights Inuit struggles to **decolonize** through creation of a unique self-government arrangement.

CASE STUDY

Nunavut: Decolonizing the North

Status Indians are not the only aboriginal people in Canada who have undergone a process of decolonization. Aboriginal peoples such as non-status Indians, Metis, and Inuit have also taken comparable steps to redefine their status and relationship within Canada's federalist system. Similarities in outlook are evident. The principle of aboriginality as a new paradigm has gained both constitutional and legislative strength in Canada's Arctic. The old paradigm, based on treaties, reserves, and outdated colonialism, was never practical for the circumpolar peoples, given geographical and demographic considerations. The evolving paradigm is squarely rooted in the principle of aboriginal rights of self-determination over their cultural and social affairs. But differences among the aims of these groups also exist. Aboriginal peoples such as Inuit and Metis each endorse different visions of what they want for historical, geographic, social, and cultural reasons. This section will highlight some of these differences by briefly examining the aspirations and progress of the Inuit of Canada's north.

THE NUNAVUT NATION

The Inuit of the Canadian Arctic have undergone considerable change in response to political and social pressures. Once isolated and without a common awareness for collective action, the Inuit have taken steps since the early 1970s to redefine themselves in relationship with each other and with the Canadian state. In the Eastern Arctic, Inuit aspirations were couched within the framework of Nunavut — The Inuktitut word for "our land" and also the name of a group of Inuit living in the Eastern Arctic. To date, the concept of Nunavut remains unrecognized in the constitution: nevertheless, the process of defining it and its ratification in 1993 allows us some glimpse into the dynamics of Canadian nation-building in the North.

The Eastern Arctic Inuit themselves number about 20,000, scattered across a tract of land the size of Argentina. Unlike status Indians in the South, the Inuit were the undisputed landlords of the North, having never entered into treaty arrangements with federal or provincial governments. Legally, however, the Inuit possessed the same status as aboriginal peoples elsewhere in Canada because of a 1939 Supreme Court ruling. Until the 1970s the Inuit did not share a common sense of peoplehood. Political, geographic, dialectical, and jurisdictional problems militated against promotion of a shared and united front under the aboriginal banner. This inability to foster a pan-Inuit identity and aboriginality undermined efforts to exert pressure on central authorities to negotiate territorial self-determination.

THE VISION OF NUNAVUT

The vision and struggle for Nunavut gathered momentum during the early 1970s. This redefining process was derived from aboriginal movements in Canada and United States as well as throughout the world. In 1976, the Inuit Tapirisat submitted its first proposal for the establishment of Nunavut. The plan sought to establish an single Inuit homeland across the Arctic, covering nearly two million square kilometres of land and adjacent offshore areas, modelled largely on the Cree land claim settlement negotiated with the Quebec government as part of the James Bay agreement. Nine years later in 1984, the agreement still unsigned, another group, the Inuvialiut Inuit signed a second land claim settlement in the Western Arctic. Having settled their grievances, the Inuvialiut Inuit were free to align themselves with either the more limited proposals of the Denedeh in the Western Arctic or broad vision of the Nunavut of the Eastern Arctic. For various political, geographical, and cultural reasons, the Inuvialiut cast their lot with the Denedeh. But in rejecting the original Inuit vision of a homeland for all the Arctic, they dampened the possibility of achieving Nunavut as reality.

What exactly does the Nunavut vision consist of? Nunavut conjures up the same emotional appeal that "mon pays" does for the Québécois. The sustaining vision of Nunavut is a society with full control over its culture and language, its resources, and environment. Equally important is the settlement of Nunavut land claims. Proposals for self-government, however, are a relatively unimportant part of the agreement. In contrast with aboriginal aspirations elsewhere, the vision of Nunavut revolves around the principle of public (not aboriginal) government in which all residents have voting rights regardless of racial or cultural background. That kind of inclusiveness makes Nunavut an appealing proposition to vote-hungry politicians.

The need for such an overarching plan was evident; the social and economic needs of the Inuit were desperate in some cases and forecasted to worsen if current trends continued and no change in governmental structure was made (Irwin 1989). Forces that were undermining efforts at cultural and language preservation were increasingly difficult to control under the territorial system. In addition, a diversified economic base was required to meet the material needs of an ever-burgeoning population.

A VISION REALIZED

The vision of Nunavut came to fruition in May of 1993 when the Nunavut Land Claims Agreement was signed by federal, territorial, and the Tungavik Federation (DIAND May 1994). Under the terms of the agreement, the Inuit will receive ownership of 350,000 square kilometres of land, including access to 36,000 square kilometres of mineral rights. The agreement provides financial compensation of $1.14 billion to be paid out over 14 years. A thirteen million dollar Training Trust Fund will be established to ensure Inuit have the skills to implement terms of the settlement. The final agreement also made provisions for the establishment of a Nunavut Territory and a "public" government which would cover about one-fifth of Canada's land mass and come into effect in 1999. The Nunavut Assembly will not resemble aboriginal self-government in the "sovereign" sense; rather, it will operate as part of the Canada's Parliamentary system, with the Inuit in effective control by virtue of the fact they comprise 85 percent of the population. The fact that they already have begun implementing wildlife harvesting rights and participating in environmental exercises suggests that the vision of Nunavut is rapidly becoming a practical reality.

Socioeconomic Status

Nearly four hundred years of sustained contact and interaction have left aboriginal-government relations in a state of disarray and despair. The imposition of a colonialistic framework in this country exerted a powerful negative effect on aboriginal peoples (Bienvenue 1985). In some cases, government policies deliberately undermined the viability of aboriginal communities in order to serve the never-ending quest for assimilation of indigenous people and the desire for land. In other cases, however, this decline came about through unobtrusive, yet equally powerful measures pertaining to education and missionization.

The combined effect has been nothing short of disastrous. No matter how they are evaluated and assessed, aboriginal peoples as a group remain at the bottom of the socioeconomic heap. Housing is inadequate or overcrowded on many reserves, failing to meet basic standards of amenities and structure. Fewer than 50 percent of aboriginal homes have sewer or water connections (Frideres 1993). Unemployment rates are three times that of average of non-native Canadians. On certain reserves, up to 95 percent of the population subsists on welfare or unemployment benefits. The awkward location of many reserves and their limited resources are a problem, as is the refusal of many residents of reserves to leave whether or not the reserve provides the tools to generate jobs or wealth. The situation is equally grim for the one-half to one-third who live in cities with few skills, high unemployment, derelict housing, and inadequate services, yet are cut off from federal funding or reserve benefits. Only a small percentage (about 20 percent) of aboriginal students even finish secondary schooling, let alone go on to postsecondary levels, although the numbers at university have increased from 200 in the 1960s to 22,000 in the mid 1990s. That so few ever make it to university is a situation many believed would have worsened if the government had fulfilled its threat to restrict post-secondary spending. Low performance levels invariably lead to low paying jobs or none at all. Of course, not all aboriginal peoples are destined to fail — even when measured by mainstream standards. Success stories abound, including the recent selection of a formerly poverty-stricken Quebec Cree community (Ouje Bougoumou) by a UN committee as one of the 50 places around the world that best exemplifies the objectives of the United Nations (Platiel 1995). Nor should success by evaluated on such narrow grounds. There are individuals who possess secure and satisfying prospects and exceptionally enriched lives without rejecting one or both cultures. As a group, however, most live under conditions that evoke images of grinding Third World poverty.

The deterioration of aboriginal cultural values has compounded the difficulties of identity and adjustment. As well, numerous aboriginal languages are currently under threat of disappearing because of the pressure of English (and French) in the schools and mass media (Fleras 1987). Equally detrimental has been the psychological effects derived from a sense of powerlessness, alienation, and irrelevance (Shkilynk 1985). As noted by David Courchene, a former president of the Manitoba Indian Brotherhood

> One hundred years of submission and servitude, of protectionism and paternalism have created psychological barriers for Indian people that are far more difficult to break down and conquer than the problems of economic and social poverty (quoted in Buckley 1992:24).

Aboriginal peoples are likely to transform this powerlessness and impotence into an expression of self-hatred. The internalization of white racism and/or indifference is reflected in violent death rates which are up to four times the national average. Infant mortality rates are about 60 percent higher than the national average. Alcohol and substance abuse are widely regarded as the foremost problems on most reserves, with alcohol-related deaths accounting for up to 80 percent of the fatalities on some reserves (Buckley 1992). Physical abuse and coercive punishment at residential schools, according to the the AFN publication *Breaking the Silence*, may be linked with social breakdowns at household and community levels. Violent deaths and suicides are also out of proportion when compared to the general population. In fact, with a suicide rate of six times the national average for certain age specific groups, aboriginal peoples represent one of the most self-destructive groups in the world at present.

Aboriginal involvement with the criminal justice system is no less imbalanced. Nearly 70 percent of status Indians have been incarcerated in a correctional centre at some point in their lives by the age of twenty-five (DuCharme 1986). Aboriginal inmates occupy 40 percent of the space in Western Canada's prisons, but only about 12 percent of the Prairie population. Some degree of cautiousness must be exercised: Statistics may be misleading since offenders may be convicted for relatively minor offences and serve time for offences that require only a fine. As well, only a small number of individuals may get in trouble with the law, but on a repeated basis (Buckley 1992). The combination of these social and cultural straitjackets has stripped many aboriginal peoples of any positive self-concept, in effect leading to self-fulfilling cycles of despair and decay. Nor can we disregard the sometimes disastrous consequences of often well-intentioned, but misguided government policies and programs (Shkilynk 1985).

To put this information into context, the "For the Record" box following (Table 7.1) provides a comparative look at First Nations in Canada and the United States. It offers a capsule summary of developments and expenditures during 1993/94 with respect to demographics, government funding, lands, government services, treaty rights, and self-government (DIAND Nov. 1993). It also furnishes an overview of how Canada compares with the United States in its treatment of the First Nations. The impression is that of greater government expenditure and involvement in Canada. Whether or not this has had a positive or negative effect can only be examined on a case by case basis.

First Nations in the Cities

Reserves were once regarded as tools of colonialism and subjugation or locales of chronic poverty. They increasingly are endorsed as sites of aboriginal identity, self-determination, and self-government (Comeau and Sandin 1990). That points to a striking ambiguity: The very isolation of these reserves fosters the "essence" of aboriginal being, both physical and psychological. The fact that they serve as a refuge from and buffer against a hostile outside world also complicates adjustment problems (Buckley 1992). Reserve communities furnish spiritual assistance and social security for aboriginal persons — even with high levels of unemployment and delapidated living conditions. Yet nearly 40 percent of the aboriginal population according to the 1986 census data prefer to live off reserve, double the number of the early 1970s (McMillan 1988). Prairie cities such as Regina and Winnipeg are characterized by high aboriginal concentrations (about 20 percent of the total population). With nearly 65,000 aboriginal peoples, Toronto is now regarded as Canada's largest reserve.

Reasons for migration are numerous, but often reflect "push" factors (lack of resources, opportunity, or excitement) and "pull" forces related to employment, education, and lifestyle. Structural (band size, proximity to urban centres), social (poor housing, unemployment), and cultural (socialization) factors are important in making the decision to leave — or return (Frideres 1993). For some the move to cities is positive. There are aboriginal lawyers, teachers, nurses, and successful entrepreneurs, many of whom earn high incomes and are actively involved in the community. For others, there are numerous difficulties in coping with the demands of a large urban centre (Moore 1995). Life off the reserve is beset with missed economic opportunities, abysmal living conditions and homelessness, exposure to substance abuses, discrimination and lack of cultural awareness, and repeated brushes with the law (Maidman 1981).

FOR THE RECORD

TABLE 7.1   First Nations in Canada and the United States:
A Comparison

	Canada	United States
Demographics		
• **Number of self-identified** aboriginal persons	1,002,675	1,906,966
• **Percentage of population**	3.7 percent	1 percent
• **Number of federally recognized** aboriginal bands/tribes	605	516
Funding		
• **Total federal expenditures**	$5.4 billion	$6.6 billion (Cdn.)
• **Target**	Status Indians on reserve and Inuit	Federally recognized tribes on reservations
• **Per capita expenditure on residents** of reserve/reservation	$13,109	$6,621 (Cdn.)
Lands		
• **Number of reserves**	2,364	287
• **Land held in trust**	1.11 million hect.	22.68 million hect.
• **Expenditure on economic development**	$347 million	$59.8 million (Cdn.)
Services		
• **(a) Health expenditure**	$836 million	n/a
• **(b) Education spending to tertiary levels**	$927.7 million	$629 million (Cdn.)
• **(c) Constitutional status**	Constitutionally entrenched aboriginal and treaty rights	No constitutional status
Treaty Rights	Peace and friendship + cessation (land and non-land) treaties	Simple land cessation treaties (none after 1871)
Self-Government	Community-based + inherent	Domestic dependent nations (internal sovereignty)

Adapted from DIAND, Nov. 1993

Imbalances in the city and on the reserve have lead some aboriginal migrants to accept dual residence (see Dosman 1972). Home in winter may be the city where welfare and heated accommodation make life bearable. Summer sees an exodus back to the reserve for the company of relatives and rural lifestyles (Comeau and Sandin 1990). The federal government, for its part, offers little in the way of services to off -reserve aboriginals, citing jurisdictional problems with the provinces as a stumbling block. Established government institutions are ill equipped (both in terms of resources or needs assessments) to provide adequate culturally-sensitive services to aboriginal clients (Maidman 1981). Many aboriginal-run voluntary agencies have been established to address issues of health care, traditional healing, shelter, and criminal justice. Nevertheless, the gap between supply and demand continues to increase.

Aboriginal Women

The plight of aboriginal women has received increased exposure. But both formal studies and personal testimonies indicate that aboriginal women rank among the most severely disadvantaged people in Canada (DIAND 1979; Silman 1987; see also Allen 1986 and Witt 1984 for similar assessment in United States). Economically, they are worse off than non-aboriginal women and aboriginal men in terms of income levels and employment options. Social hardships are numerous, and include abusive male family members, sexual assaults and rapes, inadequate housing, squalid living conditions, unhealthy child-raising environments, and alcohol and drug abuse. Levels of violence directed against aboriginal women and children is extremely high: As explained by the Native Women's Association of Canada in a 1991 brief (quoted in Razack 1994: 910):

> We have a disproportionately high rate of child sexual abuse and incest. We have wife battering, gang rapes, drug and alcohol abuse, and every kind of perversion imaginable has been imported into our lives...

Depression and self-hatred among aboriginal women is vented in high rates of suicide, alcohol dependency, or neglect of children. Nearly 6.4 percent of aboriginal children (status Indian) in 1986 were in protective care compared with only 1 percent of the general population (Comeau and Sandin 1990). Derogatory stereotypes from the past remain an ongoing problem (Witt 1984; also LaRocque 1975; 1990).

Negative images make it difficult to recognize the positive contributions of aboriginal women to community life and social change. Historical and social factors work against adequate recognition. Those who lost status because of marriage to non-aboriginal males have been penalized through deprivation of Indian rights, ostracism from involvement in band life, and exclusion from housing and jobs. Not even the repeal of the offending passage (Section 12(1)(b) of the Indian Act in 1985) has eased the barriers for some women. Their status and that of their children has been reinstated but several bands have refused membership and residence because of scarce resources. Finally, efforts by aboriginal women to do away with blatant forms of discrimination have met with resistance on the grounds that tampering with the status quo could jeopardize aboriginal status as set out in the Indian Act (Weaver 1993).

ABORIGINAL POLICY:
FROM COLONIZATION TO NATIONS WITHIN

Federal policy toward aboriginal peoples has evolved over the 125 years. An initial period of cooperation and accommodation gave way to assimilation and through residential segregation. Placement on reserves facilitated the process of resocialization (assimilation) of aboriginal peoples into independent and hardworking Christian farmers. The late 1940s resulted in yet another move toward integration and ordinary citizenship. In rejecting an agenda of wardship and control, government policies and programs sought to normalize relations with aboriginal peoples. Yet aboriginal reaction to the "termination" of federal responsibility was sharp and hostile. Policy discourse shifted again in the 1970s toward a greater tolerance of aboriginal languages and culture as well as proposed institutional control over health and education. Aboriginal-government relations continued to explore the logical consequences of a commitment to **limited autonomy** and power-sharing (Tobias 1976). A recent shift toward **inherent rights to self government** and **self-determination** suggests the possibility of a new policy paradigm.

Setting the Policy Agenda: The Royal Proclamation

Aboriginal policy in the broadest sense began with the Royal Proclamation of 1763. The Proclamation sought to establish British sovereignty over the unexplored interior of Turtle Island. Aboriginal tribes were acknowledged as "nations within," with claims to treatment as a distinct people with self-determining, self-governing rights (Clark 1990; Fleras and Elliott 1992). The Proclamation also demonstrated a willingness to recognize aboriginal land title through traditional use and ancestral occupancy (Raphals 1991). Nevertheless, Crown objectives went beyond control over settlers and land secured through treaties; it also sought to expand that power to include sovereignty over the First Nations and their territory (Boldt 1993).

Assimilation (1867-1945)

Initial contacts with French and British explorers, missionaries, and traders were reasonably cooperative and mutually beneficial. Relationships were based on a principle of co-existence involving reciprocal trade and practical accommodation in matters such as subsistence and miscegenation. All sides pursued military alliances with powerful tribes. With some obvious exceptions, this state of affairs persisted into the latter stages of the eighteenth century. This symbiotic relationship began to unravel by the turn of the nineteenth century (Purich 1986). Reciprocity and accommodation gave way to a system of internal colonialism and conquest-oriented acculturation, reflecting Britain's and France's desire for (a) political control of aboriginal populations, (b) protection of British and French interests, and (c) removal of competition for scarce resources. The end of the 1812 War with United States meant that aboriginal allies were no longer required by the British. Land-hungry settlers looked instead to aboriginal lands as open spaces for settlement and agriculture.

A policy of assimilation evolved in an attempt to subdue, transform, and control the First Nations. In 1867, the federal government assumed jurisdiction over aboriginal affairs with the establishment of Indian Affairs branch under the Secretary of State (Ponting and Gibbins 1980). Subsequent passage of the 1876 Indian Act created the legal framework for administration of aboriginal affairs under federal jurisdiction as stipulated in the BNA of 1867. The Act stripped First Nations communities of their political sovereignty, while imposing a system of indirect (elected band council) rule and pervasive segregation. Imposition of internal colonialism resulted in the denial of self-governing rights, foreclosure of social and economic opportunities, and restriction of language and cultural values. Early department activities were consistent with the mandate and provisions of the Indian Act (see next case study), with its numerous trust obligations pertaining to land claims and dictatorial intrusion into all aspects of community life (Platiel 1994b). Its colonialist/paternalistic character reflected a perception of aboriginal peoples as childlike wards of the state in need of superior guidance and protection (Ponting and Gibbins 1980; Ponting 1986). Aboriginal peoples were placed on reserves to ensure protection from lawless elements interested only in profit or amusement. Reserves were justified as "holding pens" to facilitate the resocialization of these "misguided heathen." Through a combination of incentives and sanctions, Indian Affairs sought to destroy the cultural basis of aboriginal society; transform aboriginal peoples through exposure to Christianity and arts of civilization; and assimilate (absorb) them into society as self-reliant and productive citizens.

Neither assimilation as policy nor the reserve system as practice brought about anticipated changes. Even legislation ostensibly aimed at protecting or improving the lot of aboriginal communities did not achieve much — except to keep the First Nations out of sight and under control (Frideres 1993). Federal responses to racist and evolutionary philosophies that disparaged aboriginal peoples as inferior and helpless left much to be desired (Weaver 1984). Treaty agreements signed with the federal government resulted in sometimes fraudulent arrangements and illegal land transfers. Efforts to solve the "**Indian problem**" by imposing an assimilationist gridlock upon aboriginal-government relations prevailed well into the twentieth century.

Integration (1945-1973)

Canada's treatment of aboriginal people came under scrutiny after the Second World War. An official commitment to assimilation gave way to the principles of integration as successive governments sought to redefine their responsibilities to aboriginal peoples. The collective mindset of central authorities reflected this shift toward integration by moving away from the control-and-deliver mentality that had prevailed as a blueprint since 1876. The reorganization of federal service delivery through direct band involvement began in 1956 with the funding of several local education committees. The rationale for this restructuring drew strength from three assumptions: first, that there was a real need to establish aboriginal rather than federal control over community affairs; second, that communities with proper resources were better equipped to solve local problems; and, third, that centralized structures were ineffective for problem solving when dealing with a geographically dispersed and culturally diverse people. In short, the shift toward devolution and decentralization bolstered the move toward community-based control over local jurisdictions. The government also conceded the importance of softening the harshly bureaucratic image of the Department of Indian Affairs.

Strategies to desegregate aboriginal peoples through integration into the mainstream proved increasingly attractive. By 1969, the Liberal government under Pierre Elliott Trudeau had proposed legislation for terminating the special relationship between the First Nations and the federal government (Weaver 1981). Federal responsibility would be transferred largely to the provinces. The Indian Act was to be repealed and the Department of Indian Affairs dismantled, while aboriginal assets (including lands) would be divided on a per capita basis. The **White Paper** also recommended the eventual abolition of aboriginal treaty privileges and special status as a precondition for "normalizing" entry into Canadian society. This decision to revoke federal obligations was not motivated entirely by political calculation or economic expediency. For the architect of the White Paper, Pierre Elliott Trudeau, the "just" society could not possibly materialize without guarantees of formal legal equality for everyone regardless of race or ethnicity. With the White Paper, in other words, the "Indian problem" would be eliminated by defining it out of existence as a meaningful legal construct.

Reactions from the aboriginal community caught federal policy-makers off guard. Allegations against the White Paper of cultural genocide galvanized aboriginal groups into national protest. The first national body of status Indians, the National Indian Brotherhood, was established to provide a platform for aboriginal concerns. The attainment of justice and equality on aboriginal rather than government terms was foremost on their agenda. Chastened by this collective show of strength, both government and public sectors began to display growing awareness of and sensitivity to aboriginal issues.

Limited Autonomy (1973-1990)

A general commitment to the principle of **limited autonomy** gradually evolved with the collapse of the White Paper initiatives. Federal policy for much of the 1970s (and arguably the 1980s) remained at an impasse — even to the point of paralysis — as government response moved from crisis to crisis with little or no sense of what to do except to appear responsive by mollifying public concern and squelching aboriginal outrage (Cassidy 1991). Since 1973, the Canadian government has formally, if somewhat grudgingly, acknowledged the legitimacy of **aboriginal and treaty rights**. Even more noticeable were First Nation initiatives to capture and transform the federal policy agenda. This focus on self-determination through self-government has become more politicized, assertive, and geared toward the constitutional entrenchment of collective aboriginal rights.

The commitment to devolution culminated in the late 1970s with establishment of detailed provisions for aboriginal administration of departmental programs, coupled with funding in support of basic local government programs (DIAND 1993b). A shift toward administrative devolution was consistent with political moves toward fiscal restraint, curtailment of direct federal services, political rationality, and a downsizing of the social policy agenda (see Prince 1987). In 1986, federal authorities announced a policy of community self-government negotiations as part of the reform package — for the most part consistent with Cabinet-approved guidelines for community self-sufficiency, but outside any federally-imposed blueprint. Passage of the Indian Self-Government Community Negotiations in 1987 was viewed as a means of experimenting with different approaches to self-government on a band-by-band basis (Hawkes and Devine 1991). The act was also heralded as a practical albeit interim alternative, to be pursued in conjunction with ongoing negotiations for constitutional entrenchment of inherent self-governance.

A revised social-political contract based on enlarging aboriginal jurisdiction over local affairs has achieved moderate success. Central delivery of programs has moved over for more flexible funding arrangements of decentralized administration, local decision making, and mutual accountability (DIAND 1993b). Government funding is increasingly "unconditional" as had been recommended in the Penner Report of 1983, thus allowing greater discretion (within limits) in allocating resources. Alternative funding arrangements ("comprehensive funding agreements") have proven attractive since they allow priorities and programs to be established by aboriginal groups. Responsibilities for delivery and effectiveness of local programs are localized, with band members increasingly accountable for management of who gets what. In this sense, DIAND has repositioned itself as a developmental agency for the transfer of federal funds to self-government structures in the same way that provinces receive federal block funding for programs and services.

Aboriginal-government discussions in recent years have continued to explore the potential of a limited autonomy model. Moderate reforms no longer strike a responsive chord among aboriginal leaders and activists. Out of self-defence, federal authorities have exhibited a willingness to renegotiate their relations with the First Nations. Policy initiatives have reconsidered the legitimacy of aboriginal demands for control over jurisdictions as a practical alternative. This represents a significant reversal from the previous decade when aboriginal and treaty rights were derogated as contrary to liberal-democratic values (Morse 1985). The 1982 constitutional entrenchment of aboriginal and treaty rights made Canada the first country to take such a bold step. This constitutional principle was gradually put to the litmus test. Several judicial cases during the 1980s established aboriginal rights in matters related to the procurement of wildlife foods. A series of First Minister Conferences between 1983 and 1987 sensitized decision-makers to aboriginal grievances (Brock 1990). But the notion of aboriginal rights continued to be undefined and excluded from the national agenda — as the Meech Lake talks graphically exposed.

Self-Government (1990s –)

Developments of the early 1990s point to a fundamental shift in government aboriginal policy. Current government objectives are geared to preserve "the special place of our first citizens in the country" within the constitutional framework of Canadian society. They also revolve around the four policy pillars, namely, accelerated land claims settlement; improved socioeconomic status on reserves; reconstruction of aboriginal-government relations; and fulfilment of aboriginal concerns as announced by the Prime Mininster in September of 1990. Even the thorny notion of inherency proved palatable as long as the First Nations did not declare independence or undermine Canadian sovereignty through their actions.

The move of aboriginal-state relations from the periphery to the centre of attention is quite remarkable. In 1969, aboriginal peoples in Canada were about to become an endangered group — in the same way earlier tribes (such as the Beothuk in Newfoundland) had become physically extinct. By mid-1991, arguably in response to the 1990 Oka crisis, Ottawa had officially endorsed a parallel aboriginal constitutional process that culminated in full assurances of the First Nations' historic right to negotiate with the Canadian federal authorities on a government-to-government basis. Aboriginal peoples had become solidly entrenched as Canada's first citizens despite a growing neo-conservatism among the general population. Changes had evolved to the point where aboriginal communities were poised to be recognized as a distinct tier of government, with corresponding rights to sit with Canada's First Ministers and debate constitutional reform. Section 35 of the 1982 Constitution Act had already acknowledged their possession of something called "aboriginal rights," that could be used as a potential bargaining chip for negotiation (Asch 1989). At the core of this aboriginality lay the potential for an aboriginal-controlled land base, in conjunction with a separate political jurisdication, and self-determination over a broad range of fronts. These rights, aboriginal leaders had proclaimed, were founded on original sovereignty and remained in effect despite passage of time and circumstances (Clark 1990; Raphals 1991).

The final piece in the decolonizing puzzle fell into place on August 28, 1992. A package of constitutional changes was proposed under the Charlottetown Accord; few of the changes proved as contentious as the decision to restore inherent self-governance for aboriginal peoples. Briefly, the tentative agreement concurred with most of the earlier recommendations by the Royal Commission on Aboriginal Affairs (1992): terms of agreement included constitutional entrenchment of aboriginal self-government both (a)inherent in nature and (b) sovereign in sphere, but (c) circumscribed in extent (no external sovereignty). These largely undefined aboriginal governments would represent a third tier of government alongside the provincial and federal, but remain subject to the provisions of the Charter and the Constitution The irony of the situation cannot be denied: in 1992, exactly 500 years after Columbus's "discovery" and plunder, Canada's aboriginal peoples were poised to restore their rightful status as the "nations within," with as-yet-to-be-defined sovereign rights.

Self-governing rights were to be extended to all aboriginal peoples both off and on the reserve, in addition to Metis and non-status Indians. This right would subsequently be enforced by the courts should political negotiations falter. Exact powers and precise jurisdictions were not defined in advance, but described in general, with specifics for negotiation at a later date. As counterparts of provincial government, aboriginal governments would receive federal transfer payments. They would also secure the power to override those sections of the Charter at odds with aboriginal interests (the "notwithstanding clause" allows dissenting provinces to opt out of constitutional amendments for five years if these interfere with provincial jurisdiction and power). Nor would anything in the Charter or Quebec's proposed distinct society clause detract from the integrity of aboriginal languages, culture, or tradition.

Not everyone agreed with the aboriginal provisions in the Charlottetown Accord — a situation that became academic when the Accord crashed to defeat in an October 1992 national referendum (Hall 1993). Criticisms ranged from those who dismissed aboriginal self-government as a "recipe for chaos" (a "swiss cheese landscape of over 600 principalities"), to others who queried the soundness of a system based on race and separate status. Others were leery of constitutionally entrenching anything not negotiated beforehand. Even those sympathetic to aboriginal aspirations raised concerns about the implementation, costs, and jurisdictions. Quebec, for its part, was understandably wary of any arrangement that infringed on its "territorial integrity" with respect to massive hydroelectric development projects in the James Bay region. Aboriginal peoples were equally divided in their opinion (for some, the Accord contained too much compromise; for others, not enough), with aboriginal women in particular concerned about individual equality provisions under collective arrangements. No less evident were social chasms between urban and rural aboriginal groups, as well as among status and nonstatus Indians, Metis, and Inuit.

Criticism and concerns aside, however, aboriginality as a self-governing principle embodied an idea whose time had come, and there would be no turning back the clock even with the collapse of the Charlottetown Accord. A threshold in restructuring aboriginal-state relations had been scaled: This baseline would henceforth represent the minimum starting point for future negotiations. As of 1995, the Liberal government has taken advantage of this momentum by exploring new political arrangements. On paper, the government has shifted its policy operations toward acceptance of aboriginal peoples as a "nation within" with certain rights to self-government. In the words of Minister of Indian Affairs, Ronald Irwin, "The federal government is committed to building a new partnership with Aboriginal people, a partnership based on mutual respect and trust. Working steadily towards the implementation of *the inherent right of self-government is the cornerstone of that relation* (emphasis, mine) (Government of Canada 1994). Recent Liberal proposals to delegate self-government on a community-to-community basis, with powers and jurisdiction that approximate municipal governments, would appear at odds with the lofty rhetoric of the Minister.

Many applaud the decision to recognize inherent self-government arrangements as an existing treaty right — with or without constitutional backing. These promises, however, are vague and unenforceable, as are the terms of reference and means of implementation, thus allowing the government to wriggle out of commitments if realities outstrip expectations (*Wataway News*, 7 April 1994). Moreover, conferral of inherency can also be manipulated to amplify the role of aboriginal peoples as pawns in a constitutional cat-and-mouse game between Quebec and Ottawa. The decision to experiment with aboriginal self-governments in Manitoba by abolishing the Indian Act and the Department of Indian Affairs is a tantalizing if unproven start.

In short, the points of contention between the First Nations and mainstream are not simply irritants that can solved through pious wishes or good intentions. Even reform or negotiated compromise may be inadequate. The problems are much more fundamental. The two sectors operate within institutional frameworks and sociocultural systems that have little in common or are logically inconsistent because of basically different views on land and property, authority and types of governance, social organization and patterns, and cultural values. That kind of reality gap can only complicate moves to accommodate aboriginal demands for self-determination and territorial repossession (Bedford 1994; Salée 1995).

The next case study, "The Department of Indian Affairs," provides a concrete example of this shift in aboriginal policy from its inception to the present. The case study demonstrates that the fortunes of the Department of Indian Affairs (DIAND) are intimately linked with the evolving character of aboriginal-state relations, since government policy is reflected in the mandate of the deparment and its operational procedures and priorities. The shift in aboriginal state relations — from periphery to centre — is also embedded in departmental moves from a control and delivery mentality to one consistent with partnership, aboriginal self-government, and development. With the decolonization of aboriginal-state relations a distinct possibility, the department may well become an architect (or victim) of its own misfortunes.

CASE STUDY

The Department of Indian Affairs: From Dependency to Partnership

"[T]he whole idea of the federal stewardship over aboriginal peoples — and its manifestation in the Indian Act and a Department of Indian and Northern Affairs — has been an attempt to rationalize and legitimize the relationship between colonizers and colonized" (Report, Human Rights Commission, 1994:24).

The colonialist context of European-aboriginal relations created the historical definition of indigenous populations as a "problem people" in need of control or solution by way of government intervention. A precondition of such internal colonialism was the establishment of state bureaucratic structures for the administration of government aboriginal policy (Blauner 1972). Ostensibly directed toward the well-being of indigenous populations, these "total institutions" (see Goffman 1963) were actually more concerned with national interests related to society-building. But at present, colonialist structures are no longer defensible, and aboriginal peoples everywhere are locked in struggles to sever the bonds of dependency and underdevelopment.

Such a situation exists in Canada where a federal bureaucracy has long presided over aboriginal policy and its administration by various Indian Affairs departments (Ponting and Gibbins 1980). Historically, aboriginal concerns were routinely compromised by restrictions within the Indian Act or the organizational imperatives of an expanding bureaucracy. Ponting (1986) has referred to the Department as a "money-moving" agency whose primary role was to allocate funds on the basis of compliance to organizational directives. Others have also described such government bodies as systems of containment whose bureaucratic imperatives are at odds with aboriginal needs (Fleras 1989). The fact that the Indian Affairs bureaucracy oc-cupied a world view entirely different from that endorsed communities and cultures proved extremely disruptive (Hummel 1987; Salée 1995).

But aboriginal peoples are casting about to disengage from the bureaucratic clutches of the DIAND. A rational control model that once secured aboriginal compliance with the state is being challenged by "indigenous" models for revitalizing the aboriginal agenda (Hedican 1995). Yet reaction remains mixed to the presence of an Indian Affairs bureaucracy — even one in the throes of de-bureaucratizing. The resulting debate over retention or reform has sharpened many of the contradictions intrinsic to aboriginal-state rebuilding. This controversy has also reinforced a perception of DIAND as a "paradox" between overlapping interests and divided loyalties, against a backdrop of "national interests" (Boldt 1993). Evidence, in other words, confirms the notion of aboriginal-state relations as a "contested domain" involving a protracted struggle between opposing ideologies for control over jurisdiction.

THE MANDATE: THE INDIAN ACT

Aboriginal relations with the Canadian state are mediated by a series of legislative initiatives known as the Indian Act. With passage of the Indian Act in 1876, a singular Victorian-era Act conferred sweeping power for the Department of Indian Affairs to invade, control, and regulate even the minutest aspect of reserve life — even to the point of curbing constitutional and citizenship rights (Morse 1989). Aboriginal languages, cultures, and identity were suppressed, while band communities were locked into patterns of dependency and despondency with little opportunity for escape (AFN 1992).

This legitimizing document sought to standardize and regulate ("bureaucratize") federal interaction with status Indians. As part of this bureaucratization process, the Indian Act defined who came under its provisions, what each status Indian was entitled to under the government's fiduciary obligations, who could qualify for disenfranchisement, what could be done with reserve lands and resources, and how local communities were to be ruled. Traditional leadership was replaced with elected band councils, most of whom were perceived as extensions of central authority, with limited powers subject to prior approval or to Ottawa's arbitrary whims (Webber 1994). Even economic opportunities were curtailed. Under the Indian Act, aboriginal people could not possess direct title to private property; nor could they generate revenue from the sale or lease of band property. Punitive restrictions not only deterred aboriginal property improvements, but they also precluded the accumulation of economic development capital for investment or growth (Eckholm 1994). Historically, then, bands have had difficulty in financing commercial endeavours on reserves since aboriginal land held in Crown trust was immune to mortgage, collateral, or legal seizure. (McMillan 1988).

That the spirit of the Indian Act survives into the present is a commentary on the powers of inertia. The Indian Act persists as an essentially repressive instrument of containment that subverts aboriginal control over jurisdictions of local concern. Even more remarkable is the degree of bureaucratization that pervades aboriginal-state relations because of the Indian Act. Program design and funding continue to be controlled by Ottawa, thus hampering community endeavors while federal authorities routinely reject band council bylaws on the grounds they violate Indian Act provisions (Platiel 1994b). Aboriginal men and women have soundly repudiated the Act as inflexible and restrictive, and at odds with even limited aboriginal aspirations (AFN 1992). Yet others acknowledge its usefulness in affording legal protection from outside interests (see Royal Commission 1993). Federal authorities have been no less vociferous in criticizing the Indian Act as patronizing or regressive (DIAND 1993b). Evidence suggests that the days of the Indian Act are numbered, although no one is willing to predict how or when, and with what effect it will disappear.

STRUCTURES OF DIAND

DIAND is best described as a geographically decentralized federal bureaucracy located in eleven regions across Canada. It is responsible for the well-being of aboriginal and non-aboriginals in the North West Territories and Yukon through a combination of direct program expenditures and transfer payments — not altogether different from what happens in other government departments (Report 1991). The objective of the Inuit and Indian Affairs Program is stated in Part II of the Main Estimates, 1992/93 which seeks to "support Indians and Inuit in achieving their self-government, economic, industrial, cultural, social, and community development needs and aspirations..." The Department draws its clout from control over funding and allocation. In the deft phrasing of Juanita Perley, "Indian Affairs is holding you with a noose around your neck — they've got you with just your toes on the ground — dangling that money over you (from Silman (1987:223)."

In recent years, DIAND has undergone a major shift in content, organization, and style. A partnership commitment in support of community-based self-government has displaced the concept of direct-service delivery. DIAND has endorsed a developmental and advisory orientation, with a responsibility to advance First Nations concerns; to enhance autonomy and self-reliance; to mediate relations with central authorities; and to service negotiated agreements (Weaver 1991; Boldt 1993; DIAND 1993b). Indian Affairs has also sought to simplify funding relationship with First Nations through increased flexibility and community-based initiatives (Frideres 1993). In other words, each First Nation government is now expected to assume ownership over program delivery at a pace tailored to meet specific community interests; ensure greater local control and accountability; and enhance service delivery capacities.

THE COSTS OF ADMINISTRATION

The Indian Act mandates the DIAND to provide a comprehensive range of obligations and services toward aboriginal peoples. The department has primary responsibility not only to fulfill the federal government's obligations for "Indians and lands reserved for Indians," but also to administer the Indian Act

through delivery of select programs and services (DIAND 1993b). In some cases, these programs embrace commitments specified in existing treaties. In others, the diversity of programs is comparable with those delivered to other Canadians by provincial and municipal governments. Federal programs for Indian reserve communities include services in health, education, social assistance, housing, community infrastructure, justice, culture, and economic growth. Funding and responsibility for meeting First Nations needs are not limited to DIAND. National Health and Welfare Canada is responsible for health services, while territorial governments and Newfoundland have assumed responsibilities for service delivery under a cost-sharing agreement with federal authorities (DIAND 1993b). The department also has a number of important legal responsibilities related to aboriginal estates, the resolution of outstanding comprehensive land claims, and continuing fulfilment of Canada's constitutional obligations and statutory responsibilities.

Administering aboriginal affairs has not come cheaply. Several government departments are responsible for the $5.041 billion spent on aboriginal affairs based on 1992/93 estimates, with DIAND at 72.3 percent, national health and welfare at 11.4 percent, Canadian Mortgage and Housing at 5.4 percent, and Employment and Immigration at 4 percent (DIAND 1993a). DIAND's estimates for expenditure in 1992/1993 stood at $3.646 billion, with the bulk directed at education from primary to university ($903.3 million), social development ($816.3 million), capital facilities and community services ($665.1 million), and northern affairs ($572 million).

Additional expenditures have focused on various programs for enhancing economic self-sufficiency and development on reserves under the Department's Economic Development Sector and the Canadian Economic Development Strategy. While some caution must be exercised in interpreting these data, the government will spend about $12,412 for each status Indian living on a reserve or on Crown land (DIAND 1993a).

Funding for the First Nations has grown steadily since 1975/76 when it stood at $703 million or 2.11 percent of federal expenditures (excluding debt) compared with a current figure of 4.22 percent of the government's budgetary expenditures (excluding debt). These increases may be more apparent than real because of rapid population growth (including reinstatement following Bill C-31) and inflationary effects, suggesting the possibility of decreased per capita spending (Hawkes and Devine 1991). In the past DIAND had assumed all responsibility for a centrally controlled and direct service delivery to aboriginal communities. DIAND funds were limited and conditional, subject to extensive legal and administrative barriers (Wotherspoon and Satzewich 1993). Funding to bands is now available that tolerates some degree of discretion in spending, leeway in priority-setting, and local accountability. By 1992/93, 77.3 percent of DIAND's budget was being administered by First Nations bands through various funding arrangements, an increase from 41 percent in 1984 (DIAND 1993a). Only 11 percent was applied directly by DIAND for direct service delivery, with 12 percent paid out against funding arrangements with the provinces. Funds are allocated to the First Nations on the basis of resourcing formulas (reflecting demographic information); they also reflect a system of prioritization anchored to the definition of need. Nevertheless, band budgets continue to be established by the Treasury Board, while Ottawa remains the only source of revenue for many band governments who must continue to operate within a funding ceiling as set out by agreement.

MULTIPLE MANDATES/ COMPETING AGENDAS

The Department of Indian Affairs remains a convenient target for criticism (AFN 1992; Royal Commission 1993) — despite initiatives to de-bureaucratize and indigenize the aboriginal agenda. To one side, there are calls for its outright abolition, followed by a transfer of functions and funding to government agencies or aboriginal bands. Since coming to power in 1993, the Liberal Government has proposed to scrap DIAND by transfering responsibility for services in health or policing away from federal authorities to aboriginal jurisdictions — starting with a groundbreaking agreement with Manitoba chiefs singled out as a test case for future developments (Platiel 1994a). To the other side are appeals for retention of DIAND, albeit in a a modified form, as a buffer to shield aboriginal ambitions from predatory interests.

Aboriginal dislike of the department is legendary: In the words of Phil Fontaine, Grand Chief of the Assembly of Manitoba Chiefs, "There is nothing more fundamental to our well-being at this time than getting rid of the Indian Affairs deparment" (quoted in Nagle 1994 F-10). Such an antipathy is hardly surprising in view of DIANDs reputation as an instrument of colonial domination and administrative control (Ponting 1986). DIAND has been taken to task for doing too much for aboriginal peoples, thus robbing them of initiative while deterring self-reliance though excessive red tape, top-heavy administration, and welfare-dependency. It has also been criticized for doing too little in pursuit of aboriginal needs and aspirations. Criticism is fueled by the impossibly wide mandate of DIAND; namely, to administer the provisions of the Indian Act; to provide a broad range of services and programs to status Indians; and to advance the cause of aboriginal self-sufficiency and community self-government. Nor can DIAND ignore the Northern Affairs component of its mandate, which complicates its relationships with the First Nations because of increasing pressure from multinational companies interested in northern natural resources such as minerals and timber (Wotherspoon and Satzewich 1993). Charges also stem from the departments central function as a regulatory agency with responsibilities for allocating funds to aboriginal groups and organizations, a situation conducive to allegations of abuse, favoritism, and paternalism. Finally, DIAND's low-priority status within government decision-making caucus — a small wobbly Indian wheel in the federal machinery, as described by Menno Boldt (1993:109) — has also hindered its effectiveness as a forum for aboriginal grievances.

Much of the criticism fails to acknowledge the difficult circumstances in which the bureaucracy finds itself. On the one hand, the department is required by an Act of Parliament to operate with a mandate that is better suited for the nineteenth century (Report 1991). On the other, many shortcomings reflect DIANDs status as a bureaucracy in charge of a culturally diverse and geographically dispersed people. The logic behind departmental decisions is no different that of other bureaucracies; namely, the pursuit of rational control by (a) reinforcing rules (go by the book), (b) enforcing proper communication and standardized procedures (get it in writing), (c) encouraging of conformity (don't make waves), and (d) creating a pervasive hierarchy (up through the channels) (see Weber 1947; Hummel 1987). Meaningful interaction suffers when relationships are institutionalized into patterns of impersonal and hierarchical authority, formal rules, rigid proceedings, a complex division of labour, and standardized procedures. Under these circumstances, decisions of the administration conform with bureaucratic dictates rather than aboriginal sensibilities (Miller 1989; Report 1991).

Nor can DIAND's functions be separated from state functions in a capitalist society, including the need to reproduce the social order through social control (Panitch 1977; Wotherspoon and Satzewich 1993). That being the case, the primary (if latent) function of DIAND continues to focus on the containment and control of aboriginal peoples. Instead of power-sharing and resource allocation, the devolutionary process represents an excuse in off-loading federal responsibility for the delivery of programs and services. Not only does this dis-empowerment reinforce the system of control; it also ensures that many aboriginal people remain trapped within structures of domination, both removed and remote. In other words, neither maliciousness nor conspiracy can account for the strain in aboriginal-state relations. Rather, as Menno Boldt (1993) points out, blame rests with the state's unwillingness to accommodate aborigi-

nal needs when these digress from so-called national interests.

SOURCE: Adapted from Fleras 1996.

RESTRUCTURING ABORIGINAL-STATE RELATIONS WHOSE PROBLEM?

Aboriginal peoples continue to perform poorly in Canadian society despite federal expenditures. Both aboriginal policy and administration have contributed to the marginality of First Nations communities, by intent in some cases, inadvertently in others (Shkilynk 1985). Many aboriginal people find themselves impoverished and disempowered, as well as alienated by their failure to reconcile competing demands of the past with the present. Internal difficulties are one thing; external relations are yet another. Aboriginal relationships with society at large can be charitably described as one of dependency and underdevelopment — a not surprising conclusion given the pervasiveness of colonialist structures and mindsets. The poverty and powerlessness make it easy to analyze aboriginal peoples as a social problem. They are depicted in the media as a people whose pesky problems require costly solutions by way of government intervention (Fleras 1996). Their demands and activism are also seen as creating problems that threaten to rip apart Canada's social order. This kind of labelling should elicit several question: What precisely do we mean by the so-called "Indian problem"? Who is responsible? How did it come about? Who decides when First Nations constitute a social problem? In what ways do varying definitions of the problem lead to different proposals for solution (Weaver 1981, Hedican 1995)?

Answers to these questions suggest that social problems are social constructions rather than accurate reflections of reality, and this section will examine more carefully the nature of such constructed realities. Logically, two types of answers to the questions are possible: One, the problems that First Nations confront are essentially "Indian problems"; they alone should take responsibility for problems and solutions. Second, the "Indian problem" is essentially a **white problem** of domination, control, and exploitation of the indigenous populations. The interaction of these two responses is complicated by the interplay of culturally different and competing sectors. Any solution to the problems of First Nations peoples must take into account this ongoing interaction.

The Indian Problem?

The difficulties encountered by aboriginal peoples have historically been described as an "Indian problem." Wax and Buchanan (1975) speculate on how this may have come about:

> To the extent that Indians possessed resources that whites wanted, they were considered "an Indian problem." When they lost those resources and became impoverished and ecologically disoriented, but managed tenaciously to endure, they were also "a problem" — a moral problem to whites who had acquired or inherited that which once had been Indian."

In Canada, the perception of aboriginal peoples as a social problem in need of a solution has animated the rationale behind aboriginal policy, and secured its assimilationist objectives and implementation. In the now legendary words of a senior bureaucrat to Parliament in 1920: "I want to get rid of the Indian problem...Our objective is to continue until there is not a single Indian in Canada that has not been absorbed." (Duncan Campbell Scott, Superintendent-General of Indian Affairs, quoted in Miller 1989).

Those who endorse a belief in the Indian problem subscribe to some version of the **modernization thesis**. This position argues that the world has become increasingly modernized in response to the forces of consumerism, technology, knowledge, mass communication, reason, and science. Any group whose social and cultural values are at variance with the demands of modernization will experience difficulties in adjustment. Only external intervention by way of government programs or spending, proponents argue, will smooth the transition. This line of reasoning can be applied to the aboriginal peoples of Canada. Failure to acquire the skills and values necessary for modernization has perpetuated their marginal status. In order to avert further decline, government agencies have assumed responsibility for hastening their transition into the modern mainstream.

The federal government in Canada, under the Department of Indian Affairs, has launched a variety of programs and projects in the belief that First Nations constitute a problem whose cultural and social idiosyncracies preclude a smooth absorption into society. Central to this so-called Indian problem is the prevalence of poverty at physical, social, cultural, and psychological levels (Shkilnyk 1985). Only elimination of this poverty is thought to make any appreciable diminution of the "Indian problem." Removal of barriers to development and growth has entailed a variety of strategies, two of which prevail. First, aboriginal peoples have been encouraged to move off the reserve (which are dismissed as nothing more than breeding grounds for violence, apathy, and alienation). Exposure to modern values and institutional involvement is extolled as crucial for facilitating this transition. Second, the government has been anxious to modernize reservations by upgrading facilities and infrastructures. If this transformation is successful, the hypothesis holds, the reserves will provide the resources necessary for renewal. If not, the reserve system will continue to siphon away taxpayer resources without eliminating the root causes of poverty and rebellion. A prime example of such a mindset occurred in a Northern Ontario reserve — with predictable and unfortunate consequences.

INSIGHT

Poisoned Policies

Nowhere are the dilemmas and difficulties associated with the so-called "Indian problem" more eloquently stated than in Anastasia Shkilnyk's ethnography, *A Poison Stronger Than Love*. A series of historical factors and ecological disasters combined with misguided government initiatives to bring about the near destruction of an Ojibwa aboriginal reserve near Kenora, Ontario. The intrusion of the outside world and its paternalistic attempts to improve reserve life led to the systematic dismantling of the community infrastructure, with a disconnecting effect on social patterns and cultural values — not all at once, but by a slow, cumulative process that eventually overtook and subdued the Grassy Narrows Ojibwa. Of particular significance in contributing to the social breakdown:

1) The DIAND's modernization philosophy which sought to eliminate any social and cultural barriers precluding an economic improvement of the Grassy Narrows Reserve. The relocation policy in 1963 that aligned the reserve community along a direct route to Kenora was especially stressful.

2) The virtual destruction of their lifestyle and means of livelihood following the mercury poisoning of the English-Wabigoon river system by local pulp and paper industries.

The impact of these two events (in addition to the long-term effects of missionization, education, and consumerism) proved as immediate as it was devastating. A relatively self-sufficient Grassy Narrows community collapsed into a state of despondency and dependency on welfare, unemployment cheques, and federal handouts. The reserve lost its sense of community and family life, resulting in growing rates of antisocial behaviour such as child abuse, suicide, and violence. Psychologically, the people grew increasingly passive and listless: Shkilnyk describes them as sleepwalking through the motions of life because of boredom, alienation, and a sense of irrelevance. Admittedly, as Shkilynk herself confesses, the situation was overstated to make a point. Moreover there has been some improvement since the mid 1980s. Both the government and the paper mills compensated the Grassy Narrows Ojibway a total of over $17 million for social and economic improvement. A temporary ban on alcohol at the reserve also resulted in noticeable shifts in the quality of community and family life. Whether the amelioration process can be maintained is less promising in light of a recent decision to revoke the liquor ban.

Reading Shkilnyk's book makes it easier to understand why some First Nations are in such a predicament. Many resent the continuation of federal programs that are designed and implemented in a manner at odds with community aspirations or levels of development. Shkilynk also demonstrates why they are mistrustful of government efforts to solve their marginal status in Canadian society. Too much of what passes as a solution to the "Indian problem" are decisions by remote and disinterested bureaucrats, many of whom are motivated by self-promotion or national interests. This is not to imply that deliberate bureaucratic miscalculation or political expediency account for aboriginal problems. There is no proof of a government orchestrated conspiracy to destroy the aboriginal populations. Negative impacts may stem instead from the logical consequences of well intentioned programs that are based on faulty assumptions ("progress through development") or inaccurate reading of the situation ("eliminate poverty by throwing money at the problem") or cultural misunderstanding ("they want to be like us"). Projects and decisions based on different cultural understandings only complicates the problem. Finally, the broader implications of her work cannot be ignored. In a world where acid rain and ozone depletion are threatening our very existence as a biological species, we may never recover from the poisoning of our environment — with disastrous consequences for the next generation.

A White Problem

There is a second way of interpreting the dilemmas that confront Canada's First Nations: they may be perceived instead as a white problem. Put bluntly, First Nations have been victimized by a system of internal colonialism that was imposed on them by European conquest and settlement (Bienvenue 1985). This model argues that Indian problems must be placed squarely within colonialistic terms and analyzed within the framework of domination, control, and exploitation. Four factors stand out in the colonization process: (Blauner 1972):

1) The indigenous populations are directly exploited for control over land, resources, and labour power. Indirectly they are exploited because they lack opportunities for economic self-development — given the constraints inherent in the Indian Act and its administration by federal departments. As a result, aboriginal peoples constitute the underdeveloped component of Canadian society, reflecting in part their dependency on the government and the economic stagnation on reserves.

2) The government has sought to undermine First Nations cultures and lifestyle. Foremost in terms of tactics are the assimilationist pressures through absorption into the education system or conversion to Christianity. Equally devastating is the modernization philosophy which guides government actions for improvement of the economic status of Native Indians.

3) First Nations cultures have been disparaged as primitive, irrelevant, and counterproductive for social and economic progress. Only adherence to the modern values of the dominant sector (a belief in progress, competition, individualism) will salvage First Nations survival.

4) First Nations lives are controlled and constrained by government bureaucrats. Although ostensibly to assist and protect, the latent functions of government involvement are nothing less than the continued domination, control, and exploitation of the target population.

Many observers have supported the internal colonialism model in analyzing root cause underlying the Indian problem (Bienvenue 1985). What we have is a white problem, generated in part from the competitive struggle over scarce resources between a militarily powerful sector and an equally resilient aboriginal resistance. Tensions arise from the clash of culturally different lifestyles — one based on the principles of consumerism, competition, and progress, the other on a commitment to spiritual values, community, and consensus. Further difficulties are created by the imposition of the capitalist system on a non-capitalist population.

CASE STUDY

A "White Collar" Crime

The harm that befalls communities does not necessarily stem from malevolent motives or sinister conspiracies. Even the best intentions when based on bloodless objectives, or false assumptions can lead to suffering and death. The coerced relocation of aboriginal peoples from one community to another provides an example of how "helping" can dissolve into "hurting." It also alerts us to the possibility of rethinking who is the guilty party in the so-called "Indian" problem.

Aboriginal communities have been afflicted by about a hundred forced removals since Confederation. In some cases, aboriginal communities shifted closer to urban centres in order to cut costs; in other cases, they were relocated farther away to reduce negative contact with whites or to reestablish traditional patterns of self-sufficiency. In all cases, aboriginal communities experienced disruptions of sort because they were rarely consulted about or deprived of resources to make the transition.

Take the case of the Inuit. In 1953, southern bureaucrats dispatched ten ill-equipped Inuit families mostly from Quebec to a life of northern hardship in a bleak and inhospitable environment. The 85 Inuit were identified by dog tags, kept in the cargo hold like livestock throughout the 2,000 kilometre trip, separated from their families, abandoned on desolate beaches to confront harsh Arctic conditions, left in near starvation conditions for many years, and discouraged from returning home. Such second-class treatment confirmed their status as "wards" of the state — little more than Nanooks of the North who rubbed noses, lived in igloos, and ate walrus blubber. The fact that the Inuit had little say in what was happening reflected a callous and arrogant indifference at odds with Canada's increasingly vaunted reputation on the global stage.

The rationale behind this and resettlement reflected a combination of factors. These included political expediency, economic cost cutting, and human compassion — all justified within the framework of "national interests." Within the bureaucracy, the resettlement was viewed as an "experiment" to determine whether the Inuit had gone "soft" or could survive when reunited with a wilderness environment. The government saw Inuit settlements as a bulwark in defence of a de facto sovereignty over the northernmost limits of Canada — a not inconsequential challenge given the fears of a cold war between Russia and the United States, with only 140 permanently-stationed Canadians to provide a buffer.

The relocation was also viewed as a way of paring government costs. The Inuit in Quebec had become increasingly dependent on government handouts. The solution lay in providing an environment where the Inuit could once again become self-sufficient through resumption of traditional living patterns. Such initiatives also reflected the last major initiative of the traditionalists who wanted indigenous peoples to return to the land rather than follow the assimilationist route of sustained exposure to education, employment, and modernity. Relief costs were underwritten largely by the Inuit families who subsidized their own victimization through exorbitant prices and reduced pelt prices at gov-

ernment supply stores. Efforts to improve the Inuit situation through relocation also reflected an activist mentality among Canadian bureaucrats, many of whom were anxious to experiment at a time when public service was seen as a calling rather than a career.

The injustice of relocation is rarely disputed. The Inuit were little more than pawns in experiments in Canadian society-building. The lack of cultural sensitivity to a people who were deeply attached to their homeland contributed to the sorry outcome. They were powerless to resist, and this powerlessness continues to plague many aboriginal communities. Even more unjust is the refusal of the government to provide an apology or a measure of redress commensurate with the gravity of this white collar crime.

SOURCES: Calamai *Ottawa Citizen* 5 March 1994, Aubry *Ottawa Citizen* 5 March 1994. Marcus 1995.

Clearly, then, the source of the problem is not a cultural one only. It emanates instead from the structural imperatives of a capitalist society (Wotherspoon and Satzewich 1993). This insatiable appetite preserving power and privilege has unleashed the forces which have set into motion the process of subordination, underdevelopment, and dependency of aboriginal peoples. Contributing to this marginalization is the paternalistic and controlling presence of the Department of Indian Affairs. Unless a massive restructuring of aboriginal-state relations is in store, the essentially white problem will continue to subvert aboriginal aspirations and efforts at improvement.

ABORIGINAL SOLUTIONS

Aboriginal leaders reject the label of First Nations as a social problem (although they acknowledge the many difficulties that confront aboriginal communities).

Physical poverty, they contend, is not necessarily responsible for aboriginal marginalization in Canadian society. Powerlessness associated with colonization is far more worrying. Strategies that involve "throwing money" or "calling in the experts" are likewise criticized. Also rejected are stereotypes of aboriginal peoples that portray them as slaves of a materialist and consumer lifestyle. Equally dismaying are notions of aboriginal cultures as barriers to the modernization process. The First Nations strongly refute the idea that aboriginal cultural values are impediments to a secure and satisfying coexistence in Canadian society. Retention of aboriginal cultural values not only provide a source of identity and resourcefulness, but also serve as a basis for a community-based renewal or healing.

The First Nations have attempted to counteract the vicious cycle of exclusion and demeaning clientelism that has historically entrapped them (Salée 1995). Three themes are recurrent throughout this process: first, conferral of "citizen-plus" status; second, promotion of self-determination through inherent self-governance and territorial repossession; and third, acknowledgement of aboriginal and treaty rights.

Citizen Plus

What do aboriginal peoples want? The most direct response is, the same things as all Canadian citizens. All aboriginal peoples want to live in a just and equal society wherein (a) their cultural lifestyles and language are protected from assimilationist pressure, (b) select elements of the cultural past can be incorporated within the realities of the present, (c) bureaucratic interference within their lives is kept to a minimum, (d) they are not victimized by racism or by indifference among politicians, bureaucrats, state agents, or general public, (e) there is reliable and culturally appropriate delivery of government services, (f) there is a collective access to power and resources, and (g) they retain meaningful involvement in decision making and power sharing. Most of us would agree that these objectives are similar to those of all Canadians.

Aboriginal peoples have also expressed a desire to be different. They want to transcend the constraints of formal citizen status and explore novel ways of redefining Canadian citizenship. In conjunction with the concept of "citizen-plus," they espouse a decided preference for treatment that is cognizant of rights that flow from their unique legal status. Recognition of unique status is paramount. Equal opportunity or equality before the law is necessary, but insufficient. As pointed out elsewhere, the promotion of mathematical equality is tantamount to freezing the status quo. Treating everyone the same merely entrenches the prevailing distribution of power and societal resources. In the belief that equal standards cannot be applied to unequal situations without perpetuating the inequality, aboriginal leaders have reinforced the commitment to unique status and equivalent treatment.

In other words, aboriginal peoples have claimed the right to be different as well as the right to be the same (hence the expression, citizen-plus). They want equality of treatment ("formal equality") as befitting all citizens, yet demand special concessions ("equality of outcomes") because of their unique legal status as original occupants. Aboriginal peoples do not see any contradiction in making these demands. As far as they are concerned, aboriginal peoples paid for these concessions with the loss of land, lives, livelihood, and cultural lifestyles. Nor do Canadian politicians and policy-makers dispute the validity of aboriginal arguments for unique status and equivalent treatment. Debate continues over the magnitude and scope of these rights with respect to specifics such as costs and jurisdictions.

Self-Determination

Five centuries after European colonization nearly destroyed the original occupants of Turtle Island (North America), the First Nations of Canada are in the midst of a drive to regain control over their lives and life chances (Alfred 1995). Central to this reconstruction process is the notion of **aboriginal self-determination**. The concept of self-determination rejects the legitimacy of existing political relations and mainstream institutions as a framework for attainment of indigenous goals. Proposed instead is the restoration of an indigenous-based nationhood through the revitalization of select aboriginal customs and institutions according to the shifting demands of an evolving political environment. Key elements in this renewal and reconciliation process include control over the process and power of local governance, the attainment of cultural sovereignty, and a realignment of political relations as expressed by formal self-governing arrangements in key jurisdictional areas related to power, resources, and status (Mercredi and Turpel 1993).

Aboriginal leaders have endorsed self-determination as essential to cracking the cycle of deprivation and dependency. Some degree of aboriginal control is imperative to achieve meaningful decision-making powers over issues of relevance to them. The rationale for this argument is based on several lines of reasoning. Arguments for self-determination encompass the principle that (a) all aboriginal peoples have the right to control their destiny; (b) international law (to which Canada was a signatory in 1967) stipulates the right for all peoples to self-determination; and (c) aboriginal control is necessary to avert the further loss of traditional social and cultural patterns. The commitment to self-determination is invariably linked with questions about jurisdiction (who controls what). Put candidly, First Nations are seeking to expand control over internal matters in the same way the Québécois are seeking a certain level of autonomy. Patterns of jurisdiction are open to negotiations ranging from shared arrangements, to exclusive tribal control over land ownership and membership up to and including autonomous political structures (inherent self-government) and cultural sovereignty as long as these reflect a community-derived legitimacy and the will of the people. This is not to say that all aboriginal communities possess the jurisdictional capacity to fully engage in self-government, but many do and are looking for ways to establish arrangements that will divest all vestiges of internal colonialism in exchange for "nations within" status.

The concept of **inherent self-government** is central to aboriginal self-determination. There is growing resolve to exercise control over political, cultural, economic, and social issues of concern to them. Constititionally entrenched provisions for recognition of inherent aboriginal self-governing rights are perceived as creating the kind of foundation that will enhance the status of First Nations as a founding people and partners in Confederaton (Penner 1983; Little Bear et al. 1984; Cassidy 1991; Royal Commission 1993; Mercredi and Turpel 1993; Chartrand 1993). The concept of self-government is not self-explanatory. Precise definitions are virtually non-existent — and most calls for clarification have generated more heat than light. Consensus regarding an ideal self-governing model is nearly absent within each side, though major differences can be discerned between aboriginal and government perceptions of aboriginal self-governing models.

Self-governing models will be varied, and are expected to evolve in accordance with community needs and local circumstances. Some will reflect a government model; others an aboriginal model; and still others will combine elements of both. Four self-governance possibilities exist (O'Regan 1994), (a) sovereign, maintaining complete independence and no external influence; (b) nationhood, within the framework of society yet retaining authority and jurisdiction over internal matters; (c) community-based, retaining control over internal affairs by way of parallel institutions but limited by interaction with comparable mainstream bodies; and (d) participatory, having meaningful decision making powers through representation and involvement in the general political and institutional order. Table 7.2 summarizes these possibilities.

General patterns can be discerned from a reading of aboriginal models (Mercredi and Turpel 1993). First, self-governing structures are envisaged as genuine political units which encampass a distinct order of government alongside the federal and provincial levels. The right to self-government is not delegated by federal authority or Canadian law. These rights are inherent, in other words, and rooted in the reality of aboriginal rights that have never been extinguished. Elijah Harper (Royal Commission, 1992:19) expressed it succinctly when he said:

"Self-government is not [something] that can be given away by any government, but rather...flows from Creator. Self-government ...is taking control and managing our own affairs, being able to determine our own future and destiny....It has

TABLE 7.2   Four Levels of Self-Government

Sovereign	Nationhood
"internal + external autonomy"	"internal autonomy"
Community-Based	**Participatory**
"limited internal autonomy"	"institutional accommodation"

never been up to the governments to give self-government. It has never been theirs to give."

Jurisdisctional matters are expected to vary from band to band, but are likely to include (a) control over the delivery of social services such as policing, education, and health and welfare (institutional autonomy); (b) control over resources and use of land for economic regeneration; (c) control over the means to protect and promote the distinct cultural values and language systems; (d) control over band membership and entitlements; and (e) control over federal expenditures according to aboriginal priorities rather than those of the government or bureaucracy. Also anticipated are political structures that reflect local decision-making (consensual) styles as well as a workable division of labour between the different levels of government. Lastly, strategies to sustain the legitimacy of self-governing doctrines will need to be devised.

The concept of an inherent right to aboriginal self-government can also be discussed in terms of what it is *not*. Contrary to popular belief, most aboriginal proposals do not advocate making a total break with Canadian society. Aboriginal demands for sovereignty are not identical to claims for political independence or territorial autonomy except in the minds of a few activists. The claims for nationhood reflect more closely the domestic dependent nations status of First Nations in the United States. American First Nations do not possess external sovereignty (for example, they cannot raise an army); nevertheless, as "domestic dependent nations," they retain considerable control over internal sovereignty, subject to certain restrictions at the federal and state level. Not all First Nation communities want to go that route in Canada. Complete autonomy is not feasible for many aboriginal communities considering the costs and obligations associated with complete and sovereign status. What is promoted instead is the concept of "sovereign-association" (first popularized by the Québécois during the 1970s) with relatively autonomous powers over political, economic, cultural, and social domains.

Finally, inherent self-governance is associated with talk of aboriginal nationhood (Levin 1993). Aboriginal endorsement of a "nations within" status is part of the decolonizing process. Aboriginal leaders categorically reject the view of themselves as individual Canadian citizens who happen to live on reserves. Unlike refugee or immigrant groups who are looking to "put down roots" or "remove discriminatory barriers," aboriginal peoples assume the politically self-conscious stance of a "nation" when they go beyond cultural concerns and physical survival (Fleras and Elliott 1992). The additional step consists of the assertion that they possess a special relationship with the state, along with a corresponding set of collective rights entitlements that flow from inherency and first principles — including the right to deal with federal authorities on a government-to-government basis. The distributive ideals associated with aboriginality are varied, but typically involve demands for aboriginal sovereignty over land, resources, culture, and identity. Failure to achieve these nationalist rights to self-government indicates further struggles are in store for collectively redefining the nations within.

Aboriginal and Treaty Rights

The third component of aboriginal aspirations revolves around the recognition, definition, and constitutional entrenchment of aboriginal and treaty rights. The First Nations have refused to be labelled as another ethnic or immigrant minority. They prefer instead to define themselves as a sovereign entity whose collective rights are guaranteed by virtue of their ancestral occupation. The concept of individual rights are rejected as insufficient to meet historically-defined collective aspirations (Boldt and Long 1984). Nor are aboriginal peoples anxious to be integrated as an ethnic component into a Canadian multicultural mosaic, with a corresponding diminishment of their claims. What has been proposed instead is recognition of their sovereign status as the original occupants of Canada, as well as a founding nation, not unlike that of the French in Quebec. Claims to sovereignty are defended either by appeal to natural law or by reference to spiritual grounds (Ahenakew 1985). As the original occupants whose inalienable rights have never been extinguished by treaty or conquest, aboriginal claims against the state are defended as *intrinsic* and basic rather than *contingent* on government largesse or political decree.

Underlying this notion of aboriginal rights are fundamental assumptions that strike at the core of aboriginal-government relations. First and foremost is the notion of aboriginality. The principle of aboriginality is essentially a statement about power. Aboriginality asserts a special relation between First Nations and the state, along with a corresponding set of rights and powers that have never been extinguished but flow from this relationship. Aboriginality, in other words, encapsulates a politicized set of claims and entitlements against the state with respect to the redistribution of power and resources. This claim is manifest in calls for self-government over agendas pertinent to aboriginal realities. Of particular importance is the establishment of institutional autonomy over aboriginal education and criminal justice procedures. Programs and policies that apply to other Canadian minority groups are dismissed as inapplicable — even counterproductive — in light of unique historical-legal status and special aboriginal concerns.

INSIGHT

The Politics of Aboriginality

The restructuring of aboriginal-government relations has not proceeded smoothly. State initiatives are rarely cohesive or fully rational. Expediency is paramount as vested interests jockey for position or control. At the core of this impasse is failure to appreciate the politics of aboriginality as a politicized ideology for radical change. Aboriginality is political in that choices about who gets what are *politicized* and out in public for debate. These debates are concerned with rules of engagement and patterns of entitlement with respect to the allocation of powers and resources (Sharp 1990). The discourse is political as well because aboriginal demands constitute grievances against the state. Initiatives that once focused on cultural preservation and formal equality before the law are now channelled into struggles for jurisdictional control along the lines of the "nation within" (Levin 1993b).

Even the tabling of aboriginal demands is inherently political. Political parties became entangled in controversies dealing with aboriginal issues. The state itself is implicated in these controversies when its legitimacy as a territorial sovereignty is directly challenged. This political aspect is embedded not only in the partisan sense of political parties and party agendas. It is also manifest in the broader sense of value judgements about the preferred vision of society. Strategies for containment have varied in the past, but most called for the placement of racial and ethnic minorities as subordinates into a settled hierarchy of status and roles, with all sectors sharing a common goal and an agreed upon set of rules (Sharp 1990). The politicization of aboriginality has overturned the dynamics of the governing process: It draws the state into the most contentious of all relations; namely, the shifting and openly contested relationship between equals in the political arena, with each claiming intrinsic authority and separate jurisdiction over powers, resources, and status (Sharp 1990).

Aboriginal peoples in Canada and throughout the world have taken the initiative in politicizing their demands for a radical restructuring of society along the lines of the "nations within." Resistance has shifted from a focus on survival and consolidation to the restructuring of aboriginal-state relations within a reconstituted state. Many Canadians understandably are alarmed by the radical nature of aboriginal proposals. Contrary to popular belief, however, aboriginal demands are not radical in the conventional sense. Their demands rarely invoke the overthrow of Western-styled values or institutions. They do not actively espouse the dismemberment of Canadian society or the imposition of aboriginal cultural values on society. What they do entail is a fundamental redistribution of power and resources. That in its own right is perceived as a threat to Canadian survival or vested interests. But if these demands appear threatening to Canadians as a whole or if they seem unrealistic in light of contemporary realities, one must ask what the alternatives are. A continuation of ineffectual government interference and paternalistic handouts is not the answer. Nor is throwing more money at the problem or expanding the legion of experts in this field. In other words, the costs of restructuring may be formidable: The costs of doing nothing or carrying on as before will be even more prohibitive.

Restructuring: A Contested Site

Moves to restructure aboriginal-state relations are increasingly common. But numerous barriers exist, each with potential to scuttle the decolonization process. Much is at stake in the reconstruction process: On the side of government, both political and private interests prefer a benign colonialist arrangement with continuing government control over the aboriginal agenda. Access to natural resources under the control of aboriginal groups is of paramount concern. By contrast, aboriginal sectors are anxious to decolonize their relationship with the state. For them, this restructuring is a prelude for charting a new course based on the entitlements that rightfully belong to them as the "first peoples."

What emerges from this intersection of competing perspectives is a "contested site" model of aboriginal-state relations involving a struggle between competing groups and opposing ideologies (Pearson 1990). Aboriginal definitions are increasingly salient to the restructuring process. Yet there is equally compelling evidence within government circles for compartmentalizing aboriginal aspirations into manageable formats. This dynamic between resistance and control provides the impetus for aboriginal-government restructuring in Canada and elsewhere.

Closer analysis suggests the rhetoric of reform is compelling, but premature. Aboriginal efforts to redefine their relationship with the state in Canada, Australia, United States, and New Zealand are fraught with ambiguity and deception in light of competing paradigms and entrenched interests (Fleras and Elliott 1992). Governments understandably are opposed to the creation of fundamentally separate structures with a distinctive power base. They prefer to accommodate aboriginal assertiveness through greater institutional flexibility and delegated responsibility. Compromises and negotiations that prove expensive in political or economic terms may be abandoned when costs mount or public interest wanes because of excessive media exposure. Inasmuch as the intent is to simply rearrange the furniture without major adjustments to the floor plan, the government's aboriginal agenda is more concerned with appearances than with substance or content.

Equally important for renewing aboriginal-state relations is the enforcement of federal treaty obligations. Treaties are regarded as ongoing and organic agreements that reaffirm the special legal status of aboriginal nations. They also serve as a basis for meaningful political interaction at government-aboriginal levels (Hall 1989). Aboriginal leaders have long upheld treaties as semi-sacred and binding documents. Land and resources were exchanged in the past for treaty rights and access to goods and services in perpetuity. As far as these leaders are concerned, the government remains bound to honour the contractual obligations of these treaties. Access to benefits and services (such as free education and tax exemptions) is not a charitable handout. Nor should it be regarded as a benevolent gesture on the part of an enlightened authority. Rather, treaty benefits derive from a legally binding exchange which aboriginal groups have paid for over and over again, not only by the expropriation of land and resources, but also through the loss of their lives and lifestyle.

Two type of treaty rights exist: specific and comprehensive claims. Specific claims arise from Canada's lawful obligations regarding the fulfilment of treaties pertaining to land administration and band funding signed by central authorities and specific aboriginal groups. Most grievances revolve about accusations related to the loss of reserve lands without adequate compensation. They also stem from the misappropriation of aboriginal monies from government sale of resources or mineral rights.

Comprehensive claims consist of modern day treaty arrangements over land whose ownership is under dispute. The goal of comprehensive claims is to clarify the rights of who controls the access to and ownership of land and resources that have not been finalized through treaty or superseded by law (DIAND May 1994). Securing aboriginal ownership and control over land and resources is imperative: Only a solid economic base can secure the basis for social and cultural renewal. Negotiated settlements provide aboriginal communities with protection for traditional land based interests related to wildlife harvests, resource management, some subsurface mineral rights, and regulated development. Economic benefits can be derived by renting out lands and resources at rates that are favourable to aboriginal interests. They also can be achieved through local development (in tandem with public or private interests) at a pace that reflects community priorities and developmental levels. In short, any fundamental changes in the status of aboriginal people can only be achieved when negotiating from a position of economic strength and the political power that sustains it.

Ten comprehensive claims settlements have been concluded since 1973, while others are in various stages of settlement. Consider the Yukon claim which was settled in the early 1990s after 21 years of negotiation. The settlement process itself was best seen as a kind of transaction in which aboriginal rights (largely unspecified but constitutionally entrenched) were exchanged for specific rights related to payments and territory (Cassidy 1991). The Yukon claim provided 14 bands with 41,439 square kilometres of land (nearly 8.6 percent of Yukon's land mass), including 25,900 square kilometres of Category A land (that is, complete control of land and ownership of resources) and the rest in Category B (with more limited and shared rights). A payment of $242.6 million (in 1989 dollars) will be spread across 15 years. In return for substantial wildlife harvesting rights and guaranteed representation on various land and resource boards, the eight thousand First Nations members will surrender certain aboriginal rights such as tax exemption status. This agreement and others like it suggest that lasting relationships can be built only on a nation-to-nation basis and in a spirit of generosity and accommodation. Yet troubles may be brewing since such treaty arrangements entail the extinguishment of aboriginal rights — hardly a minor consideration when one realizes that perhaps up to 50 percent of Canada (and up to 80 percent of British Columbia) may be under aboriginal ownership (Cassidy 1991).

To Sum Up: Aboriginal demands are consistent with their image as a unique nation within a federalist framework. Central to their aspirations is the **middle way** — to strike a balance between extremes. The First Nations don't want to separate from Canada in the territorial sense, but they also reject any move toward assimilation that includes a corresponding diminution of aboriginal identity and pride. A commitment to self-governing status is endorsed as a compromise between the extremes of separatism and absorption. Second, they don't want to preserve their cultural lifestyle in amber for the edification of purists or tourists. Nor do they do not want to impose their vanishing lifestyles on the non-native group. But many refuse to abandon their language and culture in exchange for an alien and incompatible set of eurocentric values and beliefs. Rather they prefer to select and reinterpret relevant elements of the past, then apply them to the realities of the present (Alfred 1995). They want to be modern, in other words, but not at the expense of what makes them unique. Third, aboriginal peoples are pragmatists who wish to achieve a working balance between the cultural and spiritual values of the past without rejecting the technological benefits of modern society. Fourth, achievement of political and economic power is viewed as critical in order to rebuild their communities into flourishing centres of meaningful activity. Yet these goals are unacceptable if attained at the cost of undermining their social obligations, collective and community rights, and cultural/spiritual values.

PUTTING PRINCIPLES INTO PRACTICE

It is one thing to promote aboriginal goals as related to citizen-plus status, self-determination through self-government, and the territorial repossession through entrenchment of aboriginal and treaty rights. It is quite another to put these goals into practice. Aboriginal leaders have relied on various tactics and strategies to get the message across. Political authorities, ever fearful of losing power or control, have responded with obfuscation and delay tactics.

Aboriginal Initiatives

Generally speaking, aboriginal leaders prefer to press for change through conventional avenues (Mercredi and Turpel 1993). They tend to rely on normal channels of dialogue, consultation, and persuasion with central policy structures. These include recourse to parliament, the existing court system, public opinion polls, and special interest/lobby groups such as the Assembly of First Nations. Constitutional forums have been employed for redress of historical inequities and promotion of collective interests. A series of First Ministers conferences in the 1980s sought to clarify the specific nature of aboriginal rights, but made little headway in collectively redefining aboriginal-government relations, outside of issue recognition (Brock 1991). Aboriginal leaders have also relied on international bodies and agencies for assistance. They have gone to the United Nations, to Britain, and to the Vatican in hopes of putting international pressure on the Canadian government for broken promises, miscarriages of justices, and pervasive paternalism. These tactics have attained a degree of success, partly because of Canada's vulnerability to international criticism over aboriginal rights violation.

Failure of political and constitutional forums to adequately address local grievances and national concerns have prompted alternative strategies. Aboriginal leaders have advocated a variety of activist measures, ranging from civil disobedience to threats of violence in some cases. They also have turned to flamboyant and staged events involving the mass media. Recourse to media-hyped events is viewed as a reliable method of upsetting a publicity-conscious government. The use of negative publicity to embarrass the government is especially effective in Canada with its strong commitment to human and individual rights (see Marcus 1995). This strategy has taken the form of a hunger strike by aboriginal youths in defiance of federal cutbacks to tertiary education spending for Native students. The blockade set up by the Lubicon Indians in Northern Alberta in protest of government failure to acknowledge their grievances proved successful in capturing national and international attention in the late 1980s. Finally, there have been occasional threats to employ violence if necessary in defence of aboriginal demands. With few exceptions such as Oka, threats of violence and forced separation have remained at the level of rhetoric. How long this will remain the case is open to conjecture, given the urgency of aboriginal grievances, aspirations, and claims.

Federal Reaction

Central authorities for the most part have stumbled in responding to aboriginal demands for indigenizing aboriginal-state relations. The promises of lofty rhetoric notwithstanding, there remains a noticeable lack of political will for implementing much of this rhetoric (Weaver 1993; Macklem 1993). A willingness to acknowledge aboriginality as a negotiating principle is counter-balanced by fears of tearing the social fabric of Canadian society (Levin 1993; Webber 1994). Government officials prefer to endorse aboriginal self-government as a political concession, both **contingent** ("qualified") and delegated on a band-to-band basis, with accountability to Parliament and the Constitution, rather than as an inherent right derived from natural or spiritual law (Tennant 1985). Nor should we ignore the element of calculation. Federal initiatives do not necessarily spring from a sense of outrage or injustice; they stem from a self-serving need to off-load Departmental functions under the guise of aboriginal empowerment (AFN 1992; Seguin 1994). Nowhere is the rift more evident than in competing perspectives on self-government where the regulated municipal model espoused by political sectors stands in sharp contrast with the inherent and expansive models proposed by aboriginal leaders.

Policy officials are understandably wary of dissolving once habitual patterns of domination for uncharted waters of aboriginal nationhood or sovereignty (Levin 1993a). A fundamental duality appears in shaping federal reaction to aboriginal demands. On the one hand, political authorities appear receptive to aboriginal claims — if only to avert a crisis of legitimacy and restore some semblance of political tranquility. Also evident is political willingness to negotiate over issues related to self-determination and self-government, albeit not to the extent of condoning territorial secession and dismemberment of the state (Boldt and Long 1985). A revised social-political contract based on the principle of aboriginal self-government has achieved modest success with the implementation of agreements among among the Naskapi-Cree of James Bay in 1975, the Nishnawbe-Aski Nation of Northern Ontario, and the Sechelt in British Columbia, with negotiations currently underway elsewhere. Table 7.3 summarizes aboriginal and government perspectives on aboriginal self-government.

Yet governments have sought by varying means to defuse, perhaps even circumvent, aboriginal challenges to the prevailing social order. They seem reluctant to address aboriginal concerns outside the framework of central policy structures or the liberal-democratic state (Fleras 1989; 1991). There remain grave misgivings about any aboriginal agenda that asks Canadians to move over and share power. The principle of aboriginality and aboriginal rights are criticized as vague and amorphous, and against Canada's national interests. Nevertheless, few politicians can afford to cavalierly dismiss aboriginality or the existence of aboriginal rights. What are debated instead are ideas over defining their limits, and how best to concede these rights without destroying the social fabric of society in the process. Reflecting this fundamental ambivalence, in other words, policy officials are understandably less than enthused about radically proposals for redefining the "nations within."

TABLE 7.3   Perspective on Self-Government

	Aboriginal	Government
Level	distinct order of self-government with unlimited, provincial-like powers	municipal-type government with limited powers
Powers	powers defined by constitutions, with specifics worked out later	powers defined by negotiations/legislation, then constitutionally entrenched
Authority	collective aboriginal rights prevail	strict application of Canadian Charter of Rights and Freedoms
Scope	institutional autonomy and total ownership of resources	limited ownership and restricted autonomy
Accountability	self-government accountable to aboriginal nations	self-government accountable to laws of Canada
Source of Governance	inherent	delegated

THE 1990s: PARADIGM MUDDLES

"Before we had to play a sort of poker. But the civil servants dealt us our cards face up, kept theirs close to the chest and asked us how much we wanted to bet. But we Natives don't have to play poker any more because we've learned how to play **bridge** (emphasis mine)."(Gene Rheaume, commenting on the Mohawk blockade of the Mercier Bridge in Montreal during the Oka crisis quoted by Viola Robinson in National Proceedings, 1993:38.)

As Canada lurches into the twenty-first century, it may well be perched on the threshold of an aboriginal paradigm shift. The rhetoric of revolution is compelling, but premature despite an atrophying of colonialist structures. Aboriginal efforts to redefine their relationship with the state in Canada (as well as in Australia, the United States, and New Zealand) are fraught with ambiguity and deception in light of competing paradigms and entrenched interests (Fleras and Elliott 1992). Aboriginal peoples in Canada have taken the initiative to sever the bonds of colonialist dependency and underdevelopment (Bienvenue 1985). In the space of just over two decades, aboriginal peoples have recoiled from the brink of social extinction to occupy a pivotal status in the reconstruction of Canadian society. Such a reversal originated and gained legitimacy when the "costs" of excluding aboriginal peoples from the national agenda proved unacceptably high to the mainstream in social, political, and economic terms (Fleras and Krahn 1992).

But the politics of restructuring often conceal hidden agendas and contested realities. Calls to improve aboriginal-state relations through devolution and decentralization are strewn with administrative landmines. The fundamental objective of various Indian Affairs departments — to eliminate the aboriginal "problem" through local self-sufficiency — has not wavered over the years (Ponting and Gibbins 1986). Only the means have altered, with crude assimilationist strategies giving way to more sophisticated channels that co-opt aspects of aboriginal discourse for self-serving purposes (see Bull 1994). The establishment of a "community negotiation process" and modified block funding arrangements may bolster DIAND's commitment to reduce band dependency, broaden reserve decision-making powers, improve effectiveness, and enhance mutual accountability (DIAND 1993b). It may also have the effect — however inadvertent — of advancing the assimilationist agenda (Pearson 1993).

Governments have endorsed the idea that aboriginal peoples (a) are a distinct society, (b) possess a threatened culture and society (c) depend on government trust responsibilities for survival, (d) desire more control in line with local priorities, and (e) prefer to achieve their goals in partnership with central authorities (Government of Canada 1992). Yet many in the government camp understandably are opposed to the creation of fundamentally separate structures with a distinctive power base and parallel institutions. As principle or practice, aboriginality poses an unprecedented challenge to the balancing act in any society constructed around a series of compromises. Central authorities prefer instead a benign neo-colonialist arrangement that compartmentalizes the aboriginal platform into packages of institutional flexibility and delegated responsibility. Nor are they particularly enthused with the prospect of reconciling aboriginal nationhood with the realities of Canadian society-building. Central authorities are reluctant to relinquish jurisdiction unless such concessions are consistent with "national" or "sectarian" interests" (Boldt 1993; see Wotherspoon and Satzewich 1993). They are even more hesitant to assert aboriginality as a basis for redrawing powers for fear of destabilizing Canada's legitimacy as a sovereign state. The interplay of these contested positions shapes the dynamics at the "heart" of aboriginal-state restructuring. Barriers must be removed and innovative arrangements implemented under an evolving set of rules. Inasmuch as the intent is to simply rearrange the furniture without altering the floor plan, the government's aboriginal agenda is more likely to focus on appearances rather than substance.

Aboriginal-state relations in Canada are currently under assessment at policy and administration levels. A proposed paradigm shift is gathering momentum — partly in response to escalating aboriginal pressure and prolonged public criticism, and in other part to deflect a growing crisis in state legitimacy. But the widely heralded realignment of jurisdictions is riddled with inconsistencies and contradictions as competing interests lock horns over a new aboriginal agenda. The usefulness of the bureaucratic paradigm rooted in the pursuit of "law," "formality," and "control" (Weaver 1990:15) is drawing to a close, but remains firmly entrenched. A new decolonizing paradigm based on empowerment and renewal has not yet taken hold, in spite of its lofty ideals of promoting national reconciliation through "justice," "adaptation" and "workable inter cultural relations" (Weaver 1990:15). This juxtaposition of bureaucracy with indigenization has proven both contradictory and confrontational, as new ways of thinking collide with the old without displacing them. It also confirms the notion of aboriginal-state relations as a **contested site** that involves an ongoing struggle between different groups for control over the aboriginal agenda.

Instead of a paradigm shift, in other words, what we appear to be witnessing is, arguably, a paradigm muddle. Aboriginal-state relations are characterized by pervasive degrees of ambivalence as colonialist paradigms grind up against new patterns of thought (Weaver 1991). It is not that the old paradigm refuses to disappear gracefully and make way for the new. Rather, diverse viewpoints are on collision course, as perspectives slide into each other, past each other, around each other, and over or under each other in a manner not unlike plate tectonics and continental drift. Neither paradigm is strong enough to dislodge its conceptual opponent, with the result that the renewal process consists of discordant amalgams of progressive and traditional. The clash of competing paradigms resonates throughout the policy and administrative fields as formal initiatives tinker with symbol and rhetoric at the expense of content, suggesting illusion rather than substance.

This would appear to be the case in Canada. Despite new images and discourses, aboriginal-state relations continue to revolve around an assimilationist nexus. Yet a restructuring is now in place with potentially profound implications for Canadian nation-building along pluralistic lines. Such a state of tension and conflict is likely to persist until such time as conventional thinking accepts a vision of Canada as an assymmetrical pluralism of three founding peoples — aboriginal, French-, and English-speaking — sovereign in their own right, but Canadians nevertheless.

CHAPTER HIGHLIGHTS

- Canadian race and ethnic relations revolve about the interplay of three major forces. Aboriginal nations, Charter groups, and multicultural minorities are actively involved in the competition for power and scarce resources.

- Each of these forces occupies a distinct relational status in Canadian society, with a correspondingly different set of problems, strategies for solution, and prospects.

- The construction of state-aboriginal relations is conducted through official policy and administration, yet secured at the level of tacit assumptions and reinforced through patterns of entitlements, symbols, and discourses.

- The aboriginal peoples (including status and non-status Indians, Metis, and Inuit) constitute one of these forces. The depressed social and economic status of many aboriginal peoples has earned them the title of a "social problem" or as "having problems" in need of solution through government intervention. State initiatives for managing the "problem" of aboriginality have varied over time and place, but invariably concentrate on containment through government policy and bureaucratic structures.

- The so-called "Indian" problem can be interpreted from two perspectives. Either the First Nations are responsible for the problem, or the problem that confronts aboriginal communities is largely the result of "white" colonialism.

- Government policies and programs have largely failed to hasten the decolonization of aboriginal marginal status. Aboriginal peoples subsequently have sought to politicize their relationship with the government through political, constitutional, and judicial channels.

- Foremost in terms of this redefinition have been the (a) promotion of self-determination through self-government within the framework of Canadian federalism; (b) recognition of aboriginal and treaty rights; and (c) acceptance of aboriginality as a cornerstone of Canadian society-building. Clearly, then, aboriginal resistance has jumped from a focus on cultural survival and formal equality, to a highly politicized demand for radical renewal and power-sharing reform.

- Much of the tension underlying aboriginal-government relations reflects debate over the politics of the "nations within" concept. This clash of competing paradigms — nationhood versus statehood — will continue to resonate throughout the corridors of policy and power.

- The current crisis in aboriginal-state relations is generated by competing claims over who controls what with respect to self-government, land claims, and treaty rights.

- The restructuring of aboriginal relations with the state is propelled by a mutual commitment to "indigenize" the aboriginal agenda by "de-bureaucratizing" the interactional basis of aboriginal policy administration over those it serves.

- Initiatives to accommodate aboriginality as a basis for claims making are flawed, primarily because First Nation aspirations are perceived as a direct challenge to the legitimacy of the Canadian state control over aboriginal jurisdictions.

- Recent attempts to redefine the aboriginal "problem" have encountered difficulties, partly because the "rational control" of bureaucracy tends to neutralize aboriginal demands for a radical renewal. Ambiguities in reshaping (indigenizing) the aboriginal agenda have sharpened the contradictory role of the Indian Affairs bureaucracy vis-a-vis the First Nations.

- Efforts to decolonize the aboriginal agenda are widely anticipated as necessary and overdue; nevertheless, proposals for indigenizing this agenda along post-colonialist lines must contend with political and bureaucratic interests, both of which resist fundamental change for fear of destabilizing state functions.

- Attempts to indigenize aboriginal policy and administration are fraught with ambiguity and deception since political and aboriginal perspectives diverge over problem and solutions, underlying rationale, and anticipated outcomes. Tradition-bound governmental mindsets are challenged by newer visions more consistent with the goals of national reconciliation.

KEY TERMS

Aboriginal and Treaty
   Rights
Aboriginal Peoples
Aboriginal Self-determi-
   nation
Citizen plus
Contested Site
Decolonize
Department of Indian
   Affairs and Northern

Development
Indian Problem
Inherent Rights to Self-
   government
"Inherent" versus
   "Contingent" Rights
Internal Colonialism
Inuit
Limited Autonomy
Metis

Modernization Thesis
Paradigm Muddles
Relational Status
Status' versus 'Non-sta-
   tus' Indians
The Principle of
   Aboriginality
White Paper
White problem

REVIEW QUESTIONS

1) Compare and contrast the three major forces in Canada in terms of their legal status, core problem, proposed solution, and anticipated outcome.

2) Provide a brief description of the social, economic, political, and cultural problems that confront aboriginal communities. Who is responsible for these problems? Justify your answer.

3) Demonstrate how an internal colonialism model can provide insights into the current status of aboriginal peoples.

4) With regard to government policy, briefly trace the stages in the evolution of aboriginal-government relations in Canada from early contact up to the present.

5) Outline the current demands of the aboriginal peoples with respect to improving their relational status in Canadian society. How do aboriginal demands compare with the solutions proposed by federal government?

6) Why do political authorities have such difficulty with aboriginal demands?

7) The concept of aboriginal self-determination through inherent aboriginal self-government is contentious in Canada. What is meant by this concept? How is it justified? What does it propose to accomplish? How does it differ from government proposals in this area?

8) Discuss how and why aboriginal-government relations can be described as existing in a "muddled" state.

CHAPTER 8

CHARTER GROUPS: RESTRUCTURING FRENCH-ENGLISH RELATIONS

INTRODUCTION: THE TWO SOLITUDES

The previous chapter demonstrated how an interplay of opposing forces is re-shaping aboriginal-government relations. Cumulative pressures, from cultural conflicts to colonialist exploitation, have contributed to the marginal status of Canada's indigenous occupants. Fundamentally different agendas have brought the state into conflict with the First Nations; they also have complicated efforts at renewal. Hostilities and mistrust continue to fester despite a political climate that is increasingly receptive to accommodation and change. Numerous barriers preclude a mutually acceptable political arrangement, including balky politicians, entrenched bureaucracy, historical inertia, and vested interests. Such a politicized arena serves only to remind us that majority-minority restructuring does not arise out of a vac-uum, but in a real world of historical circumstances and political constraints.

A similar assessment can be applied to the realm of charter group interaction. As privileged and Charter members of Canadian Confederation, with a right to establish agendas consistent with their concerns, French-English relations have coexisted uneasily since 1841 when Upper and Lower Canada combined into an incipient nation-state — a situation nicely described by Lord Durham as "two na-tions warring in the bosom of a single state." Interaction has vacillated from stretches of sullen isolation ("two solitudes"), to periods of convulsive social change, with occasional flashes of violence in between ("two scorpions in a bottle"). The points of conflict are varied and numerous, including provincial-federal squab-bling, but tend to focus around Quebec as a "distinct society." That is, the Québécois constitute a powerful political community of people who in the name of **ethnic na-tionalism** claim some degree of autonomy by virtue of shared history, a collective vision, a set of grievances, common goals, and whose distinctiveness as a nation-ality is derived from perceived descent or ancestry (see Juteau 1994).

The potential for misunderstanding is complicated by issues related to lan-guage. Recent efforts at redefining French-English relations have revolved around

the politics of language renewal within a federalist framework of official bilingualism. But debate over bilingualism has infuriated and divided the country as
few other issues. Francophones throughout Canada have depicted English-speaking Canadians as insensitive to language and cultural aspirations. English Canada
is perceived as hostile toward Quebec's legitimate interests. Not surprisingly, many
saw the federally-mandated closure of Canada's only French-speaking military
training academy, Collège Militaire Royal de Saint-Jean, despite widespread Quebec
opposition, as politically motivated rather than economically driven (Bourgault
1994; also Commissioner of Official Languages 1995). Sensitivities are further inflamed when the English-speaking media pounce on minority issues to portray
Quebec as harsh and intolerant (Sniderman et al. 1993) — in effecting contributing to a siege mentality and a defensive attitude among Quebeckers. Anglophones
have dismissed the Québécois as rabid nationalists, with little or no respect for liberal values or individual rights, much less any concern with Canada's "national
interests." Quebeckers are accused of treating Canada as a treasure trove for plunder rather than a community to nourish. For example, while Quebec receives 34
percent of the federal immigration budget to assist in the settlement of new
Canadians, its decision to reduce the intake of immigrants from 25 percent to 16 percent (since 1991 Quebec has the right to choose who it will accept) of Canada's total
has not sat well. Quebec receives $2200 from Ottawa per immigrant; by contrast,
Ontario's total is $820 per immigrant or 39 percent of the total funding despite
receiving 55 percent of the immigrants (Simpson 1994c; *Kitchener-Waterloo Record*,
Editorial, 7 July 1994).

In short, both sectors continue to seethe over the seemingly unrealistic demands and expectations each has of the other. Quebec has made some important
gains as part of a restructuring of Quebec-Canada relations, yet continues to chafe
under pressures from federal containment (Gagnon 1993). English-speaking
Canadians appear increasingly opposed to any admission of the emergent realities
of Quebec's development, preferring a status-quo federalism of equal provinces
(McRoberts 1993). Rather than easing, the sparring has escalated even further
with the entrenchment of official bilingualism as a linchpin of national unity. The
Québécois dismiss bilingualism as an act of appeasement bereft of any shift in
power; English Canadians bristle at the inconvenience associated with bilingualism.
Many are outraged by Quebec's commitment to French unilingualism: Consider only
the rash of English-only moves by some 50 Ontario municipalities in 1990 in
protest against Quebec's Bill 178 to entrench French as the sole language of business and service. Quebeckers, in turn, are infuriated by the lack of adequate protection for a homeland of last resort.

What we have, then, is a breakdown in communication at the most fundamental level. Failure to foster a rapprochement cultivates the potential for conflict at interpersonal and intergroup levels. The forging of a workable accommodation
between Ottawa and Quebec is overdue, but unlikely without a major rethinking
of Canada's federalism. Quebec's demands for self-determination along the lines of
a "distinct society" status appear to be increasingly accepted although the scope

of this concession is open to debate. Proposals for a more flexible ("assymetrical") federalism has drawn attention to (a) the polarization of Canadian society along linguistic lines; (b) the socially constructed dimensions of national unity and identity; (c) a proposed restructuring of federal-provincial relations; and (d) debate over individual versus collective rights in a liberal democracy. Responses to these perennial concerns provide many of the dynamics underlying Ottawa-Quebec relations. They also furnish insights into "what is really going on between the French and English"; "what do the Québécois really want"; and "how feasible are Québécois demands in light of competing realities."

Chapter Content

This chapter examines the political dimensions of Québécois ethnicity by exploring the logic behind the ongoing renewal of French-English relations. This analysis of the politics of ethnicity is framed within the broader context of Canadian federalism on the one side, the process of Canadian society-building on another, and Quebec's nation-building moves on yet another. Charter group interaction is discussed as a distinctive configuration of intergroup relations that have coalesced around the issues of sovereignty and language as well as ethnic nationalism and collective rights. Emphasis is on the patterned interaction that has evolved as the English and French continue to jockey for control over respective agendas. Particular attention is paid to *how* language strikes at the heart of Québécois ethnicity, followed by *why* language issues have assumed such a profile in Quebec-Ottawa restructuring — even if concerns related to power and jurisdiction are perhaps more fundamental. Much can be gleaned from re-examining recent constitutional efforts to further bolster Quebec's claim as a "distinct society" with a corresponding right to preserve and promote its unique status. Prospects for arriving at a mutually satisfactory solution remain elusive because of radically different visions of Canada and Quebec's place in it. With the spectre of Quebec separatism clearly before us, further procrastination has potential to rend asunder what history has carefully cobbled together.

The chapter is divided into five sections. The first provides a brief look at language and the centrality of symbols in advancing the nationalist aspirations of incipient nations (Gagnon 1993). An overview of language policies and laws in Canada is laid out next. Of central concern are provincial and political responses to the entrenchment of two official languages in Canada. The following section deals with language of politics/the politics of language in Quebec. The role of language as an agent of social change is examined by way of its influence in politicizing Québécois aspirations. Language conflicts in Quebec are also considered within the context of an emergent ethnic nationalism. The fourth section examines English-French relations against the backdrop of Canadian federalism and conflicting visions of Canada — namely as contract or as compact, with a "three-nations" view gathering momentum. In the fifth and final section, we discuss the content and implications of restructuring Quebec along the lines of a distinct society. The emergent notion of Canada as a three-nation state has further complicated the balancing act in a society constructed around compromises.

A Word of Caution

French- and English-speaking relations are subject to different interpretations. For example, this relationship can be analyzed as a federal-provincial issue or a constitutional debate or even a case of regionalism. We have preferred to couch the debate within the context of ethnicity and ethnic nationalism. French and English-speaking interactions are portrayed as relations of inequality in the competition over scarce resources and jurisdictional control. Language politics are central to these power struggles: Language serves as a key ethnic marker that not only reflects Quebec's distinctiveness, but also provides a vehicle for conveying political and economic aspirations. In short, the politics of language animate the dynamics of French-English restructuring, and this chapter is devoted to exploring the "whys" and the "hows."

A note on terminology. The chapter makes repeated references to anglophones and francophones, as well as to Québécois and Ottawa. Its contents are focused primarily on the relationship of French-speaking Canadians in Quebec (the "Québécois" or "Quebeckers") to the rest of Canada (ROC). Some attention is paid to the 1.6 million French speaking persons outside of Quebec, including the 500,000 Franco-Ontarians and 300,000 Acadians in New Brunswick who occupy a different legal status than Québécois. Francophones outside of Quebec face a different set of challenges as an official language minority. While the concerns of the Québécois revolve about power-sharing, jurisdiction, and language survival, other francophones are more likely to worry about assimilation without adequate guarantees of French-speaking educational or provincial services (Gray 1994). A reluctance by Quebec to endorse the struggles of francophone communities in other provinces attests to divergences of outlook and aspirations.

The term "English speaking" also requires some clarification. Rather than an ethnic group, this category refers to a rather broad description of those Canadians who reside primarily outside Quebec and rely on English as the primary language of communication. English-language minorities who live in Quebec are often called anglophones. Those anglophones who meet the criteria as stated in Section 23 (1a) of the Charter qualify as the "official language minority" and are certified to educate their children in English:

> Citizens of Canada whose first language learned and still understood is that of English or French linguistic minority populations of the province in which they reside... have the right to have their children receive primary and secondary school instruction in that language in that province (S 23(1a).

Immigrants and refugees in Canada whose first language is neither French nor English are called allophones. Finally references to the term "Ottawa-Quebec" (or Quebec-Canada) relations are employed as a convenient shorthand to describe the politics of English-French interaction.

THE LANGUAGE OF ETHNICITY/THE ETHNICIZATION OF LANGUAGE

Canadians appear to possess a remarkably high threshold for debate on language issues. Passage of the Official Languages Act in 1969, followed by promotion of multiculturalism as government policy since 1971 have contributed to the controversies. The existence of two-tier language policy (official + non-official) is no less contentious: French and English constitute the official and equal languages of public commmunication. Both heritage languages and the 53 different languages of the First Nations comprise the unofficial sector. It is common knowledge that French- and English-speaking relations are driven by language politics. But Canadian language debates are not confined only to the realm of official languages (Fleras 1993). Diverse language groups such as the Ukrainians in Western Canada have lobbied hard to entrench non-official languages ("heritage languages") across the school system, on the assumption that official multiculturalism is inseparable from linguistic diversity. Aboriginal peoples have also taken steps to avert the decline of indigenous tongues including the establishment of aboriginal language preschools and related salvage measures (Hall 1986; Fleras 1987).

Nor are language conflicts restricted to Canada. Language controversies culminating in violence and bloodshed are surprisingly common throughout the world. Efforts to accommodate minority language groups are evident in European countries such as Belgium and Switzerland as well as in African and the South Pacific countries. Developing nations that are anxious to purge themselves of imperialist stigmas have replaced colonialist English with indigenous languages. The institutionalization of Swahili throughout central Africa is a clear example of linguistic engineering in support of nationalist endeavours. Language chauvinism also plays an important role in furthering nationalist ambitions in powerful nation-states such as France. The French are proud of their language and envision it as a sign of intelligence and sophistication as well as a prelude to social acceptance and career advancement. The French Language Academy is under constant pressure to maintain the purity of French by purging it of contaminations from English "junk" culture. Even that bastion of English speakers — the United States — is not immune to language politics. Lobbying by the group "U.S. English" has entrenched English as the official language in nineteen states. The lobby group has also attempted to constitutionally enshrine English as the sole official language of the country.

What is it about language that gives it such appeal in cases of interethnic strife? Any ethnic group that wants to remain distinct must activate certain symbols to express and preserve its uniqueness. Language fits the bill. It is proven as an agent of social and political change with respect to the competition for scarce political and economic resources. Language conflicts have the capacity to sharpen political objectives by raising levels of awareness over majority-minority relations. Debates about language also have the potential to camouflage and conceal when necessary.

Language and Ethnic Politics

Efforts to restructure ethnicity are increasingly dependent on the powerful role of language (Taylor and Giles 1979; also Kramarae 1984; Shkilynk 1986). Such a linkage is to be expected, given the intimate relationship between language, identity, and ethnicity (Kennedy 1983; Edwards 1985). The link between language and identity is a powerful one for mobilizing individuals in pursuit of collective interests (Edwards 1985). It is also important for shaping the perceptual reality and social cohesion of otherwise disparate populations (Bourhis, Giles, Leyens, Tajfel, 1979; Ross 1979). A common language allows minority members to become situated in a web of satisfying relationships and meaningful activities (Rubin 1983). The Supreme Court of Canada has stated as much even overruling Bill 101. While critizing provisions in the Bill, the Court has endorsed the salient role of language as highly visible manifestations of a people's aspirations, self-hood, cultural distinctiveness, world view, and aesthetics (also Nadkarni 1983; Sutcliffe 1986):

> Language is so intimately related to the form and content of expression that there cannot be true freedom of expression by means of language if one is prohibited from using the language of one's choice. Language is not merely the means or medium of expression; ...[it is] a means by which a people may express its cultural identity.

In other words, minority languages serve as a vessel for sustaining ethnic consciousness and interaction (Harries 1983; Hewitt 1986). Leaders will capitalize on threats to minority language as a way of galvanizing an otherwise inchoate group into protest action. Minority languages can compress subordinate group aspirations into manageable proportions for political expression. The recasting of political concerns into linguistic issues can transform the often abstract demands of minority sectors (for example, "distinct society" or "self-government") into something central policy structures can understand (Fleras 1987).

Majority languages are often devalued as viable communication in highly politicized contexts (Watson 1983). They are also viewed as as unacceptable for expressing minority concerns. Rather than neutral vehicles for conveying impartial information, dominant languages are perceived instead as ideological extensions for majority rule and cooptation. Certain racial or class biases are inherent within majority speech habits. These distortions render them inappropriate for nationalist movements (Bones 1986). Minority use of dominant speech patterns is dismissed as disloyal and counterproductive to the movement (Rubin 1983). In short, language debates are not about the freedom of personal expression, but rather about the politics of power in societies undergoing social change.

Those whose language is secure may not appreciate the emotion and passion evinced by minority language aspirations. Many are oblivious to the symbolic and emotive properties associated with minority language use. Since theirs is a universally accepted lingua franca that is rarely threatened or challenged, English-speaking individuals, like fish in water, tend to be blasé about its value and power. English is treated as little more than a routine and tacitly accepted form of communication. Only under threatening conditions (such as that which confronted the anglophone community in Quebec) is English embraced as a symbol of anglo-identity and distinctiveness.

CASE STUDY

World Languages: Towers of Babel or Bridges to Prosperity?

Canada strikes many as a complicated, even ungovernable society. Its sprawling size and regional distinctions contribute to this image, as does an ongoing struggle to cope with the competing concerns of racial, ethnic, and aboriginal minorities. Though daunting, the challenges confronting Canada are intrinsic to any modern and diverse democracy. Multiculturalism in Canada has evolved as one way to address the pressures to accommodate diversity. Policy objectives are not the promotion of minorities per se: the focus instead is on the creation of a coherent society in which differences co-exist as legitimate and integral components within a framework of shared values and common institutions (Fleras 1994).

The role of non-official language (sometimes called world or heritage language) rights have been ambiguous throughout Canada's society-building process (Cummins and Danesi 1990). The preservation of world languages is widely endorsed as beneficial to (a) minority individuals (in terms of intellectual development and academic success), (b) ethnocultural communities (with respect to survival), and (c) Canadian national interests (within an interdependent global economy). Others disagree, and see world languages as complicating the natural unscrolling of

Canada as a bilingual society (Parel 1992). Minority language maintenance is also denounced as a costly luxury for a cash-strapped economy, and having the potential to dismantle the country if left unchecked. Government support for world languages has faltered because of these political worries or economic costs, both real or imagined, despite statutory regulations to "preserve and enhance the use of languages other than English or French…" (Multiculturalism Act, July 1988).

That world language rights are arguably part of Canada's multicultural package is reasonable enough—even if federal support can be described as long on principle, short on practice. Failure to secure ethno-language rights under federal multiculturalism may stem from contradictions within the diversity agenda rather than from negligence or conspiracy. Paradoxes that underlie the logic behind Canada's language policies need to be examined in light of broader political developments and the politics of society-building. This case study explores how world languages constitute a renewable resource of inestimable value to Canada; nevertheless, a combination of factors has colluded to cramp their potential. Until these factors are brought into line, the potential for renewal is limited.

CANADA'S LANGUAGE POLICY CONTEXT

The concept of Canada's world languages can only be understood within the context of the state's language policy. A two-tier system prevails at present, although a third tier may emerge because of First Nations pressure to avert the alarming decline of Canada's 53 different aboriginal languages (Fleras 1987; Hassan 1995).

Tier 1 — Official Languages

The first tier consists of Canada's official languages. French and English stand in a privileged position as the official languages of political and public discourse. By virtue of the 1969 Official Languages Act, both French and English are equal in the institutional sense: that is, French and English represent the languages of communication in domains under federal jurisdiction. All individuals are entitled to federal services in either French or English where significant demand exists. Federal employees not only have the option to communicate in preferred official language in the workplace; they also have the right to equitable employment and promotional opportunities regardless of their language of choice (Annual Report 1992).

In keeping with Canada's language duality, official language minorities (namely, French-speaking Canadians outside Quebec; English-speakers in Quebec) are accorded equal protection under the Charter of Rights and the Official Languages Act of 1988. But bilingual realities are less impressive at the provincial level. Twenty-five years after passage of the Official Languages Act only the province of New Brunswick is officially bilingual. All other provinces are unilingual, with English monolingualism predominant across Canada outside of Quebec and New Brunswick. In fairness, official language minorities have managed to secure limited control over provincial services in designed areas across Canada (*Language and Society* 1994), but not without controversy or resistance, as evidenced by the occasional outbursts of English-only dissidents (for example, the Association for the Preservation of English).

Tier 2 — World Languages

The second tier consists of non-official languages (languages other than French or English or aboriginal), sometimes called "community" or "international" or "heritage" languages. World languages are a formidable presence in Canada. According to Statistics Canada (1992), 59.9 percent of the population in 1991 indicated English as their mother tongue (language first learned at home during childhood and still understood), 24.1 percent reported French as first language, and 14.8 percent identified a non-official language — up from 12.2 percent of the single responses in 1981. In terms of home language (language spoken most often at home), 67.5 percent spoke English, 23.0 percent spoke French, and 7.7 percent spoke a non-official language, an increase from 6.6 percent in 1981 (see also *Annual Review* 1992). The most frequently reported home languages other than French or English were Chinese (430,000), Italian (288,000), Portuguese (153,000), Spanish (145,000), aboriginal languages (138,000), and German (134,000). The proportion of those relying on home language other than English or French was highest in Toronto (23 percent) and Vancouver (18 percent) (Statistics Canada 1992). As might be expected, ethno-language use and identification is highest among new Canadians, but declines sharply for subsequent generations (see Kralt and Pendakur 1991). With immigration totals currently at post-war highs, language diversities are likely to escalate, with or without official support.

The prevailing discourse about world languages is centred on the theme of survival. Three strategies for world languages survival exist in varying degrees across Canada (see Cummins and Danesi 1990; Cummins 1994; also Fleras and Elliott 1991). *First,* there are the bilingually-based world language programs. World languages are employed as languages of instruction through their incorporation into the school curriculum. The Prairie provinces have long supported such bilingual programs for transitional or maintenance purposes: Up to 50 percent of the classroom instruction may be conducted in a world language—mainly German or Ukrainian, but also Yiddish and Mandarin in cities such as Edmonton. The *second* type of program is conducted within the school system, but outside the core curriculum. Instruction may be held after class hours, as part of an extended school day, or outside school hours such as on weekends. For example, Ontario under its 1977 Heritage Language Program is obligated by law to implement school-based heritage language programs in response to requests by community groups who can supply a minimum of 25 pupils (Cummins 1994). But instruction remains outside the normal school day,

even with enrolment figures at nearly 120,000 students in 60 languages across Canada. The *third* type consists of heritage language programs under the auspices of ethnocultural communities. Ethnocultural communities have underwritten such classes for a century or more, yet government funding has materialized only in the past fifteen years (Cummins 1994). These largely private initiatives may utilize school resources but are only remotely plugged into the educational system.

Canada's world languages are subject to negotiation and containment. Proposals for mainstreaming them have elicited both criticism and praise as opponents and proponents alike clash over world languages as (a) a social problem; (b) a multicultural right; or (c) a renewable resource for Canadian society (Cummins 1991). The challenge that awaits the Canadian state is relatively straightforward: how to expand the scope of world languages, without incurring the debilitating costs of such an accommodation.

BALANCING THE TIERS

Promotion of non-official languages poses a perennial challenge to a democracy that attaches value to diversity. A comprehensive multiculturalism is almost inconceivable without a world languages component—even in a society that is officially bilingual—since language and culture are intertwined (Dore 1993). The symbolic importance of language for indigenous and ethnic minority groups goes beyond political interests or commercial value (Edwards 1985; Fishman 1989). An ethno-language is revered as a satisfying means of communication—especially when alternate outlets of expression are unacceptable (see Fleras and Elliott 1991 for fuller explanation). A language heritage serves as a highly visible manifestation of a people's aspirations, self-hood, world view, and aesthetics (Laurin 1978). It not only symbolizes cultural distinctiveness and identity, but also facilitates ethnic boundary maintenance and intra-group solidarity in contexts both changing and diverse (Bourhis et al. 1979; Fleras 1987; Henderson 1993).

But what binds together may also rend asunder unless appropriate safeguards are secured. That thought alone should underscore the perils of balancing world languages with Canada's linguistic duality (Yalden 1993). To one side, access to world languages is endorsed as a basic human right (Yalden 1993). Minorities in Canada are entitled as individuals to employ the language of their choice in personal settings, within their own communities, in creative capacities, and for school instruction on occasion. Nor can Canada afford to openly discriminate against world languages. To do so by violating constitutional guarantees for protection would pose a grave risk to our national self-image and international obligations.

Yet outright support for world languages is equally disruptive. Consider only the chaos in communication from a linguistic free-for-all. Even more mind-boggling are the economic costs and crippling administrative burdens incurred by a totally non-discriminatory policy. World language programs have drawn flak for being "socially divisive," "excessively costly," and "educationally retrograde" (Cummins and Danesi 1990). Others condemn world languages as

likely to (a) balkanize the school system, (b) detract from the school curriculum, (c) shortchange minority children in the outside world, (d) foster linguistic and cultural barriers, and (e) deter newcomers from learning English or French and becoming Canadian. With such an array of criticism, who can be surprised by government tentativeness in this area.

In short, what sounds good in theory may not work in practice. This is particularly true in Canada where a multiplicity of languages are contesting for social space. The Canadian state is ensnared in a paradox: It must strike a balance between competing forces by reconciling the human rights principle that all languages are equal, with the realization that some languages are manifestly *unequal* when it comes to social utility or public power. A compromise that acknowledges a distinction between the "ideal" and the "real" is plausible enough, provided that the discriminatory effects of such a distinction constitute a reasonable limitation on individual rights (Yalden 1993). That said, there is much to commend Canada's language policy of "multilingualism within a bilingual framework." Canada retains a reputation for fair and reasonable treatment toward world languages despite the looming realities of two language majorities. Does this assessment hold up to scrutiny in light of historical developments?

POLICY AND DEVELOPMENTS

Historically, heritage languages did not count for much in Canadian society-building. The prevalence of racist and assimilationist agendas undercut immigrant language aspirations (Elliott and

Fleras 1991). Ethnocultural communities—particularly those outside the Prairie provinces—had one of two options open to them. Many sacrificed their ethnolinguistic heritage in exchange for anglo-conformist citizenship. Others continued to embrace their first language, but only in private and without expectations of government support (Cummins and Danesi 1990). Even the relaxation of assimilationist policies did not automatically catapult world languages into prominence. Nor did passage of official multiculturalism in 1971 prove to be an immediate windfall. Although Canada had no official culture, as Prime Minister Pierre Trudeau claimed in his Parliament speech in October of that year, only French and English stood as official and equal as expressed by the Official Languages Act of 1969. Three stages can be discerned in the evolutionary development since then:

Tentative Acceptance

A significant outcome from the 1971 multiculturalism policy statement led to a commissioned study of world languages. The Non-Official Languages Study of 1976 (O'Bryan et al. 1976) uncovered substantial ethnocultural support for world language teaching within the primary school system. Then as now, ethnocultural communities sought government support for world languages as a *right* bestowed by official multiculturalism. World languages were depicted as a national resource with considerable economic clout abroad and political benefits at home (Cummins 1991). Not everyone agreed with this assessment. Berry and his associates (1977) found considerable public opposition to the

principle of publicly funded minority language instruction. Even the massive 1991 survey on general attitudes by Multiculturalism Canada underscored public resentment of heritage language funding (Angus Reid 1991; also Berry and Kalin 1993). Such mixed messages have sharply altered the government's language agenda.

Celebrating Language

Canada's world languages policy originated in the context of official multiculturism. The folkloric multiculturalism of the 1970s leaned heavily toward cultural preservation. The rationale for this support reflected a key multicultural assumption, that is, individuals who feel good about their ethnic culture will extend a similar right to others (Berry et al. 1977; Berry and Kalin 1993). That kind of thinking was parlayed into government support for world languages as a basis for society-building. This commitment was further entrenched by the pivotal role of German and Ukrainian lobbies who argued tirelessly for their protection and promotion.

Language retention policies did not materialize until the creation of the Cultural Enrichment Program in 1977. This program made provisions for a variety of initiatives, including supplementary school assistance, heritage language teaching aids, and teacher training support—all on a shoestring budget; for example, the world languages component of the multicultural grants program under the Secretary of State received $3,398,785 for the fiscal year 1987/88 (Pal 1993). However modest such expenditures, the use of government monies to legitimize world languages symbolized a radical departure from the assimilationist agenda of the past (Cummins 1994).

World languages enjoyed a further boost with passage of the Multiculturalism Act in 1988. The Act sought to preserve and enhance the use and importance of world languages without detracting from official languages. Additional assistance stemmed from a federal department of Multiculturalism and Citizenship when it established a Heritage Cultures and Languages Division, with its focus on identity, the mainstreaming of ethnic artists, and promotion of language and ethnoculture. The 1988 act also cleared the path for a proposed Canadian Heritage Language Institution in Edmonton, although this institute continues to languish in some Byzantine limbo for lack of political will, despite receipt of royal assent (Pers Comm., Canadian Heritage, 4 November 1993).

Relapse—or Re-prioritization?

Recent policy initiatives are less encouraging. The first blow was the collapse of Multiculturalism Department in 1993 into a superministry of Canadian Heritage (including Parks Canada, Amateur Sports, etc.). A corresponding shift in priorities has dealt another blow to the world languages program. Direct financing of world languages instruction has given way to the principle of indirect funding *in support of* teaching and learning. Attention is focused on the need to "support and promote innovative approaches to the learning of heritage languages"…"to develop expertise and teaching materials for heritage language classes"…"to research and promote heritage language" (Annual Review 1993:11). Government efforts to justify this move toward "referral" or "facilitator" as a shift in responsibilities rather than outright abandonment have not proven convincing. The fact that federal spending for world languages has fallen to about $750,000 for 1993-94 does not bode well for the future (*Multiculturalism* 1993). Compare this anomaly in expenditure with the current $1.1 million as a base grant for Basketball Canada, or the estimated $600 million for implementing official bilingualism. The decision in 1990 to eliminate the Cultural Retention Program as part of an overall budget-crunch is equally foreboding.

WORLD LANGUAGES AS A RENEWABLE RESOURCE

The role and status of world languages has fluctuated in response to prevailing ideologies in society. This relationship between multiculturalism and world languages is neither fixed in time nor monolithic across space. Ideally each of the multicultural discourses (from celebrating differences to managing diversity) entertains a distinctive outlook on the relevance of world languages (Fleras 1993). Official multiculturalism in recent years has drifted away from an endorsement of language and cultural heritage, preferring instead a commitment to anti-racism and institutional accommodation. Predictably world languages initiatives have been cast adrift by this switch in priorities.

Yet signs point to growing support for world languages. This renewal can be attributed to the profusion of intercultural contacts at domestic and international levels. Consider only the composition of urban school environments: over half the school population in Toronto and Vancouver possesses a non-English, non-French speaking background (Cummins (1991). Capitalizing on this diversity for curriculum or pedagogical purposes may represent a necessity rather than an option or luxury. As well, much of the fear once associated with second language acquisition is vanishing. Evidence suggests that second language learning does not interfere with dominant language acquisition, much less detract from cognitive development and general academic performance (Cummins 1994). If anything, studies reveal, the opposite is true as general language and conceptual skills may be bolstered by transfer through second language learning.

Another factor in this renewal entails the rapidly changing social realities of a global economy. In terms of international competitiveness, Canada is heavily dependent on a culturally adept and linguistically diverse citizenry for maximizing export trade and globalized investment (Cummins 1991). Canada can learn from the experiences of other countries; for example, Australia has also concurred with the importance of community languages as a basis for improving international competitiveness in trade and commerce—as confirmed by a 1990 federal report (quoted in *Annual Review* 1992:21):

> It is incorrect to describe English as the international language of business. English is only one of nine major languages used by the business and scientific community.

Monolingual speakers are disadvantaged in the international community...since those persons who speak one of the major international languages together with English have access to greater information resources. This disadvantage may be part of the explanation for the relative lack of exporting success of Australia, New Zealand, the U.S.A., and the UK since the growth of other major non-English-speaking economies.

Yet another factor in this reconciliation may stem from a reconsideration of those multicultural priorities that divide rather than unite. Properly managed, multiculturalism can be employed as a social glue for binding all Canadians into a coherent, prosperous, and distinct society. With all trends pointing to even more diversification because of high immigration to counter the effects of low birth rates and an aging population, pressure will mount to accommodate diversity in ways that are sensible and helpful to newcomers. A productive world language component is but one response to pressures for rebuilding Canada along pluralistic lines. The cross-linkages and shared commitments implicit within a world languages program may also secure the basis for the long-awaited global re-ordering. Rather than a tower of babel, in other words, world languages may play a key role in bridging those differences that threaten to partition or provoke.

Note: A version of this paper was presented at the "Languages in Collision" Conference, University of Ottawa, November 1993.

The Politics of La Langue Française

Nowhere are the **politics of language** more evident than in Quebec where the Québécois have relied on language legislation to repel English-speaking threats to their existence. Promotion of French is justified for various reasons (Laurin 1978). Language represents a complex and powerful system of communication: It not only reflects the foundation of their cultural existence ("ground under their feet"), but also serves as a repository of past values and historical beliefs. As well as a symbol of identity and nationhood, the French language provides a buffer against central authority intrusion. Political objectives are clearly established through the manipulation of these symbols of protest. With its capacity to inflame passions and to trigger demonstrations of public support, the French language allows Quebec leaders to retain the upper hand in negotiating with federal authorities.

Language issues have become even more important because of cultural changes. French-English differences are widely assumed as self-evident. For example, market surveys indicated that French Canadians prefer Pepsi over Coke. Others point to differences in personality. The Québécois are seen as animated and exuberant, with a penchant for creativity and spontaneity. The *anglais* by contrast are viewed as rational and staid. Still others such as Fournier (1994) point to more substantial differences: The French and English belong to different nations and draw upon different traditions. That invariably brings them into conflict over opposing orientations and aspiring lifestyles (see also Chodak 1994).

What is shared between them is no less impressive than the differences between the French and English. Cultural convergence is reflected in mutual endorsement of democratic and liberal values, a commitment to protect human rights and freedoms, and willingness to address a pluralist agenda in a way that accommodates diversity without undermining the centre. Differences are rapidly vanishing because of consumerism and mass technologies. Only language remains a distinct feature to be nurtured and protected. That alone exerts additional pressure for protective measures.

Even more intriguing is the capacity of the French language to disguise concerns pertaining to the Quebec economy. The conflict between Quebec and Ottawa is not about language per se, but about power and control. The economic rather than ideological intent of Bill 101 was expressed by Guy Rocher, a University of Montreal sociology professor, who claimed:

> The key element when we were writing it was to francicize the economic structure so that francophones could work in French and have access to senior positions. We wanted to change the workplace from an anglo-dominated hierarchy.

With passage of Bill 101, the rules of Quebec's economic game underwent change. The new rules were slanted exclusively toward French language speakers. Such a competitive handicap resulted in a massive flight of English-dominant companies such as Sun Life Insurance. A number of anglophones at middle and upper management levels also fled. The subsequent vacuum created by these departures enabled the French middle class to move in. Control of the economy subsequently moved from being predominantly in English hands to almost exclusively those of the French.

In short, language plays a dual role in Quebec's politics. Language issues possess a kind of visceral appeal to the Québécois, as they do for many minority groups, including English speakers. That alone makes language an effective symbol for mobilizing the masses in defence of minority interests. Yet language as a trump card can be overplayed. Primary contests in Quebec are not necessarily about language or ethnicity. They are equally concerned with power and resources, as well as control over jurisdictions that "rightfully" belong to Quebec, though the threat of mass insurrection because of language grievances may be manipulated for leverage against Ottawa. The symbols of language and ethnicity provide an emotionally charged vehicle for politicizing the more practical concerns of the Québécois in a manner both socially acceptable and easily identifiable.

OFFICIAL BILINGUALISM: SOCIETY-BUILDING OR SOCIETY-BASHING?

Canada can be described as a linguistic duality whose national language policies are simultaneously a source of comfort and a force for confrontation. Problems in communication and language accommodation can be expected in a country of two official languages with three-quarters of the population speaking one language, one-quarter the other. A series of responses known as official bilingualism have evolved to address the national unity crisis created by perpetual sniping between the French and English. Bilingualism itself comes in different shapes and sizes. Under **individual bilingualism**, each person is expected to become proficient in one or more languages in the country. **Territorial bilingualism** is another option, and reflects a division of language use along geographical lines. For example, Belgium and Switzerland are divided into regions where one of the other official language predominates. Finally, there is **institutional bilingualism** with its focus on bilingual workplaces and delivery of services.

Canada is characterized by all three types. There is an unofficial territorial bilingualism, namely, Canada is divided into two language heartlands — Quebec and the rest of Canada — with a limited number of bilingual districts such as Ottawa or New Brunswick. Many people are attracted to this type of bilingualism, but the sprawling expanse of this country may render such a solution inadequate for society-building. Individual bilingualism also exists in Canada; nearly 16 percent of the total population possesses fluency in both languages. Officially, however, Canada endorses institutional bilingualism. It acknowledges the equal and official status of French and English as languages of communication in federal institutions across the country. A second tier of languages, both heritage and aboriginal, also receive federal support, but do not qualify for official status as languages of public discourse (Yalden 1993; Fleras 1993). How, then, do we assess official bilingualism in a country renown for society-building through compromises?

Federal Bilingualism: Institutional-Style

Canada's experiment with federal bilingualism began in the 1960s. Efforts to strengthen French language rights in exchange for social peace resulted in the right of federal public servants in 1966 to conduct business in either French or English. Passage of the **Official Languages Act** in 1969 formalized linguistic duality as a fundamental characteristic of Canadian society. Implicit in this formula for relations between the two main language groups was a vision of Canada that allowed speakers of either language to feel comfortable in all parts of the country (Goldbloom 1994b; Commissioner of Official Languages 1995). No less implicit were political goals: That is, to "cool out" troublesome Québécois dissidents without any fundamental restructuring of Canada's power relations (McRoberts 1989).

Provisions of the Act acknowledged the presence and legitimacy of both French and English as official and equal languages throughout Canada. The courts and Parliament, in addition to the central offices of all federal government institutions, were to be bilingual. The rights of official-language minorities would be protected in English Canada and Quebec. The act stipulated that official language minorities were entitled to federal services in either French or English — in areas where numbers warranted or demand was significant. It also confirmed the right of federal employees to work in the official language of their choice. Equal opportunities for French and English speakers in the public service were guaranteed as well. Bilingualism was expressed in federal documents, signs in national parks, parliamentary proceedings, court cases, and federally chartered passenger vehicles from Air Canada planes to shuttle buses at Pelee National Park. Recent efforts to update the Official Languages Act (1988) to conform with the 1982 Charter's equality provisions have reaffirmed Ottawa's commitment to bilingualism by strengthening official language minority control over education and school boards (parents who speak one of the official languages have a right to educate children in the preferred language) where they constitute viable communities.

Reaction to Bilingualism

Nearly thirty years of official endorsement have complicated the the verdict on bilingualism. Both political and public responses are polarized, involving an admixture of support, rejection, expediency, and indifference. Critics tend to exaggerate the magnitude and scope of official bilingualism. A favorite target is bilingualism within the federal civil service. Consider, however, the facts. In 1993, according to a report from the Official Languages Commissioner, 30 percent or 64,086 federal civil service jobs had been designated as bilingual in order to accommodate significant demand for two-language services. About 50 percent of the bilingual placements were in Quebec; by contrast, only 8,791 out of 115,780 jobs in the rest of Canada outside of Quebec were posted as bilingual — including only 3 percent of the federal civil jobs in western Canada. Still, the costs of bilingualism are not insignificant: Ottawa spends about $300 million in promoting official bilingualism through training programs and incentives; it also spends another $300 million for official language programs to meet the obligations of the Official Languages Act.

INSIGHT

Myths and Facts about Bilingualism

Many myths and half truths circulate around official bilingualism — each of which has the potential to blunt its society-building potential. To clarify them, here are some facts:

1) Corn flake boxes have been bilingual since 1907. So much for the theory that French is "being crammed down our throat because of current government policy."

2) A person cannot receive English or French services on demand anywhere in Canada. Most bilingual and official language minority services are offered only where numbers warrant or there is a significant demand. In other words, one is not likely to receive bilingual postal services in tiny Tobermory, Ontario except perhaps via a 1-800 telephone line.

3) Official bilingualism does not mean that everyone has to be fluent in French or English. With the exception of some federal civil servants, federal bilingualism means that *no one* except people in certain federal postings need be bilingual for information or services.

4) The provision of information and services in two languages applies only to the federal sector. The provinces are exempt from federal initiatives because of a constitutional division of jurisdiction.

5) All federal jobs do not require a proficiency in French. Only 7 percent of federal jobs require French only, while 60 percent demand a knowledge of English only and 30 percent are designated bilingual.

6) Why don't we all speak English? Well, nearly 4 million francophones speak no English. If we exclude the island of Montreal, 83 percent of Quebeckers do not speak English. 90 percent of English-speaking Canadians do not speak French. The existence of these two solitudes creates a strong need for bridging devices.

7) Canadians do not hate bilingualism. Much depends on how survey questions are phrased. Surveys suggest that many Canadians like the idea of two official languages and believe that people deserve to receive services in their own language rather than having to learn a new language just because they happen to live in certain part of the country.

8) Official bilingualism and protection of official language minorities do not come without cost. In 1992/93, total expenditures came to $631.5 million or 0.5 percent of government spending.

Levels of support for bilingualism vary with the phrasing of questions on national surveys. A slight majority of Canadians appear to support Canada's language duality, the principle of bilingualism, and the provision of bilingual government services as a blueprint for intergroup relations — at least when issues are couched in terms of responsiveness and accommodation rather than government intervention

(Commissioner of Official Languages 1995). Popular too is the extension of French language social services into areas of high francophone concentration. As well, highly motivated parents across Canada have enrolled their children in French immersion programs, thus bringing the number of bilingual Canadians from 2.9 million in 1971 to 4.4 million in 1991 (16.2% of the population) (*The Globe and Mail*, 11 January 1992).

Bilingualism and the Provinces

Federal and provincial structures have wavered in their endorsement of official bilingualism. Generally speaking, the reality of bilingualism is restricted to (a) federal institutions, (b) communities with a high proportion of French-speaking residents such as Eastern and Northern Ontario, (c) the delivery of some essential provincial services, and (d) some school children in larger urban centres. Only New Brunswick among the provinces is officially bilingual. Even here, hostilities arise between French-speaking Acadians who want to expand French language services versus the English-speaking majority who prefer the status quo. The Northwest Territories has also acknowledged French and English as official languages; official status has also been extended to six aboriginal languages for a total of eight official languages.

The other six provinces are nominally unilingual. English is the de facto language of communication in the delivery of service, although French language concessions have been introduced for a variety of reasons. Ontario is a good example of a province that has moved toward limited French language services. The French Language Services Act (Bill 8) in 1986 enshrined the delivery of French language services when warranted by numbers (namely, where the French-speaking population reaches a total of 5,000 or represents 10 percent of the population). London, Ontario by virtue of its 5,100 francophone inhabitants became the twenty-third region to qualify for bilingual provincial services. These and related concessions are largely politically motivated: Only five percent of the province is French speaking, but most franco-Ontarians are sufficiently compressed in the north and east to attract electoral concern.

Despite this extension, Ontario refuses to constitutionally guarantee bilingual rights across the province. Ontario's 15,000 French-speaking university students do not have a French-speaking university; yet the existence of four bilingual universities as well as five French speaking community colleges in the north and east should not be casually discounted. Only 102 of Ontario's 398 French language schools are francophone controlled, despite a Supreme Court ruling in 1990 to put that arrangement into effect. Several provinces, including Nova Scotia and British Columbia, have not even implemented minimal concessions to official minority language education — despite constitutional guarantees that suggest otherwise (Goldbloom 1994a). Elsewhere, Franco-Manitobans have experienced difficulty in having their constitutionally entrenched rights recognized. Not surprisingly, with the exception of the bilingual belt (those parts of Ontario and New Brunswick that straddle Quebec) (Joy 1970), the strength of French language has shown a gradual decline (McRoberts 1989).

How do Canada's 978,000 francophones in other provinces deal with agendas inconsistent with their political interests? Without going into detail for each province, certain general propositions are apparent. For francophones outside Quebec, the situation is grim because of assimilationist pressures (Gray 1994). Radio Canada is the lifeblood of francophones across Canada. In 1989, only two French newspapers were published daily, along with approximately 20 weeklies. With the exception of New Brunswick, moreover, true institutional completeness is not a lived-in reality for the francophone minority (Denis 1990). Provincial francophone associations are unified at the national level as the Fédération des Francophones Hors Québèc. The FFHQ is concerned with identifying and alleviating the institutional and legislative obstacles to their survival. Access to education as an official minority charter right is a primary concern. Parents in provinces outside Quebec have gone to court to gain recognition of their educational rights. That several provinces refuse to abide by these constitutional guarantees is cause for concern.

Uneven best describes provincial support for official bilingualism and official language minorities. Tolerance levels for official language minorities and official bilingualism dwindle as we move outside central Canada. Provinces such as Quebec have rejected the legitimacy of federal bilingualism as yet another clumsy government intrusion into a foreign domain. Quebec continues to provide its official language minorities with guaranteed services in English. Plebiscites and city councils in parts of Ontario (see the case study below) have voted to establish English-only municipalities for fear of absorbing costly French language service. An English-only lobby group, "The Alliance for the Preservation of English in Canada," has campaigned vigourously to curb the expansion of French in the public realm because of needless expense, inefficiency, and perceived unfairness (Andrew 1988). Even moves to update the Official Languages Act met with pockets of opposition within the ruling Conservative Party. In most cases resentment over official bilingualism is couched in economic terms ("too costly"), political terms ("too divisive"), cultural terms ("too irrelevant"), and social terms ("too undemocratic"). What happens when worries translate into action?

CASE STUDY

Language Grievances in Ontario: Genuine or Spurious?

Language conflicts are an inevitable dynamic in culturally and racially diverse societies. Even in United States with its overwhelming English-speaking majority, at least nineteen states (including California) have passed resolutions that specify English as the only official language. Canada is no exception to these language wars. Canadian unity has once again been put to the test in the aftermath of incidents involving bigotry and language intolerance. A recent crisis was engineered by a city council resolution in Sault Ste. Marie which declared itself an official English-only municipality. A petition of nearly 25,000 signatures and support from another English language lobby group (known as the Society for the Preservation of English in Canada) prompted "Soo St. Mary" to join ranks with over 40 other Ontario municipalities and counties (another 31 are officially bilingual) in declaring English the sole official language of business. No matter how justified the decision to preserve English usage in the conduct of municipal affairs, these actions have come across as a slight to the vision of bilingual Canada where all Canadians can communicate freely in the official language of their choice.

These mean-spirited actions were activated by public reaction to Ontario's French Language Services Act that came into effect in November of 1989. This law obligated the province to provide French-language services in provincial government ministries across 23 designated areas. Municipal services are clearly exempt from this ruling; nevertheless, there remains widespread anxieties about a creeping imposition of forced bilingualism. In defence of the actions of those municipalities that preemptively declared English as the formal language for delivery of local service, many of the councillors have taken pains to disassociate their initiatives with any anti-French sentiment. Economic reasons related to start-up and implementation costs have been put forward instead, as well as concerns over English-speaking access to provincial civil service jobs.

This resurgence of language tensions in Ontario cannot be separated from the politics of language in Canada and Quebec. Municipal efforts to circumvent the spread of French language services are widely condoned as revenge against passage of Bill 178 which in essence has prohibited the use of any language but French on commercial signs. Anglophones throughout the country condemned Bourassa's use of the "notwithstanding clause" to override a Supreme Court ruling on the unconstitutionality of French-only sign law. Many felt the law not only contravened the spirit of the Official Languages Act, but also infringed on fundamental and basic individual rights. Even the passage of time has not diminished anglophone resentment over this snub — as events in the Sault graphically demonstrate.

The latest sequence of moves by Ontario municipalities might well be interpreted as retaliation (a "quid pro quo") against Québécois nationalists. Municipalities such as the Sault can now condone their reprisals as no less discriminatory than comparable moves by Quebec to suppress English signage. After all, if authorities in Quebec can revoke English speaking rights, surely Ontarians possess an equal right to clamp down on French in Ontario. As the mayor of one English-only municipality was quoted as saying in a Toronto paper: "I don't think our council is against French, but a number of people feel that its get even time with the French Canadians." This raises of the question of whether the actions in Ontario and Quebec are similar in logic or intent? Can we justify francophone language restrictions in the Sault as similar to those in Quebec? Is there a separate logic at work despite surface similarities in form? Appearances in this case have been deceiving.

The turn of events in Quebec and Ontario are not equivalent, reflecting as they do, different political consequences and social contexts. Quebec's actions to restrict anglophone language rights must be analyzed from within a broader framework of North American society, rather than at the level of provincial discourse. Put simply, Quebec prefers to promote itself as a French-speaking enclave of 8 million, surrounded by a continental mass of 267 million English speakers whose assimilationist designs (largely inadvertent but deliberate in some cases) are foreboding. Arguing that Quebec is the homeland of last resort for a threatened language, the government has had little recourse but to invoke special measures. Although anglophone rights have been imperilled to some extent, the restrictions are seen as "reasonable, legal, and justified" in pursuit of Quebec's collective right to survival. Besides, the English in Quebec already possess an enviable set of constitutional guarantees pertaining to education and social services.

Can a similar assessment be applied to predominantly English-speaking Ontario? Has the violation of anglophone rights in Quebec set a precedent for Francophone "bashing" in Ontario? English is hardly a threatened language in Ontario, notwithstanding moderate concessions to Franco-Ontarians and heritage language groups. Both French and heritage language groups have lost ground to English as the preferred

speech at home and outside. The necessity for special measures to protect and promote English would appear to be an overreaction. It would be equally far-fetched to justify English-only resolutions as a "reasonable restriction" on an already threatened language base.

The decision to restrict English-speaking rights in Quebec cannot be compared with the dismissal of potential French language services in Ontario. The suspension of language rights in one jurisdiction is arguably not a violation of individual rights in another, given differences in circumstances and consequences. One set of actions is based on a concern over collective survival as a "distinct society." The other deals primarily with pragmatic issues over costs, resource allocation, and spending priorities. It is also concerned with reversing the tide of French language inroads in a province undergoing rapid and confusing changes. To many, Ontario is no longer the province it used to be. The recent influx and growing assertiveness of Third World immigrants have combined to create an astonishingly complex, diverse, and demanding society. Under these conditions, the mounting of English-only resolutions is aimed at securing a reassuring line of defence against what is unknown and threatening.

Fears and frustrations are not the only dynamic at work. As Canadians we take pride in our open and tolerant attitudes toward multicultural minorities. However, our historical record is littered with openly racist actions and discriminatory restrictions towards Asians, blacks, and First Nations. Recent trends indicate our racism has taken on increasingly subdued and polite overtones. This is to be expected in a climate where racial bigotry is no longer socially or legally acceptable. The emergence of a new moral order compels us to disguise our intolerance by appeals to a higher moral principle ("equal treatment for all," "Canadian unity," "no double standard") or practical constraint ("costs," "needs," "priorities"). The decision to ban French in Ontario municipalities may camouflage a thinly veneered but deeply entrenched racism toward outgroups. Evidence to this effect is substantiated by a recent incident reported in the Sault where an anglophone store clerk was overheard admonishing a francophone customer to "speak white."

Three provinces are now officially unilingual in opposition to the spirit of the Official Languages Act. Alberta and Saskatchewan have passed legislation making English the official provincial language. This decree ensures the primacy of English for business, commerce, administration, and provincial court activities. In fairness, there exists limited but inconsistent access to French language services. It might be noted that ethnically powerful groups such as the Ukrainians have been successful in incorporating their language into the school curriculum in certain regions throughout Western Canada.

The third unilingual province is Quebec. Quebec has endorsed official unilingualism since passage of the French Language Charter (Bill 101) in 1977. French is the only language of communication, although Quebec's 667,000 anglophones or almost 9.7 percent of the population benefit from guaranteed services in health and education. On the surface Quebec's unilingual language laws appear to contravene constitutional and statutory guarantees for official language minorities. Section 23 of the Charter stipulates that the "official language minority has the right to instruction in their mother tongue, the right to autonomous homogeneous school facilities, and the right to the management and control of these schools." Nevertheless, the unilingual nature of Quebec has been defended on a variety of grounds which will be examined shortly.

Summing Up: Bilingualism as Society-Building?

The ability to speak more than one language is widely recognized as an important personal resource. That makes Canada's stubborn resistance to language diversity difficult to explain (Clift 1989). Opponents argue that the concurrent use of two or more languages is a recipe for social disaster, unless one is relegated to the realm of the private and non-official. Others suggest that public commitment to bilingualism provides a solution to many problems that confront a dual society:

How does official bilingualism contribute to or detract from Canadian society-building? Kenneth McRoberts (1989) suggests official bilingualism originated in large part to counter the surge of nationalism in Quebec. It arose to restore national unity by offering Quebec the promise of participation and opportunity througout all of Canada. As a "society-saving" strategy, this national language policy responded to Quebec's discontent and threat of separation, not by power-sharing, but by de-politicizing the language components of the struggle. In the words of William Thorsell, editor in chief of *The Globe and Mail*, March 30, 1991,

> In essence, Ottawa tried to dilute Quebec nationalism by dispersing it across Canada, most obviously in the form of official bilingualism. The strategy was basically this: Ottawa would deny Quebecers additional powers in their own province in exchange for additional rights in Ottawa and all the other provinces.

The intent was purely political: Official bilingualism sought to allay public fears by securing language policy reforms within English Canada in exchange for Quebec's compliance with Canadian federalism. Establishing official bilingualism sought to make Quebec francophones feel at home across Canada without wholesale power-sharing or promotion of collective rights.

There is much to commend in this view of official bilingualism as a conflict management device to solve Canada's national-unity crisis. However effective in keeping Canada together during the 1970s and 1980s, recent events and polls indicate an unravelling of federal bilingualism as a relevant response to Québécois assertiveness. What has evolved instead is a **"twinned bilingualism"**: That is, an institutional bilingualism across Canada and a territorially based bilingualism split along French- and English-speaking cleavages (with a bilingual belt along the Ontario-Quebec-New Brunswick borders). In other words, efforts to integrate Quebec into the national political community by way of language policies rather than power sharing appear to be self-destructing. The singular lack of effectiveness has shown that federal bilingualism is necessary but insufficient. It must be supplemented by constitutional amendments that ensure Québécois mastery of their house.

REDESIGNING QUEBEC: MAITRES CHEZ NOUS

Language wars strike at the core of Canadian society-building. The genesis of language conflicts can be discerned from a brief history of Quebec in its evolution as a French-speaking nation within Canada. From 1841 onwards, when Upper (Ontario) and Lower (Quebec) Canada were united, French-English relations have displayed a tendency toward disagreement and open hostility (Rioux 1973). The seemingly opposed forces of federalism and nationalism have co-existed uneasily in response to regional and national forces. The forces of modernization and economic growth have created equally ambiguous effects (Whitaker 1993). They not only enhanced the desire and capacity for small nationalisms to construct cultural and political space for themselves, but also proved a catalyst for a new round of French-English confrontations.

A Dormant Society

Prior to 1960, Quebec represented a rural backwater of Canadian society; it was dominated by Roman Catholic clergy and controlled by a Montreal-based English elite. Serving for the most part as cheap and unskilled labour, Quebeckers had little say in the running of the economy. Schools emphasized religious instruction and classical curricula. Exceptionally high reproduction rates diminished the capacity of most families to provide higher education or other opportunities for their children. Unprepared for competition and lacking requisite resources and skills, many francophones were unable to penetrate middle or upper management levels in commerce, industry, or government services. The threat of cultural assimilation with the broader English-speaking group was an additional concern among French nationalists (Laurin 1978). Equally worrisome was the reluctance of many immigrants to Quebec to learn French as their working language in recognition of the distinctive French character of that province. The combination of these pressures, together with a falling birth rate magnified Quebec's insecurity. This resentment and hostility eventually fueled another surge in nationalist sentiment.

The Not-So-Quiet Revolution

The Liberal Party in 1960 under Jean Lesage introduced a series of internal reforms that have come to be known as the **Quiet Revolution**. Under the slogan "*Il fait que ça change,*" the Quiet Revolution not only rejected the policies and priorities of the Union Nationale government. A series of important social and political changes was also initiated that culminated in the restructuring of Quebec society. Lesage pushed to transform Quebec into a modern and urban society by combining an ethnic with a territorial basis of identification (Juteau 1994). The modernization and expansion of Quebec society focused increasingly on the homeland of Les Québécois rather than francophones across Canada. The quest for Quebec's nationalism emphasized blood ties and ancestry, with particular attention on citizenship, identification of the state with economy, and a pluralistic ideology. Prosperity lay in modernizing major political and economic institutions, without a corresponding loss of identity, language, and culture. Survival of Quebec as a distinct society also was dependent on government involvement in accelerating social change. Quebec's central authorities modernized and improved the delivery of educational and social services, introduced planned economic reforms such as nationalization of key industries, and channelled the increasingly assertive aspirations of Québécois nationalists into socially productive outlets.

Notwithstanding these efforts at modernization, the English "tail" continued to wag the French "body". English domination and control persisted at the direct expense of francophones who chaffed at occupational and promotional restrictions (Laurin 1978). English continued to prevail as the language of public communication. The francophone middle class was further dismayed by the 1972 Gendron Commission on the Status of French and Linguistic Rights. The vernacular appeal of French may have remained intact, yet provincial surveys revealed a declining French-speaking presence in parts of the province. Not only did anglophones possess negative attitudes toward the francophones, the report claimed, immigrants also snubbed their French hosts by enrolling children in English-speaking schools. A host of separatist initiatives sprang up within this context of nationalist ferment and a bleak demographic future. Foremost was the Front du Libération de Québec with its open advocation of violence and terrorism. The Parti Québécois provided a political forum for articulating separatist inclinations.

Unilingualizing Quebec

Response to mounting linguistic insecurities resulted in passage of **Bill 22** in 1974 by Premier Bourassa of the Liberal Party. Fears over a language in crisis proved pivotal, even if these perceptions did not necessarily match reality:

> Hostility towards the English language surfaced at the moment when French society was losing its distinctiveness and as it was moving closer to the attitudes and lifestyle of the rest of Canada. As language became the only significant point of difference, French Quebec was gripped by a panic...and found expression in politics. (Clift 1989).

Two parallel movements arose: one for independence and the other for legislative curbs on the use of English (Clift 1989). Bill 22 made French the sole official language of the province as well as the preferred language of work, education, and commerce. The primacy of French was promoted in administration, business, education, and all important spheres of Quebec's institutional life including advertising, job placement, government contracts, and career enhancement. Immigrant parents were deprived of access to English schools although English speaking parents educated in Quebec retained this option. Even with Bill 22, however, Quebec remained nominally committed to bilingualism. Because it did not expressly prohibit the use of English, the act itself stopped short of withdrawing support of the official languages. It merely asserted the primacy of French as a system of public communication.

It took the Parti Québécois under the late René Levesque to transform Quebec into an official unilingual province. Elected in 1976 amidst growing disillusionment over federal bilingualism, the Parti Québécois reinforced the need for a Quebec homeland with a corresponding territory, language, culture and identity, institutional autonomy, history, and collective purpose and will to exist (Laurin 1978). Proposals to secede from Canada were softened through appeals for **sovereignty-association**. Political independence remained a priority, albeit within the institutional framework of Canadian federalism. Passage of **Bill 101** in 1977 completed the initiatives of Bill 22: namely to prohibit the use of English from the public sphere. Also called the **French Language Charter**, it asserted French as the sole official language on the grounds that French was increasingly threatened by (a) the influx of non-francophone immigrants, (b) a declining provincial birth rate, and (c) the threat of assimilation. The government acknowledged its responsibility to uphold the primacy of French across all levels of internal operations and communication (McRoberts 1989). English would be permitted in certain constitutionally designated realms such as education and health. But for all intents and purposes, English was restricted to informal and private domains — thereby restricting its usefulness as a language of power (Daost-Blais 1983).

The impact of Bill 101 was far reaching. Most notable was its capacity to define the basis of Quebec society. The province's social order was transformed into one which made Quebec as French as the other provinces were English. Quebec shifted from a de facto bilingualism to official unilingualism at odds with the federal language policy. By making French the language of work and communication, Bill 101 sought to impress upon immigrants (and anglophones) the reality of Quebec as French. It fortified French as the language of business, administration, advertising, public announcements, and education — to the virtual exclusion of English. A series of penalties and sanctions were devised to ensure compliance with the French Language Charter.

Public response to Bill 101 was polarized. At one pole stood those who viewed the French language law as critical to Quebec's collective rights for survival as a distinct society. Opposed were those who perceived such legislation as a discriminatory infringement on constitutionally guaranteed individual rights. In between were intermediate positions that regretted the move as a necessary evil. Even anglophones in Quebec — incensed and humiliated by the sacrifice of their rights in order to advance nationalist goals — have come around to accept the principle of francophone language rights in Quebec. What they find repugnant are the seemingly undemocratic means to achieve this goal.

Reactions to Bill 101 crystallized over the exclusive use of French on commerical and storefront signs. Two Quebec Superior Court decisions eventually ruled aspects of Bill 101 to be in violation of the Charter Rights and Freedoms. A similar ruling was made by the Canadian Supreme Court in 1988. Yet Quebec's Liberal party under Robert Bourassa moved cautiously in rescinding the offending clauses, despite electoral promises to do so in 1985, for fear of appearing soft on Québécois nationalism. Relying on the "notwithstanding clause" (allowing the provinces to exempt themselves from federal constitutional arrangements and Charter rights for a period of five years) to override the Supreme Court and the Charter resulted in the contentious "inside-outside" compromise (French outside, bilingual inside) Passage of the inside-outside proposal provided Canadians with an opportunity to witness the clash of competing rights — individual versus collective — when applied to a practical context. The case study, "Conflicting Rights and Competing Realities," illustrates this.

CASE STUDY

Conflicting Rights and Competing Realities

Many of the language issues that confront Canadians are based on efforts to reconcile conflicting rights as well as competing realities. Continued discussion and disagreement over Bill 101 constitutes one example. Another is the recent controversy over **Bill 178** and its ruling on bilingual storefront signs in Quebec. Much of this conflict reflects the politics over language in Quebec.

In 1985, Robert Bourassa regained power on a platform to promote the French face of Quebec from inside a framework of bilingual federalism. The Liberals pledged to revoke the French commercial signs provisions of Bill 101 and institute bilingual storefront signs as decreed by Quebec's Superior Court and the Supreme Court of Canada. Both court decisions acknowledged Quebec's right (by way of Bill 101) to take necessary steps in promoting French as the working language of the majority in that province. But banning the use of English on storefronts was ruled both unconstitutional and in violation of Canadian human rights. To be sure, the courts ruled that the Quebec government could promote the prominence of French on commercial signs. But the National Assembly could not expressly prohibit the use of other languages such as English without grossly violating official language minority rights.

Bourassa responded by invoking the notwithstanding clause within the Constitution to override both the Canadian and Quebec Charter of Rights and Freedoms. French-only signs were permitted outside an establishment; bilingual signs were allowed inside provided the presence of French prevailed. Few were satisfied by Bourassa's inside-outside compromise for reconciling the demands of Quebec nationalists and anglophone federalists. Nationalists scorned any concession to the hated *anglais* as appeasement. Anglophones by contrast resented the supercedence of Quebec's collective rights over individual language rights. Protective measures were justified for survival of French, but surely not by trampling on the constitutional rights of official language minorities.

Passage of Bill 178 followed by the demise of the Meech Lake accord ignited a resurgence of Quebec nationalism. The Parti Québécois was resurrected from the political graveyard as a legitimate force in provincial politics. The fact that it currently sits in power is indicative of the turnaround in separatist forces since publication of Kenneth McRobert's ill-timed words (1989:9):

> By most appearances, the dramatic and prolonged crisis into which Quebec nationalist movement propelled Canadian politics has run its course.

In addition, there has been considerable debate on whether the bill dovetails with the principles of **individual rights** and minority language protection. How justified were the Québécois in passing a law that violated not only the spirit of official bilingualism but also the individual equality provisions of the Canadian

Charter of Rights and Freedoms? Does suppression of English language rights by the Quebec legislation constitute a justifiable limit on individual rights in a free and democratic society?

Answers to these questions seem to begin with, it depends. Right or wrong depends on whose perspective is taken into account. From an anglophone perspective, Bill 101 is a serious infringement on individual rights and the right of official language minorities for protection as guaranteed by the Canadian Constitution and Charter. Anglophones perceive francophones as a majority in the province who prop up their linguistic and cultural insecurities by eroding minority individual rights. They are of a conviction that no democratic government has the right to prohibit the use of another language in public — even if certain concessions may be possible under limited circumstances.

From Quebec's point of view, the promotion of **collective rights** as implicit within Bills 101 and 178 is justified. Proponents have stoutly defended Bill 101 as the minimum necessary to neutralize the impact and assimilative pressures of an English-speaking continent. Language laws have brought about improvements in the francisation of the province and institutions of the province, with the vast majority of students enrolled in French, most companies under French control, and French as the indisputable language of work and public communication (Fournier 1994).

Several lines of argument are employed. First, the Québécois define anglophones as part of a huge English majority in Canada and United States scarcely in need of protection despite their minority status in Quebec. By con-

trast, the 8 million Québécois see themselves as imperilled by a continental tide of 267 million North Americans with designs (both conscious or by consequence) to remove the French face of Quebec. The precarious status of French in the homeland of last resort demands special measures to promote Quebec's collective rights — even if these should infringe on anglophone individual rights. For francophones, the clause which prohibits English on Quebec storefront constitutes a reasonable restriction for the preservation of its French character. Even anglophones agree that special language policies are permissable. But these constraints must be designed in a way that recognizes federal bilingualism, the Official Languages Act, and protection of basic human rights for freedom of expression.

Second, with passage of Bill 101, Quebec is doing only what other provinces have historically done, namely, to deny the official language minority their language as a basis for public communication. Besides, they argue, Quebec's treatment of its anglophone minority is no worse and, in many cases, much better than what the other provinces confer on the French-speaking minority. While the Canadian Charter allows official language minorities to be educated in French or English, the option exists only where numbers warrant the expense. With nearly 500,000 franco-Ontarians in the province, Ontario refuses to guarantee access to French speaking schools or the delivery of social services except in designated areas where numerically warranted. By contrast, the anglophone minority in Quebec is guaranteed access to these services by way of law, not just a privilege which can be revoked at a government whim.

Third, those who regard Bill 101 (and Bill 178) as blatant violations of the Charter's equality provisions have had to rethink the application of abstract individual rights in contexts of inequality. For the Québécois, the protection of its French culture and language is prior to individual rights. Without this collective guarantee there is no context for the expression of individual rights. The promotion of collective over individual rights is thus justified under certain circumstances. Both Brian Mulroney and Robert Bourassa have defended the collective right of francophones to protect their language because of their status as a cultural enclave in North American society. This override of collective rights is permitted as long as the promotion is reasonable, set out in law, and demonstrably justified in a free and democratic society. Violations of anglophone rights to free speech are not a serious concern since the survival of English is not at stake. Moreover, as noted earlier, anglophones already possess the best constitutional protection of official minority rights in Canada — unlike the French in other parts of Canada where services depend on provincial political whims.

Fourth, even the relevance of individual rights in majority-minority contexts has come under criticism. Evidence indicates that rich and powerful groups can afford the luxury of promoting individual rights. That is not necessarily a viable option for minorities. Collective rights may be endorsed by those whose cultural and social existence is threatened and requires group defence. For francophones, a formal respect for individual rights means nothing if the social and economic conditions surrounding these rights are disregarded (Laurin 1978). Protection of individual rights under these circumstances (including formal bilingualism) is likely to enhance pressures for assimilation (McRoberts 1989). For that reason, both the constitution and charter of rights will continue to straightjacket Quebec's aspirations until recognition that (a) Quebec is not a province *commes les autres*; (b) the Charter of Rights cannot supersede Quebec's National Assembly; (c) Quebec needs a constitutional veto; and (d) English-speaking authorities cannot define the fate of North America's only French speaking society (Gagnon 1993b).

Postscript In late 1993, Quebec passed Bill 86 following the expiry of the notwithstanding exemption for Bill 178. Bill 86 watered down some of the controversial provisions of Bill 178 by allowing languages other than French on commercial signs — as long as the French was dominant (Picard 1994). Outstanding charges against merchants who violated the French only commercial sign law were dropped as a gesture of good faith. The Bill also abolished the so-called language police *"Commission de Protection de la Langue Française."* These compromises were rooted in pragmatism rather than ideology, according to Quebec's Language Minister, Claude Ryan. The fact that these changes, unlike the inside-outside compromise in 1988, were greeted with a minimum of public fanfare points to a new dynamic in Quebec society.

The case study reveals how the Québécois confront a curious paradox: In their province, they are a majority that exerts power and control. Outside the province, however, they are a linguistic minority. The interplay of these dramatically opposed dynamics has a way of fueling language tensions. The passage of time does not appear to have eliminated language tensions in Quebec or outside. They simply go underground. Yet recent events suggest an escalation of language conflicts in different parts of the country. What is it about language that evinces such passion and emotion?

CLASHING VISIONS OF QUEBEC: PROVINCE OR PEOPLE?

Language and culture are widely conceded as vital ingredients in defining Quebec's distinctiveness. Debates over Quebec's relational status within Canadian federalism are also inseparable from language. Charter group relations rotate around several visions of Canada that have been expounded countless times since the signing of the British North American Act (1867). These visions include **federalism as a contract**, **federalism as partnership**, and **federalim as compact**. A fourth vision — Canada as a **three-nations state** — is slowly gaining acceptance. The coexistence of these competing visions generates much of the dynamic underlying French-English relations.

Canada as Contract

Canada constitutes a federalist system of ten provinces and a central authority in Ottawa. A contract exists between the provinces (of which Quebec is one) and the federal government. The provinces (including Quebec) as well as the federal government are sovereign within their own jurisidiction as set out in the constitution; neither can usurp the authority or powers of the other. The British North America Act in 1867 specified the limits and scope of provincial versus federal powers.

Provinces are equal to each other, under the Canada-as-contract vision, but subordinate in status and power when compared with central governing structures. Conferral of priority status on the federal government is justified because of its responsibility for advancing Canada's national interests both at home (through comprehensive social programs) and abroad (through diplomatic or military initiatives). This bestowal of first-among-equals status upon central authorities can be defined as a federalist position. Pierre Elliott Trudeau stands out as a confirmed centrist whose espousal of Canadian federalism put him on collision course with Quebec's leaders.

Canada as Partnership

A second vision involves a partnership relation involving relatively autonomous provinces who have freely entered into accord with the federal government. Under terms of the agreement, Ottawa has assumed those duties and responsibilities which the provinces were unable — or unwilling — to carry out. As a result of this freely agreed upon division of power, all eleven players are equal within Canadian confederation. The federal sector is one of eleven partners within Canadian federalism — no better, no more valuable — with distinctive duties as outlined by constitutional decree. Canadian history can be interpreted as a struggle by provinces and federalist forces to secure and maintain power at the expense of other.

The relationship of Quebec to this federal-provincial system is variable. Quebec is perceived by some as equal to the other provinces in legal status; all individuals are also legally equal with each sharing similar rights and entitlements regardless of the province they live in. Others, however, acknowledge Quebec as simultaneously a province among provinces as well as a distinct society with special powers to pursue its language and cultural objectives, even if these should regrettably interfere with fundamental Charter rights (Chodak 1994).

Canada as Compact

There is a third position at odds with the previous perspectives. This perspective is strongly endorsed by the Québécois who reject views of themselves as ethnics or Canadians who happen to speak French and live in Canada. Many even reject the notion of Quebec as a province in the conventional sense. Canada is not an union of one central authority with ten equal provinces, of which Quebec is but one province. In rejecting contract or partnership interpretation, this position endorses Canadan federalism as a **compact** between the French (Quebec) and English (Ottawa). Canadian society is based instead on a fundamental dualism that is rooted in constitutional law and longstanding political agreement. The BNA recognized the right of Quebec to promote its distinctive cultural and language heritage without undue interference from Ottawa except in cases involving national concerns.

A compact perspective endorses a vision of Quebec as a nation within the Canadian state whose self-governing powers are equivalent to those of English Ottawa. Quebec does not like to be viewed as just another province with equal rights and privileges. Nor does it want to be treated as an ethnic group or racial minority with needs that can be solved through government intervention and assistance. Also rejected is the idea that Québécois are really Canadians with similar values and outlooks, but who just happen to speak French. Rather, they are a people with a shared language and culture and occupying a homeland of last resort. Quebec entered into Confederation with assurances that it would retain its status as a nation and, as founding peoples, retain this entitlement and special citizenship in perpetuity. As co-contributors to Canadian nation-building but citizens of Quebec first, they possess a constitutional and legal right to exercise control over their land, language, and identity. These self-governing powers include the right to establish immigration policies as well as the right to conduct foreign policy and initiate bilateral agreements which fall under provincial jurisdiction.

Interpreting of French-English relations as a "compact" enables us to appreciate the logic underlying Quebec's aspirations, concerns, and political moves. As noted, the English are perceived as politically and economically powerful agents for assimilation. English-speaking Canadians are seen as federalists with a sense of national citizenship and community that transcends provincial identities while embracing federal institutions. Ottawa is viewed as a force anxious to centralize its powers at the expense of the provinces. Moves to strengthen federalism are frequently interpreted as assimilationist in intent if not by consequence. Not surprisingly, Quebec's leaders have looked to strengthen the boundaries between Ottawa and Quebec. They have sought ways to transfer power and resources from Ottawa for fulfillment of Quebec's ambitions. Public support must be galvanized to legitimate their nationalist policies as well as to strengthen their hand in dealing with central authorities. This raises the questions: How do leaders attract the constituencies they need in order to substantiate their claims with federal authorities? What resources can they rely on to draw attention to and justify Quebec's grievances? What is the best way of convincing central policy structures of the necessity for power-sharing?

A variety of channels may be utilized to mobilize public attention and support. But recourse to language policy is especially valuable in securing legitimacy and authority in this area. As noted earlier, language possesses the emotive properties to elicit nationalistic passions and galvanize people into protest action. It can address a variety of issues in a simple, direct fashion without resorting to convoluted arguments. By virtue of its potency, Québécois leaders have capitalized on the public's inclination to equate language issues with the state of French-English relations. Widespread public support for language policy is thus manipulated as leverage for extracting various concessions from the federal government. The rejected **Meech Lake Accord** to constitutionally enshrine Quebec as a distinct society with rights to protect its distinctive character represents but yet another example of the power of language to simultaneously unite and divide, to define as well as to undermine.

CASE STUDY

Constitutional Discords

The relational status of Quebec within Canada's federalist system has undergone change in response to constitutional developments. In 1982, Canada patriated its constitution from Britain. All provinces agreed to the terms except for Quebec which felt certain provisions contravened its broader interests. Quebec resented the strong federalist /centrist dimensions implicit within the Constitution. The leading architect for patriation, Pierre Elliott Trudeau, balked at any notion of Quebec as a formally distinct society. When Levesque and

Trudeau failed at a compromise, Quebec subsequently refused assent (although it remained bound by the provisions of the Constitution and the Charter of Rights and Freedoms which came into effect in 1985).

Five years passed before another round of talks addressed Quebec's constitutional boycott. During this interval, the social and political climate underwent change: French-English tensions eased, Quebec's interests shifted from politics to business, and the sovereignty-association option was defeated in a provincial referendum in 1980 on the strength of Ottawa's promise to renew federalism. With this end in sight, an agreement subsequently known as the Meech Lake Accord (reflecting the name of a government-owned resort in the Gatineaus) was hammered out in June of 1987 by provincial and federal first ministers.

Amendments in the Meech Lake Accord were written to secure Quebec's signature to the 1982 constitution. At the core of these proposals was recognition of Quebec as a distinct society within Canada; the coexistence of French and English across Canada (including Quebec) as a fundamental characteristic, the obligation of Ottawa and the provinces to preserve the linguistic duality of Canada; and the role of Quebec to preserve and promote its distinct identity. With these provisions, the accord took what was essentially a sociological reality — that Quebec is indeed a cultural and linguistically distinct society with a right to pursue and protect its French charter — and transformed this fact into a prescriptive statement at the highest levels of decision-making (*The Globe and Mail*, 29 March 1988).

The Meech Lake Accord generated widespread controversy regarding the relational status of Quebec vis-a-vis federalism in Canadian society. Much of the debate dwelt on the ultimate significance of the accord for French-English relations: did the accord represent a device for integrating Quebec into Canada by explicitly acknowledging the obvious? Or was the accord primarily a rule of interpretation for assisting the courts to interpret the constitution "in a manner consistent with" the recognition that "Quebec constitutes within Canada a **distinct society**." To what extent did the accord bequeath sovereign power to Quebec enabling it to override the equality provisions of the Canadian constitution (*The Globe and Mail*, 29 December 1987). Conversely, did the accord merely confirm the existing powers of Quebec without broaching the realm of federal or Parliamentary powers?

Answers to these questions proved elusive, largely because of the term, distinct society (*The Toronto Star* 22 January 1989). For francophones, the concept is tantamount to separate and independent status, with attendant power to foster its French face. For anglophones, however, the concept simply acknowledges Quebec as different from the rest of Canada, but having no new powers and maintaining continued primacy of the Constitution and Charter. Equally troubling was the dissonance between distinct society and individual versus collective rights. While the Canadian charter has ensured protection of individual rights, the Meech Lake provisions have threatened to undermine these provisions by upholding the collective priorty of Quebec's distinct society status. Still, even with the Constitution and the

Charter as the supreme law in Canada, there is no guarantee future Quebec governments will not renege on equality provisions by invoking the notwithstanding clause. Concern has also been expressed over the redistribution of power. In contrast with the centrist thrust of the Canadian Constitution, the accord has advocated a significant dispersal of power for the provinces (but especially Quebec) in setting agendas that may run counter to the federal or constitutional priorities.

All of this turned out to be academic. Both Manitoba and Newfoundland refused to ratify the accord, plunging the country into yet another round of re-criminations and threats. Perhaps Meech Lake tried to do too much by attempting to reconcile the unreconcilable: centralization versus decentralization; duality versus multiculturalism; collective versus individual rights; and universality versus special treatment (Fournier 1994). Another attempt to resolve Quebec-Ottawa relations by constitutional means went down to defeat following a national referendum in October 1992. By playing on this notion of federalism as inimical to Quebec's interests, the Parti Québécois rode to power on the strength of this well intentioned but ultimately flawed constitutional fiasco.

Canada as a three-nation state

A new and challenging vision of Canada is slowly gaining ground. Canada is neither a contract between Ottawa and the provinces, nor a compact between Ottawa and the French. The preferred view of Canadian society is leaning toward a three-nation state model. Canada comprises three separate founding nations with overlapping citizenships, each of which possesses rights and jurisdictions within their sphere (Kaplan 1993; Webber 1994). The survival of Canada will hinge on our ability to acknowledge and incorporate a plurality of ways of belonging because of deep diversities (Taylor 1993). The final chapter in this book will examine this issue more carefully. Suffice it at this point to point out that the belated recognition of First Nations as a nation within and a distinct society will complicate an already complex relationship that exists between the two charter groups. An Applications box, "Competing Nationalisms/Intersecting Sovereignties," at the end of this chapter provides an inkling of what may be in store.

SOVEREIGNTY WITHOUT SECESSION

Le Quebec, ma patrie, le Canada, mon pays. (Quebec is my homeland, Canada is my country.)

Lysiane Gagnon (*The Globe and Mail* 4 April 1992).

French-English tensions appear to have escalated in reaction to Meech Lake and Charlottetown constitutional failures. The national-unity pot has come to a boil with resentment over Bill 178 in Quebec, coupled with mounting concern over the costs of bilingualism at federal, provincial, and municipal levels. The unthinkable — the spectre of Quebec separating from Canada — is now actively pondered as a result of the growing estrangement between two of Canada's founding nations. Polls conducted since the early 1990s point to a similar conclusion: A majority of Quebeckers are attracted to some form of renewal within the present federalist system. Far fewer appear to be inclined toward any outright separation, suggesting that independence may be a burning issue only for elites. Several prominent businesspeople also hint of Quebec's dissassociation from the rest of Canada in light of that province's economic strength, abundance of human and natural resources, and the need to stabilize the present political and investment climate.

A healthy skepticism toward polls and statistics is called for. Yet we can hardly dismiss the significance of these projections for the viability and future of Canadian society. Three scenarios are possible: We are presiding over a turbulent period of intensive social change from which Canada will emerge a strengthened and restructured union; second, we are currently witnessing the breakup of Canadian society, fractured, as it were, by a series of relatively autonomous political entities along the lines of the European Common Market bloc; Canada as we know it will never be the same; third, it will be business as usual once all the sabre rattling and politics of brinkmanship subside. We cannot predict which scenario is the most feasible, but we can ask, what, then, do the Québécois want, and what is being done to address the demands of Quebec's ethnic nationalism?

What Does Quebec Want?

It is unfair to imply that the Québécois have a uniform set of expectations and aspirations. To the question, what does Quebec want, the range of responses may vary from those who prefer only moderate changes, to those who wish to radically restructure Quebec's relationship with Canadian society at large — up to and including outright secession. Terms such as sovereignty or separation are hazy and misleading, with meanings that vary among contexts and people, and the way people respond to them is contingent on the wording of the questions. The distinction between separation and sovereignty is subtle but valid. Sovereignty is what the Québécois already possess, as far as many Quebeckers are concerned, because of its Charter group status and evolution as a distinct society. Separation is something that perhaps only a small percentage of Québécois are willing to entertain. Thus, sovereignty is not merely a softer version of separation, much less a sign of confusion in the minds of a confused electorate, but a nuanced reading of Canadian federal system and Quebec's place in a globalizing and interdependent world (*The Globe and Mail*, 11 March 1994).

Responses to the "Quebec question" do not always reflect a perfect consistency; ambiguities often prevail that reflect situational circumstances. For example, many may like the idea of cultural security and political determination; nevertheless, the economic disadvantages of severing ties with Canada are no less compelling and provide a powerful incentive for the status quo. In other words, the Québécois want the best of both worlds; or as quipped by Yvon Descamps, a French-Canadian comedian: "They want an independent Quebec within a united Canada" (*The Globe and Mail*, 18 June 1994).

Generally speaking, all Quebeckers are anxious to maintain the French character of their society. They want to create conditions, both political and economic, with which to protect and preserve the distinctiveness of Quebec as the homeland of last resort for French in North America. Quebec's nationalism is rooted ultimately in the desire of the Québécois to exist collectively and to have this collective existence recognized at political levels (Balthazar 1993). But agreement over goals has not translated into agreement over means (Fournier 1994).

On the one side are the *moderates* who generally prefer to stay within Canada by strengthening Quebec's position within the federalist system — in large part by reinforcing Quebec's presence in Ottawa and in other part by expanding Quebec's access to power and resources. A new constitutional division of powers is also anticipated to ensure that each level of government controls what it does best (Johnson 1995). Moderates may even define themselves as **sovereigntist yet disagree with the principle of separation**, preferring instead a kind of flexible federalism with sovereign control over internal jurisdictions of relevance. Quebeckers may not want to quit Canada, but neither do they want to appear weak or surrender in the battle for constitutional change. In short, the moderates can be described as federalists who endorse a kind of civic nationalism and affiliation with Canada as their country, yet who continue to identify first and foremost with Quebec as their homeland.

Radical perspectives revolve about some degree of separation from Canada. Many independantistes are tired of being labelled a minority group who English-Canadians define as a costly problem people. They prefer a space that Quebecker can call their own, where they are the majority and call the shots. Quebeckers want to be in the "big leagues" — a state within a state — not just an administrative subunit of Canada (Latouche 1995; also Salée 1995). Or as put by Louise Beaudoin of the Parti Québécois "I want to be a majority in my own country" (*The Globe and Mail*, 1 March 1995). The high risk of being permanently outmaneouvered (tyranny of the majority) is sufficient to justify a fundamental shift of power from the federal to provincial levels as confirmed by a a Globe/Leger poll (*The Globe and Mail*, 20 May 1994). The transfer is as critical as it is radical, and was recognized a generation ago by a Canadian national-unity commission:

> Quebec is distinctive and should, within a viable Canada, have the powers necessary to protect and develop its distinctive character. Any political solution short of this would lead to the rupture of Canada.(Task Force on National Unity *Pepin-Roberts Report*, 1977-1979).

Many are also weary of English-speaking Canadians who appear unwilling to accept even minimal concessions to confirm Quebec's distinctiveness. English-speaking insensitivity stems from failure to discard a conqueror's mentality. It also arises from a lack of cultural identity. While Québécois know who they are, English-speaking Canadians are perceived as bereft of common vision or grand design, except in opposition to something else, thus inhibiting their capacity to accept Quebec for its differences and history. Others argue that the federal system is no longer viable: Quebec cannot possibly associate itself with a system that is incapable of dealing with its own problems (Castonguay 1994). Federalism does not pay; rather, staying in Canada extracts a heavy economic cost because of extra layers of governance and the perpetual gridlock between Quebec and Canada (Fournier 1994).

Separatists believe Quebec is ready to make a move: It has a broad industrial base, a healthy government financial structure, a reduced dependency on federal government, and autonomous sources of revenue. To be sure, secessionist moves come in different packages, from outright separation to sovereignty association, but most proposals veer toward some degree of political independence (including control over culture and language), without loss of close economic ties such as free trade and common currency (Laxer 1994). All agree on the need to enhance Quebec's control over language and culture. A secure economic base is equally important to reduce Quebec's dependency on Canada while improving its position in the North American common market (Fournier 1994). This dependence on natural resources as a springboard for economic progress has brought Quebec into conflict with the First Nations who also occupy Quebec. This encounter has raised questions about the legitimacy of secession, and whether Quebec's threat to leave Canada can supercede the wishes of those who wish to stay. It also raises the issue of whether Quebec's nationalism can create a modern nation-state incorporating a territorial (rather than an ethnic) dimension through inclusion of all its people and diverse ethnic components (Balthazar 1993; Latouche 1993). The chapter concludes with a case study that highlight some of the paradoxes that arise when sovereignties collide.

INSIGHT

Competing Nationalisms/Intersecting Sovereignties

If there is one thing sacred in Quebec, as in any country, it is territory.
                                       Lucien Bouchard, Leader of the Bloc Québécois

In terms of legitimacy, the aboriginal peoples, the aboriginal nations on this territory, are quite ahead of the francophones in Quebec, the anglophones of Quebec, and all the Europeans and other nationalities on this territory.
                                       Daniel Turp, Legal Advisor, Bloc Québécois

The Cree people are neither cattle nor property, to be transferred from sovereignty to sovereignty or from master to master. We do not seek to prevent the Québécois from achieving their legitimate goals. But we will not permit them to do so on Cree territory and at the expense of our fundamental rights, including our right to self-determination.

Mathew Coon Come, Chief, James Bay Cree Nation quoted in *This Magazine*, June, 1994.

If Quebec can separate, so can the Indians.
Kahn-Tineta Horn, quoted in *Windspeaker*, Nov.6, 1994.

Ethnic nationalisms threaten the territorial integrity of every nation-state. Central authorities fear the balkanizing effect of ethnic nationalisms, with their capacity to fractionalize the country like pieces of a jigsaw puzzle. Consider Canada as portrayed by the sample of quotes above. The people of Quebec may be politically divided, but many are unhappy with the current federalist arrangement that treats them as one of ten relatively equal provinces rather than one of two(!) founding nations. Federalist and nationalist forces may agree on Quebec as a distinct society, with a unique and distinctive assemblage of cultural and linguistic characteristics. Disagreements tend to reflect different means — flexible federalism or secession — for preservation of Quebec as a French-speaking homeland.

Quebec is not alone in pushing for distinct society status. The indigenous occupants of Quebec have also staked a claim for ownership. The seeds of this discontent were planted with the Oka crisis and energetic opposition to Hydro Quebec's megaprojects. Quebeckers were forced to discard folkloric images of the first inhabitants as museum pieces or subject matter of anthropological study, and confront instead questions about autonomous governments by those claiming to be legitimate owners of the land and resources (Leger 1994). The furor over Quebec's future has escalated further following the election of the Parti Québécois in 1994, with its promise of a future referendum to determine the relational status of the Québécois. At the core of this debate are the politics of recognition (Salée 1995) and the desire of ethnic minorities for acknowledgement and respect of their particular identities, followed by inclusion of these differences, on their *own* terms rather than that dictated by central authorities.

Contested Claims

The ten nations that comprise the 60,000 strong First Nations in Quebec (including the Cree, Inuit, Mohawk, Huron, and Algonquin) are no less adamant that Quebec does *not* have a legal claim to their lands. They see themselves as no less sovereign as nations, with as much right to remain in Canada as Quebec has a right to secede. According to the the indigenous peoples, up to 80 percent of Quebec is under aboriginal control: Certain lands have never been ceded while others are up in the air because of yet unresolved treaty or aboriginal rights claims.

The Quebec government disagrees. Quebec's boundaries are inviolate, as far as the Québécois are concerned, and its territoriality is sovereign and beyond negotiation or dismemberment. Aboriginal rights to Quebec's land no longer exist; instead they were extinguished when the Canadian state transferred Ungava to the province at the turn of the century. The James Bay Agreement in 1975 also signed away aboriginal "interests" (although a federal act in 1977 also said that Cree and Inuit would retain the "benefits and rights of all other [Canadian] citizens." A hardening of their position is understandable. On the one hand Quebec's treatment of aboriginal peoples is seen as second to none, given the government's willingness to recognize aboriginal self-government (within Quebec society), ownership of land and resources, and protection of language and culture (Gourdeau 1993). On the other Quebec can hardly afford to appear weak, and risk the loss of enormous reserves of hydro-electric power. Aboriginal lands are rich in natural wealth: ownership of this potential treasure trove is a necessary asset for any newly independent state in search of economic viability. Without a resolution or at least a compromise, moreover, the international community would be slow to acknowledge the sovereignty of Quebec.

The Canadian state is precariously perched between these intersecting yet rival nationalisms. It stands to lose because neither of these sovereignties is compatible with national interests. The federalist strategy rests with playing one group off the other in hopes of neutralizing the combined impact. Ottawa sees the Cree as allies and a negotiating chip in bargaining with Quebec — even if the government has spent the last decade subverting international approval for inherent aboriginal rights to self-determination. John McGarry, a political scientist from The University of Western Ontario writes: [T]hey will be happy to use the Native position on Quebec as a club with which to beat the separatists, and a convenient tool to minimize the amount of territory they can take from Canada (*The Globe and Mail*, 15 October 1994).

Whose Rights? The Politics of Jurisdiction

What does international law have to say in sorting out the validity of these contested claims? Under international law, colonial peoples (those who live in a defined territory but under a foreign power) have the right to secede. This right to independence and self-determination does not apply to either Quebec or the Cree because secession under international law applies only to "salt-water" (overseas) colonies. Since both international law and the United Nations are constructed around the inviolability of sovereign states, an expansive interpretation of sovereignty to include internal colonies is seen as de-stabilizing the community of sovereign states, as far as the international community is concerned, with predictable consequences for world political and economic order. The obligation to respect minority rights but not to the extent of secession is clearly outlined in this passage from a UN declaration:

> States shall protect the existence and the national or ethnic, cultural, religious, and linguistic identity of minorities within their respective territories and shall encourage conditions for the promotion of that identity... Persons belonging to national or ethnic, religious, and linguistic minorities ... have the right to enjoy their own culture, to profess and practise their own religion and to use their own language, in private and in public, freely and without interference or any form of discrimination...States shall take measures where required to ensure that persons belonging to minorities [are able] to express their characteristics...except where specific practices are in violation of national law and contrary to international standards...**Nothing in the present Declaration may be construed as permitting any activity contrary to the purposes and principles of the United Nations, including sovereign equality, territorial integrity and political independence of states** (emphasis added). UN Declaration on the Rights of Persons Belonging to National or Ethnic, Religious and Linguistic Minorities.

In other words, a "people" have the right to self-determination and autonomy; a province does not, and it most certainly does not have a right to force any people to secede along with it.

Between a rock and...

Both Quebec and the First Nations are recognition seekers. The politics of recognition is steeped in the struggle for control over jursidictions related to power and resources. Their relationship is complicated by competing efforts to draw the attention of the Canadian state to their respective grievances and identity claims (Salée 1995). But dangers await whatever course of action federal authorities choose. Siding with the Québécois against aboriginal nationalism could spark a First Nations backlash that could make Oka seem a light-hearted romp. That may explain recent statements by Ron Irwin, Indian Affairs Minister, in defence of First Nations rights: "The separatists say that they may have a right to leave, then why don't the aboriginal people who have been here 20 times as long have the same right. It only seems logical to me." Yet cuddling up to the First Nations might play into Québécois hands. In either case, the interplay of intersecting nationalisms will profoundly reconfigure the contours of Canadian society.

SOURCES: *The Globe and Mail* 19 October 1994. *The Globe and Mail* 15 October 1994. Kitchener-Waterloo Record 10 June 1994; Monohan *The Globe and Mail*, 19 May 1994. Salée (1995).

The picture at present is in transition. Aboriginal claims to land and self-government may not be compatible with Quebec's nationalistic aspirations — even if the latter is shifting from a purely ethnic based nationalism to one more inclusive and cosmopolitan (Latouche 1993). Neither of the nationalisms may be consistent with Canada's society-building aspirations. Nor can Canada hope to survive the social cleavages engendered by the deep diversities of a three-nation state — with or without the possibility of different ways of belonging to society.

Yet there is room for a guarded optimism. Canada's federal system is remarkably flexible in its capacity to endlessly tinker with the balance of power between Ottawa and provinces. As part of this **flexible federalism**, de facto (informal) arrangements have been worked out that recognize the distinctiveness and relative autonomy of certain provinces. Quebec, for example, has its own pension plan, has its own system of private law, levies its own income tax, and exercises a degree of control over immigration that is unprecedented for any federal system (Black and Hagan 1993). In fact, Quebec ressembles a quasi state, according to Stephane Dion, a political scientist at the University of Montreal, with most of the powers it needs to be a key player in setting priorities and controlling jurisdictions (Stewart 1994). With or without constitutional guarantees, Quebec is acting as if it were a distinct society by exercising powers of a relatively sovereign nation. Ad hoc arrangements, in other words, do not appear to be the problem. The stumbling block rests in moves to legally recognize Quebec's distinct society status. As Charles Taylor (1993) notes, English-speaking Canadians may be willing to accept negotiated and pragmatic arrangements but many balk at the idea of formalizing those concessions that that run counter to conventional views of Canada (as a social contract), violate certain values related to formal equality (the principle of equal provinces), and create imbalances within Canada's federal system because of preferential treatment. There may be an additional barrier: Formal recognition may also restructure Quebec-Canada relations in a way that complicates that quintessential of Canadian questions "What is a country for?" (Taylor 1993:83).

CHAPTER HIGHLIGHTS

- Canada represents a multicultural and bilingual society whose French-English duality constitutes a fundamental and powerful characteristic. The French and English represent two of Canada's founding nations or Charter groups who are privileged members with the right to formulate Canada's political agenda.

- However basic this duality, it is an uneasy coexistence since French-English relations originated in conquest, are inflamed by cultural differences and the centralizing tendencies of the federal system, and involve federal-provincial squabbles.

- The politics of language reflect and reinforce the tempestuous character of French-English relations. Yet linguistic efforts to resolve this problem have proven inadequate. Federal bilingualism is viewed as appeasement without power; Québécois language rights come across as blatant power exercises that insufficiently appease the official language minority in Quebec.

- Bilingualism has not caught on in the other provinces of Canada (except New Brunswick). Three provinces are now officially unilingual. Nevertheless, all provinces are constitutionally bound to respect official language minority rights, although the magnitude of concessions can vary from one province to another.

- Language debates may prevail in Quebec but many of the language issues are ultimately about power, access to resources, and control over jurisdiction.

- A central question in this chapter asks, what is really going on in terms of Quebec-Ottawa relations"? Answers to this question suggest the necessity to see Canada from a variety of diverse perspectives, including Canada as a contract, a partnership, a compact, or a three-nations cacophony.

- The second question asks, what do the Québécois want? While answers are varied and reflect a certain ambiguity, consensus points to a need to protect, preserve, and promote the conditions that will enhance the distinct and sovereign character of Quebec's identity, language, and culture. Ambiguities in response may reflect the diverse means employed to achieve these goals, including those of moderates who are willing to work within the federalist system on one side, and those of radicals who want to scrap federalism in exchange for some degree of separation on the other.

- Quebec-Ottawa relations are currently a contested site. Opposing interests are locked in a struggle to define the nature of the relationship of Quebec with Ottawa, and decide how best to restructure this relationship in a way that each acknowledges the agendas of the others without necessarily capitulating to their entire package.

- Competing ethnic nationalisms continue to complicate politics in Canada. Quebec's First Nations argue for the right to stay in Canada if they choose, should Quebec decide to secede. As one might expect, given who makes the rules, international law appears to be siding with the First Nations and the Canadian state.

KEY TERMS

Bill 22
Bill 101 (French
    Language Charter)
Bill 178
Collective versus
    Individual rights
Distinct Society
Federalism as Compact
Federalism as Contract

Federalism as
    Partnership
Flexible Federalism
Institutional bilingualism
Meech Lake Accord
Notwithstanding Clause
Politics of language
Sovereignty versus
    Separation

Sovereignty without
    Secession
Sovereignty-Association
Territorial Bilingualism
The Official Languages
    Act
The Quiet Revolution
Three-Nations State
Twinned Bilingualism

REVIEW QUESTIONS

1) With reference to the struggles of French-speaking Canadians, indicate why language issues appear to elicit such strong passions in the competition for scarce resources.

2) Briefly outline the recent history of Quebec's language legislation in terms of what it is trying to do and why.

3) Quebec's demand for distinct society status strikes at the core of the debate between ethnic nationalism on the one hand and society-building on the other. Explain.

4) Compare and contrast the differing visions of Canada and its relationship to Quebec. Which do you think is the most correct reading of Canadian society?

5) In what ways does the French language controversy (such as that manifested by Bill 101) focus on the issue of collective versus individual rights? Which of these interpretations is justified in light of the current situation in Quebec?

6) If someone were to ask you, "what is really going on in Quebec today," how would you answer in light of text material?

7) What do the Québécois want with respect to the their status in Canada? Expand on the concept of sovereignty without secession as an answer. Can you speculate as to what English-speaking Canada wants with respect to Quebec?

8) Indicate the nature of the debate that is going on between Quebec secessionists and the First Nations in Quebec.

9) Demonstrate how Québécois nationalism reflects many aspects of ethnicity as covered in Chapter 6. In your answer, concentrate on the definition of ethnicity, why the surge in ethnicity, its manifestation, and its implications for Canadian society.

CHAPTER 9

MULTICULTURAL MINORITIES

INTRODUCTION

The previous two chapters discussed how Canada's aboriginal and charter groups, the so-called first and second forces, possess a distinctive sense of who they are and what they want. National agendas have been constitutionally constructed to protect and promote the linguistic and cultural priorities of the French and English. The concerns of the First Nations have also leapt to the forefront in keeping with their distinguished status as a founding nation. Solving the challenges of Canada as a three-nation state promises to keep the political pot boiling for years to come.

Canada's multicultural minorities occupy an entirely different status, both historically and legally. Their relational status is not derived from "first principles"; it is based instead on their status as immigrants or descendents of immigrants. That may explain their preoccupation with concerns of equality and institutional accommodation in contrast with the more political demands of Canada's "ethnic nationalisms (Kymlicka 1995)." Many from this multicultural sector have encountered formidable barriers in adapting to a country whose agenda caters to the first and second forces. Yet Canada's multicultural minorities are rarely in a position to present a coherent and united front to central policy structures. Social cleavages are prevalent because of geographic dispersal, cultural heterogeneity, political powerlessness, public unease, and general lack of economic clout. This assessment applies to both native-born and foreign-born (immigrants and refugees) Canadians. Much to their relief, the entrenchment of multiculturalism in Canada has established a collective platform for articulating issues of relevance to this sector. It is from the perspective of inequality and power — in terms of what, why, and how — that we attend to this chapter on the third force.

Chapter Content

This chapter deals with multicultural minorities as an emergent and evolving third force at the forefront of society-building in Canada. The chapter is not concerned with studying racial or ethnic minority groups per se. Rather, multicultural minorities are examined as a distinct social category whose relational status is distinguished from others on the basis of needs, concerns, entitlements, and aspirations.

Particular emphasis is placed on immigrants and refugees as emergent social actors not only in the competitition for scarce resources, but also in the vanguard of society-building. A review of immigration policy and practices, in addition to a look at the pros and cons of immigration, confirms what many have suspected: The relationship of multicultural minorities with "mainstream society" are riddled with inequality. Efforts to isolate, challenge, and transform these unequal relations are fraught with tension and ambiguity as competing sectors struggle for control of the national agenda. The fact that many new Canadians encounter a less than hospitable climate in adjusting to the demands of Canadian society suggests the possibility of a long haul before multiculturalism becomes a reality in Canada.

The chapter begins with an overview of Canada's multicultural minorities in terms of demographic composition and geographical distribution. This is followed by a closer look at the collective transformation of Canada by means of past and present immigration trends. Policies and principles that have governed the movement of immigrants into Canada are examined next. Also open for discussion are some of the issues and challenges associated with immigration as different sectors of Canada square off to determine who will come in, on what grounds, from where, and at what level of acceptance. We will also look at the recent flow of refugees into Canada with respect to public reaction and policy responses. A number of misconceptions and half-truths about immigration and immigrants are dissected and debunked. The final section will deal with the problems and the pressures that multicultural minorities confront in securing an adjustment to Canadian society.

Cautions and Caveats

A note on terminology. There is no one term that adequately encapsulates all Canadians in the non-British, non-French, and non-aboriginal sector. It is inaccurate, for example, to speak of the third force as "immigrants" since the label designates a foreign-born status and, with the possible exception of the First Nations, we are all immigrants in status and entitlements. Likewise, it is not entirely satisfactory to speak of "racial" or "ethnic minorities" as synonymous with the third force. Sociologically speaking, a minority is not a numerical designation but a social relation in which one party lacks power or access to scarce resources. While such groups exist in this category, not all ethnic sectors can be considered as disadvantaged minorities — consider only the English in Canada or the French within the context of their provincial homeland. What about "ethnic group"? The expression is too broad since the term "ethnic group" could technically include aboriginal and charter peoples — even though these sectors do not see themselves this way. Other expressions such as "visible" and "nonvisible" are widely accepted as administrative labels but have limited emotional appeal. Terms such as "world majorities" have yet to catch on. We have tried to resolve this terminological dilemma by referring to the third "diversity" as **multicultural minorities.** This category includes those whose legal endowments are derived from their status as immigrant or descendent of immigrants. Collectively, they look to official multiculturalism in addition to citizenship rights as a source of entitlements.

Even the concept of multicultural minorities requires some clarification. Multicultural minorities can refer to those Canadians who are native-born as well as to new (foreign-born) Canadians, namely immigrants and refugees. **Immigrants** refer to persons born overseas, with permanent residency in Canada, including successful refugee claimants, but not temporary residents such as "foreign students." Immigrants constitute about 16 percent of Canada's total population — a figure that has remained unchanged since 1951. By contrast, **multicultural minorities** (or racial and ethnic minorities) can refer to both immigrants from Europe or developing countries, as well as native-born Canadians who possess some non-British, non-French, non-aboriginal ancestry. This figure has increased dramatically in recent years, including a jump from 37.5 percent of the population in 1986 to 45 percent in 1991. The category is further divisible into **people of colour** (or **visible minorities**) and **European (or "white") ethnics.** The term visible minority refers to an official government category of native- and foreign-born, non-white, non-Caucasoid individuals, including: blacks, Chinese, Japanese, Koreans, Filipinos, Indo-Pakistanis, West Asians and Arabs, Southeast Asians, Latin Americans, and Pacific Islanders.

A chapter on multicultural minorities could not possibly hope to engage all topics about this diversity without stretching its resources to the point of superficiality and gloss. We have decided to focus primarily on foreign-born Canadians from so-called non-conventional countries of origin. Particular emphasis is centred on immigrants and refugees with respect to their movement and transition into Canadian society under a bewildering array of policy circumstances and social pressures. Those interested specifically in people of colour in the context of Canadian society, both foreign and native born, are advised to consult Chapter 6, "The Ethnic Experience." The chapter on gender and race, Chapter 5, provides a more thorough account of the issues and challenges, needs and concerns, that confront both women and men of colour in Canada.

This chapter will not deal extensively with specific groups per se. Our intent is to provide a useful overview of multicultural minorities as if they comprised a relatively uniform category for analysis in terms of their relationship to Canadian society. This *ideal-typical* stance runs the risk of oversimplification or omission of detail. Others might argue that minority voices are being silenced by this reliance on analysis. There is some validity to these charges. For example, references to blacks can descriptively include those of both Caribbean and African origins. It can also encompass African-Americans who happen to live in Canada or African-Canadians with long roots in Canadian society. Consider also the category of South Asians: The category can incorporate Indo-Pakistanis from the Indian subcontinent as well as from Pakistan, Bangladesh, and Sri Lanka. The subcontinent in turn is partitioned into Punjab, Bengali, and South India. Major religious affiliations divide into Hindu, Sikh, Moslems, Christians, Buddhists, and Jains. The term Indian also refers to those of Indian ancestry by way of Africa, Britain, Trinidad and

Guyana. Nor should we soft-pedal the charges that immigrants exhibit a broad range of internal diversity because of age, gender, culture, socioeconomic status, length of residence, and country of origin. Patterns of adaptation and rates of success differ considerably for middle class versus underclass members of a multicultural minority group, for men versus women, and for youth versus adults.

Despite a common classification, each of these sectors is anxious to establish its own identity and social space in Canadian society. All possess a unique set of social and historical circumstances that constrains and defines their collective interests. The content of these experiences is varied, of course, but common ground exists. Underlying principles are evident throughout in shaping the dynamics of group interaction at this level. Our intent is to examine the nature of these commonalities by virtue of their shared experiences as new Canadians. Our focus also remains fixed on the social construction of patterned and unequal relations within competitive contexts.

FOR THE RECORD

IMMIGRATION FACTS AND FIGURES

1. An average of 180,000 immigrants came to Canada each year in the decade between 1910 and 1919. Since 1990, an average of 245,000 immigrants per year have come to Canada. The record for annual intake was 400,870 immigrants in 1913; by contrast, the record low was 7,576 immigrants in 1942.

2. With a population of 27 million (1991) and an annual rate of 245,000 immigrants per year, Canada's acceptance rate stands at 8.8 immigrants per 1000 population. Compare this level of acceptance with Australia at 7.6 per 1000 and USA at 2.5 per 1000.

3. Since 1981, about 75 percent of the immigrants to Canada have arrived from Asia, Africa, the Caribbean, and Central America. The other 25 percent come from Europe or the United States. These figures were reversed in 1966. A total of 27,873 immigrants arrived from Hong Kong in 1992. China was next with 22,131, followed closely by India, Philipines, Sri Lanka, and Poland. India provides the largest number of family class immigrants.

4. Of the 256,000 immigrants to Canada in 1993, 24,000 arrived as independents; another 8,000 as business class, and 13,000 as sponsored refugees. Only 15 to 20 percent of immigrants are handpicked for the credentials required to excel in a changing and globally competitive market.

5. The percentage of visible minorities in Toronto Census Metropolitan Area in 1971 was about one percent.

The percentage of visible minorities in Toronto at present is approximately 25 percent. The projected total for 2001 is 45 percent (*Marketing* V97,23, 1992).

6. A total of 1.2 million refugees sought landed status in Western countries in 1993. 500,000 went to Germany (which does not have a formal immigration system); 400,000 went to the USA; and 20,000 to Canada (down from 36,000 in 1992). Canada accepts 68 percent of refugee claims, with only about 10 to 15 percent ever deported as fraudulent. The acceptance rate for the next 15 countries is between 5 and 15 percent.

7. A long-term study of 1,348 Southeast Asian refugees that began in 1981 indicates that 78 percent are employed, 18 percent own businesses or are self-employed, two-thirds feel at home in Canada, with no strong desire to return, and 99 percent have taken out Canadian citizenship. On the downside, two-thirds are unhappy with their command of English.

8. The average immigrant household paid more in taxes ($22,528) in 1990 than they took out in public services ($10,558). The average Canadian born household paid $20,259 in taxes, and received $10,102 in services. According to Professor Ather Akbari, an economist at Saint Mary's University in Halifax, the $1,813 difference between immigrant and Canadian-born households results in $2.6 billion transfer from immigrants to native born Canadians.

9. The more things change....From 1885 onwards, immigrants from China were expected to pay a head tax that reached a sum of $500 by 1923. In February of 1995, the government imposed a right-of-landing fee on each adult immigrant, on top of the $500 administrative fee that each pays at present. A family of four must pay $3,150 to gain entry into Canada — the equivalent of a year's pay for an accoutant from El Salvador.

10. The United States is also experiencing some major upheavals in immigration. Records from the US Bureau of the Census reveal a total of 1,827,167 legal immigrants in 1991, compared with a 1980s average of about 600,000 per year. Between 1983 and 1991, Asia supplied nearly 2.6 million immigrants while Mexico contributed 2.4 million. By contrast, only 600,000 Europeans arrived. The American population at present stands at 75 percent white, 12 percent African-American, 9 percent Latino, 3 percent Asia, and 1 percent Native Americans.

11. What's in a name? A federal department for immigration has experienced several name changes that reflect government values, including Canadian Immigration and Quarantine Services (1867-1892); Immigration Branch: Department of the Interior (1892-1917); Department of Immigration and Colonization (1917-1936); Immigration Branch: Department of Mines and Resources (1936-1950); Department of Immigration and Citizenship (1950-1966); Deparatment of Manpower and Immigration (1966-1977); Canadian Employment and Immigration Commission (1977-June 1993); (two departments- Department of Public Security and Human Resources (June 1993- November 1993); Department of Immigration and Citizenship (November 1993 to present) (*The Globe and Mail* 2 November 1994).

DEMOGRAPHICS OF MULTICULTURAL MINORITIES

Canada embraces a diverse collection of immigrants and refugees from different parts of the world. The movement of East Asian populations across the Bering Strait as far back as 50,000 years ago inaugurated the first of many waves. Both French and English traders/adventurers/explorers comprised the second wave of immigrants. These colonizers eventually displaced the aboriginal populations and assumed status as the official founding nations of Canada. The third wave consisted of various non-English- and non-French-speaking immigrants who arrived en masse during the twentieth century to assist in Canadian society-building.

Canada's demographic composition has turned on its head during the last 125 years. Only 8% of Canada's population was not British or French at the time of Confederation in 1867 (Palmer 1975). Between 1896 and 1914, the balance began to shift when up to 3 million immigrants — many of them from Central and Eastern Europe — arrived to domesticate the west. Immigration increased substantially prior to and just after World War I, reaching a peak of over 400,000 in 1913. Another wave of Eastern European immigrants during the 1920s brought the non-British, non-French proportion up to 18%. The post-Second World War period resulted in yet another influx of refugees and immigrants from the war-torn European theatre. Similar increases occurred during the baby boom era, culmi-

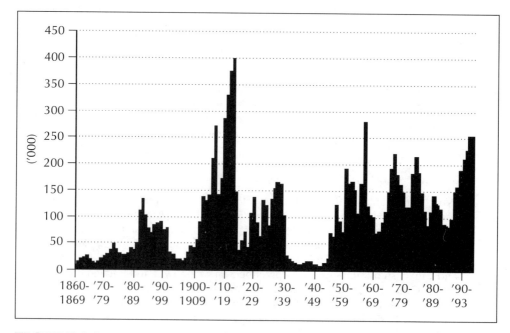

FIGURE 9.1   A Historical Look at Immigration to Canada

SOURCE: Department of Citizenship and Immigration

nating with 282,000 entrants in 1957 and 218,000 as recently as 1974 (see Figure 9.1).

The number of immigrants to Canada in recent years has matched the post-World War II peak periods. The decade between 1981 and 1991 accumulated the largest number of immigrants to Canada — with little or no reason to assume that the 1990s will be altogether different. Sources of immigration have also shifted toward so-called non-conventional countries such as Asia, the Caribbean, and South and Central America. Equally significant has been the unprecedented influx of refugees many of whom have landed in Canada without sponsorships or prior clearance. This infusion of visible minority immigrants and Third World refugees has rekindled controversy over the direction of Canada's immigration policies and programs. It has also fostered considerable debate regarding the role of multicultural minorities in forging Canadian identity and unity.

Multicultural Diversity in Canada

Canada's multicultural diversity is manifest by the demoghrapic figures (see Figures 9.2a, 9.2b). Of Canada's total population of just under 27 million according to the 1991 Census Canada figures, about 45 percent of all Canadians report having some non-British or non-French ancestry. Thirty-one percent reported no British or French background. Those reporting European origins comprised the largest percentage of such persons at 15 percent of the total population. Persons with Asian origins represented 5.1 percent of the total population, up from 3.5 percent in 1986. Interestingly 2.8 percent indicated Canadian as their ethnic origin (Badets and Chui 1994). Those with British-only roots stood at 28 percent of the population, French at 23 percent, British and French at 4 percent, and British and French and another ethnic origin at 14 percent.

Table 9.1 provides a breakdown of those reporting non-British and non-French ethnic origins. Total responses indicated that those of German background rank highest (with 2,793,780), with Italians next (1,147,775), followed by Ukrainian (1,054,295) and aboriginal (1,002,675). With the exception of Quebec and Ontario where Italian-Canadians dominate, those of German descent are the most frequently reported ethnic origin in the other provinces. No less impressive has been the rapid growth of visible minorities. Their proportion in relation to the general population has expanded from 6.3 percent in 1986 to 9.1 percent of the population in 1991, with predictions suggesting double digit figures by the year 2000. Those of Chinese origins are the most populous people of colour with a total of 652,645 persons. Regional and municipal variations in ethnic composition are noticeable. Ontario has the largest number of persons with non-British, non-French origins at 4 million. This is followed by British Columbia and Alberta with just over 1.5 million each, and Quebec with just under 1 million. The Atlantic provinces have relatively small totals. Arguably, then, multicultural minorities have evolved to the point where by sheer numbers alone they occupy a formidable status in Canadian society.

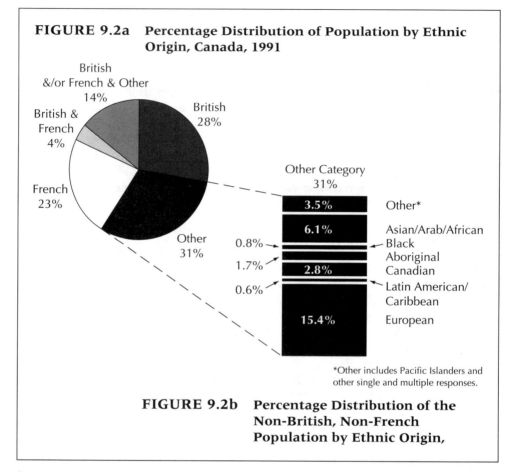

FIGURE 9.2a   Percentage Distribution of Population by Ethnic Origin, Canada, 1991

British &/or French & Other 14%

British & French 4%

British 28%

French 23%

Other 31%

Other Category 31%

3.5% — Other*

6.1% — Asian/Arab/African

0.8% — Black

1.7% — Aboriginal

2.8% — Canadian

0.6% — Latin American/Caribbean

15.4% — European

*Other includes Pacific Islanders and other single and multiple responses.

FIGURE 9.2b   Percentage Distribution of the Non-British, Non-French Population by Ethnic Origin,

[4] Asian origins includes South Asian, East and South East Asian single responses.

SOURCE: Statistics Canada, *Ethnic Origin*. 1991 Census of Canada, Catalogue No. 93-315

Multicultural minorities continue to reside in large urban regions. Both absolute numbers and relative percentages make Montreal, Toronto, and Vancouver more diverse than provincial or national averages. Just over 1.5 million of those who reported ethnic origins other than (or in addition to) French or English live in Toronto. Another half-million are found in each of Vancouver and Montreal. These three metropolitan regions are also important centres for visible minorities: Toronto's figure is now at 25 percent of the total population (up from 1 percent in 1971), with future projections pegged at 45 percent by 2001. The vast majority of visible minorities reside in major urban centres for reasons related to opportunity, sociability, and transition. That concentration, in turn, proves irresistable as a magnet for the next wave of immigrants and refugees.

TABLE 9.1   **Selected Ethnic Origins Other than British, French, Canadian, as Reported for Canada, 1991**

Ethnic Origin	Total Responses	Single Responses	Multiple Responses
German	2,793,780	911,560	1,882,220
Italian	1,147,775	750,055	397,720
Ukrainian	1,054,295	406,645	647,650
Aboriginal	1,002,675	470,615	532,060
Dutch	966,595	358,180	608,415
Polish	740,710	272,805	467,905
Scandinavian	717,200	174,375	542,825
Chinese	652,645	586,645	66,000
South Asian	488,370	420,290	68,080
Jewish	369,565	245,840	123,725
Black	351,665	224,620	127,045
Portuguese	292,185	246,890	45,295
Hungarian	213,700	100,725	112,975
Balkan	198,650	131,440	67,210
Arab	194,880	144,050	50,830
Greek	191,480	151,150	40,330

SOURCE: 1991 Census of Canada, Prepared by Policy & Research, Multiculturalism and Citizenship Canada.

Immigrants: Patterns and Trends

Canada is home to approximately 4.33 million foreign-born Canadians. The proportion of immigrants relative to the population at large (16%) has remained stable since 1951. The top five countries of birth for all immigrants are United Kingdom (717,745), Italy (351,620), United States (249,080), Poland (184,695), and Germany (180,525) see Table 9.2. Between 1981 and 1991 a total of 1.24 million immigrants came to Canada — an unpredented ten year total — but likely to be superseded during this decade. Heading the list of immigrants who arrived this decade include those from Hong Kong (96,540), Poland (77,455), China (75,840), India (73,105), and United Kingdom (71,365) (see Table 9.2). In 1992, 48 percent of immigrants were from Asia and the Pacific, while 18 percent came from Europe. Compare this with 1965 when 73 percent came from Europe, only 10 percent from Asia and the Pacific (see Figure 9.3). The top immigrant sources in 1992 were Hong Kong, the Philippines, India, Sri Lanka, and Poland.

Provincial and regional figures vary in terms of immigration totals. Most immigrants (54.6%) live in Ontario, even though the province contains just 37 percent of the country's population (see Figure 9.4). This is followed by B.C. with 16.7 percent, Quebec at 13.6 percent (but about 25 percent of the population) and the Prairies with 13.3 percent. Atlantic Canada ranks far behind at 1.7 percent.

TABLE 9.2   Top 10 Countries of Birth for All Immigrants and Recent Immigrants [1], Canada, 1991

	All immigrants			Recent Immigrants [1]	
	Number	%		Number	%
Total	**4,342,890**	**100.0**	**Total**	**1,238,455**	**100.0**
1. United Kingdom	717,745	16.5	1. Hong Kong	96,540	7.8
2. Italy	351,620	8.1	2. Poland	77,455	6.3
3. United States	249,080	5.7	3. People's Republic of China	75,840	6.1
4. Poland	184,695	4.3	4. India	73,105	5.9
5. Germany	180,525	4.2	5. United Kingdom	71,365	5.8
6. India	173,670	4.0	6. Viet Nam	69,520	5.6
7. Portugal	161,180	3.7	7. Philippines	64,290	5.2
8. People's Republic of China	157,405	3.6	8. United States	55,415	4.5
9. Hong Kong	152,455	3.5	9. Portugal	35,440	2.9
10. Netherlands	129,615	3.0	10. Lebanon	34,065	2.8

(1) Immigrants who came to Canada between 1981 and 1991.

SOURCE: 1991 Census of Canada, unpublished data.

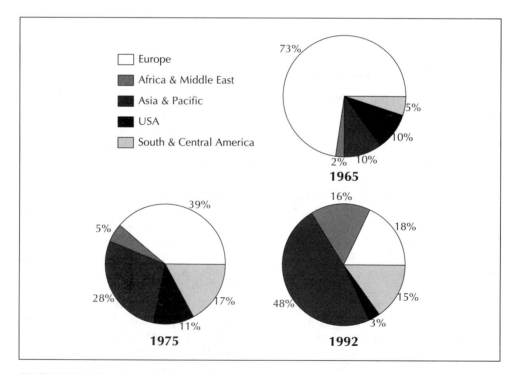

FIGURE 9.3   Immigration by Source Area 1965, 1975 and 1992

SOURCE: Immigration Canada, 1994.

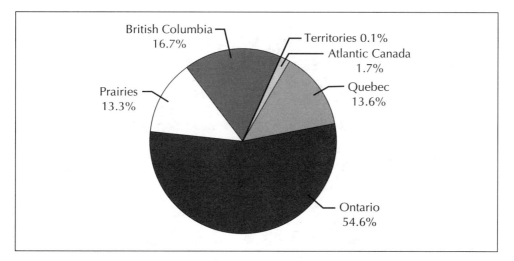

FIGURE 9.4 **Distribution of Foreign-born Population in Canada by Province and Territory**

SOURCE: Statistics Canada 1991 Census.

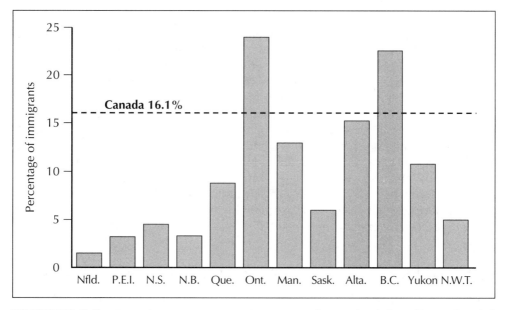

FIGURE 9.5 **Immigrants as a Percentage of Provincial and Territorial Populations, 1991**

SOURCE: Statistics Canada, *Immigration and Citizenship*. 1991 Census of Canada, Catalogue No. 93-316.

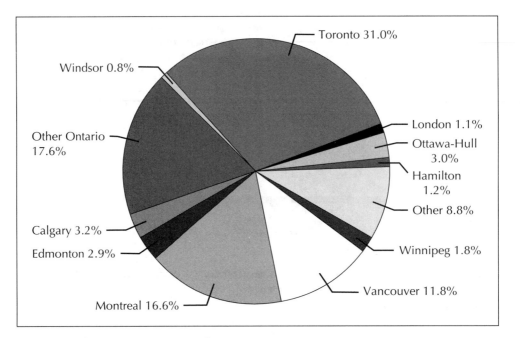

FIGURE 9.6   Immigration by Metro Area, 1992

SOURCE: Immigration Canada, 1994.

Immigrants constitute nearly 25 percent of the total population in Ontario and B.C., but less than 5 percent in each of the Atlantic provinces (see Table Figure 9.5).

Finally there are urban-rural differences. Nearly three-quarters of all immigrants prefer to live in cities for various reasons. Most also prefer larger urban centres: Immigrants may constitute 16 percent of Canada's population, but immigrants represent 39 percent of Toronto's population, 30 percent of Vancouver's, 24 percent of Hamilton's, 22 percent of Kitchener's (see Figure 9.7). Chicoutimi-Jonquière ranks last with about 1 percent. This trend is likely to continue. Of all immigrants by metro area in 1992, 31 percent landed in Toronto followed by Montreal at 16.6 percent and Vancouver with 11.8 percent (see Figure 9.6). With nearly 57 percent of all immigrants packed into the three major centres, Canada be best described as a relatively homogeneous society, interspersed with pockets of immigrant and native-born diversity (see Shifrin, *Toronto Star*, 23 January 1989).

CANADIAN IMMIGRATION: POLICIES AND PATTERNS

Canada is frequently praised — or pilloried — as a country of immigrants. As one of the three primary immigrant countries in the world (United States and Australia

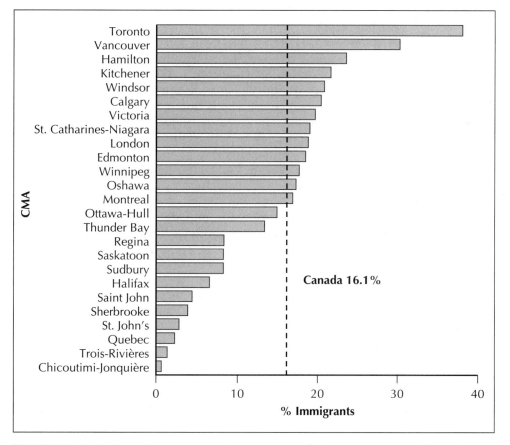

FIGURE 9.7 **Immigrants as a Percentage of Census Metropolitan Areas, 1991**

SOURCE: Statistics Canada, *Immigration and Citizenship*. 1991 Census of Canada, Catalogue No. 93-316.

being the others), immigration has played a pivotal role in our national development. With the exception of the First Nations, all Canadians are immigrants or descendents of immigrants. Yet Canadians seem curiously ambivalent about immigration and immigrants. Antipathy toward new Canadians borders on the xenophobic at times, with calls for Rights of Landing Fees, DNA testing, and vigorous deportation procedures. Nor has immigration as policy and practice received the kind of attention it deserves (Whitaker 1991). The next section will attempt in a small way to atone for that neglect by exploring patterns in Canada's immigration policies and practices as they existed in the past, are expressed at present, and are projected into the future.

Early Policy and Trends

Canadian immigration policies have shifted noticeably since Confederation (Knowles 1992). Policy content and objectives were shaped historically by a combination of ideological considerations, political expediency, international obligations, and economic requirements. Outcomes were decided by an interplay of racism and ethnocentrism; the agricultural bias of Canada's early immigration policies; the pivotal role of private interests; immigration trends as alternately taps-on or taps-off; the contested character of the national agenda; and the expediency and calculation that has characterized policy-decision making.

Initial policies could be described as essentially racist in orientation, assimilationist in objective, and nativist in content. As much energy was expending in keeping out certain "types" as there was in encouraging others to settle (Whitaker 1991). A "racial pecking order" (Lupul 1988) sorted out potential migrants on the basis of racial affiliation and capacity for assimilation. Preferred categories of immigrants were drawn from the so-called superior stock of Great Britain or northwestern Europe. Immigration from "white" countries was encouraged to ensure the British character of Dominion. This category was virtually exempt from entry restrictions except for certain visa formalities (Abella and Troper 1991). The non-preferred class consisted of immigrants from mid European countries (such as Austria) and Russia. The special permit class was aimed at Jews and Mediterranean populations.

Attempts to settle the prairies saw preferential treatment extended to more "assimilable" Europeans once preferred sources shrivelled up. It took a lot of convincing to get people to come. Even more inducements were required to make them stay. Many new Canadians promptly left for the United States — in effect reinforcing a perception of Canada as little more than a transfer point (Whitaker 1991) between the United States and Europe. Canada's first Immigration Minister, Clifford Sifton, made virtue of necessity in 1896 when he encouraged immigrants from eastern Europe despite a chorus of criticism about introducing foreign or alien "bohunks" into a "white mans country." Clifton resolutely opposed the import of urban factory workers, many of whom were seen as degenerate, subject to economic unrest, or fodder for radical agitors. The agricultural bias of early immigration was eloquently expressed when Clifton mused about "stalwart peasants in a sheepskin coat, born on the soil, whose forefathers had been farmers for ten generations, with a stout wife and a half-dozen children" (quoted in Whitaker 1991:7).

The decision to promote immigration from across Europe provoked debate about Canada's national identity (Lehr 1987). Political parties engaged in endless polemics over who was desirable or assimililable. But they all agreed the survival of Canada was dependent on the absorption of alien groups into Anglo-Celtic culture. Strangely enough, the government did not play a prominent role in making immigration decisions. Once the framework for development was established, according to Reg Whitaker (1991), the state was content to leave the actual process to market forces and private companies. Transportation companies benefitted enor-

mously from this arrangement (Abella and Troper 1991): The CPR actively recruited immigrants since profit margins required a stable, captive population willing to pay going freight rates (Simpson 1994). In its role as agents for the
government, the CPR established a Department of Colonization and Immigration
for expediting the movement and settlement of new Canadians — in effect confirming the view that immigration was"...simply part of the economics of transportation in a developing country dependent on staple extraction within a wider
imperial framework" (Whitaker 1991:5). The government's involvement in immigration was restricted largely to issuing visas and doing medical checks. Corporate
interests declined only with the collapse of Prairie small-scale farming in the 1930s
and 1940s.

Asian immigrants such as the Chinese and Indians were tolerated only as cheap
labour for Canadian capitalist expansion. The Asian tap was turned off when their
usefulness disappeared upon completion of nation-building activities. Immigrants
from non-conventional sources were expected to accept unobtrusively Anglo ideals
while toiling way in regions and at tasks (for example, railways, mines, lumber
camps, domestic work) below the dignity of native-born Canadians. Restrictions for
entry were imposed, ranging from head taxes to restrictive quotas. Case studies
in earlier chapters featuring the Chinese, Indo-Pakistanis, and Jews described the
racist and nativist dimension of Canada's early immigration policies. German and
Ukrainian immigrants (and native-born Canadians of German and Ukrainian descent) were rounded up as potential subversives during World War I, then interned in remote labour camps across Canada. This pattern was repeated again
during World War II with the forced relocation of Japanese Canadians, many of
whom lost all possessions and property. The level of state coercion reflected the
sometimes contradictory and always contested aspects of immigration. Business
and powerful transportation companies conspired to inflate immigration levels;
by contrast organized labour and public sentiment generally favoured a restriction
of number and type (Whitaker 1991). Short-term economic interests came into
conflict with long-term national development strategies and goals. The government was sandwiched in between, sometimes taking the high ground, other times
capitulating to private or public interests as the circumstances dictated.

Early immigration policies were based on practical considerations that dovetailed
with Canada's economic needs. Immigrants were selected on the basis of their
ability to fill slots in the expanding economy. The resulting taps-on and taps-off
approach reflected and reinforced a cautious estimate of Canada's absorptive capacity.
Western settlement required large numbers, with immigration peaking at 400,870
in 1913; wars and Depression conditions resulted in lower figures, bottoming out
in 1942 at 7,576 immigrants. This stop-and-go mentality exposed Canada to criticism that it was merely operating a guest-worker system: that is, foreigners were
welcome when the economy boomed, but were turfed out when recession set in.

Depressed rates of immigration accompanied both the Depression and Second
World War, but annual rates skyrocketed in the wake of Canada's post-war boom
economy. Even with the demands of labour-starved industries, post-war immi-

gration reflected a preference for northwestern Europeans, many of whom were selected from DP (displaced persons) camps under international supervision. A new Department of Immigration and Citizenship was established in 1950. It introduced immigration reforms related to a **family reunification class** (called sponsorship) and a shift toward skilled non-agricultural workers, but with orders to maintain a strict eye on Canada's absorptive capacity (Whitaker 1991). Strict quotas remained in place for most non-Europeans.

Towards Reform

In 1962, Canadian immigration laws underwent a major shift. Canada became one of the first countries to remove overt racial criteria from its immigration policies (Hawkins 1974). **Independent-class immigrants** were admitted on the strength of their capacity for self-reliance, productivity, and contribution to Canadian society. **Sponsored immigrants** included close relatives of permanent residents, whereas the **nominated class** of more distant relative was subject to certain restrictions. Clauses were inserted, however, to prevent Asians or African-Canadians from sponsoring distant relatives.

The criteria for entry underwent further reform in 1967. Canada's expanding economy required educated and skilled labour; yet economic recovery in Europe had sharply curtailed Canada's favourite taproot. Skilled immigrant labour could only be found in those quarters of the world that historically fell afoul of Canadian customs and practice (Whitaker 1991), so that immigration pipelines opened to non-conventional sources, including countries in Asia and Africa, South and Central America. A **points system** of evaluation was introduced by which independent applicants were ranked according to possession of language, skills, and resources. Establishing a formally colour-blind immigration policy minimized the salience of racial or ethnic criteria for entry. Still, the system was not free of bias because of systemic discriminatory barriers against the acceptance of poor or the different. The point system also confirmed the link between immigration and the employment market, with the Canadian economy's absorptive capacity the key variable in regard to immigration.

Contemporary Policy

Canada has never had a clearly articulated national consensus about immigration and its relationship to society-building (Knowles 1992). The closest thing to it was expressed by the 1976 Immigration Act, with minor amendments in 1989 and 1993. The Act attempted to specify the economic, humanitarian, and legal objectives of Canada's immigration commitment, and included the following political, demographic, social, and cultural dimensions:

- Family reunification
- Protection of legitimate refugees

- Enhancement of Canada's prosperity and global competitiveness
- Preservation of Canada's integrity

Amendments have focused primarily on the removal of abuses within the system (ranging from illegal immigrants to smugglers); improvement of the refugee determination system by replacing the two-stage hearing process with a single hearing before members of the **Immigration and Refugee Board (IRB)**, and introduction of procedures to eliminate backlogs (Annual Report 1994; Government of Canada 1993).

Admissable immigrants could can apply under three categories: Family, Independent, and Refugee. The **family reunification class** recognizes the need for families to stay to together if only to stabilize the process of integration into Canada. Immediate members of the family, namely a spouse and dependent children under 19, are automatically allowed into Canada provided they are of good health and unblemished character. Until recently, parents and grandparents were also included; a separate entry stream is currently under consideration. More distant relatives must top up with points for entry into Canada. The vast majority of family-class immigrants come from India (at 17,081 in 1993), followed by Hong Kong, Philippines, China, Vietnam, and Jamaica according to Citizenship and Immigration Canada (24 Oct. 1994). Currently, the family reunification category accounts for about 45 percent of all immigration to Canada, a figure that is expected to remain intact for the next five years.

The second class consists of individuals who apply as **independent-class immigrants**. They are assessed under a point system that emphasizes the suitability of the candidate on the grounds of job-related skills, age, official language knowledge, and education, as well as a personal assessment by an immigration officer (see Table 9.3). The number of points required for entry varies: Business class (both investor and entrepreneur) requires only 25: self-employed and skilled workers need 70, although they are automatically entitled to a large bonus because of

TABLE 9.3 The Immigrant Selection System

Factor	Maximum Units
Education	16
Specific Vocational Preparation	18
Experience	8
Occupational Demand	10
Arranged Employment or Designated Occupation	10
Demographic Factor	8
Age	10
Knowledge of Official Language(s)	15
Personal Suitability	10

Source: Immigration Canada, 1994.

their talents. Assisted relatives also receive credit as nominated immigrants, but required additional points elsewhere to qualify for the necessary 70 points. Currently, the independent category accounts for about 45 percent of all immigration, with an anticipated increase to just over 50 percent within the next five years.

Refugees comprise the third category. The point system does not apply to the refugee category but their acceptance is dependent on health and security considerations. They are accepted as part of Canada's humanitarian and legal obligations to the world community. The category includes both sponsored refugees who are selected abroad by government or private agencies and those who are sponsored by private individuals, clubs or church agencies in Canada, with sponsors obligated to provide support for up to ten years. Both government and privately sponsored refugees receive landed immigrant status before arriving in Canada and assistance through government programs once they arrive (Jackson 1991). A large and controversial category consists of **refugee claimants** who arrive unannounced by foot, boat, or plane, and claim refugee status upon arrival to Canada. Refugee claimants are not entitled to some of the social services that Canadians take for granted; until recently, they were also ineligible for work until an initial hearing, thus imposing an additional burden on cash-strapped provinces. Of the 52,751 refugees who arrived in 1992, the vast majority were refugee claimants ("inland") with 37,152, followed by sponsored refugees at 14,726. (see Table 9.4). This category now accounts for about 20 percent of all immigration to Canada (Annual Report 1994) (see Table 9.5 for overview). Figure 9.8 provides an overview of Canada's immigration policy.

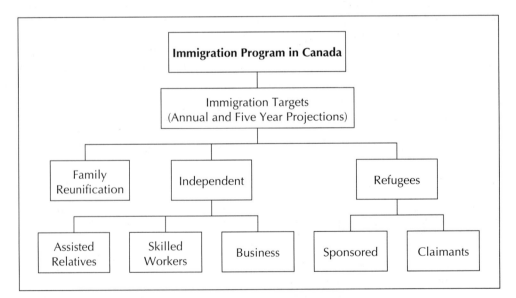

FIGURE 9.8   Overview of Canada's Immigration Policy

TABLE 9.4   Refugee and Humanitarian Landings, 1979-1993*

| | Refugee** | | Special | |
	Abroad	Inland	Measures***	Total
1979	27,240	500	—	27,740
1980	39,922	718	—	40,640
1981	14,502	558	—	15,060
1982	15,840	1,162	12	17,014
1983	12,955	1,107	679	14,741
1984	14,324	1,229	2,518	18,071
1985	15,482	1,518	2,562	19,562
1986	17,709	1,776	2,625	22,110
1987	20,148	1,802	2,845	24,793
1988	26,059	1,053	2,040	29,152
1989	35,460	1,899	2,468	39,827
1990	31,862	8,328	3,323	43,513
1991	24,601	29,092	2,404	56,097
1992	14,726	37,152	873	52,751
1993*	9,646	16,519	3,321	29,486
Total	**320,476**	**104,413**	**25,668**	**450,557**

* 1993 is approximately ten months' data.
** Convention Refugees or members of Designated Classes (including the Backlog Clearance Program).
*** Special Measures are humanitarian family reunification programs in place at various times for citizens of El Salvador, Guatemala, Iran, Lebanon, Sri Lanka and former Yugoslavia.
Source: Immigration Canada 1994.

Canada's immigration policy extends to the settlement and integration of new Canadians. A total of about $270 million is allocated by the government for immigration settlement. Direct assistance is provided by non-profit organizations who specialize in language training, employment counselling, and translation services. The objective is to ensure immigrants become self-sufficient and contributing members of society. It should be noted that the federal government exercises primary responsibility in this area; nevertheless it shares jurisdiction with the provinces through consultations over immigration levels and settlement measures. Only Quebec at present possesses powers of immigration selection. (Annual Report 1994).

Not all immigrants and refugees stay in Canada. Some decide to return to their country of origin for various reasons. Others are asked to leave because of a failure to meet minimum criteria. Still others are deported for breaking the law. Procedures for deporting undesirables serve to protect Canadians and uphold the integrity of the system, but implementation has proven erratic. The immigration department had issued a total of 26,000 unexecuted deportation orders by the early 1990s, with a total of 9,300 removals (see Figure 9.9) Some failed claimants have been ordered out of the country but are allowed to stay because of dangerous conditions in their homelands.

TABLE 9.5   Immigration Levels, 1991-1994

Component	1992 Actual	F
Family Class		
Spouses and Dependent Children	54,824	
Parents and Grandparents	41,399	
Total Family Class	**96,223**	
Percent of total	**(44%)**	
Refugees		
Refugees Landed in Canada	21,389	
Government-assisted Abroad	6,259	
Privately Sponsored	8,960	
Total Refugee	**36,608**	
Percent of total	**(16%)**	
Economic: Independents		
Skilled Workers–Principals	20,136	
–Dependents	15,754	
Assisted Relatives–Principals	6,628	
–Dependents	11,806	
Live-in Caregivers	N/A	
Retirees	5,479	
Total Independents	**59,803**	
Business–Principals	6,991	
–Dependents	21,152	
Total Economic	**87,946**	
Percent of total	**(40%)**	
Total Immigration	**220,777**	
Estimated out-migration	**50,000**	

Source: Immigration Canada, 1994.

Current immigration policy reflects a commitment to moderate and controlled growth. It also embraces a balance of the enlightened with the practical to ensure fairness without loss of control (Knowles 1992). Family reunification remains the core of Canada's immigration policy. The number of family members eligible for sponsorship under the family class has expanded and contracted in line conventional definitions of a Canadian family. Refusal to drastically reduce refugee and family re-unification classes suggests a firm commitment to humanitarian values. The practical aspects of Canada's immigration policy are manifest in different ways. Only those with requisite skills and resources are allowed entry when applying as in-dependents. Particularly noticeable is the creation of the business or entrepre-neural class of immigrants. Those immigrants who are willing to invest in Canada through creation of employable industries are actively courted. The need for cheap

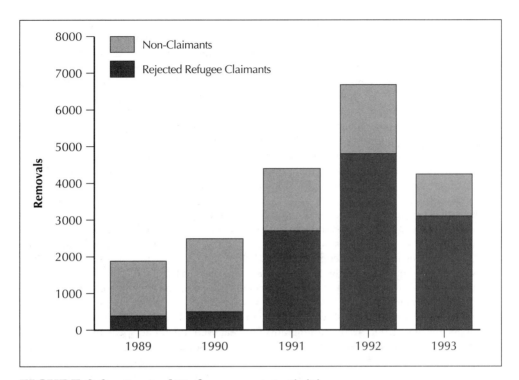

FIGURE 9.9 **Control/Enforcement Activities**
January 1, 1989–July 31, 1993

SOURCE: Immigration Canada, 1994.

disposable labour also is critical. Current examples include the importation of migrant workers on a cyclical basis from the Caribbean to handle fruit and agricultural pursuits, as well as the Domestic Workers scheme to alleviate the crisis in child-care.

Not surprisingly, Canada has been accused of poaching the best and brightest from depleted overseas countries. Canada, of course, is not the only country whose immigration practices reflect political calculation and economic expediency. European countries have demonstrated all too readily their willingness to accept immigrants to feed a labour-starved economic boom, but an equal disdain for them when the downturn returns.

INSIGHT

Fiddling with the Figures: Immigration Towards 2001

The unfolding of the 1990s coincided with growing perceptions of Canada's immigration program as "out of control." Many people were alarmed by the sheer volume of immigrants: From a post-war low of 84,302 in 1985, immigration had peaked at 254,321 in 1993. Between 1990 and 1993, immigrants averaged 244,793 per year (Simpson 1994a), compared with 125,982 during the 1980s, 144,491 in the 1970s, and 136,903 in the 1960s. Even Canada's most celebrated decade in immigration, the 1910s, only drew about 180,000 per year.

Historically Canada's immigration reflected economic needs, from filling up the Prairies to fueling the post-war boom. Between 1945 and 1990, Canada's immigration totals exceeded 200,000 only three times: in 1957 when unemployment was 3.8 percent, in 1967 when unemployment was 3.8 percent, and 1974 when it stood at 5.3 percent (Sudol 1994). Conversely low points in immigration have coincided with economic downturns; for example, less than 100,000 in the mid 1980s when unemployment peaked at 11.8 percent. This link, however, was snapped by the Conservative government under Brian Mulroney (Gwyn 1994) when 255,725 new Canadians were allowed entry in 1993 and 218,976 in 1994, despite double digit unemployment rates.

Canadians were also concerned by the type of immigrants: Many thought Canada had lost control over who could enter and why. In 1994, a total of 138,300 immigrants were drawn from the family and refugee class (over which Canada has little control in terms of skills), while only 110,700 came from the independent class. Jeffrey Simpson, a senior writer with *The Globe and Mail*, pointed out that even with the independent class, a total of 35,200 consisted of assisted relatives; another half consisted of dependents (spouses, children, and parents) who accompanied the main applicant. As many as 43,000 parents and grandparents accompanied their children, even though most were unlikely to contribute directly to the economy without the necessary skills. Up to 58,000 immigrants per year were unable to speak either French or English, according to Don DeVoretz, an economics professor at Simon Fraser University and a recognized expert in this field. In cities such as Toronto, the family class outnumbered the independent immigrant by a ratio of 2 to 1, with predictable consequences on the region's social and welfare programs. Finally, Canadians expressed concern over the high proportion of immigrants from Third World countries. The absorptive capacity of Canada would be stretched to the limit by excessive numbers, it was argued. (Ontario, which receives the majority of new Canadians, had lost 300,000 jobs to the recession/restructuring but gained 700,000 new welfare/unemployment caseloads.) Others worried about the demise of Canada's social cohesiveness and cultural identity.

With a backlash mounting against the previous government's immigration program, the Liberal government had little choice except to respond to this crisis of legitimacy. Tougher measures were proposed not only to foster the impression of control over the immigration process, but also to restore electoral confidence by appeasing conservative elements. It established a national consultation process that culminated in a set of reforms that sought to reassure Canadians that immigration is "being managed" (Sergio Marchi, quoted in Gwyn 1994). The Liberals unfurled a long-range immigration plan that focused on four key issues with respect to numbers, criteria, and accountability:

- Immigration levels would be reduced from 256,000 in 1993 to 215,000 from 1995 and onwards to 2000, without necessarily losing sight of the eventual target of 1 percent of Canada's population (or nearly 280,000).

- Immigration would focus increasingly on independent immigrants rather than family reunification. Independent immigrants would comprise 53 percent of the totals by 2000 from a current 43 percent, while family class would decline from 51 percent to 44 percent. (See Figure 9.10) The process of selection would be modified to ensure a doubling of points for education and official language skills.

- The number of refugees would be increased to approximately 32,000 per year.
- Permanent residents who sponsor relatives may be asked to post a bond or collateral of sorts to ensure continuing support.

An economic spin was apparent from these projections. The welcome mat was out for well educated and highly skilled immigrants, who were proficient in French or English, and who could contribute to the economy without exerting undue stress on the social services system. The Liberal party argued that a change in the mix and match of immigrants was overdue. The nature of the economy had changed, Canada no longer being in need of vast pools of unskilled labour. As well, the immigration minister argued, the fiscal picture made it clear the government could no longer afford to spend huge sums on immigration settlement and integration. Nor could the government afford to bail out those immigrants whose sponsors defaulted on support payments — perhaps as high as $700 million in 1993.

Reaction to the proposed changes was swift and varied. Some saw the changes as going to far, others not far enough. A few saw the reforms as fundamental, others as modest or cosmetic. Supporters lauded the changes as overdue and consistent with Canada's national and global interests rather than pandering to the demands of immigrants or their lobbies (Gwyn 1994). Critics were not impressed. Proposals to reduce family reunification were denounced as inhumane, contrary to international convention, and disruptive to the integration process. Immigrant and church groups, as well as immigration lawyers, deplored the racist implications.

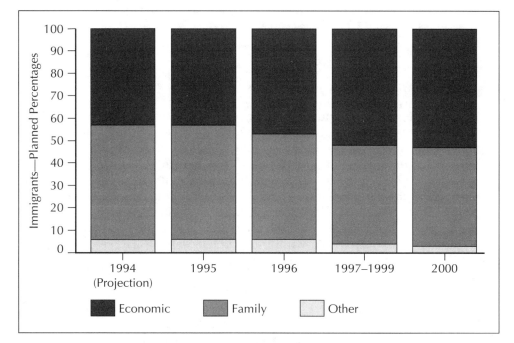

FIGURE 9.10   1996–2000 Immigrant Plan

SOURCE: Immigration Canada, 1994.

Maria Shin, the Executive Director of the Canadian Ethnocultural Council, claimed the Liberals had caved in to racist and right wing groups:

> The real reason why people want to limit immigration is racism. There is still a prevailing mindset in this country that real Canadians are only those who are descended from British or French stock (Quoted in *The Toronto Star*, 2 Nov 1994).

Others saw it as sexist and racially discriminatory. According to Kike Roach of the National Action Committee on the Status of Women (*The Toronto Star* 2 Nov.1994), "It seems as if Sergio Marchi is marching to the drum of right wing policies and what's left, unfortunately, resonates with discrimination and racism. The message it sends is our door is open, but it's open to rich white men. It's open to Europeans, but not others." The decision in 1995 to slap a $975 landing fee on each adult immigrant further reinforced this perception.

At the other end of the spectrum of reaction was the Reform party who claimed the policy was all smoke and mirrors, full of fury but signifying nothing. Despite rhetoric and number manipulation, there remained a fundamental commitment to business as usual, with nearly 80 percent of immigrants still not selected for skills or costs to Canada. In between were those who felt the facts did not justify a reduction in discrimination. However the government could hardly afford to ignore the backlash; instead it sought to silence critics by proving once again that Canada was tough on immigrants and in control of its boundaries.

SOURCES: Gwyn *Toronto Star* 2 Nov 1994; *Kitchener-Waterloo Record* 2 Nov. 1994; Gombu *Toronto Star* 2 Nov 1994; Samuel *Toronto Star* 3 Nov 1994; Cardozo *Toronto Star*, 17 October 1994. *Kitchener-Waterloo Record* 3 Oct. 1994; Simpson *The Globe and Mail* 25 October 1994a; Simpson *The Globe and Mail* 26 Oct 1994b; Simpson *The Globe and Mail* 27 Oct 1994c.

IMMIGRATION: PRO OR CON?

All indicators suggest a continuation of Canada as a favourite destination for those fleeing political oppression, ethnic conflicts, demographic pressure, and economic stagnation. Canada is widely praised for imposing a balancing between compassion and order on a potentially sensitive issue (Gherson 1994). Immigrants and refugees are not only "pushed" from their homeland, but also "pulled" to Canada because of its opportunities and potential. Invariably this raises the question of whether immigration provides a benefit or extracts a cost. Canadians have reacted to the who, why, from where, and what costs of immigration in different ways. Similar questions are circulated within the United States (Bean et al. 1989) and Australia (Adelman et al. 1994).

Pro

Increased immigration into Canada has been justified on various grounds. We are a land of immigrants whose prosperity and identity is dependent on the perpetual influx of immigrants and refugees (Tepper 1988). Studies in other parts of the world, such as Australia and United States confirm the notion that, on balance, immigrants are a net contributor to society (Cardozo 1994; Samuel 1994). The same conclusions exist for Canada: These outcomes, however, are not distributed equally, with provinces such as B.C. compared with Ontario receiving a disproportionate slice of benefits because of a larger business class sector (Matas 1994).

Many tout the economic perks of immigration. Immigrants create more jobs than they take; as consumers they provide markets for Canadian goods, they are more likely to start businesses thean other Canadians, are better qualified in terms of education, and pay more in taxes than they receive in social services. They not only ease labour shortages during phases of capitalist expansion, but also find employment in jobs that Canadians dislike. The entrepreneurial class alone invested nearly $180 million and created some 8000 jobs for Canadians since its inception in the late 1980s. Rather than hurting a stagnant economy, in other words, immigrants are more likely to provide a much needed kick start. The demographics of Canada also work in favour of increased immigration. An aging population pyramid with declining birthrate totals (that dip below replacement rate of 2.1) puts the onus on younger immigrants for future support of social programs. Finally, most immigrants are enthusiastic and hardworking and do not soak up welfare rolls or commit a disproportionate amount of crime. To the contrary, with the possible exception of one or two groups, they are less likely to end up in the criminal justice system or engage in criminal activity despite irresponsible media sensationalism. Immigrants are also likely to integrate into Canadian society. Controversies that do occur often involve modest demands or outwardly superficial symbols such as the contentious turban, rather than any fundamental shift in power or resources.

Certain myths about Canada's 4.3 million immigrants have been exploded in a recent report entitled *Canada's Changing Immigrant Population*, based on 1991 census data and published by Statistics Canada (Mitchell 1994). Rather than a population of criminals and layabouts, StatsCan argues, immigrants tend to be harder working, better educated, and more socially stable than native-born Canadians. A greater proportion of adult immigrants (14%) held university degrees than those born in Canada (11%). The median number of years in school for immigrants was 12.8 compared to 12.5 years for the Canadian born. To be fair, the study is not entirely clear or even-handed. For example, it is difficult to determine whether the study refers only to economic immigrants who come under the independent class. And the study underplays the fact that more immigrants (19%) compared with native-born Canadians (13%) possess less than grade nine education. Still, the signs look promising. Immigrant men were more likely to hold managerial (15%) and professional jobs (17.1%) compared with Canadian-born men at 13.6 percent. Even social stability factors favored immigrants. Immigrants were more likely to be married (66.2 percent) compared with Canadian born at 51.9 percent, while 4.9 percent of immigrants were divorced compared with 6.3 of Canadian born.

Con

Public acceptance of immigration is mixed (Knowles 1992). Canadians as a whole possess ambivalent attitudes toward the presence of immigrants and refugees. Many people are supportive of immigrants and refugees as hardworking and positive contributors to society. But others dislike what they see as threats to Canada's economy and cultural identity. Still others resent immigrants who they see as failing to adapt to Canada or making unreasonable demands on Canadian society. Still other people, criticise what they believe is makers whose muddled thinking about immigrants and their relationship to society. Thses people have certain assumptions, including:

- That Canada possesses a distinctive culture;
- That this culture is superior and should supersede immigrant cultures;
- That immigrants are "guests" in this country, and they should fit into Canada rather than the other way around;
- That immigration should be shaped by national needs rather than by immigrant wants or ethnic lobby groups pressure;
- That Canada should be able to cut back on immigration when it chooses to do so;
- That immigrants ought to be free to retain their culture, provided it is compatible with Canada's and does not drain public monies;
- That immigrants know their place in society; they must prove themselves by starting at the bottom and working their way up. (adapted from Ted Bayfield, *Financial Post*, 18 July 1994)

The ideas may reflect concerns of many Canadians. Many believe there is too much immigration of the wrong kind at the wrong time. Canadians as a rule may accept the necessity or inevitability of immigrants and refugees, but bristle at legislative loopholes and unscrupulous stakeholders, with the result that even dysfunctional government policies are resistant to change because of a small number of vocal clients ("clientele capture") with a vested interested in preserving the status quo (Stoffman 1994). Some resent what they see as excessively generous concessions to increasingly demanding immigrant sectors. Others take exception to the economic costs of immigrants (for instance, the costs for language training and welfare can reach nearly 1 billion per year according to the *The Globe and Mail* 2 Nov 1994:A-6); still others are concerned about the "problems" that new Canadians bring with them to Canada. This include allegations that immigrants are using their ties abroad to establish illegal international distribution systems for illegal drugs, loan sharking, prostitution, and smuggling of illegal aliens into Canada, while victimizing those already in Canada through extortion rackets (Madely 1994). Finally, there is growing fear of undermining the WASP-ish character of Canadian society through unrestricted entry.

Why, then, do high levels of immigration occur when the electoral odds are not in favour of such a position? How do we account for such levels in the perceived

absence of any demographic or economic rationale? Michael Valpy (1994) provides one answer when he writes of the different sectors that can gain benefits
from immigration:

> They serve ethnic groups who want easy access to the country for their rela-
> tives...They serve capitalism's desire for cheap labour. They serve immigrant
> lawyers' desire for a steady supply of customers. They serve the intellectual con-
> victions of those who believe virtually everyone outside Canada can qualify as a
> refugee.

Perhaps Richard Gwyn (1994) put it best when he announced:"Most immigrants
vote Liberal; Marchi is a Liberal; End of in-depth analysis."

THE REFUGEE CRISIS: WHOSE CRISIS?

Debate over refugees has provoked Canadians as few issues have in recent years.
This is not surprising given the magnitude of the problem. At present there are up
to 25 million refugees world wide, an increase of from 2.5 million during the 1970s.
Another 25 million are displaced from their homes but still inside their country
in makeshift government-sponsored camps with few amenities and even fewer
prospects for placement. Most refugees have fled from war-torn countries; others
from regimes who routinely violate human rights as state policy. Establishing a
fair and just system to cope with this human crisis would appear a simple enough
challenge. Yet the refugee question remains complex and convoluted with perennial concerns over "who is a refugee," "how do we find out," "is the system working," and "how many can Canada handle" (Bauer 1994). Answers to these questions
will provide a springboard for discussion.

A Beacon of Hope

The first refugees to Canada to qualify under compassionate grounds did not arrive
until the 1920s. Since World War II, Canada has officially admitted over half a
million refugees. Large numbers of refugees were admitted from Hungary in 1956
(37,000), Czechoslavakia (12,000) in 1968, Uganda (7,000) in 1973, Chile (17,000)
since 1973, Lebanon (10,000) between 1976 and 1978, and Poland (10,000) during the 1980s. From late 1970s onwards, Canada has accepted some 120,000
Indochinese refugees, many by way of Vietnam after the fall of Saigon. Primary
sources at present include Sri Lanka, Iran, Afghanistan, Somalia, Lebanon, and El
Salvador. The number of sponsored refugees has hovered in the vicinity of 12,000
to 15,000. By contrast, the number of refugee claimants has varied from 10,000 to
38,000 since the mid 1980s. For example, 37,720 refugees claimants arrived in
Canada in 1992. Of these 17,437 were accepted, 9,871 were rejected, and 1,869
withdrew their application (*Kitchener-Waterloo Record* 5 March 1994). The remainder presumably were in the pipeline.In 1993, the IRB heard 20,500 claims; it is
expected to hear upwards of 30,000 in 1994.

Canada's apparent generosity and support of international refugee programs has been amply documented. Receipt of the Nansen Medal in 1986 — the the first country ever to be bestowed such an honour by the United Nations — can attest to that. Its contribution to international humanitarian agencies, including $67 million in 1988/89, is consistent with this tradition (*The Globe and Mail*, 10 April 1990). Canada has fared well by comparison with countries who deny basic human rights or routinely deport refugees as part of a general crackdown. Canada received a combined total of 56,000 refugees (sponsored and claimants) in 1991 — a figure that had declined to 31,963 in 1994. The refugee acceptance rate stands at an impressive 68 percent in 1994, up from 55 percent in 1993. Even passage of stringent and controversial laws to curb the flow of illegal refugees into Canada, namely Bill C-55 and C-84, has not been much of a deterrent. Not that Canada's record is unblemished (Abella and Troper 1991). But compared with other countries, Canada is a beacon of hope even when grappling with knotty issues about who is eligible and what will happen if people are turned away.

The Politics of Definition

Defining a refugee is not as straightforward as it might appear. According to the United Nations Human Rights Convention of 1951 (to which Canada is a signatory) and Canada's Immigration Act of 1976, refugees constitute a class of individuals who have left their country and cannot return because of a well-founded fear of persecution for reasons of race, religion, nationality, group membership, or political opinion. These criteria are not absolutely reliable: For example, the distinction between outright persecution and ordinary discrimination is fuzzy. As a result even those who have fled famine or civil wars, in some cases suffered hardship or death of family members, may not qualify as refugees under Canadian law if they have not been singled out for persecution because of their affiliation to a particular religion, race, nationality, political opinion, or group membership (Bauer 1994). Nevertheless, the political dimension separates refugees from immigrants who migrate primarily for social or economic reasons.

There are exceptions to this law. Refugees who have committed crimes or atrocities are normally not allowed refugee status in Canada. Those refugees who have travelled through a safe country are denied a haven in Canada. Others who do not conform with the letter of the refugee law are accepted, however, including those who experience refugee-like conditions such as political oppression or environmental disaster (Government of Canada 1993). Politics also play an important part: Historically those who fled communist regimes were happily accepted as refugees, while those escaping from right wing coups loyal to America such as that in Chile in 1973 have received a cool reception since they lacked "Cold War legitimacy" (Whitaker 1991:22). Refugee status is now being claimed on gender grounds, such as in cases of abusive domestic situations, exposure to mutilation, or forced marriage and sterilization. Canada became the world's first country in 1993 to recognize gender persecution as legitimate grounds for entry. A total of 195 women were settled in 1995, prompting some critics such as Audrey Kobayashi (in Simone 1994) to label the refugee process as hostile to women's concerns, largely because of male bias in qualifying for refugee status. Finally, refugee claimants whose applications have been rejected and appeals exhausted are not being deported because of dangerous or unstable conditions (Thompson 1994).

Sorting out Refugees

Up to 36,000 refugees per year claim status in Canada. That is about twice the number the system was designed to handle, with the result that refugee workers are overworked and claimants encounter lengthy delays (Eve 1991). In 1977 a total of 500 refugee claims were made: During the 1980s the number of "undocumented" refugees skyrocketed, with many countries inundated by those seeking entry to a new life (Hawkins 1991). Even those who are highly critical of government restrictions concede that Canada cannot possibly open its doors to every refugee: The sovereignty and prosperity of Canadians depends on securing the integrity of the system.

Arrival at Canada's borders activates a set of procedures. A lengthy process may be required to determine if the claimants in question qualify as bona fide refugees under the 1951 Geneva Convention statutes (Jackson 1991). The old system of refugee determination proved cumbersome, involving a seven step process that culminated in delays of five years. Bottlenecks ensued, with an 80,000 person backlog by 1988 despite an administrative review to clear unprocessed applications. A new streamlined two-step refugee determination system was put in place on January 1, 1989 not only to clear up the refugee backlog but also to fast-track current claims.

The current system consists of a simplified procedure. Within 72 hours of entry, a refugee claimant is interviewed and assessed by a senior immigration official. If the claim is upheld as credible, the refugee is then expected to attend a more detailed hearing by the Immigration and Refugee Board — a quasi-independent tribunal created in 1989 after a scandal involving political and diplomatic interference in the refugee determination process. Claimants are given a month or so to provide basic data in support of their claim (Bauer 1994). They also are entitled to legal aid in preparing a case or filing an appeal. Those claimants who are almost certain of entry are conferred what is called an "expedited hearing" to speed things up and prevent a backlog. If claimant is not given expedited treatment, another hearing is held in several months with a two-member panel from IRB in one of its offices across Canada. The support of one of two panel members is required to confer refugee status to the claimant; a unanimous decision in writing is required for a rejection. That entire process may take up to three years if appeals are exhausted.

Is the System Working?

Two mindsets prevail about refugee claimants (Plaut 1989). Many Canadians recognize and accept Canada's humanitarian commitments to those less fortunate.

This sector is inclined to see the refugee process as protecting the lives of endangered human beings. The objective of a humane policy is to cast as wide a net as possible for refugees, then dispose of those who don't fit — keeping in mind that refugees from a disordered society are not like immigrants who can follow a prescribed pattern of structured behaviour and regulations (Plaut 1989).

An opposing view sees the refugee process as a potential threat to the integrity of Canada's immigration system. This sector approaches refugees as frauds, and favours an approach that deports as many refugees as possible while winnowing out genuine refugees for settlement in the process. Rather than treating each claim as potentially truthful and going from there, refugees are perceived as fakes anxious to take Canada for a ride. Loopholes are exploited by these refugees through (a) inadequate measures to implement and monitor refugee activities; (b) shady immigrant lawyers and self-interested ethnic organizations, and (c) undesirables who jump queues and create havoc. Is Canada's system capable of standing up to this criticism?

The refugee determination system is working as well as can be expected, given the complexities of making life and death decsions. The refugee determination process was never intended to handle large numbers of people. From as few as 500 in the late 1970s, the volume of refugees had grown to proportions never envisaged by the Immigration Act, with an unprecedented swell of refugee backlogs that have proven embarassing (Whitaker 1991). The Immigration and Refugee Board (IRB) is processing up to 3,000 cases per month, with some claimants waiting up to 10 months for an initial hearing or paper screening to determine if they have a credible basis for their claim. Another two years may pass before a final decision. The costs of this lengthy and expensive process are a burden to everyone: Until recently, refugee claimants could not work, forcing most onto welfare rolls. The 27,000 refugee claimants on Ontario's welfare rolls cost about $155 million in 1991-92 (Eve 1991). Since 1994, refugee claimants have received a work permit upon arrival. But they remain ineligible for language and training services until their status is resolved. The stresses that accompany refugee claimants are compounded by their language difficulties, shame at their inability to work, and low self-esteem due to loss of control over destiny. Even after they secure a work permit, refugees still suffer from lack of Canadian experience, are vulnerable to recession or restructuring in the workplace, encounter discrimination at work, and must cope with language barriers.

Critics of the system, such as William Bauer (1994) take a jaundiced view of the current system. Bauer concedes the system is effective in identifying genuine refugees; however, the system is ineffective in weeding out and deporting fraudulent claimants and criminals. As far as he is concerned, only about 35 percent are genuine refugees, but the system takes in 80 percent — though his figures are inconsistent with the 68 percent acceptance rates (up from 55 percent from the previous year) reported in other circles. The system is open to abuse, Bauer argues, primarily by unscrupulous lawyers, gullible refugees, scheming refugee and ethnic organizations, and incompetent IRB members. He also accuses the 211 member IRB of bending to political pressure, especially in the area of increasing the number of successful applicants for electoral and public relations purposes. The fact that as many as half the 211 membership are recently appointed refugee advocates has done nothing to counter the criticism of favoritism. To those who believe the IRB should ensure the maximum number of refugees are accepted, he retorts that the board is mandated to examine the facts and to ensure that decisions are made objectively as they apply to law. Even the refugee appeal process has come under criticism as arbitrary and irrational, as well as costly and insensitive, in a recent government-sponsored report (*Kitchener-Waterloo Record* 14 May 1994). Most surprising is international condemnation of Canada's refugee policy in offending diplomatic friends, military allies, and important trading partners (Shallot 1994). Canada's decision to accept refugees from Mexico and China (important trading partners), Israel (diplomatic allies), and Turkey (military allies) has not sat well with most of these countries — none of which like to be singled out as possible human rights violators. Finally, the system is unworkable, critics claim, because the government refuses to make tought decisions about deporting false claimant. This waffling is seen as undermining public confidence in our ability to control our borders.

INSIGHT

Setting the Record Straight: A Dialogue with Immigration

The field of immigration and ethnicity is littered with clichés, contradictions, and half-truths. One way of cutting through this clutter is by isolating certain *points of contention* for analysis and assessment. This dialogue will attempt to separate fact from fantasy by engaging the reader in conversation about issues of perennial concern in immigration. As various issues are addressed, it will become apparent that criticism is cheap; constructive criticism is considerably more difficult. Moreover, few solutions are of an either-or variety. A balance is often required, with national interests on the one side and the needs of those in search of opportunity or freedom on the other. The middle ground is the challenge before us.

1) *Does Canada accept too many immigrants?*
   Critics say that Canada is stretching its "absorptive capacity" by accepting too many immigrants and refugees. Current immigration into Canada is currently in the 250,000 range: Some argue for an increase in numbers to about 300,000 (reflecting one percent of Canada's population); others propose 150,000 as the preferred figure (it brings Canada in line with its postwar average and with worldwide proportions). What figure is acceptable? What is "too much" and how can we determine the acceptable figure? When is the absorptive capacity stretched to the limit? What kind of criteria do we employ to justify any proposed levels?

2) *Does Canada take in too many Third World immigrants?*
   The largest percentage of immigrants to Canada have come from Asia, averaging between 43 to 52 percent per year since 1981. The totals for Europe and the United States have declined to about 25 percent, with the remaining from Africa and Latin America. What is

the proper proportion? How would you arrive at a better mix, keeping in mind that Canada no longer has complete freedom in choosing who it admits. How would you justify your choice?

3) *Does Canada have the wrong "class" of immigrants?*
Canada's immigrant quotas are divided roughly between the family reunification class and the independent class, with each contributing approximately 45 percent of the intake. Refugees comprise the other 10 percent. Some argue that we need more independent immigrants with the social and economic skills to contribute directly to Canada. Others believe that the integrity of the family is uppermost in building a strong Canada, and that family class increases are in order. How do you sort out who is right or wrong? On what basis do you justify this answer?

4) *Are immigrants good for the economy?*
Immigrants are perceived by some as an economic deficit. They are accused of taking jobs from Canadians or contributing less to the economy than they take out. Opposed to this view are those who see immigrants as positive contributors to Canada: On balance, they pay more taxes than they receive in social services; they create jobs and bolster consumer demand; they tend to be better educated and more socially stable then native-born Canadians; they will replenish our aging and diminishing population; they possess drive and vitality, and a willingness to take risks; and they can capitalize on international links to improve Canada's competitive position in a global economy. In between these positions are those who conclude that the economic impact of immigrants is relatively negligible. Which position is correct? How do you find out? Do different classes of immigrants contribute in a different way?

5) *Do we need more skilled immigrants?*
Conventional wisdom dictates that we select those who are most qualified in terms of credentials, expertise, and educational levels. A post-industrial Canada within an intensely competitive global market no longer requires a pool of cheap manual labour. With 10 percent unemployment and underemployed graduates, does Canada really need highly skilled competitors in a downsized economy? Perhaps immigrants are required for the kind of work (from service jobs to manual labour) that many native-born regard with contempt. How would you respond to this dilemma, keeping in mind the need to balance national with self interest?

6) *Are refugees abusing Canada's generous refugee policy?*
In a world awash with 25 million refugees, Canada is not exactly swamped with refugees (at least compared to countries such as Germany or the USA). Canada's acceptance rate is second to none, however. Canada currently accepts 68 percent of refugee claimants; those rejected can pursue a lengthy and costly appeal process. Perhaps only 10 to 15 percent are ever deported. This suggests that the vast majority of refugees are genuine. Conversely it could also suggest that Canada's system is absurdly generous, with numerous loopholes and vulnerabilities. That being the case, why not accept all refugee claimants, and dispense with the costs involved in deporting the few that fail to meet our standards. In other words, the key question is how much is not enough, and on what grounds. Perhaps we need to rethink the bottom line: It is not that Canada accepts too many refugees: more to the point, other countries accept too few (Bergman 1994).

7) *Are immigrants are subverting Canadian culture?*
Many believe that Third World immigrants represent a threat to Canada's identity and

core values. Admittedly, the Canada of today is different from the one of a generation ago. However it seems a bit unsporting to blame immigrants while ignoring a host of other factors, ranging from passage of Canada's first Citizenship Act in 1947 to the globalization of Canada's market economy. Moreover some might counter that there is nothing to undermine in a country reknown for lacking strong central values. Canadian identity is not a "thing" cast in perpetuity but a process that must be reinvented every generation in response to changing circumstances. Alternately, rather than detracting from Canada's identity and culture, immigrants have contributed to the construction of a cultural mindset, both receptive to diversity and willing to agree to disagree without resorting to reprisals.

8) *Are immigrants not adapting?*
   There is an underlying perception that immigrants are making an inadequate effort to become Canadian. They are seen as religiously holding on to their culture while huddled together in ethnic enclaves. Reality suggests otherwise. Immigrants do not come to Canada to perpetuate a way of life that many are trying to escape. Many (but especially the young) are anxious to be Canadian as quickly as possible — without necessarily abandoning everything that provide a sense of meaning or continuity. Those who do settle into ethnic communities often leave for the suburbs after an initial adjustment period, leaving behind the members who lack the resources and resourcefulness to cope with the outside.

9) *Are immigrants hastening the social decay of Canada?*
   Everyone has heard of immigrants or refugees who are a disgrace to Canadian society. The media seem particularly obsessed with ferreting out stories on immigrants in trouble with the law, or who interfere with the rights of others, or who take advantage of Canada's social security system. This kind of reporting (and the mindset associated with this kind of thinking) reflects a conservative agenda that fixates on the negative for ulterior purposes. Sure, there are immigrants and refugees that are not making any contribution to Canada. There are native-born Canadians who are no less guilty. But the overwhelming majority of new Canadians want to establish roots as productive and self-reliant citizens.

10) *Should Canada accept immigrants?*
    There are a lot of people who wonder why we accept immigrants or refugees. The vulnerability of Canada's economy, coupled with the allegedly fragile state of its social and cultural fabric, would dictate against such rash generosity. On balance, however, immigrants and **society-building** are strongly linked. Immigrants provide economic benefits, they enrich Canadians through diversity, and the foster international reputations and global linkages. Besides, one might ask whether Canada has a moral right to keep out those less fortunate because of circumstances beyond their control. On what grounds can we justify securing our privilege while others must suffer and perish?

IMMIGRATION SETTLEMENT: CHALLENGES AND PROSPECTS

Certain immigrant and refugee groups have experienced difficulties in making an adjustment to Canadian society. Problems may arise not only because of personal shortcomings related to culture shock, lack of political power, loss of economic well-being, and personal isolation, but because of discriminatory barriers that preclude entry or acceptance. Compounding these adjustment problems are those Canadians who resent the minorities, and lash out at the prospect of moving over and making space. To be sure, many immigrant and refugees appear to be relatively satisfied with the quality of life in Canada, the opportunities and services available to them and their children, and the freedom and tolerance of a liberal-democratic society (*The Toronto Star* Report 1986). Many arrive with higher post-secondary education levels than native-born Canadians; they as a group are proportionately represented in certain occupations such as management and professions (Badets and Chui 1994). Nevertheless, most confront a series of problems that they have brought with them into Canada or encounter upon entry and settlement. These problems are in some ways similar to, yet also different from, those experienced by native-born multicultural minorities.

Immigrants, for example, have long endured racial abuse and discrimination in the field of employment, education, housing, and government services (Report, Equality Now, 1984; Henry and Tator 1985). Licensed occupations including medicine or dentistry continue to impose restrictions that have the effect of blocking the entry of immigrants with foreign degrees or credentials outside Canada. New Canadians find themselves segregated in menial and unskilled occuptions with little in the way of security or prospects for promotion. Their visible status may preclude a smooth transition into Canadian society, while public reaction to their physical appearance and cultural differences can only complicate the settlement process.

Canadians for the most part have not yet fully confronted the reality and challenges of a racially and cultural diverse society (Whitaker 1991). Reluctance to endorse measures that encourage inclusiveness and accommodation is one sign of this denial. Growing anti-immigrant sentiment is another — even though any backlash will be constrained by (a) human rights codes that restrict the public articulation of racist views, (b) a pervasive liberalism within the political cultures, and (c) a lack of institutional base with both labour unions and churches on board the immigration express. Nor is there much likelihood of reverting to an openly racial basis for selection of immigrants or treatment of Canadians once in Canada. Still, there is room to impose restrictions on minorities that have a discriminatory effect.

Criticism in recent years has been directed at the police for failure to respond appropriately to demographic, political, and social trends in urban centres. This criticism is especially vocal in Toronto where a series of incidents has created a crisis in the management of diversity at frontline levels.

INSIGHT

The Crisis in Police-Minority Youth Relations

Police-minority relations provide us with an insight into the dynamics and logic underlying race and ethnic relations in general. The combination of demographic, political, and social changes has strained this relationship to the point where it is fraught with ambiguity and distrust. Police shootings of African-Canadian males in Montreal, Toronto, and Mississauga in the late 1980s have drawn further attention to this growing crisis in police-minority relations. On the one hand, community activists have been outraged by what they perceive as racist and violent acts against a vulnerable and oppressed target. On the other, the police have defended their actions on grounds of the existence of excessive violence within certain minority communities. Efforts to smooth out the hostility and mistrust through various task forces and public inquiries have served only to infuriate both the police and minority communities. The cost is steep in deepening the loss of public confidence in policing.

Crisis in Community Relations

Nowhere is the breakdown in police-minority relations more conspicuous than in the Birchmount-Jane-Finch corridor in north Toronto. Over 38,000 residents — many of them immigrants and nearly a third under nineteen years of age — are squeezed into less than five square kilometers of concrete and cramped income assisted housing. With few public amenities to absorb interests or attention, minority youth find themselves in a situation where negative contact with the police occurs on a regular basis.

Reports of breakdowns in police-minority youth interaction are almost legendary. Minority youths have long complained about harrassment by an overzealous and less than impartial police force. They criticize the police for random checks and strip searches which are conducted for no apparent reason. Police stereotyping of them as hustlers, pushers, or pimps has done nothing to improve interaction. Any item of personal wealth is assumed by the police to be derived from illegal actions. Minority youths who may be engaged in relatively harmless activities are provoked because of overpolicing, racial taunts, and verbal abuse. The act of sticking up for one another against an authority that threatens their rights is likely to result in further charges for obstruction or assault. Finally, police stereotyping and discriminatory policing increases the likelihood of being charged and arrested, sentenced and convicted, more often and for longer durations than those from the mainstream. Not surprisingly, the police are *perceived* as an occupying army — defenders of a white status quo with its prevailing distribution of power and privilege.

The police deny the accuracy of these claims, saying they are distortions and half-truths. They defend their actions by emphasizing the need for monitoring a vicious drug problem in certain minority enclaves. Increased surveillance and stepped-up enforcement is the price the community must pay. Community activists are dismissed as malcontents who do not represent the general community, but who act on hidden agendas and have political axes to grind. Minority youths are described as arrogant, assertive, defiant, uncooperative, and clannish — thus making enforcement that much more difficult for the police. In short, a problem exists that sabotages any possibility of sustainable police-minority interaction in a complex and rapidly changing social context.

What is the Problem?

Much of the difficulty in restructuring relations represents a failure to agree on the fundamental problem. Do we have a drug problem, or are drugs merely the manifestation of a system that fails to provide employment opportunities for minority youth? This is particular true with regards to the nature of "black crime." Are minorities more likely than white youth to commit crime? Or does the greater visibility and distinctive cultural lifestyles culminate in higher rates of detection and arrest?

Two issues must be kept in mind. Minorities as a group are often members of a social and economic underclass. Crimes committed by this sector — whether black or white — tend to come to the attention of the police. Contrast this with "white-collar" crime that may be no less pervasive but not nearly as visible or as easily detected. Second, certain minorities are subject to prejudice, stereotype, and discrimination because of their visibility. They are not necessarily more criminal than other groups, but they are more likely to be apprehended and charged. They also see themselves as victimized by a police force that is culturally insensitive and openly discriminatory in their actions. Failure to understand minority social patterns and cultural values has contributed to this gap. For instance, minority youth may be taught to challenge authority if its exercise infringes on their rights. The police, in turn, represent authority figures who expect deference and respect. Confrontation with minority youths becomes almost inevitable under these circumstances.

For the police, their actions are justified in light of their mandate to enforce the law and maintain law and order in society. As professional crime fighters, they have an obligation to apply the law equally to all sectors of society regardless of cultural differences or social circumstances. The very nature of policing may make it difficult to relate to racial diversity. Problems of cross-cultural understanding are compounded by a policing subculture (with its emphasis on defensiveness and suspicion toward the community) and a para-military bureaucracy that tends to minimize meaningful contact with constituents of any sorts.

Bridging the Gap

Efforts to improve police-community relations in general are now standard. A number of reforms and initiatives have been implemented in an attempt to bridge the gap (Fleras and Desroches 1989). Police executives have taken a resolute stand against any form of racist or discriminatory behaviour against ethnic minorities. Initiatives have been aimed at making the police more accountable for their actions, more accessible to culturally different groups, and more sensitive to special community needs. Yet the message has been slow in trickling down to the rank and file who must deal with highly volatile situations involving diverse publics on a daily basis (see Gould 1995). To be sure, the police cannot be expected to clear up problems which they are not responsible for. Nevertheless, it is incumbent on the police to deal with at the least the precipitating (if not the root) causes of problems that hinder the creation of more inclusive and accommodative policing.

Immigrants are often victimized by inequities in the planning and delivery of social services. Educational instititutions have long come under attack for continued insensitivity to their needs and aspirations (Alladin 1996). Immigrant and refugee school children may perform poorly because of racial stereotyping, low teacher expectations, curriculums and textbooks at odds with minority experiences, and lack of positive role models among school staff. Many youth experience social dislocation as they drift apart from the senior generation, women chaffe over traditional roles and pervasive paternalism, and elites become estranged from the rank and file. Nor should we trivialize the impact of cultural shock because of exposure to radically different lifestyles, expectations, rapid social change, and inhospitable climates. Additional problems can arise from concern over the gradual loss of cultural identity — especially among the young who appear anxious to spurn the past, but may struggle to find acceptance in their present situation. Traumatized by emotional and psychological abuses enroute to Canada, refugees are expected to adapt to the unique social, cultural, or geographic climate with only minimal outside assistance.

Non-English speaking immigrant women encounter additional problems because of gender and race constraints (Ng and Ramirez 1981). Many women of colour find themselves restricted to the lower echelons of the Canadian labour force where they are slotted into low paying job ghettoes such as manufacturing, service industries, and domestic work. (Anderson and Lynam 1987). Domestic workers on two year probationary periods are particularly vulnerable to exploitation and abuse. Women of colour are also victimized by policies and programs that keep them illiterate, isolated, and vulnerable to abuse. Melody Neufeld-Rocheleau and Judith Friesen (1987) write on the suffering experienced by immigrant women in Canada.

> The loneliness stemming from isolation (limited language, lack of training opportunities, childrearing and school-related problems, underemployment, lack of "Canadian" experience, limited services to cater to their unique situations) often experienced by immigrant women can be devastating. For them Canada becomes a cage.

In an attempt to organize for change that reflects their distinct needs and experiences, immigrant women have begun to look for support outside conventional feminist groups (hooks 1984; Rhodes 1989).

In Summary

Generally speaking, the primary concerns of immigrants and refugees are practical and survival-related. They want to "put down roots" and to "fit in" to Canadian society, without necessarily severing ties with their cultural tradition. More specifically, their needs can be summarized as follows:

1) The elimination of all forms of discrimination, racism (including stereotyping), and exploitation in the workplace.

2) The expansion of opportunities in the labour and education market as well as ease of access to services in housing, government institutions, and mass media.

3) Conferral of full citizenship rights including the right to pursue interests and activities without undue bureaucrataic interference or central surveillance.

4) Access to the best Canadian society has to offer without diminishing their children's sense of cultural identity. Immigrants should be capable of expressing themselves in terms of their identity, yet possess the capacity to construct a successful world around them.

In short, immigrants and refugees want the best that both worlds have to offer. They are anxious to participate in the modern as well as the traditional without foresaking either. In seeking to merge the old and the new, they want belong to the present as well as to retain an identity with the past. Culture, history, and language are important, but no more so than meaningful involvement in the wider sector. They desire equality (to be treated the same) and full citizenship rights, but they also want recognition of their cultural worth if they choose to identify with their traditions, without necessarily being labelled as less than Canadian in the process. Yet the division of society into "us" and "them" can have a damaging effect on the "other" as we shall see.

VOICES

Immigrant: A Label that Sticks for Life

With the exception of First Nations people, everyone living in Canada has immigrated here.

However, for those of us who are black, the word immigrant lasts infinitely longer than its paper life. Long after becoming citizens, we continue to carry the burden of being immigrants—with all the negative connotations of job-stealer, criminally inclined and diseased.

At best, our darker skins become badges, advertising to the world that either we or our ancestors came here from somewhere else; at worst, that we don't truly belong in Canada.

Two recent high-profile killings in Toronto have linked issues of immigration to those of crime. In what now has come to be described as the Just Desserts robbery and killing, one of the accused, Oneil Grant, had been ordered deported, appealed and was allowed to remain in Canada.

In the killing of Metro police Constable Todd Baylis, the accused, Clinton Gayle, also a landed immigrant, also was ordered deported. He appealed, lost his appeal and, through bureaucratic errors, was never deported.

The media have had what can only be called a field day with these issues, repeatedly emphasizing that, had Gayle been deported, Baylis would not have been killed. Immigration Minister Sergio Marchi, in Toronto for public hearings about the future direction of immigration, had to deflect criticism that immigration is out of control and that the wrong kind of immigrant is being allowed in. On the surface, these two crimes provide all the evidence needed to support these allegations.

That the due process of the law as it exists did not take place in the case of Gayle is quite clear. Having failed at his appeal, Gayle should have been deported. That there may have been an erroneous judgment call in the case of Grant is also a likelihood, if he is found to be guilty in the Just Desserts robbery. That the immigration bureaucracy needs to be overhauled is, in all likelihood, also true.

The media have, however, chosen to ignore that both these men came to Canada as children—Grant at age 12 and Gayle at ate 8. Contrary to the impression given by the media, these men are not recent immigrants.

Gayle could have been a Canadian citizen of several years standing long before he had his first brush with the law some 11 years after his arrival in Canada. Why the families of these men did not apply for citizenship on their behalf, which they could have done some five years (now three) after arrival in Canada, will probably never be known. The fact remains, however, that these African Canadian men have been shaped and formed by Canadian society and Canada needs to accept responsibility for that shaping process.

The present system of immigration and citizenship allows an individual, provided they meet all the requirements, to become a citizen after three years of being in Canada legally. If that person commits a crime in their fourth year, immigration status cannot be used as an issue. If, however, someone fails to apply for citizenship, as in the case of these men, and commits a crime, even after a decade in Canada they will still be discussed in terms of being an immigrant, with all the negative implications that arise from that.

For the media and public to insist on an irrevocable link between the so-called immigrant status of Grant and Gayle and their criminality is to fuel the flames of an anti-immigrant sentiment. It is a sentiment spreading like bush fire around this city and country, one that barely masks the underlying racism. The fact that both victims were white—in one case a female, in the other a male police officer—and both accused are black, has only served to inflame these sentiments. Any cursory check of open-line shows over the days immediately after both shootings confirmed a disturbing level of racism against blacks.

The experience of both these men and the many, many others like them who have not come to the public's notice in quite the same way, ought to make us as a society ask questions about how and why young people—particularly

young, black people—turn to crime. The trail of those questions will lead us unswervingly to Canadian society, and to institutions such as the education system in which, as in Gayle's case, young immigrants would have spent most of their young lives, before first running afoul of the law. Not to mention an economy that offers little hope of work for young, black males.

The shooting of a police officer always is startling and newsworthy. However, the overwhelming result of the way in which the media portrayed the killing of Baylis, and the way the public understood it, was as an unusually significant event and one symbolic of some deeper and foreign malaise in Canadian society—a malaise bred by darker-skinned immigrants and uncontrolled immigration?

How then do we explain that in the last year there have been two other police officers killed in Ontario—one in Minden last July, and one in Sudbury last October? In both these killings the accused are white men. Does that explain why public outrage was minimal in both these cases? Is that why the flag at Queen's Park did not fly at half-mast? And what of the media's role in all this? Why wasn't Baylis's killing put in the context of these two recent killings—*not* in large metropolises like Toronto, but in a small, rural town and a medium-sized city? Does it matter less if a white person kills a white police officer?

To link crime to immigration as has been done over the last several weeks in Toronto is a false and dangerous ploy; it ill serves the memory of those who lost their lives in unfortunate circumstances and sows a seed bed of racism from which one can harvest only yet more hate. More than anything else, such linkages serve to remind those of us with black skins—lest we forget—that being immigrant is an immutable quality. But perhaps *the* most tragic consequence of this is that attention is detracted away from the many deep-seated problems within our society, like racism, a flagging economy, and a school system that fails too many of its black students.

Instead, Canadians are being provided with simplistic, knee-jerk solutions to complex problems that often pander to the more base instincts within society.

As a society, we are all diminished by this.

SOURCE: Marlene Nourbese Philip

IMMIGRATION, MULTICULTURAL MINORITIES, AND SOCIETY-BUILDING

Immigration has emerged as one of the pivotal issues for the 1990s. Its importance and significance goes beyond the question of dollars and cents or demographic imbalances. Canada has evolved as an immigrant country and immigrants continue to fuel the spark for building Canada. The words of the Minister of Immigration and Citizenship are mindful of this relationship: "Immigration is fundamentally about nation-building — about deciding who we are as Canadians and who we want to become....we need a clear and practical vision of the kind of nation we want to build" (Sergio Marchi, Annual Report, p.iii 1994).

The role of immigration in redefining Canada is no less important than the re-structuring of aboriginal-state relations along the lines of the "nations within" or Ottawa-Quebec relations with respect to the politics of "distinct society." The ambiguities inherent in immigration, the Third force, are no less confusing than those of the first and second forces. Immigration is vital in shaping Canada's prosperity and social well-being; on the whole Canada has become a more vibrant and dynamic society because of immigrants, and for the most part has embraced this migration with the kind of civility and openmindedness that is becoming a trademark of Canada (Editorial *The Globe and Mail* 3 Nov 1994). Immigration can also pose a threat to the integrity and character of Canadian society. Many have grown wary of immigrants, wary of making changes to accommodate diversity, and concerned whether a deficit-soaked government can afford the costs. These oppositional dynamics cannot be readily resolved. What has become increasingly clear is Canada's emergence as a world nation (Gwyn 1994) — a society whose character is not defined by a specific history or set of national values but by the contribution of immigrants in pursuit of opportunity and freedom. The relevance of immigration in the re-construction of Canada is reflected in the kind of questions invariably raised by immigration, including:

- What does it mean to be a Canadian?

- What kind of country do we want to live in?

- What is Canada's absorptive capacity with respect to the volume and diversity of immigrants?

- What core values must be protected, and which values are open for negotiation?

Answers to these questions require careful deliberation. Responses also demand a broader understanding of immigration within the context of Canadian society, both past and present, rather than some limited samples within a restricted time frame. The next chapter explores the issue from a multicultural perspective.

CHAPTER HIGHLIGHTS

- Multicultural minorities occupy a relational status in Canada at variance with the legal status of First Nations and the Charter members with respect to history, problems, solutions, entitlements, and outcomes.

- The relationship of multicultural minorities to society can be analyzed in different ways. A focus on immigrants and immigration provides a useful organizational device that acknowledges the unequal relations of multicultural minorities with society.

- The demography of contemporary Canada reveals an increasingly diverse society. According to the 1991 Census Data, 45 percent of all Canadians possessed some non-British, non-French ancestry. Thirty-one percent had no French or British background, with the greatest numbers from Europe at 15 percent of the total population and people of colour ("visible minorities") at nearly 10 percent.

- Immigration currently stands at about 250,000 per year, with the vast majority arriving from Asia, Africa, South and Central America. Most immigrants move to Ontario, with Quebec and Alberta next; Atlantic provinces are not a favourite destination. Large urban centres, mainly Toronto, Vancouver, and Montreal, are primary destination points.

- Several themes can be discerned to describe Canada's immigration policies and practices. Historically, immigration selection was racist and nativist, geared toward agricultural needs, highly contested with business and labour competing for control of the agenda, reflecting a stop-and-go mentality, and rooted in an interplay of economic calculation and political expediency sprinkled with a dash of compassion.

- Canada's Immigration Act, 1976, is committed to the principle of family reunification, Canadian economy, protection of refugees, and preservation of Canada's integrity.

- Immigration selection is divided into three categories. Family reunification is based on sponsorship of close and distant relatives; independent class based on the point system as it applies to skilled workers, investors, and entrepreneurs; and refugee class, both sponsored and claimants.

- Recent changes to the immigration policy have focused on reducing total levels to about 200,000, placing more emphasis on the independent rather than family class, increasing the number of refugees, and securing more responsible sponsorships. The rationale is that Canada no longer needs unskilled immigrants; nor is Canada prepared to accept the escalating costs of immigration settlement and integration.

- Immigrant needs and aspirations have been misportrayed. Few, if any, want to establish ethnic enclaves or to change Canada to suit their images. Most want to put down roots in their adopted country, contribute to its growth, receive benefits that all Canadians are entitled to, and get the best for their children without necessarily losing that which provides a line of continuity with the past.

- Police-minority relations remain as hotly contested as ever. Breakdowns occur because of cultural misunderstanding and miscommunication. The nature of policing in an unequal society also contributes to the problem. Efforts to bridge the gap between police and minority communities has shown only modest progress.

- Immigration can be used as a force for society-destroying or society-building. The emergence of a global community suggests that immigration will continue to benefit Canadian society.

KEY TERMS

Family Reunification Class
Immigrants
Immigrants and Society-building
Immigration Act 1976
Immigration and Refugee Board

Independent-Class Immigrants
Multicultural Minorities
Point system
Police-Minority Relations
Refugee Claimants
Refugees

Sponsored Refugees
Visible versus nonvisible minorities

REVIEW QUESTIONS

1) Briefly review the trends and premises underlying immigration policies in the past and at present.

2) Discuss the benefits and drawbacks of increased immigration to Canada.

3) Briefly describe the changing nature of Canada's demographic composition.

4) Compare and contrast the aspirations of multicultural minorities in terms of needs and goals?

5) Indicate why the problems associated with police-minority relations are inherent in modern Canadian urban contexts? What if anything can be done about the looming crisis?

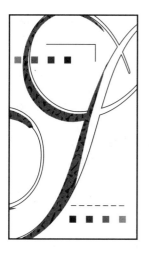

PART 3

MULTICULTURALISM
AND
SOCIETY-BUILDING

The upsurge of racial pride and ethnic affiliation has been widely documented in Canada (Reitz 1980; Richmond 1988; Herberg 1989) and elsewhere (Glazer and Moynihan 1975; Spoonley et al. 1991). Central authorities have responded to this unprecedented surge in a variety of ways, ranging from indifference and rejection on the one hand, to its acceptance and promotion as a potential society-building asset on the other. Countries such as Australia (Vasta 1993; Goot 1993; Adelman et al. 1994) and New Zealand (Pearson 1991;1993) have also implemented strategies to address (a) the influx of immigrants, (b) the popularity of ethnicity, (c) the tenacity of racism, and (d) and ascendancy of nationalist aboriginal movements. Traditional initiatives related to assimilation or segregation are losing their moral authority for managing diversity. Race and ethnic relations have been recast instead within the framework of multicultural policies and practices as governments and minorities alike struggle for equality, extension of human rights, recognition of culture, and access to scarce resources (Pearson 1993; Fleras and Elliott 1992).

Of those societies at the forefront of managing diversity, few can match Canada's pace-setting properties. Canada is widely admired for its commitment to multi-culturalism as a bedrock for the management of race and ethnic relations. Under the banner of multiculturalism, this country has implemented a bold and largely unprecedented strategy to secure a society, both united and diverse. Official multi-culturalism has served admirably as a conflict resolution device for defusing majority-minority conflict. Its role as a blueprint provides Canadians with a map for sorting out issues as varied as cultural retention and social equality on the one hand, with that of societal integration and national unity on the other. Entrenchment at constitutional and statutory levels has also contributed toward our collective sense of who we are as a society. To be sure, Canadians are not nearly as multi-cultural as our collective pride would imply; in some ways we are less diversity-minded than exponents of the American melting pot (Reitz and Breton 1994). Still, the promotion of multiculturalism has propelled a reconstruction of Canadian society in ways that have evoked international acclaim and global envy.

ESTABLISHING BOUNDARIES

The concept of multiculturalism has an uncanny ability to mean different things to different people. Multiculturalism may strike the casual observer as an empty category in which many meanings can be tossed around without much fear of contradiction or consistency. Such flexibility can pose problems of consensus or debate; it may also endow multiculturalism with the resiliency it needs to adapt and evolve. A cursory overview of cross-national initiatives reveal recurrent themes in the multicultural management of diversity. One or more of the following objectives is evident (Hudson 1987):

• to harmonize group relations through intercultural exchanges;
• to eliminate discrimination, both personal and systemic;
• to reduce minority disadvantage at social and economic levels;
• to expand minority opportunities through institutional participation;
• to assist individuals in preserving their cultural identities;
• to (re)educate the public about the virtues of tolerance and cultural diversity;
• to foster a transformation of the social world.

It should be obvious that multiculturalism encompasses a process of social change that entails a multitude of subprocesses and interrelated dimensions — all under a single umbrella term. Multiculturalism is linked with the goals of cultural identity, social justice, citizenship, national unity, societal integration, and equality as a basis for reconstructing society (see Goot 1993). As a social movement, multiculturalism has the potential to provide an alternative way of viewing the world, thinking about society, experiencing reality, and relating to diversity. It also provides an official framework for the reconstruction of majority-minority relations, with an eye toward mutual accommodation and coexistence. This revised and more inclusive relationship represents a significant departure from the past when philosphies of assimilation, integration, or segregation prevailed — to the detriment of minority survival.

But multiculturalism as an official doctrine remains vulnerable to criticism (Goldberg 1994). Debates over multiculturalism have unmasked a number of political or economic agendas, many of which may compromise minority concerns and aspirations. Ambiguity and conflict are likely to prevail in these pluralist contexts, as both political and minority sectors apply different spins to multiculturalism by improvising self-serving lines of action. The downside of multiculturalism may include the following consequences or motives:

- imposing social control;
- cultivating social cleavages;
- encouraging ethnic conflicts;
- appeasing minorities;
- reinforcing the status quo;
- enhancing symbols rather than substance;
- entrenching inequality;
- fomenting racism;
- dismembering a country.

The charges against multiculturalism are as compelling as arguments in its favour. That raises a key theme in this section: To what extent does multiculturalism contribute to or detract from society-building, and how do we weigh the evidence for one position rather than another?

Section Overview

This final section deals with the concept of multiculturalism as a society-building strategy for accommodating the challenges of diversity. The policy context of multiculturalism provides a conceptual framework for discussion and analysis: What is official multiculturalism; how did it originate as a policy and why does it continue to exist; how is it manifest; what is its impact on unequal relations; and what are its implications for Canadian society. Multiculturalism is analyzed from different viewpoints — in part as a specific government policy in response to political and demographic changes; in other part as a resource for shoring up political and minority interests. The relationship of multiculturalism to society is paramount. Multiculturalism is acknowledged as a bold yet ambiguous social experiment in the management of race and ethnic relations along pluralist lines. Multicultural initiatives are shown to have transformed the diversity agenda in ways both innovative and integrative, yet fractious and controversial. The extent to which multiculturalism enhances the transformation of Canada along pluralist lines completes the analysis.

The first chapter in this section, Chapter 10, examines official multiculturalism as a compelling if imperfect strategy for the management of race and ethnic relations. Interest will focus initially on conceptual issues related to policy, perspectives, problems, reactions, and prospects for accommodating diversity in Canada. Chapter 11 will emphasize the practice of multiculturalism in terms of putting diversity to work at institutional levels. Multicultural principles do not necessarily translate into practice because of barriers created by institutional structures and individual mindsets. Gaps in the management of diversity at institutional levels, including the police, the media, or education, not only say a lot about who we are as Canadians, but failure to address these omissions may detract from the vitality and future survival of Canada.

CHAPTER 10

MULTICULTURALISM IN CANADA

INTRODUCTION

People overseas are intrigued by two dimensions of Canada. First, some ask, how can Canada maintain its indepedence and integrity despite proximity to the world's most powerful economic and military machine? That Canadians have retained their distinctiveness and autonomy under the shadows of this colossus, yet managed to secure an enviable standard of living, is a testimonial to the resiliency and tenacity of its people. Second, some ask, how can Canada remain united and prosperous when confronted by such daunting levels of diversity. For example, English-speaking Canadians seem to be perpetually embroiled with the Québécois over language issues; aboriginal assertiveness has culminated with violence at Oka; and Canada accepts thousands of immigrants and refugees with radically different cultures. Responses to these questions are diverse and complex, but surely the term "multiculturalism" must be factored into most answers.

Canada represents one of several democratic societies that has taken advantage of diversity as a basis for national identity and society-building. Multiculturalism since 1971 has served as a formal means for defining government policy and programs at federal and provincial levels. Originating in part to ensure social harmony among competing forces, in other part to forge virtue from necessity (Palmer 1975; Hawkins 1975; Burnet and Palmer 1988), multiculturalism has been perpetuated for a variety of political and economic considerations related to state functions. A combination of demographic and political upheavals in recent years have not only defined the government's multicultural agenda, but the cumulative effect of these changes has also altered Canadian society-building in a direction scarcely conceivable even a generation ago.

This chapter will deal with multiculturalism in terms of policy, perspectives, problems, and prospects. The chapter will focus on the politics of multiculturalism as a strategic device for the management of Canada's racial and ethnic diversity. Primary attention will aim at official multiculturalism in terms of its relationship with a changing and diverse society. The first part of the chapter provides a working definition of multiculturalism. This is followed by a look at its general properties and characteristics, with special attention devoted to multiculturalism at different levels of meaning, including fact, ideology, policy, and practice (see Kallen 1982; Fleras and Desroches 1986; Fleras and Elliott 1992). Failure to separate these different levels of multicultural discourse has generated confusion and back-lash. Special attention is aimed at official multiculturalism as official government pol-icy; its origins and evolutionary development from a focus on culture to that of equality and citizenship; and its role as a widely acclaimed and renewable resource in promoting both political and minority interests. Multiculturalism is hardly im-mune to criticism; nevertheless, a reassessment of this criticism provides an op-portunity to debunk many of the myths that hobble its effectiveness or acceptance. A sense of balance is required here: Multiculturalism is neither the root of all evil nor the source of all solutions to Canada's problems, but a social experiment that straddles a position somewhere in between the poles of bad and good. The chap-ter concludes with an extended case study that explores a perennial challenge in a multicultural society: that is, the question of where to draw the line between ac-ceptance or rejection.

DEFINING MULTICULTURALISM

Multiculturalism continues to elude any simple and straightforward definition. Such an admission may strike the reader as unusual, even paradoxical, given the profile of multiculturalism in Canada (and more recently the United States). Part of the problem is related to the definitional process itself: Should a definition em-phasize what a thing or process looks like (structure) or what it should do (func-tion) or what it really does (process). Another part of the problem reflects failure to make an analytical distinction between multiculturalism as a "thing" or as a "process" or as a "condition." Inconsistent application of the term to a variety of sit-uations and contexts only adds to definitional woes.

Many like to define multiculturalism around its promotional qualities. That is, multiculturalism is equated with promoting ethnic diversity or traditional cul-tures. A commitment to acceptance and mutual coexistence is critical to most of these definitions. But any definition that ignores the political dimensions of an unequal context is insufficient. Multiculturalism is inseparable from issues related to un-equal power relations, and its role in supporting or challenging these inequities cannot be ignored. Any definition that excludes a dynamic and contested compo-nent is also questionable. Too static an interpretation of multiculturalism such as that conveyed by "mosaic" or "quilt" or "smorgasbord" cannot capture what is forma-tive and evolving. The dynamism and clamour attending contemporary multicul-turalism is aptly captured by Amyn B. Sajoo (1994:17) who writes:

> Ours is more like an orchestral symphony, complex and energetic in its flow. If the result sometimes strains harmony, blame it on tough rehearsals by an ambitious if relatively young orchestra.

At its broadest, multiculturalism can be defined as a process for accommodating diversity. The accommodation of diversity is concerned with improving the relational status of racial and ethnic minorities in the same way that the principles of assim-ilation and or segregation offered competing frameworks for the management of race and ethnic relations. More specifically, multiculturalism consists of an official doctrine, along with a corresponding set of policies and practices, for promoting the related goals of cultural differences, social equality, societal integration and national unity. A definition by V. Seymour Wilson (1993:654) comes closest to what we are saying:

> [Multiculturalism] is a doctrine that provides a *political framework* for the official promotion of *social inequality* and *cultural differences* as an integral component of the social order (emphasis in the original).

Several points require clarification: Multiculturalism is not about promoting minorities or ethnocultural differences. Multiculturalism is concerned instead with creating a political climate in which diversity is incorporated as a legitimate and equal component of society, without sacrificing the interconnectedness of the parts that hold a society together. Diversity is endorsed to the extent that it allows individuals to identify with the cultural tradition of their choice, provided this affilation does not violate human rights or laws of the land. These parameters are implicit in our definition of multiculturalism, and will be discussed later.

DISCOURSE ON MULTICULTURALISM

How would you respond to the question:

"Is Canada a multicultural society?"

   (a) Yes _____

   (b) No _____

   (c) It Depends _____

We believe the last response (c) provides the kind of answer most useful for analysis. The open-endedness of this response implies the possibility of different meanings associated with multiculturalism. **Multiculturalism** can be interpreted at the level of (a) **empirical fact**, (b) an **ideology** with a corresponding set of ideas and ideals, (c) an explicit government policy and programs, and (d) a **process** for promoting political and minority interests (see Table 10.1). Failure to separate these different levels of meaning invariably leads to misunderstanding.

Multiculturalism as Fact

As fact, multiculturalism makes an empirical statement about "what is." It may be stating the obvious but the obvious is sometimes overlooked for precisely that reason: nearly all countries are composed of race and ethnic groups whose identities are stoutly defended. Many of these groups wish to remain culturally distinct, yet are equally anxious to enjoy the benefits of full societal involvement. Employed in the descriptive sense of the term, few would dispute the notion of Canada as a multi — cultural society. The existence of aboriginal, charter, and multicultural

TABLE 10.1   Levels of Interpretation of Multiculturalism

Multiculturalism as Fact	Multiculturalism as Ideology	Multiculturalism as Policy	Multiculturalism as Process
Empirical description of ethnic reality in Canada	Prescriptive statement of what ought to be — a set of ideas and ideals that extol the virtues of tolerance and diversity	Accommodation diversity through explicit state initiatives: (a) celebrating differences (1971-), (b) managing diversity (1981-), and (c) citizenship and belonging (1991-)	Manipulation by political sectors (multiculturalism means business) and minority sectors (culture + equality)

minorities attests to this sociological fact (Elliott 1983). Adding to this variety are over one hundred culturally different ethnic groups whose presence can no longer be ignored. Recent immigration patterns suggest Canada will continue to be multicultural in outlook, and increasingly multiracial in terms of population composition. (See Chapter 9, "Multicultural Minorities.")

Multiculturalism as Ideology

Unlike its descriptive counterpart outlined above, multiculturalism as an ideology refers to a normative statement of "what ought to be." It prescribes a preferred course of thought or action with respect to how a society should be organized. This prescriptive state of affairs is modelled after liberal virtues of freedom, tolerance, and respect for individual differences.

Several assumptions underly a multicultural ideology. First and foremost is a belief that minority cultures can constitute living and lived-in realities that impart meaning and security to adherents at times of stress or social change. Cultural differences are not disparaged as incompatible with national goals, but endorsed as integral components of a national mosaic, a reflection of the Canadian ideal, and a source of enrichment and strength. Towards that end, multiculturalism points to a utopian state of affairs whereby the integration of minority differences create a unique but unified whole as people become aware of each other's differences.

Second, multiculturalism does not downgrade diversity as contrary to the goals of national unity or socioeconomic progress. Ethnocultural affiliation does not imply an element of mental inferiority, stubbornness, or lack of patriotism. Rather these differences can be woven into a workable national fabric with a common set of overarching values ("unity-within-diversity"). Universalizing the right to a particular identity acknowledges that people are more than individuals, but social beings whose well-being depends on a shared identity within the cultural framework of an ethnocultural group (see Angus 1995). They are allowed the right to voluntarily affiliate with the ethnocultural tradition of their choice without fear of penalty as long this affiliation does not violate laws or interfere with the rights of others.

Multiculturalism as a set of ideas and ideals is employed somewhat differently in Canada than in the USA. Canadian usage of the term generally implies a folding of cultural differences into the whole without loss of distinctiveness among the constituent units. The term multiculturalism in the USA is often employed as a code for "who controls American national culture?" Identity politics and radical social change are part of this tug of war, involving minority demands for separate yet equal recognition of cultural differences within academic or cultural institutions (Turner 1994). Efforts to collectively empower all disempowered identities challenge the cultural hegemony of the Eurocentric and androcentric dominant sector. The objective is to understand the world from diverse perspectives in hopes of forging a more inclusive and democratic common cultural base. These ideals are not altogether absent from the Canadian context but rarely match the highly political nature of American multiculturalism.

Third, a multicultural ideal builds upon the principles of cultural relativism. Multiculturalism foster an open-minded philosophy firmly grounded on the principles of tolerance and mutual respect. This doctrine holds that all cultural practices are relative to a particular time and place. No cultural lifestyle is regarded as superior to another. If anything, cultural relativism reinforces the equality of customs when examined in their historical and environmental context. That is not to say that everything *is* equality good; nor is anyone espousing the philosophy that "anything goes." Rather, for purposes of analysis or understanding, diversity must be treated *as if* it were an equally valid expression of the human experience. Secure in the knowledge of *thoughtful relativism*, a commitment to multiculturalism reflects the premise that those confident in their cultural background will concede a similar tolerance to others (Berry et al. 1977).

In short, attainment of multicultural ideals is contingent on (a) enhancing individual self-esteem through strong cultural identification, (b) eliminating prejudice and racism through sensitivity to others, and (c) fostering improved intercultural exchanges through increased empathy and understanding. As Robert Hughes writes in his otherwise scathing indictment of multiculturalism (*The Culture of Complaint* 1994):

> [The premise of multiculturalism is] that people with different roots can co-exist, that they can learn to read the image banks of others, and they can and should look across the frontiers of race, gender, language, and age without prejudice or illusion... It proposes — modestly enough — that some of the most interesting things in history and culture happen at the interface between cultures.

There is no guarantee of satisfactorily solving that perennial conundrum of "us" versus "them." But multicultural ideals are aimed at negotiating such a relationship by emphasizing our commonality and shared values, not only our differences.

Multiculturalism as Policy

In terms of policy, multiculturalism consists of specific government initiatives to transform multicultural ideals into practice. A new symbolic order is constructed under multicultural policies, along with a corresponding mythology that helps to paper over inconsistencies at odds with present realities (Breton 1984; Stasiulis 1988; Helly 1993). Multiculturalism as a policy can also consist of a broader framework that justifies the design and implementation of diversity-driven programs without inciting public concern over the possibility of creeping socialism or cultural apartheid.

Policy considerations lie at the core of official multiculturalism. Governments throughout the world have embarked on strategies for controlling immigration, managing ethnic relations, and integrating ethnocultural minorities into the mainstream. Multiculturalism represents but one of the policy options open to central authorities for coping with diversity. Other devices such as assimilation or integration have been tried, but found inadequate in balancing societal needs with those of diversity. A multicultural arrangement recognizes the reality of cultural diversity and validates its legitimacy at cultural, political, economic, and social levels. Multiculturalism also concedes the possibility of different types of belonging. Individuals are expected to display primary affiliation as citizens of the state: They also have the option of secondary identification with the cultural tradition of their choice, with no inconsistency envisioned by this dual identity as long as priorities are kept intact. Some people are dismissive of government policies as "symbolic" or superficial. Others recognize that conferral of official legitimacy bolsters the status of minorities by including them in the national agenda while providing a platform to articulate grievances and demand entitlements (Webber 1994). The next box, Dealing With Diversity, explores the relationship between the state and diversity as mediated by official multiculturalism.

INSIGHT

Dealing with Diversity: Perspectives from the State

There are different ways of looking at multiculturalism. Our preference rests with the genesis, development, and impact of multiculturalism as official policy as it pertains to social equality, cultural retention, societal integration, and national unity (see also Dorais et al. 1994). This focus on multiculturalism as a series of government initiatives for managing diversity invariably draws us into the politics of social control.

Debates about managing diversity invariably raise questions about the role of the state in spearheading initiatives. Though extremely complex in formulation, two theories appear to have monopolized perspectives on state-minority relations (Simmons and Keohane 1992; Wolfe 1989). A Marxist analysis situates the state within the framework of a capitalist economy (Panitch 1977). Capitalist systems are driven to fulfill two basic, sometimes contradictory functions (Offe 1984). First, they must create conditions necessary for capital formation, namely, transport infrastructure and so on. Second, a social climate conducive to accumulation must be fostered — in part by ameliorating the social costs of private production. These functions serve to facilitate ruling class interests with respect to wealth accumulation and social reproduction. State policies pertaining to multiculturalism are closely linked with the need for social control in a profit-oriented society (Simmons and Keohane 1992).

A second interpretation is more consistent with Weberian analysis in acknowledging power, wealth, and status as social catalysts. The state is defined as a relatively independent actor (or at least must be perceived as reasonably neutral), with considerable scope for pursuing policy interests — albeit within the constraints imposed by the forces of production (Miliband 1973; Poulantzas 1975). Policies for managing diversity arise from the interplay of varying forces, rather than from mechanical responses to economic pressures. The state actively seeks to reinforce its presence in minority policy fields because of its ongoing quest for legitimacy and control in the face of opposition, diversity, and change (Simmons and Keohane 1992). Even with a self-serving agenda, however, state policy continues to be distorted by the imperatives and practices of a capitalist economy (Offe and Ronge 1982).

Other issues are equally salient in sorting out state-minority relations. The policy process is complicated by high levels of internal diversity and interdepartmental conflict. Most typically this entails competition between ministries, between subgroups within government and administration, and between politicians and bureaucracy with each possessing distinct world views regarding efficiency, constraints, and long term objectives (Hummel 1987; Fleras 1989). State policies for accommodating diversity must also incorporate demands from a host of competing groups and opposing ideologies. Competition for supremacy in the policy arena transforms policy into a contested terrain between unequally endowed and diverse sectors, each jockeying to impose its definition of the situation on others. Managing diversity for the state becomes an exercise in dealing with a broad but conflicting spectrum of demands without losing control of its internal agenda. The state is expected to defuse these crises and challenges to its legitimate authority, as well as exert control over the outcomes by silencing opposition, discrediting critics, deflecting criticism, and preempting the threat of confrontation as much as possible (Habermas 1976; Fleras and Elliott 1991).

Despite contradictions and disagreements, the state tends to pursue three diffuse interests: economic security for itself and society at large; a rational-bureaucratic agenda (Weber 1947); and legitimacy in the face of growing competition and conflict. The concept of legitimacy is especially pressing. The state may be powerful in its capacity to set agendas and fix outer limits of debate, yet its hegemony is never secure in defending its "turf" against intruders. Even with power and resources at its disposal, the state has few options except to exercise eternal vigilance in neutralizing any potential threat to its credibility (Habermas 1976). Interests groups are willing and able to confront the state in concerted attempts to undermine legitimacy or to wrench concessions from it, and in recent years have openly contested the distribution of power and resources. Not unexpectedly, what passes for a state policy position is often a balancing act of last resort involving a workable accommodation through negotiation, consultation, and compromise (Simmons and Keohane 1992).

The pursuit of legitimacy and control are integral to state efforts to manage diversity. The state confronts a notoriously daunting challenge in its quest for legitimacy since proposals for minority-state restructuring are uneasily perched between disparate values and conflicting interests. This dual function of control and legitimacy engages the state in a series of proactive measures as one way of deflecting potential criticism away from itself. It also results in a series of rear guard actions in hopes of shoring up strengths and camouflaging weaknesses. This is especially true of Canada where failed constitutional reforms have left the state especially vulnerable to second guessing, threats, and blackmail. State concessions to the three major forces must address the extenuating circumstances of a post Meech Lake/Charlottetown constitutional crisis (Simmons and Keohane 1992). The inclination to build bridges and appease potentially troublesome constituents is preferred over brooking further opposition or dealing wtih outright confrontations. It is within this context of multiculturalism as a formal device in defense of state interests that rivets our attention.

Folkloric Multiculturalism ("Celebrating Differences") (1971–)

The policy of multiculturalism has undergone many changes since inception in 1971. An initial focus on "celebrating differences" as a means of eradicating prejudice and securing acceptance was superseded by an emphasis on "accommodating diversity" through institutional accommodation and removal of discriminatory barriers. The ground has again shifted in recent years to concerns about citizenship and belonging. For the sake of simplicity these shifts can be partitioned into three stages, including **folkloric** , **institutional**, and **civic multiculturalism** — keeping in mind that overlap and juxtaposition are the rule rather than exception.

Pre-Second World War governments in Canada did not address the issue of cultural diversity in any systematic fashion. Central policy structures overlooked ethnic heterogeneity as inimical to broader interests. To be sure, religious and cultural differences were tolerated as private matters, but deemed divisive or dangerous when foisted on the public. Governments instead relied on time-honoured strategies that embraced the virtues of assimilation as essential for national unity and prosperity. Expressions of assimilation reflected a commitment either to Anglo-Canadian conformity or to a melting pot (or "fusion") in the American sense of the term (Hudson 1987). Anything that departed from the standards of God, King, and Empire was contemptuously dismissed as incompatible with national identity or loyalty to the Dominion.

Canada's self-image remained steadfastly rooted in Anglo-American ideals until mid-century. National consensus, however, began to crumble with the subsequent influx of immigrants from Europe and later from Third World countries (Hawkins 1989; also Castles et al. 1988). If only to assist in the integration of immigrants and to foster community harmony, successive governments sought to modify the existing concept of Canada in line with new demographic realities. These changes forced a rethinking of Canada's character and the place of the "other ethnics" in the evolving configuration of Canadian society. Pressure to create a new symbolic order was further heightened by the forces of Québécois nationalism in the aftermath of the Quiet Revolution (Breton 1989). The multicultural nod to ethnic minorities was endorsed as a counterbalance to an excessively dualistic view of Canada (Webber 1994).

A shift in priorities occurred with publication of the Report of the Royal Commission on Bilingualism and Biculturalism in 1969. Various ethnic minority groups, especially the Ukrainian and German lobbies, had argued strenuously that their language and culture were vital and empowering components of the Canadian mosaic rather than inconsistent with national goals (Wilson 1993). A compromise solution was eventually struck to take "into account the contribution made by the other ethnic groups to the cultural enrichment of Canada" (see Jaworsky 1979). A policy of multiculturalism within a bilingual framework was articulated by the Liberal government when Prime Minister Pierre Elliott Trudeau rose in Parliament and declared on October 8th 1971:

> There cannot be one cultural policy for Canadians of British or French origins, another for the originals, and yet a third for all others. For although there are two official languages, there is no official culture. Nor does any cultural group take precedence over another.... We are free to be ourselves. But this cannot be left to chance... It is the policy of this government to eliminate any such danger and to safeguard this freedom.

This all-party agreement sought to assist those ethnic minorities who were relatively new to Canada by integrating them into the mainstream of Canadian national life (Parel 1992). In the government's own words, multiculturalism would "strengthen the solidarity of the Canadian people by enabling all Canadians to participate fully and without discrimination in defining and building the nation's future." Four major principles prevailed in this commitment (MacLeod 1983):

- *Equality of status;* Canada does not have an official culture, but all cultures including French and English are equal to each other.
- *Canadian identity;* diversity lies at the heart of Canadian identity.
- *Personal choice;* the ability to choose lifestyles and cultural traits is a positive factor in society.
- *Protection of individual rights;* no discrimination is allowed that interferes with equality and full participation.

Government initiatives would aim to (a) assist those cultural groups which have demonstrated a desire and effort to continue to develop, a capacity to grow and contribute to Canada, as well as a clear need for assistance; (b) assist the members of all cultural groups to overcome cultural barriers to full participation in Canadian society; (c) promote creative encounters and interchange among all Canadian cultural groups in the interests of national unity; and (d) assist immigrants to acquire at least one of Canada's official languages in order to become full participants in Canadian society. A folkloric dimension was particularly noticeable: An Anglo-French bias had infiltrated traditional support of arts and culture, and multiculturalism would be a corrective measure for alternative support outside existing agencies (Li 1994).

Funds were also set aside for specific initiatives in securing language and culture, cultural sharing, official language learning, and removal of cultural barriers to equality (Stasiulis 1993). A multicultural directorate within the Department of

Secretary of State was instituted in 1972 for the promotion of multicultural ideals, social integration, and racial harmony (Report, "Equality Now," 1984). Efforts were directed at consolidating human rights, strengthening Canadian identity, preventing discrimination, fostering citizenship involvement, reinforcing national unity, and promoting cultural diversity. To assist federal authorities, the Canadian Consultative Council on Multiculturalism was established in 1973. The Council was later restructured and renamed Canadian Ethnocultural Council in 1983 in hopes of improving its advisory, research, and monitoring capacities. Later developments included the creation of a Ministry of Multiculturalism to monitor government departments. A federal Department of Multiculturalism and Citizenship was established in 1991 with passage of the **1988 Multiculturalism Act**, but subsequently scrapped in 1993. Currently federal multiculturalism stands as one of many portfolios (including Parks and Amateur Sport) within the superministry of Canadian Heritage.

Most Canadian provinces have formally endorsed the principles of multiculturalism as a guideline for government-minority relations. Saskatchewan was the first province to become officially multicultural when it established its Multicultural Council and Multicultural Directorate in 1974. Quebec is also committed to a nonfederal variation of multiculturalism, known as "interculturalism" with its objective the integration of allophones into French language and culture as revealed by this passage:

> ... *Désireux que toutes communautés culturelles et les nations autochtones du Québec puissant continuer de s'épanouir et contribuer pleinement a l'édification et au progrès d'une société regnant paix et harmonie.* (in translation) All cultural communities and aboriginal nations in Quebec should be able to continue to flourish and fully contribute to the building and progress of a society in which peace and harmony reign. (Robert Bourassa et al. 1986).

Federal multiculturalism has been rejected by Quebec as a calculated plot to transform a founding people into another folkloric ethnic minority. Under interculturalism, however, French is the official language and culture, with diversity tolerated and accepted only to this point (Talbani 1994). The promotion of this "diversity within unity" theme includes the learning of French as the language of communication; the right of minorities to full and equal institutional participation; and creation of a pluralistic society in which cultural minorities are integrated as full-fledged Québécois (Helly 1993). The priority of French makes Quebec more like most countries in not claiming to be neutral with respect to the dominant language and culture, but active in their defence and support of one ideal (Walser 1992).

The government of Ontario is equally committed to multiculturalism. A major element of this commitment is the recognition of all citizens, regardless of racial or religious background, as equal before the law with full political rights and equal access to government services. Procedures and tribunals were established at the provincial level to facilitate attainment of multicultural objectives. The Ontario Human Rights Commission, for example, was created to promote multicultural understanding in compliance with the Ontario Human Rights Code. Part of its mandate includes an obligation to develop and conduct programs of public information and education; to review statutes in conflict with the Code; to inquire into incidents leading to racial conflict or discrimination; and to take appropriate steps to alleviate sources of interethnic tension. All important government announcements and advertisements are conveyed through existing ethnic presses to ensure equality of opportunity. Thus, like their federal counterparts, the Ontario government has recognized the right of individuals to retain their cultural tradition if they so choose without sacrificing access to social and economic equality.

Institutional Multiculturalism (1981-)

Federal multiculturalism had experienced a discernible shift in focus by the early 1980s. Political discourse evolved from a focus on cultural preservation to concerns about social incorporation and economic equality. Changes in Canada's immigration and demographic patterns contributed to this rethinking (Webber 1994). Pre-1970s immigrants shared with their hosts a broad commitment to European ethos; by contrast, the legacy of cultural assimilation could not erase the prejudice and discrimination associated with the sometimes incompatible differences of the Third World immigrants (Sajoo 1994). An institutionally-based multiculturalism shed its folkloric roots to accommodate this demographic revolution. The principles of equality and participation prevailed under institutional multiculturalism, with a corresponding commitment to managing diversity through anti-racism, removal of discriminatory (rather than prejudicial) barriers, and institutional accommodation.

Subsequent developments further heightened the multicultural profile. The role of multiculturalism in shaping Canadian life through litigation was enhanced following its emergence as a principle of interpretation in the 1982 Charter of Rights (Parel 1992). Its prominence was further advanced when Canada became the first country to formally endow multiculturalism with legal authority. The Multiculturalism Act in 1988 sought to promote cultures, reduce discrimination, and accelerate institutional accommodation through the "preservation and enhancement of Canadian multiculturalism." It also specified the right of individuals to identify with the cultural heritage of their choice, yet retain equal access to institutional involvement. The principle of institutional accommodation proved pivotal. The Act obligated federal institutions to accommodate diversity in a manner consistent with Canada's multicultural character.

The government has parlayed its principles into hard cash. Funds totalling $192 million for five years were set aside to (a) promote harmonious race relations, (b) enhance cross-cultural understanding, (c) preserve heritage languages and cultures, (d) ensure full and equal participation of ethnic minorities, and (e) foster cross-government commitment for all federal institutions (News Release, Multiculturalism, 30 May 1988). Government funds are no longer absorbed by the 3 "D"s (diet, dance, or dress) (Knowles 1992). For the 1993/94 fiscal year, grants from federal multiculturalism totalled $25.5 million, with $13.3 million earmarked for community support and participation (to help social services access new Canadians), another $6.5 million for public education and anti-racism, and $5.5 million to heritage cultures and languages (Thompson 1994).

Passage of the Multiculturalism Act did not occur without acrimony or incident (Parel 1992); yet its significance cannot be underestimated. The Act rationalized government objectives by reaffirming within a statutory framework what existed previously as de facto policy. It also embued multiculturalism with the cloak of legal authority and the weight of Canadian law. Official endorsement made multiculturalism less vulnerable to political party politics or electoral whims (Report, Multiculturalism, 1987). It has also endowed multiculturalism with the legitimacy to co-exist in harmony with (and equal to) the principle of bilingualism in Canada. Finally, multiculturalism is woven into the Canadian Charter of Human Rights and Freedoms which came into effect in April of 1985 (see Beckton 1987). Its emergence as a tool of interpretation at the highest levels of national decision making reinforces a fundamental multicultural right in Canadian society — that is, the right to be different (culture) as well as the right to be the same (equality).

Civic Multiculturalism (1991 –)

Multiculturalism continues to attract adherents for celebrating differences. Its commitment to managing diversity is no less important, and is manifest in the mainstreaming of key institutions to ensure minority access, representation, and equitable treatment. Equally evident is a trend toward twinning multiculturalism with citizenship, a relationship that was consummated during the short-lived arrangement under the Department of Multiculturalism and Citizenship. Even the current arrangement aligns Multiculturalism with the Citizenship and Canadian Identity portfolio of Canada Heritage. Civic multiculturalism is oriented toward society-building through citizenship (See also Chapter 12 for a closer examination of citizenship). Its scope is aimed at society at large rather than at racial or ethnic minorities only. Fostering a sense of belonging and a shared sense of Canadian identity is pivotal to paving the way toward participation and inclusion of all Canadians. Table 10.2 compares and contrasts the different dimensions of Canada's multiculturalism.

Multiculturalism as Process

A raft of platitudes about celebrating and sharing cannot disguise the pragmatic components of multiculturalism. Multiculturalism as a process refers to its manipulation by both political and ethnic sectors to promote respective goals and ambitions. Its use as a resource transforms multiculturalism into a vehicle for the attainment of profit and advantage. This focus on multiculturalism as a process will enable us to examine its role as a renewable resource in the ongoing reconstruction of Canadian society. We are reminded that the expression "mosaic" is catchy but unhelpful if it reinforces the view of cultures as fixed in space and sep-

TABLE 10.2   Styles of Multiculturalism

	Folkloric Multiculturalism (1970s)	Institutional Multiculturalism (1980s)	Civic Multiculturalism (1990s)
Focus	Celebrating Differences	Managing Diversity	Society-Building
Frame of Reference	Culture	Structure	Society
Mandate	Ethnicity	Race Relations	Citizenship
Magnitude	Individual Adjustment	Institutional Accommodation	Participation/ Membership
Problem Source	Prejudice	Systemic Discrimination	Exclusion
Problem Solution	Cultural Sensitivity	Employment Equity	Inclusion
Key Metapnhor	"Mosaic"	"Kaleidoscope"	"Belonging"

arated by grouting (Gates Jr. 1994). It also serves to remind us that multiculturalism is "first and foremost a political program with very defined political aims along with the means to accomplish these aims" (Peter 1978).

Politics and Politicking

If politics is the process of conflict resolution, (Van Loon and Whittington 1981), then multiculturalism is indeed political because of its inseparability from government management of minority relations. Politicians and bureaucrats look upon multiculturalism as a resource with economic or political potential to be exploited at national or international levels for practical gain. Multiculturalism originated from the customary interplay of good intentions and political opportunism (Gwyn 1994). It sought to shore up electoral strength in urban Ontario, to counterbalance Western resentment over perceived favouritism toward the Québécois, and to preempt the encroachment of American cultural values (Burnet and Palmer 1988). It sprang from a political responsibility to encourage public sensitivity to new Canadians as well as to ease the cultural shocks of integration and participation. It hoped to ensconce a new founding myth of Canada as land of opportunity and equality for all Canadians (from ethnic hierarchy to national mosaic) that would unite all Canadians at a time of political turmoil, yet do so without any fundamental redistribution of power (Helly 1993). The governing apparatus of the Canadian state also relied on multiculturalism to fulfil a variety of legitimating functions revolving around national unity, economic prosperity, and electoral survival. Such resourcefulness on the part of central authorities bolstered the political dimensions of multiculturalism.

At the simplest level of political endorsement is a belief in ethnic support as relevant for (re-)election. The vast majority of Canada's multicultural minorities are concentrated in major urban centres such as Toronto, Montreal, and Vancouver —

a trend likely to be amplified by future immigration patterns. The growing heterogeneity of Canada's population has compelled all political parties to capture the multicultural vote through promises of increased representation, funding, and affirmative action at federal levels. Response to minority pressure may have led to the passage of the Employment Equity Act in 1986 with its focus on visible minority representation in federally regulated business. Minority pressure may also account in part for continued high levels of immigration into Canada despite a swell of growing concern.

The society-building potential of multiculturalism is widely endorsed by politicians. Federal government policy has increasingly shifted toward a focus on practical concerns, away from the folkloric dimensions of the past. Rather than simply doling out money to ethnocultural organizations or events as was the case, authorities have embraced the principle of multicultural involvement in commercial activities, especially when promoting Canadian exports. Then Prime Minister Brian Mulroney outlined this challenge in a speech at the "Multiculturalism Means Business" conference in 1986 at Toronto when he stated:

We, as a nation, need to grasp the opportunity afforded to us by our multicultural identity to cement our prosperity with trade and investment links the world over and with a renewed entrepreneurial spirit at home... But our multicultural nature gives us an edge in selling to that world... Canadians who have cultural links to other parts of the globe, who have business contacts elsewhere are of the utmost importance to our trade and investment strategy (Report, Secretary of State, 1987).

Multiculturalism is currently promoted as a desirable Canadian export with marketable value in the same way staple products were in the past (Moodley 1983; Crane 1995). By enhancing Canada's sales image and competitive edge in a global economy, multiculturalism is touted as having the potential to harness lucrative trade contracts and penetrate export markets, both at home and abroad (Multiculturalism/Secretary of State 1993). This resource value is succinctly expressed with reference to international linkages and mutually profitable points of contact. Even the key to local and regional markets is focused increasingly on serving the needs of a multicultural population (Stinson 1994).

CASE STUDY

Multiculturalism versus Multinationals: Friend or Foe?

The concept of multiculturalism has evolved into a contemporary concern. At the core of this paradox are competing perspectives on the relevance of diversity for contemporary society-building. Some continue to condone the supremacy of Eurocentric values and institutions, not only as the measure of progress, but also as a standard by which to guide, evaluate, and justify. Others prefer the virtues of a new social and intellectual order, with its rejection of Eurocentrism and acceptance of diversity as morally equivalent and socially valid. Few by now can be surprised by the intensity of these clashes over the primacy of monoculturalism versus multiculturalism. Both positions (and those in between) attract a mix of adherents who, for various reasons, refuse to budge or compromise.

Equally intriguing are debates over the usefulness of multiculturalism in a globalizing economy. The paradox can be rephrased as follows: Can a pluralistic ideology be reconciled with the realities of a world pervaded by multinational corporations? This is not an idle question when applied to Canada. Support for multiculturalism may be dismissed as irrelevant or counterproductive in an intensely competitive environment. Multiculturalism represents an added cost and government intrusion at a time of downsizing and cost-cutting. Nowhere is this more evident than in debates over free trade. Doubts continue to linger over the wisdom of integrating Canada's multiculturalism into the proposed trilateral agreement with Mexico and the United States. In other words, multicultural principles are perceived as incompatible with a multinationally-driven global economy.

To what extent can multiculturalism be folded into multinationalism without dimishing Canada's global stature?

DISCOURSES IN COLLISION

Multiculturalism or multinationals? What could be further opposed than these legendary foes? To one side are the forces of multiculturalism, with their focus on the unique and particular. To the other are the universalizing forces of globalization and multinationalism. Like it or not, Canada is increasingly implicated in an integrated global economic order where competition is fierce, the profit motive reigns supreme, and free markets are the rule. With the collapse of the Soviet Union, the world has become even more compressed into a single comprehensive marketplace — in effect making a shambles of sovereign boundaries and national identities. Multinational companies and stateless corporations are spearheading this transformation of Canada. From the clutches of a predominantly branch-plant economy, both regulated and protected, Canada's current status is that of a link in a vast global productive loop where labour (jobs) and capital (in the form of goods, services, investment, and markets) are under intensive pressure to compete with less costly producers. The net result? Traditional labour and capital are tempted to abandon Canada for the less costly confines of Mexico and southern United States. Not only does this flight imperil Canada's ability to underwrite social programs but the subsequent loss of control over resources and autonomy also inhibits the creation of a multicultural social climate.

On the surface, the concepts of multiculturalism and multinationals appear opposed. In its conventional sense of "celebrating differences," multiculturalism emphasizes the acceptance of diversity in the face of conformist pressures. The post-multicultural sense of "managing diversity" involves the creation of policies and programs for institutional accommodation through removal of discriminatory barriers. Multiculturalism establishes a society in which diversity can flourish as a legitimate component, without sacrificing the interconnectedness at the core of a coherent system. Thus, multiculturalism represents a political compromise that mediates the poles between equality and diversity, in effect "defusing" the full impact of a competitive market economy.

Compare this logic with that behind multinational corporations. Business is rapidly becoming a global affair as reflected in where multinationals decide to locate, how they pursue markets or extract resources, and when they decide to vacate. With far-flung companies for consolidating buying power and negotiating deals, multinationals prefer to conduct business in a culture-free environment — unfettered by government intervention or by the destabilizing intrusion of diversity. They also wish to avoid the costly combination of social programs, national borders, and state sovereignties that, collectively, might interfere with the relatively unimpeded flow of goods and services. In short, the competitive challenges of multinational-driven global economy would appear at odds with the humanistic concerns of multiculturalism. The one acknowledges and supports diversity; the other veers toward uniformity of standardized production and global consumerism.

So much for conventional wisdom, however. This opposition between diversity and uniformity is not always a foregone conclusion. Perfectly sound reasons exist for advancing an alternate thesis, namely, that multiculturalism can coexist — even thrive — under the glob-

ality of multinationals. The opposition between multinationals and multiculturalism is less tenable in an evolving global economy. What has emerged instead is a "functional symbiosis" since neither multiculturalism nor multinationals can survive without the other. Multiculturalism will prosper or perish depending on its capacity to address real needs and evolving concerns. Similarly, world capitalism and multinationals can no more ignore the consumer potential of expanding diversity than it can overlook the bottom line. Put bluntly, the multicultural dimensions of multinational business encourages a reciprocal relationship — by default if not necessarily by design.

MULTICULTURALISM MEANS GLOBAL BUSINESS

The thesis of multinationals and multiculturalism as "partners" is gaining some publicity. An interesting paper by David Rieff in the August (1993) issue of *Harper's* advanced a case for multiculturalism as capitalism's silent partner in a changing and diverse global economy. Erstwhile foes are now forging friendships of convenience. The popularity of multiculturalism in corporate boardrooms around the world is but one indication of this growing diversification of markets, investments, and resources. How is this possible?

First, multiculturalism provides an opening for new areas of consumerism and market penetration (Gates Jr. 1994). Cultural diversity as a consumer resource in its own right is justified under the notion of multicultural marketing. Benetton has graphically shown how ethno-racial sensitivities can be marketed as progressive or chic. African-American symbols such as Kente cloths are now employed by Miller Breweries for boosting sales of malt liquor to targetted consumers. The demographics demand no less. World majorities now comprise around 30 percent of the population in the United States, 9 percent in Canada. The spending power at their disposal has yet to be fully realized. More lucrative still is the vastly untapped markets of Asia. Far too much is at stake for multinationals to ignore this market by failing to address diverse consumer preferences. That much was conceded in a recent Annual Report by Molson's Canada. A single global market that transcends traditional markets no longer exists, according to the company president. What exists instead is a worldwide integration of distinct and diversified markets with local tastes and requirements. Thinking globally, but managing locally, may well emerge as the twenty-first century buzzword.

Second, multiculturalism provides a tool for managing workplace diversity. This commitment is especially striking with the introduction of strategies for participatory management, quality circles, and frontline empowerment. A diverse workforce can improve corporate productivity and company performance if properly harnessed. Creativity may be enhanced by tackling the problem from different perspectives or through alternate solutions. Flexibility can also be bolstered if sufficient time is allocated to surmounting preliminary difficulties or to fostering lines of cooperation.

Third, there is an additional way for welding multiculturalism with multinationalism. The concept of ethnicity and immigration is key here. Contrary to their popular images as insular or backward-looking, ethnic groups across the world embrace the virtues of self-sufficiency, hard work, and solidarity — qualities that are frequently associated with consumer success. These global "tribes" appear conveniently poised to profit from a global economic network because of world-wide business ties and cultural networks. This ethnic advantage has been employed in Canada as a cutting edge for improving its global competitiveness. Under the motto of "multiculturalism means business," multicultural initiatives have aimed at securing external markets (through joint ventures) while enhancing Canada's sales image abroad. The returns are not clear as yet; nevertheless, this mainstreaming of diversity into corporate Canada can only enhance this country's pool of "human capital."

Multiculturalism, in other words, is not an enemy of capitalism, much less a threat to contemporary capitalist offshoots, namely, multinationals or global free-market forces. The new capitalism thrives on diversity in its unremitting search for profitable sites of production or investment. Anything that can enhance its capacity to penetrate largely untapped markets at home and abroad will be coopted without much concern for ideological purity. Even official multiculturalism is not necessarily a problem, provided these initiatives foster a political environment conducive to hefty returns. By exploring new areas of consumerism, including the consumption of culture, multinationals rely on multiculturalism as the thin edge of the wedge for market entry and profit making.

CAPITALIZING ON DIVERSITY

Talk about multiculturalism within the confines of a single society is increasingly obsolete. Knowledge of events in Canada can only make sense within the global context of free market economies, trading blocs, and multinationals. The world is being pushed together by the globalizing forces of multinationals; at the same time it is being pulled apart by nationalist demands for autonomy and self-determination. Canada has not been spared this turmoil. The interplay of various demographic, social, and political changes has contributed to a rethinking of rules that have loosened Canada's conventional moorings and set it adrift in a sea of uncertainty.

Such a perspective points to multiculturalism as an innovative if somewhat flawed political experiment for social progress. It also reinforces the salience of multiculturalism in economic terms. Canada's "world majorities" are increasingly part of the economic mainstream, as argued recently by Raymond Chan, federal minister for Asia Pacific Rim; they also are conducting Canada's business in a language other than French or English. Recognition of this reality must be interpreted against the backdrop of global multinational order where the primacy of an isolated sovereign state with non-porous borders and distinct identities is under seige. Advancements in transportation and the telecommunications superhighway have seen to that. No less clear is the repackaging of the planet into a "village" marketplace of diverse vendors and buyers. This globalization of economies has ushered in a multiculturalism of the market, with its anchor in diversity-driven consumerism and a commercial mosaic.

The restructuring of Canada along global as well as plural lines is fascinating in its own right. The fact that capitalism has taken a potential disadvantage (that is, multiculturalism) and transformed it into an advantage attests to the resilience of the market economy as an adaptive force. The fact that multiculturalism can thrive within the confines of multinationally-driven globalism is no less remarkable. The fact that multinationalism and multiculturalism are not necessarily mutually exclusive, even if they have different reasons for collusion, is an encouraging sign for Canada's future as a distinct but prosperous society.

SOURCES: Krotkin 1992 as reviewed in the *New York Times Magazine,* March 8, 1993); Laxer 1993; Rieff 1993; Ujimoto 1992; Satzewich, ed. 1992; Watson 1993 as reviewed in the Economist, 7 August 1993. This case study was adapted from Nelson and Fleras 1995.

The mantra of multiculturalism continues to be invoked to maximize the benefits of diversity without incurring the costs of disruption (Samuel 1995). Nowhere is this more evident than at the level of institutional responses (Tepper 1988). The need for institutional adjustment has become increasingly urgent with the infusion of diversity through immigration, the political and constitutional response to this influx, and the emergence of a revised moral order based on the principles of moving over and making space. Efforts to improve both workplace dynamics and the delivery of services to minorities has led to an anticipated restructuring of federal institutions toward increased representivity, equity, and access (Samuda et al 1984; Tepper 1988).

Minority Perspectives

Multiculturalism in Canada was directed initially at the ethnic sector, namely, those landed immigrants primarily from Europe who claimed neither French nor English ancestry. It sought to enhance social status through symbolic affirmation of their language and culture. It also sought to improve participation in society through removal of prejudicial attitudes. The focus of multiculturalism has shifted recently to embrace the more equity-focused concerns of Third World immigrants and people of colour. The earlier cultural emphasis has inched toward institutional accommodation through removal of discriminatory barriers at structural levels. This distinction between culture or equality can be overstated: Both visible and invisible minorities are equally supportive of a more encompassing view that incorporates culture (the right to be different) as well as equality (the right to be the same). Each is concerned with culture, yet equally anxious to enjoy the benefits of full societal involvement. Nevertheless, differences are apparent.

On the surface, people of colour and recent Third World arrivals are inclined to see multiculturalism as a resource for attaining practical goals (Burnet 1981). They are increasingly reliant on formal mechanisms to combat discrimination and to secure their multicultural rights to be different, yet the same. Needs are basic: they want to become established, to expand economic opportunities for themselves and their children, to eliminate discrimination and exploitation, and to retain access to their cultural heritage without loss of citizenship rights. Multiculturalism is employed as a tool for opening up economic channels as well as for eliminating discrimination in areas of employment, education, housing, and criminal justice (Report, Equality Now, 1984). Recourse to multicultural principles has been instrumental in securing redress from the government for past wrongs, namely the 1988 compensation package to Japanese Canadians for violation of their rights during World War II.

The resource value of multiculturalism is evident in other ways. Multicultural minorities are often unable to influence central policy structures because of geographical dispersal, cultural heterogenity, and negligible negotiatory powers. With multiculturalism, an otherwise powerless sector now possesses the leverage to prod, embarrass, and provoke central policy structures by holding it accountable for failure to practice what it preaches. Issues over power-sharing, resource-distribution, and meaningful decision making take precedent over food courts, folkdancing, and ethnic festivals. Appeals to multiculturalism are thus calculated to extract public sympathy and global sympathy — in the same way aboriginal groups in Canada have relied on the United Nations as a bargaining chip against the federal government.

Other minorities are equally receptive to multiculturalism, but for different reasons. European ethnics appear more interested in cultural promotion and language maintenance than socioeconomic status (Burnet and Palmer 1988). The focus is on sponsoring folk and arts festivals, promoting heritage language programs, and securing ethnic presses and publications. Towards that end, multiculturalism is endorsed not only for advancing expressive interests, but also for diversifying Canadian cultural institutions along multicultural lines. Government funding in these areas is positively received in part because of the political legitimacy conferred by federal support of a wide variety of ethnic concerns and activities.

To Sum Up: Racial and ethnic minorities have turned to multiculturalism as a useful resource in competing with a crowded agenda. With the entrenchment of multiculturalism in Canadian society, a new set of rules have evolved around the concept of who gets what. Revisions to the national agenda imply the creation of a new moral authority that portrays minorities as legitimate contenders in the competition for power and resources. Redefining the rules governing government-minority relations has enhanced minority access to social, legal, and political claims that otherwise might lie beyond their grasp (Philip 1995). Minority groups are now empowered with yet another resource in staking out their claims and articulating their demands alongside those of the first and second force.

ATTITUDES TOWARD MULTICULTURALISM

Interviewer: Are you against multiculturalism?
Respondent: Yes.
Interviewer: Do you know what multiculturalism is?
Respondent: No.

(from Goot 1993:228)

Public perception of multiculturalism in Canada continues to elicit a wide variety of responses. Some Canadians are in vigorous support; others are in total rejection; still others couldn't care less; and yet others know nothing or next to nothing about multiculturalism. The majority are caught somewhere in between depending on their reading of multiculturalism and its role in building a certain kind of society (Goot 1993). Variables such as age, income, levels of education, and place of residence are also critical in gauging support, with higher levels of support among younger, more affluent, better educated, and urban individuals.

National surveys on multiculturalism suggest a support base of between 60 to 70 percent (Angus Reid 1991; Fleras and Elliott 1992; Berry 1993). Canadians generally endorse the principles of multiculturalism as long as costs are low and demands reasonable. Some see multiculturalism as an attempt to redefine national identity, while catering to the principles of fairness and equality; others perceive it in opposition to bilingualism and perceptions of Canada as a two-nations state (Parel 1992). Yet others resent any policy that encourages minorities to challenge the symbols of Canadian identity or to encroach on the country's cultural landscape

(White and Samuel 1991). Public resentment may be fueled by the prospect of government interference or spending in domains that many feel belong to the personal or private (Bissoondath 1994). Criticism may also arise from confusion over what multiculturalism is, what it is trying to do, and how it hopes to accomplish these goals. To the extent that multiculturalism originated — and persists — as a political program to achieve political ends, and should prepare us against any unrealistic benefits.

Sectoral Reaction

Official multiculturalism is unevenly supported across Canada. Residents of Ontario and Western Canada appear receptive, yet the Québécois (Bourassa 1975; Ryan 1975) and First Nations (Sanders 1987) have demonstrated less enthusiasm. As others have noted, it is doubtful if multiculturalism can handle the concerns of a people who belong to Canada through membership in their own national communities.

Quebec in particular has rejected any federal multiculturalism that glosses over Quebec's collective rights as a distinct society. Federal multiculturalism is denounced as yet another centralizing intrusion into Quebec's internal affairs. Instead of the federal mosaic, Quebec endorses a "tree" version of multiculturalism in which minority branches are grafted onto a Québécois trunk (see Webber 1994). Official multiculturalism is also rejected as a calculated federal effort to undermine Quebec's charter status by transforming a founding people into yet another multicultural minority. In its place Quebec pursues instead a lively multiculturalism policy in its own right, known as interculturalism, with its focus on affirming the cultural plurality and equal participation — without compromising the non-negotiable primacy of French language and culture, sovereignty of the National Assembly, a secular state, and equality between sexes (Hudson 1987; Helly 1993; Webber 1994).

The First Nations are likewise skeptical of multiculturalism as a solution to their problems. Like the Québécois, they make no claims to be part of a pluralistic society but a distinct people with shared history and a common homeland (see also Carter 1994). The levelling provisions within multiculturalism are perceived as a threat to cultural survival (Kallen 1987). Worse still, multiculturalism is criticized as downsizing aboriginal status to that of a minority/ethnic group, thereby foreclosing the fiduciary relationship between First Nations and central authorities (Sanders 1987). Federal attempts to promote aboriginal cultural preservation from outside a general framework of self-determination and aboriginality are dismissed as inadequate. That being the case, aboriginal peoples, like the Québécois, prefer to negotiate from within a bicultural framework that recognizes their collective right to special status and distinct entitlements.

Public Criticism

Many observers of Canada's political scene have chastized the government's initiatives in this area (Peter 1978; Kallen 1982; Burnet 1984; Bibby 1990; Thobani

1992; Das Gupta 1994; Bissoondath 1994; Falding 1995). What started out as a good idea with noble intentions (to assist newcomers into Canada) has evolved into a flashpoint for tension and hostility when the government foisted the concept of Canada as a mosaic on an unsuspecting public (Field 1994). Scholarly opinion has been dismissive of multiculturalism as a colossal hoax perpetuated by vested interests to ensure minority cooptation (see also Stasiulis 1993). Critics on the left have pounced on multiculturalism as ineffective except to provide symbolic redress to minorities; those on the right repudiate it as costly drain of resources. Those in the middle define multiculturalism as a form of ideological indoctrination whose social control functions include conflict resolution or public relations. Public awareness of cultural diversity has been heightened, critics contend, but little has been done to reduce overt economic inequalities for racial minorities (Ramcharan 1982). Minorities are ghettoized instead into certain occupational structures and residential arrangements, thereby preserving the prevailing distribution of power and wealth (Porter 1965; Anderson and Frideres 1981; Moodley 1983).

Others have argued that government is willing to lavish funds on folk festivals and ethnic performing arts, but is reluctant to support minority demands for collective rights or socioeconomic enhancement (Kallen 1987). Cultural solutions, critics argue, cannot possibly solve structural problems related to discriminatory barriers and systemic racism. This in turn raises questions of whether multiculturalism represents an authentic policy alternative or an interim measure for easing minorities into the mainstream. Writer and author, Neil Bissoondath (1994) is especially vocal in his condemnation. He likens multiculturalism to a shibboleth that has been shamelessly manipulated by politicians and ethnic opportunists for ulterior purposes. Our obsessive preoccupation with accommodating diversity, he argues, may embolden minorities to demand that Canada adapt their customs and languages, rather than the other way around, in effect fanning the flames of hatred and tribalism while undermining Canadian unity, identity, and culture. Not only is multiculturalism impervious to criticism; it also comes across as condescending paternalism in a country where the prevailing mindset endorses British and French as real Canadians, while regarding others as not-quite-Canadians. Multiculturalism fosters sentiments that exclude minorities from full and equal participation, trivializes minority contributions, stigmatizes minorities as foreigners or outsiders, and diminishes minorities as inferior or incapable of accomplishment without outside assistance. Multiculturalism also commodifies cultures while freezing them in time or romanticizing them as exotic, in effect compartmentalizing minorities into ethnic ghettoes (for criticism of Bissoondath, see Joseph 1995; Philp 1995).

Few should be surprised by levels of resistance to multiculturalism. Public expectations around multiculturalism are unrealistic in some cases. Multiculturalism is expected to balance the diverse claims for state versus minority rights on the one hand, as well as group versus individual rights on the other. Claims for special measures must be attended to without infringing on minority demands for social and economic equality. Individual rights must be protected, yet recognition of collective rights is no less important for social or economic progress to occur. Reluctance to delve more deeply into the nature of the criticism has only inflamed public confusion about multiculturalism. Multiculturalism (and immigration) are tarred as scapegoats for Canada's social and economic woes (Bissoondath 1994), in effect diverting attention away from real issues that have a destablizing effect on individuals and society such as racism, unemployment, recession, Free Trade, and cut backs to social services (Philip 1995). The box, "Muddling Through Another Multicultural Crisis," reveals some of the muddles that invariably accompany efforts to sort out multiculturalism in Canada.

INSIGHT

Muddling Through Another Multicultural Crisis

The harm that people do does not necessarily spring from evil dispositions or malevolent design. Injury can also result from the logical, often unanticipated, consequences of even well-intentioned actions. The banality of such systemic evil was confirmed recently by a national survey on racial attitudes. Even Canadians who routinely dote on gloom and despair were dismayed by the findings. In 1994, a year already marred by headlines about "bogus" refugees and "system-bashing" immigrants, the news print media confirmed the worst: "Canadians 'Frustrated' With Traditional Cultural Mosaic" (*Kitchener-Waterloo Record*), "More Immigrants Must Adapt, Survey Says" (*The Toronto Star*), and "Canadians Harbor 'Latently Racist' Attitudes: Poll" (*Montreal Gazette*). But a closer look yielded another story, one more consistent with the emergent realities of a multicultural Canada.

The poll was commissioned by the Canadian Council of Christians and Jews (CCCJ) in hopes of gauging public perception of racism in Canada. Data was collected through the polling firm Decima Research between October 23rd and 28th, 1994 by telephone with 1,217 adults, 18 years and older. With respect to the national picture, 68 percent said that one of the best things about Canada is its acceptance of people of all races and ethnic backgrounds. Yet 72 percent agreed that "people should adapt to the value system and way of life of the majority in Canadian society." Another 55 percent believed that some racial and ethnic minorities "don't make enough of an effort to fit into Canada." In terms of immigration, 54 percent concluded that current immigration policies and practices were "just right." By contrast, 41 percent felt immigration allowed "too many people of different races and cultures." Responses to questions about racism were no less ambiguous: An impressive 86 percent were aware of racism in Canada; 74 percent thought racism to be a serious problem in this country; and 53 percent perceived it to be on the rise. Only about one in four had witnessed or experienced a racial incident. Still, 50 percent were "sick and tired of some groups complaining about racism being directed at them." Another 41 percent were "tired of ethnic minorities being given special treatment."

There is no need to quibble about the survey results if taken as a "snapshot" of Canadian racial attitudes. What was more contentious, however, were the official interpretations, many of which took liberties with the raw data by casting multiculturalism and race relations in an unflattering light (see also Cardozo 1995). Most commentaries were highly critical of multiculturalism as Canada's legendary approach to managing race relations. The president of the CCCJ concluded that Canadians were frustrated with the ethnocultural ideals of a multicultural mosaic, preferring instead the virtues of an American-style melting pot as a basis for homogeneity and harmony.

Attitudes toward immigrants and racism were no less charitable, according to his assessment of the survey. References to "hostility to immigrants," "hardening attitudes," and "racist undercurrents" were liberally sprinkled about in his remarks to bolster the argument. The conclusion? Canadians are openly racist in some cases, politely racist in others, and implicitly racist in still others — despite social sanctions that inhibit the acting out of such views.

Reading between the survey lines proves enlightening. First and foremost, one is struck by the superficiality of people's knowledge of race relations in Canada. Consider, for example, the statement that some minorities are not making enough of an effort to embrace "Canadian values" or the "way of life of the majority." Instead of accepting this assertion at face value, we should be deeply skeptical of such a claim, then retaliate with a series of counter-questions such as: What proof is there to substantiate such a statement? Who are these unassimilable groups? Who says they are not adapting and on what grounds? What constitutes satisfactory adaptation? Even the reference to Canadian values demands a rebuttal: What precisely do we mean by Canadian "values" or "way of life"? Are we talking about some mythical 1950s ideal enshrined in an Anglocentric patriarchy? Or does "our" Canada include a respect for difference, a tolerance for agreeing to disagree, freedom of expression, and commitment to equality for all? The questionnaire didn't ask any of these questions.

On the contrary, the evidence suggests a different conclusion: The vast majority of new Canadians are not repudiating Canada. They want to put down roots and become accepted, if only out of a sense of national obligation or because of social pressure. That some do not make this transformation is to be expected, often reflecting differences in age or socioeconomic status. Likewise, a bumpy transition may stem from differing perceptions about the nature of belonging as a Canadian citizen. Failure to adapt may also be attributable to the exclusionary forces of prejudice and discrimination. To be sure, not all racial or ethnic minorities are enthusiastic boosters of Canada. But that is hardly an excuse to label all minorities as lukewarm participants or outright subversives, intent on hijacking the Canadian agenda for self-serving purposes.

A second set of claims was equally shaky. The survey thought it discerned a growing disenchantment with official multiculturalism, coupled with a glowing endorsement of the American melting pot. According to the polls, multiculturalism had outlived its usefulness in Canada, with 72 percent of the respondents demanding more conformity from racial and ethnic minorities. Yet this type of conclusion only emphasizes the muddled thinking about multiculturalism as policy and practice. Contrary to popular belief, multiculturalism is not about promoting minorities per se. Rather it is concerned with creating a society in which diversity can flourish as a legitimate and positive component, without undermining the interconnectedness of the whole. Paradoxically, the rejection of multiculturalism may deter Canadians from full and equal participation. With its emphasis on settlement and integration, multiculturalism is more relevant than ever to society-building in Canada.

A third set of survey conclusions took a swipe at the pervasiveness of prejudice and racism in Canada. Prejudice and racism are known to assert themselves during hard times, especially against easily targetted scapegoats. Once again, what was left off the questionnaire proved more fascinating than what was asked: Are racism and prejudice on the rise or is it merely public perception that is increasing? Do increases in perception reflect growth in the number of incidents, or simply a greater public awareness coupled with a willingness to remember or report? Does increased awareness signify a downward spiral or a first step toward solution? True, those who have followed national trends concede the tenacity of prejudice among most Canadians. And yes, Canada is a racist society, although the magnitude and scope of this racism depends on its definition. But what is perceived by some as a backlash or bigotry may be seen by others as a starting point for positive change, namely, a growing willingness among Canadians to admit that a problem exists. Given our legendary reputation for denying the reality of prejudice and racism, this open admittance may herald the first step toward renewal and reform.

Response to Criticism

There is a growing chorus of boos directed at multiculturalism. Much of the criticism ignores the multidimensional nature of multiculturalism. Multiculturalism can be liberating yet marginalizing, unifying yet divisive, inclusive yet exclusive (Vasta 1993). Its symbolic value is rubbished by some, but praised by others as a paradigm shift of not insignificant value (Breton 1984). On the one hand, multiculturalism provides minorities with a platform with which they can participate in society without the imposition of heavy-handed government tactics. On the other, minorities get drawn into the dominant culture since measures to improve access or participation often have assimilationist consequences. Even efforts at resistance are perceived as self-defeating exercises that absorb minorities into the very system they are rejecting (Pearson 1993).

In short, multiculturalism can be interpreted as a two-edged sword that can be swung in either direction (see also Dorais et al. 1994). In the same way that ethnicity can empower or divide depending on one's frame of reference, so too can multiculturalism enhance and accommodate yet sow the seeds of internal strife. Positive and negative effects coexist uneasily, with one prevailing because of circumstances, but its opposite ready to reappear under different conditions. Even operationalizing the terms "effective" or "beneficial" can be difficult, in many ways reflecting observer bias and competing visions of society. Table 10.3 below illustrates the hydra-headed character of multiculturalism by indicating how criticism and rebuttal are not mutually exclusive but complementary yet oppositional.

Criticism can also distort the goals of multiculturalism in a liberal-democratic society. Multiculturalism as a government policy is not geared toward the retention of ethnic groups as relatively self-sufficient ongoing entities. It is not directed at the maintenance of minority customs or ethnic values, much less that of parallel institutions with a separate power base and collective rights. In this modern age of superpowers and multinational corporations, it is doubtful if any society could — or would want to — survive as a kaleidoscope of culturally diverse enclaves (Castles 1988). Rather, multiculturalism is concerned with creating a pluralistic and productive society in which diversity can be incorporated as a legitimate component without undermining social unity and national identity. Multiculturalism tolerates diversity but only to the extent that it does not contravene the laws of the land or violate the rights of others. That said, criticism should focus not on what people think multiculturalism should do, but on what it can realistically accomplish compared with other strategies for managing diversity.

TABLE 10.3   Cons and Pros of Multiculturalism

Cons	Pros
Divisive — undermines Canadian unity and identity through endorsement of diversity ("balkanization")	**Unifying** — promotes unity and coherence by de-politicizing diversity ("society-building")
Regressive — ghettoizes minorities and keeps them in their place	**Progressive** — provides platform for articulation of interests and stepping stone for success
Symbolic — without substance, full of fury signifying nothing except preservation of the status quo	**Substantive** — symbols can move mountains by legitimizing diversity as part of the national agenda
Fraudulent — instrument of control that deludes, conceals, evades, and distorts; that is, it promises a lot, but delivers little	**Catalytic** — instrument of opportunity through creation of a social climate for diversity to flourish

DRAWING THE MULTICULTURAL LINE

One of the nice things about living in Canada is our general willingness to agree to disagree without resorting to threats or fear of reprisals. Multiculturalism is famed for its promise to accommodate diversity within the framework of Canadian society. The accommodation process is simple enough when the differences are superficial. Shall we order Chinese tonight? How about Italian? Anyone care for Middle Eastern? Things get more complex when fundamentally different and mutually opposed values come into contact. They become even more complicated when one set of values prefers to disagree with our commitment to agree to disagree. The Salmon Rushdie case (in which a Muslim writer is under a death sentence by members of his own religion because some of his writings are considered blasphemous) is a primary example of the paradoxes when groups threaten to *disagree* to *agree*. The resolve for compromise and adjustment stiffens visibly when cultural differences are counter to fundamental Canadian values such as gender equality or secular pluralism. Consider the controversies created by the Sikh turban in the halls of Canadian Legions and among the RCMP. The wearing of the hijab, a head covering (or scarf) worn by some Muslim women, has also provoked debate for violating school dress codes in a predominantly secular school environment. The limits to multiculturalism are stretched even further with customs such as female genital mutilation that are totally at odds with core Canadian values. Do we impose Eurocentric values in outright condemnation, or do we capitulate to social chaos because of our failure to agree on what is disagreeable even when human rights abuses are involved? Such dilemmas raise the issue of what is tolerable in a multicultural society. Where do we draw the line between what is acceptable and what is not? Are there limits to tolerance within Canada's multiculturalism commitments? The case study, "Putting Multiculturalism into Christmas," explores this issue more fully.

CASE STUDY

Putting Multiculturalism into Christmas

Another Christmas has come and gone. Instead of tranquility and good cheer with people of all colours, Christmas festivities were marred by rancour and misunderstanding over tradition versus diversity. The source of the conflict went beyond the mere formality of grafting diversity onto traditional Christmas activities. Controversies erupted over the politics of preservation, with adherents of traditional Canadian symbols squared off against proponents of an inclusive multicultural mosaic. Sorting through these issues will help us to dissect the substance — and the fallacies — behind drawing the multicultural line.

THE ISSUE

At the crux of this controversy are decisions by a growing number of schools (and public institutions) to abolish Christian symbolism from Christmas pageants or public displays. References to Christianity such as the Nativity scene have been purged or downplayed, even to the point of renaming Christmas festivities as a winter solstice or mid-winter holiday. Christmas carols have also been banned from annual concerts for fear of offending non-Christian pupils. Friendship trees have replaced Christmas trees so as not to tweak dissenting opinions. Even the venerable symbol of Santa has endured a dose of debunking.

Reaction to this "interference" has varied, but invariably is hostile or confused, in effect reminding us that even in a predominantly secular society religious symbols still have the power to provoke and partition. Consider the spectrum of opinion: For some, the celebration of a Christian Christmas is a fundamental characteristic of Canada, and deserving of its special place in the school system. Those who want to banish Christ from Christmas are accused not only of excessive political correctness or "bad faith," but also of pandering to immigrants with hidden agendas and subversive interests. Others disagree: For them, a traditional Christmas is quintessentially a Christian practice with no justification in a publicly-funded, pluralistic school system. Not only are non-Christian children offended by exposure to Christian icons; many also are robbed of access to their own religious sentiments. As a compromise, Christmas may be tolerated, albeit in a less doctrinaire way, possibly by incorporating other religious practices such as the Jewish Hanukkah or the Hindi Diwali. Yet others doubt whether a multi-faith diversity can be incorporated into a predominantly Christian society (According to the 1991 Census, 80 percent of all Canadians (or 23,252,000 of the total) identify with Christianity (both Catholic and Protestant), another 1 percent are Jewish (318,065), about 0.8 percent are Muslims (253,265) and 0.5 percent are Buddhist (163,420). Another 11 percent declare no religious affiliation.) Finally, the cynics have managed to capture an intermediate position. The very act of linking Christmas with Christ, they argue, is nothing short of hypocritical — given the pervasiveness of commercialism and consumerism. The only practical solution consists of expunging Christmas from any spiritual connotations — Christian or non-Christian — for the sake of consistency.

THE SOLUTION(S)

It is obvious that public celebrations of Christmas have become a contested site, involving a struggle for supremacy among competing groups with opposing agendas. Is there a correct answer to this growing debate? Should Christianity retain its primacy during Christmas, or should all faiths be included as part of a pan-tribal celebration? Alternately, should references to spirituality be abolished in pursuit of a purely secular ritual?

The simplest answer would be one of strict impartiality. No religious symbols of any type should be tolerated or endorsed in multicultural public, lest offence be created. That precisely is the route employed by governments in Canada and the United States, many of whom are taking seriously the necessity to protect the state from religion for political reasons (rather than vice versa as was formerly the case). But equality before the law is not a compromise to everyone's liking. Nor is it necessarily consistent with multicultural principles. Multiculturalism is not about strict neutrality where nothing goes; conversely, it is not about a smorgasbord-style morality where everything goes. Multiculturalism does not categorically deny the validity of mainstream Canadian practices any more than it blindly endorses minority customs. Multiculturalism is about compromises, instead, and any solution to the

Christ-in-Christmas crisis must unearth a multicultural middle ground that balances competing rights. Public preference for one religion rather than another violates that principle of neutrality. Multiculturalism reminds us that, however treasured and traditional, conventional patterns may be rendered irrelevant — even superfluous — by changing circumstances. Social practices are not cast in stone: More realistically, they should be subject to discussion and debate, not because of their inferiority, but because of their irrelevance as time goes on.

IMPLICATIONS: THE BIG PICTURE

What are the implications of folding multiculturalism into Christmas? First, there is no evidence whatsoever of an orchestrated plot by minorities, much less by the fictitious "thought police," to delete Christmas from the public realm. Look around! It's business as usual. Secular symbols of Christmas remain as formidable as ever, judging by the sound of jingling cash registers and the ubiquity of shopping mall Santas. Any concessions to diversity must be seen in this light. Nor can anyone seriously entertain the charges that special minority interests are hijacking Canada's agenda for self-serving purposes. The placement of a few non-Western ornaments on a public Christmas tree is no more a threat to cherished traditions than the addition of a few "token" minorities within corporate boardrooms. In both cases, the prevailing distribution of power remains intact.

Second, changes to a traditional Christmas are consistent with developments elsewhere. Evidence by sociologists such as Reginald Bibby reveals what many have suspected: Organized religion is losing its mass appeal. In its place is growing popularity of conservative evangelical sects or, alternately, personal spiritual arrangements between consenting adults in private, as the sociologist Peter Berger has commented elsewhere. Furthermore, what has happened in private is also taking place in public. Central authorities are looking to enhance the secular impartiality of key institutions for effectiveness and legitimacy. For example, Ontario banned the mandatory recital of the Lord's prayer in public schools in 1988. The province later abolished religious instruction from the daily curriculum in exchange for detached analysis and cross-cultural study. Likewise, the American Supreme Court ruled against organized prayer in a public place as a violation of the First Amendment, arguing that the state is not against religion per se or its abolition but that the state has no right to impose a view of how people should pray or worship (Carter 1994). In short, the decision to de-politicize religion (or their symbols) is neither accidental nor abitrary. It represents "good politics" in the same way official multiculturalism and bilingualism are used as a way of **de-politicizing diversity**. Similarly, the decision to diminish the salience of a Christian Christmas is consistent with broader trends to sanitize religion from society in pursuit of a civic and secular nationalism.

Third, much of the Christmas controversy is misleading. The issue is not necessarily about Christmas as an exclusively Canadian tradition. Many new Canadians have also selectively embraced aspects of a traditional Christmas.

They have done so because of a sense of national obligation to their adopted country, also because of a desire to fit in and to put down roots. The issue is concerned with the primacy of Christian symbols in a publicly-funded domain. Even here care must be exercised. Minorities are not "grinches" out to steal Christmas. No one is questioning the right of all Canadians to celebrate a traditional Christmas, with all the religious trimmings, within the confines of their own home, place of worship, or private business. Multiculturalism, after all, is not concerned with what people do in private; it can only address what happens in public where the appearance of neutrality is uppermost to secure political tranquility.

Fourth, federal multiculturalism recognizes no official culture. However it allows each person to identify with the cultural tradition of their choice, provided this neither violates the rights of others nor contravenes the laws of the land. Similarly, Canada's Constitution does not acknowledge the existence of an official religion — Christianity or otherwise. Taken together, this suggests that no cultural practice — or religious symbols in this case — should have priority of placement in public. To concede space to one rather than another contravenes the principle of strict neutrality inherent in most (but not all) versions of multiculturalism. Why is this neutrality so important? Society-building does not come naturally to a pluralistic society such as Canada. The pursuit of national unity is anchored on the construction of a civic nationalism, both tolerant in process and secular in outcome. Attainment of this political goal depends on de-politicizing those aspects of society that have proven detrimental to society-building elsewhere. Towards that end, central authorities have gradually stripped the public order of religious symbols as a precaution against ethnic or religious strife. Herein, then, lies the rationale behind the move to de-Christianize Christmas: Canada's survival depends on witholding any overt displays of favouritism for fear of disturbing the social peace.

RESOLUTION

Not everyone will agree with this interpretation of multiculturalism and Christmas. That's understandable, considering the range of opinion spanning what multiculturalism is and what it should do. Disagreements over multiculturalism often reflect different visions of Canadian society. Our assessment builds on a belief that multiculturalism goes beyond promoting minorities. Nor is it directed at displacing Canadian traditions for those of other ethnocultural groups. Multiculturalism in the final analysis is about creating a society that is accommodating of diversity, primarily to: (a) foster a social climate receptive to diversity as a legitimate and positive contributor to society; (b) preserve the interconnectedness of Canadian society without offending the constituent ele-

ments comprising the national mosaic; and (c) establish a sense of belonging and participation in a moral community. With its commitment to belonging and inclusiveness, in other words, the message of multiculturalism may not be altogether different from the original meaning of Christmas.

The resentment generated by this now all-too-familiar fiasco cannot be lightly dismissed. Canadians appear to be polarizing into competitive camps, with traditionalists at one pole and multiculturalists at the other. Fallacies and misconceptions abound, yet keeping open the lines of communication is essential to a multicultural society. An ongoing dialogue about the Christmas crisis provides Canadians with an opportunity to challenge conventions and customs. It also draws attention to the challenges of putting multicultural principles into practice in changing and uncertain times. There is yet another theme of importance. For those who truly are concerned about the meaning of Christmas perhaps they should redirect their venom toward the real "grinches" behind the Christmas caper. We could do worse than examine the materialist underpinnings of a consumerist mentality with its capacity to dismantle the spirituality at the core of a multicultural society.

DEBUNKING MULTICULTURAL MYTHS: THE GOOD, THE BAD, AND THE IN-BETWEEN

As the cutting edge for progressive social change, multiculturalism has attracted its share of criticism. National shortcomings for some reason tend to polarize and be magnified around minority relations. Much of this criticism tends to be misguided or misplaced since it overlooks the context and consequences of multiculturalism. Part of the problem originates from highly inflated expectations about what multiculturalism can or should do. Just as multiculturalism cannot be blamed for all social problems in Canada, so too should it be exempt from lavish and undeserved praise as the solution to all our ills. Its influence exists somewhere in between: Rather than a magical formula for success, it is but one component — however imperfect — for managing diversity in a a complex yet unequal context.

The in-between quality of multiculturalism is manifest in yet another way. Politically speaking, Canadian society can be envisaged as socially constructed around a series of national compromises. These national compromises range in scope from regional equalization concerns and charter group dynamics, to a perpetual rebalancing of individual and collective rights. In such a system of checks and balances, multiculturalism is aptly suited as a mediator for working the area between opposing ethnocultural forces. A system of compromises in its own right, multiculturalism provides a counterbalance for reconciling ambiguities inherent in a diverse and changing society. A capacity for speaking the language of "in-between" enables it to secure the priority of the whole without destroying the constituent elements in the process. A commitment to multiculturalism furnishes a symbolic rationale for reconciling what otherwise would lapse into dismemberment and chaos. It also steers a path between the conflicting demands of state sovereignty on the one hand and those of ethnic tribalism on the other (*The Economist* 1993).

The objectives, scope, and limitations of multiculturalism must be clearly articulated if its full potential as a workable concept is to be realized. Yet Canadians remain curiously misinformed about what multiculturalism is; what it does or is supposed to do; why; and how it goes about doing its job. One way of separating fact from fiction is by responding to popular misconceptions:

Fiction   Multiculturalism is ineffective.

Fact   Who says so, and by what criteria? Multiculturalism possesses neither the power nor resources to "move mountains." As policy or program, it cannot singlehandedly eliminate discrimination or racism. Nor can it automatically improve minority opportunities and life chances. Its strength resides in a capacity to foster a social climate responsive to diversity as a legitimate and integral component of society-building.

Fiction   Multiculturalism ghettoizes minorities.

Fact   Multiculturalism is not about ghettoizing minorities. To the contrary, multiculturalism seeks to accommodate differences through sharing, interaction, and participation. Institutional accommodation and removal of discriminatory barriers are two additional initiatives for improving involvement.

Fiction   Multiculturalism forces minorities to choose between ethnicity and equality.

Fact	Multiculturalism neither constrains minority aspirations, nor does it lock people of colour into a vertical mosaic. Racial and ethnic stratification long predated the appearance of multi-culturalism, and it will continue to flourish as long as cultural solutions are applied to structural problems. More accurately, multiculturalism provides a conceptual framework that encourages individuals to identify with their cultural background without sacrificing access and equitable participation.
Fiction	Multiculturalism encourages an anything goes mentality because it fudges the line between what is acceptable or not.
Fact	Multiculturalism does *not* endorse a mindless relativism in which anything goes in the name of tolerance. Multiculturalism is clear about what is permissable in Canada. It rejects any customs that violate Canadian laws, interferes with the rights of others, offends the moral sensibilities of most Canadians, or disturbs central institutions or core values
Fiction	Multiculturalism is about promoting minorities.
Fact	Multiculturalism is *not* about promoting minorities. It constitutes an exercise in society-building by which minorities are incorporated as legitimate and distinctive contributors without forfeiting the goals of a united and progressive society.
Fiction	Multiculturalism encourages diversity.
Fact	Multiculturalism does not encourage diversity per se. More accurately it seeks to *de-politize* this diversity by channelling potentially troublesome conflicts into relatively harmless avenues pertaining to identity or culture. To be honest, multiculturalism has never quite figured out how either to make everyone *different* but in the same kind of way or to recognize that people are the *same* but in different kind of way.
Fiction	Multiculturalism promotes ethnic groups.
Fact	Multiculturalism does *not* promote ethnic communities. No society could survive by actively fostering collective group rights, with parallel institutions and separate power base. What multiculturalism emphasizes instead is *identity*: that is, the right of *individuals* to identify with select aspects of their tradition — preferably in private and in accordance with Canadian laws.
Fiction	Multiculturalism is undermining Canadian culture.
Fact	Multiculturalism can hardly undo what we may not have ever had. There is *no* definitive Canadian culture except in the most abstract sense. The existence of First Nations cultures and lived-in ethnicities such as the Hutterites will attest to that.

Nor is there any all-encompassing vision of what Canadian culture should be like. The only thing we may have in common, culturally speaking, is our differences.

Fiction   Multiculturalism is destroying shared values.

Fact   The concept of shared Canadian values is open to debate. Either these values never existed and never will, or consensus is impossible to achieve because of our deep diversities. Alternatively, these core values are so resilient and secure that modest multicultural adjustments pose little or no threat. Perhaps our core value is that we don't have any central values except a basic decency, a respect for rule of law, and a commitment to individual equality (see Sajoo 1994).

Fiction   Multiculturalism excludes and divides.

Fact   Multiculturalism is hardly the cause of division or exclusion. The real culprit is racism with its power to shunt minorities to the sidestream for reasons unrelated to merit. Multiculturalism is a beginning in patching over these divisions through removal of exclusionary barriers.

Fiction   Multiculturalism is an act of political expediency.

Fact   It is that but it is also much more. Multiculturalism may have originated as a cynical Liberal ploy for balancing power in Canada, yet people should never underestimate the power of ideas to move nor the creativity of people in taking advantage of policies that may not have had their interests at heart (Phlip 1995).

Fiction   Multiculturalism is an example of meddlesome government interference.

Fact   Multiculturalism operates on the assumption that diversity needs to be actively managed if conflicts are to be avoided, and benefits gained. Neither the market nor voluntary compliance have made much headway in accommodating diversity. Government intervention is required instead, and certain costs are inevitable in forging a social climate conducive to inclusiveness.

Fiction -   Multiculturalism is an expensive luxury during times of fiscal restraint.

Fact -   Multiculturalism is not expensive: Federal spending on multiculturalism stands at $25 million, most of which is directed at anti-racism, settlement and integration, and cultural sharing. Compare this with the $700 million expended for official bilingualism. To put it another perspective: Multiculturalism in

1992-93 received less than one percent of the government (both federal and provincial) spending allocated for arts and culture.

Fiction   Multiculturalism has been a failure.

Fact   Equating multiculturalism with the label of failure raises the questions of "compared to what" and "on what grounds." The fact that Canada appears to be working vindicates the relative success of multiculturalism. The fact that Canada remains a pacesetter in managing race and ethnic relations is a hopeful sign.

Fiction   Multiculturalism is destroying Canada.

Fact   What proof is there of Canada falling apart because of multicultural minorities? Multiculturalism is arguably a key component in binding together Canadians. It is interesting to note that the two non-multicultural communities in Canada, the First Nations and the Québécois, may pose a graver threat to Canada's long term survival than multiculturalism.

Fiction   Multiculturalism is experiencing a backlash.

Fact   Criticism of multiculturalism is mounting. But that of its own right does not signal a backlash. Disgruntlement may stem from discontent that is growing among the already disenchanted rather than the result of growing disenchantment. A small but vocal minority may be the source behind this anti-multiculturalism, emboldened, as it were, by a social and political climate conducive to criticism without public censure.

Fiction   Canadians dislike multiculturalism.

Fact   Its possible that most Canadians have certain qualms about multiculturalism. Many may agree with the principles of multiculturalism, but are irked by its association as formal government policy, with a publicly funded set of programs and practices. Others may be hostile toward the diversity agenda in general, including employment equity and immigration, with multiculturalism swept along because of guilt by association.

Fiction   Multiculturalism is dated and irrelevant.

Fact   The kind of multiculturalism associated with folklore is slowly losing its political grip. In its place is a growing commitment to a multiculturalism that acknowledges a world that is global, competitive, information-based, and technology-driven. Diversity in its own right will not produce benefits in this kind of environment: it must be actively managed to bring about results.

Fiction	Multiculturalism is only a symbol.
Fact	Many have criticized multiculturalism as a kind of addendum to the national agenda established by the founding peoples. Yet multiculturalism provides minorities with a legitimate platform within the national agenda for making claims and airing grievances.
Fiction	Multiculturalism conflicts with a Canadian identity.
Fact	National identities are not fixed in concrete but evolving and created anew with each generation. Multiculturalism provides the basis for a new post-modernist identity based on the realities of change, diversity, and uncertainty. This shift in mindset may foreshadow a citizenship of the future: that is, citizens bound not by a powerful national ideal but by shared commitments within a common geographical space in a "just-in-time" world (see Gwyn 1994). Or as expressed by Michael Adams, president of Environics Research Group: "Ours is a population that is resigned to — and may even take some pride in — the relatively weak attachments that bind us to each other. It is my feeling that we will continue on much as we have...forever pragmatic, forever flexible, forever Canadian.

MULTICULTURALISM: IS THERE ANOTHER CANADIAN WAY?

Canada's commitment to multiculturalism has contributed to its image as an open, secular, and largely tolerant society. Some measure of proof is gleaned from Canada's lofty status (as deemed by various UN panels) as a socially progressive society with an enviable standard of living. Multiculturalism has proven a beacon of tolerance in a largely intolerant world: Compared to a utopia Canada falls short of the mark; compared with the grisliness of reality elsewhere, we stand as a paragon of virtue. The fact that Canada has avoided much of the ethnic strife that currently convulses as many as 48 countries speaks well of its stature in managing diversity and society-building (*New York Times* 1993).

The worldwide reputation for tolerance that Canada enoys is largely deserved (Bricker 1994). The majority of Canadians, especially the young and the well-educated, are relatively open to diversity and proud of our multicultural heritage, despite undercurrents of fear and hostility toward certain newcomers. Even wholehearted support, however, is no excuse for glossing over its imperfections. However potent a mechanism for managing diversity, the principle and practice of official multiculturalism remains riddled with inconsistencies. Everyone agrees that there are enough loopholes in federal multiculturalism to dishearten even the most optimistic. Few would deny its vulnerability to manipulation by politicians and minority leaders. Fewer still would dismiss its potential to deter, divide, diminish, or digress. But criticism is one thing; proposals for alternatives to multiculturalism are quite another. Critics may be relentless in their attacks on multiculturalism as an after thought to the national agenda established by the founding parties. But most critiques rarely offer *constructive* criticism. Our stand is unequivocal: Multiculturalism is hardly an option in a modern Canada with deep diversities and competing citizenships. There are *no* alternatives to multiculturalism (see also Sajoo 1994). Neither assimilation nor integration stand much chance of survival in a post-multicultural era. A much touted return to traditional values as a glue for cementing Canadians into a unified and coherent whole sounds good in theory (Bibby 1990; Bissoondath 1993, 1994). In reality such wishful thinking also may camouflage a hidden agenda for a return of the "good old days" when minorities knew their place in society.

A sense of perspective is overdue. Multiculturalism is not the cause of Canada's problems, any more than it can be the cure-all. This country is not going to unravel because of multiculturalism. The politics of "distinct society" and the "nations within" will see to that first. Nor should we get worked up over the absence of a common culture — as if multiculturalism destroyed what we never had in the first place. Diversity not commonality *is* Canada's strength: To expect otherwise is unrealistic in a society organized around overlapping citizenships of the First Nations, the Québécois, and multicultural minorities (Kaplan 1993; Kymlicka 1994). A shared set of core values about who we are or want to be is far more important than a common culture. Disagreement and conflict are inevitable in such a context. Just as shared ethnicity does not entail a unanimity of vision, as Bissoondath (1994) reminds us, so too can a multicultural society survive on a "multiplicity of voices and visions, or the interplay of conflicting views" — provided that, within limits, we agree to disagree.

Multiculturalism, in short, remains the policy of necessity if not of choice for a changing and diverse Canada. As policy or practice, it symbolizes an innovative if imperfect social experiment for managing diversity. Multiculturalism has excelled in rescuing Canada from being an Anglocentric outpost, to its much ballyhooed status as a trailblazer in the enlightened management of race and ethnic relations. Under the circumstances, it is not a question of whether Canada can afford multiculturalism. More to the point, Canada cannot afford *not* to embrace multiculturalism in its relentless search for political unity, social coherence, economic prosperity, and cultural enrichment.

CHAPTER HIGHLIGHTS

- This chapter has focused on the concept of Canadian multiculturalism. Multiculturalism is properly examined as a technique for accommodating diversity within the context of Canadian society-building with the potential to expand government-minority relations in hitherto unexplored realms.

- With traditional styles of race-relations management (including assimilation or integration) on the decline, multiculturalism has emerged as the key option in the pluralistic package for coping with the challenges of diversity.

- Multiculturalism is defined as a policy and practice concerned with creating a society that accommodates diversity as a legitimate and integral component without destroying the unity and integrity of the system in the process.

- Responses to the question, "is Canada a multicultural society?" indicate the need to examine multiculturalism at different levels of interpretation; that is, as a sociological fact, an ideological system of beliefs and values, a set of policies involving government-minority relations, and a renewable resource in serving political and minority interests.

- Canadian multiculturalism has historically been concerned with improving minority equality and participation in society, initially through elmination of ethnocentric biases ("folkloric"), then through removal of multicultural discriminatory barriers and institutional accommodation ("institutional multiculturalism"), and currently through enhancing a sense of belonging to Canada ("civic multiculturalism").

- At once an asset as well as a hindrance, multiculturalism has been regarded as a source of social tension, in addition to an innovative means for minority conflict management.

- Multiculturalism is often associated with several misconceptions that are ripe for plucking, including: (a) fact: multiculturalism is not expensive (only $1 per year per Canadian in federal expenditures); (b) fact: multiculturalism is not divisive (ideally, it seeks to promote unity through preservation, participation, and integration); (c) fact: multiculturalism does not detract from national identity (Canada's collective self-image is dependent on accepting diversity); and (d) fact: multiculturalism is not a failure (Compared to what?).

- Multiculturalism is usually criticized as being divisive, regressive, a symbol without substance, and an instrument of containment. Multiculturalism can also be shown to be unifying, progressive, a symbol with substance, and social catalyst. The degree of criticism or praise may vary with a person's vision of Canadian society, and the role of multiculturalism in managing group relations. It also reflects the notion that reality cannot be carved into fixed and mutually exclusive units of good or bad.

- While official multiculturalism is riddled with inconsistencies and contradictions, critics have been unable to propose a viable alternative for managing diversity in a society that is increasingly diverse, ever changing, and more uncertain.

- The balancing act implicit in a country of compromises follows from this. Multicultural initiatives must simultaneously preserve a precarious balance of power between the imperatives of the state and majorities on the one hand, with the rights of minorities on the other. Confronted by such challenges and conflicts, liberal-democratic governments have stumbled in resolving these issues to everyone's satisfaction.

- Official multiculturalism is not simply a set of programs for splashing a dash of colour or pageantry into Canada's anglocentric agenda. For minorities, multiculturalism provides a platform that enables a transformation of the national agenda in terms of who gets what, and why (entitlement).

- Multiculturalism originated and continues to exist for a variety of social, economic, and cultural reasons, most of which uphold the legitimacy of the state in managing diversity. This perspective confirms the adage that multiculturalism is essentially a political program to achieve political goals in a politically acceptable manner.

- Multiculturalism is not a coherent set of policies or programs that are fixed in perpetuity. Multiculturalism undergoes renewal and reform through adaptation to political, social, and demographic changes. The open-ended and resilient nature of multiculturalism provides it with the flexibility to shift agendas (for example, from focus on ethnicity to equity to citizenship) as the context dictates.

- Multiculturalism is not about promoting ethnicity or diversity per se. The focus is on de-politicizing diversity by channelling it into harmless outlets, thus short-circuiting their potential for disruption. This reinforces the notion of multiculturalism as essentially a technique for society-building.

- What are the limits of multicultural tolerance? Which ethnocultural differences can be absorbed within a multicultural society without undermining incontestable values and beliefs? The dilemma is self-evident: too many differences can create anarchic conditions which inhibit the effective functioning of a social system while too many restrictions make a mockery of multicultural principles. Nevertheless, the question arises, where do we draw the line?

KEY TERMS

Christmas and Multiculturalism
Civic Multiculturalism
De-politicizing Diversity
Folkloric Multiculturalism
Institutional Multiculturalism
Multiculturalism
Multiculturalism Act, 1988
Multiculturalism as Empirical Fact
Multiculturalism as Ideology
Multiculturalism as Policy
Multiculturalism as Process
Multiculturalism as Society-Building

REVIEW QUESTIONS

1) Indicate how multiculturalism differs from other techniques for managing race and ethnic relations.

2) Compare and contrast the different phases in the development of Canada's multiculturalism policy in terms of objectives, assumptions, means, and outcomes.

3) How would you respond to the assertion "Canada is a multicultural society." Be sure to focus on the different interpretive levels of multiculturalism.

4) Demonstrate some of the benefits and drawbacks associated with multiculturalism. Defend whether or not you regard multiculturalism as a society-building process or society-destroying phenomena.

5) Multiculturalism raises a number of issues/dilemmas regarding the status of race and ethnic relations in Canadian society. It also raises questions about the possibility of achieving national unity within a framework of diversity. Provide a critique of multiculturalism that acknowledges the difficulties in implementing such a program in Canada.

6) Multiculturalism is viewed differently by diverse sectors of Canadian society. Discuss the validity of this statement by examining the responses of the aboriginal, charter, and public sectors to multiculturalism as government policy.

7) Multiculturalism is about knowing limits and drawing lines. Explain and provide an example to illustrate your answer.

CHAPTER 11

PUTTING MULTICULTURALISM TO WORK

INTRODUCTION:
TOWARD INSTITUTIONAL ACCOMMODATION

The previous chapter outlined the magnitude and scope of official multiculturalism in Canada. Historically, a tendency prevailed in Canada that shunted aside minority races and ethnocultures, not only because of prejudice and discrimination, but also because of a belief in diversity as inimical to society-building. With the inception of multiculturalism, however, response to diversity has been stood on its head. Diversity is promoted currently as an integral and legitimate component of our social fabric, with untapped potential for improving our national wealth and international standing. Racial and ethnocultural differences are no longer dismissed as a bothersome anomaly with no redeeming value outside a personal or private context. Social trends instead point to the **accommodation of diversity** as indispensible for building a strong and prosperous Canada.

Preliminary efforts at putting multiculturalism to work have proven uneven. Demographic pressures have altered the way institutions conduct their business, while reinforcing the notion that the established way of doing things is not the only way. Public and private institutions are seeking to enhance organizational effectiveness by taking into account all Canadians — not simply the more affluent or privileged. This commitment to inclusiveness is especially true for service-oriented institutions, including the mass media, formal educational institutions, and law enforcement agencies since their involvement as agencies of socialization or social control subjects them to greater accountability. Both socialization and control strike at the very core of social existence; they also influence whether or not we perceive ourselves in harmony with our communities or alienated from them. The mass media and schools furnish the means to understand our own reality through interconnections with a larger whole. The police in turn control the limits of acceptable behaviour within an ordered and diverse society. Each of these institutions has little option but to establish the necessary linkages for "bridging the reality gap." To the extent that they are successful in doing so will determine whether multicultural principles can take root and flourish in our society.

This chapter is concerned with the theme of putting multiculturalism to work. It examines how major institutions such as the mass media, educational, and law enforcement agencies are responding to the challenges of accommodating diversity. The chapter explores programs and policies aimed at managing institutional diversity both internally (in terms of organizational procedures and workforce) and externally (with respect to service delivery and client relations). Each institution is analyzed in terms of the problems that confront it in adapting to a multicultural society; what has been accomplished to date in managing diversity at organizational levels; and what should be done to improve patterns of accommodation. Also discussed are the challenges, the dilemmas, and concerns associated with the multicultural management of diversity. The police, formal education, and mass media are employed as illustrative examples to accentuate the advances and the pitfalls for mainstreaming, diversity. First, however, we need to explore the concept of institutional accommodation to determine the institutional lay of terrain for study and evaluation.

INSTITUTIONAL ACCOMMODATION

It is one thing to encourage the diversification of Canada through immigration. It is another thing to promote a multiculturalism policy that endorses the principle of diversity as a legitimate component in Canadian society-building. It may be something altogether different to take these principles and put them into practice in a way that makes an appreciable difference. The danger signals are everywhere for those impervious to the demands of diversity. Consider only the damage to personal careers and institutional reputation. Better still, consider the potential for social strife unless minorities are made to feel as if they have a stake in Canada's system. The flashpoint at Oka and the protracted inner city problems of minority youth are just two of the indicators of a system in trouble. The fact that the latter scenario is routinely enacted in the United States, with deadly and costly results, should serve as warning to Canadians. Unless we move over and make institutional space for all Canadians, our much vaunted multicultural mosaic will shatter into shards too numerous to recombine.

Defining the Concept

What is meant by the term **institutional accommodation**? Institutional accommodation can be defined as a process by which organizations incorporate diversity at the level of structure, function, and process. Five components would appear uppermost in specifying the limits of accommodative institutions, including *representation, institutional rules and operations, workplace climate, service delivery* and *community relations*. First, an institution's workforce should be representative; that is, relatively proportional to the composition of the regional labour force — taking into account both social and cultural factors as extenuating circumstances. Such a numerical accommodation applies not only to entry-level jobs. It also is concerned with all levels of management, access to training, and entitlement to rewards. Second, institutional rules and operations cannot hinder the recruitment, selection, training, promotion, and retention of minority personnel. This commitment to root out systemic bias demands a carefully scrutiny of company policy and procedures. Third, the institution must foster a working climate conducive to minority health and productivity. At minimum, such a climate cannot tolerate harassment of any form; at best, diversity is accepted as normal, even beneficial, to effective functioning. Fourth, an accommodative institution ensures that delivery of its services is community-based and culturally-sensitive. This multicultural commitment entails both a varied workforce and a sense of partnership with the community at large. Fifth and finally, institutions do not operate in a social or political vacuum. Nor can they hope to remain outside community control and public accountability if success is anticipated. Institutions must establish meaningful relations with all community members to ensure open and productive lines of communication.

In short, institutional accommodation is all about compromise. These compromises are not concerned with promoting diversity or minorities per se. Rather they deal with creating institutions that are receptive to diversity as legitimate and integral without abdicating their traditional role of service delivery. Accommodation is necessary but not at the expense of institutional coherence and interconnectedness. A dual focus is required to create an institition that is representative of and accessible to minorities, as well as equitable in treatment and culturally sensitive. The adjustment process must occur at the level of institutional structure as well as within individual mindsets. It must also concentrate on the relationships within (the workplace environment), in addition to relationships without (clients). The magnitude of this list should confirm how the challenge of change and accommodation is a formidable one.

Barriers to Accommodation

Numerous barriers exist that interfere with the accommodation process. Stumbling blocks include *people, hierarchy, bureaucracy, corporate culture*, and *occupational subcultures*. People themselves are a prime obstruction. Institutional actors are likely to resist any appeal to change when they do not understand what is going on and why. That revelation should come as no surprise: Few individuals are inclined to relinquish power without some kind of struggle, or to voluntarily share privilege. The dimension of hierarchy will also inhibit accommodative adjustments. Those in higher echelons may be highly supportive of institutional change for a variety of reasons, ranging from genuine concern to economic expediency, with an eye toward public relations in between. Yet those in position of power may be long-winded on platitudes but short-minded on practice or implementation. Middle and lower management may be less enthusiastic about changes, preferring to cling to traditional authority patterns instead, since this level of management is most likely to be affected by institutional adjustments. Bureaucratic structures can also inhibit institutional accommodation. Larger systems operate on bureaucratic principles of hierarchy and rational control. Such an imperative is not conducive to adjustment and accommodation, especially if the reform process interferes with conventional wisdom. Institutional cultures are no less inimical to change. The operational philosophy as well as instititional imperatives may not be conducive to adjustment when perceived as a threat to the bottom line or the goal of efficiency. Finally, occupational subcultures may sabotage the best intentions of an accommodative institution (Nelson and Fleras 1995). Subcultural values of front line workers may differ from that of management because of differences in experiences or expectations. This slippage may prove fatal to the accommodative process.

Management of diversity at institutional levels is confronted by an array of personal and social barriers. Debate in this field is further complicated by those who advocate change without much thought to the costs and difficulties, versus those who are resolutely opposed and resist change at all costs. Implementing institutional changes is not like installing a new computer technology. Institutions are complex, often baffling landscapes of domination and control as well as resistance and sabotage. Conservatives and progressives are locked in a struggle for power and privilege. Conventional views remain firmly entrenched as vested interests balk at discarding the tried and true: Newer visions are compelling yet lack the singularity of purpose or resources to scuttle traditional paradigms. The interplay of these juxtapositions can be disruptive as the **institution** is transformed into a **"contested site"** involving competing worldviews and opposing agendas.

Our position rests somewhere in between these extremes: We believe that instititional accommodation is necessary and overdue; yet we also acknowledge the tenacity and logic of organizational inertia. The diversification of Canada's population demands a rethinking of traditional ways of doing things — if not for social justice, then for institutional effectiveness. We also believe that institutional accommodation is workable once the impediments to adjustment and change are isolated and challenged. Institutions and the people who inhabit them are not entirely rigid and unbending. Compromises and adjustments will materialize if there is a promise of payoff. The next sections will examine how three key institutions have addressed the notion of institutional accommodation, in the process revealing the perils and pitfalls — and successes and benefits — of putting multiculturalism to work in a multicultural society.

MINORITIES AND THE MEDIA

Canada is universally proclaimed as a multicultural society whose commitment to managing diversity at institutional levels is globally admired and occasionally copied. But these accolades gloss over discrepancies between reality and rhetoric (Cummins and Danesi 1990). Criticism by academics (Bibby 1990) and authors (Bissoondath 1994) has proliferated with charges of multiculturalism as irrelevant, wasteful, divisive, counterproductive, expedient, naive, decorative, and misplaced

(Fleras and Elliott 1991). Failure by major institutions to incorporate ethno-racial minorities into the institutional "mainstream" has made them particularly attractive targets of criticism. Few institutions, however, with the possible exception of schools and police agencies, have attracted as much criticism and concern as the mass media.

The mass media have been singled out as visibly negligent in responding positively to Canada's aboriginal and racial diversity. Passage of the Multiculturalism Act in 1988 has obligated all government agencies such as the CBC to improve access, equity, and the representation of minorities — both within the organization (in terms of hiring, promotion, and training) and outside through delivery of culturally-sensitive services to a diverse public (Secretary of State 1988). But media treatment of minorities in Canada remains mixed at best, deplorable at worst (Fleras 1994). The mass media have been reproached for an biased and inaccurate coverage of aboriginal and racial minorities, many of whom continue to be insulted, stereotyped, and caricaturized, when not actually ignored. This criticism applies across the board, from workforce composition and employment opportunities on the one hand to media portrayals of minorities on the other. The cumulative impact of such **media race role stereotyping** is unmistakably clear: Failure to improve the presentation of minorities will squander the benefits of Canada's multicultural potential.

Media and Society

Freedom of expression is one of our cherished ideals. The media are central to the construction of a democracy that is dependent upon an informed citizenry. In the interests of a free and impartial media, professional journalists appear objective and balanced in their presentation of the news. But have you ever asked yourself, what constitutes news? Is news something out there for the dispassionate journalist to uncover; or is news a socially constructed product that reflects the organizational interests and commercial priorities of the mass news media? How, then, can the media adequately cover the news to include everyone? Can television programming reflect the realities of all Canadians or only those favoured as primary consumers? To what extent can advertising encompass the entire multicultural spectrum of diversity? That answers to these questions are as inconclusive as ever is reason for worry (Fleras 1995).

Providing multicultural coverage is complicated by economic considerations. Advertising revenue is necessary to sustain the operation of both alternative and the main stream media—either print or electronic. What are the potential implications of a media dependent for survival on advertising revenue? Advertising sponsors and media owners are interested in mass circulation to boost sales and market share. As large an audience or readership as possible is a primary goal. The tastes of the majority are pandered to by the selection of news and entertainment. Advertisers target the largest segment possible for their message. Advertisements tend to be bland and sanitized so as not to offend anyone as well as to encourage consumer identification and needs. Promotional messages are as likely to conceal, evade, mis-inform, and confuse as they are to reveal, confront, inform, and enlighten. An advertising account may be cancelled if controversial programming is shown or if audience ratings drop. Thus, the media, in order to survive, must not only compete in the market place of ideas but in the economic marketplace as well.

The consequences of being ignored by the media are two-fold. First, the informational needs of a minority are ignored. The second consequence may be potentially the more serious of the two. The mass media serve as both a window on the world in terms of what is or should be, and as a mirror in which cultural values and priorities are reflected. While the media do not directly determine behaviour, they are likely to create a cultural climate in which certain persons or objects are defined as acceptable and desirable. These images and cultural frames of reference become the basis for defining what is right or wrong, good or bad. Excluding minority issues from the media tends to deny their importance or even existence. The consequences reflect poorly on Canada. If the media represent a mirror that reflects an image of society, we still have a long way to go in achieving a multicultural "looking glass self" (Desbarats (1987/1988:23).

The media arbitrate what is important, normal, and acceptable in society. This function is referred to as "reality construction" (see Harris 1993). Reality construction is doubly articulated: The media *construct* the images around which reality is created. The media confer legitimacy on the "news" by the sheer act of selecting an event for presentation — regardless of the slant or bias (see also Muhherjee 1992). The values and priorities inherent within the media impose a cultural context for framing our experiences of social reality. Conversely, the media *are constructed* by powerful forces to reproduce the social order by "manufacturing consent" (Herman and Chomsky 1988). The owners of the media as well as their commercial sponsors are pivotal players in this reality construction process. The media are also constructed through hegemonic activities — the process of consenting to one's own domination through everyday actions. Ruling class interests are better served by the media than working class needs. Minority interests are compromised by a pervasive Eurocentrism, a process whereby cultural differences are forced into a single perspective that elevates European traditions (related to values, institutions, realities, and accomplishments) as the standard by which others are judged and found wanting (Shohat and Stam 1994).

Media Mistreatment

What precisely is the nature and scope of this relationship? Certain patterns can be discerned if we look closely at mass media themes and trends. Put bluntly, racial and aboriginal minorities tend to be portrayed (a) as invisible; (b) in terms of race-role stereotyping, (c) as problem people, and (d) in decorative poses (Fleras 1991; 1994; 1995). This interpretation holds up to scrutiny on balance, whether applied applied to print or electronic media. It also applies across the board to news, advertising, or television programming.

Media portrayals of minorities tend to fall into one of the following four objectionable categories. First and foremost, minorities tend to be either *peripheral* to the central message or ignored altogether. Minorities are excluded from coverage unless there is a compelling reason to include them. Robert MacGregor in 1989 concluded that women of colour remained largely invisible in Canada's national newsmagazine (*Maclean's*) if measured by the number of appearances in ads and articles during a 30-year span, with most images restricted to a limited set of roles as well as a narrow range of goods and services — an observation also made nearly a decade earlier in a study by Doreen Indra (1981) of minority women depictions in the Vancouver presses. When featured in the media, the portrayal tends toward the negative or unflattering. Violence and tragedy will entice media coverage, as will events dealing with entertainment or sports since that creates safe places for the media to explore.

Second, minorities tend to be pigeonholed into race or gender role *stereotyping*. Aboriginal women are depicted as "princesses or squaws" (Harris 1993); African Canadians are seen as entertainers, or athletes or crooks; Asian Canadians come across as scientific wizards or mathematical geniuses; and Arab-Canadians as hot-blooded terrorists. Mass media stereotyping has shown only marginal improvement in recent years. Newscasting prefers to situate minorities in context of conflict or tragedy. Rarely are they portrayed as average people in the process of making a living and getting along, much less as experts who make a positive contribution to society. Television's ratings game excludes any complex depiction of minorities at odds with prevailing stereotypes. Minorities are sanitized and bleached of any discomfiting attributes for fear of alienating consumer expectations. Portrayal of minorities within the framework of "jokes," "jiggles" and "jolts" may ensure audience approval, but at considerable cost. In advertising, minorities are type-cast with certain products or services, presumably on the basis of market-driven research that reinforces a natural association for the product in question (see Barr 1994). Who better to hype foreign airlines, chamber-maid service in quality hotels, or high cut gym shoes? Through stereotypes, in other words, minorities are put down, put in their place, or put up as props for the edification of the mass audience. That in turn makes it difficult for people of colour to break free of such limiting confines.

Third, minorities are depicted either as *social problems* or as having problems in need of political attention or scarce national resources. As **problem people**, they are chided for making demands that may imperil Canada's unity or public coffers. Consider the case of Canada's aboriginal peoples: Time and again they are portrayed as (a) a threat to Canada's territorial integrity (the Lubicon blockade in 1988 or the Oka Mohawk confrontations in the summer of 1990) or to national interests (the Innu protest of the NATO presence in Labrador), (b) a risk to Canada's social order (the violence between factions at the Akwesasne Reserve), (c) an economic liability (the costs associated with massive land claims settlement or recent proposals to constitutionally entrench inherent self-governing rights), (d) a crisis throughout the criminal justice system (ranging from the Donald Marshall case to disproportionate numbers within the penal system), and (e) social deviants (who engage in cigarette smuggling, gaming establishments, or wildlife hunting). Immigrants and native-born minorities are also subject to mistreatment. Media reporting of refugees is normally couched in terms of illegal entry and associated costs of processing and settlement. Immigrants are routinely cast as potential trouble-makers who steal jobs from Canadians, violate rules for entry, engage in illegal activities involving drugs and guns, or deter Canada's search for identity. In all cases minority plights are sensationalized rather than situated within an historical or contemporary context. Seldom are minority problems placed in the framework of the larger society that condones, if not encourages, them in the first instance.

Fourth, minorities are exploited as *adornments* by the entertainment-driven media industry. This decorative effect is achieved by casting minorities as entertainment with which to amuse or divert the audience as villains, or victims, buffoons, or folksy sitcom types (Fiske 1994). Only rarely do they appear as heroes, overtly sexual beings, or perceptive critics of society. Minority women's bodies are gratuitously paraded to sell everything from exotic fashions to sensual perfumes (see Graydon 1995; Creedon 1993). The putting down of minorities through comic relief and cheap humour enables the larger society to elevate its own status by distancing itself from the "other." This "token" effect has a negative influence on taking minorities seriously (Wilson and Gutierrez 1995).

Accounting for the Problem

In short, minorities are reduced to invisible status through underrepresentation in programming, staffing, and decision making. Conversely they are overrepresented in areas that count for less including tourism, sports, international relief, or entertainment. Even substantial presentation in the media may be misleading if minorities are slotted into a relatively small number of programs such as TV Ontario's "Polka Dot Door" or reduced to victim/assailant in reality-based programming. No less disturbing than media "whitewashing" is the absence of minorities in creative roles such as producer, director, editor, or screenwriter. Fewer still are destined to attain the upper levels of management where key decision making occurs (see Fleras 1994 for fuller discussion). Slanted opinions of minority groups are but one consequence of such one-sided coverage. Instead of empowerment on the basis of their experiences, minority realities are refracted through the prism of a white-controlled media.

Neglect of minorities in the media may occur for a variety of reasons. Excuses may span the range from hard-boiled business decisions that reflect market forces, to a lack of cultural awareness and and deep-seated prejudice among media personnel. Certain working assumptions about racial minorities may also inhibit progressive action. People of colour are rarely depicted in the context of beauty care and personal hygiene, so entrenched is the image of "whiteness" as the preferred standard of beauty (Bledsloe 1989). Reluctance among advertisers to employ people of colour is further fueled by anxiety of a white boycott over products exclusively identified with minority ("lower class") consumption. Advertisers also fear the loss of sophistication and exclusiveness of up-scale products when linked with minority use.

Does media mistreatment of minorities imply the presence of personal prejudice or overt discrimination? Is it a case of unwittingly cramming minority realities into Eurocentric categories as a basis for evaluation, engagement, or entitlement (Shohat and Stam 1994)? Or does it reflect a preference to act out of self-interest and the dictates of market place — especially during economic recessions and periods of corporate restructuring (Jhally and Lewis 1992)? Key personnel may be unsure of how to integrate racial minorities into the media without the whiff of paternalism or tokenism. Advertising personnel may fear making mistakes that could attract negative product publicity or incite a consumer boycott. Minorities themselves may be reluctant to enter media professions because of low status associated with such employment (Khan 1989). Answers to these questions are critical, but elusive. Nevertheless, studies in this area suggest that media-minority relations are tainted by incidents of discrimination and traces of racism — at times deliberate, at other times inadvertent as the case study, "Media as Systemic Discrimination" acknowledges.

INSIGHT

Media as Systemic Discrimination

How do the media discriminate systemically? At the core of media actions is a commitment to Eurocentrism — a belief so pervasive as to be undetectable yet powerful in sanitizing the West while inferiorizing the rest of the world (Shohat and Stam 1994).

Minorities as a group are ignored or rendered irrelevant by mainstream presses. Otherwise coverage is animated by the demands of crisis or calamity, involving natural catastrophes, civil wars, and colourful insurgents. While such events do occur, the absence of balanced coverage results in distorted perceptions of minority needs, concerns, or aspirations. This distortion may not be deliberately engineered. Rather, the misrepresentation is systemic in light of media preoccupation with readership and advertising revenues. The flamboyant and sensational are highlighted to satisfy audience needs and sell copy, without much regard for its effects on racial minorities. The mass media may not be aware of its discriminatory impact, arguing they are reporting only what is news. Nevertheless, the resulting outcome paints an unflattering portrayal of racial minorities as subhuman and hardly worthy of our sympathy or foreign aid (Elliott and Fleras 1991; Omi: 1989).

The use of language can reflect a systemic bias in how media issues are framed. For example, reference to the expression "Oka Crisis" is part of our vocabulary. Its use as a convenient media shorthand has the effect if not the intent of localizing aboriginal concerns into one irrational flashpoint, while ignoring a history of aboriginal grievances across Canada. Or consider the language employed by a Toronto columnist who described the funeral of Georgina Leimonis (accidently shot in a robbery at a neighbourhood restaurant called Just Desserts) as a ritual of innocence: "Four young women in white, each holding a single white rose, lead a gleaming white coffin to the alter. A wedding dress and a veil; a corpse as pale as the moon..." Compare this with her assailant — a bearded brown man with a facial mole and a dangling earring (see also Irshad Manji "Nation's Newsroom a Pale Reflection of our Diverse Society" *The Toronto Star* 9 August 1994). There is no malevolent intent here to verbally bash minorities. Rather a clear dichotomy of good versus evil is inadvertently conveyed in a world where primary access to reality is through image and representation. The combined impact of these images tends to demonize minorities by racializing crime while criminalizing minority groups.

Mainstreaming the Media

What have the media accomplished by way of improving their relationship with minorities in Canada? What do minorities want in terms of institutional accommodation? To what extent are these demands consistent with organizational priorities and operations?

Minority Demands

Racial and aboriginal minorities are displeased with their treatment by the media. They advocate instead a media that reflect the diversity in Canada, and take responsibility for advancing minority concerns in a multicultural society. Responsible coverage of minority interests and concerns is predicated on the need to stop (a) selective and sensationalistic accounts, (b) images and words that demean and malign, (c) portrayals that are biased and unbalanced while lacking any sense of context, and (d) stereotyping that inflames hatred and fear (Rees 1986). In a society where the media claim to represent the general public and to be representative of public interest, racial and aboriginal minorities are determined to exert some degree of control over the who, why, what, how, and where of media-minority relations. Patterns for self-determination are proposed at all levels of operation and organization, ranging from the collection of news items to its layout and dissemination (Fleras 1994).

Institutional Responses

The media in Canada are under scrutiny to make appropriate adjustments. Racial and aboriginal minorities have asked some tough questions of the media regarding the reality and richness of Canada's cultural diversity combined with the legal and moral responsibilities of the Canadian broadcasting system (Abu-Laban 1981). Proposed changes include the incorporation of minority perspectives into the media process, multicultural programming, balanced and impartial newscasting, and sensitivity training for journalists and decision makers. Alternate arrangements include the creation of separate minority networks for enhancing minority input into the media process and outcomes (see also Spoonley and Hirsch 1990).

Changes are already in progress. The government Task Force on Broadcasting Policy co-chaired by Gerald Caplan and Florian Sauvagneau in 1986 singled out the need to include aboriginal peoples and racial minorities (Currents 1987; Raboy 1988). The 1988 Broadcasting Act has come out in favour of "cultural expression" by expanding air time for ethnic and racial minorities. Reforms include sensitivity training for program and production staff, language guidelines to reduce race-role stereotypes, and monitoring on-air representation of racial minorities. Rules are in place to deter abusive representations of individuals on the basis of race or ethnicity, as well as age, gender, religion, or disability. In short, the programming of multicultural minorities in a positive manner is an enlightened and overdue commitment.

The expansion of the "third media" (including ethnic presses and non-English, non-French broadcast programs) is a prime example of minority inroads (Taborsky et al. 1986). Over 200 ethnic periodicals were accounted for in 1980 with a readership of over 2 million (Black and Leithner 1987). There are 2000 hours a week of third language programming divided among 8 multilingual radio stations, CFMT Toronto — the world's only full time commercial television station to feature multicultural programming, 8 television stations with some language programs, 60 radio stations that offer ethnic programming, 3 pay and specialty services, and community-based programs on cable television (Report, National Proceedings 1988).

Reforms are also evident in the private sector where Toronto's CITY-TV station and on-air programming are addressing multicultural issues. Aboriginal communities especially in the far north have been successful in gaining control of the media as one means of empowerment through language and culture (Higgins 1993). Finally, people of colour are appearing more frequently across a broader range of advertised products and services. International companies such as Benetton that utilize diversity are now perceived as sophisticated and cosmopolitan; all-white counterparts tend to come across as staid and dated. Governments too have cast about for the right mix of racial minorities in their ads, although some people view the final product as forced and contrived (Allen 1991). In general, then, evidence from the past twenty years has confirmed what ethno-racial minorities have long protested: media changes are slow. Yet efforts to improve the situation are criticized as not enough and unconvincing. That sets the stage for further conflict of interests.

To Sum Up: The mass media play an influential role in defining what is socially desirable or normal. This is accomplished in large part by laying down a specific cultural framework that provides a reference point for acceptance or validity. So embedded and pervasive is a commitment to Eurocentrism in everyday life that it often is unnoticed — let alone challenged or debated (Shohat and Stam 1994). As a primary channel of communication, the mass media have the potential to articulate a powerful statement about the legitimacy of diversity in our society. Yet they are equally likely to inculcate and defend the economic, political, and social agenda of the privileged classes. At the core of this redefinition process is power. Until the issue of power is resolved — in terms of who owns it, who has access to it, and whose values will dominate — media-public relations will remain riddled with ambiguity and fraught with frustration.

MINORITIES AND EDUCATION

The educational system has for the most part reflected a fundamental commitment to monoculturalism. Historically, education was inseparable from the amalgamation of cultures into the mainstream. This conformist ideology sought to absorb immigrant children directly into Canadian society by stripping them of language and culture (Berryman 1988; Allingham 1992; McAndrew 1992; Moodley 1993). All aspects of schooling, from teachers and textbooks to policy and curriculum, were folded into the principles of anglo-conformity. Anything that veered outside this anglocentric framework was ignored as irrelevant or dangerous. Special curricula or references to other languages or cultures were rejected as inconsistent with the educational needs of Canadian society-building. Aboriginal children were sent to residential schools and punished for speaking their own languages. An exception to this assimilation-through-exposure ethos lay in the exclusionary segregation that until recently existed by law in Ontario and Nova Scotia, as described in "Segregated Education."

INSIGHT

Segregated Education

Taken from *Chronicle of Milestones in Canadian Multiculturalism* (1987): ...black Canadians in Ontario and Nova Scotia...were progressively restricted from access to schools attended by white children and were forced into segregated educational systems. These segregated systems did not totally disappear in this country until the mid-1960s....

By the 1850s, segregated public schools could be found operating in both Nova Scotia and Ontario. Segregated schools had been legalized throughout the Province of Canada in 1849 by a statute that permitted municipal councils to establish separate schools for blacks. The practice was reinforced by the Separate School Act of 1859, which provided that any five black families could petition local school officials to establish schools for blacks. What appeared on paper as a voluntary procedural device became in fact a means to force black children out of white local schools. Court decisions reinforced this segregation in Ontario where, for example, in the 1860s it was decreed that black children could be legally assigned to a segregated school regardless of the distance from home.

In Ontario, separate black schools began to disappear after 1910 more because of a lack of students than because of an enlightened and tolerant attitude on the part of the white community. But it took until May 7, 1964, for the references to separate education for blacks to be removed from Ontario's school laws, and until September 1965 for the last black school in that province to close. Meanwhile, legally segregated education ended in Nova Scotia in 1963, although some schools still have an all- black student body because they serve an all-black rural community.

The explicit assimilationist model that once prevailed within educational circles is no longer officially endorsed (Fleras and Elliott 1992). The impetus for multicultural education differs from the past educational initiatives in both its form and content. The new focus in education is increasingly to be responsive to diversity, and to create a learning environment that acknowledges the culture of its students (Henry et al. 1995). These initiatives wrap themselves around the rhetoric of "cross-cultural communication," "racial awareness and sensitivity," and "healthy identity formation." Yet there is a sense in which the public school system is failing certain minorities by not giving them the proper education (*Toronto Star* Feb 11, 1995) A closer look at these policies reveals a set of functions associated with formal education that are not altogether dissimilar from the mass media.

Both the media and education are secondary agents of socialization whose social functions are often at odds with formal mandates. The following functions of education prevail in society: (a) socialization, or transmission of culture (b) self-actualization and individual self-development (c) preparation for workplace, consumerism, and citizenship (d) improvement in Canada's competitive edge, and (e) reproduction of the social order. Education plays both a conservative and progressive role in society depending upon the level of education under examination. For example, elementary school education serves a conservative function whereby cultural assumptions are tacitly inculcated along with the three Rs. Postsecondary education, by contrast, endorses debate and knowledge as a basis for progressive change. Yet the a tacit commitment to assimilation remains a central objective. Alok Mukherjee (1992:73) writes:

> Traditionally, the school has been a conservative institution. Its function, on the one hand, is to legitimize the dominant social, political, economic, and cultural ideas of society and, on the other, to perpetuate existing relations. The ownership, organization, and activities of the school reflect this dual role.

From daily routines to decision making at the top, education is organized to facilitate cultural indoctrination and social control of students. These reproductive functions can be accomplished in a direct manner by the selection of textbooks that reflect mainstream experiences or values. The streaming of minority students into lower level programs, as well as diminished teacher expectations, restricts these students' access to higher education and useful employment. Indirect and largely unobtrusive measures are also employed. For example, the widely accepted practice of grading students often has been accused of reinforcing competitive individualism to the exclusion of prosocial values. Through schooling, in other words, the reproduction of the ideological and social order is realized without much public awareness or open fan fare. Nor are administrators or decision makers necessarily aware of the systemic bias inherent within the institution itself. This "hidden curriculum" is nicely described by Apple and Franklin (1979):

> Schools...help control meaning. They preserve and distribute what is perceived to be "legitimate knowledge" — the knowledge that "we all must have." Thus schools confer cultural legitimacy on the knowledge of specific groups. (quoted in Muhherjee 1992:76)

Deliberate or not, the school system screens out certain information by projecting some views of the world while rejecting others. In linking power with culture, the school ends up perpetuating the social status quo and prevailing power distributions (Apple 1987).

The notion of social reproduction puts constraints on multicultural education. A receptivity to diversity and change within the context of equality is doubly difficult in a milieu where assimilation and monoculturalism prevail. Powerful forces and entrenched interests are unlikely to tolerate significant changes without considerable resistance. Changes when they do occur may be relegated to the cosmetic realm, and away from the key domains of decision making, agenda setting, and power sharing. The largely conservative orientation of education ensures some degree of opposition to change unless the change serves vested interests. This factor alone should warn against any excessive expectations regarding the potential of multicultural education. Still, the fact that pluralist initiatives have materialized at numerous schools suggests that **multicultural education** is an idea whose time has arrived.

Multicultural Education

Multicultural education encompasses a variety of policies, programs, and practices for managing diversity within the school setting. It can encompass the study of many cultures or an understanding of the world from diverse perspectives or convey how power and politics are inextricably connected with unequal group relations (see Schuman and Olufs 1995). Additional perspectives include healthy identity formation, cultural preservation, intercultural sensitivity, racism awareness, and cross-cultural communication. Issues related to social equality and equity are also recognized, in theory if not always in practice. The impact and implications of these shifts cannot be taken lightly. The introduction of multicultural education has redefined how schools relate to the presence of diversity. Its introduction has also raised questions about the form, function, and processes of formal education in a racially and culturally plural society.

What, then, are the specific objectives or functions of multicultural education? Two main perspectives emerge — enrichment and empowerment. **Enrichment multicultural education** is aimed at all students, not just ethnic minority students. Students are exposed to a variety of different cultures to enhance a knowledge of and appreciation for cultural diversity. The curriculum is enriched with various multicultural add-ons. Special days are set aside for multicultural awareness; projects are assigned that reflect multicultural themes; and specific cultures are singled out for intensive classroom study. A desirable side effect of the enrichment process is greater tolerance, enhanced sensitivity, and more harmonious inter-cultural relations. A less beneficial consequence is a failure to initiate wholescale institutional changes — much less to challenge the racism both within and outside the school.

A second model which is not necessarily incompatible with the first is **empowerment multicultural education**. This perspective calls for sweeping changes in the curriculum — not simply a tinkering with multicultural concessions. An empowerment perspective deals with issues related to the control and exploitation of minorities. The targets are not only pupils (minority and otherwise), but also decision makers from principals to superintendents. The school itself is seen as part of the problem with concerns aimed at hiring policies, teacher training, textbook selection, and curriculum development. Even pedogogical style may come under scrutiny as explained in, "Schooling Aboriginal Children."

INSIGHTS

Schooling Aboriginal Children

One variation of the empowerment model is directed essentially at the perceived needs of the minority student. The minority-focus model is controversial because not everyone necessarily shares the initial assumption about the nature and scope of the problem upon which the model is based.

An example of multicultural education as empowerment can be seen in the struggle by aboriginal peoples to gain control of aboriginal education. Since the early 1970s, the First Nations have sought to implement a variety of changes revolving around the need to (a) decentralize the educational structure, (b) transfer funding control to local authorities, (c) devolve power from the centre to the community, and (d) empower parents to assume increased responsibility for their children's education. Aboriginal grievances and concerns over education are understandable. Historically, the government's educational policies have embraced a explicit commitment to assimilate aboriginal children through segregation and indoctrination. Federally-directed native education sought to disrupt the cultural patterns of aboriginal children, then expose them to the values and priorities of the West, often in schools off the reserve and away from community, friends, and relatives. The abusive consequences of residential schools have been widely documented. Other consequences are less direct but no less real in denying aboriginal experiences, as the Metis scholar, Paul Chartrand (1992:8-9) says, "It is easy to assert power over others if they are made to feel they have no identity, they have no past, or at least no past that matters."

The aims of aboriginal-controlled education are two-fold. First, it seeks to impart those skills which aboriginal children will need to succeed in the outside world. Second, it hopes to immerse children in an environment that is unmistakeably aboriginal in content, style, and outcome. Only a relatively separate education system controlled by aboriginal people for aboriginal people is viewed as a corrective to these historically imposed disadvantages. The key is to produce children who possess a strong sense of who they are and where they came from, without foresaking skills for the dominant sector. Various strategies have been put into place to foster the goals of culture, identity, and equality. These include (a) greater reliance on aboriginal styles of learning and teaching, (b) increased dependence on aboriginal tongues as languages of instruction not just subjects on the curriculum, (d) improved teacher training and sensitivity to aboriginal customs and experiences, and (e) moves to purge textbooks and curriculum of bias and distortion. It remains to be seen if the aboriginal educators can solve the dual dilemma of an education system that delivers both culture and equality for native pupils.

The empowerment model addresses such topics as power, agenda setting and decision making. The objective is to redesign the educational institution from the bottom up. Modifications include (a) school policies and politics, (b) the school culture and "hidden" curriculum, (c) languages — official, heritage, and other, (d) community participation, (e) assessment, testing procedures, and program tracking, (f) instructional materials, (g) the formal curriculum, (h) the ethnic composition of the teaching staff, (i) and teacher attitudes, values and competency. Table 11.1 provides a succinct comparison and contrast of the focus of enrichment versus empowerment educational styles (adapted in part from Henry et al. 1995).

To sum up: How might one assess the enrichment and empowerment models? The enrichment model is generally acceptable to all because of its status as a pleasant diversion. It is non-threatening in its initial assumptions and program delivery. Yet the enrichment model has been criticized as too static and restrictive in scope. It tends to focus on the exotic components of a culture, rather than values and beliefs, and is sometimes taught by poorly trained teachers who inadvertently may trivialize or stereotype (Henry et al. 1995). Diverse cultures are studied at the level of material culture, stripped of their historical context and discussed from an outsider's point of view (Mukherjee 1992). There is also a danger of over-romanticizing minorities or of damning them as social problems if discussion dwells on conflict or racism. Finally, since not all cultures can receive equal time, how is the selection process handled? Even sensitive presentations must grapple with dilemmas as varied as (a) discussing elements of other cultures that are fundamentally opposed to Canada's democratic principles; (b) emphasizing the positive features of minorities and overlooking the problems many confront; (c) focusing on those aspects of culture (for example, the material components) that everyone can relate to yet ignoring more substantial issues; (d) presenting differences without reinforcing stereotypes or an "us" versus "them" mentality; and (e) teaching the idea that everyone is basically different in the same kind of way or, alternatively, everyone is fundamentally the same in radically different ways (see MacAndrew 1992).

TABLE 11.1 Styles of Multicultural Education

	Enrichment	Empowerment
Focus	attitudes	behaviour
Objectives	prejudice	discrimination
Goals	diversity	disparity
Outcome	lifestyle ("heritage")	life chances
Means	culture	race relations
Style	accommodation	opposition
Magnitude	reactive	proactive
Scope	individual	organizational

To date, both models have had only partial and limited application. Rarely do schools seriously contemplate the changes that must occur at the level of curriculum, language, and culture programs for children, placement and assessent, employment and promotion, teacher training, and relations with community to apply them fully (McAndrew 1992). Ad hoc adjustments are more common than radical restructuring. Nor does there appear to be any wholesale move to reject the assimilationist ethos of the school system (Cummins and Danesi 1990). Discriminatory structures are not easily dismantled in the light of entrenched interests and ideologies. The education system is only one institution among many, reflecting the values and attitudes that prevail in the larger community. Only when all institutions act in unison can genuine reform be implemented (Bhatnagar, 1983).

Anti-Racist Education

Two styles prevail in accommodating diversity within schools: multicultural and/or anti-racist (Fleras and Elliott 1992). Multicultural education refers to a philosophy for celebrating differences. It consists of activities or curricula that promote an awareness of diversity in terms of its intrinsic value to minorities and/or society at large (Ministry of Education and Training 1993). The aim of multicultural education is largely attitudinal; that is, to enhance sensitivity by improving knowledge about cultural differences. Strategies are varied, spanning the spectrum from museum approaches to immersion programs, with cross-cultural enrichment in between.

Anti-racist education differs from multicultural education as an ideal type. While multicultural education is merely intolerant of racism in its practice, anti-racism seeks to actively eradicate racism through awareness, challenge, and confrontation. At one level anti-racist education is concerned with equalizing minority presence in the centre of the curriculum; providing a platform for minority stories to be told in their own voices; the acquisition of critical tools to understand and challenge racism and inequality; questioning the white-centredness of school knowledge as the only legitimate form of culture; and employing this knowledge as a basis for action (Allingham 1992; Mukherjee 1992; McCaskill 1995). At another level, anti-racism is concerned with the identification and removal of discriminatory barriers, both personal and systemic, at interpersonal and institutional levels. Minority underachievement is not necessarily caused by cultural differences; nor will cross-cultural understanding contribute to any fundamental change. Improving minority status is contingent on removing the behavioural and structural components of racial inequality, along with the power and privileges that sustain racism through institutional policies, practices, and procedures (Ministry of Education and Training 1993). Table 11.2 provides a summary comparison between multicultural versus anti-racist education in terms of *focus, objectives, concerns, scope,* and *outcomes.*

TABLE 11.2 Multicultural and Anti-Racist Education: Comparisons and Contrasts

	Multicultural Education	Anti-Racist Education
Focus	Culture	Structure
Objectives	Sensitivity	Removal of Discriminatory Barriers
Concerns	Ethnocentrism	Systemic Racism
Scope	Ethnicity	Race
Outcomes	Understanding	Equality

Two styles of anti-racist strategy can be discerned: one is concerned with modifying individual behaviour; the other with removal of discriminatory structural barriers through institutional reform. Anti-racism at *individual* levels concentrates on behaviour modification through education and training (Stern 1992). *Institutional* anti-racism strategies are aimed at dismantling the structural basis of school racism. These systemic biases are most apt to occur at the level of mission statement, culture and subculture, power and decision making, structures (including rules, roles, and realationships), and distribution of physical, financial, and human assets. These two-pronged anti-racist initiatives sound plausible in theory; their implementation may prove another story. The case study, "Toward Anti-Racist Campus," illustrates this dilemma.

CASE STUDY

Toward an Anti-racist Campus

It is taken as axiomatic that racism is a pervasive feature of Canadian institutions (Henry et al. 1995). The magnitude and scope of this racism, as well as its intensity and intent, are expressed in different ways. Yet its impact tends to be the same, regardless of who, what, why, or how. People of colour are put down or put in their place in a society that professes multiculturalism but doesn't always match the words with actions (Fleras and Elliott 1992).

Educational institutions are no exception to this rule. Both primary and secondary schools have been criticized as sites of racism and discrimination, in effect sullying Canada's reputation as pacesetter for progressive social change (Mukherjee 1993). Considerable energy has gone into the design and implementation of appropriate anti-racist policies; since 1992, for example, school boards in Ontario have parlayed anti-racist and ethnocultural equity programs into everyday practice (Ministry of Education and Training 1993). By contrast, post-secondary initiatives for mainstreaming diversity through anti-racist measures have been inconsistent at best, non-existent at worst. Policies and programs tend to be motivated by a preference for crisis management or public relations, rather than a commitment to fundamental change.

This seeming indifference to campus racism beyond the symbolic or token cannot be taken lightly. The demographic revolution of the past twenty years has had a profound effect on post-secondary schooling. The composition of the student body has been irrevocably altered; course content is increasingly contested; minority faculty are growing in numbers and assertiveness; Eurocentric pedagogical styles are under review; and university operations can no longer abide by conventional rules, roles, and responsibilities (Price 1993; Schuman and Olufs 1995; Henry et al. 1995). Rather than being above the fray, as popularly depicted, colleges and universities are no less susceptible to change around equity issues of race and gender then any other institution (Exum 1980; OFS 1991; McCaskill 1995).

THE PROBLEM

Survey studies provide some data that describe the magnitude and scope of campus racism (Ramcharan 1991). The results of these studies have been published elsewhere (Fleras 1995), but the following points appear consistent across Canadian universities and community colleges.

- The number of *reported* race-related incidents on postsecondary campuses is not especially high, averaging from about 20 to 120 per year at certain Canadian universities and community colleges.

- Most of the incidents that come to the attention of authorities do *not* involve physical retaliation, but consist of verbal slurs (from innuendos to stereotypes) and ethnic jokes.

- Students (because their of their numbers) are predominantly involved in most racial encounters, with most incidents occuring in residences, pubs, cafeterias, and classrooms.

Some tentative conclusions can be drawn from these surveys, though total reliance on statistics can distort our understanding of magnitude and scope. First, the numbers themselves may say more about the survey instrument than about campus racism. The recording of an incident as race related or racial is not necessarily proof of racism; it may reflect interpersonal conflict that entails a racial dimension because people of different backgrounds are involved. Increases in reported incidents may convey a greater willingness to report racial violations rather than a collapse of society. Second, there may be a strong tendency to under-report racial incidents — partly from fear of reprisals or from being branded a malcontent. Minorities may be deterred from coming forward with legitimate concerns because of worries that a complaint could be dismissed as frivolous if not upheld (McGill 1994). They risk being stereotyped as hypersensitive and overreactive, with a tendency to exaggerate or create problems. Such labelling has the effect of diminishing the force of their claims. Visa minority students may disregard racial incidents altogether, even when directly confronted, for fear of losing their visa status or compromising academic standing (Ramcharan 1991). Many whites are still incapable of recognizing racism in its varied forms, let alone in reporting it to proper authorities (University of Guelph 1994). For whites, racism consists of deviant actions by malevolent persons; for minorities, racism is about patterns of *power* and *privilege* that are locked into the structures of society (Blauner 1972). Many individuals are unsure of where or when to report an incident, in some cases preferring the security of confiding only among friends.

Numbers cannot possibly convey a victim's humiliation or sense of betrayal. Minorities routinely encounter mistrust or hostility, in addition to distorted perceptions and polite putdowns, all of which combine to intensify feelings of isolation or exclusion (OFS 1991). Unless victimized themselves, few can appreciate either the pain inflicted by racist grafitti or the paralyzing fear imposed by hate groups and racist literature. Even a seemingly harmless prank or thoughtless remark can create psychological distress every bit as emotionally devastating and socially debilitating as open bigotry (Stern 1992).

DISSECTING CAMPUS RACISM

Racism exists on postsecondary levels even if its magnitude and scope cannot be adequately assessed. Discrimination may be blatant at times; at other times discriminatory actions veer toward the polite, with most overt expressions (slurs or jokes) restricted to classrooms or student residences and cafeterias. More common still is *systemic* discrimination.

Systemic discrimination rests on the belief that higher education operates on principles that deny or exclude even if the individuals themselves are free of prejudicial intent. It refers to the adverse yet unintended effect of applying apparently neutral institutional rules but with dissimilar consequences. Policies and programs that appear neutral on the surface may rest on structures and patterns that distribute rewards unequally (Schuman and Olufs 1995). Take, for example, an Eurocentric curriculum as a tacitly assumed point of departure for class content and conduct. This exclusiveness may be systemically discriminatory, regardless of motive, in that alternative perspectives never appear. This monocultural agenda not only excludes or invalidates minority experiences; such exclusionary reference points also have a detrimental effect on those who fail to comply with the game plan (OFS 1991).

However defined, campus racism continues to be perceived as a social problem. Racial discrimination is created and is secured by official policies and practices, incorporated into structures and operations as normal or necessary, and sustained through ideologies that rationalize inequities as aberrations from an otherwise fair and open system of competition (Chesler and Crowfoot 1989). Yet campus racism is anything but incidental or accidental, much less individual or attitudinal. Nor is it "idealist" in the sense that underachievement stems from cultural differences, with its implicit commitment to "blame the victim" as a central explanatory variable (Hick and Santos 1992). As Blauner (1972: 276-278) puts it in defining the nature of campus racism:

...[F]or the liberal professor...racism connotes conscious acts, where there is an intent to hurt or degrade or disadvantage others because of their color or ethnicity...He does not consider the all-white or predominantly white character of an occupation or institution in itself to be racism. ... acts of omission, indifference, and failure to change the status quo.

The true nature of ivory tower racism is neither sporadic nor random; nor is it restricted to the deranged actions of a few social misfits. Campus racism is not so much about what happens but more with what doesn't happen. Racism is properly located in the systemic and institutionalized, with deep roots in organizational structures and dynamics that disempower and exclude. Eurocentric (and patriarchal) values tend to prevail with respect to underlying assumptions, mission statements, culture and subcultural values, power relations, organizational structure, operating principles, reward systems, and intended outcomes (Chesler and Crowfoot 1989; McIntyre 1993; Schuman and Olufs 1995). The sheer invisibility of systemic racism renders it difficult for whites to recognize the institutional inequities that confront people of colour. Those in the dominant sector are often oblivious to the privileges and social advantages associated with whiteness as the preferred norm and taken-for-granted standard (McIntosh 1988). As Robert Blauner (1972:277) notes: the university is racist because people of color are and have been systematically excluded from full and equal participation and power — as students, professors, administrators, and, particularly, in the historic definition of the character of the institution and its curriculum."

THE SOLUTION

Perceptions of racism in the ivory towers have elicited responses ranging from denial to bandwagon acceptance. Few, however, would doubt the realities of campus racism even if its intensity and tone are subject to dispute. Wishing to prevent or respond to racial incidents, many universities have instituted policies and offices expressly for diversity issues (Montgomery and MacDonald 1991). Others have implemented harassment codes and anti-discrimination guidelines in conformity with provincial Human Rights Codes. Students too have been at the anti-racism vanguard through mobilization at different campuses (Hick and Santos 1992). Yet administrative initiatives may border on the misguided or cosmetic. To date, many anti-racist concessions are seen as devices for calming "troublesome constituents" through conflict management or damage control. Nor can we be sure that solutions will fall into place even when people agree on the problem and program objectives (Queen's 1991:3); nevertheless, consensus is growing around proposed solutions to improve minority-university relations.

Reactive Strategies

Post-secondary institutions have conceded the ineffectiveness of ad hoc responses to racist incidents. Impromptu solutions are prone to magnify tensions rather than dampen hostilities. Indecisiveness can be fatal when the administration stands accused of footdragging in censuring racist actions (Stern

1992). Failure to act quickly with zero tolerance can escalate a crisis by fostering an impression that anti-racism has a lower priority than pandering to contented alumni. To avoid either chaos or institutional paralysis, two types of response mechanism have been articulated.

Reactive strategies concentrate on crisis management through damage control and conflict resolution. Rules and procedures are put in place to deal with racist incidents as expeditiously as possible for the preservation of campus peace and order. Reactive response plans consist of rehearsed contingency measures about what to do in an emergency, and who should do it. Formal mechanisms are instituted to open the lines of communication and grievance resolution. Resource persons are appointed to provide advisory and consultative services for students in need. Recruitment of committees from a cross-section of the campus may assist in planning policy and procedures for worst-case scenarios. Disciplinary codes are implemented as a last resort for punishing offenders or to deter would-be offenders.

Proactive Strategies

Proactive measures concentrate on prevention and problem-solving. Universities and community colleges across the country have conducted research and drawn up plans to identify and solve problems (Gray 1993). Formal positions have been instituted such as a Race Relations Office or Human Rights Committee as a means of grievance resolution or conflict mediation. In conjunction with these support committees are formalized mission statements and reports that denounce campus racism.

Recommendations from these reports tend to follow a common script by focusing on proposals related to policy, offices, committees, admissions, hiring and rewards, equity measures, and complaint procedures (Queen's 1991; UWO 1993; McGill 1994; O'Neill and Yelaha 1994). More specifically:

(a) Facilitate the participation of members from underrepresented groups at institutional levels of decision making. Foster equity in terms of recruitment and minority hiring within acceptable time frames; in addition, establish clearly articulated guidelines about appointment, promotion, and tenure. Review all procedures, policies and practices to ensure they are free of systemic bias. Indicate that those in positions of authority are answerable for failure to implement race relations programs or improve employment opportunities for minorties.

(b) Encourage the entry of aboriginal and minority students through more flexible admission requirements and the removal of hidden barriers. Institute procedures for the "care and feeding" (counselling or financial advice) of minority students.

(c) Include non-Eurocentric perspectives and minority concerns across the entire post-secondary spectrum, from governing bodies to classrooms, curricula, resource centres and library, ethics, and research. Accomodate minority religious observance within the demands of scheduling. Construct minority-friendly student and support services as well as a classroom climate consistent with Canada's multicultural principles.

(d) Investigate complaints. Reduce incidents of discrimination and racism on campus by dealing firmly with violations through consultation or counselling. Recommend corrective action. Ensure persons in authority are accountable for actions that violate the spirit of anti-racist initiatives.

(e) Foster a supportive university climate for work and study that is free of discrimination and racial harassment. Introduce race relations awareness education for all university members. Provide skills training programs that assist in addressing racial problems. Pursue positive community relations as a preventative measure.

(f) Design workshops to assist departments in promoting an environment free of discrimination or harassment. Establish appropriate procedures for implementation of race relations programs. Publicize an awareness of complaint procedures and disciplinary channels that are universally accessible, free of reprisals from peers or authority, and complainant-friendly without infringing on the principles of due process.

Universities and community colleges appear to be moving in the right direction. Policy and mission statements are increasingly commonplace — nearly 20 documents were in place by late 1993 (Gray 1993) — with a broad array of chairs, committees, advisors, and offices for advising, consulting, monitoring, recommending, and initiating disciplinary action. All share certain outlooks; namely, a desire to uphold the right for everyone to study or work in an environment free from racial discrimination for reasons unrelated to ability or skills (CAUT 1994). Most are also convinced of the need to educate students and staff about racism — its causes and consequences as well as manifestations and solutions (CAUT 1994).

Admittedly the effectiveness of these offices and policies are open to conjecture (Henry et al. 1995): Solutions lean toward moderate reforms such as additional courses or sensitivity training, all of which provide a temporary departure from conventional norms, but do not disrupt institutional structures, curricular content, academic freedom, standards of merit, and hierarchies that shore up entrenched interests. Effectiveness of agencies and initiatives depend on their location within the academic structure (Chesler and Crowfoot 1989). Access to resources is no less critical than their degree of involvement in decision-making. There are additional risks: The establishment of offices and officers may help individual victims, but it also increases the chances of individualizing racism rather than galvanizing support against the systemic but assymetrical power relations in society that are reproduced in the ivory towers (Carniol 1991: Hick and Santos 1992; also Bartolome 1994). In other words, despite a spate of administrative concessions and reforms, the question remains as baffling as ever: How willing are universities to go the anti-racist route, given its potential to provoke or partition different groups?

PROSPECTS

Institutions of higher learning are expected to comport themselves in an exemplary fashion. They are looked upon as bastions of enlightenment; yet they are saddled with the messy responsibility of spearheading progressive social change. Their mission and objectives related to teaching and research must somehow strike a balance between empowering the dispossessed and enhancing excellence in understanding (Proceedings 1993; Schuman and Olufs 1995). The problem is common to all institutions: How to appear progressive and liberal-minded without changing the foundational core of the system (McIntyre 1993). How can diversity be accommodated without undermining the interconnectedness of the constituent parts? Whether or not these institutions can meet this challenge without capitulating to conflicting demands will hinge on how contemporary roles and responsibilities are reassessed.

Evidence is mounting that minorities want institutional changes and meaningful inclusion rather than token acceptance at the margins of higher learning (McIntyre 1993). Efforts to address campus racism through inclusiveness will require the cooperative efforts of all stakeholders — from president to custodian, from students to staff, from boardrooms to classrooms — by way of forums, presidential statements, and campus debate (Stern 1992). Responding to this challenge will entail both political will and financial muscle, at a time of fiscal restraint and minority assertiveness. It will demand personal courage to stand up to charges of "political cor-

rectness" for speaking out against racism and sexism (Richer and Weir 1995). Compromise and commitment will be sorely tested in balancing the apparent clash between quality and equality, freedom and inclusiveness. This restructuring process is not intended to fragment or needlessly diversify higher education. Rather the aim is to create a post-secondary culture in which diversity can flourish as a legitimate organizational component, without repudiating the principles that animate higher education and propel its mission (Arthurs 1993).

IMPLICATIONS

The issue of campus racism and anti-racist universities and colleges raises a host of questions about the form and function of post-secondary education for the twenty-first century. A shared set of values are urgently needed to address the identity crisis confronting contemporary higher education. Yet the questions loom ever larger: Who will participate in redefining the role and responsibilities of postsecondary education; what values will predominate; and whose interests will they serve (Banks 1992)?

Inclusiveness is one key in the reconstruction process. Racism itself is a social and cultural phenomena, as well as a political and economic issue, and must be confronted accordingly, namely through creation of an egalitarian and inclusive political culture (Arthurs 1993). Anti-racism is *not* merely an add-on that can be compartmentalized or isolated, then dusted off for public relations or crisis intervention. Rather the incorporation of anti-racism as philosophy and practice is potentially revolutionary, with its promise to radically redefine the entire postsecondary enterprise from teaching to tenure. Such a re-inventing will prove formidable in a political environment where diverse interests compete for scarce resources. Debates about the role of higher education are really about power and control — who

has it, who wants it, and who is going to do something about it (Schuman and Olufs 1995). Despite costs and disruptions to "the way things are done around here," the benefits from this struggle will be worthwhile with respect to post-secondary institutions, both inclusive and equitable, in a world increasingly global in outlook and postmodernist in practice.

POLICING AND MINORITIES

The criminal justice system should be no less responsive to the demands of accommodation than other institutions in our society; for this reason the slow and erratic nature of the response is cause for concern. This indictment is especially evident at the level of policing and law enforcement where miscalculations are not always measured by inconvenience but in deadly consequences. The police have been accused of underpolicing (slow response rates), in addition to overpolicing (excessive and oppressive coverage). The consequences of such discrimination tend to racialize crime in Canada while criminalizing minorities (Henry et al. 1995).

Both political and community pressure have drawn widespread attention to aspects of police-minority relations that are at odds with Canada's multicultural ethos. An increasingly fractious policing environment is evolving, given the combination of changing demographics, new legislation, diverse ethnocultural communities, minority activism, and public demands for accountability. A so-called crisis in police-minority relations has gained intellectual currency in recent years, in the process undermining the confidence of certain publics in Canadian policing. Police initiatives to stem this loss of public confidence and restore legitimacy to policing functions need to be acknowledged. Authorities at various levels have cast about for ways to ease the tension, calm troublesome constituents, patch up the crisis, and improve police-minority relations without impairing the effectiveness of the police. Initiatives related to community-based, multiculturally-sensitive policing are an important step toward easing the crisis. The fact that each step forward is counteracted by another step backward provides some insight into the challenges and complexities of institutional accommodation.

Crisis in Policing

Police-minority relations are undergoing a profound reassessment that borders on crisis and a withdrawal of legitimacy from the police in multiracial communities. The sensibilities of many Americans and Canadians were deeply offended by the riots that left over 50 people dead in Los Angeles in early May of 1992. The fact that a similar, smaller-scale riot was reenacted in Toronto with considerable property damage on the fabled Yonge Street strip proved even more distressing to those Canadians who believed that America was the land of interracial conflict. Shock, outrage, and sadness greeted news of the destruction in what many had regarded as one of the model cities in the multicultural management of multiracial cities. Elsewhere across Canada the police came in for sometimes scathing criticism. In Montreal, a coroner's inquest castigated the police for the callous and racist indifference to human life following a display of sheer incompetence in the bungled shooting of an unarmed black male. Police in Halifax and Vancouver also confronted racial animosities. This breakdown in police-minority relations and the proposed solutions to heal the rift need to be examined more carefully (Baker 1994).

The crisis in police-minority relations stems from incidents involving young urban male African-Canadians. In the greater Toronto conurban area, a total of eight young blacks were shot by the police between 1988 and 1992, compared with 10 whites, even though African-Canadians comprise only a small percentage of the total population of the metropolitan area. Of the 10 people shot in Montreal between 1988 and 1993, five were black, and three were Hispanic. Minority parents and community leaders did not see these shooting incidents as isolated cases, but a pattern of police harassment, brutality, and oppression, in the same way Marc Lepine's shooting of 14 women in Montreal in 1989 is often interpreted as a logical extension of male violence toward women. There is a widespread perception that blacks are harassed more often and subject to double standards, as well as charged and arrested at a rate far beyond their proportion in the community. Police are accused of intense presence on the grounds that they believe minorities are predisposed to crime ("overpolicing") or conspicious by their absence when needed ("underpolicing") (Henry et al. 1995). Not surprisingly, the police have been criticized as acting as an "occupying army" in a state of undeclared war in defense of white interests.

The police would dispute this assessment of their relationship with certain minority communities. The spate of shootings is perceived as isolated and coincidental events, reflecting increased incidence of gun and drugs in the city. Racially motivated actions may exist, they concede, but apply only to a small number of "bad apples" in a blue barrel rather than to institutionalized racism within the organization. The apprehension of minority youths is not a case of discriminatory policing, as far as the police are concerned, but a situation where street cultures are likely to bring these youths into collision with law enforcement agents whose job it is to impartially uphold law and order.

What we have, in other words, is a failure to connect because of contrasting perceptions of the problem — and proposed solutions. The police believe that the shootings reflect irresponsible behaviour on the part of dissaffected youths and the community in general. African-Canadians for the most part see racist and trigger-happy police as primarily responsible for the carnage on the street. Opinion is also split within the African-Canadian community since blacks themselves are internally divided into opposing camps including indigenous blacks who arrived as far back as the eighteenth century, Caribbean blacks, many of whom are relatively new Canadians, and finally African blacks such as recent refugees or immigrants from Ethiopia and Somalia.

The fact that neither side can trust or understand the other exacerbates the potential for crisis. The police circle the wagons even more securely against what they perceive as unwarranted attacks by community activists, an unsympathetic press, and opportunistic politicians. Many bristle at the prospect of relinquishing more power to civilian control or public accountability. Minority youth, in turn, become more bitter and alienated from the system, living in constant fear of their lives and having little hope of improvement for the future.

Conflicting Perspectives

How do these perceptions stack up in reality? There is little doubt that certain minority youth possess a lifestyle and pattern of behaviour that invites confrontation with the police. Minority youths may identify with "nonwhites," and define themselves in opposition to a white society and everything that it stands for or tries to do (Henry 1994). Subcultural patterns that may emphasize bravado or loyalty to others in the group creates a situation ripe for police charges and arrests. The criminalization of minority street behaviour amplifies the labelling of youth as potential troublemakers. Their reaction also has the effect of perpetuating the cycle of arrest-perception-more-arrests.

Perceptions abound that police have never shaken stereotypes of blacks as exotic, victimized, and as threats to the social order, thus trivialing minority concerns and criminalizing their lives. As a result, many minority youth find themselves in a no-win situation: For many, their lives are filled with hopelessness and despair with little or no possiblity of improvement in the future. There is a gnawing sense of having no stake in a system that essentially treats them as disposable and dispensible, yet continues to uphold the necessity of the good life rooted in material satisfaction. A lifetime of crime and deviance may be inevitable where few viable alternatives exist. Even those minority youths who possess the skills and resources to be successful are often harrassed because they don't fit the image of a typical minority youth. In other words, what we have here is a no-win situation that ensures hostile encounters with the police (see Henry 1994).

Police perceptions of minority youths are reflected in the job and organization in which they are employed. The gaps in perception create a situation of misunderstanding that undermines virtually all efforts at meaningful communication. There is little doubt that the police work under unbearable pressure, having to make split-second decisions over matters of life and death in a hostile environment that rarely appreciates the pressures of policing in a modern, heterogeneous community. Police officers are frequently estranged from the community because of the nature of **conventional policing** with its emphasis on incidents, combativeness, patrol cars, and gadgetry. Each of these is likely to isolate police from the community they serve and to interfere with effective community relations. Efforts to improve lines of communication with the community by way of **community-based policing** have been moderately successful, but attempts to initiate positive reform in preventative policing are undermined by entrenched subcultural values among police that revel in a John Wayne mentality of authoritarian police officers who expect deference and respect for laying their lives on the line to perform their duty.

A democratic society expects its law enforcement agents to be answerable for their actions and accountable to the community. Yet the police as an institution appear to be hostile toward community involvement, preferring to remain isolated from and closed to the public (Henry et al. 1995). An openness to the public is not enhanced by bureacratic structures with their emphasis on conservatism, distance from the community, hierarchy, division of labour, and a paramilitary chain of command. Any potential for positive police-minority relations is diminished by the nature of incident-driven policing, with its focus on charges and arrests. Interactional patterns are further hampered by ineffective race and ethnic relations training. What little they receive has been conducted by poorly trained, sometimes unmotivated officials. Much of the education has been geared toward cultural sensivity, yet invariably has reinforced stereotyping while doing little to improve police engagements with minorities (Ungerleider 1992). Few police forces have the resources — or the courage — to conduct anti-racist training that deals with the racist and discriminatory aspects of police behaviour.

Bridging the Gap: Towards Multicultural Policing

The police for their part have attempted to bridge this gap through **multicultural policing**, if only to ensure open lines of communication and to prevent any further deterioration in their relationship with the public in complex urban contexts. Reliance on minority police officers is widely heralded as a first step in restoring community confidence in law enforcement. Specific initiatives have been designed and implemented to secure a proportional balance of visible minority officers. Initiatives have sought to increase visible minority numbers to the point where they are proportional with the local population. Strategies have included (a) comprehensive advertising campaigns through the mass media (such as ethnic publications, posters, radio, TV, and public transit); (b) career day and recruitment sessions at secondary and post-secondary schools; and (c) direct appeals to visible minority organizations within the community. Visible minority police officers are also encouraged to actively recruit members by virtue of their community links. This reliance on personal encounters and in-depth follow-ups (involving home visits and consultation) reflects the belief that sustained contact with potential recruits is necessary to diffuse community misperceptions about the police. Yet there is no assurance that minority police officers are anxious to serve in these communities, given the potential for conflicts of interests and competing loyalties. Nor is there any proof that minority policing is any more effective in minority communities even if the potential for communication and cultural sensitivity may be improved.

CASE STUDY

C*O*P*S: Community-Oriented Policing Service

Community policing is widely touted as the wave of the future. No longer an option or a luxury in light of emergent realities and diverse publics, community policing has evolved an operational style and organizational content whose principles are at variance with conventional policing. A fundamental restructuring of police-community relations lies at the core of this paradigm shift in how policing is defined and assessed. The police are moving away from a professionally elitist and technologically-driven style to one that embraces partnership in crime prevention. Reactive and remote organizations are criticized for lacking (a) the human dimension and sensitivity to vulnerable minorities, (b) accountability and responsiveness to citizens in the agenda-setting process, and (c) partnership perspectives in alleviating public fears and community disorders. Progressive police forces are shifting organization and operations away from the ideal of efficiency (measured by response times and charges cleared) to the goal of effectiveness, from crime-control and law enforcement to peacekeeping and public safety, and from autonomy (crime as exclusive propert of the police) to interdependence and consultation (Normandeau and Leighton 1990). In short, community policing is now poised on the brink a new era in redefining police-community relations along innovative lines.

Police forces across Canada have responded in diverse ways to this push for

change. They have introduced programs and initiatives consistent with the principles of community-based and culturally-sensitive policing (Fleras 1992). Experimental police training programs such as the Police Intercultural Education Pilot Project were devised in Vancouver and Ottawa (Ungerleider and Echols 1985; Scotti and Miller 1985; Miner 1986). Numerous programs have been initiated to foster better relations with Toronto's expanding and diverse population. In addition to the establishment of police mini-stations and foot-patrols, a team of ethnically-mixed police officers called an ethnic relations squad has been organized for response to racial conflicts. Due to better recruitment techniques, ethnic minority officers are increasingly visible within the department. Equally significant has been the establishment of police-ethnic community organizations. Designed to defuse conflicts and promote interaction on a continuous basis, these committees serve as two-way channels for communication, liaison, and mediation. Minorities can utilize these formal channels to inform the police of their concerns. The police in turn rely on them to (a) educate minorities about law and methods of enforcement, (b) peacefully resolve ethnic disagreements by bringing the disputants together for discussion, (c) caution participants against violations of the law; and (d) be present at activities in which a possibility of racial conflict exists (Fleras and Desroches 1989).

PERILS AND PITFALLS

What has been done to date has not been a resounding success story, keeping in mind that levels of expectations have increased exponentially. What formerly was ignored as part of the job is now singled out for scrutiny and criticism by the media, minorities, and the police services themselves. What more can be done to improve police-minority relations in such a way as to prevent crime, ensure integrity of the police, and equality under the law for racial minorities?

First, it is important to understand that police-minority relations have always involved discrimination and racism. One only needs to have seen signs in police stations that once warned "Jews and Catholics need not apply." Police antipathy toward gays is legendary, and many senior police officials recall the days when gay bars were routinely trashed by officers on patrol. In fairness, the police were not acting any differently than the majority of Canadians who held equally racist and discriminatory attitudes toward those who were different, especially those from Asia and Eastern Europe. A cross-section of the police population should reveal a similar proportion of racism to that of the general population, perhaps even higher if we are to believe studies that suggest authoritarian personality types are more likely to join the service.

Secondly, the relationship between the police and minority communities is not necessarily a law-and-order issue. This would appear to be a miscalculation by many officials in dealing with the crises in Los Angeles and Toronto, most of whom appear more anxious to quell further disturbances and protect white interests from minority hooliganism. What we have is a social problem, that is, a minority and dispossessed underclass created by social conditions that ensure poverty and neglect. The solution to this problem must then follow along these lines, that is, development of programs that focus on the social causes and origins. Ironically, then, the police are expected to deal with victims of a system that generates reactions from powerlessness and despair, to resentment and outrage.

Third, it is important to distinguish between root and precipitating causes of the crisis in police-minority relations. Conflict exists because of personalities and circumstances related to policing and police work. Yet it is quite evident that the underlying causes behind such disturbances are much deeper and rooted in the structures of a capitalist society. For effective change, it is critical that a holistic approach be seriously considered, rather than one that focuses only on the immediate psychological attitudes of the police or the protesters.

Fourth, just as police-minority relations are not a law and order issue, so too are they not necessarily a racial issue but one of class relations in an inner city environment. The media prefer to focus on the racial dimension, but an equally plausible case could be made for analyzing police-minority relations as a class conflict with the police sandwiched in between.

TWO STEPS FORWARD...

The police play a crucial role in securing the social order around which a multicultural society is organized. But the police have found it difficult at times to respond effectively to changes in Canada's racial and cultural composition (Hill and Schiff 1986). Police-community relations are already nearing a breaking point in parts of Canada, and have already assumed critical proportions in large urban centres. There is a constant sense of crisis in the air as we hover on the threshold of one police-minority confrontation after another. One misunderstanding has the capacity to undo years of carefully cultivated progress, thus fostering the impression of events beyond our control. The general lapse in public confidence in the police is fueled primarily (but not exclusively) by negative police interaction with minority and aboriginal groups. As well, communities are concerned about expanding police budgets at a time when booming crime rates appear impervious to personnel or resource increases. Paradoxically, many police departments continue to uphold the old professional crime-fighting image, in the process revealing more about organizational inertia and subcultural tenacity than any commitment to policing excellence. Nevertheless, there is a growing chorus of support for community-based and community-driven service as one way of bringing the police closer to the public, both physically and psychologically (Asbury 1992).

WHERE TO NOW?

This chapter makes it clear that the principle of institutional accommodation is here to stay. Institutions can no longer afford the luxury of remaining aloof from the demographic and cultural revolutions taking place in Canada. Conventional ways of doing things — from working with others to delivery of a service or a product — are less acceptable than in the past. The combination of minority pressure and government edicts have compelled many institutions to redefine themselves in a way that makes them more inclusive and equitable. Barriers continue to plague the transformation process since those in positions of power and privilege dislike the prospect of losing it all. Institutional subcultures and organizational procedures may not lend themselves to accommodative change. Yet the benefits of accommodation cannot be dismissed. The extent to which Canada can "move over and make space" will largely determine the direction and pace of society-building in Canada.

We conclude the chapter with a case study of putting multiculturalism to work. The recent settlement of grievances among Japanese-Canadians for mistreatment during the Second World War is particularly instructive of the revised rules that govern engagement and entitlement. The politics of resolution also reveal that "mainstreaming diversity" is not necessarily driven by altruism or commitment to justice. More important is the need to secure a stable social order while defusing threats to the legitimacy of the Canadian state.

CASE STUDY

Righting Japanese-Canadian Wrongs

On September 22, 1988 the federal government issued a formal apology to Japanese Canadians who were stripped of their rights, uprooted, and interned in substandard camps during the Second World War. In addition to acknowledging this violation of Japanese citizenship rights, each of 12,000 survivors received a tax-free payment of $21,000 as a "symbolic individual redress." Another $12 million was set aside for the Japanese-Canadian community as well as $24 million for the establishment of a new Canadian Race Relations Foundation to foster inter-racial harmony. While some regarded this comprehensive redress settlement totalling $291 million as inappropriate, many people embraced this gesture of atonement as a step toward removing the stigma of disloyalty (*Toronto Star*, 23 September 1988).

The events leading up to the internment occurred in the aftermath of the Pearl Harbour bombing in late 1941. Reaction to public pressure and the perceived presence of "enemy aliens" along Canada's west coast resulted in the enactment of the War Measures Act. Approximately 22,000 Japanese Canadians, mostly in British Columbia, were forcibly removed or evacuated from coastal regions as precaution against collusion. A few were arrested and nearly 4,000 were deported to Japan after the war. Most were dispersed to relocation or POW camps across Canada and forced to work at hard labour for the duration of the hostilities. Property was confiscated and auctioned off without consent

as a way of raising funds for the war effort. Rights of citizenship were not restored until 1949; still, compensation and apology eluded the Japanese community until Mulroney's historic address.

The compensation did not match the levels proposed by the firm involved in calculating appropriate amounts (Price Waterhouse) or by the National Association of Japanese-Canadians. Yet the package deal was remarkably similar to one by the American government as compensation for the removal and dispossession of its Japanese population. Each of the 120,000 survivors received a tax-free lump sum of $20,000. Another $300 million were earmarked for a general community fund to promote collective goals in areas such as eduation. The American government also admitted the error of its ways, attributing the transgression to racial prejudice and wartime hysteria. It is interesting to note that in both Canada and the United States sustained government surveillance failed to detect any sign of Japanese disloyalty or subversiveness.

To what extent was the abrogation of Japanese civil rights the result of (a) a threat to national security, (b) wartime hysteria or (c) a blatant act of racial discrimination? Was internment justified in the context of a war whose outcome was unknown? Are reparations necessary for difficult decisions that were made under such pressures? Were government actions the inevitable byproduct of pervasive anti-Oriental sentiments at the time? (Leo 1988) Given the longstanding antipathy of Canadians toward Asian populations, the racist explanation is compelling. No Canadian citizens of Japanese ancestry were ever accused of sabotage, espionage, or of disloyalty to the Canadian government. No other groups were systematically interned during the war. The Japanese, however, proved to be convenient targets of in alleviating a growing public crisis of confidence in the government's handling of the war effort. In short, the suppression of basic human rights was caused by racist antipathy, wartime hysteria, and ineffective political leadership by the Mackenzie King government.

We should not overlook the significance of this historical redress. The government for its part has admitted wrongdoing in its treatment of certain minorities, and acknowledges that such mistreatment is inconsistent with Canada's multicultural character. The repudiation of the past has also confirmed that minorities in Canada are now entitled to the same rights as all Canadians, as well as special rights because of earlier difficulties or grievances. The government has also acknowledged its responsibility in a multicultural society to mediate and intervene in those situations which have the potential to undermine the national fabric. Finally, the compensation of Japanese-Canadians has established a legal and moral precedent for resolving related acts of injustice. For example, the Ukrainian-Canadian Committee has demanded and received symbolic redress for the 8,000 Ukrainians interned in two dozen camps across Canada as slave labour during the First World War for 25 cents a day. Many were released blind or partially maimed. Another 80,000 were branded as enemy aliens and compelled to report to the police on a regular basis. During World War II, 700 Italian-Canadians were sent to internment camps for up to three years, while another 17,000 were labelled as enemy aliens. None were ever charged, despite compulsory registration, house searches, and surveillance. Similarly, 3,000 Germans in World War I and 700 in World War II were interned and their property confiscated (*Toronto Star* 27 Dec. 1994). The Chinese Canadian National Council is also seeking redress for the 81,0000 who paid a $23 million 'head tax' for entry into Canada between 1885 and 1903. Until these and additional reparations are addressed by the federal authorities, government-minority relations will continue to fester over past indiscretions. This puts the onus on all Canadians to strike a compromise that accommodates diversity in a manner both workable and fair.

CHAPTER HIGHLIGHTS

- The concept of putting multiculturalism to work is concerned primarily with the "mainstreaming of diversity" through institutional accommodation. Endorsement of multicultural principles is one thing; efforts to manage diversity and to operationalize multiculturalism on behalf of Canada are quite another.

- The mass media, education, and police services are but three of the institutions that are called upon to respond to social, demographic, and political pressures in a society that is changing, diverse, complex, and uncertain.

- Institutional change is evident not only at the level of organization and delivery, but also in terms of initial assumptions and goals. Without diminishing the impact of the changes which have taken place, the gap between expectations and reality remains a cause for concern.

- The concept of institutional accommodation is concerned with improving an organization's representation, workplace climate, operational procedures and rules, and service delivery in a multicultural society.

- The most common barriers to institutional accommodation include people, hierarchy, bureaucracy, corporate culture, and occupational subculture.

- Canada's mass media industry has been remiss in responding to the challenges of diversity and institutional accommodation. Such an omission creates problems since the media possess the cultural capacity to define what is acceptable and good in society.

- Media mistreatment of minorities falls into one of four categories, regardless of medium (print versus electronic) or outlet (advertising, news, TV programming). Minorities tend to be portrayed as invisible, as stereotypes, as social problems, and as ornaments.

- Recent initiatives to put multiculturalism to work are to be applauded. But accommodation is slow and gradual, in part because of resistance created the commercial logic of the media.

- There are three approaches to education and diversity: assimilation, multiculturalism, and anti-racist. Educational agendas have historically revolved around the principles of assimilation, creating a challenge to the development of an institution that is receptive to diversity under the multicultural umbrella.

- Two types of multicultural education are shown to exist. Enrichment multicultural education is concerned primarily with celebrating differences. Empowerment education is focused on informed and critical understanding of Canadian race, ethnic, and aboriginal relations. One variant of empowerment education is creation of separate schools for racial or aboriginal minorities.

- Anti-racist education differs from multicultural education. Anti-racist education is concerned with isolating and challenging expressions of racism (both personal and institutional) through direct action.

- Police-minority relations are currently experiencing a crisis. The sources of the problem are varied but invariably include problems of perception, communication, lifestyle differences, and authority patterns in society. That gap in power suggests that police are in a difficult position when asked to solve problems that lie beyond their jurisdiction.

- Multicultural policing represents an effort to close the institutional gap between the police and minority communities. Initiatives in this area tend to ignore the social context in which police-minority relations are constructed and maintained.

- Community-based and culturally-sensitive policing are riding a popular wave at present. The principles are widely accepted, but much more difficult to implement because of bureaucracy and occupational subcultures.

KEY TERMS

Accommodation of Diversity
Anti-Racist Education
Community Based Policing
Conventional Policing
Empowerment Multicultural Education

Enrichment Multicultural Education
Institutional Accommodation
Institutions as Contested Site
Media as Systemic Discrimination

Media Race Role Stereotyping
Minorities as Problem People
Multicultural Education
Multicultural Policing

REVIEW QUESTIONS

1) Compare and contrast the enrichment and empowerment models of multicultural education in terms of assumptions, objectives, and intended effects.

2) Compare and contrast anti-racist education with multicultural education with respect to focus, objectives, concerns, scope, and outcomes.

3) How are minorities (both racial and aboriginal) portrayed by the mass media? Why? How does this present a problem in a multicultural society such as ours?

4) What are the basic problems underlying police-minority minority relations in Canadian metropolitan regions? What steps have been taken to alleviate these problem areas?

5) What is community policing and how does it hope to improve minority-police relations? What problems may interfere with its implementation?

6) What do we mean by institutional accommodation? What are the components that comprise an accommodative institution? What barriers exist that may preclude the accommodation of diversity within institutions?

CHAPTER 12

CONCLUSION: RECONSTRUCTING CANADA

Twenty five years ago, Canadian sociologist John Porter (1965) aptly defined Canada as a huge demographic railway station....The time has come to change the metaphor as Canada now ressembles a busy construction site, where not only one but many nations are being constructed, deconstructed, and reconstructed. (Juteau 1994)

INTRODUCTION:
THE CHALLENGE OF SOCIETY-BUILDING

It is not overly dramatic to suggest that Canada is at a crossroads with regard to its future as a diverse society. Recent events confirm that society-building in Canada involves a series of interrelated yet competing national projects (Juteau 1994). First and foremost is the still unfinished business of constructing a cohesive and over-arching Canadian society. Contemporary society-building entails nothing less than the creation of a moral community rather than an aggregation of self-seeking in-dividuals. The accommodation of diversity at different levels is foremost on the list of do's.

Equally important as a national project is the sorting out of jurisdictions and entitlements as they pertain to various subnational units. The First Nations are clearing the way for a complete revamping of their collective status, from one of a colonized dependency to one of a "nation within." All eyes are focused on how far developments in aboriginality can be explored before a public apathy or polit-ical backlash interrupts this restructuring process. A parallel situation exists at the level of charter groups where Ottawa-Quebec relations are nearing collapse. A deepening polarization has become apparent as each side engages in acts of brinkmanship to see who blinks first. With the spectre of separation clearly be-fore us, it remains to be seen whether we can forge a workable Canadian society that reflects the legacy of the *deux nations* motif. At an equally critical juncture is the evolving prominence of Canada's "multicultural force." The interplay of political, demographic, and social changes has initiated a fundamental shift in the collective status of this once ignored sector. With the growth of multiculturalism, racial and ethnic minorities are poised to emerge as major societal players, with the capacity to catapult Canada into as yet uncharted realms.

Few of these developments have occurred without conflict or controversy. That much can be expected in a society where minority relations are essentially relationships of inequality in need of attention. Canada is currently in the midst of a social revolution so profound that it threatens to destroy conventional patterns of engagement and entitlement. What once were vices are now embraced as virtues, while weaknesses become strengths as the postmodernist process scuttles traditional assumptions about right and wrong. The lurching about from one diversity crisis to another has left many Canadians in a quandry over where to go next. Certain sectors have applauded these challenges to Canadian society-building. A three-nations-state concept within a framework of multiculturalism may provide Canada with the flexibility it requires to withstand the stresses of uncertainty and change. Others disagree, however, and continue to embrace attitudes inconsistent with any renewal or reform. In trying to turn back the clock, they want a Canada fortified against the realities and pressures of the world at large. Still others are mentally predisposed for change but dismayed by the prospect of dealing with tomorrow's problems by way of yesterday's solution. With minority assertiveness unlikely to diminish in the near future, Canada's society-building skills will be sorely tested in seeking to balance the often competing demands of race, aboriginal, and ethnic relations.

Where, then, do we go from here? The subtitle of this chapter, "Reconstructing Canada," may provide some illumination. The concept of "reconstructing" society can be applied in different ways. Interactionist perspectives portray Canada as a socially constructed and contested site—that is, a diverse and complex yet unequal society undergoing constant change and adjustment in response to internal pressures and external forces. Group dynamics are being reshaped by the interplay of three major forces, each with competing agendas, unique histories, distinct legal status, and different entitlements. Society-building in this "adventure called Canada", as Governor General Vincent Massey once deftly put it, is complicated by factors as disparate as geography, history, regionalism, a proximity to the USA, the presence of deep diversities, and the temperament of its population. Over time, Ottawa has responded to the challenge of diversity with a package of compromises that continue to elicit admiration—or invoke wrath—at both national and international levels. That these initiatives consolidate Canada's reputation as a pacesetter for managing diversity is accurate enough. Whether they go far enough in guaranteeing Canada's survival remains to be seen.

It would be folly to underestimate the magnitude of the problem confronting Canada. Formidable barriers are strewn about in the ongoing reinvention of Canada along more pluralistic lines. Consider only these questions: How will central authorities respond to the increasingly assertive demands of the three major forces without compromising Canada's survival? Are policy structures capable of addressing these competing demands without unravelling the social fabric or territorial integrity? Canada's future will depend on our government's ability to meld this diversity into a workable and cohesive unit. Our international prestige as well as our trading links will also depend on sustaining the policies and agendas that endorse diversity without undermining national unity and order.

In this concluding chapter we set out to explore the possibilities for Canada at a critical juncture in its society-building process. Mindful of shifting tides and competing principles of group interaction, we hope to isolate and expand on the recurrent patterns in the reconstruction of Canada along aboriginal, charter group, and multicultural lines. Historical themes in the management of majority-minority relations are explored and contrasted with contemporary trends. The chapter also examines some of the reasons—political, social, ideological, and demographic—behind these transformations for managing diversity. These themes not only provide an overview of the subject matter; they can also be employed, albeit speculatively, as a basis for predicting future trends. In other words, it's important to know where we have been, where we are at present, and what the future holds in store, as Canada struggles to secure its lofty status in the progressive management of race, ethnic, and aboriginal relations.

THE PAST: KEY THEMES, EVOLVING ISSUES, EMERGENT TRENDS

Debate over racial, aboriginal, and ethnic diversity has assumed a relatively high profile in contemporary liberal-democratic societies such as Canada (MacNeill 1986; Driedger 1989). The very politicization of this diversity signals a shift from earlier eras when government policies routinely endorsed the superiority of majority values and institutions. Minorities are no longer willing to bide their time on the sidelines; they are actively and openly competing for scarce resources. Minority struggles in the competition to advance collective interests has had the effect of reversing many conventional rules and relationships in a remarkably short period of time. The periphery is moving into the centre as a result of these upheavals, while the centre is under pressure to move over and make space. Transformations of that magnitude make it doubly imperative to delve into what is going on, and why. The following trends appear foremost.

From Assimilation to Diversity

Canadian race, aboriginal, and ethnic relations have undergone numerous changes in policy content, style, and scope. Historically, government-minority relations were structured around lines of assimilation and absorption into the mainstream. Loyalty to the Empire defined anglo-Canadian identity, and minorities were expected to fall into line. This assimilationist orientation was consistent with evolutionary philosophies and racial doctrines that extolled the virtues of Western progress, but

denigrated the lowly status of non-Western populations as irrelevant to society-building. At times, government efforts to stamp out diversity bordered on the explicit and
ruthless. For example, consider the removal of aboriginal children from communities
and placement into federal schools. At other times, assimilationist philosphies were
consistently applied (if not always explicitly articulated) to achieve national goals.
At still other times, the principles of assimilation were tacitly assumed, implicit
within or derived from the consequences of government actions. The end result was
predictable regardless of technique: the creation of a white anglo-Canadian society
that upheld the virtues of God, Empire, and the Dominion. Differences, when tolerated, were relegated into the realm of the private or personal, or restricted to
the folkloric dimension.

Diversity burrowed its way into Canada's political discourse after World War II.
A vocabulary evolved that stratified Canadians into majority-minorities, immigrants, visible minorities, and refugees, implying an unequal social and political
status yet recognizing the need for equal opportunities regardless of race or origin (Talbani 1994). Explicit assimilationist agendas began to erode in the face of national and international pressures. Canada's three major forces awakened to the
prospect of redefining their relational status within Canadian federalism. Aboriginal
organizations attacked the racist assumptions and objectives underlying government policies. Eschewing the colonialist mentality of the past, aboriginal leaders displayed a marked preference for negotiating from the framework of aboriginal and
treaty rights. Likewise priority was assigned to the principle of self-determination
through self-government structures. By the late 1980s, one could detect a general
drift toward a fundamental restructuring of aboriginal-state relations.

Elsewhere, Quebec's demands for quasi-independence burst into open confrontation with federal authorities during the 1960s. In rejecting the value or legitimacy of official bilingualism and federal multiculturalism to Quebec's needs,
provincial authorities pounced on the issue of cultual survival and ethnocultural diversity through demands to control the selection, socialization, and integration of
immigrants into a French-speaking Quebec community (Talbani 1994). Separatist
leanings were diffused only with passage of controversial language laws that ensured
French ascendancy in the homeland of last resort. Nevertheless, the constitutional
basis of Quebec-Ottawa relations faltered for lack of consensus. The elusiveness
of a workable partnership became painfully evident with the failure of English
Canada to consider even Quebec's moderate demands for distinct society status.

Adjustments in the relational status of the multicultural force are no less noticeable. Much of this shift can be attributed to a major overhaul in Canada's immigration policies in favour of so-called non-conventional (non-European) sources.
Further adjustments in redefining the national agenda stemmed from the introduction of multiculturalism as government policy in 1971, and as a statute in 1988.
Promotion of multiculturalism acknowledged the usefulness of diversity as a basis
for national identity and unity. It also confirmed the salience of diversity rather
than assimilation as a basis for society-building in Canada.

From Exclusion to Stakeholders

Racial, ethnic, and aboriginal minorities were routinely perceived as fringe players in the unfolding of Canadian society. The First Nations in particular were deemed expendible—on occasion even as obstructionist—for society-building purposes. It took a crisis at Oka to startle policy-maker from their complacency and indifference, to belatedly recognize First Nations as key actors in any reconstruction of Canada.

A similar line of reasoning was applied to multicultural minorities. Minorities may have been important in the settlement of Canadian society, but their role was limited primarily to agricultural pursuits or factory labour. Under the "new multiculturalism" (with its post-multicultural focus on equality, accommodation, and race relations), ethno-racial diversity is now recognized as a legitimate and integral component of Canada's identity and society-building. Multicultural minorities are entitled to make demands upon the Canadian state that acknowledge their right to equal as well as equivalent treatment—that is, the same rights as all Canadian citizens as well as equity rights for remedying the effects of past discrimination. Institutions are under pressure to become more inclusive through a closer examination of rules and procedures that relate to minority representation, access, and equitable treatment.

To be sure, there is little tangible proof that multiculturalism has dramatically improved minority-majority relations in areas such as the delivery of service or income distribution. What multiculturalism provides, however, is a supportive social climate where diversity initiatives can be implemented without undue fear of backlash or electoral reprisals. A commitment to inclusiveness for all stakeholders ensures the funnelling of most multicultural spending into race relations and anti-racism, removal of discriminatory barriers, and immigrant access and participation.

From Problem to Resource

Through policy and practice, Canada perceived itself as a Dominion of white settlers. Minorities were routinely defined as a social problem or as a problem people with deficiencies that consumed government resources. Government efforts were directed at eliminating these differences that interfered with mainstream institutions, customs, and values.

With the growing legitimacy of multiculturalism as law, policy, and constitution, the third force has now emerged as a key player with power to influence and shape Canada's destiny. Minorities are no longer cavalierly dismissed as a problem—at least in theory if not necessarily in practice. Difference are viewed instead as resources or assets with sizable potential for enhancing Canadian prosperity both at home and abroad.

From Inequality to Equity

At one time Canada espoused a racist system that routinely denied political equality and civil rights to racial, aboriginal, and ethnic minorities. Inequality was endorsed as normal and natural in the sorting out process that determined who got what. Even an assimilationist commitment did not appear sufficient to dislodge the ideals of a socially ingrained hierarchy.

By the 1960s another shift was apparent. The concept of formal equality was extended to include all individuals regardless of colour or ethnic background. Discrimination would no longer be allowed in a system where everyone was equal before the law. But notions of equality underwent a shift in emphasis when it became clear that inequality was deeply entrenched. Formal equality with its emphasis on equal (as in similar) treatment before the law was insufficient for people of colour. Nor was a straightforward equality of opportunity an answer to the removal of discriminatory barriers. Rather, both expressions perpetuated the problem since applying formal equality to unequal situations had the effect (however unintended) of freezing the status quo. In applying the metaphor of a competitive footrace with staggered starting blocks, it was obvious that not all contestants—especially those historically disadvantaged by race or ethnic origins—were in a position to compete equally in a rigged labour market. What was required instead was a substantive equity, that is, one that recognized that minorities had different needs and experiences for consideration in creating a more egalitarian society. Equal opportunities were important in opening the competition, in other words, but no less so than a commitment to equality of outcomes or conditions.

The emergence of new equality rules has proven disconcerting to many Canadians. Many have only recently come around to the principle of formal equality as a basis for treatment and opportunity. Now they are under pressure to accept the notion that equality can mean treating others differently, as well as treating them the same when the situation dictates. Under these conditions of uncertainty or confusion, the current spate of hostilities and misunderstandings between groups is understandable, if somewhat unfortunate.

From Laissez Faire to Government Involvement

The government (or state) has historically played a passive role in the management of Canada's race, ethnic, and aboriginal agenda. Its role was restricted to that of disinterested neutrality—to improve access and eliminate discrimination by ensuring a level playing field for all the contestants. All minorities were expected to assimilate into the mainstream without any government assistance. Certain adjustment problems were inevitable throughout the transition; nevertheless, minority relations would be sorted out through the interplay of market forces and voluntary compliance.

With the diversity agenda firmly in tow, the state has become critically involved in designing more accommodative institutional structures. Federal multicultural initiatives have appeared that seek not only to ensure an equality of outcome through participation and involvement, but also to preserve ethnicity and support intercultural sharing. Passage of the Employment Equity Act in 1986 has also confirmed government commitment to engineering social change. The government is now entitled to enact special measures for hiring and promotion in the workplace if these are employed to overcome historically imposed disadvantages for certain minorities.

From Culture to Structure

It was widely assumed that cultural differences interefered with minority adaptation into Canada. Minorities endorsed cultural values at odds with the needs of a progressive, productive society. These values and customs, though quaint, were irrelevant or regressive, and had to be discarded or compartmentalized into folkloric or personal levels. The elimination of these cultural barriers paved the way for acceptance and incorporation. Even the mainstream was expected to display a degree of forebearance toward differences until prejudicial attitudes were laid to rest.

By the early 1980s a paradigm shift was in progress (Agocs and Boyd 1993). The rapid increase of visible minorities through more liberal immigration policies exerted considerable pressure for a rethinking of strategies for managing diversity. Cultural and attitudinal solutions could not solve what essentially was a structural problem. Impediments to advancement were not derived entirely from prejudice and culture, but from structural constraints within institutions, both systemic and chronically embedded (Asbury 1992). The free market contributed to the problem because of numerous barriers related to segmented labour fields, racial division of labour, dual labour markets, and systemic structures of discrimination. These structures combined with relations of power to constrain minority opportunities and life chances. The onus, in other words, lay on the removal of these structural barriers—not as a form of special treatment—but as "equivalent measures" to ensure equitable access, treatment, and outcomes.

From Colour-Conscious to Colour-Blind (and Back Again)

Canadian society has experienced a fundamental transformation in its treatment and assessment of racial differences. At one time colour (racial) criteria were manipulated to justify the exclusion of certain minorities from full institutional involvement. The aftermath of the American civil rights movement resulted in the replacement of racially-based exclusion with a colour-blind policy that guaranteed mathematical equality for all irrespective of racial background.

The salience is colour is undergoing change again. A colour-blind commitment was once endorsed as a humane improvement over colour-conscious discrimination. Such a commitment may now be condemned as a subtle form of systemic bias and white privilege in support of the status quo. In place of colour-blindness has appeared a new colour-conscious philosophy that singles out racial affiliation as a basis for entitlement or social engagement. Unlike in the past, this colour-coded consciousness is not intended to deny or exclude. It is endorsed instead as an equivalence measure for overcoming disadvantage. In short, colour-coded differences now constitute a an "attribute" that entitles certain individuals to compete more equitably in society.

From Individual to Collective Rights

With several exceptions, Canada has not been receptive to the notion of collective rights. Canadian society was steeped in a kind of liberalism that elevated the individual as the basis of our productivity and progress (Gwyn 1994). Society was envisaged as a collection of individuals in need of only limited state protection from the excesses of the market or government to exercise their rights and obligations. Anything that enhanced the group at the expense of the individual was viewed as retrograde.

There is a growing commitment to balancing individual rights with those of collective and even group rights. The sacred compact between individuals and society state is being contested by special interest groups engaged in a struggle for control over rights and entitlements. Minorities are concerned that individual rights are a luxury that only those in positions of dominance can afford. Minority marginal status is deepened by failure to safeguard advantages for the disadvantaged on the basis of collective rather than individual rights. Collective rights can be defined as rights accorded to individuals as members of specific multicultural communities. That is, each member of a racial or ethnic minority has the right not only to identify with the cultural tradition of her choice but also to qualify for special rights as a member of that collectivity. Group rights by contrast consist of rights afforded to groups as a community largely independent of the individuals that form them (Baker 1994; Kymlicka 1994). The rights of individuals may be superceded or balanced in order to preserve group solidarity or identity in the face of internal or external pressure. Group rights apply to such nations as the Québécois or the First Nations, both of whom possess both the mandate and resources for parallel institutions and a separate power base (that sets them apart from multicultural communities).

Recognition of certain collective/group rights has altered the internal dynamics of Canada. Individualism as a source of entitlement is being tempered by a vision of Canada as divisible into natural groups (subnational forces or multicultural minorities) whose distinctiveness provides the basis for achievement of equality (Gwyn 1994). Government priorities are leaning toward giving the advantage to the previously disadvantaged as a distinct group with specific rights rather than just individuals with universal rights. That alone complicates the society-building process: Efforts to forge national unity from social disunity must balance the rights of individuals, the group rights of nations within, and the collective rightsof multicultural minorities. Predictably, then, central authorities find themselves in a political quagmire in attempting to cope with this balancing act as a basis for new concept of Canadian citizenship (Kymlicka 1992).

From Universal to Particular

Passage of Canada's first Citizenship Act in 1947 served notice that Canada would no longer serve as another British outpost. Citizenship articulated a statement of Canada's history and its hopes, its common principles, and common values (Sergio Marchi, Citizenship and Immigration Canada News Release, April 14, 1994). It conferred statutory rights and equal obligations to all citizens without distinction or favoritism, on the assumption that citizenship is a universal category that transcends all particular backgrounds and beliefs in deference to the whole (the state). Individual citizens may be entitled to many beliefs and identities, but only one civic identity in public affairs (see Kauffman 1990). The social dimension of citizenship is no less important. Citizenship is concerned with establishing a relationship, between individuals and the state, with mutual rights and obligations.

But the abstract rationality of nineteenth century citizenship may be incompatible with Canada's contemporary needs for the management of diversity. The dominance of a unified civic citizenship has been challenged by previously excluded and marginalized groups. The fragmented and decentered nature of these "identity" movements have combined to weaken the universalizing tendencies of a citizenship-based politics. Practitioners of identity endorse affiliation with race, aboriginality, or ethnic as a basis for engagement with the state—or beyond the state in some cases (Kauffman 1990).

Such a contemporary reading of citizenship has a profound effect on Canada. For citizenship to mean anything in a postmodernist, post-multicultural society, it must expand from its universal focus to incorporate the identity demands of deep diversities. A revised citizenship must address not only individual rights and responsibilities, but also the placement of members from racial, ethnic, and aboriginal groups in society *without denying differences in the process.* Such a challenge is formidable—especially when the members in question desire a different way of belonging than that envisioned by central authorities (Kaplan 1993; Cairns 1993).

The next case study examines whether Canada can come around to the notion of an inclusive (one identity folded into another) citizenship. Many Canadians are baffled by a citizenship in which individuals can identify with the whole yet "belong" to subnational units without fear of contradiction. The extent to which we can accept this shift in mindset will say a lot about Canada's future survival.

CASE STUDY

Reconceptualizing Citizenship

Nowhere are the shifts in Canadian society-building more evident than in the debates about redefining citizenship for the twenty-first century. What do we mean by citizenship? Why in a pluralistic society is there a relationship between citizenship and creating a sense of belonging and commitment? How is this relationship expressed? In what way does citizenship within a multicultural framework contribute to the goals of national identity and societal unity as well as those of social equality and cultural retention? We will attempt to answer these questions by exploring the concept of a redefined citizenship as a tool for remaking Canadian society. Not everyone will agree with our notion of citizenship as (a) overlapping and situational, (b) accommodative of differences and radical ways of belonging, and (c) responsive to individual and collective rights. But a multi-dimensional view of citizenship not only provides the basis for reconstructing a distinct Canadian identity, it also confirms Canada's status as a pacesetter in the creation of possibly the world's first postmodernist society.

WHAT IS CITIZENSHIP?

Defining citizenship is not as simple as it might appear on the surface. As with multiculturalism, the concept of citizenship can be interpreted from different vantage points, depending on context or intent. Citizenship in general refers to rules of engagement, that is, the mutually reciprocal set of duties, rights, and obligations that define a relationship between society (the state) and individuals. It is also concerned with the patterns of entitlement in terms of who gets what and on what basis as part of this social contract. A social contract spells out what both parties are entitled to under an arrangement, what each must give up as part of the transaction, and the basis for terms of the agreement. Citizens look to the state for protection of basic rights

pertaining to security, opportunity, and survival. The state, in turn, expects citizens to abide by the laws of the country even when this entails sacrifices and restrictions. Fostering a sense of community, identity, and purpose—a kind of national esprit de corps—is of paramount state concern especially when diversity is involved. Citizenship is concerned with the integration of previously excluded minorities, in the hope of fostering a shared loyalty and society-building commitment to the whole of which they are part. Failure to achieve the goal of a uniform citizenry has long been predicted as a ticket for self-destruction. There is much to lose unless those who were once culturally excluded are encouraged to identify with the values and institutions of the host society and to experience a sense of belonging and full participation. Not unexpectedly, the rationale behind citizenship in Canada (and elsewhere) has historically condoned the stamping out of differences in pursuit of the common good.

Dealing with diversity is a formidable challenge in any plural society. This challenge is further complicated in countries such as Canada where groups are racially and culturally different. How can liberal democratic societies preserve political integrity and societal interconnectedness when conventional ways of belonging and accommodation (based on the principle of society as a voluntary aggregation of individual interests) lose their salience in the presence of racial and ethnic groups whose membership is defined involuntarily and ascribed at birth. Strategies that may have worked in the past have proven inadequate to address the highly politicized and collective claims of ethnic nationalism. The game is changing, so that traditional rules are inapplicable. Yet new rules have yet to be defined that ensure societal cohesion and national identity, while bolstering the legitimacy of the state (Williams 1995). In short, we need to rethink the concept of citizenship in response to a changing and diverse society.

CITIZENSHIP IN CANADA: THE CHALLENGE OF DIVERSITY

Until 1947 and passage of the Citizenship Act, there was no such thing as a Canadian citizen apart from a Commonwealth context. All persons in Canada were regarded as British subjects, with an obligation to conduct themselves in a manner that upheld the language, culture, and identity of England. The Citizenship Act established the framework for creating a new kind of citizen, consistent with Canadian rather than Anglocentric realities. The need to construct an indigenous citizenship became even more urgent with the diversification of Canadian society. Hundreds and thousands of emigrants from war-torn Europe had arrived in hopes of rebuilding shattered lives. The rights of previously disenfranchised minorities—from African- to Japanese- and Chinese-Canadians—were restored in the rush to put democratic principles into practice. Even aboriginal peoples shook off a once dormant status in exchange for political activism with the goal of reclaiming their rights. For central authorities, the challenge was unmistakable: This diversity had to be "managed" in a way that accommodated differences, yet did not interfere with the construction of a united, identifiable, and prosperous Canada. The challenge

lay in cultivating a sense of community, with a common sense of purpose and identity as unifying principles. It is in this context that citizenship blossomed as an integrative device for society-building.

Canada, as most modern nation-states, must address the challenges of diversity within the framework of full and equal citizenship. How does a liberal-democratic society create a common citizenship (with its sense of shared loyalty and political unity) when confronted by the centrifugal forces of diversity? There are two conventional answers to that question (Lyman 1994): Some would argue that recognition and acceptance of differences are key to national unity. Efforts to deny differences or to exclude minorities because of language or cultural differences have not worked in the past, and there is no reason to believe in the appeal of assimilation at the present. This view endorses instead as a basis for citizenship an official recognition—no matter how symbolic—of minority differences coupled with institutional support (funding, language rights protection, political representation, and so on). This leads to what Iris Young (1989) has called "differentiated" citizenship. Disenfranchised groups are entitled to special rights and collective entitlements commensurate with their distinct identities, unique circumstances, and evolving aspirations. The meshing of these differences into an integrated whole provides a rationale for exploring new styles of citizenship.

Others disagree with this view. They argue that citizenship differentiated into this and that cannot possibly fulfill its basic functions of creating shared loyalty, common identity, and patriotic commitment. What is required instead is a type of citizenship in which every person is treated equally before the law. Pluralistic citizenship, with its special and collective rights, cannot fit the bill because it leads to the demise of a common culture and corresponding loss of unifying symbols for bonding citizens into a single framework. In short, only a unitary citizenship holds the promise of social unity and national identity.

There are other problems with a diversified the concept of citizenship. Specifying certain minorities for special treatment raises questions about who is entitled to the largest concessions, and why. The distribution of rewards may become a problem without a practical way—such as a so-called misery index—for sorting out who gets what. Second, can differentiating citizens on the basis of need be applied to groups that are dispersed or partially assimilated? Or must this concession be restricted to groups that are compact, self-conscious, territorially intact, institutionally complete, and culturally complete? Does such a preferred citizenship make sense extended only to populations such as aboriginal peoples and the Québécois who entered into formal agreement that created Canada on the condition that they retain some degree of self-determination over land, language, and identity? Finally, there are time concerns that need to be addressed. Are special, group-based rights to last only as long as groups experience marginality, then removed when no longer required? Or do these rights exist in perpetuity to ensure equity? That these and related questions have not been adequately answered (at least to everyone's satisfaction) suggests that the issue is more complex than repeated mantras about "unity within diversity" convey.

THE STRANDS OF CITIZENSHIP

Contradictions are inherent in the "unity within diversity" equation. Too much uniformity can culturally exclude minorities; too much diversity can rend unity asunder. One way of solving the problem is through promotion of liberal individualism and "universal" citizenship. An alternate way is by embracing cultural pluralist principles, with a commitment to "differentiated" citizenship. A third way falls between universal and differentiated, and is consistent with the principles of multiculturalism and "inclusive" citizenship.

Universal Citizenship

There are few ideals as widely admired by Canadians as the principles of universal citizenship and liberal individualism. One of Canada's foremost sociologists, John Porter, endorsed a version of citizenship that treated everybody alike, with formal legal rights and equality before the law at the core of this universalism. In emphasizing the priority of individual rights, a universal citizenship rejects any type of entitlement rooted in collective or group rights. Rejected outrights are claims for preferential treatment derived from membership in a particular racial or ethnic group. The problems of inequality and cultural exclusion must be addressed—not by affirmative action plans for aggrieved groups, but through removal of discriminatory barriers followed by gradual elimination of those cultural (and linguistic) traits that inhibit full institutional participation. Emphasis is placed on the prejudice and racism that created the problem of exclusion in the first place. To be sure, a universal citizenship does not deny the free and private expression of individual (and even group) cultural identity. Endorsement of these cultural differences, however, should not affect the rights of individuals or citizenship status. Promotion of group differences on racial or ethnic grounds—even in the spirit of accommodation and progress—can only deter and distract from universal citizenship's main goals.

Differentiated Citizenship

For liberal thinkers, equality and progress stem from the renunciation of differences and conferral of universal citizenship. For cultural pluralists, the opposite is true. The accommodation of differences and recognition of group-based special needs is central to social equality and national unity. Overcoming a history of cultural exclusion requires a more "pliable" definition of citizenship; similarly, eliminating group-based exclusion points to special rights for meeting distinct needs and historical disadvantage (Kymlicka 1992). As Iris Young (1989) has argued, a universal conception of citizenship is unfair when applied to unequal contexts. The unfairness arises from treating all citizens—regardless of race, class, or gender—as individuals rather than as members of disadvantaged groups. People in groups *are* different: collectively, they have different needs, aspirations, status, and experience. What is required in such pluralistic contexts is a citizenship that is sufficiently flexible to accommodate and respond to historically excluded groups.

The rationale behind group rights is relatively straightforward. Individuals are controlled and exploited as members of a group; therefore solutions must have a collective dimension to address special needs. Refusal to recognize a citizenship that allows minorities to collectively articulate their concerns not only reinforces the priviledge of those ahead in the competitive race, it also silences the voices of those who cannot afford to renounce their particular experiences. Nevertheless, group rights can be addressed in different ways: three types of differentiated citizenship can be discerned (equity, self-determining, and multicultural), with profoundly different implications for citizenship and society-building.

(a) Equity It is widely acknowledged that racial minorities are underrepresented in many parts of Canadian society. Special means for improving institutional representation have been proposed as one way of overcoming historical marginality. For example, culturally excluded groups who are disadvantaged in the political process may require a means of explicit representation for grievance articulation. Citizenship in this case is "differentiated" because eliminating these inequities begins with recognition of minorities as having special needs beyond those of universal citizenship. This unique status entitles minorities to make special claims against the state consistent with their marginal position.

As Kymlicka (1992) notes, equity rights are usually focused around institutional access and representation, especially in the political domain, because of historical exclusion from decision-making circles. The conferral of equity citizenship rights is not meant to repudiate the principle of universal citizenship as a basis for equality. It merely confirms its insufficiency in societies where inequalities are chronic, embedded, and systemic. Nor is there any sense of permanence about these initiatives. Rather equity and affirmative action measures stay in effect until they are no longer required; that is, when citizens are not differentiated because of exclusion or inequity.

(b) Self-determining The concept of an equity-based citizenship applies largely to racial minorities (in addition to the other target groups singled out by the employment equity laws). Another type of citizenship is endorsed by aboriginal peoples and the Québécois. In this view, inherent rights coupled with the principle of self-determination are more important than rights to special, but temporary, treatment. The concept of a self-determining citizenship applies only to those who define themselves as a "people" or a "nation." The rationale is straightforward: Unlike other racial and ethnic minorities, aboriginal peoples and the Québécois are each historically a community, possess some degree of institutional completeness, occupy a territory or a homeland, share a distinct language and culture, and are encapsulated by the boundaries of a larger political community. As peoples or nations, their demands as citizen go beyond universal or equity citizenship; they include claims upon the state for control over land, culture/language, and identity; the right to self-government and jurisdiction over matters of direct relevance; and a transfer of power from central authorities ("devolution") rather than mere political representation or economic access (Kymlicka 1992).

The collective and constitutional right to survive as a group is central to this notion self-determining citizenship. Both aboriginal people and the Québécois have agreed to become part of Canada and have even transferred powers to this effect, although not at the expense of their right to self-determination over internal matters. They see Canada as a federation of equal communities, with equal rights to flourish as distinct societies within a broader framework of citizenship. Failure of the state to meet this agreement entitles the "signatories" to withdraw from the arrangement. Not surprisingly, the concept of self-determination is threatening to many Canadians; its very presence is seen as (a) superceding universal citizenship, (b) elevating special group rights for entitlement to power and resources, and (c) undermining the legitimacy of the political community at large.

(c) Multicultural In between equity and self-determining citizenship is one that focuses on multicultural rights. Immigrant-based groups are anxious to secure some degree of official support in defence of their ethnocultural heritage. Multiculturalism has emerged as a tool for that advancement. A multicultural citizenship officially confirms the validity of diversity and provides institutional support (for example, funding) for its survival. It also acknowledges ethnicity as legitimate and valuable. A long-term commitment to cultural support is balanced by universal rights to full involvement and equal participation in society. In other words, a multicultural citizenship is concerned with preserving cultural particularities without, however, hampering access and equality in

political or economic fields (Kymlicka 1992).

The distinction between self-determining and multicultural citizenships is instructive. The discourse on multiculturalism is not about self-determination (with its connotation of a separate power base and parallel institutions). It connotes instead a willingness to work within the system to attain a degree of integration and acceptance. It accepts and takes for granted the authority of the larger community, provided that some degree of accommodation is enforced for "mainstreaming" institutional diversity. Conversely, equity and multicultural citizenship converge. The focus is on special measures and the accommodation of differences as necessary for equality and unity. However, unlike equity measures, which are seen as temporary in the march to a universally equal society, multiculturalism acknowledges that cultural differences need to be permanently entrenched as something useful and worth preserving (Kymlicki 1992).

Inclusive Citizenship

The conferral of universal citizenship with its entitlements derived from formal individual rights is one thing; a differentiated citizenship with a focus on collective group rights and special treatment for minorities is quite another. With its capacity to straddle the extremes of differentiated and universal citizenship, a multicultural citizenship is uniquely positioned to ply the area in between. Under multiculturalism, each citizen is entitled to an "inclusive" citizenship that is made up of two strands. One of these strands emphasizes uni-

versal citizenship rights, with rights to individual equality and similar treatment. The other strand focuses on citizenship rights that accommodate differences as a legitimate and integral component of citizenship. That clashes are likely to arise under these circumstances is to be expected. But the integrative functions of overlapping citizenship cannot be casually dismissed.

Universal and differential citizenships are not mutually exclusive. Universal citizenship is claimed by all or most Canadians; similarly, aspects of differentiated citizenship are also sought after by those who demand more than one kind of right. This confirms that citizenship in Canada is not only overlapping but situational in responding to demands of the diverse contexts. Consider this: in a comprehensive poll of Quebec residents done by *L'Actualité* in July, 1992 (and reported on by Will Kymlicka [1992]), just over 50 percent of the respondents identified themselves as Quebeckers, about 30 percent as Canadians, and 20 percent as both Quebeckers and Canadians. Being a Quebecker was important to 89 percent of respondents, yet 71 percent also considered being a Canadian as integral to their identity. For some purists, this mishmash of figures is contradictory and a sign of public confusion. Others may apply a different spin. Citizenship is overlapping and situationally adjusted according to the needs of the situation without fear of dissonance or despair. One can identify with Quebec without necessarily relinquishing an affiliation and identity with Canada. These "nested" identities range in scope from the universal to the differentiated, and provide the basis for an inclusive citizenship.

Central to the concept of inclusive citizenship is the notion of a shared identity. A shared identity is based on two principles: First, all Canadians must come around to a sense of "peoplehood," with a pride in "things Canadian" such as respect for cultural differences. To do this, Canadians must concede the insufficiency of surface diversity (such as ethnic dances or foods). Instead there must be a willingness to tolerate differences that are substantial and deep. That is, Canadians must recognize and accept different ways that each group expresses its citizenship and belonging to Canada. This distinction is important for unity to happen. Tolerance of differences is less important for citizenship rights than respect for a diversity of approaches to diversity. Unity is thus derived from a shared commitment not only to value diversity but to value it in a different way and in different spheres of life (Kymlicka 1992).

An inclusive citizenship acknowledges the desire for recognition as an important animating dynamic in society (Salee 1995; Gutman 1992). People want particular identity claims to be acknowledged and respected by central authorities. They also want an official commitment to ensure an adequate resource base in support of their claims for an inclusive citizenship. Problems arise, however, when minorities want concrete policy measures to satisfy the goal of inclusion of their differences *on their own terms*. Liberal democratic societies are poorly equipped to respond to demands for recognition of otherness when these take the form of autonomous territories or separate power bases. How then can unity and national identity be constructed in a society where "deep diversities" prevail (Taylor 1992; 1993)?

A NEW BELONGING

The politics of citizenship in Canada make one thing very clear: citizenship is neither uniform nor homogeneous but diverse and evolving. Each strand of which citizenship is comprised offers a different set of entitlements about who gets what, and why. Entitlements are justified in part on (a) the magnitude of need (formal equality versus special rights), (b) the status of group members (racial, ethnic, or indigenous), (c) the relationship to society at large (collective versus individual), and (d) on the nature of the claims against the state (inherent versus conferred). The concept of entitlement by group affiliation has further implications for citizenship. Some groups are disadvantaged because of underrepresentation within the community, therefore, they require equity citizenship; others who are disadvantaged because of community nonresponsiveness to cultural diversity need multicultural citizenship; still others disadvantaged because of more than one political community demand self-determining citizenship.

There is much to be said for conceptualizing citizenship as a rope of different yet interwoven strands. Admittedly, a citizenship of many rights poses problems related to social unity and national identity. But proponents of a differentiated citizenship reply that an adherence to universal citizenship runs the risk of needless conformity in unequal contexts, thus further freezing out the historically unpriviledged. Under inclusive citizenship, minority identities (values, needs, concerns, and aspirations) are affirmed in the symbols, institutions and political arrangements of society. The accommodation of differences under a differentiated citizenship holds out a chance for coherence and solidarity.

Unity in a pluralistic society thrives in a citizenship environment that upholds the principle of agreeing to disagree. For example, aboriginal and Québécois approaches to citizenship may not concur with ours. Prescriptions for managing diversity among racial and ethnic minorities may vary from the mainstream. But the survival of a multicultural society is dependent on creating different ways of relating as citizens of Canada. This is no time for the modernist notion of a unitary Canadian citizenship, with a dash of multicultural colour thrown in for good measure. What we need instead is a postmodernist

Canada—a country that is moving ahead not in the conventional way of stamping out differences in exchange for a uniform citizenship, but that can accommodate diversity within an enlarged citizenship. The viability of an inclusive citizenship, both universal and differentiated, yet within a shared identity, is open to debate. People are alike in different kinds of ways; they also are different in similar ways. We will have to learn to respect both of these dimensions and attempt to live together with such paradoxes.

SOURCE: This case study is based largely on Will Kymlicka, "Recent Work in Citizenship Theory," Multiculturalism and Citizenship, Ottawa, 1992.

The overview makes it clear how social developments have altered the operational basis of Canada's society-building process. Many reasons lie behind this transformation of the national agenda, some of which will be examined in the next section. Table 12.1 provides a summary overview of these emergent trends by comparing past and present in terms of *ideal types* related to official policy, objectives of government policy, level of government involvement with respect to managing race and ethnic relations, the focus of government intervention, the preferred type of relationship within Canada's social organization, the terms of entitlement with respect to who gets what, citizenship, and the status of human rights. As is the case with any endeavour to reduce complex information into simple charts, the possibility of overgeneralization is one that the reader must consider.

NEW RULES, NEW GAME, NEW STAKES

Demographic, political, ideological, and social changes have contributed to upheavals in Canadian race, ethnic, and aboriginal relations. Each of these changes is powerful in its own right; they become even more potent in impact when combined. The fact that these changes are still in the process of working themselves through will have an even more profound effect on society-building.

TABLE 12.1   Emergent Trends

	Past	Present
Official Policy	assimilation	diversity
Objectives	exclusion	inclusion/accommodation
Level of Government Involvement	"hands off"	"hands on"
Focus of Intervention	culture	structure
Status of Diversity	problem/deficit	resource/asset
Social Organization	unequal+ equality of opportunity	equity + equality of outcomes
Terms of Entitlement	colour-blind	colour-coded
Human Rights	individual	individual+collective
Citizenship	universal	inclusive

1) *Demographic Changes*   Racial and ethnic minorities with ancestries other than those of French or English exclusively now constitute nearly 45 percent of Canada's population. Equally significant is the growing percentage of visible minorities. People of colour now comprises about 9.5 percent of Canada's total population, up from the 5.1 percent in 1981. Much of the increase can be attributed to recent changes in immigration patterns between 1981 and 1991 when approximately half of immigrants arrived from "non-conventional" sources. With no foreseeable reversal anticipated, Canada's visible minority population could climb to about 17 percent by the twenty-first century.

2) *Demographic Concentrations*   Over half of the visible minorities who arrive in Canada reside in Ontario. Half of that group is drawn to the greater Toronto region. As a result, visible minorities constitute about 25 percent of Toronto's total population. Although other urban regions (with the exception of Vancouver and Montreal) are less attractive to visible immigrants, the impact and implications of these patterns are reflected in increased public awareness of race-related incidents and proposed efforts to deal with these before and after they occur.

3) *Political Reactions*   Liberal societies have reacted to diversity in one of three ways (see Raz 1994). First is by way of tolerance. Minorities are allowed to conduct themselves as they please without penalty as long as this diversity does not interfere with the culture and public space of the dominant sector. Second is by way of non-discrimination. A non-discriminatory commitment upholds the principle that minorities have a right to be free from discrimination on grounds unrelated to merit. They also possess an inalienable right to equal opportunity as a natural extension of the individual rights. Third is the response of multiculturalism. Multiculturalism can consist of situations where different cultures coexist in territorially separate units (for example, the Inuit in

Canada). More commonly, however, it will refer to situations where individuals must share the same common space. That being the case individuals of different cultural backgrounds are accorded full and equal participation in society, in effect reinforcing this commitment to equality through accommodation of differences. As well, they are entitled to maintain (within limits) their cultural differences as a valid or valued contribution to society (Raz 1994). None of this detracts from political attention to suppress (de-politicize) those aspects of diversity at odds with the principle of secular tolerance (Sen 1993).

4) *Policy Responses*   Central authorities have endorsed diversity as normal and necessary. Cultural and racial diversity is now recognized and legitimized as an integral component of Canada's identity and nation-building. Passage of the world's first Multiculturalism Act in 1988, preceded by the constitutional entrenchment of multiculturalism in the Charter of Rights and Freedom, has reinforced the growing status and power of the Third Force. The First Nations and the Québécois have also made strides in ensuring a national discourse consistent with their nations within status.

5) *Institutional Initiatives*   Government efforts to "mainstream" federal and provincial institutions are clearly in the ascendancy. Both private and federal institutions must comply with diversity principles to ensure accommodation through measures that enhance minority access, treatment, and outcomes. More important, however, is growing institutional recognition of diversity as a potential asset in a market both global and competitive. The movement of diversity from sidestream to mainstream will leave institutions no choice except to move over and make space in the relentless quest for profit or advantage.

6) *Social Reaction* Passage   of the Constitution Act in 1982 and the Charter of Rights and Freedom in 1985 has elevated public awareness of individual and collective rights. Citizens are now better informed, more demanding, and increasingly articulate about their rights throughout the entire criminal justice system. Minorities do not hesitate to exercise laws and policies that are designed to enhance justice and equality.

7) *Ideological Changes*   We live in what is popularly known as a postmodernist society. That is, society is no longer organized around conventional rules of engagement or entitlement. Postmodernist philosophies reject the priority of uniformity and order, best exemplified in the Enlightenment's obsession with universal progress through reason and science and expressed in architectural circles by buildings that look like cereal boxes. Postmodernists acknowledge the lived experiences of Canadians as fragmented and eclectic, with no obvious centre, except perhaps in an endorsement of diversity, change, and uncertainty as real and unavoidable. A profound cultural shift has resulted, in other words, that has moved us away from Canada's eurocentric society. It has also brought about a reassessment (de-construction) of what formerly was considered historically and politically correct" What once were virtues are now vices (for example, "might is right"), and vice versa. This pluralist ("postmodernist")critique

of conventions and values has catapulted diversity to the point where it commands public attention and political concern.

Certain patterns can be discerned from this brief review. Government–minority relations are poised for entry into a new era, characterized in part by the growing assertiveness of the three major forces, in other part by political willingness to address these demands. The reasons behind this shift are complex and not always easy to decipher. Invariably, however, they will cast the future foundation for Canada's social landscape.

RESISTANCE AND REACTION

That we live in a period of convulsive social change is surely beyond dispute. Everything is changing so quickly that nothing is certain or predictable except a pervasive sense of confusion or uncertainty. The combination of feminist and civil rights movements has rocked the very foundations of society, in the process loosening the moorings that formerly secured a scripted Canadian society. What once were endorsed as universal truths and self-evident virtues are no longer accepted as morally valid. The rules of the established order, in addition to the structures and values around hierarchy and control, are openly challenged and resisted. The impact of this postmodernist tumult is unshakeable: Canadian society is increasingly a "contested site," that is, a kind of battleground involving a struggle between opposing groups in constant competition over power, status, and resources.

Not everyone is conceding ground to the inevitability of these changes. Established interests have resorted to a variety of measures for reasserting the priority of "traditional values" and "Canadian identity." An anticipated backlash by angry white males threatens to revoke many of Canada's initiatives in the progressive management of race, ethnic, and aboriginal relations. That vested interests have chosen to roll back social advances is hardly a surprise, given the assumption that nobody voluntarily relinquishes power or privilege without a struggle. What is more surprising are the means employed, means that often manipulate the language and concerns of the historically disadvantaged to the advantage of the traditional elites.

It is within this postmodernist context of power politics that the phrase "political correctness" has leapt into the forefront of contemporary discourse. The charge of "political correctness" can be variously interpreted, but most commonly in terms of a conservative reaction to contemporary social changes, in which those with the most to lose are casting about for scapegoats to cut back losses (Richer and Weir 1995). Those accused of political correctness are charged with imperilling free speech and critical thought in a misguided attempt at gender inclusiveness and racial accommodation (Abramowicz 1991). The politically correct have been caricaturized for their bullying tactics in making people afraid to say what they think for fear of being censured by the so-called "thought police" (see Brennan 1991; also *The Economist* 1993). Not surprisingly, the expression continues to be bandied about indiscriminantly by the left and the right—even to the point of abuse—as a tactic to silence the opposition or to terminate debate. What then is the history and current status of political correctness, and how does it relate to the reconstruction of Canada along pluralist lines?

CASE STUDY

Rights in Collision: The Politics of Political Correctness

"Political correctness" is one those curious turns of phrase that somehow manages to sound superficially positive even when the underlying message is negative or contemptuous (Trillin 1993). The concept itself is difficult to define, much less to defend, because of its lack of tangible referents. Nobody has ever defined themselves as politically correct although many take a perverse delight in sticking it to others. To make matters worse, political correct is neither an identifiable ideology (such as Marxism) nor a coherent social movement (such as feminism). As a noun the concept may symbolize the "thin edge" of a shift from Eurocentrism to inclusiveness; as an adjective it refers to a person who stands on a particular side of this seismic shift. In the final analysis, political correctness means whatever a person wants it to mean, for as James Raskin (1992:31) concludes:

> As a description of political ideas, "political correctness" expresses, literally nothing. It is an empty vessel of a signifier into which meaning is poured on a purely expedient and ad hominem basis.

Mindful of the disarray and the slippery terrain, any working definition of political correctness is likely to meet resistance. We prefer to define political correctness as a *term of derision,* for this is what it has become, as used by the neoconservative right for slandering those in the vanguard of a more inclusive society. Political correctness can also be defined within the context of a right wing backlash against "institutional accommodation" when active steps to improve minority access and treatment are seen as violating conventional patterns of speech and free expression. Those labelled as politically correct are denounced as "stooges" in defence of this proposed social/moral order; they also are castigated for their aggressiveness and rigidity in suppressing debate over goal attainment. At the core of this notion of political correctness is reaction and resistance—a kind of struggle between those who want to defend tradition versus those who want a new kind of society. Such a reactionary stance was not the case in the early days of usage.

GENESIS

The concept "political correctness" originated among socialist and middle-class social movements during the 1960s (Kohl 1991; Weir 1995). Once employed in a mildly-deprecating sense among leftists for occasional lapses into rigidity or dogma, the phrase evolved into a kind of in-joke within radical circles for chiding ideologues who approved of the party line even in the face of contradictory evidence (McGillivray 1992). The term was expanded to single out commitment from hypocrisy. Among cohorts, it provided a gently reproving way of admonishing those who mistakenly associated progressive political engagement with puritanical language codes, flamboyant posturing, and correct poses (Raskin 1992). The label was occasionally reserved for those "designer" radicals who sported all the right "buttons" or slogans, but rarely put principles into practice when confronting militarism or repression. The reproach also drew attention to inconsistencies in the lives of do-gooders, the same ones who protested against foreign injustice in some remote corner of the world, but who thought nothing of abusing their partners or ripping off the system at home. In short, to be rebuked as politically correct within leftist circles was not a case of being too radical, but rather of too much liberalism—that is, a level of engagement consisting of "frozen politics of empty gestures" with a surplus of "preachy self-righteousness, but a deficit of analysis and courage" (Raskin 1992:31).

FROM IRONY TO PUTDOWN

The gist of political correctness as "cosmetic commitment" and "doctrinaire rigidity" has lingered into the present. There remains a sense of political correctness as a kind of commitment to change in the abstract, well-intentioned perhaps, but devoid of conviction or consequence. Yet there is no mistaking the more strident, even sneering, tone associated with the putdown as it is now used. The term is applied in a disparaging way to slander individuals who ape an activist party line or rigidly adhere to a leftist political orthodoxy without critical reflection or any sustained commitment. The politically correct are skewered by the right as shallow, unbending persons who robotically hop aboard any trendy cause because of social pressure or impression management. By contrast, those who disagree with the politically correct dogma portray themselves as courageous and critical in reaction to such mealy-mouth timidity and cowardice, as expressed in this self-serving phrase "...this may not be politically correct, but..." (see Trillin 1993).

The revival of political correctness as a term of derision can be properly understood within the context of a conservative backlash against the forces of diversity and change. Stripped of its irony and applied to smear any progressive change, the concept has been coopted by neoconservatives who wrap themselves around the flag of free speech to discredit as tyrannical the anti-racist initiatives for assisting the historically disadvantaged (Richer and Weir 1995). Conservative elements have appropriated this expression as a semantic club with which to bash the credibility of the progressives, in the same way the phrase "knee jerk liberalism" once denounced everyone who hopped aboard every chic-leftist issue for personal rather than for political reasons (Raskin 1992). What we have in other words is a case of "theft" and "inversion" (Brennan 1991). The conservative right has turned the tables on its enemies in an effort to discredit activism or stifle intellectual dissent without appearing reactionary in the process.

HIGHER EDUCATION AS POLITICAL CORRECTNESS

The labelling of activists as well meaning, yet woefully misguided and potentially dangerous zealots, is not unprecedented. The conservative right already has a prior record of appropriating the language of the left (consider the expression, "reverse discrimination") to justify retention of traditional values. What perhaps is novel is its application to postsecondary education. The concept of political correctness has been twisted to incorporate the spectre of a conspiracy, both sweeping and coercive, to suppress debate and enforce a politically motivated rewriting of curricula, pedogogy, and administration.

Conservatives have rebelled against criticism of American colleges and universities as repositories of entrenched orthodoxy. What once were "ivory" towers (pure, white, male, and shining) are now exposed ("de-constructed") as implicitly racist and systemically sexist, with curricula geared around "pale male" priorities and anti-minority hiring practices. Authors such as the late Allan Bloom or Dinesh D'Souza lamented the introduction of women's studies departments and multicultural curricula as warning signs of an impending demise of everything "good" about liberal education (see McCormack 1991). The issue that rankled these writers was not the criticism of injustice or unfairness; after all, everyone concurs with a more inclusive environment. The object of dissaffection were the means employed to achieve

that goal. Especially galling was the perceived chilling effect on free speech and academic freedom. Faculty and administration have pounced on activists as modern day puritans whose obsession with correct conduct (with respect to what is taught and how) constitutes an infringement on a fundamental cultural value.

Conservatives intuitively recognize this threat to power and entrenched privilege. Postmodernism is much more than a exercise in deconstructing poetry, prose, or architecture. It is not about professors' right to say what they like in class or even about the cultural wars in the educational curricula. In the final analysis, postmodernism and its expression in political correctness is part of a social revolution in which structures and values that once endorsed hierarchy and domination are being contested andchallenged. The issue is ultimately about power and dominance, about who gets what in society and why, and a redefinition of who we are as a people (Kohl 1991).

THE NEW SILENCERS? WHO IS SILENCING WHOM?

That political correctness is often associated with censorship of free speech is a curiosity in its own right. The politically correct are portrayed as the new "silencers," at the sinister edge of a new wave of repression and intolerance with respect to the free marketplace of ideas. Yet it might be argued that the opponents of politically correctness are equally guilty of free speech infringement in their zeal to defend privilege and the status quo. The anti-P.C. platform is no less anxious to restrain serious social analysis through reliance on disparaging labels to silence and deter (Raskin 1992). Strangely enough, the politically correct credo—that you can change the world by changing how you talk about it, since after all, the power to define is the power to rule—has been turned back upon the movement itself. This is evidenced by a host of unflattering references such as the Thought Police, the new Puritanism, the Silencers, the new McCarthyism, the Kindly Inquisitors, the new conformists, the Intimidators, and the Multiculturalists.

Speech codes are linked with political correctness as a social weapon in the cultural wars between tradition and inclusiveness. Political correctness is defined by the new Concise Oxford English Dictionary as "the avoidance of forms of expressions that exclude, marginalize, or insult racial or cultural minorities." For example, people who are seen as politically correct may prefer the term "individual with disabilities" rather than the expression "disabled person." The distinction, they believe, is important. The former expression focuses on the individual first, the disability second. The latter reverses the order and puts the disability first—in effect (if not in intent) reinforcing "ablism," that is, discrimination in favour of the able bodied. Those who think the distinction is irrelevant may not appreciate the role of language in the social construction of language (but see Berger and Luckman 1967). Yet use of one expression rather than another says a lot about others and their relationship to society. It may say even more about the speaker and his or her politics—whether we are aware of it or not.

This suggests a new spin on the debate. The struggle is not about political

correctness and something else, but between competing versions of political correctness (Fish 1994). Nor is the clash about ends—everyone agrees on equality and justice. The means are central to the debate, and the politically correct are accused of using the same repressive measures that created the problem in the first place (see also *The Economist* 1993). The politically correct are also accused of undermining everything that is superior about western civilization, as well as unravelling the social fabric that bonds the disparate parts of society into a coherent whole. Yet the anti-politically correct faction is no less political or politicized. Instead of criticizing the reality of racism and sexism in society, conservative right factions prefer to unload their fears on the agents of change by referring to them as rigid, dogmatic, lacking in humour, and superficial.

IMPLICATIONS: STICKS AND STONES MAY BREAK MY BONES, BUT WORDS...

Political correctness as a concept can embrace either a putdown or a critique. It symbolizes a struggle between groups over competing visions of society: on the one hand, efforts to shore up the distribution of power supported by the ideology of formal equality; on the other, the challenges of those in favour of substantive equality (McIntyre 1993). Either way, there are several misconceptions associated with political correctness in need of clarification. Those associated with political correctness do not automatically condemn white male privilege as the root of all evil. But the inclusiveness associated with political correctness does demand that those of privilege move over and make room for the other 90 percent of world. Nor is political correctness a threat to erode excellence on campus. But it does raise the issues of what exactly constitute standards of excellence, who says so, why, on what grounds, and what precisely constitutes a liberal (as in critical and informative) education?

The forces of political correctness are not anti-free speech or against academic freedom—except in cases where free speech acts as a cover for hate speech (Fish 1994). There is no such thing as absolute free expression: restrictions exist by definition. Under political correctness, the concept of free expression is subjected to further negotiation and restriction, in the belief that the world can be changed by changing how you speak about it. In the final analysis, restricting the right of free expression for the powerful may secure the rights and freedom of those who historically have been excluded from full participation.

One final thought: The protest against postmodernist changes, with its most visible expression in political correctness, is not simply about the questioning of conventional knowledge (McCormack 1991). It goes beyond saying the right word at the right time. Put candidly, the phrase politically correct has evolved into a symbol about the politics of power—who has it, and who wants it. In a society contested by the left and right, the charge of political correctness is directed against the critics of the established agenda as a criticism for what they say and how they say it. On the well-founded assumption that power is never freely surrendered, political correctness represents the sharp end of the stick for empowering the once powerless through direct action. Herein lies the dilemma: Free speech debate is not between a good versus an evil, but rather between two mutually exclusive yet equally valid goods. On the one hand are many who endorse the sanctity of free speech, and who view any effort at curbing it as nothing short of a civil liberty violation. On the other are those who believe that the current climate is inappropriate in a changing and diverse society, and are looking for ways to make it more inclusive even if certain restrictions need to be imposed in the process. The fact that both positions are "right" provides political correctness with its animating properties.

RETHINKING RACE, ETHNIC, AND ABORIGINAL RELATIONS: MAKING VIRTUE FROM NECESSITY

Canada sits among a handful of modern countries including Australia and New Zealand which are in the vanguard of constructing a coherent yet pluralistic society (Hudson 1987; also Pearson 1991, 1993). Yet Canada's status among the leaders beacon in managing diversity does not allow Canada to rest on its laurels. Canada is currently entangled in the throes of a massive, unprecedented restructuring. In shifting from a predominantly monocultural system to one consistent with pluralist principles and egalitarian practices, the canvas of Canada as a bilingual, three-nation state, within a multiculturalism framework is being contested through upheavals in state-minority relations. This transformation is manifest at different levels. The ongoing decolonization of Canada's aboriginal peoples has evolved to the point where the reality of inherent aboriginal self-government is at hand. The proposed renewal in Quebec-Ottawa relations along "distinct society" lines remains a pressing priority, especially if the threat to secede materializes. No less evident is the restructuring of Canada's race relations agenda where the principles and practices of cultural pluralism have catapulted official multiculturalism to the forefront of strategies for managing diversity (Fleras and Elliott 1991). Few Canadians have been untouched by these diversity initiatives: nevertheless, the threat of a growing backlash against diversity may deprive Canadians of a key resource in forging the world's first "postmulticultural" society (Fleras 1993).

The challenge confronting liberal democracies such as Canada should not to be underestimated. The objective is the creation of a moral community of communities to be nurtured. Equally important is a political union with a sense of shared core values, a common vision, a sense of belonging and commitment, a workable citizenship, and a sense of collective purpose. On balance, Canada appears to have been relatively successful in balancing the demands of society-building with minority rights—even if the juggling act tends to be wobbly at times. Nevertheless, moves to strengthen the society-building process are contested as central authorities struggle to secure state legitimacy in the face of opposition and group conflict (Simmons and Keohane 1992; also Lewycky 1993).

External pressures complicate the challenge of fashioning unity from diversity. We are living in a world engulfed by two mutually exclusive yet extremely powerful forces (Nelson and Fleras 1995). On the one hand are the universalizing (and homogenizing) forces of globalization and global market economies. Transnational movements of goods and services, as well as jobs and investments, are conducted with little regard for societal boundaries. Advances in information technology have also rendered national borders nearly impossible to monitor or control. On the other hand are the fragmenting forces of ethnicity with equally formidable potential to dismember and destroy. Radical ethnicities and ethnic nationalisms are largely indifferent to the legitimacy of the nation-state. Many are willing to jettison this arrangement for parochial interests (Ignatieff 1993). This interplay of centrifugal and centripetal forces promises to reconfigure the political landscape of societies large and small. It also promises to alter the meaning of sovereignty toward the affirmation of cultural identity and away from statehood as a politically autonomous site of social regulation and economic activity (Cox 1992).

Two scenarios prevail because of these opposing forces. The first suggests that a decentralized Canada may collapse because it lacks any coherent centre. The demise of Canada could also result from failure to mend social fissures both old and new (Simpson 1993). Critics of multiculturalism (Bissoondath 1994), for example, are skeptical of Canada's prospects. Any policy that encourages diversity, they argue, creates conditions for ethnic strife rooted in a sense of psychological separation. Others disagree with such a gloomy scenario. According to Richard Gwyn, in a address to the D.G. Willmot Distinguished Lecture Series at Brock University, St Catharines, and reprinted as "The First Borderless State" (*Toronto Star* 26 November 1994), Canada stands on the cusp of becoming the world's first postmodernist, postmulticultural society. In a world that is rapidly changing, and increasingly uncertain and diverse, Gwyn asserts, Canada will continue to be a trailblazer for the management of race and ethnic relations, as well as a prototype for the ideal twenty-first century society. The fact that Canada represents a political union born out of economic necessity rather than national spirit created out of violent struggle may also work in its favour (Simpson 1993; Eisler 1994). In short, Canada will prosper because of its alleged weaknesses.

We, too, believe that Canada will survive and prosper even if proof of this is somewhat elusive. Like it or not, diversity is an integral part of reality because of massive global migrations. Countries that are wired for dealing with diversity will have an enormous competitive edge. Canada's precedent in coping with diversity—from French-English duality to the society-building virtues of immigration—provides an advantage. Much can be gleaned from the interlocking nature of this diversity. The three major forces are interdependent to the point where talk of secession can be interpreted as a negotiating gambit. Each has a vested interest in maintaining order, avoiding disruptive social change, encouraging flexibility and accommodation, and discouraging rigidity when confronted by difficult decisions (Barth and Noel 1972). This mutual dependency tends to promote an element of pragmatism and cooperation for the achievement of goals beyond the scope of each group alone.

Canada's pacesetting abilities may stem from yet another unexpected source. Canadians are frequently accused of lacking shared values or national character; our nationalism is muted, it is lamented, while our sense of peoplehood is fractured along regional and ethnic lines, without any root in history and homeland. This dispassionate, self-effacing nature should not be interpreted as an indifference to Canada, as Richard Gwyn notes (1994). A recent survey indicated that 94 percent of Canadians agreed that Canada was the best place in the world to live (the highest ranking among all industrialized societies). Even Quebeckers came in at a 90 percent approval rating of Canada. Our multiple and nested identities will allow us to shift without necessarily experiencing contradiction or dissonance.

In a world of diversity and change, in other words, Canadians may possess the kind of temperament best suited for the indeterminacies of the twenty-first century, namely, a dedication to pragmatism, civility and tolerance, an openness to negotiation and a willingness to compromise as a way of muddling through. Our historical experience of muddling through problems collectively rather than having solutions imposed by authoritarian regimes paves the way for negotiated settlements between seemingly incompatible aspirations while rejecting false dichotomies and polarities in favour of interplay and compromise. In a world where rules are being turned on their heads, our threshold for uncertainty and tolerance for ambiguity may stand us in good stead. In a world where a passionate attachment to homeland or culture can maim or destroy, we may benefit from our inability to define precisely who we are and what it means to be a Canadian in terms of rights, principles, obligations, character, and rules of engagement (MacQueen 1994).

It is in this sense that Canada represents the world's first postmulticultural, postmodernist society. The decentralization within Canada, long thought a bane of our existence, may hold up well in a world where calls for self-determination threaten to fragment and dismember countries. Diversity, reviled in the past, represents a potential resource. Through the management of its race, ethnic, and aboriginal agenda, Canada has transformed former weaknesses into contemporary strengths in a way that may consolidate its unity and integrity while securing a competitive edge in a global economy. Perhaps this penchant for snatching virtue from vice will further promote the progressive—if somewhat contested—management of Canada's race, ethnic, and aboriginal relations.

CHAPTER HIGHLIGHTS

- With the First Nations, Charter groups, and multicultural minorities vying for power and scarce resources, it is not farfetched to describe Canada as the contested site of a struggle between opposing forces and competing agendas.

- The interplay and impact of rapid change, growing diversity, and increased uncertainty has contributed to this notion of Canada "at the crossroads" with respect to building a modern and progressive society.

- The reconstruction of Canada along pluralist lines will entail imaginative ways of addressing minority concerns and balancing the competing demands of Canada's three major forces.

- Key themes and evolving trends can be discerned in this reconstruction process. Foremost in terms of managing race, ethnic, and aboriginal relations is the shift from a monocultural, assimilationist framework to the accommodation of diversity not only as an important national resource, but also as a basis for government policy and institutional change.

- Other shifts are also noticeable, particularly with respect to changing definitions of equality (from formal to substantive), increased government involvement in managing in/equality, a growing focus on the structural determinants of equality, a commitment to accommodate differences and colour-conscious programs, and recognition of the importance of balancing individual with collective rights.

- Many of these contemporary changes are reflected in and reinforced by debates over citizenship as a basis for redefining minority-state relations. The case study makes it clear that conventional ways of thinking about citizenship ("universal citizenship") will need to expand into more inclusive styles if Canada hopes to survive.

- Talk is one thing when it comes to reconceptualizing citizenship: action is another. It remains to be seen whether the deep diversities envisioned by a more inclusive citizenship can be incorporated into the society-building process without irreparable damage to Canadian distinct society status.

- Canada is increasingly drawn into playing a set of largely untested rules because of demographic, political, ideological, and social changes. As a result, what once were virtues are increasingly regarded as vices, while former weaknesses are now interpreted as potential strengths.

- Not everyone is hopping aboard the diversity bandwagon. Resistance and reaction are symbolized by debates over political correctness. Political correctness can be defined as a struggle between those who want progressive change by altering how people think or talk, versus those who regard demands for inclusiveness and power-sharing as a threat to core cultural values, individual freedom, and national prosperity.

- The challenges associated with society-building should not be underestimated. Conflicting demands and opposing agendas complicate the process of reinventing a three-nations society, bilingual and multicultural in both policy and practice.

- Canadians possess a relatively high threshold for ambiguity and change because of historical precedents. Such flexibility may enable Canada to emerge as the world's first postmodern and postmulticultural society in the progressive management of race, ethnic, and aboriginal relations.

KEY TERMS

Citizenship	Political Correctness	Society-building
Differentiated Citizenship	Postmodernist Society	Universal Citizenship
Inclusive Citizenship	Postmulticulturalism	
	Reconstructing Canada	

REVIEW QUESTIONS

1) What are the challenges that await the reconstruction of Canada along pluralist lines?

2) How can Canada be transformed into an inclusive society that is both safe for diversity and safe from diversity?

3) Briefly outline the key themes and emergent trends in the management of Canada's race, ethnic, and aboriginal relations.

4) Discuss the demographic, political, ideological, and social changes that have altered the contours of Canada's social landscape.

5) Compare and contrast the different types of citizenship that are brought to bear in managing diversity.

6) What are the issues that surround the political correctness debate?

7) Evidence suggests that Canada may be advantageously positioned to redefine itself as the world's first postmodern, postmulticultural society. Comment.

GLOSSARY

Aboriginal Peoples: Aboriginal peoples such as the New Zealand Maori, Australian aborigines, the Saami of Scandinavia, and Native Americans in United States, represent the original ("indigenous") occupants of a particular country or territory. Canada's aboriginal peoples regard themselves as (a) first among equals whose collective entitlements have never been extinguished, (b) entitled to special considerations because of their original occupancy, (c) in possession of a special relationship with the state, and (d) a relatively independent "nation within" the framework of Canadian federalism. Also called *indigenous peoples.*

Aboriginality: A political statement that establishes a unique and irrevocable relationship between aboriginal peoples and the state, and embodies a corresponding set of entitlements, powers, and privileges that flow from this special relationship. Aboriginality can also mean the restoration of unextinguished rights that belong to indigenous peoples because of original occupancy.

Affirmative action: Affirmative action in the United States consists of policies and programs which, since the late 1960s, have sought to improve minority status in the workplace through preferential treatment and special programs. These programs tend to rely on quotas and deadlines as one way of complying with federal laws. Also called *Employment equity.*

Anti-racism: A commitment to identify, isolate, and challenge racism in all its forms through direct action.

Apartheid: Until recently apartheid represented the official race relations policy in South Africa. Derived from the Dutch word meaning "separate," apartheid involved a system of laws and procedures that segregated whites from non-whites. Central to the notion of apartheid was the creation of semi-autonomous black homelands whose primary purpose was to provide centres of cheap and disposable labour for white-owned industry. Also included under apartheid was a pervasive belief in the virtues of racial purity and white supremacy. Apartheid was officially abolished in 1993.

Assimilation: The concept of assimilation is derived from the biological process whereby nutrients are absorbed by a living organism. Sociologically speaking, assimilation consists of a complex and dynamic process in which minorities begin to lose their distinctiveness through absorption into the ongoing activities and objectives of the dominant society. As a policy, assimilation can refer to specific and formal government directives for the transformation and incorporation of minority populations; it can also encompass an overarching political framework for introducing, promoting, and justifing program initiatives for amalgamation. Assimilation processes may (a) entail forced or voluntary compliance with laws and institutions, (b) proceed at varying rates of change or scope, (c) involve explicit or implicit policy guidelines and (d) consist of outward compliance rather than wholesale conversion. The impact of assimilation can also vary depending on whether the process of change occurs at the level of culture, social structure, individual, or group. Also known in the context of this book as *Anglo-conformity.*

Bilingualism: Bilingualism, the coexistence of two languages, can be expressed at territorial, institutional, or individual levels. Canada is officially bilingual at institutional levels: Both French and English are legally and constitutionally entrenched as official and equal languages. Official bilingualism is applied primarily to federal institutions: that means that people have the right to work in or receive services in French or English. Parliament and federally underwritten organizations (from Air Canada to Parks Canada) are bilingual for public service purposes. Official Language minorities are also entitled to certain guarantees in areas where numbers warrant concessions. Only New Brunswick among the provinces is officially bilingual. Approximately 16 percent of all Canadians regard themselves as bilingual speakers.

Capitalism: Capitalism can be defined as an economic (and social) system dedicated to the rational pursuit of profit. It is also characterized by (a) the presence of exchange (involving money) and market relations (including class relationships), (b) the organization of production and distribution of goods at prices determined by the laws of supply and demand, and (c) the use of modern technology and machinery to bolster the production process.

Charter groups: The French and English are the Charter groups who comprise the second major force in Canadian society. The 1867 British North America Act acknowledged and enshrined the rights of the French and English settlers/colonizers as founding ("charter") and privileged members of Canadian society, and having the right to establish agendas and define priorities. Much of the current political crisis revolves around competing visions of Canada as compact or contract or three-nations state.

Charter of Rights and Freedoms: Canada passed the Charter of Rights and Freedoms in 1982. The Charter constitutionally entrenched the right of individuals to be free from discrimination on irrelevant grounds; it guaranteed individuals freedom from unnecessary state intrusion; and endorsed the concept of collective rights putting reasonable limits on individual rights when taking into account the common good.

Citizenship: The reciprocal rights and duties that exist between a person and the state they live in. Universal citizenship has historically included the concept of treating everyone the same through conferral of similar rights and obligations. The concept of *universal citizenship* is currently contested by the notions of *differentiated* and *inclusive citizenships,* each of which recognizes that different kinds of belonging can exist without necessarily undermining a commitment to the whole.

Civic nationalism: This term is usually employed to indicate state initiatives in society-building. Civic nationalism is concerned with creating a society that is made up of a community of individuals in whom reside ultimate authority (sovereignty of the people). Under civic nationalism all people who are citizens (a) possess equal rights, (b) are conferred citizenship on the basis of common loyalty to shared values and institutions; and (c) coexist with their differences in a cosmopolitan state. See *ethnic nationalism*.

Class: An aggregate of persons who occupy a similar position in society because of similarities in power, wealth, or status. Theorists of a Marxist persuasion prefer to see class as the division of society in terms of people's relationship to the means of production and private property. Those who own productive private property are the ruling class; those who must sell their labour power to survive are called the working class. Those of a Weberian bent tend to see class as a complex interplay of factors, not all of which coincide, in effect leading to different class systems, including one which divides a society into the ever-popular categories of upper, middle, and lower class.

Collective definition: A distinct, if somewhat underutilized, approach to the study of race and ethnic relations. It endorses a view of race and ethnic relations as dynamic and contested, involving competing sectors within both the dominant and subordinate groups, each of which defines the situation differently and acts accordingly. The end result is a view of society in a state of flux that ranges from cooperation or cooptation to open confrontation and conflict. See *dualisms*.

Colonialism: Refers to a specific era of European expansion into overseas territories from the sixteenth to the mid twentieth century. It entailed the process whereby a European power took control of and exploited an in-

digenous people by appropriating land and resources, extracting wealth, and capitalizing on cheap labour. Racial doctrines that reinforced patterns of superiority were often invoked to justify, explain, and promote the blatant exploitation of indigenous groups. White settlement often accompanied the colonialist enterprise; that in turn led to the displacement of indigenous populations who were seen as barriers to progress of the white settlers.

Compact: Refers to an interpretation of Canadian federalism as a special union between the French and English rather than a contract of federal and provincial subunits. According to the compact vision, the Québécois are not an ethnic minority and Quebec is not just another province. The Québécois are a distinct people with a common homeland, culture, language, and identity who have a status equivalent to that of the English as a founding (Charter) group. See *Charter groups*.

Conflict theory: One of several sociological perspectives that can be applied to a study of race and ethnic relations. Conflict theory takes as its starting point the idea that confrontation and change are critical components of society. Race and ethnic relations are interpreted as the interplay of different groups who compete for scarce resources in contexts that favour some groups, not others. See also *internal colonialism*.

Contested site: Conventional ways of thinking and doing are increasingly being challenged because of demographic, social, and political changes. The concept of a contested site captures this notion of societal domains as battlegrounds on which opposing groups struggle to impose their agendas and priorities at the expense of the others. The outcome of the struggle is open to debate and rarely entirely resolved. For example, the contemporary university can be interpreted as a contested site involving those who wish to (a) retain its ivory tower status, (b) move it closer to a business enterprise, and (c) engage higher education in progressive social change.

Cultural relativism: Cultural relativism consists of a belief that cultural practices should be evaluated on the grounds of their relationship and contributions to the social context in which they exist rather than by some arbitrarily selected external criteria. It is widely (but incorrectly) thought that in the absence of absolute standards cultural relativism embraces all cultural practices as good and valid, even when in violation of basic standards of human decency. But cultural relativism is not a blanket endorsement of all cultural practices. Proponents of a thoughtful cultural relativism argue instead that cultural practices can be evaluated as if equally good and valid for purposes of understanding, without necessarily condoning them.

Culture: Social scientists employ the concept of culture in a more comprehensive sense than non-academics. The concept of culture can be defined as a complex and socially constructed system of rules, meaning, knowledge, artifacts, and symbols that (a) guide human behaviour, (b) account for pattern regularities of thought and action, (c) provide a standard for right or wrong, good or bad, and (d) contribute to human social and physical survival. More specifically, culture can refer to the integrated lifestyle of a particular group of people who differ from others in terms of beliefs, values, world views, and attitudes.

Discourse: A conceptual framework with its own internal logic and underlying assumptions that may be readily recognizable to the audience is called a discourse; it involves a distinct way of speaking about some aspect of reality. For example, approaching race and ethnic relations as relationships of inequality is one kind of discourse; another is the analysis of race and ethnic relations within the framework of the assimilation cycle or theories of prejudice is another. See also *paradigm*.

Discrimination: Discrimination represents a denial of equal treatment to some group or member of a group because of race, ethnicity, gender, or disability. Often viewed as the behavioural counterpart of prejudice or attitudes, discrimination consists of actions that have the effect (whether deliberate or not) of denying or excluding a person because of that person's inclusion in a socially devalued category. Diverse types of discrimination can be discerned, ranging from the personal, intentional, and direct, to the impersonal, inadvertent, and systemic. See also *racism*.

Dominant group: The collectivity of people in society who have both power and authority to preserve and promote the prevailing distribution of privilege in society. It represents that part of society that has the capacity to define itself and its culture as the standard or norm by which others are evaluated. Competition over the good things in life is likely to propel the dominant sector into conflict with those who are excluded for one reason or another.

Distinct society: The concept of distinct society is usually applied to describe the political aspirations of the Québécois, that is, an historical people with a unique language, culture, and identity, whose homeland of last resort is Quebec. The notion of distinct society does not necessarily mean outright separation from Canada, but some kind of association that acknowledges Quebec's distinctiveness and its right to self-determination over internal matters. See *nations within*.

Dual labour market: The observation that the labour market is not uniform or homogenous but divided along major racial lines is called the dual labour market. It proposes that patterns of employment involving racially different groups in urban areas can entail qualitative differences that reflect advantage and relative disadvantage. The primary market (usually associated with the priviledged sectors of the labour force) provides high wages and career opportunities, in contrast with the reduced opportunities and rewards of the secondary labour market.

Dualism: This is a term at the core of collective definition perspective. The concept of dualism suggests a series of binary divisions (factions) within society. One faction within the dominant sector is anxious to incorporate minorities into the mainstream; another faction prefers to maintain a degree of separation between the competing groups. Within the subordinate sector are those who endorse closer ties with the dominant sectors; others want to remain separate. The interplay of these dualisms imparts the dynamic quality to pluralist societies.

Egalitarian: The term egalitarian does not mean that everyone is or should be the same. It conveys instead the idea that the everyone has relatively equal and unimpeded access to the basic necessities of life as defined by society. Egalitarian may also imply a more equitable distribution of scarce resources.

Employment equity: Employment equity is a concept that can be interpreted as a principle, a law, and a set of practices. As a principle, employment equity embraces the notion of institutional accommodation by improving the hiring and treatment of minorities. As law, employment equity refers to legislation such as the Employment Equity Act of 1986 that enshrined equity principles as formal government initiative. The law is aimed at providing equitable employment opportunities for all Canadians through removal of discriminatory barriers and implementation of proactive measures to accommodate differences. As practice, employment equity consists of formal programs and procedures by which companies draw up plans to hire and promote targetted minorities (namely, women, people of colour, individuals with disabilities, and aboriginal people) in compliance with federal or provincial laws. Unlike affirmative action in the United States, companies in Canada have only to establish goals and timetables rather than quotas and deadlines. They are also expected to exhibit reasonable progress toward attainment of these particular goals, although penalties for not doing so remain unclear. See also *affirmative action*.

Entitlement: The conferral of certain rights and privileges (who gets what) to a particular group or category of groups by virtue of their collective and relational status in society. Canada's First Nations, for example, are entitled to additional consideration from the federal government because of their status as the original occupants whose rights to culture and land have never been extinguished.

Equality of outcome: A pattern of distribution by which the good things in life (wealth, power, and privilege) are allocated on the basis of people's needs rather than on market skills or ability to generate revenue. Compare this egalitarian pattern of allocation with the concept of equal opportunity and its focus on individual competition and abstract merit as the basis for sorting out who gets what.

Equity: A belief that each individual is entitled to a fair share of scarce resources. Attainment of equity may entail treating people differently and recognizing collective rights.

Ethnic: The largely ascriptive identity of a group of individuals who see themselves as having a shared cultural affiliation because of their identification with a common language, ancestry, homeland, and historical and cultural symbols.

Ethnic boundaries: The "membrane" that keeps an ethnic group in and unwanted influences out. It consists of socially constructed divisions that are negotiated and adjusted between groups to ensure a sense of "peoplehood" among the different members. Certain beliefs and practices that people have in common are employed as symbols to demarcate one group from another and from society at large. Boundaries between groups can also be maintained through certain practices such as prohibition of mixed marriages, rules regarding exit and entry, and establishment of ethnic institutions for catering to member needs.

Ethnic group: Ethnic groups consist of a kinship-based community of individuals with an awareness of a common identity and cultural symbols. Key characteristics include: (a) common ancestry, (b) awareness of an historical past, (c) identification with select cultural elements as symbolic of their peoplehood, (d) a set of related experiences, interests, origins, and de-

scent, (e) potential to interact with others up to and including the point of a community, and (f) an awareness of themselves as a people. The viability and persistance of an ethnic group as a community depends to some degree on the level of boundary maintenance, cultural strength, institutional completeness, and shared interests.

Ethnic nationalism: See also *nationalism*. The beliefs of those who share an ascriptive ethnic identity and are mobilized into an action group (social movement) for attainment of certain goals related to land, recognition, honour, or revenge. Ethnic nationalism entails a community of like-minded people whose attachments reflect defence of the homeland rather than loyalty to society at large or universalistic principles of equality or human rights. On occasion, associated with "ethnic cleansing" or doctrines of racial purity. See *civic nationalism*.

Ethnic surge: This concept refers to the explosion of ethnicity in recent years. It reflects the growing assertiveness of minorities who have utilized cultural or racial symbols as strategic resources in the competition over scarce resources. From the status of marginal groups at the edge of society, ethnic minorities throughout the world have shifted to a position as a force to be reckoned with in competition with the nation-state as the basis of a morally legitimate political community.

Ethnic stratification: A hierarchical ranking of racial and ethnic minorities in ascending/descending order on the basis of the criteria of income, education, or social class. Canadians of British or northwestern European background have historically ranked near the top of the hierarchy. Groups such as aboriginal First Nations and certain visible minorities occupy the bottom of the hierarchy, with others in between.

Ethnicity: A principle by which people are defined, differentiated, organized, and rewarded on the basis of commonly shared physical or cultural characteristics. Ethnicity can consist of a consciously shared system of beliefs, values, loyalties, and practices of relevance to group members who regard themselves as different and apart. The salient feature of ethnicity lies in its self-definition and self-identification as a distinct and unique people (peoplehood). Other characteristics and traits that symbolize and reinforce this shared system—including religion, language, and homeland—can vary in importance or strength depending on the nature of the situation.

Ethnicity and culture: The two are not synonymous despite some overlap. Culture refers to an integrated whole that is lived naturally and organized around tacitly accepted beliefs and practices of a community. Ethnicity, by contrast represents a self-conscious expression of culture that not only is subject to manipulation and open articulation, but also depends on open competition with other cultures for its existence.

Ethnocentrism: A tendency to see reality from a person's own cultural perspective. It also includes a belief that one's culture or cultural inventory is necessary, normal, and superior to other practices or values. It includes a corresponding inclination to dismiss or denigrate others as inferior or irrelevant. Incorrectly applied, ethnocentrism can interfere with a person's capacity to understand or empathize with others. Refusal to see the world outside one's own "filter" can also breed intolerance and bigotry toward others because of their differences.

Eugenics: A social movement and so-called science that attained considerable popularity during the first part of the twentieth century, eugenics was concerned with improving the quality of the human species through selective reproduction. Eugenics involved encouraging the creation of large families among the socially superior, while discouraging breeding within so-called inferior stock (that is, the poor or minorities). Eugenic-type organizations remain in existence today, often underwriting persons or agencies that embrace racism or racist codes.

Eurocentrism: A belief that European thought and practices are morally superior and should be the norm or standard by which others are judged and interpreted. European values and institutions are viewed as the apex of human development, while European achievements are rarely thought to be linked with developments in other parts of the world.

Everyday racism: Racism that is expressed and reinforced in the minutae of daily life and interaction. Everyday racism can be interpreted as an interplay of actions involving the individual (beliefs), the systemic (organizational rules and priorities), and culture (social values).

Genocide: An orchestrated effort by members of a society to eradicate members of a devalued group. Genocide can be open, deliberate, and violent; it can also be systemic and nonviolent in process.

Group: This concept has been widely and indiscriminately employed to encompass a broad range of meanings. It can be applied to include anything from statistical categories of persons who may be unrelated to each other except for some single unifying characteristics, to a relatively cohesive social community with a distinctive cultural pattern, social norms, and common identity.

Hegemony: That constellation of everyday practices by which the prevailing distribution of power and resources in society are secured and maintained without people's awareness of their involvement. For example, the participation of boys in organized team sports reinforces certain values that are conducive to perpetuating a certain type of masculinity as a cherished ideal. Compare hegemony with the different types of "isms" that constitute intellectual explanations of the world.

Heritage languages: See *world languages.*

Identity politics: Also known as *politics of recognition,* the expression is used in two ways. First, it acknowledges the desire of groups to have their identities recognized and accorded respect *on their own terms* rather than the conditions espoused by central authorities. Second, it concedes that certain issues involving aggrieved minorities are claimed as the exclusive jurisdiction of those who are directly victimized. For example, only a person of colour can identify and talk about the experience of racism. Both variants impart a key dynamic to contemporary politics.

Ideology: Defined in its broadest sense, ideology refers to a system of ideas that attempt to explain, justify, legitimate, and perpetuate a specific set of circumstances. Ideology can be employed in the Marxian sense as a complex of ideas underlying particular material (class) interests that distort and falsify an account of the real world. Thus, racism is construed as an ideology es-

tablished by the ruling class to justify and extend the exploitation of the working class.

Immigrant: Refers to any person born outside Canada (foreign-born), but who is seeking or has received permanent status. Immigrants include those who are seeking family reunification or improvement in economic status. Refugees are seen as special category of immigrants (fleeing because of fear of persecution), while visa students would not normally be included since their status is temporary. With the exception of the First Nations, all Canadian are immigrants or descendents of immigrants. About 16 percent of Canada's population is foreign born (that is, immigrant) —a figure that has remained relatively constant since the early 1950s.

Integration: Integration involves a set of policy ideals that oppose the principles of segregation or separation. As policy or practice, integration is concerned with incorporating minorities into the mainstream so that they can participate as equals. In theory, integration differs from assimilation as a technique for the management of race and ethnic relations. Assimilation involves a one-way process of minority compliance or conformity with majority beliefs and practices; integration by contrast allows the adaptation and acceptance of the minority without sacrifice of their cultural identity. In practice, however, the difference between assimilation and integration in terms of impact is more nominal than real.

Institutional accommodation: The idea that mainstream institutions must move over and make space for the historically disadvantaged. Both the Employment Equity Act of 1986 and the Multiculturalism Act of 1988 specify the need to hire and promote minorities through removal of discriminatory barriers and introduction of proactive measures to improve minority representation, treatment, and equity. See also *inclusiveness.*

Institutional racism: Institutional racism involves an explicit set of discriminatory policies, priorities, and practices that openly deny and exclude minorities from full participation within the organization.

Internal colonialism: Internal colonialism refers to control and domination of indigenous (aboriginal) groups by a settler colony. A colonized indigenous minority is forced to live in a society not of its own making, but one where (a) their political and social involvement is curtailed, (b) the cultural basis of society is undermined, and (c) bureaucratic structures are constructed to regulate movements or aspirations of the indigenous group.

Ku Klux Klan: The Ku Klux Klan originated in United States after the Civil War in reaction to the conferral of legal and political rights to blacks. The organization sought to uphold white supremacy and the purity of white Anglo-Saxons. Terrorist threats and violent actions accompanied the Klan's efforts to unilaterally keep minorities in their place. Targets included not only blacks but also Jews, Catholics, communists, and Mormons. The KKK remains a formidable presence in Canada, Britain, as well as the USA; its underground status makes it difficult to assess its organizational strength or scope.

Mainstreaming: A process whereby minorities are incorporated into institutions as legitimate and integral contributors. The term is employed in opposition to "sidestreaming," a process

that relegates minorities to the margins of society. See also *inclusiveness.*

Melting pot: A metaphor that is used to describe the preferred ideal in American race and ethnic relations. The concept of a melting pot suggests the fusion of minority differences to create a new and improved national culture. The ideal, however, does not match the reality for many racial minorities who by choice or circumstances remain unmeltable. See *mosaic.*

Merit/Meritocracy: The act of rewarding a person on the basis of credentials or achievement. Three features make a judgement meritocratic: the measurement of achievement against a commonly accepted scale is applied to all candidates; measurement is impersonal, that is, on the basis of performance rather than identity; and a reliance on examiners who are selected on the basis of their excellence and impartiality.

Minority group: The concept of minority group does not refer to numbers or statistical proportions. Sociologically, the concept of minority refers to any group (whether based on race, ethnicity, or gender) that is disadvantaged, underprivileged, excluded, discriminated against, or exploited. This socially defined category of individuals are perceived as different and treated accordingly by the majority, They have a disproportionately small share of resources because of a lack of power, discriminatory barriers, and denial of opportunity. The one thing all minorities have in common is their lack of access to wealth, power, or privilege.

Mosaic: A metaphor to describe the ideal arrangement of various racial and ethnic groups in societies such as Canada. The proposed image is that of disparate and distinct elements arranged into a patterned, cohesive whole. Proponents admire the positive images associated with the mosaic; detractors denounce it as a gross distortion that neither fits reality nor escapes the conceptual trap of cultural coexistence both fixed in time and separated by inequality.

Multicultural minorities: One of the three major forces in Canada, multicultural minorities are comprised of those Canadians who are immigrants or descendants of immigrants. Multicultural minorities have the same citizenship rights as Canadians at large, in addition to special rights because of inclusion under official multiculturalism. Both visible minorities and European ethnics are known to possess a distinct set of problems and to have proposed a set of solutions consistent with this problem definition. Their goals are less political than that of the First Nations or Québécois, and tend to focus on institutional accommodation, removal of discriminatory barriers, and establishment of cultural space. Also known as racial or ethnic minorities.

Multicultural thinking: What does it mean to think like a multicultural person? Such thinking reflects a pattern of thought that is non-judgemental, informed, and critical; flexible, multidimensional, and complex. Multicultural thinking sees diversity not as a threat or irrelevant, but as something to be enjoyed for its own sake and as a way of learning about ourselves and the world at large. In contrast, ethnocentric or stereotyped thinking is judgemental, morally evaluative, unbending, static, uncritical, and dismissive of alternatives cultures.

Multiculturalism: Multiculturalism can be used in different ways as a technique for the management of race and ethnic relations. The different levels of multiculturalism include fact, ideology, policy, and practice. We prefer to define multiculturalism as a doctrine and corresponding set of practices that officially acknowledges and promotes a society in which diversity is viewed as legitimate or integral without necessarily undermining the interconnectedness of the parts that hold it together.

Nation: A nation consists of people who share a common homeland, language, identity, set of grievances, and cultural and historical symbols. Both Quebec and the First Nations prefer to see themselves as "nations" within Canadian federalism.

Nations within: A term normally employed to describe aboriginal ambitions for self-determination in Canada. The "nations within" concept acknowledges the relative autonomy of the First Nations, but does not advocate outright secession as an independent state with control over external affairs. See *self-government.*

Nationalism: Nationalism entails the notion of a world divided naturally into identifiable and distinct populations, each with the right to self-determination over territory, institutions, and values. Nationalism evolved into a formidable political force in Europe during the nineteenth century and provided the basis for the creation of nation-states in the twentieth. Paradoxically, nationalism now competes with the civic notions of a nation-state—to the detriment of stability and conventional world order.

Notwithstanding clause: Canada possesses a written constitution with provisions that apply equally to all provinces. It also retains clauses that allows a province to override these provisions if they are perceived as detrimental to that province's well-being. The notwithstanding clause in Section 33 of the Constitution allows provinces the right to opt out of the Charter agreements for up to five years without a court challenge, provided the province is explicit that the purpose of the suspension of civil liberties is to pursue collective goals.

Official Languages Act: The *Official Languages Act* of 1969 officially declared Canada a bilingual society (see *bilingualism*). The Act was updated in 1988 to consolidate changes since 1969 as well as to strengthen the rights of official language minorities.

Official language minorities: The *Official Languages Acts* of Canada (1969/1988) offer protection to speakers of Canada's official languages. French-speaking Canadians who live outside Quebec and English-speaking Canadians who reside in Quebec have certain rights that not only allow them access to services in their language, but enable them to exercise control over institutions such as education.

People of colour: Those Canadian who have nonaboriginal, nonwhite, and non-Caucasion origins, and are defined as such by the government or have agreed to be defined as such for employment or census purposes. People of colour have one attribute in common: they generally lack access to power, wealth, or privilege compared with the dominant sector.

Plural society: First popularized by Furnvival in his study of Dutch overseas colonies, the concept focuses on societies where settler domination of subordinate groups leads to social, political, and cultural separation. Only the marketplace allows these groups to come together for the purposes of exchange involving goods, services, and labour. Without a common or unifying consensus, plural societies are held together by the threat of force or heavy-handed ideological indoctrination.

Pluralism: Pluralism can be defined as an environment in society in which culturally different groups coexist. This cultural coexistence is achieved through the creation of an overarching set of values or institutions. A commitment to multiculturalism represents one variant of pluralist society.

Politically correct: A term of derision employed by conservative thinkers to criticize as rigid or undemocratic those people who wish to enhance inclusiveness to society by transforming how people talk and think. *Political correctness* can also be employed as a symbol to describe the struggle between the traditional order and a new, more inclusive society.

Politicization: The process by which issues are taken out of the personal or private domain and situated instead within the public domain for the express purpose of competing for scarce resources.

Postmodernism: A term that does not lend itself to a quick definition. We prefer to see postmodernism as a discourse that rejects the modernist belief in a unified and organized way of thinking about the world from a fixed and objective point of view, exposing instead a more open, flexible acceptance of multiple points of view. Postmodernism shares much with the principles of a radical cultural relativism, making it suitable for addressing the challenges of diversity and change, and the uncertainties that accompany such transformations.

Postmulticulturalism: A term employed in two senses. First, it recognizes that celebrating cultural differences is no longer central to Canada's multiculturalism, having been replaced by commitments to inclusiveness and belonging. Second, it implies the appearance of diverse approaches to accommodating diversity and society-building rather than a single cookie-cutter formula.

Power: Power refers to the capacity of dominant groups (or at least the elites within the dominant sector) to enforce a degree of compliance (obedience) in accord with their needs and aspirations. A key concept in the study of race and ethnic relations, power can be acquired and applied in different ways, ranging from the exercise of physical coercion to the construction of ideologies that sustain the prevailing patterns of power and privilege. Power is not a thing, but a relationship within a context.

Prejudice: Prejudice is a set of biased and generalized prejudgements about outgroups derived from inaccurate and incomplete information. It represents a dislike of others based on faulty and inflexible generalizations, involving an irrational and unfounded set of assumptions that influences a person's ability to treat minority groups in an impartial or equitable manner. Prejudice can be "framed" as a social construction rather than a purely psychological phenomenon that originates when the dominant sector invokes negative ideas to justify and entrench its power and privilege over the subordinate sector.

Refugee: A refugee is defined by the UN as a person who flees his or her country because of a well-grounded fear of persecution. Currently there are about 25 million refugees in the world, with Canada accepting around 20,000 to 40,000 each year. Canada distinguishes between sponsored (hand selected by private agencies or the government) refugees and refugee claimants who arrive unannounced and request asylum. The grounds for admittance have expanded in recent years; for example, Canada now extends refugee status to those who face gender-based persecution.

Race: Race is currently defined as an arbitrary classification of persons into categories on the basis of real or imagined physical characteristics such as skin colour. According to racial classifications, the world is divided into fixed number of immutable groups of individuals (from 2 to 160) who are differentiated on the basis of inherited biological (and sometimes sociological) traits. Race is generally regarded as having no empirical validity or scientific merit. It exists instead as a social construction that which is manipulated to define and reinforce the unequal relations between dominant and subordinate groups.

Race and ethnic relations: Race and ethnic relations consist of those recurrent and unequal patterns of interaction that evolve between groups who are defined as biologically or culturally different. Race and ethnic relations are inseparable from relationships of inequality, and this puts the onus on sociologists to determine how these inequities are constucted, maintained, challenged, and transformed within contexts of control and exploitation.

Racial types: Racial types invoke the social construction of categories of persons who share one or more physical properties according to some system of classification. Each racial type is usually assigned a set of social, moral, and psychological characteristics as well.

Racial typologies: The concept of racial typologies includes a process whereby racial groups are evaluated and hierarchically arranged in ascending and descending orders of superiority or inferiority. Racism becomes inevitable when racial typologies are employed to justify patterns of privilege and power.

Racism: Racism consists not only of a relatively complex and organized set of ideas and ideals (ideology) that asserts the natural superiority of one group over another in terms of entitlements and privilege; it also consists of the power to put these beliefs into practice in a way that denies or excludes those who belong to a devalued category. The components of racism are often summarized in this popular equation: racism = prejudice + discrimination + power. It is important to discern different types of racism, from the personal and direct to the impersonal, institutional, and systemic. Racism also exists at different levels, including the individual, the institutional, the cultural, and the everyday.

Racism as hatred/racism as power: It is useful to make a distinction between variants of racism. Employed in the narrow sense of hatred, racism involves the belief that biology is the primary determinant of group attitudes and the entitlements they deserve. The term may also be employed in the broader sense of power and privilege that one group has over another.

Reconstructing Canada: This concept acknowledges that Canada constitutes an "unfinished business" that is continually in the process of re-inventing itself to meet new challenges. See also *society-building.*

Scapegoating: A process by which a particular group is singled out and un-justly blamed for the misfortunes, failures, and shortcomings of another.

Self-determination: A claim made by a particular group of people to assume control over jurisdictions (or domains) of immediate concern to them.

Segregation: The process and practice of separating groups on the basis of race or culture. This separation can occur voluntarily or involuntarily and can be formal or informal.

Self-government: A term that is usually employed in the context of aboriginal demands for inherent self-determination rights. The First Nations argue that they continue to possess a Creator-given right to take control of their destinies at political, economic, social, and cultural levels. Self-government is the political expression of this demand for control over internal jurisdictions. The types of self-government will vary from those that resemble provincial governments to those that operate along community-based municipal governments to those that confer aboriginal control over the delivery of social services within cities. Demands for self-government are invariably tied with restoration of aboriginal lands, not simply out of justice but to provide a viable resource-base for renewal and healing.

Society-building: The challenge that confronts contemporary societies as they attempt to create a political and moral community through the accommodation of diversity.

Sovereignty: A term that can mean whatever the context allows or the author wants to convey. It generally refers to the attainment of some degree of autonomy for the distinct society aspirations of Quebec. The concept can apply to a variety of political arrangements, ranging from more flexible federalist arrangements to outright secession with only minimal ties to Canada.

Stereotype: A stereotype is a shorthand way of classifying social reality into convenient categories on the basis of common properties. As a generalization, it provides an oversimplified or exaggerated version of the world based on preconceived and unwarranted notions that extends to all members of a group—for example, Germans are industrious; blacks are natural athletes. Stereotypes become harmful when individuals are judged and evaluated according to the norms of their group rather than on personal merit. They can also be damaging if employed to deny equality of opportunity or participation.

Stratification: Stratification is the division of society into layers or "strata" that can be ranked according to certain criteria in ascending or descending order. This suggests that inequality is not random or fleeting, but is patterned and predictable, and tends to cluster around certain devalued categories related to race or ethnicity.

Substantive equality: Substantive equality is based on the idea that differences sometimes have to be taken into account in order to achieve genuine rather than formal equivalence. This colour-conscious approach to equality appears to be at variance with colour-blind practices in which everyone is treated the same (mathematical equality). See also *equality of outcome*.

Symbolic ethnicity: Symbolic ethnicity (also *situational ethnicity*) constitutes a process in which an individual retains a cognitive or emotional affiliation with a cultural past. Involvement in the daily and organizational life of that particular ethnic group is kept to a minimum without necessarily abdicating any

sense of belonging or attachment. This type of ethnicity has been popular in Canada, reflecting as it does a type of continuity with the past that is voluntary and without the costs and sanctions of primary group participation. Canada's official multiculturalism policies are based on endorsement of symbolic ethnic affiliation. It remains to be seen if Canada can accommodate the "deep" ethnicities at the core of contemporary society-building processes.

Systemic discrimination: Systemic discrimination is based on the principle that inequality is often be built into the institutional system in a way that hinders minorities without much awareness of this effect. It can be defined as any action that has the effect (rather than intent) of denying or excluding persons because of their membership in devalued groups. An action is systemically discriminatory if it indirectly impacts on some group because of inappropriate standards or tacit assumptions within the workplace.

Three major forces: For analytical purposes, Canada can be divided into three major racial and ethnic groups or forces. Each of these groups (including the original Native Peoples, the Charter groups, and the others) differs from the others in its legal status, major problem, proposed solutions, and anticipated outcomes.

Three-nation state: A term that reflects the emergent reality of Canada as a society of three founding nations—the French, the English, and the First Nations. Each of these groups possesses the privilege of contributing to the political agenda as it relates to Canada's national interests.

Visible minorities: Also *people of colour*. The term visible minority is used to designate non-white, non-Caucasian racial minorities in Canada who have distinctive physical characteristics, especially pertaining to skin colour. The government recognizes about ten geographic areas from which visible minority immigrants or refugees come. Not everyone is happy with this expression; after all, the concept is arbitrary, subjective, reductionist, simplistic, unrealistic (Synnott and Howes 1994). However imperfect, the term represents an improvement over other terms that have pejorative connotations; it also has the bonus of acknowledging the common problems encountered by this category because of its visibility.

Vertical mosaic: A twist on the notion of Canada as a multicultural "mosaic," the term originated with publication of the book ***Vertical Mosaic*** by the eminent Canadian sociologist, John Porter. According to Porter, Canada's multicultural mosaic is organized and aligned along a system of stratification that is disadvantageous to certain racial or ethnic minorities. Porter contends that any policy or program which promotes diversity would only serve to entrench and perpetuate the hierarchical notions of racial or ethnic inequality. See *stratification*.

World languages: Those non-French, non-English, and non-aboriginal languages associated with multicultural minorities. Canadian governments tend to be supportive of world languages, in part from principle, but also from economic expediency. This support, however, remains constrained with the framework of two official languages as public systems of communication.

References

Abella, Irving 1989 *A Coat of Many Colours: Two Centuries of Jewish Life in Canada.* Toronto: Lester and Orpen Dennys.

Abella, Irving 1995 "Anti-Semitism is Declining." *Kitchener-Waterloo Record.* May 18.

Abella, Irving and Harold Troper 1991 *None is Too Many: Canada and the Jews in Europe 1933-1948.* 3rd Edition. Toronto: Lester and Orpen Dennys.

Abramowicz, Lenny 1991 "Why Isn't It Wrong to be Correct?" *The Globe and Mail.* December 30.

Abu-Laban, Yasmeen and Daiva K. Stasiulis 1992 "Ethnic Pluralism Under Seige: Popular and Partisan Opposition to Multiculturalism." Canadian Public Policy XVIII(4): 365-386.

Adam, Heribert 1989 "Contemporary State Policies toward Subordinate Ethnics." in *Multiculturalism and Intergroup Relations.* James Frideres (ed.). p.19–34. New York: Greenwood Press.

Adam, Heribert 1992 "Ethnicity, Nationalism and the State." in *Beyond Multicultural Education. International Perspectives.* Kogila A. Moodley (ed.). p.14–22. Calgary: Detsilig Enterprises Ltd.

Adams, Howard 1985 "The Metis." in *Racial Oppression in Canada.* B. Singh Bolaria and Peter S. Li (eds.). p.61–80. Toronto: Garamond Press.

Adelman, Howard, Allan Borowski, Meyer Burnstein, and Lois Foster (eds.) 1994 *Immigration and Refugee Policy. Australia and Canada Compared. Volume 2.* Toronto: University of Toronto Press.

Adorno, T.S. et al. 1950 *The Authoritarian Personality.* New York: Harper and Row.

Agòcs, Carol and Monica Boyd 1993 "The Vertical Mosaic Revisited." in *Social Inequality.* 2nd Edition. Jim Curtis (ed.). Scarborough: Prentice Hall.

Aguirre, Jr. Adalberto and Jonathan Turner 1995 *American Ethnicity: The Dynamics and Consequences of Discrimination.* New York: McGraw Hill.

Ahenakew, David 1985 "Aboriginal Title and Aborginal Rights: The Impossible and Unnecessary Task of Identification and Definition." *The Quest for Justice: Aboriginal Peoples and Aboriginal Title.* Menno Boldt and J. Anthony Long (eds.). p.24–30. Toronto: University of Toronto Press.

Alberta Report 1994 "Last Rites for White Writers' Rights." April 25.

Alfred, Gerald Robert 1995 *Heeding the Voices of Our Ancestors: Kahnawake Mohawk Politics and the Rise of Native Nationalism in Canada.* Toronto: Oxford University Press.

Alladin, Ibrahim 1996 "Racism in Schools: Race, Ethnicity, and Schooling in Canada." in *Racism in Canadian Schools*. I. Alladin (ed.). p.4–21. Toronto: Harcourt Brace.

Allen, Dianne 1991 "What's Wrong with these Pictures." *Toronto Star* January 5.

Allen, Paula Gunn 1986 *The Sacred Hoop: Recovering the Feminine in American Indian Traditions*. Boston: Beacon Press.

Allingham, Nora Dewar 1992 "Anti-Racist Education and the Curriculum – A Priviledged Perspective." in *Racism and Education: Different Perspectives and Experiences*. Canadian Teachers Federation (ed.). p.15–29. Ottawa.

Allport, Gordon 1954 *The Nature of Prejudice*. New York: Doubleday and Company.

Anctil, Pierre 1986 "La Société Québécoise Face au Multiculturalisme." Paper presented to the Canadian Ethnological Society.

Anderson, Alan and James Frideres 1981 *Ethnicity in Canada: Theoretical Perspectives*. Toronto: Butterworths.

Anderson, Joan M. and M. Judith Lynam 1987 "The Meaning of Work for Immigrant Women in the Lower Echelons of the Canadian Labour Force." Canadian Ethnic Studies XIX(2): 67-90.

Andrew, J.V. 1988 *Enough! (Enough French, Enough Quebec)*. Kitchener, Ontario: Andrew Books.

Angus, Ian 1995 "Multiculturalism as a Social Ideal." Paper presented to the Learned Society Meetings (CSAA) at Montreal. June.

Angus, Murray 1990 "And the Last Shall be First." *Native Policy in an Era of Cutbacks*. Ottawa: Aboriginal Rights Coalition.

Angus Reid Group Inc. 1991 Multiculturalism and Canadians: Attitude Study, 1991. National Survey Report Submitted to the Department of Multiculturalism and Citizenship.

Annual Report 1992 *Annual Report of the Commissioner of Official Languages*. Ottawa: Minister of Supply and Services.

Annual Report 1993 *The Operation of the Canadian Multiculturalism Act*. Annual Report 1991/1992. Ottawa: Minister of Supply and Services.

Apple, Michael 1993 "Series Editor's Introduction." *Race, Identity and Representation in Education*. C. McCarthy and W. Crichlow (eds.) pp. vii–ix. New York: Routledge.

Armstrong, M. Jocelyn 1987 "Interethnic Conflict in New Zealand." in Ethnic Conflict. Jerry Boucher, Dan Landis, Karen A. Clark (eds.), p.255–278. Newbury Park: California: Sage.

Arthurs, Harry. 1993 Keynote Address. *National Symposium for University Presidents on Institutional Strategies for Race and Ethnic Relations at Canadian Universities*. Report of a symposium held at Queen's University at Kingston. February 2-4, 1992.

Asbury, Kathryn E. 1992 "Building Police-Community Partnerships With Culturally, Racially, and Linguistically Diverse Populations in Metropolitan Toronto." Published by the Council of Race Relations and Policing. Toronto.

Asch, Michael 1984 *Home and Native Land: Aboriginal Rights and Canadian Constitution.* Toronto: Methuen.

Asch, Michael 1989 "To Negotiate Into Confederation: Canadian Aboriginal Views on Their Political Rights." in *We are Here. Politics of Aboriginal Land Tenure.* Edwin N. Wilmsen (ed.). Berkeley: University of California.

Asch, Michael 1993 "Aboriginal Self-Government and Canadian Constitutional Identity: Building Reconciliation." in *Ethnicity and Aboriginality. Case Studies in Ethnonationalism.* Michael D. Levin (ed.). p.29–52. Toronto: University of Toronto Press.

Assembly of First Nations 1992 "To the Source." *The First Nations Circle on the Constitution.* Commissioners Report. Ottawa.

Badets, Jane and Tina W.L. Chui 1994 *Canada's Changing Immigration Population.* Catalogue No 96–311E. Published by Statistics Canada and Prentice Hall Canada Inc.

Bailey, Ronald 1987 "Black-White Relations in Mississippi." Jerry Boucher, Dan Landis, and Karen Arnold Clark (eds.). pp.140–181. Newbury Park, California: Sage.

Baker, Donald (ed.) 1994 *Reading Racism and the Criminal Justice System.* Toronto: Canadian Scholars Press.

Baker, Judith (ed.) 1994 *Group Rights.* Toronto: University of Toronto Press.

Balthazar, Louis 1993 "The Faces of Quebec Nationalism." in *Quebec. State and Society* 2nd Edition. Alain G. Gagnon (ed.) pp.2–17. Scarborough: Nelson.

Banks, James A. 1992 "A Curriculum for Empowerment, Action, and Change." *Beyond Multicultural Education. International Perspectives.* Kogila Moodley (ed.). pp.154–170. Calgary: Detsilig Enterprise Ltd.

Bannerji, Himani, Linda Carter, Kari Dehli, Susan Heald, and Kate McKenna 1991 "Introduction" in *Unsettling Relations. The University as a Site of Feminist Struggles."* H. Bannerji et al. (eds.). Toronto: Women's Press.

Banton, Michael 1967 *Race Relations.* London: Tavistock Publications.

Banton, Michael 1979 *The Idea of Race.* London: Tavistock Publications.

Banton, Michael 1987 *Racial Theories.* London: Cambridge University Press.

Barkun, Michael 1994 *Religion and the Racist Right. The Origins of the Christian Identity Movement.* Chapel Hill NC: University of North Carolina Press.

Barrett, Stanley R. 1987 *Is God a Racist? The Right Wing in Canada.* Toronto: University of Toronto Press.

Barth, Frederick 1969 Ethnic Groups and Boundaries. Boston: Little, Brown.

Bauer, William 1994 "How the System Works." *The Globe and Mail.* November 12.

Baureiss, Gunter 1985 "Discrimination and Response: The Chinese in Canada." in *Ethnicity and Ethnic Relations in Canada.* Rita M. Bienvenue and Jay E. Goldstein (eds.). pp.241–262. Toronto: Butterworths.

Bean, Frank; Georges Vernez and Charles B. Keely 1989. *Opening and Closing the Doors. Evaluating Immigration Reform and Control.* Washington: The Rand Corporation/The Urban Institute.

Beckton, Clare F. 1987 "Section 27 and Section 15 of the Charter." in *Multiculturalism and the Charter: A Legal Perspective.* Canadian Human Rights Foundation (ed.). pp. 1–14. Toronto: Carswell.

Bedford, David 1994 "Marxism and the Aboriginal Question: The Tragedy of Progress." *The Canadian Journal of Native Studies* XIV (1): 101-117.

Behrens, Gerd 1994 "Love, Hate, and Nationalism." *Time Magazine.* March 21.

Bell-Fialkoff, Andrew 1993 "Ethnic Conflict." *The World and I* July: 465-477.

Berger, Brigitte 1993 "Multiculturalism and the Modern University." *Partisan Review.* pp.516–530.

Berger, Thomas R. 1981 *Fragile Freedoms: Human Rights and Dissent in Canada.* Toronto: Clark Irwin.

Berger, Thomas R. 1991 *A Long and Terrible Shadow.* Vancouver: Douglas and McIntyre.

Bergman, Brian 1994 "Points of Contention." *Macleans.* February 7.

Berry, John W., Rudolph Kalin, and Donald M. Taylor 1977 *Multiculturalism and Ethnic Attitudes in Canada.* Ottawa: Ministry of Supply and Services in Canada.

Berry, John and Rudolph Kalin 1993 "Multiculturalism and Ethnic Attitudes in Canada: An Overview of the 1991 National Survey." Paper Presented to the Canadian Psychological Association, Annual Meetings. Montreal. May.

Berton, Pierre 1975 *Hollywood's Canada: The Americanization of our National Image.* Toronto: McLelland and Stewart.

Best, Carrie M. 1977 *That Lonesome Road: The Autobiography of Carrie M. Best.* New Glasgow, Nova Scotia: Clarion.

Bettelheim, Bruno and Morris Janowitz 1949 "Ethnic Tolerance: A Function of Social and Personal Control." *American Journal of Sociology* 55: 137-146.

Bibby, Reginald W. 1987 "Bilingualism and Multiculturalism: A National Reading." in *Ethnic Canada: Identities and Inequalities.* Leo Driedger, (ed.). pp.158–169. Toronto: Copp Clark Pitman.

Bibby, Reginald W. 1990 *Mosaic Madness. The Potential and Poverty of Canadian Life.* Toronto: Stoddart.

Biddiss, Michael D. (ed.) 1979 *Images of Race.* New York: Holmes and Meier Publishers.

Bienvenue, Rita M. 1985 "Colonial Status: The Case of Canadian Indians." in *Ethnicity and Ethnic Relations in Canada.* Rita M. Bienvenue and Jay E. Goldstein (eds.). pp.199–216. Toronto: Butterworths.

Billingsley, B. and L. Musynzski. 1985 No Discrimination Here... Toronto.

Bissoondath, Neil 1993 "A Question of Belonging: Multiculturalism and Citizenship." in *Belonging. The Meaning and Future of Canadian Citizenship.* William Kaplan (ed.). pp.367–387. Kingston/Montreal: McGill-Queen's University Press.

Bissoondath, Neil 1994 *Selling Illusions. The Cult of Multiculturalism.* Toronto: Stoddart.

Black, Jerome H. and David Hagan 1993 "Quebec Immigration Politics and Policy: Historical and Contemporary Perspectives." *Quebec. State and Society.* 2/e. Alain-G. Gagnon (ed.) pp. 280–303. Scarborough: Nelson.

Blauner, Robert 1972 *Racial Oppression in America.* New York: Harper and Row.

Blauner, Rob 1994 "Talking Past Each Other: Black and White Languages." *Race and Ethnic Conflicts.* Fred L. Pincus and Howard J. Ehrlich (eds.) pp. 18–28. Boulder CO: Westview Press.

Bledsloe, Geraldine 1989 "The Media: Minorities Still Fighting for Their Fair Share." *Rythym and Business Magazine.* March/April: 14–18.

Blumer, Herbert 1965 "Industrialisation and Race Relations." in *Industrialisation and Race Relations: A Symposium.* Guy Hunter (ed.). London: Oxford University Press.

Blumer, Herbert 1969 *Symbolic Interactionism: Perspectives and Methods.* Englewood Cliffs, NJ: Prentice Hall

Blumer, Herbert and Troy Duster 1980 "Theories of Race and Social Action." in *Sociological Theories: Race and Colonialism* UNESCO (ed.). pp.211–238. Paris.

Bolaria, B. Singh and Peter S. Li 1988 *Racial Oppression in Canada.* 2nd Edition. Toronto: Garamond Press.

Boldt, Edward D. 1985 "Maintaining Ethnic Boundaries: The Case of the Hutterites." in *Ethnicity and Ethnic Relations in Canada.* Rita M. Bienvenue and Jay E. Goldstein (eds.). p.87–104. Toronto: Butterworths.

Boldt, Edward D. 1989 "The Hutterites: Contemporary Developments and Future Prospects." *Multiculturalism and Intergroup Relations.* James Frideres (ed.) pp. 57–72. New York: Greenwood Press.

Boldt, Menno 1993. *Surviving as Indians: The Challenge of Self-Government.* Toronto: University of Toronto Press.

Boldt, Menno and J. Anthony Long 1984 "Tribal Traditions and European-Western Political Ideology: The Dilemma of Canadian Native Indians." *Canadian Journal of Political Science.* 17: 537-554.

Boldt, Menno and J. Anthony Long (eds.) 1985 *The Quest for Justice: Aboriginal Peoples and Aboriginal Rights.* Toronto: University of Toronto Press.

Bonacich, Edna 1972 "A Theory of Ethnic Antagonism: The Split Labour Market." *American Sociological Review* 37: 547-559.

Bones, Jah 1986 "Language and Rastafaria." in *The Language of Black Experience.* David Sutcliffe and Ansel Wong (eds.) pp.37–51. Oxford: Basil Blackwell.

Boulding, Elise 1976 *The Underside of History: A View of Women Through Time.* Boulder, Colorado: Westview Press.

Boulding, Kenneth E. 1962 *Conflict and Defense: A General Theory*. New York: Harper and Row.

Bourassa, Robert 1975 "Objections to Multiculturalism." Letter to *LeDevoir*, November 17 1971. Reprinted in Howard Palmer 1975 .

Bourgault, Pierre 1994 "The Sacking of a Military College." *The Globe and Mail* November 11.

Bourhis, R.Y. and H. Giles, J.P. Leyens, H. Tajfel, 1979 "Psycholinguistic Distinctiveness: Language Divergence in Belgium." in *Language and Social Pyschology*. H. Giles and R.N. St. Clair (eds.). pp.158–185. Oxford: Basil Blackwell.

Bowker, Gordon and John Carrier (eds.) 1976 *Race and Ethnic Relations. Sociological Readings*. London: Hutchinson.

Boyd, Monica et al. (eds.) 1985 *Ascription and Attainment: Studies in Mobility and Status Attainment in Canada*. Ottawa: Carleton.

Boyd, Monica 1987 "Migrant Women in Canada: Profiles and Policies." Research Division, Immigration Canada and Status of Women Canada. Ottawa.

Boyd, Monica 1993 "Gender Issues in Immigration and Language Fluency."

Brennan, T. 1991 "PC and the Decline of the American Empire." *Social Policy.* Summer 16–29.

Breton, Raymond 1964 "Institutional Completeness of Ethnic Communities and the Personal Relations of Immigrants." *American Journal of Sociology* 70: 103-205.

Breton, Raymond 1984 "The Production and Allocation of Symbolic Resources: An Analysis of the Linguistic and Ethnocultural Fields in Canada." *Canadian Review of Sociology and Anthropology.* 21(2): 123-140.

Breton, Raymond 1988 "The Evolution of the Canadian Multicultural Society." *Canadian Mosaic, Essays on Multiculturalism*. A.J. Fry and Ch. Forceville (eds.) pp. 25–47. Amsterdam: Free University Press.

Breton, Raymond 1989 "Canadian Ethnicity in the Year 2000." in *Multiculturalism and Intergroup Relations*. James Frideres (ed.) pp. 149–152. New York: Greenwood Press.

Breton, Raymond 1991 "The Political Dimensions of Ethnic Community Organization." in *Ethnicity, Structural Inequality, and the State in Canada and the Federal Republic of Germany.* Robin Ostow (ed.). New York: Peter Lang.

Breton, Raymond, Wsevolod W. Isajiw, Warren E. Kalbach, and Jeffrey G. Reitz 1990 *Ethnic Identity and Equality: Varieties of Experience in a Canadian City*. Toronto: University of Toronto Press.

Bristow, Peggy (coordinator), Dionne Brand, Linda Carty, Afua A. Cooper, Sylvia Hamilton, and Adrienne Shadd 1993 *We're Rooted Here and They Can't Pull Us Up: Essays in African Canadian Women's History*. Toronto: University of Toronto Press.

Brock, Kathy L. 1990 "Aboriginal Self-Government By Comparison." Presented for the Indigenous Peoples and the Law Conference, Ottawa.

Brock Kathy L. 1991 "The Politics of Aboriginal Self-Government: A Paradox." Canadian Public Administration 34(2): 272-285.

Brown, David 1989 "Ethnic Revival: Perspectives on State and Society." *TWQ* 11(4): 1-17.

Browne, Malcolm W. 1994 "What is Intelligence, and Who Has It?" *New York Times Book Review.* October 16.

Brownmiller, Susan 1975 *Against Our Will: Men, Women, and Rape.* New York: Simon and Schuster.

Brunt, Stephen 1994 "It's all There in Black and White." *The Globe and Mail* November 12.

Brym, Robert (ed.) 1985 *The Structure of the Canadian Capitalist Class.* Toronto: Garamond Press.

Brym, Robert J. 1991 "Ethnic Group Stratification and Cohesion in Canada: An Overview." in *Ethnicity, Structural Inequality, and the State in Canada and the Federal Republic of Germany.* Robin Ostow (ed.). p.49–78. New York: Peter Lang.

Brym, Robert J., William Shaffir, and Morton Weinfeld (eds.) 1993 *The Jews in Canada.* Toronto: Oxford University Press.

Buckley, Helen 1992 *From Wooden Ploughs to Welfare: Why Indian Policy Failed in the Prairie Provinces.* McMillian Collier: Toronto.

Buckner, H. Taylor 1993 "Minorities on Minorities. How Canada's Ethnic Minorities View Selected Canadian Minority Groups." *Working Paper. Centre for Community and Ethnic Studies.* Concordia University.

Bull, Sam 1994 "Federal Government Pursues Assimilation Policies Through Devolution Process." *Solidarité.* Newsletter by Aboriginal Rights Coalition. Vol. 4 No. 2.

Bullivant, Brian 1981 "Multiculturalism: Pluralist Orthodoxy or Ethnic Hegemony." Canadian Ethnic Studies XIII (2):1-22.

Burger, Julian 1987 *Report From the Frontier. The State of the World's Indigenous Peoples.* New Jersey: Zed Books.

Burnet, Jean 1981 "The Social and Historical Context of Ethnic Relations." in *A Canadian Social Pyschology of Ethnic Relations.* Robert C. Gardiner and Rudolph Kalin (eds.). p.17–36. Agincourt, Ontario: Methuen.

Burnet, Jean 1984 "Myths and Multiculturalism." *Multiculturalism in Canada.* Ronald J Samuda, John W Berry and Michael Laferriere (eds.), pp. 18–29. Toronto: Allyn and Bacon Inc.

Burnet, Jean 1986 "Looking Into My Sister's Eyes." Toronto: Multicultural History Society of Ontario.

Burnet, Jean 1989 "Taking Into Account: the Other Ethnic Groups and the Royal Commission on Bilingualism and Biculturalism." in *Multiculturalism and Intergroup Relations.* James Frideres (ed.) pp. 9–18. New York: Greenwood Press

Burnet, Jean and Howard Palmer 1988 "Coming Canadians." *An Introduction to the History of Canada's People.* Toronto: McLelland and Stewart in conjunction with the Multicultural Directorate within the Secretary of State.

Burrell, G. and G. Morgan 1979 *Sociological Paradigms and Organizational Analysis* London: Heinemann.

Caldwell, Gary and Eric Waddell 1982 "Les Anglophones du Québèc: De Majoritaires à Minoritaires." Quebec: Institut Québécois de Recherche sur la Culture.

Cardozo, Andrew 1994 "On GUARD for Multiculturalism." *Canadian Forum.* April 14–18.

Carniol, Ben 1991 "The Way We Respond Can Become an Issue." Paper presented at the Remedies for Racism and Sexism Conference. University of Western Ontario, London.

Carter, Stephen L. 1995 "Let Us Pray." *New Yorker.* January pp.60-62.

Carty, Linda 1991 "Black Women in Academia: A Statement from the Periphery." *Unsettling Relations: The University as a Site of Feminist Struggles.* Himani Bannerji et al. (eds.). pp.13–44. Toronto: Women's Press.

Carty, Linda 1993 "African Canadian Women and the State." *We're Rooted Here and They Can't Pull Us Up: Essays in African Canadian Women's History.* Peggy Bristow et al. (eds.). Toronto: University of Toronto Press.

Carty, R.W. and W.P. Ward (eds.) 1981. *National Politics and Community in Canada.* Vancouver: University of British Columbia Press.

Cashmore, E. Ellis (ed.) 1984 *Dictionary of Race and Ethnic Relations.* London: Routledge and Kegan Paul.

Cashmore, E. Ellis and Barry Troyna 1983 *Introduction to Race Relations.* London: Routledge and Kegan Paul.

Cassidy, Frank 1991 "First Nations Can No Longer Be Rebuffed." *Policy Options* May 3-5.

Cassidy, Frank 1994 "British Columbia and Aboriginal Peoples: The Prospects for the Treaty Process." *Policy Options.* March: 10–13.

Castles, S. and B. Cope, M. Kalantzis, M. Morrissey 1988 "The Bicentenary and the Failure of Australian Nationalism." *Race and Class* XXIX(3):53-68.

Castonguay, Claude 1994 "Why More Quebec Voices Aren't Arguing for Federalism." *Globe and Mail.* July 25.

CAUT "CAUT Calls on Ontario Gov't to Withdraw 'Framework." *CAUT Bulletin ACPPU.* P.1. June 1994.

Chagnon, Napolean 1992 *The Yanomamo.* 4/e. New York: Holt Rinehart.

Chartrand Paul 1992 "Aboriginal Peoples, Racism, and Education in Canada: A Few Comments. in *Racism and Education: Different Perspectives and Experiences.* Ontario Teachers Federation (ed.) Ottawa pp.7–14.

Chartrand, L.A.H. Paul 1993 "Aboriginal Self-Government: The Two Sides of Legitimacy." *How Ottawa Spends. A More Democratic Canada...?* Susan D. Phillips (ed.) pp. 231–256. Ottawa: Carleton University Press.

Chesler, Mark A. and James Crowfoot 1989 *Racism in Higher Education 1: An Organizational Analysis.* PCMA (Program in Conflict Management Alternatives) Working Paper No. 21. November.

Chodak, Simon 1994 "Review Essay: Voices on National Divorce." *Canadian Journal of Sociology.* 19(3):379-389.

Clark, Bruce 1990 *Native Liberty, Crown Sovereignty: The Existing Aboriginal Right of Self-Government in Canada.* Kingston: McGill-Queen's University Press.

Clement, Wallace 1975 *The Canadian Corporate Elite.* Toronto: McClelland and Stewart.

Clift, Dominique 1989 *The Secret Kingdom. Interpretations of the Canadian Character.* Toronto: McClelland and Stewart.

Cohen, Abner 1969 *Custom and Politics in Urban Africa.* Berkeley: University of California Press.

Cohen, Percy 1976 "Race Relations as a Sociological Issue." in *Race and Ethnic Relations. Sociological Readings.* Gordon Bowker and John Carrier (eds.). pp.9–26. London: Hutchinson.

Collins, Randall 1975 *Conflict Sociology: Toward an Explanatory Science.* New York: Academic Press.

Commissioner of Official Languages 1995 *Annual Report 1994.* Ottawa: Minister of Supply and Services Canada.

Comeau, Pauline and Aldo Santin 1990 *The First Canadians. A Profile of Canada's Native People Today.* Toronto: James Lorimer and Sons.

Connor, Walker 1973 "The Politics of Ethnonationalism." *Journal of International Affairs.* 27(1):1-21.

Connor, W. 1972 "Nation-Building or Nation-Destroying." *World Politics* 24(3).

Cook, Peter 1995 "In South Africa." *The Globe and Mail.* February 8.

Cornell, Stephen 1984 "Crisis and Response in Indian-White Relations: 1960-1984." *Social Problems* 32: 44-59.

Cornell, Stephen 1988 *The Return of the Native: American Indian Political Resurgence.* New York: Oxford.

Cose, Ellis 1994 "Color-Coded 'Truths.'" *Newsweek.* October 24.

Coser, Lewis A. 1956 *The Functions of Social Conflict.* New York: Free Press.

Coser, Lewis A. 1967 *Continuities in the Study of Social Conflict.* New York: Free Press.

Cox, Robert 1992 "Global Perestroika." *Socialist Register* Ralph Miliband and Leo Panitch (eds.). pp.26–43. Merlin.

Cox, Oliver C. 1948 *Caste, Class, and Race: A Study of Social Dynamics.* New York: Doubleday.

Crane, David 1995 "Canada Should Capitalize on its Multicultural Society." *Toronto Star.* January 14.

Creedon, Pamela J. (ed.) 1993 *Women in Mass Communication.* 2/e. Newbury Park: Sage.

Cryderman, Brian, Chris O'Toole, and Augie Fleras (eds.) 1992 *Policing, Race, and Ethnicity. A Guidebook for the Policing Services.* Toronto: Butterworth.

Cummins, Jim 1991 "Heritage Languages in Canadian Schools: Fact and Fiction." *Lectures and Papers in Ethnicity* No. 6. November. University of Toronto Press.

Cummins, Jim 1994 "Heritage Language Learning and Teaching." in *Ethnicity and Culture in Canada. The Research Landscape* by J.W. Berry and J.A. Laponce (eds.). pp.435–456. Toronto: University of Toronto Press.

Cummins, Jim and Marcel Danesi 1990 *Heritage Languages: The Development and Denial of Canada's Linguistic Resources.* Toronto: Garamond Press.

Cuneo, Carl and James Curtis 1975 "Social Ascription in the Educational and Occupational Attainment of Urban Canadians." *Canadian Review of Sociology and Anthropology.* 12:6-24.

Curtis, James, Edward Grab and Neil Guppy (eds.) 1993 *Social Inequality in Canada.* Scarborough: Prentice Hall.

Dahrendorf, R. 1959 *Class and Class Conflict in Industrial Society.* London: Routledge and Kegan Paul.

Dalhousie 1989 *Breaking Barriers: Report of the Task Force on Access for Blacks and Native Peoples.* September.

Daost-Blais, Denise 1983 "Corpus and Status Language Planning in Quebec: A Look at Linguistic Education." in *Progress in Language Planning.* Juan Cobarrubias and Joshua K. Fishman (eds.). pp.207–234. New York: Moulton Publishers.

Darder, Antonia 1990 *Culture and Power in the Classroom: A Critical Foundation for Bicultural Education.* Critical Studies in Education and Culture Series. edited by Henry A. Giroux and Paulo Freire. New York: Bergin and Garvey.

Darroch, Gordon A. and Wilfrid G. Marston 1984 "Patterns of Urban Ethnicity: Toward a Revised Ecological Model." in *Urbanism and Urbanization. Views, Aspects, and Dimensions.* Noel Iverson (ed.). pp.127–162. Leiden: E. J. Brill.

Darroch, Gordon A. 1979 "Another Look at Ethnicity, Stratification, and Social Mobility in Canada." *Canadian Journal of Sociology.* 4:1-25.

Das Gupta, Tania 1994 "Multiculturalism Policy: A Terrain of Struggle for Immigrant Women." *Canadian Woman's Studies.* 14(2):72-76.

Dashefsky, Arnold. 1975 "Theoretical Frameworks in the Study of Ethnic Identity." *Ethnicity.* 2(1):1-15.

Davidson, Janet M. 1981 "The Polynesian Foundation." in *The Oxford History of New Zealand* W.H. Oliver and B.R. Williams (eds.). pp.3–27. Wellington N.Z.: Oxford University Press.

Davidson, Basil 1994 "Government by Massacre." *The Times Higher Education Supplement.* October 7.

Davis, Kingsley and Wilbert E. Moore 1945 "Some Principles of Stratification." *American Sociological* Review 5:242-249.

Davis, Angela 1989 *Women, Culture, and Politics.* New York: Random House.

Dei, George 1996 "Black/African-Canadian Students' Perspectives on School Racism." in *Racism in Canadian Schools.* I. Alladin (ed.) pp.42–61. Toronto: Harcourt Brace.

Dei, George J. Sefa 1993 "The Challenges of Anti-Racist Education in Canada." *Canadian Ethnic Studies* XXV (2):36-49.

Delacourt, Susan 1995 "Finally, To Be a Somebody." *Globe and Mail.* May 20.

Deloria Jr., Vine and Clifford Lytle 1984 *The Nations Within. The Past and Future of American Indian Sovereignty.* New York: Pantheon.

Denis, Wilfrid B. 1990 "The Politics of Language." in *Race and Ethnic Relations in Canada.* Peter Li, (ed.) pp.148–185. Toronto: Oxford University Press.

Desroches, Frederick J. and Augie Fleras 1986 "Immigration and Ethnicity in Canada." in *Police, Race, and Ethnicity: A Guide For Law Enforcement Officers.* Brian K. Cryderman and Chris N. O'Toole, (eds.). pp.25–38. Toronto: Butterworths.

de Toro, Fernando "Ontario's Zero-Tolerance Policy or the End of Academic Freedom: Between the Reign of Intellectual Terrorism and University Cleansing." *CAUT Bulletin ACPPU.* p.15. June 1994.

DeVoretz, Don 1988 "Bad Economics: Irrational Racism." Speech to a conference on Policing in Multicultural/Multiracial Ontario.

Dewes, Koro 1968 "The Place of Maori Language in the Education of the Maoris." Paper presented to the 40th ANZASS Congress, Christchurch, New Zealand.

Diamond, Jared 1989 "Everything Else You Wanted To Know About Sex...But That We Were Afraid That You Would Never Ask." in *Anthropology 89/90.* E. Angeloni (ed.). Guilford Conn: The Dushkin Publishing Group.

DIAND 1993a "Growth in Federal Expenditures on Aboriginal Peoples." Published under the authority of Hon. Tom Siddon, Minister of Indian Affairs and Northern Development. Ottawa.

DIAND 1993b "DIAND's Devolution From Direct Service Delivery to a Funding Agency." Published under the authority of Hon. Pauline Bowes, Minister of Indian Affairs and Northern Development. Ottawa.

DIAND 1993c "Indians in Canada and the United States." Information Sheet No 37. November. Ottawa.

DIAND 1994 "DIAND Programs and Services for Indians and Inuit." *Information Sheet No. 15.* Indian and Northern Affairs, Canada. November.

DIAND 1994 "Tungavik Federation of Nunavut (TFN) Comprehensive Claim: Northwest Territories. *Information Sheet No. 8.* May.

Dickason, Olive Patricia 1992 *Canada's First Nations: A History of Founding Peoples from Earliest Times.* Toronto: McClelland and Stewart.

Dickman, Howard *The Imperiled Academy.* Transaction Publishers. 1993.

Dorais, Louis-Jacques, Lois Foster, and David Stockley 1994 "Multiculturalism and Integration." in *Immigration and Refugee Policy: Australia and Canada Compared.* Howard Adelman et al. (eds.). pp.372–404. Toronto: University of Toronto Press.

Dore, Lyette 1993 "Official Languages and Multiculturalism: Choices for the Future." Notes for a conference speech, "Linguistic Rights in Canada: Collisions or Collusions?" Canadian Centre for Linguistic Rights. University of Ottawa. November 5.

Dosman, Edgar 1972 *Indians: The Urban Dilemma.* Toronto: McClelland and Stewart.

Drakich, Janice, Marilyn Taylor, and Jennifer Bankier 1995 "Academic Freedom is the Inclusive University." *Beyond Political Correctness* S. Richer and L. Weir (eds.). pp.118–135. Toronto: University of Toronto Press.

Draper, P. 1983 "Muses Behind Barbed Wire: Canada and the Internal Refugees." in *The Muses Flee Hitler.* J. Jackman and C. Bordens, (eds.). pp.271–281. Washington: Smithsonian Institution Press.

Driedger, Leo (ed.) 1987 *Ethnic Canada: Identities and Inequalities.* Toronto: Copp Clark Pitman.

Driedger, Leo 1989 *The Ethnic Factor: Identity in Diversity.* Toronto: McGraw Hill Ryerson.

Driedger, Leo, C. Thacker, and R. Curry. 1982 "Ethnic Identification: Variations in Regional and National Preferences." *Canadian Ethnic Studies* 14:57-68.

DuCharme, Michele 1986 "The Canadian Origins of South African Apartheid?" *Currents.* (Summer): 2.

DuCharme, Michele 1986 "The Coverage of Canadian Immigration Policy in the Globe and Mail 1980-1985." *Currents.* (Spring):6-11.

DuCharme, Michele 1986 "The Segregation of Native People in Canada: Voluntary or Compulsory." *Currents.* (Summer): 2–3.

Duley, Margaret I. 1986 "Toward a Theory of Gender Stratification: Selected Issues." in *The Cross-Cultural Study of Women: A Comprehensive Guide.* Margaret I. Duley and Mary I. Edwards, (eds.). New York: The Feminist Press.

Dworkin, Ronald 1977 *Taking Rights Seriously.* London: Duckworth.

Dyck, Noel (ed.) 1985 *Indigenous People and the Nation-State. Fourth World Politics in Canada, Australia, and Norway.* St John's, Newfoundland: Memorial University.

Dyck, Noel 1985 "Aboriginal People and Nation-States: An Introduction to Analytical Issues'. in *Native Power: The Quest for Autonomy and Nationhood of Indigenous Peoples.* Jens Brosted (ed.). pp.155–171. Universitetsforlaget AS.

Dyer, Gwynne 1994 "High Immigration Countries Avoid Economic Stagnation." *The Globe and Mail.* November 9 1994.

Eckholm, Erik 1994 "The Native and Not-so Native American Way." *New York Times Magazine.* February 27:45-52.

Economist 1993 "Three Other-Visioned Mice." April 17. pp. 89–90.

Edwards, John 1985 *Language, Society and Identity.* London: Basil Blackwell.

Edwards John and Lori Doucette 1987 "Ethnic Salience, Identity and Symbolic Ethnicity." *Canadian Ethnic Studies* XIX(1):52-62.

Eidheim, Harald 1985 "Indigenous Peoples and the State: The Sami Case in Norway." in *Native Power: The Quest for Autonomy and Nationhood of Indigenous Peoples.* Jens Brosted, (ed.). pp.155–171. Oslo: Universitets forlaget AS.

Eisler, Dale 1994 "The Coming Cross-Canada Debate is Overdue." *Kitchener-Waterloo Record* December 30.

Elkin, F. 1971 "The Employment of Visible Minority Groups in Mass Media Advertising." A Report Submitted to the Ontario Human Rights Commission.

Elliott, Jean Leonard (ed.) 1983 *Two Nations, Many Cultures. Ethnic Groups in Canada.* Scarborough: Prentice-Hall.

Elliott, Jean Leonard and Augie Fleras 1990 "Immigration and the Canadian Mosaic." in *Race and Ethnic Relations in Canada.* Peter S. Li (ed.). Toronto: Oxford University Press.

Elliott, Jean Leonard and Augie Fleras 1991 *Unequal Relations. An Introduction to Race and Ethnic Dynamics in Canada.* Scarborough: Prentice Hall.

Employment and Immigration Canada 1988 "Annual Report to Parliament on Future Immigration Levels." Ottawa. Communities. October 14-16.

Engels, Frederick 1972 *The Origins of the Family, Private Property, and the State.* Revised Edition by E.B. Leacock. New York: International Publishers.

Environment Canada 1990 *The Free People — Otipemisiwok.* Ottawa: Canadian Government Publishing Centre.

Epstein, Rachel 1983 "Domestic Workers: The Experience in BC." in *Union Sisters.* Toronto: The Women's Press.

Eve, Donelda, K. 1991 "Refugee Claimants and Canadian Bureaucracy." *Perception* 15(3):4.

Exum, William H. "Plus ça change...? Racism in Higher Education." Paper presented at the Annual Meetings of the American Psychological Association. September 2-6, 1980. Toronto: OISE.

Eyoh, Dickson 1995 "From the Belly to the Ballot: Ethnicity and Politics of Africa." *Queen's Quarterly* 102(1):39-52.

Eysenck, H.J. 1971 *Race, Intelligence, and Education.* London: Temple, Smith.

Falding, Harold 1995 "Multiculturalism — A Great Shibboleth. *Policy Options.* March: 42-47.

Feagin, Joe R. 1984 *Racial and Ethnic Relations.* 2nd edition. Englewood Cliffs: Prentice Hall.

Feagin, Joe R. and Clairece Booher Feagin 1993 *Racial and Ethnic Relations.* 4/e. Englewood Cliffs, NJ: Prentice Hall.

Field, Dick 1994 "Multiculturalism Undermines Values Held by Canadians." *Toronto Star.* December 23.

Fish, Stanley 1993 "Reverse Racism. How the Pot Got to Call the Kettle Black." *The Atlantic Monthly.* November: 128–136.

Fish, Stanley 1994 *There's No Such Thing as Free Speech and It's a Good Thing, Too.* New York: Oxford University Press.

Fisher, Robin 1980 "The Impact of European Settlement on the Indigenous Peoples of Australia, New Zealand, and British Columbia: Some Comparative Dimensions. *Canadian Ethnic Studies.* 12:1-14.

Fishman, Joshua 1989 *Language and Ethnicity in Minority Sociolinguistic Matters.* Clevedon, Eng: Multilingual Matters.

Fiske, John 1994 *Media Matters.* Minneapolis: University of Minnesota Press.

Fitzgerald, Thomas K. 1977 *Education and Identity: A Study of the New Zealand Maori Graduate.* Wellington: New Zealand Council for Educational Research.

Fitzgerald, Thomas K. 1989 "Coconuts and Kiwis: Identity and Change Among Second-Generation Cook Islanders in New Zealand." *Ethnic Groups* 7: 259–281.

Flanagan, Thomas 1985 "The Manufacture of Minorities." in *Minorities and the Canadian State.* N. Nevitte and A. Kornberg, (eds.). pp.109–110. Oakville Ontario: Mosaic Press.

Fleras, Augie 1984 "Monoculturalism, Multiculturalism, and Biculturalism: The Politics of Maori Policy in New Zealand." *Plural Societies.* (15): 52-75.

Fleras Augie 1987 "Aboriginality as a Language Issue: the Politicization of 'te Reo Maori' in New Zealand." *Plural Societies.* 17 (2):25-51.

Fleras, Augie 1987 "Redefining the Politics over Aboriginal Language Renewal. Maori Language Schools as Agents of Social Change." *Canadian Journal of Native Studies* 7(1): 1–40.

Fleras, Augie 1989 "Inverting the Bureaucratic Pyramid: Debureaucratizing the Maori Affairs Bureaucracy." *Human Organization.* 48(3):214-225.

Fleras, Augie 1990 "Race Relations as Collective Definition: Aboriginal-Government Relations in Canada." *Symbolic Interaction.* 13(1):19-34.

Fleras, Augie 1990 "Towards a Multicultural Reconstruction of Canadian Society." *American Review of Canadian Studies.* XIX(3):307-320.

Fleras, Augie 1991 "Beyond the Mosaic. Racial Minorities and the Mass Media in a Multicultural Society." *Communications in Canadian Society.* Benjamin D. Singer (ed.). pp.344–367. Scarborough: Nelson.

Fleras, Augie 1991 "Tuku Rangatatiratanga: Devolution in Iwi-Government Relations." in *Nga Take. Ethnic Relations and Racism New Zealand.* Paul Spoonley, Cluny McPherson, and David Pearson (eds.). pp.171–193. Palmerston North, NZ: Dunmore Press.

Fleras, Augie 1991 "Aboriginal Electoral Districts for Canada: Lessons from New Zealand." in *Aboriginal Peoples and Aboriginal Reform in Canada.* Rob Milen (ed.). pp.67–104. Toronto: Dundurn Press.

Fleras, Augie 1992 "From Force to Service: Toward Community Policing in Canada." in *Policing, Race, and Ethnicity.* Brian Cryderman et al. (eds.). pp.87–111. Toronto: Butterworth.

Fleras, Augie 1992 "Managing Aboriginality: Canadian Perspectives: International Lessons." Paper presented to the Australian and New Zealand Association for Canadian Studies. Victoria University in Wellington, N.Z. December 6.

Fleras, Augie 1993 "From Culture to Equality: Multiculturalism as Ideology and Policy." *Social Inequality in Canada.* 2nd Edition. James Curtis, Edward Grab, and Neil Guppy (eds.). pp.330–352. Scarborough: Prentice-Hall.

Fleras, Augie 1993 "Heritage Languages in Canada. A Post-Multicultural Outlook." Paper Presented to the Conference on Linguistic Rights in Canada: Collisions or Collusions? University of Ottawa. November 5-7.

Fleras, Augie 1994 "Doing What is Workable, Necessary, and Fair. Multiculturalism in Canada." *Contemporary Political Issues.* Mark Charlton and Paul Barker (eds.). pp.25–40. Scarborough: Nelson.

Fleras, Augie 1994 "Walking Away From the Camera." in *Ethnicity and Culture in Canada. The Research Landscape.* J.W. Berry and Jean Laponce (eds.) pp.340–384. Toronto: University of Toronto Press.

Fleras, Augie 1995 "Please Adjust Your Set: Media and Minorities in a Post-Multicultural Society." *Communications in Canadian Society.* 4th Edition. Benjamin Singer (ed.). pp.281–307. 1995.

Fleras, Augie 1996 "Behind the Ivy Walls: Racism and Antiracism in Academe." in *Racism in Canadian Schools* I. Alladin (ed.). pp.62–91. Toronto: Harcourt Brace.

Fleras, Augie 1996 "The Politics of Jurisdiction." in *Visions of the Heart.* David Long and Olive Dickason (eds.). Toronto: Harcourt Brace. Forthcoming.

Fleras, Augie and Frederick J. Desroches 1986 "Multiculturalism: Policy and Ideology in the Canadian Context." in *Police, Race, and Ethnicity: A Guide for Law Enforcement Officers.* Brian K. Cryderman and Chris N. O'Toole (eds.). pp.17–24. Toronto: Butterworths.

Fleras Augie and Frederick J. Desroches 1989 "Bridging the Gap: Towards a Multicultural Policing in Canada." *Canadian Police College Journal.* 13(3):153-164.

Fleras, Augie and Jean Leonard Elliott 1992 *Multiculturalism in Canada: The Challenge of Diversity.* Scarborough: Nelson.

Fleras Augie and Jean Leonard Elliott 1992 *The Nations Within: Aboriginal-State Relations in Canada, the United States, and New Zealand.* Toronto: Oxford.

Fleras Augie and Vic Krahn 1992 "From Community Development to Inherent Self-Government: Restructuring Aboriginal-State Relations in Canada." Paper presented at the Annual Meetings of Learned Societies. Charlottetown, P.E.I. June.

Ford Clyde W. 1994 *We Can All Get Along.* NY: Dell Publishing.

Fournier, Pierre 1994 . *A Meech Lake Post-mortem: Is Quebec Sovereignty Inevitable?* Montreal: McGill-Queen's Press.

Fraser, Graham 1994 "For Poor Blacks the Road Leads to Nowhere." *The Globe and Mail.* January 22.

Fraser, John 1988 "Refugee Riddles, Dark Mirrors, and the National Honour." *Saturday Night.* March: 7-8.

Fraser, John 1989 "The Embarrassing Case of Rushton and Rushdie." *Saturday Night.* June: 11–14.

Freudenberg, William R. and Robert Gramling 1994 "Bureaucratic Slippage and Failures of Agency Vigilance: The Case of the Environmental Studies Program." *Social Problems* 41(2):214-233.

Frideres, James S. 1983 *Native Peoples in Conflict.* Scarborough: Prentice-Hall.

Frideres, James 1990 "Policies on Native Peoples in Canada." *Race and Ethnic Relations in Canada.* Peter S. Li (ed.). Toronto: Oxford University Press.

Frideres, James 1991 "From the Bottom Up: Institutional Structures and the Indian People." in *Social Issues and Contradictions in Canadian Society.* B. Singh Bolaria (ed.). Toronto: Harcourt Brace and Jovanovich.

Frideres, James S. 1993 *Native Peoples in Canada: Contemporary Conflicts.* 4th Edition. Scarborough: Prentice-Hall.

Frideres, James (ed.) 1989 *Multiculturalism and Intergroup Relations.* New York: Greenwood Press.

Fry, A.J. and C. Forceville (eds.) 1988 *Canadian Mosaic: Essays on Multiculturalism.* Amsterdam: Free University.

Fukuyama, Frances 1994 "The War of All Against All." *New York Times Book Review.*

Furnivall, J.S. 1948 *Colonial Policy and Practice.* London: Cambridge University Press.

Gaertner, Samuel L. and John F. Dovidio 1986 "The Aversive Form of Racism." in *Prejudice, Discrimination, and Racism.* John F Dovidio and Samuel L. Gaertner (eds.). pp.61–90. New York: Academic Press.

Gans, Herbert J. 1979 "Symbolic Ethnicity: The Future of Ethnic Groups and Culture in America." *Ethnic and Racial Studies.* 2:1-20.

Gates Jr. Henry Louis 1994 "Goodbye, Columbus? Notes on the Culture of Criticism." in *Multiculturalism: A Critical Reader.* D. T. Goldberg (ed.). pp.203–217. Cambridge, Mass.: Basil Blackwell.

Gelfand, Donald E. and Russell D. Lee 1973 *Ethnic Conflicts and Power: A Cross-National Perspective.* New York: John Wiley and Sons.

George Brown College 1990 *Race and Ethnic Relations Policy.* January.

Gherson, Giles 1994 "Playing Gatekeeper to a World That is Forever Pleading for Admission. *The Globe and Mail.* July 12, 1994.

Gibbins, Richard and J. Rick Ponting 1986 "Faces and Interfaces of Indian Self-Government." *Journal of Native Studies.* VI:43-62.

Ginzberg, Effie 1986 "Power Without Responsibility: The Press We Don't Deserve." *Currents* (Spring):1-5.

Giroux, Henry E. 1994 "Insurgent Multiculturalism and the Promise of Pedagogy." in *Multiculturalism: A Critical Reader.* D.T. Goldberg (ed.). pp.325–343. Cambridge Mass: Basil Blackwell.

Glazer, Nathaniel and Daniel P. Moynihan 1970 *Beyond the Melting Pot.* Cambridge, Mass.: MIT Press.

Glazer, Nathaniel and Daniel P. Moynihan 1975 *Ethnicity. Theory and Experience.* Cambridge: Harvard University Press.

Globe and Mail 1994 "Canadian Languages." *Editorial.* April 14.

Goar, Carol 1995 "Unequal Shares of the American Dream." *Toronto Star.* May 14.

Gold, Gerald L. (ed.) 1984 *Minorities and Mother Country Imagery.* St. John's: Institute of Social and Economic Research, Memorial Univesity.

Goldberg, David Theo 1993 *Philosophy and the Politics of Meaning.* Oxford: Basil Blackwell.

Goldberg, David Theo 1994 "Introduction: Multicultural Conditions." in *Multiculturalism: A Critical Reader.* D.T. Goldberg (ed.). p.1–44. Cambridge Mass.: Basil Blackwell.

Goldbloom, Victor 1994 "Ottawa Urged to Support Bilingualism?" *Globe and Mail.* April 13.

Gonick, Cy 1987 *The Great Economic Debate: Failed Economics and a Future For Canada.* Toronto: James Lorimer.

Goot, Murray 1993 "Multiculturalists, Monoculturalists and the Many in Between: Attitudes to Cultural Diversity and Their Correlates." *Australia and New Zealand Journal of Sociology.* 29(2):226-254.

Gordon, Milton M. 1964 *Assimilation in American Life.* New York: Oxford University Press.

Goudar, Ruth 1989 "Adjusting the Dream." *Saskatchewan Multicultural Magazine.* 8(3):5-8.

Gould, Terry 1995 "Line of Fire." *Saturday Night.* February 35-41.

Government of Canada 1958 Department of Citizenship and Immigration. *A Review of Activities. 1948-1958.* Indian Affairs Branch.

Government of Canada 1969 "White Paper." *Statement of the Government of Canada on Indian Policy.* Department of Indian Affairs and Northern Development.

Government of Canada 1992/93 *Main Estimates. Part II.* Government of Canada.

Government of Canada 1993 *Canadian Immigration Law.* Ottawa: Minister of Supply and Services.

Government of Canada 1994 . "Federal Government Begins Discussions on Aboriginal Self-Government." News Release 1-9354.

Granastein, J.L. 1994 "Universities Strangled by 'PC.' Politicians." *Canadian Speeches: Issues of the Day.* July, 2-8.

Gray, John 1994 "The Vanishing." *Globe and Mail.* December 10.

Gray, Kathy, "Racism Policies." *Memorandum to Canadian Universities Employment Equity Network.* September 10, 1993.

Grayson, J. Paul "'Visible Minority' Problematic for Students of Chinese Origin." *Institute for Social Research.* Vol. 9 (3) Fall.

Green, Joyce 1989 "Untitled Paper." presented to the Panel on Political Issues, National Symposium on Aboriginal Women in Canada, University of Lethbridge, Lethbridge, Alberta.

Greenfield, Meg 1994 "Falling Back on Fatalism." *Time Magazine.* March 14.

Greenland, Hauraki 1984 "Ethnicity as Ideology." in *Tauiwi. Racism and Ethnicity in New Zealand.* P. Spoonley, C. MacPherson, D. Pearson, and C. Sedgewick (eds.). pp.86–102. Palmerston North, New Zealand: Dunsmore Press.

Guelph, 1994 *Final Report of the President's Task Force on Anti-Racism and Race Relations.* University of Guelph (Summer).

Gutman, Amy (ed.) 1992 *Multiculturalism and the Politics of Recognition.* Princeton University Press.

Gwyn, Richard 1994 "Our Refugee System Less Generous Than Extravagant Government." *Toronto Star.* June 22.

Gwyn, Richard 1994 "The First Borderless State." *Toronto Star* November 26.

Habermas, Jurgen 1976 *Legitimation Crisis.* Boston: Beacon.

Hacker, Andrew 1993 "'Diversity' and Its Dangers." *New York Times Review of Books.* pp. 21–25. October 7.

Hale, Sylvia 1993 "Using the Oppressor's Language: A Study of Women and Development." in *Human Rights: Issues and Trends.* Abdul Lohdi and Russell McNeilly (eds.). pp.167–178. Toronto: Canadian Scholars Press.

Hall, Anthony J. 1986 "The N'ungosuk Project. A Study in Aboriginal Language Renewal." Unpublished paper.

Hall, Tony 1986 "Self-Government or Self-Delusion? Brian Mulroney and Aboriginal Rights." *Journal of Native Studies* VI:77-89.

Hall, Tony 1993 "The Politics of Aboriginality." *Canadian Dimension.* January-February, pp.6-8.

Harries, L. 1983 "The Nationalisation of Swahili." in *Language Planning and Language Change.* Chris Kennedy, (ed.). pp.118–131. London: George Allen and Unwin.

Harris, Debbie Wise 1993 "Colonizing Mohawk Women: Representation of Women in the Mainstream Media." *RFD/DRF* 20 (1/2) 15–20.

Harvey, Edward B. 1988 *Information Systems for Employment Equity: An Employers Guide.* Don Mills Ontario: CCH Canadian Limited.

Harvey, Jim 1992 "Multicultural Education: An Undetheorised Romanticism." *Multicultural Teaching* xi (3): 5–7.

Hassan, Marwan 1995 "Articulation and Coercion: The Language Crisis in Canada." *Border/Lines.* 36:28-35.

Havel, Vaclav 1994 "Needed: A New Spirit for a New World." *The Globe and Mail.* February 28.

Hawkins, Freda 1972 *Canadian Immigration: Public Policy and Public Concern.* Montreal: McGill-Queen's University Press.

Hawkins, Freda 1975 "Recent Immigration Policy." in *Immigration and the Rise of Multiculturalism.* Howard Palmer (ed.). pp.71–75. Toronto: Copp Clark Publishing.

Hawkins, Freda 1982 "Multiculturalism in Two Countries: The Canadian and Australian Experience." Journal of Canadian Studies (17): 64–80.

Hawkins, Freda 1988 "Canadian Multiculturalism: The Policy Explained." *Canadian Mosaic. Essays on Multiculturalism.* A.J. Fry and Ch. Forceville (eds.) pp. 9–24. Amsterdam: Free University Press.

Hawkins, Freda 1991 *Critical Years in Immigration: Canada and Australia Compared.* 2nd Edition. Montreal/Kingston: McGill Queen's University Press.

Hayes, Rose D. 1975 "Female Genital Mutilation, Fertility Control, Women's Role, and the Patrilineage in Modern Sudan." *American Ethnologist.* 2(4):617-633.

Hayes-Bautista, David E. "Academe Can Take the Lead in Binding Together the Residents of a Multicultural Society." *The Chronicle of Higher Education.* October 28, 1992.

Hawkes, David C. (ed.) 1989 *Aboriginal Peoples and Government Responsibility: Exploring Federal and Provincial Roles.* Ottawa: Carleton University Press.

Hawkes, David C. and Marina Devine 1991 "Meech Lake and Elijah Harper: Native-State Relations in the 1990s." in *How Ottawa Spends.* pp.33–63. Ottawa: University of Carleton Press.

Hechter, Michael 1975 *Internal Colonialism: The Celtic Fringe in British National Development.* Berkeley: University of California Press.

Hedican, Edward J. 1995 *Applied Anthropology in Canada. Understanding Aboriginal Issues.* Toronto: University of Toronto Press.

Helly, Denise 1993 "The Political Regulation of Cultural Plurality: Foundations and Principles." *Canadian Ethnic Studies* XXV (2): 15-31.

Henderson, James [sakej] Youngblood 1993 "Governing the Implicate Order: Self-Government and the Linguistic Development of Aboriginal Communities." Paper presented to the conference on Linguistic Rights in Canada: Collisions or Collusions? University of Ottawa. November 5-7th.

Henry, Frances 1968 "The West Indian Domestic Scheme in Canada." *Social and Economic Studies.* 17(1)83-91.

Henry, Frances 1994 *The Caribbean Diaspora in Canada.* Toronto: University of Toronto Press.

Henry, Frances and Carol Tator 1985 "Racism in Canada: Social Myths and Strategies for Change." *Ethnicity and Ethnic Relations in Canada.* 2nd Edition. Rita M. Bienvenue and Jay E. Goldstein (eds.). pp.321–335. Toronto: Butterworths.

Henry, Frances and Carol Tator 1993 "The Show Boat Controversy." *The Toronto Star.* May 28.

Henry, Frances, Carol Tator, Winston Mattis and Tim Rees 1995 *The Colour of Democracy.* Toronto: Harcourt Brace.

Henry, Frances and E. Ginzberg 1984 *Who Gets the Work: A Test of Racial Discrimination in Employment Toronto.* Urban Alliance on Race Relations and the Social Planning Council of Toronto.

Henry, Frances and Effie Ginzberg 1993 "Racial Discrimination in Employment." in *Social Inequality in Canada.* James Curtis et al. (ed.). pp.353–360. Scarborough: Prentice-Hall.

Herberg, Edward 1989 *Ethnic Groups in Canada: Adaptation and Transition.* Scarborough: Nelson.

Hewitt, Roger 1986 *White Talk, Black Talk.* New York: Cambridge University Press.

Hick Stephen and Ron Santos 1992 *Anti-Racism Student Organizing in Canadian Universities.* Sponsored by the Race Advisory Committee, School of Social Work, Carleton University, Ottawa.

Hill, Daniel G. 1981 *The Freedom Seekers. Blacks in Early Canada.* Agincourt Ontario: The Book Society of Canada.

Hill, Jennifer Leigh 1992 "Accessibility: Students with Disabilities in Universities in Canada. *The Canadian Journal of Higher Education.* Vol. XXII (1):48-67.

Hiller, Harry 1986 *Canadian Society. A Macro Analysis.* Scarborough Ontario: Prentice-Hall.

hooks, bell 1984 *Feminist Theory: From Margin to Centre.* Boston: South End Press.

hooks, bell 1992 *Black Looks.* Toronto: Between the Lines.

Hooten, E.A. 1946 *Up From the Ape.* New York: Macmillan.

Hosek, Chaviva 1987 "How Women Fought for Equality." in *Women and Men: Interdisciplinary Readings on Gender.* Greta Hofmann Nemiroff, (ed.). pp.493–514. Markham Ontario: Fitzhenry and Whiteside.

Hostetler, John A. and Gertrude Huntington 1967 *The Hutterites in North America.* New York: Holt Rinehart Winston.

Hudson, Michael R. 1987 "Multiculturalism, Government Policy and Constitutional Enshrinement — A Comparative Study." in *Multiculturalism and the Charter: A Legal Perspective.* Canadian Human Rights Foundation (ed.). pp.59–122. Toronto: Carswell.

Hughes, Robert 1992 "The Fraying of America." *Time.* pp.40–46. February 3.

Hummel, Ralph 1987 *The Bureaucratic Experience.* New York: St Martins Press.

Hunn, Jack Kent and John M. Booth 1962 *The Integration of the Maori and Pakeha in New Zealand.* Study Paper No. 1. Published in conjunction with the Department of Maori Affairs and the Government Printer. Wellington, New Zealand.

Hurtado, Aida 1989 "Relating to Privilege: Seduction and Rejection in the Subordination of White Women and Women of Colour." *Signs* 14(4):833-855.

Ignatieff, Michael 1994 *Blood and Belonging: Journeys into the New Nationalism.* Viking.

Ignatieff, Michael 1995 "Nationalism and the Narcissism of Minor Differences." *Queens Quarterly* 102(1): 1-25.

Irwin, Colin 1989 "Lords of the Arctic: Wards of the State." *Northern Perspectives* 17(1). Ottawa: Canadian Arctic Resources Committee.

Isajiw, Wsevolod W. 1977 "Olga in Wonderland: Ethnicity in Technological Society." *Canadian Ethnic Studies* IX(1): 77-85.

Isajiw, Wsevolod W. 1982 "Occupational and Economic Development." *A Heritage in Transition: Essays in the History of Ukrainians in Canada.* M. Lupul, (ed.) pp. 59–84. Toronto: McClelland and Stewart.

Isajiw, Wsevolod W. 1990 "Ethnic - Identity Retention." *Ethnic Identity and Equality.* R. Breton et al. (eds.) pp. 34–91. Toronto: University of Toronto Press.

Jackson, Kirsty 1991 "The Refugee Determination System." *Perception* 15(3):11-13.

Jacques, Rulx-Leonel 1990 "Reflexions sur l'avenir des Relations Inter-ethniques au Canada et au Québec." Paper presented to the Canadian Council on Community and Race Relations. Ottawa.

Jain, Harish C. 1988 "Affirmative Action/Employment Equity Programs and Visible Minorities in Canada." *Currents* 3-7.

Jain, Harish C. and Rick D. Hackett 1989 "Measuring Effectiveness of Employment Equity Programs in Canada: Public Policy and a Survey." *Canadian Public Policy* XV(2): 189-204.

Jakobsh, Frank 1994 "Racist Foundations." *Kitchener-Waterloo Record.* September 3.

James, Carl 1994 "The Paradoxes of Power and Privilege: Race, Gender, an Occupational Position." *Canadian Women Studies* 14(2):47-51.

James, Carl 1995 *Seeing Ourselves: Exploring Race, Ethnicity, and Culture.* Toronto: Thompson Publishing.

James, Carl and Adrienne Shadd (eds.) *Talking About Differences. Encounters in Culture, Language, and Identity.* Toronto: Between the Lines.

Jaret, Charles 1995 *Contemporary Racial and Ethnic Relations.* Scarborough Ont: Harper Collins.

Jaworsky, John 1979 *A Case Study of Canadian Federal Government's Multicultural Policies.* Unpublished MA Thesis. Political Science. Ottawa: Carleton.

Jenkins, Richard 1994 "Rethinking Ethnicity: Identity, Categorization, and Power. *Ethnic and Race Relations* 17 (2):197-223.

Jensen, Arthur R. 1969 "How Much Can We Boost IQ and Scholastic Achievement?" *Harvard Educational Review* 39:1-123.

Jhally, Sut and Justin Lewis 1992 *Enlightened Racism. The Cosby Show, Audiences, and the Myth of the American Dream.* Boulder CO: Westview Press.

Jhappan, C. Radha 1990 "Indian Symbolic Politics: The Double-Edged Sword of Publicity." *Canadian Ethnic Studies* XXII(3):19-19-39.

Johnson, Daniel 1995 "Daniel Johnson Urges Flexible Federalism." by John Gray *Globe and Mail* January 19.

Jones, B. 1978 "Nova Scotia Blacks: A Quest For a Place in the Canadian Mosaic." in *Black Presence in Multi-Ethnic Canada.* V.D'Oyley, (ed.). pp.81–96. Vancouver: Faculty of Education, University of British Columbia.

Jordan, Deidre F. 1987 "Aboriginal Identity: The Management of a Minority Group by the Mainstream Society." *Canadian Journal of Native Studies.*

Joseph, Gloria I. and Jill Lewis 1986 *Common Differences: Conflicts in Black and White Feminist Perspectives.* Boston: South End Press.

Joy, Richard 1971 *Languages in Conflict.* Toronto: McClelland and Stewart.

Kallen, Evelyn 1982 "Multiculturalism: Ideology, Policy, and Reality." *Journal of Canadian Studies* (17): 51-63.

Kallen, Evelyn 1987 "Multiculturalism, Minorities, and Motherhood: A Social Scientific Critique of Section 27." *Multiculturalism and the Charter: A Legal Perspective.* Canadian Human Rights Foundation (ed.) pp. 123–138. Toronto: Carswell.

Kallen, Evelyn 1989 *Label Me Human. Minority Rights of Stigmatized Canadians.* Toronto: University of Toronto Press.

Kallen, Evelyn 1995 *Ethnicity and Human Rights in Canada.* 2nd Edition. Toronto: Oxford University Press.

Kanter, Rosabeth 1977 *Men and Women of the Corporation.* New York: Vintage.

Kaplan William (ed.) 1993 *Belonging: The Meaning and Sense of Citizenship in Canada.* Montreal and Kingston. McGill-Queen's University Press.

Katz, Irwin, Joyce Wackenhut, and R. Glen Hass 1986 "Racial Ambivalence, Value Duality, and Behavior." in *Prejudice, Discrimination, and Racism.* John F. Dovidio and Samuel L. Gaertner (eds.). pp.35–60. New York: Academic Press.

Kauffman, L. A. 1990 "Citizenship. Democracy in a Postmodern World." *Social Policy:* Fall 1990: 7-11.

Keating, Michael 1993 "Two Faces Under One Flag." *The Times Higher Education Supplement.* September 24. p.19.

Kelsey, Jane 1986 "Decolonization in the 'First World.' – Indigenous Minorities Struggle for Justice and Self-Determination." *The Windsor Yearbook of Access to Justice* 5:102-141.

Kennedy, Chris (ed.) 1983 *Language Planning and Language Education.* London: George Allen and Unwin.

Kessler-Harris, Alice 1992 "Multiculturalism Can Strenthen, Not Undermine a Common Culture. *The Chronicle of Higher Education.* October 21, 1992.

Khayatt, Didi 1994 "The Boundaries of Identity at the Intersections of Race, Class, and Gender. *Canadian Women Studies* (14)(2):6-13.

Kilgour, David 1988 *Uneasy Patriots: Western Canadians in Confederation.* Edmonton: Lone Pine.

Killian, Lewis M. 1970 "Herbert Blumer's Contributions to Race Relations." in *Human Nature and Collective Behavior.* Papers in Honor of Herbert Blumer. Tamotsu Shibutani (ed.). pp.179–190. Englewood Cliffs, N.J: Prentice-Hall.

King III, Martin Luther 1994 "Forward." in *We Can All Get Along.* Clyde W. King (ed.). pp.ix - x. NY: Dell Publishing.

King, Deborah 1988 "Multiple Jeopardy, Multiple Consciousness: The Context of Black Feminist Ideology." *Signs* 14(2): 42-49.

Kinloch, Graham C. 1977 *Sociological Theory: Its Development and Major Paradigms.* Toronto: McGraw Hill.

Kinsella, Warren 1994 *Web of Hate: The Far-Right Network in Canada.* Toronto: Harper Collins.

Kitchener-Waterloo Record 1994 "Partial Victory." March 26.

Kitchener-Waterloo Record 1994 "Foreign Education Less Valued." June 20.

Kitchener-Waterloo Record 1994 "Quebec Obtains Money for Nothing." July 7.

Kitchener-Waterloo Record 1994 "46% of Black Children are Poor in Canada." September 15.

Kleinman, S. 1978 "Female Premarital Sexual Careers." in *Shaping Identity in Canadian Society.* Jack Haas and William Shaffir, (eds.). pp.101–115. Scarborough, Ontario: Prentice-Hall.

Knight, David B. 1985 "Territory and People or People and Territory? Thoughts on Postcolonial Self-Determination." *International Political Science Review* 6: 248-272.

Knowles, Louis L. and Kenneth Prewitt 1969 *Institutional Racism in America.* Englewood Cliffs, N.J.: Prentice-Hall.

Kohl, Herbert 1991 "The Politically Correct Playground. Multiculturalism and the Schools." *Social Policy.* Summer 33–40.

Kohl, Howard 1994 "Service with a Sneer." *New York Times.* November 6.

Kostash, Myrna 1988 "Domination and Exclusion: Notes of a Resident Alien." in *Ethnicity in a Technological Age.* Ian H. Angus (ed.). pp.57–66. Edmonton: Canadian Institute of Ukrainian Studies, University of Alberta.

Kralt, John and Ravi Pendakur 1991 "Ethnicity Immigration & Language Transfer." *Policy & Research. Multiculturalism Sector.* Multiculturalism and Citizenship, Ottawa.

Kramarae, Cheris 1984 "Introduction: Toward an Understanding of Language and Power." in *Language and Power.* Cheris Kramarae et al. (eds.). pp.9–22. Beverley Hills: Sage Publications.

Kromkowski, John A. 1995 "To the Reader." *Race and Ethnic Relations. Annual Editions.* Sluice Dock Conn: Dushkin Publishing.

Krotkin, Joel 1992 *Tribes. How Race, Religions and Identity Determine Success in the New Global Economy.* New York: Random House. (As reviewed in the New York Times Magazine. March 8, 1993.)

Krotz, Larry 1990 *Indian Country: Inside Another Canada.* Toronto: McClelland and Stewart.

Kulchyski, Peter (ed.) 1994 *Unjust Relations. Aboriginal Rights in Canadian Courts.* Toronto: Oxford University Press.

Kymlicka, Will 1995 "Misunderstanding Nationalism." *Dissent* (Winter): 131–137.

LaPiere, R. 1934 "Attitudes Versus Action." *Social Forces* 13: 230-237.

LaRoque, Emma 1975 *Defeathering the Indian.* Agincourt, ON: Book Society of Canada.

LaRoque, Emma 1990 "Preface, or Here are Our Voices - Who Will Hear?" *Writing the Circle: Native Women of Western Canada.* Jeanne Perreault and Sylvia Vance (eds.) pp. xv–xxx. Edmonton: NeWest.

Laurin, Camille 1978 "Charte de la Langue Française/French Language Charter." *Canadian Review of Sociology and Anthropology* 15(2).

Latouche, Daniel 1993 "Quebec, See Under Canada: Quebec Nationalism in the New Global Age." *Quebec. State and Society.* 2/e. Alain-G. Gagnon (ed.) pp. 40–63. Scarborough: Nelson.

Latouche, Daniel 1995 "To Be or Not to Be a Province." *The Globe and Mail.* February 17.

Laxer, James 1993 "Buying Into Decline." *Canadian Forum.* April: 5–7.

Laxer, James 1994 "Canada Can't Survive as a Union of 10 Equal Provinces." *Toronto Star.* August 7.

Leah, Ronnie 1989 "Race, Class, Gender: Bonds and Barriers." *Socialist Studies/Etudes Socialistes* 5:174-205.

Lehr, John C. 1987 "Government Perceptions of Ukrainian Immigrants to Western Canada 1896-1902." *Canadian Ethnic Studies* XIX(2):1-13.

Lemarchand, Rene 1993 *Ethnocide as Discourse and Practice.* New York: Cambridge University Press.

Leo, John 1988 "An Apology to Japanese Americans." *Time Magazine.* May 2.

Levin, Michael, D. (ed.) 1993a *Ethnicity and Aboriginality: Case Studies in Ethnonationalism.* Toronto: University of Toronto Press.

Levin, Michael, D. 1993b "Introduction." in *Ethnicity and Aboriginality: Case Studies in Ethnonationalism.* Michael pp.3–8. Toronto: University of Toronto Press.

Levin, Michael, D. 1993c "Ethnicity and Aboriginality: Conclusions." in *Ethnicity and Aboriginality. Case Studies in Ethnonationalism.* pp.168–179. Toronto: University of Toronto Press.

Levin, Michael D. 1995 "Understanding Ethnicity." *Queen's Quarterly* 102(1):71-89.

Levitt, Howard 1994 "Employment Equity Act Ill-Conceived." *Toronto Star.* July 18.

Lewis, Oscar 1964 "The Culture of Poverty." in *The Explosive Forces in Latin America."* J. Tepaske and S. Fisher, (eds.). pp.149–173. Columbus: Ohio: University Press.

Lewycky, Laverne 1993 "Multiculturalism in the 1990s and into the 21st Century: Beyond Ideology and Utopia." In *Deconstructing A Nation. Immigration, Multiculturalism and Racism in 90s Canada.* Vic Satzewich (ed.). pp.359–402. Halifax: Fernwood Press.

Li, Peter S. 1988a *The Chinese in Canada.* Toronto: Oxford University Press.

Li, Peter S. 1988b *Ethnic Inequality in a Class Society.* Toronto: Wall and Thompson.

Li, Peter S. (ed.) 1990 *Race and Ethnic Relations in Canada.* Toronto: Oxford.

Li, Peter S. 1994 "A World Apart: The Multicultural World of Visible Minorities and the Art World of Canadians." *Canadian Review of Sociology and Anthropology.* 32 (4): 367-398.

Lipset, Seymour Martin and Earl Raab 1995 *Jews and the New American Scene.* Harvard University Press.

Little Bear, L., Menno Boldt and J. Anthony Long 1984 *Pathways to Self-Determination: Canadian Indians and the Canadian State.* Toronto: University of Toronto Press.

Louder, Dean and Eric Waddell 1983 *Du Continent Perdu a L'archipel Retrouvé: le Québec et l'Amérique Française.* Quebec: Presses de l'Universite Laval.

Lupul, M.R. 1988 "Ukrainians: The Fifth Cultural Wheel in Canada." in *Ethnicity in a Technological Age.* Ian H. Angus (ed.). pp.177–192. Edmonton: Canadian Institute of Ukrainian Studies, University of Alberta.

Lupul Manoly R. 1994 "Multiculturalism, Ethnic Studies, and the Present Economic Crisis in Alberta. *Shevchenko Lecture.* University of Alberta, March 24.

Lyman, Stanford M. 1984 "Interactionism and the Study of Race Relations at the Macro-Sociological Level: The Contribution of Herbert Blumer." *Symbolic Interaction* 7(1):107-120.

Lyman, Stanford M. 1994 *Color, Culture, and Civilization. Race and Minority Issues in American Society.* Chicago: University of Chicago Press.

Lyman, Stanford M. and William A. Douglas 1970 "Ethnicity: Strategies of Collective and Individual Management Impression." *Social Research* 40:344-365.

Lyons, Christopher and Mona Farraell "Teaching Tolerance." *McGill Journal of Education.* Vol. 29(1):5-14

Macionis, John, Juanne Nancarrow Clarke and Linda M. Gerber 1994 *Sociology. Canadian Edition.* Scarborough: Prentice-Hall.

Mackie, M. and M. Brinkerhoff 1984 "Measuring Ethnic Salience." *Canadian Ethnic Studies.* 16: 114-131.

Mackie, Marlene 1978 "Ethnicity and Nationality: How Much Do They Matter to Western Canadians?" *Canadian Ethnic Studies.* 10:118-129.

Mackie Marlene 1985 "Stereotypes, Prejudice, and Discrimination." in *Ethnicity and Ethnic Relations in Canada.* 2nd Edition. Rita M. Bienvenue and Jay E. Goldstein, (eds.). pp. 119-159. Toronto: Butterworths.

Macklem, Patrick 1993 "Ethnonationalism, Aboriginal Identities, and the Law." in *Ethnicity and Aboriginality: Case Studies in Ethnonationalism.* Michael D. Levin (ed.). pp.9–28. Toronto: University of Toronto Press.

MacLeans 1991 "The Silencer." May 27.

MacQueen, Ken 1994 "I am a Canadian. Don't Let Me Screw Up." *Kitchener-Waterloo Record.* April 23.

Madely, Steve 1994 "Immigration and Crime." *Ottawa Sun.* July 20.

Mandel, Ernest 1979 *Introduction to Marxism.* Whitstable Kent: Whitstable Litho.

Maori Synod of the Presbyterian Church 1961 *A Maori View of the Hunn Report.* Christchurch: Presbyterian Bookroom.

Marcus, Alan Rudolph 1995 *Relocating Eden. The Image and Politics of Inuit Exile in the Canadian Arctic.* Hanover NH: The University Press of New England.

Marger, Martin N. 1994 *Race and Ethnic Relations. American and Global Perspectives.* 2/e. Belmont CA: Wadsworth.

Marger, Martin N. and Phillip J. Obermiller 1987 "Emergent Ethnicity Among Internal Migrants: The Case of the Maritimers in Toronto." *Ethnic Groups* 7:1-17.

Marin, Peter 1995 "Secularism's Blind Faith." *Harpers.* September: 20–22.

Martin, James G. and Clyde W. Franklin 1973 *Minority Group Relations.* Columbus Ohio: Charles E. Merrill Publishing Company.

Martin, Jerry 1993 "The Postmodern Argument Considered." *Partisan Review.* pp.638–646.

Marx, Karl 1951 *The Woman Question.* New York: International Publishers.

Matas, Robert 1994 "Putting a Price on Immigration." *The Globe and Mail.* February 11.

McAndrew, Marie 1992 "Combatting Racism and Ethnocentrism in Educational Materials: Problems and Actions Taken in Quebec. in *Racism and Education. Different Perspectives and Experiences.* Ontario Teachers Federation (ed.). pp.49–60. Ottawa.

McBride, Stephen and John Shields 1993 *Dismantling a Nation: Canada and the New World Order.* Halifax: Fernwood.

McCall, George J. and J.L. Simmons 1978 *Identities and Interactions. An Examination of Human Associations in Everyday Life.* Revised. New York: Free Press.

McCarthy, Cameron and Warren Crichlow (eds.) 1993 *Race, Identity, and Representation in Education.* New York: Routledge.

McCaskill, Tim 1995 "Anti-Racist Education and Practice in the Public School System." *Beyond Political Correctness.* S. Richer and L. Weir (eds.). pp.253–272. Toronto: University of Toronto Press.

McConohay, John B. 1986 "Modern Racism, Ambivalence, and the Modern Racism Scale." in *Prejudice, Discrimination, and Racism.* John F. Dovidio and Samuel L Gaertner (eds.) pp.91–126. New York: Academic Press.

McCormack, Thelma 1991 "Political Correct?" *The Canadian Forum.*

McFarlane, Scott 1995 "The Haunt of Race." *Fuse* 18(3): 18–31.

McGarry John and Brendan O'Leary 1994 "The Political Regulation of National and Ethnic Conflict." *Parliamentary Affairs* pp.94–115.

McGill 1994 *Anti-Racism and Race Relations.* Prepared by Monique Shebbeare. McGill's Equity Office. July.

McGillivray, Don 1992 "Meanings Can Move Between Right and Left." London Free Press March 2.

McGregor, Robert M. "The Distorted Mirror: Images of Visible Minority Women in Canadian Print Advertising." *Atlantis* 15(1).

McGregor, Roy 1989 *The Fearless Vision of Billy Diamond.* Markham Ontario: Viking.

McIntosh, Peggy "White Privilege and Male Privilege: A Personal Account of Coming to See Correspondences Through Work in Women Studies." *Working Paper No. 189* Wellesly College, Centre for Research on Women, MA.

McIntyre, Sheila 1993 "Backlash Against Equality: The 'Tyranny' of the 'Politically Correct.' *McGill Law Journal/Revue de Droit de McGill* 38(1):3-63.

McKague, Ormand (ed.) 1991 *Racism in Canada.* Saskatoon: Fifth House Publishing.

McKenna, Ian 1994 "Canada's Hate Propaganda Laws - A Critique." *British Journal of Canadian Studies:* 15–42.

McLemore, S. Dale 1994 *Racial and Ethnic Relations in America.* 4th Edition. Toronto: Allyn and Bacon.

McLeod, Keith A. (ed.) *Multiculturalism, Bilingualism, and Canadian Institutions.* Toronto: University of Toronto Guidance Centre.

McMillan, Alan D. 1988 *Native Peoples and Cultures of Canada.* Vancouver/Toronto: Douglas and McIntyre.

McNeill, William H. 1986 *Poly-Ethnicity and National Unity in World History.* Toronto: Butterworths.

McRae, K.D. 1974 *Consociational Democracy: Political Accommodation in Segmented Societies.* Toronto: McClelland and Stewart.

McRoberts, Kenneth 1989 *Quebec Social Change and Political Crisis.* 3/e. Toronto: McClelland and Stewart.

McRoberts, Kenneth 1993 "English-Canadian Perceptions of Quebec." *Quebec. State and Society.* Alain-G. Gagnon (ed.) pp. 116–129. Scarborough: Nelson.

Mead, Margaret 1963 *Sex and Temperament.* New York: Dell.

Mead, Walter Russell 1993 "This Land is My Land." *New York Times Book Review.* November 7.

Medjuck, Sheva 1988 "From Self-Sacrificing Jewish Mother to Self-Centered Jewish Princess: Is This How Far We've Come." *Atlantis: A Women's Studies Journal* 14(1):90-97.

Mercredi, Ovide and Mary Ellen Turpel 1993 *In the Rapids: Navigating the Future of First Nations.* Toronto: Penguin Books.

Metge, Joan 1976 *The Maoris of New Zealand: Rautahi.* London: Routledge and Kegan Paul.

Miles, Robert 1982 *Racism and Migrant Labour.* London: Routledge and Kegan Paul.

Miles, Robert 1993 *Racism after Race Relations.* New York: Routledge.

Miles, Robert and Ann Phizacklea 1984 *White Man's Country: Racism in British Politics.* London: Pluto Press.

Miliband, Ralph 1973 *The State in Capitalist Society.* London: Quartet Books.

Miller, Barbara D. 1981 *The Endangered Sex: Neglect of Female Children in Rural North India.* Ithaca N.Y.: Cornell University Press.

Miller, J.R. 1989 *Skyscrapers Hide the Heavens: A History of Indian-White Relations in Canada.* Toronto: University of Toronto Press.

Miner, Michael 1986 *Police Intercultural Training Manual.* Published by the Canadian Association of Chiefs of Police with the support of the Multicultural Directorate of the Secretary of State. Ottawa.

Ministry of Education and Training, *Antiracism and Ethnocultural Equity in School Boards. Guidelines for Policy Developent and Implementation.* Toronto.

Ministry of Municipal Affairs 1988 *Employment Equity.* Toronto.

Mitchell, Alana 1994 "Study Debunks Immigration Myths." *The Globe and Mail.* July 13.

Mitchell, Alana 1995 "Members of Minorities Hold More Degrees." *The Globe and Mail.* June 14.

Money, J. and A.A. Ehrhardt 1972 *Man and Woman, Boy and Girl: The Differentiation and Dimorphism of Gender Identity From Conception to Maturity.* Baltimore: John Hopkins Univerity Press.

Montague, Ashley 1943 "The Myth of Blood." in *Race, Individual, and Collective Behavior.* E. T. Thompson and E.R. Hughes (eds.) Glencoe: The Free Press.

Montgomery, Moses and W. G. MacDonald 1991 "Human Rights and Race Relations Policy in Canadian Universities and Colleges. *International Education Magazine.* pp.8–16, 22.

Moodley, Kogila 1984 "Canadian Multiculturalism as Ideology." *Ethnic and Race Studies.* 6(3): 320-332.

Moodley, Kogila (ed.) 1992 *Beyond Multicultural Education. International Perspectives.* Calgary: Detsilig Enterprises.

Morse, Bradford, W. (ed.) 1985 *Aboriginal Peoples and the Law.* Ottawa: Carleton University Press.

Mukherjee. Alok 1992 "Educational Equity for Racial Minorities and the School: The Role of Community Action. in *Racism and Education: Different Perspectives and Experiences.* Ontario Federation of Students (ed.). pp.73–81. Ottawa.

Mukherjee, Alok 1993 "Educational Equity for Racial Minorities and the School: The Role of Community Action." in *Human Rights. Issues and Trends.* Abdul Q. Lodhi and Russell A. McNeilly (eds.). p.135–144. Toronto: Canadian Schools Press.

Mulroney, Brian 1985 "Statement by the Prime Minister of Canada to the Conference of First Ministers on the Rights of Aboriginal Peoples." *The Quest for Justice: Aboriginal Peoples and Aboriginal Rights.* pp.148–156 in Menno Boldt and J. Anthony Long (eds.). Toronto: University of Toronto Press.

Murphree, Marshall W. 1988 "The Salience of Ethnicity in African States: A Zimbabwean Case Study." *Ethnic and Racial Studies* 11 (2).

Nadkarni, M.V. 1983 "Cultural Pluralism as a National Resource: Strategies for Language Education." in *Language Planning and Language Education.* Chris Kennedy, (ed.). pp.151–159. London: George Allen and Unwin.

Nagel, Joane 1994 "Constructing Ethnicity: Creating and Recreating Ethnic Identity and Culture." *Social Problems* 41(1):152-170.

Nagel, Joane and Susan Olzak 1982 "Ethnic Mobilization in the New and Old States: An Extension of the Competition Model." *Social Problems* 30 (2):127-142.

Nagle, Patrick 1994 "Manitoba Takes First Steps to Axe Indian Act." *Toronto Star* April 24th.

Nelson Adie and Augie Fleras 1995 *Social Problems in Canada: Conditions and Consequences.* Scarborough: Prentice Hall.

Neufeld-Rocheleau, Melody and Judith Friesen 1987 "Isolation: A Reality for Immigrant Women in Canada." *Saskatchewan Multicultural Magazine* 6(2):12-13L.

Nevitte, Neil and Allan Kornberg 1985 *Minorities and the Canadian State.* Oakville, Ontario: Mosaic Press.

Newsweek 1995 "Holes in the Glass Ceiling Theory." March 27.

Ng, Roxana 1988 *The Politics of Community Services: Immigrant Women, Class, and the State.* Toronto: Garamond Press.

Ng, Roxana 1989 "Sexism, Racism, Nationalism." in *Race, Class, Gender: Bonds and Barriers.* Jesse Vorst (ed.). Toronto and Winnipeg: Between the Lines and the Society for Socialist Studies.

Ng, Roxanna 1994 "Sexism and Racism in the University: Analyzing a Personal Experience." *Canadian Women Studies* 14(2):41-46.

Ng, Roxanna and Judith Ramirez 1981 *Immigrant Housewives in Canada.* Toronto: The Immigrant Women's Centre.

Nicks, T. and K. Morgan 1985 "Grande Cache: The Historical Development of an Indigenous Alberta Metis Population." in *The New Peoples: Being and Becoming Metis in North America.* J. Peterson and J.S.H. Brown (eds.). Winnipeg: University of Manitoba Press.

Northfield, Stephen 1993 "No Middle Ground." *The London Free Press.* March 20.

O'Bryan, K.G., J. Reitz, and O. Kuplowska 1976 *The Non-Official Languages Study.* Ottawa: Minister of Supply and Services.

Olmstead, A. 1983 "The Mixed Bloods in Western Canada." in *Native Indians in Conflict.* James S. Frideres, (ed.). Scarborough: Prentice-Hall.

Omi, Michael 1989 "In Living Color: Race and American Culture." *Cultural Politics in Contemporary America.* Ian Angus and Sut Jhally (eds.) pp. 111–122. New York: Routledge.

Omi, Michael and Howard Winant 1993 "On the Theoretical Concept of Race." *Race, Identity and Representation in Education.* C. McCarthy and W. Crichlow (eds.) pp. 3–10. New York: Routledge.

O'Neill Brian J. and Shankar A. Yelaja 1994 "Multiculturalism and Postsecondary Education." in *Ethnicity and Culture in Canada. The Research Landscape.* J. W. Berry and J. A. Laponce (eds.). pp. 483-506. Toronto: University of Toronto Press.

Ontario Council of Regents, 1992 *Report on Harassment and Discrimination in Ontario Colleges of Applied Arts and Technology.* Submitted by the Harassment Task Force of the Ontario Council of Regents, May.

Ontario Federation of Students. 1991 *Whitewashed: Institutional Racism in Ontario Post-Secondary Education.* Toronto.

Ontario Women's Directorate 1989 *Making Connections: Regional Employment Equity Network in Ontario: A Practitioners Resource Guide.* Toronto.

Oommen, T.K. 1994 "Race, Ethnicity and Class: An Analysis of Interrelations." *International Journal of Social Sciences.* February: 83-94.

Paine, Robert 1985a "Ethnodrama and the 'Fourth World': The Saami Action Group in Norway, 1979-1981." *Indigenous Peoples and the Nation-State: Fourth World Politics in Canada, Australia and Norway.* pp.190–235 in Noel Dyck (ed.). Social and Economic Papers No. 14. St John's, Newfoundland Memorial University.

Paine, Robert 1985b "The Claim of the Fourth World." *The Quest for Autonomy and Nationhood of Indigenous Peoples.* Jens Brosted (ed.) pp. 49–66. Bergen: Universitesforlaget AS.

Pal, Leslie 1993 *Interests of State. The Politics of Language, Multiculturalism,and Feminism in Canada.* McGill-Queen's: Montreal and Kingston.

Palmer, Howard (ed.) 1975 *Immigration and the Rise of Multiculturalism.* Toronto: Copp Clark Publishing.

Panitch, Leo 1977 "The Role and Nature of the Canadian State." in *Canadian State: Political Economy and Political Power.* Leo Panitch (ed.). pp.3–27. Toronto: University of Toronto Press.

Parel, A. J. 1992 "Multiculturalism and Citizenship." in *George Grant and the Future of Canada.* Yusuf K. Umar (ed.). p.139–150. University of Calgary Press.

Parillo, Vincent N. 1990 *Strangers to These Shores: Race and Ethnic Relations in Canada.* New York: MacMillan.

Park, Robert E. 1950 *Race and Culture.* New York: Free Press.

Parsons, Talcott 1951 *The Social System.* New York: Free Press.

Parsonson, Ann 1981 "The Pursuit of Mana." in *An Oxford History of New Zealand.* W.H. Oliver and B.R.Williams (eds.). pp.140–167. Wellington, New Zealand: Oxford University Press.

Payment, Diane 1989 "La Vie en Rose? Metis Women at Batoche 1870-1920." Paper presented to the National Syposium of Aboriginal Women, University of Lethbridge, Lethbridge, Alberta.

Pearson, David 1990 *A Dream Deferred. The Origins of Ethnic Conflict in New Zealand.* Wellington: Allen and Unwin.

Pedraza, Silvia 1994 "The Sociology of Immigration, Race, and Ethnicity in America." *Social Problems* 41(1):1-6.

Penner, Keith 1983 *Indian Self-Government in Canada.* Report of the Special Committee chaired by Keith Penner. Ottawa: Queens Printer for Canada.

Pentney, W.F. 1987 "Race Relations: The Legislative Basis." Foundation Paper, Conference on Canada 2000. Race Relations and Public Policy. Ottawa: Carleton University.

Peoples, James and Garrick Bailey 1994 *Humanity. An Introduction to Cultural Anthropology.* 3/e. St. Paul/Minneapolis: West Publishing.

Peter, K. 1978 "Multi-cultural Politics, Money, and the Conduct of Canadian Ethnic Studies." Canadian Ethnic Studies Association Bulletin 5: 2-3.

Petrone, Penny (ed.) 1983 *First People, First Voices.* Toronto: University of Toronto Press.

Petrone, Penny (ed.) 1990 *Native Literature in Canada: From the Oral Tradition to the Present.* Toronto: Oxford University Press.

Pettigrew, Thomas F. 1994 "New Patterns of Prejudice: The Different Worlds of 1984 and 1964." *Race and Ethnic Conflict.* Fred L. Pincus and Howard J. Ehrlich (eds.) pp. 53–59. Boulder CO: Westview Press.

Pettman, Jan 1987 "Combatting Racism within the Community." in *Prejudice in the Public Arena: Racism.* Andrew Markus and Rahda Rasmussen (eds.). Monash University, Victoria University: Centre for Migrant and Intercultural Studies.

Philip, M. Nourbese 1992 *Frontiers. Essays and Writings on Racism and Culture.* Stratford ON: Mercury Press.

Philip, M. Nourbese 1995 "Signifying Nothing." *Border/Lines* 36:4-27.

Picard, Andre 1994 "Quebec Drops Old Sign-Law Changes." *The Globe and Mail* April 13.

Pincus, Fred L. and Howard J. Ehrlich (eds.) 1994 *Race and Ethnic Conflict. Contending Views on Prejudice, Discrimination, and Ethnoviolence.* Boulder CO: Westview Press.

Pineo, Peter C. and John Porter 1985 "Ethnic Origin and Occupational Attainment." in *Ascription and Achievement: Studies in Mobility and Status Attainment in Canada.* M. Boyd et al. (eds.). pp.357–392. Ottawa: Carleton University Press.

Platiel, Rudy 1994a "Chretien Objects to Federal Paternalism in Indian Act. *The Globe and Mail.* March 11.

Platiel, Rudy 1994b "Talks to Focus on Mohawk Communities." *The Globe and Mail.* April 6.

Platiel Rudy 1994c "Ceremony to Alter Canada's Course." *The Globe and Mail.* December 7th.

Platiel, Rudy 1995 "Natives Make Little Headway." *The Globe and Mail.* January 11.

Platiel, Rudy 1995 "UN Praises Quebec Cree Band for Setting Fine Example." *The Globe and Mail.* June 20.

Plaut, Rabbi W. Gunther 1989 "Unwanted Intruders or People in Flight." *Perception* 13(2):45-46.

Ponting, J. Rick 1986 *Arduous Journey: Canadian Indians and Decolonization.* Toronto: McClelland and Stewart.

Ponting, J. Rick and Roger Gibbins 1980 *Out of Irrelevance: A Socio-Political Introduction to Indian Affairs in Canada.* Toronto: Butterworths.

Porter, John 1965 *The Vertical Mosaic.* Toronto: University of Toronto Press.

Price, Christopher 1993 "Schools of Thought." *New Statesman and Society.* August 20th.

Priest, Lisa 1989 *Conspiracy of Silence.* Toronto: McClelland and Stewart.

Prince, Michael J. 1987 "How Ottawa Decides Social Policy: Recent Changes in Philosophy, Structure and Process." in *The Canadian Welfare State: Evolution and Transition.* Jacqueline S. Ismael (ed.). Edmonton: University of Alberta.

Proceedings 1992 *Challenges of Measuring an Ethnic World: Science, Politics, and Reality.* Joint Canadian-United States Conference on the Measurement of Ethnicity. Cosponsored by Statistics Canada and the U.S. Bureau of the Census. Washington: U.S. Government Printer.

Proceedings 1993 *National Symposium for University Presidents on Institutional Strategies for Race and Ethnic Relations at Canadian Universities.* Report of a symposium held at Queen's University at Kingston February 2-4 1992.

Puddington, Arch 1995 "What to do About Affirmative Action." *Commentary* June 22-28.

Purich, Donald 1986 *Our Land: Native Peoples in Canada.* Toronto: James Lorimer.

Queens University "Towards Diversity and Equity at Queen's: A Strategy for Change." Final Report of the Principal's Advisory Committee on Race Relations. *Queen's Gazette Supplement.* April 8, 1991.

Ramcharan, Subhas 1982 *Racism: Nonwhites in Canada.* Toronto: Butterworths.

Ramcharan, Subhas, James Chacko and Roxanne Baker. 1991 *An Attitudinal Study of Visible Minority Students at the University of Windsor.* Windsor, Ontario.

Rashkin, James 1992 "The Fallacies of "Political Correctness": 1." *Z Magazine.* January: 31-36.

Raz, Joseph, 1994 "Multiculturalism: A Liberal Paradox." *Dissent* Winter 67-80.

Raza, Racheel 1994 "Silent Shame." *Toronto Star* August 5.

Razack, Sherene 1994 "What is to be Gained by Looking White People in the Eye? Culture, Race, and Gender in Cases of Sexual Violence. *Sign* Summer: 894-922.

Regional Municipality of Waterloo 1986 *Equal Employment Opportunity. Phase 1.*

Reitz, Jeffrey and Raymond Breton 1994 *The Illusion of Difference: Realities of Ethnicity in Canada and the United States.* Toronto: C.D. Howe Institute.

Reitz, J.G. 1980 *The Survival of Ethnic Groups.* Toronto: McGraw-Hill Ryerson.

Rensberger, Boyce 1994 "The Case for One Race." *Toronto Star.* December 24th.

Report 1984 *Equality Now! Report of the Special Committee on Visible Minorities in Canadian Society.* Bob Daudlin, MP Chairperson. Ottawa: Queen's Printer.

Report 1987 *Multiculturalism: Building the Canadian Mosaic.* Report of the Standing Committee on Multiculturalism. Gus Mitges, MP, Chairperson. Ottawa: Queen's Printer.

Report 1987 *Multiculturalism...Being Canadian.* Report of the Secretary of State of Canada (Multiculturalism). Ottawa: Minister of Supply and Services.

Report 1988 *Towards a National Agenda for a Multicultural Australia.* Goals and Principles Report of the Advisory Council on Multicultural Affairs. Canberra: Australian Government Publishing Service.

Report 1988 *Multiculturalism in Canada.* Draft prepared by the Policy Analysis and Research Division, Multiculturalism, Secretary of State. Ottawa.

Report 1991 *Towards Managing Diversity: A Study of Systemic Discrimination at DIAND.* Report by the Deputies Council for Change. Ottawa: Minister of Supply and Services.

Resnick, Philip 1990 *The Masks of Proteus: Canadian Reflections on the State.* Montreal and Kingston: McGill-University Press.

Rex, John 1983 *Race Relations in Sociological Theory.* London: Routledge and Kegan Paul.

Rhodes, Jane 1989 "Strategies in Studying Women of Colour in Mass Communication." in *Women in Mass Communication. Challenging Gender Values.* Pamela J. Creedon, (ed.). pp.112-116. Sage: Newbury Park.

Richardson, Laurel 1988 *The Dynamics of Sex and Gender A Sociological Perspective.* 3rd Edition. New York: Harper and Row.

Richer, Stephen and Lorna Weir eds. 1995 *Beyond Political Correctness: Toward the Inclusive University.* Toronto: University of Toronto Press.

Richmond, Anthony H. 1988 *Immigration and Ethnic Conflict.* Basingstoke, England: MacMillan.

Rieff, David 1993 "Multiculturalism and the Global Information Society." *Deconstructing a Nation: Immigration, Multiculturalism, and Racism in the 90s Canada.* Vic Satzewich (ed.) pp. 351–357. Halifax: Fernwood.

Rioux, Marcel 1973 "The Development of Ideologies in Quebec." in *Communities and Cultures in French Canada.* Gerald Gold and Marc-Adelard Tremblay, (eds.). Toronto: Holt Rinehart and Winston.

Roberts, Lance W. and Rodney A. Clifton 1990 "Multiculturalism in Canada: A Sociological Perspective." in *Race and Ethnic Relations in Canada.* Peter S.Li (ed.). pp.120–147. Toronto: Oxford University Press.

Rose, Arnold M. 1957 "Intergroup Relations vs. Prejudice: Pertinent Theory for the Study of Social Change." *Social Problems* 4:173-176.

Ross, J.A. 1979 "Language and the Mobilization of Ethnic Identity." in *Language and Ethnic Relations.* H. Giles and B. St.-Jacques (eds.). pp.1–14. Oxford: Pergammon Press.

Ross, Jeffrey A. 1982 "Urban Development and the Politics of Ethnicity: A Conceptual Approach." *Ethnic and Racial Studies* 5(4):440-456.

Roth, Lorna 1995 "(De)Romancing the North." *Border/Lines* 36: 36-43.

Rothchild, Donald and Alexander J. Groth 1995 "Pathological Dimensions of Domestic and International Ethnicity." *Political Science Quarterly* 110(1):69-79.

Royal Commission 1992, *Framing the Issues: Discussion Paper No 1.* Royal Commission on Aboriginal Peoples. Ottawa.

Royal Commission 1993 *Overview of the Second Round.* Prepared for the Royal Commission on Aboriginal Peoples by Michael Cassidy Ginger Group Consultants. Ottawa, Minister of Supply and Services Canada.

Rubin, J. 1983 "Bilingual Education and Language Planning." in *Language Planning and Language Education.* Chris Kennedy (ed.). pp.4–16. London: George Allen and Unwin.

Ryan, Claude 1975 "Biculturalism or Multiculturalism?" Speech 1972. Reprinted in *Immigration and the Rise of Multiculturalism.* Howard Palmer (ed.). Toronto: Copp Clark Publishing.

Ryan, William 1971 *Blaming the Victim.* New York: Vintage.

Sajoo Amyn B. 1994 "New Dances With Diversity." *Policy Options.* December: 14-19.

Salee, Daniel 1995 "Identities in Conflict: The Aboriginal Question and the Politics of Recognition in Quebec. *Racial and Ethnic Studies* 18(2):277-314.

Samuda, Ronald J., Berry, John W. and Michel Laferriere (eds.) 1984 *Multiculturalism in Canada: Social and Educational Perspectives.* Toronto: Allyn and Bacon.

Samuel, T. John 1988 "Immigration and Visible Minorities in the Year 2001: A Projection." Ottawa: Centre for Immigration and Ethnocultural Studies.

Samuel, T. John 1995 "Let's Make Multiculturalism Work." *Toronto Star.* January 23.

Sanders, Douglas 1985 "Aboriginal Rights: The Search For Recognition in International Law." in *The Quest For Justice: Aboriginal Peoples and Aboriginal Rights.* Menno Boldt and J.Anthony Long (eds.). pp.292–303. Toronto: University of Toronto Press.

Sanders, Douglas 1987 "Article 27 and the Aboriginal Peoples of Canada." *Multiculturalism and the Charter: A Legal Perspective Canadian Human Rights Foundation* (ed.) pp. 155–166. Toronto: Carswell.

Satzewich, Vic 1991 "Social Stratification: Class and Racial Inequality." *Social Issues and Contradictions in Canadian Society.* B. Singh Bolaria (ed.) pp. 91–107. Toronto: Harcourt Brace.

Satzewich, Vic (ed.) 1992 *Deconstructing a Nation: Immigration, Multiculturalism, and Racism in the 90s Canada.* Fernwood Publishing and the Social Research Unit. Department of Sociology, University of Saskatchewan.

Sayer, J. 1982 *Biological Politics: Feminist and Anti-Feminist Perspectives.* London: Tavistock.

Schaffly, Phyllis 1995 "Wilting Democratic Centerpiece." *Washington Times* March 18.

Schermerhorn, R.A. 1956 "Power as a Primary Concept in the Study of Minorities." *Social Forces* 35:53-56.

Schermerhorn, R.A. 1970 *Comparative Ethnic Relations: A Framework For Theory and Research.* New York: Random House.

Schlesinger, Arthur M. Jr. 1992 *The Disuniting of America. Reflections on a Multicultural Society.* New York: W.W. Norton.

Schwartz, Bryan 1985 *First Principles: Constitutional Reform with Respect to Aboriginal Peoples of Canada 1982-1984.* Kingston: Institute of Intergovernmental Relations, Queeens University.

Scotti, Rosannna and Earl Miller 1985 "National Conference on Policing in Multiracial Urban Communities." *Currents* 3(2):44-45.

See, Katherine O'Sullivan and William J. Wilson 1988 "Race and Ethnicity." in *Handbook of Sociology* Neil J. Smelzer (ed.). pp.223–242. Newbury Park, Calif: Sage.

Seguin, Rheal 1994 "Native Self-Rule Talks Plunged into Disarray." *The Globe and Mail.* May 19.

Senese, Guy B. 1991 *Self-Determination and the Social Education of Native Indians.* New York: Praeger.

Sewell, William and Robert M. Hauser 1975 *Education, Occupation, and Earnings: Achievement in Early Career.* New York: Academic Press.

Shadd, Adrienne L. 1987 "Dual Labour Markets in 'Core' and 'Periphery' Regions of Canada: The Position of Black Males in Ontario and Nova Scotia." *Canadian Ethnic Studies* XIX(2):91-113.

Shaffir, William and Cyril Levitt 1987 *Riot at Christie Pits* Toronto: Lester and Orpen Dennys.

Shallot, Jeff 1994 "Canada's Refugee Body has Freedom to Offend Friends." *The Globe and Mail* August 19.

Sharp, Andrew 1990 *Justice and the Maori.* Auckland: Oxford.

Shenk, Margot 1994 "The Role of Librarians in the Inclusive University." *CAUT Bulletin ACPPU.* p.12. June.

Shibutani, Tamotsu and Kian M. Kwan 1965 *Ethnic Stratification: A Comparative Approach.* New York: Macmillan.

Shkilnyk Anastasia M. 1985 *A Poison Stronger Than Love.* New Haven, Conn: Yale University Press.

Shkilnyk, Anastasia M. 1986 *Progress Report - Aboriginal Language Policy Developments.* Unpublished Report for the Assembly of First Nations.

Shohat Ella and Robert Stam 1994 *Unthinking Eurocentrism. Multiculturalism and the Media.* New York: Routledge.

Siegel, Fred 1991 "The Culture of Multiculturalism." *The New Republic* Feb 18: 34–39.

Silman, Janet (ed.) 1987 *Enough is Enough. Aboriginal Women Speak Out.* Toronto: Women's Press.

Silvera, Mikeda 1983 *Silenced.* Toronto: Williams-Wallace Publishers.

Simmel, G. 1950 *The Sociology of George Simmel.* Kurt Wolff (ed.). Glencoe, Ill: Free Press.

Simmons, Alan B. and Kieran Keohane 1992 "Canadian Immigration Policy: State Strategies and the Quest for Legitimacy." *Canadian Review of Sociology and Anthropology* 29 (4):421-452.

Simmons, Dale 1994 "How the West Won." *Faces* (Saskatchewan Multicultural Magazine) Winter: 12-14.

Simone, Rose 1994 "Immigration Act Criticized as Sexist." *Kitchener-Waterloo Record* October 15.

Simpson, G.E. and J.M. Yinger 1972 *Racial and Cultural Minorities: An Analyis of Prejudice and Discrimination.* New York: Harper and Row.

Simpson, Jeffrey 1993 *Faultlines. Struggle for a Canadian Vision.* Toronto: Harper-Collins.

Sinclair, Keith 1971 "Why are Race Relation in New Zealand Better Than in South Africa, South Australia, or South Dakota?" *New Zealand Journal of History.* 5:121-127.

Singer, Benjamin (ed.) 1983 *Communications in Canadian Society.* Don Mills Ontario: Addison-Wesley.

Sleeter, Christine E. 1991 *Empowerment Through Multicultural Education.* Albany: State University of New York Press.

Smelser, Neil 1993 "Contested Boundaries and Shifting Solidarities." *ISA Bulletin.* pp.58–59.

Smith, A.D. 1994 "The Problem of Nationalist Identity: Ancient, Medieval, or Modern." *Ethnic and Race Relations.*

Smith, Bobbi Jo 1992 "Curbing Racism on Campus." *Campus Scene*. pp.12–15.

Smith, Dorothy 1979 "Using the Oppressor's Language."*Resources for Feminist Research*. Special Publication no 5. pp.10–18.

Smith, Michael G. 1965 *The Plural Society in the British West Indies*. Berkely: University of California Press.

Smith, S. 1991 *Report: Commission of Inquiry on Canadian University Education*. Ottawa. Association of Universities and Colleges in Canada.

Sniderman, David, David A. Northrup, Joseph Fletcher, Peter Russell, and Philip E. Tetlock 1993 "Psychological and Cultural Foundations of Prejudice: The Case of Anti-Semitism in Quebec." *Canadian Review of Sociology and Anthropology* 30(2):242-267.

Snyderman, Mark 1994 "How to Think About Race." *National Review* September 12. pp.78–80.

Sowell, Thomas 1989 *Preferential Policies: An International Perspective*. Morrow.

Spoonley, Paul, David Pearson and Cluny Macpherson (eds.) 1991 *Nga Take. Ethnic Relations and Racism in Aotearoa/New Zealand*. Palmerston North, NZ: Dunmore Press.

Stagner, Ross 1987 "Foreward." in *Ethnic Conflict*. Jerry Boucher, Dan Landis, and Karen Arnold Clark (eds.). pp.7–16. Newbury Park, California: Sage.

Stamm, Robert 1993 "From Stereotype to Discourse: Methodological Reflexions." *Cineaction* No 32.

Staples, Janice 1974 "Consociationalism at Provincial Level: The Erosion of Dualisms in Manitoba, 1870-1890." in *Consociational Democracy*. K.D. Macrae, (ed.). Toronto: McClelland and Stewart.

Stasiulis, Daiva K. 1980 "The Political Structure of Ethnic Community Action. A Reformation." *Canadian Ethnic Studies* XII:19-44.

Stasiulis, Daiva K. 1988 "The Symbolic Mosaic Reaffirmed: Multiculturalism Policy." in *How Ottawa Spends 1988-89*. Katharine A. Graham (ed.). pp.81–111.Ottawa: Carleton University Press.

Stasiulis, Daiva K. 1990 "Theorizing Connections: Gender, Race, Ethnicity, and Class." in *Race and Ethnic Relations in Canada*. Peter S. Li (ed.). pp.269–305. Toronto: Oxford University Press.

Stasiulis Daiva 1991 "Symbolic Representation and the Numbers Game: Tory Policies on "Race" and Visible Minorities." *How Ottawa Spends*. pp.229–253. Ottawa: Carleton University.

Stea, David and Ben Wisner (eds.) 1984 "The Fourth World: A Geography of Indigenous Struggles." *Antipodes: A Radical Journal of Geography* 16 (2).

Stepan, Nancy 1982 *The Idea of Race in Science: Great Britain, 1800-1960*. London: Macmillan Press.

Stern, Kenneth S. "Battling Bigotry on Campus." *USA Today Magazine*. pp.58-62. March 1992.

Stewart, Edison 1994 "Being No.1 Isn't Enough for Quebec." *Toronto Star.* November 13.

Stinson, Marion 1994 "Real Estate Spoken Here." *Globe and Mail.* October 26.

Stocking, George Jr. 1968 *Race, Culture, and Evolution: Essays in History of Anthropology.* London: Collier-Macmillan.

Stoffman, Daniel 1994 "Marchi's Big Change is to Factor in National Interests." *Toronto Star* November 5.

Stonequist, E.V. 1937 *The Marginal Man: A Study in Personal and Culture Conflict.* New York: Scribners.

Sudol, Stan 1994 "Economic Realities Demand a Reduction in Immigration Quotas." *Toronto Star.* August 16.

Sugiman, Momoye (ed.) 1992. *Jin Guo: Voices of Chinese Canadian Women.* Women's Book Committee, Chinese Canadian National Council. Toronto: Women's Press.

Sunahara, Ann G. 1981 *The Politics of Racism.* Toronto: James Lorimer.

Sutcliffe, David 1986 "Introduction." in *The Language of Black Experience.* David Sutcliffe and Ansel Wong, (eds.). pp.1–14. London: George Allen and Unwin.

Synnott, Anthony and David Howes 1994 "Visible Minority: Concept and Reality." *Working Paper. Centre for Community and Ethnic Studies.* Concordia University.

Talai, V. 1989 "Social Boundaries Within and Between Ethnic Groups: Armenians in London." Manitoba (N.S.) 21: 251-270.

Talbani, Abdulaziz 1993 "Intercultural Education and Minorities: Policy Initiatives in Quebec." *McGill Journal of Education* 28(3): 407–421.

Tambiah, Stanley J. 1989 "Ethnic Conflict in the World Today." *Ethnology* 16(2):335-339.

Taylor, Charles 1992 "The Politics of Recognition." *Multiculturalism and the Politics of Recognition.* Amy Gutman (ed.) pp. 25–74. Princeton University Press.

Taylor, Charles 1993 "The Deep Challenge of Dualism." *Quebec. State and Society.* 2/e. Alain-G. Gagnon (ed.) pp. 82–95. Scarborough: Nelson.

Taylor, D.M. and H. Giles 1979 "At the Crossroads of Research and Language and Ethnic Relations." in *Language and Ethnic Relations.* H. Giles and B. St. Jacques, (eds.). p.231–241. Oxford: Pergammon Press.

Taylor, John P. and Gary Paget 1989 "Federal/Provincial Responsibility and the Sechelt. in *Aboriginal Peoples and Government Responsibility.* David Hawkes (ed.). p.297–348. Ottawa: Carleton University Press.

Tebege, Ainamlem 1989 "Cultural Interaction of Canadians and Ethiopian Newcomers in Canada." Policy Analysis Directorate, Immigration Policy Branch. Ottawa: Employment and Immigration.

Tennant, Paul 1985 "Aboriginal Rights and the Penner Report on Indian Self-Government." *The Quest for Justice: Aboriginal Peoples and Aboriginal Rights.* p.321–332 in Menno Boldt and J. Anthony Long (eds.). Toronto: University of Toronto Press.

Tepper, Elliot L. 1988 *Changing Canada: The Institutional Response to Polyethnicity. The Review of Demography and Its Implications for Economic and Social Policy.* Ottawa: Carleton University.

Thobani, Sunera 1995 (1992) "Multiculturalism: The Politics of Containment." *Social Problems in Canada Reader.* Adie Nelson and Augie Fleras (eds.) pp. 213–216. Originally published in Aquelarre. Scarborough: Prentice-Hall.

Thompson, Allan 1994 "MPs Attack Multiculturalism." *Toronto Star* February 8.

Thompson, Allan 1995 "Economist Debunks 'Head Tax'." *Toronto Star* May 17.

Thornicroft, R. 1983 "A Multicultural Research Survey Summary."

Thorsell, William 1995 "Who Are We." *Report on Business Magazine.* January: 21-22.

Throne, Jeanette 1994 "Living with the Pendulum: The Complex World of Teaching." *Harvard Educational Review* 64(2): No Page Numbers.

Tinker, George 1993 *Missionary Conquest. The Gospel and Native American Cultural Genocide.* Fortress Press, Minneapolis.

Tobias, John L. 1976 "Protection, Civilization, and Assimilation: An Outline History of Canada's Indian Policy." *Western Canadian Journal of Anthropology.* 6(2):13-30.

Toronto Star 1994 "Immigrants Do Not Commit More Crime." *Editorial.* July 23.

Toronto Star 1995 "The Color of Learning." February 11.

Trillin, Calvin 1993 "Smoking Incorrectly." *The Globe and Mail.* April 8.

Troper, Harold and Morton Weinfeld 1989 *Old Wounds: Jews, Ukrainians and the Hunt for Nazi War Criminals in Canada.* Chapel Hill: University of North Carolina.

Tucker, Erin 1987 "Old Racism, New Racism." in *Prejudice in the Public Arena: Racism.* Andrew Markus and Rahda Rasmussen (eds.). pp.16–20. Monash University, Victoria, Australia: Centre for Migrant and Intercultural Studies.

Turner, Terence 1994 "Anthropology and Multiculturalism: What is Anthropology that Multiculturalists Should Be Mindful of It? *Multiculturalism: A Critical Reader.* D.T. Goldberg (ed.). pp.406–425. Cambridge Mass: Basil Blackwell.

Ujimoto, K. Victor and Gordon Hirabayashi (eds.) 1980 *Visible Minorities and Multiculturalism: Asians in Canada.* Toronto: Butterworths.

Ujimoto, K Victor and Josephine Naidoo 1986 *Asian Canadians. Contemporary Issues.* Selections from the Proceedings of the Asian Canadian Symposium, Manitoba, University of Winnipeg. June 4-7.

Ungerleider, C.S. and F.H. Echols 1985 "Police Intercultural Education Project in Vancouver and Ottawa." *Currents* 3(2)18-21.

University of Guelph 1994 *Final Report of the President's Task Force on Anti-Racism and Race Relations.* Summer.

University of Toronto 1994 *First Report of the Race Relations and Anti-Racist Initiative Office.* April.

University of Western Ontario 1989 *Survey of Race Relations at the University of Western Ontario.* Presidents Advisory Committee on Race Relations.

University of Western Ontario 1993 "Report of the Race Relations Policy Review Committee. MW Westmacott, Chair. *Western News Supplement*. September 16.

University of Windsor 1993 "Fourth Annual Report. July 1, 1992-June 30th 1993." *Ombudsperson and Race Relations Officer*. September 8.

Vallieres, Pierre 1971 *White Niggers of America*. Toronto: McClelland and Stewart.

Valpy, Michael 1994 "Mr Marchi's Flawed Doomsday Argument." *Globe and Mail* June 15.

van den Berghe, Pierre 1967 *Race and Racism*. New York: John Wiley.

van den Berghe, Pierre 1970 *Race and Ethnicity*. New York: Basic Books.

van den Berghe, Pierre 1981 *The Ethnic Pheonomenon*. New York: Elsevier.

van den Berghe, Pierre 1985 "Race and Ethnicity: A Sociobiological Perspective." *Ethnicity and Ethnic Relations in Canada* (Second Edition). Rita M. Bienvenue and Jay E. Goldstein (eds.) pp. 19–30. Toronto: Butterworths.

van den Berghe, Pierre and Karl Peter 1988 "Hutterites and Kibbutzniks: A Tale of Nepotistic Communism." Manitoba (NS) 23(3):522-539.

van Dijk, Teun A. 1987 *Communicating Racism: Ethnic Prejudice in Thought and Talk*. Newbury Park: Sage Publications.

Vasta, Ellie 1993 "Multiculturalism and Ethnic Identity: The Relationship Between Racism and Resistance." *Australia and New Zealand Journal of Sociology* 29(2):209-225.

Vidich, Arthur J. and Stanford Lyman 1985 "A Secularization of the Sociological Perspective: Herbert Blumer." in *American Sociology*. pp.209–232. New Haven, Conn: Yale University Press.

Wade, Mason 1967 *The French Canadians 1760-1945*. Vol. 1. London: MacMillan.

Wagley, Charles and Marvin Harris 1958 *Minorities in the New World*. New York: Columbia University Press.

Walker, James W. St. G. 1985 *Racial Discrimination in Canada. The Black Experience*. The Canadian Historical Association Booklet No. 41.

Walker, James W. St. G. 1989 "Race Policy in Canada. A Retrospective." *Canada 2000: Race Relations and Public Policy*. O.P. Dwivedi et al. (eds.) pp. 1–19. Guelph: University of Guelph. Department of Political Science.

Walser, Michael 1992 "Comment." *Multiculturalism and the Politics of Recognition*. Amy Gutman (ed.) pp. 99–104. Princeton University Press.

Wardhaugh, Ronald 1983 *Language and Nationhood: The Canadian Experience*. Vancouver: New Star Books.

Warren, Catherine E. 1986 *Vignettes of Life: Experience and Self-Perceptions of New Canadian Women*. Calgary: Detselig.

Waterloo 1994 "Discrimination and Harassment. A Student's Perspective. *An Educational Package for Students*. Lisa DuCharme. Office of Ethical Behaviour and Human Rights.

Watson, J.K.P. 1983 "Cultural Pluralism, Nation-Building and Educational Policies in Penninsular Malaysia." in *Language Planning and Language Education*. Chris Kennedy, (ed.). pp.132–150. London: Routledge and Kegan Paul.

Watson, Paul 1995 "Reality Bites New South Africa." *Toronto Star* January 1.

Watson, Warren 1993 "Cultural Diversity's Impact on Interaction Process and Performance." *Academy of Management Journal* 16(3). As Reviewed in the Economist, 7 August 1993.

Watts, Franklin 1975 "Introduction." in *The White Mans Burdensome Business.* Murray L. Wax and Robert W. Buchanan (eds.). pp.1–5. New York: A New York Times Book/New Viewpoints.

Weaver, Sally M. 1981 *Making Canadian Indian Policy: The Hidden Agenda, 1968-1970.* Toronto: University of Toronto Press.

Weaver, Sally M. 1983 "The Status of Indian Women." *Two Nations, Many Cultures: Ethnic Groups in Canada.* 2nd edition. Jean Leonard Elliott (ed.) pp. 56–79. Scarborough: Prentice-Hall.

Weaver, Sally M. 1983 "Australian Aborigine Policy. Aboriginal Pressure Groups or Government Advisory Bodies?" Oceania LIV: 1–22, 85–108.

Weaver, Sally M. 1984 "Struggles of the Nation-State to Define Aboriginal Ethnicity: Canada and Australia." *Minorities & Mother Country Imagery.* pp. 182–210 in G. Gold (ed.) Institute of Social and Economic Research Number 13. St. John Nfld: Memorial University Press.

Weaver, Sally M. 1985. "Federal Difficulties With Aboriginal Rights Demands." p.139–147 in *The Quest for Justice. Aboriginal Peoples and Aboriginal Rights.* Menno Boldt and J. Anthony Long (eds.). Toronto: University of Toronto Press.

Weaver, Sally M. 1988 "Public Opinion on Aboriginal Rights and Land Issues in Canada and Australia." Paper presented to the 1988 Biennial Conference of the Association of Canadian Studies in Australia and New Zealand, Canberra, Australia.

Weaver, Sally M. 1990 "Self-Government for Indians 1980-1990: Political Transformations or Symbolic Gestures." Paper read at the UNESCO Conference Proceedings on the Migration and the Transformation of Cultures in Canada.

Weaver, Sally M. 1991 "A New Paradigm in Canadian Indian Policy for the 1990s." *Canadian Ethnic Studies* XXII(3):8-18.

Weaver, Sally M. 1993 "First Nations Women and Government Policy 1970–1992: Discrimination and Conflict." *Changing Patterns: Women in Canada.* 2/e. Sandra Burt et al. (eds.) Toronto: McClelland and Stewart.

Weaver, Sally M. 1993 "Self-Determination, National Pressure Groups, and Australian Aborigines. The National Aboriginal Conference 1983-1985." in *Ethnicity and Aboriginality. Case Studies in Ethnonationalism.* Michael D Levin (ed.). pp.53–74. Toronto: University of Toronto Press.

Webber, Jeremy 1994 *Reimaging Canada. Language, Culture, Community, and the Canadian Constitution.* Montreal and Kingston: McGill-Queen's University Press.

Weber, Max 1947 *The Theory of Social and Economic Organization.* New York: Oxford University Press.

Weigel, Russell H. and Paul W Howes 1985 "Conceptions of Racial Prejudice: Symbolic Racism Reconsidered." *Journal of Social Issues 41* (3):117-138.

Weimann, Gabriel and Conrad Winn 1986 *Hatred on Trial: The Zundel Affair, the Media, and Public Opinion in Canada.* Oakville, Ontario: Mosaic Press.

Weinfeld, Morton et al. 1981 *The Canadian Jewish Mosaic.* Toronto: John Wiley.

Weinfeld, Morton 1985 "Myth and Reality in the Canadian Mosaic: 'Affective Ethnicity'." *Ethnicity and Ethnic Relations in Canada.* 2nd Edition. Rita M. Bienvenue and Jay E. Goldstein (eds.). pp.65–86. Toronto: Butterworths.

Weir, Lorna 1995 "PC Then and Now: Resignifying Political Correctness." *Beyond Political Correctness.* S Richer and L Weir (eds.) pp.51–87. Toronto: University of Toronto Press.

Whitaker, Reg 1991 *Double Standard: The Secret Story of Canadian Immigration.* Toronto: Lester and Orpen Dennys.

Whitaker, Reginald A. 1993 "From the Quebec Cauldron to the Canadian Cauldron." *Quebec. State and Society.* 2/e. Alain-G. Gagnon (ed.) pp. 18–39. Scarborough: Nelson.

White, Philip G. and Augie Fleras 1990 "Multiculturalism in Canada: Charter Group Attitudes and Responses Toward Cultural and Racial Outgroups." *Plural Societies* (forthcoming).

Wieseltier, Leon 1989 "Scar Tissue." *The New Republic.* June 5:18-22.

Will, George 1993 "Sympathy for Guinier." *Newsweek.* June 14.

Williams, Beryl 1987 "Kollantai and After: Women in the Russian Revolution." in *Women, State and Revolution: Essays on Power and Gender in Europe Since 1789.* S. Reynolds (ed.). Amherst: University of Massachusettes Press.

Wilson, Clint III and Felix Gutierrez 1995 *Race, Multiculturalism, and the Media. From Mass to Class Communication.* Thousand Oaks CA: Sage.

Wilson, V Seymour 1993 "The Tapestry Vision of Canadian Multiculturalism." *Canadian Journal of Political Science* XXIV (4).

Wilson, William J. 1978 *The Declining Significance of Race.* Chicago: The University of Chicago Press.

Winkler, Karen J. 1992 "Race, Class, Gender in American Studies: 'Mantra' or New Conception of the Field." *Chronicle of Higher Education* November 25, 1992.

Witt, Shirley Hill 1984 "Native Women Today: Sexism and the Indian Woman." *Feminist Frameworks: Alternative Theoretical Accounts of the Relations Between Women and Men.* 2/e. Alison M. Jaggar and Paula S. Rothenberg (eds.) pp. 23–31. Toronto: McGraw-Hill.

Wolfe, Morris 1994 "Dr Fabricant's Solution." *Saturday Night.* July/August. pp.11–18, 56–59.

Woodcock, George and Ivan Avakumovic 1977 *The Doukabors.* Toronto: McClelland and Stewart.

Woodsworth, James S. 1972 *Strangers Within Our Gate. Coming Canadians.* Toronto: University of Toronto Press.

Wooldridge, Adrian 1994 "Left with an Aptitude Problem." *Times Higher Education Supplement* December 2.

Wotherspoon, Terry (ed.). 1987 *The Political Economy of Canadian Schooling.* Toronto: Methuen.

Wotherspoon, Terry and Vic Satzewich 1993 *First Nations. Race, Class, and Gender Relations.* Scarborough: Nelson.

Woycenko, O. 1982 "Community Organizations." in *A Heritage in Transition: Essays in the History of Ukrainians in Canada.* M. Lupul, (ed.). pp.173–194. Toronto: McLelland and Stewart.

Yalden, Maxwell 1993 "Language, Human Rights, and the New World Order." Speech to a Conference on "Multilingualism in an Interdependent World," Sponsored by the OISIE and the Goethe Institute, Toronto, September 9. Reprinted in the *Canadian Speeches of the Day.* October 1993.

Yancey, William and E.P. Ericksen, R.N. Juliani 1976 "Emergent Ethnicity: A Review and Reformation." *American Sociological Review* 41:391-403.

York, Geoffrey 1989 *The Dispossessed: Life and Death in Native Canada.* Toronto: Lester and Orpen Dennys.

York Geoffrey 1994 "Self-Rule Discussions Yield Little." *The Globe and Mail.* March 29.

York University 1986 *Report of the Committee on Race and Ethnic Relations.*

York University 1993 "Fiscal Report, August 1992 to August." *Centre for Race and Ethnic Relations.*

Zelmer, A. and N. Johnson, 1988 "International Students in Higher Education." *Canadian Journal of Higher Education.* 18 (3).

Zerbisias, Antonia 1994 "Media Accused of Inflaming Conflicts of Language and Race." *Toronto Star* May 30.

Annotated Bibliography

CHAPTER 1. UNEQUAL RELATIONS: PATTERNS AND PERSPECTIVES

Anderson, Alan and James Frideres 1981 *Ethnicity in Canada: Theoretical Perspectives.* Toronto: Butterworths. This is a comprehensive overview of theoretical perspectives that have been brought to bear on the topic of ethnicity and ethnic relations in Canada. One of the original texts in this field and still useful for some of its conceptual insights.

Bienvenue, Rita and Jay E. Goldstein (eds.) 1985 *Ethnicity and Ethnic Relations in Canada.* Toronto: Butterworth. The passage of time may have eroded some of its relevance, but this collection of articles continues to impress with its scope and depth of coverage. Still recommended for those who want an overview of race, ethnic, and aboriginal relations in Canada by acknowledged experts in the field.

Cashmore, E.E. (ed.) 1984 *Dictionary of Race and Ethnic Relations* London: Routledge and Kegan Paul. This valuable reference work will benefit both the casual reader and serious scholar. Many of its entries are sufficiently detailed to provide a thorough introduction to the field.

Jaret, Charles 1995 *Contemporary Racial and Ethnic Relations.* Scarborough: HarperCollins. This is the book that we would like to write if commissioned to analyze race and ethnic relations in the United States. The book is intelligently written and uncovers patterns in the construction and maintenance of race and ethnicity that are of interest even to experts in the field. Its American content may be offputting to some, but much can be gleaned by exploring how others think and talk about these issues. Highly recommended!

Li, Peter S. (ed.) 1990 *Race and Ethnic Relations in Canada.* Toronto: Oxford. There is little on the market that can surpass the quality of the articles written expressly for this volume on Canadian race and ethnic relations. Its willingness to deal with challenging issues in a sophisticated manner renders the book a logical step for those who wish to expand their knowledge in this field.

Rex, John 1983 *Race Relations in Sociological Theory, 2nd Edition.* London: Routledge and Kegan Paul. A classic text on race relations written by an eminent British sociologist that emphasizes the sociological dimensions of race and ethnicity. Provides an interesting contrast with how Canadian scholars approach this field of study.

CHAPTER 2. RACE MATTERS

Allport, Gordon 1954 *The Nature of Prejudice.* New York: Doubleday. Anti-Semitism sparked this seminal work concerned with the relationship between prejudiced attitudes and discriminatory behaviour. It remains a classic within the field of social psychology.

Banton, Michael 1977 *The Idea of Race.* London: Tavistock. The intellectual inheritance surrounding the concept of race is examined from a historical and philosophical perspective.

Biddiss, Michael (ed.) 1979 *Images of Race.* New York: Holmes and Meier. Also recommended for its historical overview of race images.

Henry, Frances and Effie Ginzberg 1984 *Who Gets the Work: Racial Discrimination in Employment.* Toronto: Urban Alliance and Social Planning Council. Race matters whether we like it or not, and this assertion is confirmed by this study of employment opportunities for people of colour. The study provides insight into how racial discrimination can be measured and assessed as part of a research project.

James, Carl E. and Adrienne Shadd 1994 *Talking About Differences.* Toronto: Between the Lines. This anthology of stories is a reminder that race continues to exert a powerful influence on minority lives and life chances. The voices that are articulated in this collection provide a riveting glimpse into what it means to be a Canadian when filtered through the prism of race and ethnicity, as well as language, culture, and identity.

McKague, Ormand (ed.) 1991 *Racism in Canada.* Saskatoon: Fifth House Publishing. This collection of previously published articles furnishes a useful cross section of studies that confirm how race can still matter in a country where colour-blind ideals are the norm.

CHAPTER 3. FACES OF RACISM

Abella, Irving and Harold Troper 1991 *None is too Many: Canada and the Jews in Europe 1933-1948.* Toronto: Lester and Orpen Dennys. A major episode in open, institutional racism is documented by this historical research. Canada's immigration policy was responsible for literally turning away Jewish refugees who had arrived by boat from Nazi Germany. The book also reveals the depth of hostility harbored by many Canadians towards the Jews in terms of denial and exclusion from mainstream participation.

Barkun, Michael 1994 *Religion and the Religious Right. The Origins of the Christian Identity Movement.* Chapel Hill: University of North Carolina Press. Describes how racism intersects with the religious right in the United States.

Barrett, Stanley R. 1987 *Is God a Racist? The Right Wing in Canada.* Toronto: University of Toronto Press. Barrett, using fieldwork methodology, presents and analyzes extreme forms of racism in contemporary Canada. The continuing profile of right wing hate groups furnishes this book with a timeless relevance.

Bolaria, B. Singh and Peter S. Li (eds.) 1988 *Racial Oppression in Canada.* Toronto: Garamond. This book remains one of the best exposés and indictments of racism in Canada. Its unremitting reliance on Marxism as an analytical framework for studying Canadian race relations may not appeal to everyone but the analysis is compelling and persuasive. Each chapter is devoted to a non-white group's experience with racism in Canada. The volume ends with a consideration of racism and the labour market.

Essed, Philomena 1991 *Everyday Racism.* Thousand Oaks, California: Sage. One of the most quoted books in recent years, and for good reason. This book provides an exhaustive account of racism in general by focusing primarily on its expression and reinforcement at everyday levels. Recommended for those who still think racism as something buried deeply inside of prejudiced people or remote and far away.

Frances, Henry, Carol Tator, Winston Mathis, and Tim Rees 1995 *The Colour of Democracy*. Toronto: Harcourt Brace. An excellent introduction to racism as a social problem in Canada by experts in the field. The authors introduce a new way of thinking about racism, which they call "democratic racism," and apply this knowledge to the concept of institutional accommodation. The gap between political rhetoric and organizational reality may surprise many readers. Recommended.

Sunahara, Ann Gomer 1981 *The Politics of Racism: The Uprooting of Japanese Canadians during the Second World War*. Toronto: James Lorimer. This is an excellent account of the events leading up to the forcible relocation of Japanese Canadians from British Columbia. The impact of this internment is explored, as is its aftermath for all Canadians.

CHAPTER 4 . INEQUALITY AND STRATIFICATION

Breton, Raymond, Wsevolod W. Isajiw, Warren Kalbach and Jeffrey Reitz 1990 *Ethnic Identity and Equality: Varieties of Experience in a Canadian City*. Toronto: University of Toronto. This study puts Porter's *Vertical Mosaic* thesis to the test by asking whether race and ethnicity are a help or hindrance to minority adaptation and success. Various ethnic groups from Toronto are examined and tested, some of whom have done well both socially and economically while others have not. The authors conclude that ethnicity will not always interfere with the attainment of socioeconomic success.

Curtis et al. (eds.) 1993 *Social Inequality 2nd Edition*. Scarborough: Prentice-Hall. One of the best all-around collections on social inequality in Canada, with particular emphasis on race, ethnicity, gender, and class. Written by experts with undergraduate students in mind, these articles are sure to stimulate and provoke a new perspective on Canadian society. Recommended.

Li, Peter 1988 *Ethnic Inequality in a Class Society*. Toronto: Wall and Thompson. Using a multivariate statistical analysis, Li is able to measure the impact of racism on the economic attainment of visible minorities in Canada.

Porter, John 1965 *The Vertical Mosaic*. Toronto: University of Toronto Press. Considered by some to be the best book in Canadian sociology, Porter's research is noteworthy as it was the first, groundbreaking Canadian attempt to study the relationship between ethnic background and participation in social institutions. The study concluded that ethnicity proved a barrier to cracking the French-English monopoly on employment and corporate management. Encouraging ethnicity through multiculturalism could only aggravate the situation, Porter concluded—an assessment that continues to draw support at present.

CHAPTER 5. GENDER AND RACE

Boulding, Elise 1976 *The Underside of History: A View of Women through Time*. Boulder, Colorado: Westview. This ambitious work successfully documents the role and status of women through the ages. It is especially useful as it takes a global perspective and provides us with many nuggets of information not found in the standard historical reference works. This is "herstory" at its finest.

Bristow, Peggy et al. (coordinator) 1993 *We're Rooted Here and They Can't Pull Us Up: Essays in African Canadian Women's History*. Toronto: U of T Press. The title of this powerful volume written largely by women of colour is a good indication of what lies in store. The book allows "voices" of women to convey the struggles experienced by African-Canadian women in coping with the challenges of Canada at personal and institutional levels.

Burnet, Jean R. (ed.) 1986 *Looking into my Sister's Eyes.* Toronto: Multicultural History Society of Ontario. The pioneer history of Ontario is told from the lived experiences of women from various ethnic groups. At last the hitherto invisible contributions of our most visible ancestors are accorded center stage.

Kallen, Evelyn 1989 *Label Me Human: Minority Rights of Stigmatized Canadians.* Toronto: University of Toronto. This book picks up where the gender, ethnicity and social class chapter of this book ends. It explores the unequal relationships that many Canadians, such as people with disabilities, and gays, and lesbians have with the larger society. The focus is on the human rights of the stigmatized minority.

Silman, Janet 1987 *Enough is Enough: Aboriginal Women Speak Out.* Toronto: Women's Press. Tobique Indian women speak of the injustices they have experienced as women and their subsequent movement from consciousness to action.

CHAPTER 6. THE ETHNIC EXPERIENCE

Driedger, Leo (ed.) 1987 *Ethnic Canada: Identities and Inequalities.* Toronto: Copp Clark Pitman; 1989 *The Ethnic Factor: Identity in Diversity.* Toronto: McGraw Hill Ryerson. These collections of articles emphasize the ways in which race and ethnicity have been theorized and discussed within the context of Canadian society. Many of the readings focus upon the meaning of ethnicity in Canadian life and its consequences.

Herberg, Edward N. 1989 *Ethnic Groups in Canada: Adaptations and Transitions.* Scarborough, Ontario: Nelson. This is an exhaustive overview of ethnic group organization using census data. Of particular interest is the focus on family structure and religion.

Ignatieff, Michael 1993 *Blood and Belonging: Journeys into the New Nationalism.* Toronto: Viking. A glimpse into the forces of ethnic nationalism in several parts of the world including Quebec is a must for those in search of possible answers to contemporary problems. Discussions focus on how this radical form of ethnicity not only departs from conventional expressions, but openly confronts the civic nationalism at the core of the modern nation-state.

Kallen, Evelyn 1995 *Ethnicity and Human Rights in Canada.* Toronto: Oxford. Few books are as impressive as this volume on the ways racial and ethnic discrimination not only violate human rights but also reinforce minority-majority relations in Canada. Minority rights are discussed in terms of Canada's three major forces— the First Nations, Charter groups, and multicultural minorities. Recommended.

Li, Peter S. 1988 *The Chinese in Canada.* Toronto: Oxford. This prominent Canadian sociologist has written a comprehensive volume that articulates the historical and contemporary experiences of the Chinese immigrants in Canada. The roots of racism during the exclusion era and in the post-war period are exhumed and examined.

CHAPTER 7. FIRST NATIONS

Alfred, Gerald Robert 1995 *Heeding the Voices of our Ancestors: Kahnawake Mohawk Politics and the Rise of Native Nationalism in Canada.* Toronto: Oxford. An extremely vibrant analysis by an "insider," this book has all the potential to become a classic in the field. The book provides insights into the logic behind Mohawk claims for sovereignty. It also points out how the basis for aboriginal renewal may rest in the reinterpretation of the past to meet the needs of the present. Recommended.

Boldt, Menno 1993 *Surviving as Indians: The Challenge of Self-Government.* Toronto: University of Toronto Press. One of the best books available for analyzing the current status of the First Nations. It examines reasons why efforts to restructure aboriginal-state relations at policy and administrative levels are proceeding at a glacial pace. The concept of "national interests" is a key theme in explaining the marginalization of First Nations. Boldt's suggestion that aboriginal survival is rooted in recreating a contemporary "Indian" identity will receive favourable response. Recommended.

Dickason, Olive 1992 *Canada's First Nations: A History of Founding Peoples From Earliest Times.* Toronto: McLelland and Stewart. This highly readable book provides a comprehensive and well-researched history into the various tribes that make up the First Nations. Dickason also conveys insights into the historical basis of contemporary issues and aboriginal challenges. Her upcoming collection of articles on different dimensions of aboriginality (with David Long, and entitled *Vision of the Heart.* Toronto: Harcourt Brace 1996) should prove no less illuminating.

Levin, Michael, D. (ed.) 1993 *Ethnicity and Aboriginality.* Toronto: University of Toronto Press. Those looking to put the experiences of Canada's First Nations into an international perspective need look no further. This collection of articles furnishes a useful compendium of issues pertaining to the politics of indigenous self-determination.

Mercredi, Ovide and Mary Ellen Turpel 1993 *In the Rapids.* Toronto: Penguin. These two prominent aboriginal leaders and lawyers have written a book that will surely strike a responsive chord among those looking for answers to the question: "What do the First Nations want?" A straightforward style is used to equip the reader with an understanding of the problems that confront the First Nations, and the proposals to solve these problems in a way that reflect aboriginal realities and ambitions of leaders. The concept of inherent self-government is accorded full treatment.

Shkilynk, Anastasia 1985 *Poison Stronger Than Love.* New Haven: Yale University Press. One of the most moving and eloquent ethnographies ever published about reserve life and its gradual destruction by forces largely beyond community control. The complicity of the government, however inadvertent, in contributing to this demise should startle any reader out of their complacency about the so-called Indian Problem. If you're going to read one book on the First Nations, make this the one.

Weaver, Sally M. 1981 *Making Canadian Indian Policy: The Hidden Agenda. 1968-1970.* Toronto: University of Toronto Press. This book was voted by a major research funding agency as one of the best social science books published in Canada during the past 50 years. Read it and find out why. The book stands as a paragon of scholarship into the politics of aboriginal policy as orchestrated around the 1969 White Paper proposals by then Minister of Indian Affairs, Jean Chretien. There may never be another book quite like it, especially given Professor Weaver's untimely death in 1993.

Wotherspoon, Terry and Vic Satzewich 1993 *First Nations. Race, Class, and Gender Relations.* Scarborough: Nelson. A book that sets out to provide a unique perspective on the First Nations, and succeeds admirably. The authors employ a political economy (Neo-marxist) approach to analyzing various issues as they relate to the First Nations. Not to everyone's liking, but still a potent piece of analysis that is likely to rattle conventional scholarship about aboriginal-society relations.

CHAPTER 8. CHARTER GROUPS

Cummins, Jim and Marcel Danesi 1990 *Heritage Languages. The Development and Denial of Canada's Linguistic Resources.* Toronto: Garamond. The politics of language in a bilingual and multicultural society are explored in this slim but formidable volume. The authors take authorities to task for disregarding Canada's linguistic assets. Multiculturalism is also soundly criticized as a kind of romanticized assimilation.

Fournier, Pierre 1994 *A Meech Lake Post-Mortem: Is Quebec Sovereignty Inevitable?* Montreal and Kingston: McGill Queen's Press. This book asks whether Quebec can possibly survive any version of Canada's federalist system. The answer will not please all English-speaking Canadians; that alone makes it an imperative read.

Gagnon, G. (ed.) 1993 *Quebec: State and Society. 2nd Edition.* Scarborough: Nelson. This is one of the best books available for understanding what is going on in Quebec. A collection of articles written expressly for the volume provides a valuable introduction to the politics and perils of restructuring Quebec-Ottawa relations in the post Meech Lake era.

Vallieres, Pierre 1971 *White Niggers of America.* Toronto: McClelland and Stewart. This autobiography of a Quebec

nationalist was instrumental in communicating to English Canada the pain and pride of the Québécois in the years following the quiet revolution. Those years are shown to have precipitated Quebec's coming of age and transition from minority to majority status as summarized by the slogan: *maîtres chez nous.*

Wardhaugh, Ronald 1983 *Language and Nationhood: The Canadian Experience.* Vancouver: New Star Books. Wardhaugh calls for a "new political mechanism" to unite the Charter groups and First Nations. Though written in 1983, his message and the analysis behind it continue to resonate with relevance.

CHAPTER 9. MULTICULTURAL MINORITIES

Adelman et al. (eds.) 1994 *Immigration and Refugee Policy: Canada and Australia Compared. Vol. 2.* Toronto: University of Toronto Press. For those who want to know more about immigration as policy and practice, this is one of the better books on the market. The comparative dimension is employed to accentuate key patterns in Canada. It also provides the reader with insights into the rationale behind immigration decisions.

Burnet, Jean R. and Howard Palmer 1988 *Coming Canadians: An Introduction to the History of Canada's People.* Ottawa: Secretary of State. This is the introductory volume of the Generations Series published by the Secretary of State. Ethnic group experiences in Canada are described as are their contributions to society-building in Canada.

Henry, Frances 1994 *The Caribbean Diaspora in Toronto.* Toronto: University of Toronto Press. This book examines the experiences of Caribbeans as they struggle for dignity and survival in a racist Canadian society. The predicament of Jamaican-Canadian youths is highlighted with respect to identity and life chances. An indictment against Canada, in other words, and a challenge for Canadians to move over and make space for everyone.

James, Carl 1995 *Seeing Ourselves: Exploring Race, Ethnicity, and Culture.* Toronto: Thompson Publishing. For those who like something a bit different, this book comes as a relief to arid conceptualizing. The author interviews a group of youth from Toronto to determine how they see and think about various aspects of race and ethnic relations. Very readable and informative.

CHAPTER 10. MULTICULTURALISM IN CANADA

Berry, John and Jean Laponce (eds.) 1994 *Ethnicity and Culture in Canada: The Research Landscape.* Toronto: University of Toronto Press. This collection of original articles was commissioned by the government to assess multiculturalism as policy, principle and an institutional practice. It is analyzed and assessed in terms of its accomplishments and failures since inception in 1971. Very informative.

Bibby, Reginald 1990 *Mosaic Madness: The Potential and Poverty of Canadian Life.* Toronto: Stoddart. Those who are interested in an academic attack on multiculturalism may turn to this book.

Bissoondath, Neil 1994 *Selling Illusions: The Cult of Multiculturalism.* Toronto: Stoddart. The book that has taken Canada by storm provides an interesting if somewhat idiosyncratic critique of multiculturalism as official policy in Canada.

Bissoondath has been taken to task by many for his criticisms, even those unsympathetic to multiculturalism. This suggests it is even more important to read the book and begin a dialogue about where we are going as Canadians.

Fleras, Augie and Jean Leonard Elliott 1992 *Multiculturalism in Canada.* Toronto: Nelson. It may be self-serving on our part, but we believe this text provides the best comprehensive introduction to multiculturalism in Canada. Multiculturalism as policy and practice at institutional levels is given prominence. Attention is also devoted to national attitudes and public criticism of multiculturalism.

Palmer, Howard 1975 *Immigration and the Rise of Multiculturalism.* Toronto: Copp Clark. This volume is a compendium of excerpts from key historical speeches, newspaper editorials, and the like. It is an invaluable source of primary data essential to our understanding of both the rise of multiculturalism and the assimilative period which preceded it.

CHAPTER 11. PUTTING MULTI-CULTURALISM TO WORK

Alladin, Ibrahim (ed.) 1996 *Racism in Canadian Schools.* Toronto: Harcourt Brace. Another excellent introduction to the mainstreaming of diversity by way of anti-racist education. The problems that confront contemporary schooling are addressed and a variety of proposals for an anti-racist system from primary to post-secondary are analyzed and assessed.

Canadian Teacher's Federation 1992 *Racism and Education: Different Perspectives and Experiences.* Ottawa: This excellent collection of articles will reward the diligent reader with numerous insights into the perils and promises of accommodating diversity at the level of formal education. Emphasis is on the commitment to anti-racist education as the logical outgrowth of multicultural education.

Cryderman, Brian et al. (eds.) 1992 *Policing, Race, and Ethnicity. A Handbook for the Police Services.* Toronto: Butterworth. The articles in this volume have been written expressly to assist police officers make the transition to a pluralist and changing policing environment. The difficulties that police encounter in policing diversity are examined, as are the challenges of creating of community-based and culturally sensitive policing.

Samuda, R.J., J.W. Berry and M. Laferrier (eds.) 1984 *Multiculturalism in Canada.* Boston: Allyn and Bacon. This collection of papers examines the relationship between education and a multicultural society. It devotes attention to the ways in which multiculturalism can be incorporated into various key institutions such as the school.

Wilson II, Clint C. and Felix Gutierrez 1995 *Race, Multiculturalism, and the Media.* Thousand Oaks, Calif: Sage. Easily the best book available on the issues and challenges of accommodating diversity within the mass media. The book is based on American experiences, with particular emphasis on television and film, but it remains relevant to a Canadian audience. Recommended.

CHAPTER 12. CONCLUSION: RECONSTRUCTING CANADA

Kaplan William (ed.) 1993 *Belonging. The Meaning and Sense of Citizenship in Canada.* Montreal and Kingston: McGill Queen's Press. This extremely valuable book addresses the meaning of citizenship in Canada, along with the diverse forms of belonging that this might entail. The changing discourse on citizenship clearly reveals how belonging is no longer a unitary concept but in need of refurbishing to accommodate the diversities of identity politics.

Pal, Leslie 1993 *Interests of the State: The Politics of Language, Multiculturalism, and Feminism in Canada.* Montreal and Kingston: McGill-Queens. In order to understand what is going on, we need to know where we are coming from. This book provides a detailed analysis of government policy and administration in an effort to reconstruct a new Canadian society. A study of society-building at its best.

Richer, Stephen and Lorna Weir (eds.) 1995 *Beyond Political Correctness: Toward the Inclusive University.* Toronto: University of Toronto Press. This book addresses the concept of political correctness within the framework of a more inclusive university. Some of the authors provide a conceptual analysis about inclusiveness; others convey to reader their personal experiences in moving over and making space at the postsecondary level.

Taylor, Charles with Amy Gutman 1992 *Multiculturalism and the Politics of Recognition.* Princeton University Press. This important volume focuses on Taylor's oft quoted contribution to the literature on the management of diversity, and is supported by several commentaries that critically address his notions of deep diversity. Readers are drawn into the paradox of accommodating substantial diversity without undermining the character and strengths of Canadian society.

Index